Labour Markets, Identities, Controversies

Studies in Critical Social Sciences Book Series

Haymarket Books is proud to be working with Brill Academic Publishers (www.brill.nl) to republish the *Studies in Critical Social Sciences* book series in paperback editions. This peer-reviewed book series offers insights into our current reality by exploring the content and consequences of power relationships under capitalism, and by considering the spaces of opposition and resistance to these changes that have been defining our new age. Our full catalog of *SCSS* volumes can be viewed at https://www.haymarketbooks.org/series_collections/4-studies-in-critical-social-sciences.

Labour Markets, Identities, Controversies

Reviews and Essays, 1982–2016

Tom Brass

Haymarket Books
Chicago, IL

First published in 2017 by Brill Academic Publishers, The Netherlands.

Published in paperback in 2018 by
Haymarket Books
P.O. Box 180165
Chicago, IL 60618
773-583-7884
www.haymarketbooks.org

ISBN: 978-1-60846-928-4

Trade distribution:
In the U.S. through Consortium Book Sales, www.cbsd.com
In the UK, Turnaround Publisher Services, www.turnaround-uk.com
In Canada, Publishers Group Canada, www.pgcbooks.ca
All other countries, Ingram Publisher Services International, ips_intlsales@ingramcontent.com

Cover design by Jamie Kerry and Ragina Johnson.

This book was published with the generous support of Lannan Foundation and the Wallace Action Fund.

Printed in United States.

10 9 8 7 6 5 4 3 2 1

Library of Congress Cataloging-in-Publication Data is available.

For Amanda,
Anna, Ned and Miles;
and in memory of my parents

∵

The author convalescing, March 2016.

Contents

Acknowledgements IX

Introduction: Labour Markets, Identities, Controversies 1

PART 1
Reviews

1 Reinventing India? 33

2 Saints and Sinners 44

3 Seeing Ghosts 51

4 Brief Encounters with Class 56

5 Interns Interned 59

6 Marxist Academics and Liberal Hypocrisy 62

7 Backing into the Limelight 68

8 A Marxist Defence of Marxist Theory 73

9 Houellebecq, Anthropologist? 77

PART 2
Review Essays

10 The Struggle of/(over) Post-emancipation Rural Labour (*'At Their Perfect Command'?*) 85

11 Shifts and Stasis in Development Studies 106

12 Zomia, or a Postmodern History of Nowhere 140

13 The Populist Drift of Global Labour History 157

PART 3
Essays

14 The Sabotage of Anthropology and the Anthropologist as Saboteur 181

15 How Agrarian Cooperatives Fail
Lessons from 1970s Peru 192

16 Capitalism Bonded Labour in India: Reinterpreting Recent (Re-) Interpretations 239

17 The Unsaying of Marxism: Capitalist Accumulation and Unfreedom 292

18 Academia as Mode of Seduction, or the Elephant in the Socialist Room 312

19 The Industrial Reserve Army: What's Not to Like? 354

Bibliography 385
Author Index 425
Subject Index 433

Acknowledgements

Debates about labour markets and the identity of those who, in an economic sense, circulate within them, together with the controversies such issues generate, have in the past been confined by development studies to the so-called Third World. Now these same concerns have shifted, as the study of development has turned its attention to the way these same phenomena affect metropolitan capitalist nations. For this reason, the reviews, review essays and essays collected in this book extend from a consideration of issues such as the free/unfree labour distinction and non-class identity, along with their political and ideological effects and implications, as these have been reproduced in and examined in relation to Third World contexts (Peru, India, the Caribbean), to similar issues now evident in metropolitan capitalism (France, the UK).

This shift notwithstanding, the comparative analytical framework – applied to the so-called Third World and metropolitan capitalist nations alike – remains the same. Namely, a Marxist political economy approach based conceptually on class formation and class struggle, one which interrogates the social composition of the workforce (currently described by many observers as 'subaltern' or 'multitude'), peasant economy, traditional culture and nationalism in the name of economic development, progress, socialism and modernity. Of particular interest is why the latter concepts, all central to Marxist political economy, have more-or-less ceased to be a feature of academic debate – especially in the social sciences – which has turned its attention to other, more fashionable ideas (resistance theory, essentializing non-class identity).

The reasons for this, and the controversies generated as a result, surface in many of the reviews, review essays, and essays in the book. Among the questions raised in discussions about identity and labour markets is a one as to the fact – plus the consequences – of a continuing inability on the part of many engaged in the study of economic and political development in both metropolitan and Third World contexts to differentiate conservative forms of anti-capitalist discourse and mobilization from their leftist counterparts. Not the least important aspect of this difficulty, it will be argued here, is how and why 'new' populist postmodern theory about cultural identity has affected state policy about labour markets.

Special thanks are due to the following people. To Professor David Fasenfest, the Series Editor, for encouragement; to Rosanna Woensdregt and Debbie de Wit of Brill publishers, who guided the book through production; and to my daughter Anna Luisa Brass, who designed and drew the cover illustration. She not only drew the cover for three previous books, *New Farmers' Movements in India* (1995), *Labour Regime Change in the Twenty-First Century* (2011), and *Class, Culture and the Agrarian Myth* (2014) but also did the drawings which appear at the start of each section in the present volume. Based on late nineteenth century characters portrayed in *Old London Cries*, and engraved by Thomas and John Bewick depicting varieties of street seller operating in the capital during earlier periods, these images illustrate the themes of labour markets and identity.

Reproduced in this volume are reviews and essays, some of which appeared previously in the *Journal of the Anthropological Society of Oxford, Science and Society, Critique of Anthropology, Capital and Class, The Journal of Peasant Studies*, and *The Journal of Contemporary Asia*. Others have not been published before, and appear here in print for the first time. The larger pieces have been edited for length, a procedure which dispensed with a number of footnotes, leaving intact the main text and its argument. Gathering together and editing these contributions has proved arduous, mainly because the process was interrupted in early 2016 by surgery for a complete knee replacement (a legacy of a sporting injury at school), which entailed having to learn to walk once again (a drawing by Anna Luisa Brass during my convalescence appears here as a frontispiece to the volume). Like all my previous monographs, this one is dedicated to two sets of kin. To my family: Amanda, and Anna, Ned and Miles. Also, to the memory of my parents: my father, Denis Brass (1913–2006), and my mother, Gloria Brass (1916–2012).

Richmond-upon-Thames
June, 2016

Introduction: Labour Markets, Identities, Controversies

Radicalism, n., The conservatism of to-morrow injected into the affairs of to-day.[1]

A definition formulated around the end of the nineteenth century by AMBROSE BIERCE.

•••

Clinching evidence angers men so much that they will sometimes end by denying the obvious, rather than admit it.[2]

An observation in an essay 'On the Use of Controversy' by HILAIRE BELLOC.

∴

Most of what has been published by me over the past thirty years deals with two contentious and much-debated issues in the area of development studies: the link between unfree labour and capitalism, and the political impact of the 'new' populist postmodernism. Although such controversy applies equally to discussions about labour markets and identities, what informs academic debate about them is of additional interest here. Reformism common to both issues has its origins in academia. On the one hand the abandonment of class analysis, socialist politics and allied concepts of progress, modernity and development; on the other, the privileging of identity politics associated with the 'cultural turn', the recuperation of the agrarian myth and the championing of peasant smallholding. A theme common to most of the contributions to this volume, therefore, is the defence of Marxist theory against a variety of critiques. Hence the framing here of controversies arising from these two issues – unfree labour and the 'new' populist postmodernism – in terms not just of capitalist development but also of the barbarism-or-socialism dichotomy posed by Rosa Luxemburg.

Consequently, one of the questions raised here concerns historical reversals. What were thought to be unilinear – and thus irreversible – emancipatory

1 Bierce (1967: 235).

2 Belloc (1941: 47).

trends, as regards both labour market development and core aspects of modernity (a decline in religious, ethnic and national identity), have returned to centre stage of the historical process, each an outcome of class struggle waged 'from above'. Another question relates to changes in academia influencing debates about such reversals. Despite paying lip-service to the ideal of political plurality, the rightwards drift in western capitalism from the 1980s onwards has been accompanied by the marginalization within the academy of Marxism.[3] Both these points surface in the reviews, review essays and essays chosen for this book, which can be grouped roughly into three categories (labour markets, identities, controversies), in the process addressing both the existence and effect of the barbarism/socialism dichotomy.[4]

The themes of labour markets, identities and controversies inform – separately or together – all the contributions to this volume, which is divided into three sections: nine are reviews (1–9), four are review essays (10–13), and six are essays (14–19).[5] The distinction between them is mainly one of length, reviews tending to be short assessments as to the adequacy of a case made, while review essays and essays present a more detailed consideration of arguments relating to themes covered in this volume. However, a certain amount of repetition over all these contributions is unavoidable, given that the defence against critiques of a particular theoretical position about the importance of class relations and its forms of struggle requires the elaboration of the case defended. Where unfree labour is concerned, for example, the focus of some essays/reviews is on its link with capitalism, while others look at its connection to a socialist transition.

In each section of the book, every contribution appears in the order it was originally published, and a few have a brief postscript attached, elaborating on

3 The conclusion, as outlined in essay 18, is – and can only ever be – that because the antimony between Marxism and academia is not transcended, those who advocate revolutionary socialist theory and practice have to operate a self-denying ordinance: forgo careers in the university system and return to the streets once more.

4 What to include and exclude from among the one hundred articles and numerous book reviews published from 1980 onwards was a choice determined mainly by the following consideration. Excluded here are contributions by me to debates which elicited responses, on the grounds that to reproduce my contribution alone would make little sense in terms of what was actually a much wider discussion. When no response to my argument was forthcoming, however, meant that the piece in question remained in consideration.

5 A minor presentational difference should be noted. Whereas in the reviews section (1–9) reference to texts cited together with the relevant pagination appears in the main text, in the two subsequent sections – the review essays (10–13) and essays (11–19) – these same kinds of information are located in the footnotes. The reason for this difference is to avoid overburdening what are otherwise short reviews with large numbers of footnotes.

issues raised in terms of contextualizing information that has surfaced since its initial appearance.[6] The last two essays have not been published before. When submitted to journals to be considered for publication, the editorial response to each of them was hostile. In the case of essay 18, this was unsurprising, in that a critique of cherished self-images of radical academic engagement was always going to be unwelcome to the two different anthropological journals to which it was submitted.[7] Conceding that it was well written, the editors of a leftist political economy journal refused to publish essay 19 on the grounds that it was 'too controversial', thereby inadvertently confirming the argument it made concerning the lack of knowledge as to what constitutes Marxist theory on the part of those promoting it.

Barbarism as Vast Cemetery

As is well-known, the relation between 'barbarism and socialism' was raised in the Junius pamphlet written during 1915 by Rosa Luxemburg in response to the nationalism fuelled by the outbreak of the 1914 war.[8] One hundred deputies of German Social Democracy, the standard bearer of the European working class struggle against capitalism, had just abandoned its internationalism and agreed to vote funds for the German war effort, 'in defence of the fatherland'. It was to reassert the validity of socialist internationalism that Luxemburg outlined the barbarism inherent in this chauvinist turn, described by her as a

6 All postscripts were written in early 2016, and are attached to review 6, review essay 12, and essay 14.

7 Of the two editorial responses to this submission, one – the more thoughtful – merely observed that, whilst agreeing with the analysis, there was unease about publishing it. The other consisted of two words: I was told (and I quote) 'fuck off'.

8 Noting that it was Engels who had observed that 'capitalist society faces a dilemma, either an advance to socialism or a reversion to barbarism', Luxemburg (1970: 269) then asked: 'What does a "reversion to barbarism" mean at the present stage of European civilization?' She continued: 'We have read and repeated these words thoughtlessly without a conception of their terrible import. At this moment one glance about us will show us what a reversion to barbarism in capitalist society means…The triumph of imperialism leads to the destruction of culture…Thus we stand today, as Friedrich Engels prophesied more than a generation ago, before the awful proposition: either the triumph of imperialism, and the destruction of all culture, and as in ancient Rome, depopulation, desolation, degeneration, a vast cemetery; or the victory of socialism, that is the conscious struggle of the international proletariat against imperialism, against its methods, against war. This is the dilemma of world history, its inevitable choice…'.

betrayal 'of the most elementary principles of revolutionary Marxism without murmuring an embarrassed disclaimer'.

Almost a century after the Russian Revolution, that warning issued by Luxemburg about the choice being ultimately between 'barbarism and socialism' is if anything more, not less, relevant. Everywhere socialism has seemingly been expelled from the political agenda, even amongst those opposed to neoliberal capitalism, leaving ever larger amounts of space to be occupied by its other, barbarism.[9] The kinds of reversal she identified as constitutive of barbarism have all re-emerged over the last fifty years. Accordingly, the theme of reversals, and what these imply for socialists and socialism, informs many of the contributions to this book.[10] The notion that, once achieved, any progress was irreversible, is a fallacy embedded in much development theory, and not by any means confined simply to bourgeois social science discourse. Luxemburg demonstrated that this kind of Panglossian optimism was at best misplaced, and at worst politically naïve. However, this is a lesson that leftists have not always heeded.

Of the reversals envisaged by Luxemburg as constitutive of barbarism, perhaps the most dramatic has been the intensification of global conflict generated by inter-imperial rivalries. Less dramatic, but no less important in terms of the potential/actual conflict generated, have been the political and economic transformations in the systemic nature of capitalism itself. Here, too, aspects of the reversal-to-barbarism argument made by Luxemburg can be seen to have

9 Historically, and in a broad sense, this kind of concern has always worried commentators occupying many different points on the political spectrum. The more perceptive, such as Alexis de Tocqueville, made this very connection in the preface to his book *L'Ancien Regime*, pointing to the unsustainable co-existence of well-being for a few with impoverishment for the many. In his words (de Tocqueville, 1850: xxiv): 'Democratic communities which are not free may be rich, refined, adorned, magnificent, powerful, by the weight of their uniform mass; they may contain many private merits, good fathers of families, honest traders, estimable men of property; nay, many good Christians will be found there, for their country is not of this world, and the glory of their faith is to produce such men amidst the greatest depravity of manners and under the worst governments. The Roman empire in its extreme decay was full of such men. But that which, I am confident, will never be found in such societies, is...above all, a great people: nay, I do not hesitate to affirm, that the common level of the heart and the intellect will never cease to sink as long as equality of conditions and despotic power are combined there.' In much the same way as Luxemburg, therefore, de Tocqueville linked his warning about barbarism to visions of imperial decay in ancient Rome.

10 See, for example, reviews 4 and 5; review essays 11 and 13; and essay 18.

been vindicated. The significance of her views emerges when considered in relation to the ability of capital to reproduce itself through access to hitherto untapped sources of cheap workers drawn from an industrial reserve army of labour.[11] The latter has expanded principally as a result of four developments: rural populations driven off the land in so-called Third World contexts, the incorporation of ex-socialist counties into the international division of labour, conflict in Middle Eastern nations, and economic crisis in the European Union.

Glimpses of precisely this kind of reversal are evident in her analysis of primitive accumulation as the pre-history of capitalism.[12] Hence the importance attached by her to the way capital resorts to violence and coercion, not just to separate peasant smallholders from means of production (land) but also – once they become workers – to exercise control over their labour-power. Although she confined the element of violence/coercion to colonies, Luxemburg nevertheless recognized that capitalists would not hesitate to use such methods if the situation required them, and this is precisely what has occurred in the midst of metropolitan capitalism itself.[13] Since it entails cost advantages where competition in the global market is fierce, nowadays capitalist producers in many different contexts do indeed employ workers that are unfree.[14] In contexts/periods where/when further accumulation is blocked by overproduction, therefore, economic crisis may force capital to restructure its labour process in one of two ways: either by replacing free workers with

11 This is an issue addressed in essay 19.

12 Capitalist production, she argued (Luxemburg 1951: 362–363, 365), 'must be able to mobilize world labour power without restriction in order to utilize all productive forces of the globe…[a]ll possible methods of "gentle compulsion" are applied to solving this problem, to transfer labour from former social systems to the command of capital. This endeavour leads to the most peculiar combinations between the modern wage system and primitive authority in the colonial countries… primitive conditions allow a greater drive and far more ruthless measures than could be tolerated under purely capitalist social conditions.'

13 This issue surfaces in reviews 2, 3, 5, and 8; review essays 10, 11, and 13; and essays 16 and 17.

14 Those who insist that free labour is the *sine qua non* of a 'fully functioning' capitalism, and invoke Marx in support of this position, are confounded by the fact that Marx's views about the historical centrality of class struggle to the shaping of the accumulation process lead to the opposite conclusion. Labour-power is unfree not because capitalism is at its beginning – that is to say, where accumulation is in its early or 'primitive' stage – but much rather because it is mature. Where accumulation has a global reach, as it does currently, it could be argued capital now has the confidence and the power to dispense with the compromise with labour it has had to make in the past. Put bluntly, because they can draw upon what is now a global industrial reserve army of labour, employers no longer have to accommodate the wishes and interests of their workers.

unfree equivalents, or by converting the former into the latter. Both these kinds of transformation correspond to deproletarianization, or the economic and politico-ideological decommodification of labour-power.[15]

Analysing a twenty-first century capitalism though the lens of class struggle undermines the hitherto prevalent approach to ways of conceptualizing the labour régime.[16] Today unfree workers are more profitable to employ but no less efficient than their counterparts who are free. Deskilling combined with a reserve army that is global in scope makes it possible for capitalist producers to use many different kinds of worker, many of whom are unfree (convicts, debt peons, bonded labourers). Instead of the emancipational linearity, whereby capitalist producers automatically replace unfree labour with free equivalents, the concept of deproletarianization includes the possibility of historical reversals, understood not in a chronological but rather in an

15 Applied by me during the 1980s and since to the sale/purchase of labour-power in the capitalist system, the concept 'deproletarianization' takes its theoretical impetus from the Marxist dynamic of class struggle, arising from the need of employers to cheapen labour-power in increasingly competitive global markets. Class struggle waged 'from above' involves the employment of unfree labour, capitalist restructuring, and workforce decomposition/recomposition, all of which correspond to deproletarianization. Hence the shifting of unfreedom from permanent, unpaid and local workers to temporary, paid and migrant equivalents. Class struggle 'from below' entails strong worker opposition to restructuring, and equally forthright attempts by employers to proceed with this, in order to cut production costs. Numerous contextually and historically-specific instances exist of the central role played by unfree labour in the process of capitalist restructuring, a procedure whereby employers used it to replace free workers bargaining over pay and conditions or engaged in strike action. Further aspects of deproletarianization are considered both elsewhere (Brass, 1999, 2011a) and in most of the reviews, review essays and essays throughout this volume.

16 Many of those on the left, who subscribed to a unilinear epistemology, thought that – once implemented – an emancipatory process was irreversible. Because it ignores the fact and the impact of class struggle, however, such a view is mistaken, in that it counts without the capacity of those who own the means of production to impose or reimpose relational forms that serve their interests. Unless an equivalent kind of class struggle is also waged 'from below', ceaselessly defending gains made – however modest, and however limited in scope – the latter will be overturned in what (as long as capitalism exists) is an unending process of socio-economic conflict. This applies as much to property rights exercised by workers over their sole commodity, labour-power, as it does to other property rights (land and other resources).

emancipatory sense.[17] In short, the very barbarism that Luxemburg warned against.

Dissolving the People, (S)electing Another

During 1953 Brecht suggested in jest that the nominally socialist government of East Germany invent a new population more in tune with (and appreciative of) its objectives.[18] Nearly three-quarters of a century later, it could be argued that it is capitalism which is engaged in inventing new populations: by drawing constantly on a globally expanding industrial reserve army to serve

---

17 Because it is informed by the dynamic of class struggle, deproletarianization accepts that such a process (conflict) is waged 'from above' as well as "from below'. Consequently, just as unfree relations can be – and have been – eliminated by 'from below' class agency, so they can be – and on occasion are – reinstated or introduced by 'from above' class agency. This is the dynamic that is missing from those who interpret history as an unproblematic and irreversible progression from unfree labour that is unpaid and employed on a permanent basis to free labour in receipt of a wage and hired on a daily, seasonal or casual basis. The historical and contemporary significance of deproletarianization, and its implications for the direction taken by class struggle, as capitalism becomes global, is not difficult to discern. As Marx (1973a: 464–465) himself pointed out, it is precisely in the existence of a space between unfree and free labour and the desirability not just of a transition from one to the other but also the reproduction of proletarian selfhood once achieved, that workers are afforded the opportunity and possibility of a shift in and retention of a specifically working class consciousness, through the realization of the fact of the appropriation from them of value they produce.

18 The poem, entitled 'The Solution' (*Die Losung*), was composed by Brecht as a response to government oppression of strikers throughout East Germany, workers who were engaged in protests during June 1953 against the imposition of higher production targets for the same wages:

After the Uprising of the 17th of June/
The Secretary of the Writers Union/
Had Leaflets distributed in the Stalinallee/
Stating that the people/
Had thrown away the confidence of the government/
And could win it back only/
By redoubled efforts. Would it not be easier/
In that case for a the government/
To dissolve the people/
And elect another?/

its own needs.[19] In the face of increasing competition, therefore, a move to the right on the part of labour is an inevitable political outcome of a global *laissez faire* system. History teaches us it is precisely in such a context that populist discourse can successfully position the term 'national' in front of the word 'socialist', with predictable results: nationalism + 'socialism' = barbarism. For those of us on the left, this raises two questions about developments in the capitalist labour market, each of which has generated much controversy: claims made by exponents of the semi-feudal thesis that unfree labour is incompatible with accumulation, and the link between industrial reserve army and immigration.

Contrary to received wisdom, therefore, it is untrue that from the 1960s onwards Indian agriculture was no longer perceived by most development theorists as semi-feudal. What was being said was very different: that India was an emerging capitalist nation in which economic growth was being held up by a backward agriculture because in the latter sector 'semi-feudal' relations (= obstacles to growth) still survived. This was the academic orthodoxy of the development decade, and took many forms (e.g., 'dual economy', etc.). As such it was a view shared by bourgeois economists and Marxist exponents of the 'semi-feudal' thesis alike.[20] Those who joined the debate about economic backwardness in the decade that followed all adhered to this orthodox view.[21] The sole exception at that conjuncture was Daniel Thorner, who on the basis of a forensic analysis of the All India Agricultural Labour Enquiry, pointed to the methodological flaws hiding capitalist trends. Much the same argument was made with regard to Latin America by Andre Gunder Frank and James Petras, who were taken to task for this by Ernesto Laclau. However, most of the assumptions structuring the 'semi-feudal' thesis remained largely

---

19 As is argued in essay 19, it is noticeable that in Britain the most ardent proponents of continuing unregulated migration are nowadays big business (Nissan, Toyota, Honda) and its representatives (Confederation of British Industry, British Chambers of Commerce). In keeping with any attempt by government to increase taxes on corporations, the stock response by capital to similar attempts to regulate the labour market is the threat to disinvest and relocate elsewhere.

20 For the details about this shared view, see Brass (2002).

21 As is clear from much of what appears both in this book and elsewhere, among the many exponents of the semi-feudal thesis at that conjuncture were Pradhan Prasad, Utsa Patnaik, Terry Byres, Jan Breman, Amartya Sen, Jairus Banaji and Amit Bhaduri. Some continued to hold this view, whilst others abandoned the semi-feudal thesis when this was subject to criticism.

unchallenged, until in the 1980s an alternative Marxist view emerged based on the concept 'deproletarianization' and its role in the class struggle.[22]

The global spread and integrated nature of capitalism has indeed undermined the semi-feudal thesis. In methodological terms, semi-feudalism thrived during the 1960s, when social scientists were engaged in trying to explain why economic development had seemingly bypassed rural areas in the Third World. This generated the notion of non-capitalism (at village level) in the midst of capitalism (the city), a form of dualism common then (particularly for those discussing the mode of production) but untenable now. Even when this kind of view initially emerged, around the start of the 20th century, Rosa Luxemburg questioned its applicability, as did Trotsky. These days – one hundred years on – it simply cannot be sustained, although those (such as Harvey and Negri) who maintain what we are seeing now is a form of primitive accumulation are merely reinstating the old dualism, albeit in a different form. The politics of the latter approach are simply another way of postponing/abandoning socialism.[23]

An indicator of the theoretical contradiction generated by this seemingly incompatible process – capitalist development on the basis of unfree production relations – is the argument made by neoclassical economists defending the employment of unfree labour by agribusiness enterprises. Gangmasters and unfree migrants, we are told, are necessary because they supply a need by filling jobs no indigenous worker wants to do. What is not said by these same neoclassical economists is that such a defence in effect negates one of the central tenets advanced by *laissez faire* theory: namely, that where workers are scarce and/or not available in the desired quantities, wages should rise until this need is met, thereby establishing the equilibrium structuring the marginalist analytical framework. As Marxists have long argued, the operation of the market depends ultimately on the intervention of the state – the very

22 To the already long list of those claiming to have 'discovered' that varieties of unfree labour are, after all, perfectly compatible with modern capitalism (on which see, for example, review 7 as well as essays 16 and 17 in this volume), it now seems necessary to add the name of Žižek. Announcing the 'rise of a new slavery', he goes on to observe (Žižek, 2016: 50–51, emphasis added): 'While capitalism legitimizes itself as the economic system that implies and furthers personal freedoms (as a condition of market exchange), its own dynamics have brought about a renaissance of slavery... And *one can risk the hypothesis* that today, with the new epoch of global capitalism, a new era of slavery is also arising.' Given that the compatibility between capitalism and unfree labour has long been recognized, not least by a few Marxist theorists from the 1980s onwards, the claim that it is now possible to 'risk the hypothesis' about this link is ironic indeed.

23 See Brass (2011b).

institution and the very activity (= intervention) which neoliberalism wishes to ban from the economic sphere – both to regulate the supply of labour and to strip away legislative protections secured by workers in the course of the class struggle.

On the face of it, there seems to be a contradiction between on the one hand opposition to unfree labour, and a consequent advocacy of free labour as embodied in proletarianization, and on the other opposition to freedom in the shape of immigration: within the context of a class struggle approach, however, no contradiction exists. Hence opposition to deproletarianization – capitalist restructuring that entails replacing free labour with unfree equivalents, or converting the former into the latter – and its accompanying view that workers should be free (i.e., a proletariat), is perfectly compatible with simultaneous opposition to the expansion of the industrial reserve army of labour. One argues that the existing workforce should be composed of free, not unfree, labour; it is qualitative, and addresses the relational content of the industrial reserve army. The other is quantitative, and concerns much rather its size; it maintains simply that attempts by capital to add to the numbers of this workforce must be opposed. Both arguments have as their object the protection of the existing workforce, so that in turn its struggle with capitalist producers is not jeopardized or undermined.

In the present neoliberal economic climate, therefore, each process – either the resort to production relations that are unfree in preference to free equivalents, or, alternatively, advocacy of an expanded industrial reserve army of labour that is free – corresponds to an attempt by capital to turn the balance of power in the class struggle to its own advantage. Rather than being antithetical, and constituting different stages in the history of economic development, which is what exponents of the semi-feudal thesis claim is the case, both unfreedom in the form of deproletarianization and a quantitative increase in migrant workers entering the labour market can – and currently do – co-exist, and in terms of contributing to the accumulation process, operate simultaneously.

Central to each of them, therefore, are conflicting interests arising from class: on the one hand, the need on the part of employers for a deregulated/uncontrolled labour market, containing workers that are either free or unfree; and on the other, the need on the part of those employed for control/regulation exercised on their behalf by the state over the form/quantity of labour-power circulating in this economic context. For this reason, the sale/purchase of labour-power, or the exchange that takes place between capital and labour, is a – and perhaps even the – critical site of class struggle, waged as much 'from above' as 'from below'; in short, the dynamic that drives the reproduction of the capitalist system.

Turning to the second of the two questions that require an answer, the need for control/regulation of the labour market – a fundamental component of the class struggle waged by capital against labour – many on the political left seem unaware of what Marx and Marxism has said about capitalist dependence on the industrial reserve army of labour.[24] Consequently, they are unable to understand that, in order to oppose – never mind defeat or transcend – neoliberalism, it is necessary first to prevent capital from being able to reproduce itself, an objective that currently can only be achieved by choking off its access to cheap labour-power drawn from what appears to be an unlimited and/or unregulated surplus labour supply composed largely of migrant workers. By avoiding political economy, and framing the issue of immigration simply in terms of culture, that of the migrant him/herself, the result is an inability to challenge an economic process that provides crucial support to the capitalist system. The political risks inherent in this lies in the current ideological shift by the far right.[25] The latter have, historically, ethnicized discourse opposing foreign migrant workers on the grounds of 'cultural otherness'. Now, however, the views of the populist right focus as much on the economic role of foreign migrants as competitors with locals in the same labour market. There is still

24 Confirmation that the debate about immigration and/as the industrial reserve army is mainly about labour market competition is evident from data provided – reluctantly – by the UK government in May 2016. These data, compiled by the Office of National Statistics from the take-up of National Insurance numbers by foreign nationals, reveal that in the 2011–2015 period there were an additional 1.2 million EU migrants entering the UK in search of work than government data previously indicated. Over the past year, a period during which the overall workforce increased by only 1.3%, workers from Europe had increased by 11.7% to 224,000, accounting for nearly 7% of the UK labour force. See 'Number 10 downplays EU migrant figures', BBC News, 19 May 2016. Supporters of an open-door policy where migration is concerned attempted to explain away this 'anomaly' by claiming that the difference was down to short-term migrants (who stay for less than a year), whose absence from the official figures was due to the fact that they did not put pressure on public services. This is beside the point, since what matters is – as has been argued here – labour market competition, and it is precisely this aspect that has been underestimated hitherto.

25 The significance of the re-emergence and consolidation within metropolitan capitalist contexts of far-right movements lies not so much with the size of the support for these right-wing parties themselves as the influence of their ideology on policies adopted/implemented by conservative and/or social democratic parties. Whereas the former may remain politically marginal in terms of exercising power, this is not true of parties belonging to the latter category. The end result is a rightwards shift in what passes for the 'moderate centre' of the political spectrum, as hitherto 'unthinkable' positions/arguments are adopted by mainstream parties either in or out of – but nevertheless close to – government.

a racist sub-text but – and this cannot be emphasized too strongly – it is now one that plays on specifically economic fears concerning loss of jobs to foreign migrant workers who are cheaper to employ.

Not the least of the many contradictions raised by this issue is that those who insist on seeing migrants purely and solely as bearers of non-economic identity – as culturally 'other' subjects of a different ethnicity, in other words – are quick to categorize as racist those who do not share this perception: specifically, anyone who examines migration via a political economy framework. Seduced by the postmodern 'cultural turn', many of those on the left have – and continue to – ignore what Marxism said, namely that of the two responses to economic austerity – to stay and fight for socialism, or to flee and become part of the capitalist workforce in another country – it was the former, not the latter, that contributed to the struggle against capitalism. Joining an already over-supplied labour market, by contrast, is to hand the advantage in the class struggle to capital, in that it enables producers to heighten the levels of surplus extraction and exploitation. Moreover, because migrants are not only cheap but also 'foreign', the deployment by capitalist enterprises of such workers may additionally fuel anti-capitalist discourse that is politically chauvinistic.

Fiddling While Rome Burns

An additional focus of this book is on how the rise of postmodernism during the 1980s constituted a retreat from the concept of modernity informing ideas about the desirability of progress envisaged in the 1960s development decade. In doing so, it created an ideological space for the very forms Luxemburg argued would culminate in barbarism. Hence the return to the global arena of conflicts based on national, regional, ethnic and religious discourse: not just in the Middle East, where Palestinian ethnic/national/religious identity confronts its Israeli counterparts, but also the equivalent kinds of discourse unleashed in the Balkans and the Caucasus regions as a result of the fragmentation of Eastern European socialist bloc. The danger is that the mainstream politics of the twenty-first century will be not socialist but fascist, a trend suggested by the rise and consolidation of political parties on the far right of the spectrum. Of particular significance is that this process is currently taking place not in less developed nations, as has been the case in the past, but in the liberal capitalist democracies: the United States and Western Europe.[26]

26 The pervasive myth is that in some sense liberal bourgeois democracies are immune to far-right political influence, which as a consequence will never establish anything more

Rather obviously the theme of identity covers a wide range of issues, and features centrally in debates about the peasantry, about Marxism, about labour markets, and about postmodernism. Thus, for example, one important aspect of identity is raised by an historical debate in political economy and more recently in development studies: whether a particular subject is a peasant or a worker, and – crucially – what sort agency is based on this identity. At issue, therefore, is the extent to which perceiving oneself to be a peasant corresponds to economic reality, whereby the major portion of income derives from selling one's labour-power, not its product. It is, in short, a question of class identity, and links in turn to issues of class consciousness and class struggle. Such a view, which has been challenged historically by populism in the United States and Russia, has resurfaced in current analyses of peasant agency by those belonging to the subaltern studies project or using the 'everyday forms of peasant resistance' framework. Whereas the 'culture of poverty' view saw traditional (and mainly rural) culture as an obstacle to the economic integration required by development, this has been reversed by those making the same connection

than a superficial foothold in such contexts. Although this is, finally, coming to be seen as the nonsense it is, the fact that it is bourgeois not Marxist political theory which has propagated this myth is still not fully recognized. That Trotsky (1971) presciently linked the rise/consolidation of the far right to the capitalist crisis in 1930s Europe is grudgingly conceded. That other Marxists continued to issue such warnings, even after the defeat of fascism in the 1939–45 world war, is invariably overlooked. One such Marxist was Schlesinger (1953: ix), who prefaced his analysis of the left/right struggle in Europe with the following words: 'Some, among my readers, may reproach me for describing phenomena which they regard as characteristic only of a few individual countries in terms of a general trend of modern society. My only answer must be to endeavour to carry out my task in such a way as to make it clear that the problems discussed are not of merely historical interest, and may yet have their relevance even for Britain.' The nature of these problems is made clear in the conclusion (Schlesinger 1953: 385–386): 'What was erroneous in the Social Democratic concept was the assertion that the economic interests of the working class would necessarily be served by collaboration with the existing government; as government was controlled by forces which demanded a monopoly of power, this amounted to political suicide on the part of Social Democracy. Yet clearly the alternative to collaboration within the established system is readiness to overthrow it, at least as a last resort if it fails to satisfy certain minimum demands... The real indication of the decay of Central European Democracy was not its inability to play a leading part in a period when the historical importance of Europe as a whole is decreasing, but the completely passive character of the role assumed by [leftist] movements... The Germans' greatest author told them, a hundred and fifty years ago, that there was no choice except to be a hammer or an anvil; they have been fonder of applying this lesson abroad than at home. The results we see today.'

nowadays, for whom culture is an *alternative* to (and substitute for) economic development.

Not only is there a long history of interpreting poverty simply as an epiphenomenon of culture/nation, and thus beyond the realm of criticism, but there are also influential contemporary discourses making this same claim now. This in turn raises the question as to why postmodern discourse about identity fuses so effectively with the populist/nationalism link, not least because it explains a structural principle at work that has an important bearing on the kind of nationalism underpinning much anti-globalization discourse. Accordingly, there is a wider point to be made here, about how the subaltern studies project – a similar kind of populist ideology – emanated from what has been termed the 'Third World scholar abroad', or academics (among them Ranajit Guha and Escobar) who hold positions in metropolitan capitalist universities, where they become in effect the voice of Third World nationalism. As such, the ideas they formulate about resistance against exploitation identify not class but the nation (India, Mexico) as victim of a capitalism that is correspondingly global. The desired objective in terms of political transition undergoes a corresponding metamorphosis, from socialism that is international in scope to a 'kinder'/'caring' capitalism that is national in scope.

However, the issue is not merely that nationalism and anti-capitalism are not antagonistic, but that a space is created for radical nationalism – of which fascism is the most notorious example – which is frequently opposed to international capitalism (categorized as 'foreign' or ethnicized as 'Jewish') on the grounds that the latter erodes all components of what is taken to be a national culture that binds the different classes together and maintains the political unity of the (bourgeois) nation state.[27] This is said in order to deflect struggle from internal issues (domestic capitalist oppression, inequality) onto external issues (exploitation of the nation by the 'foreign other'). It is also an important part of the intra-capitalist struggle, between capitals of different national origin. Hence the question of identity in all its forms (institutional, economic,

27 Paul Mattick (1971, 1978, 1981, 1983) was another Marxist who warned against dismissing the possibility of a resurgent far right in metropolitan capitalist contexts during the era following the 1939–45 war. He shared a number of things with Schlesinger: a thorough knowledge and understanding of Marxist theory and debates about this; a background in labour movement politics; and an awareness of the important political and ideological effects of economic crisis. It was the latter in particular, and the fact that – sooner or later – a crisis returns that neither Keynesian demand management nor *laissez faire* supply side remedies would be able to solve, that underwrote his political analyses and adherence to the socialism/barbarism dichotomy (Mattick 1971: 341).

cultural, political, national, religious) structures not just discussion but also disagreement about what is (and what isn't) Marxism, and consequently who is (and who isn't) a Marxist.

These days much of the public debate – in which a number of self-professed socialists are participating – is about what precisely constitutes 'English', 'British' or 'American' (or, indeed, any) national identity.[28] Socialists, however, should be asking a different question: not *what* is Englishness/Britishness, but *why* Englishness/Britishness? Against the privileging by postmodernism of non-economic identities, whereby subjects appear simply as bearers of a particular cultural or ethnic form of 'otherness', socialists must continue to argue for – and organize on the basis of – the 'sameness' internationally of class identity. That is, workers globally, and also capitalists worldwide, as is argued in many contributions to this book.[29] Inevitably and symptomatically, therefore, questions raised by the epistemological collision between postmodern identity politics and Marxism emerges in relation to different interpretations about the current effect the industrial reserve army, in the form of immigration, has on the labour market.

Muddying the Waters

An attempt to address this difficulty, one faced by most of those on the left in moving the discussion about immigration from culture to political economy, from humanitarianism to labour market, and from race to class, has been raised again most recently by Žižek.[30] Lamenting 'the (deplorable near-absence of) radical emancipatory politics in our world today', he points out that grassroots concern about mass immigration is not inconsistent with a leftist viewpoint.[31] Consequently, he accepts that immigration into Europe must be

28 Among those attempting either to formulate or to recuperate a progressive – and thus ideologically acceptable – form of 'Englishness' are the contributors to the volume edited by Samuel (1989), and the monographs by Colley (1992), Paxman (1999), Kumar (2003), and Bragg (2006). Of these, Samuel and Bragg are socialists.

29 See reviews 1, 4, 5, 7, and 8; review essays 11 and 13; and essays 15, 16, 17, and 18.

30 It could be argued that, as a product of celebrity culture in late capitalism, Žižek fulfils an analogous role to that of the jester at a medieval court: tentatively highlighting shortcomings but not really challenging the system which provides him with sustenance. This is borne out by his many contradictory utterances referred to below.

31 Žižek (2016: 18–20, 35).

regulated/controlled (the 'total right to "free movement" should be limited').[32] In keeping with this, therefore, is that among the many taboos Žižek insists the left must discard is to equate the 'European emancipatory legacy with cultural imperialism and racism', thereby defending the Enlightenment project against postmodern condemnation of it as Eurocentric fundamentalism.[33] Although this argument is correct, as others have indicated previously, the difficulty facing Žižek's restatement of the problem is that his approach is bedevilled by what might be termed symptomatic contradictions, not the least important of which is his earlier – and in certain respects continuing – endorsement of postmodernism (= the 'cultural turn'), or the very theory he now (almost) recognizes as mistaken.[34]

The reason for this failure to adopt a political economy approach – let alone a Marxist one – to the immigration question, therefore, is familiar: an inability on the part of Žižek to avoid the multiple contradictions arising from his eclecticism, of which there are many examples.[35] Having insisted that global capital

---

32 Žižek (2016: 98, 103). On this, as on so much else, he appears to have had a change of mind without acknowledging it; earlier, therefore, Žižek (2014: 139) did not view immigration as a process which required control/regulation.

33 Hence the view (Žižek, 2016: 18) that 'we must discard...the all too fast equation of the European emancipatory legacy with cultural imperialism and racism: many on the left tend to dismiss any mention of "European values" as the ideological form of Eurocentric colonialism. In spite of Europe's partial responsibility for the situation from which refugees are fleeing, the time has come to drop the Leftist mantra according to which our main task is the critique of Eurocentrism.' A few of us on the left have been making precisely this case for some time now, a point Žižek overlooks when announcing his arrival at the same conclusion.

34 Like many others in academia, Žižek was not slow originally to embrace the ideas of postmodernists such as Derrida, Kristeva, Foucault and Lacan. His enthusiasm for the psychoanalytic views of the latter remains intact. For recent sympathetic invocations of postmodernism, see Žižek (2014: 7, 111, 168). As is clear from a number of contributions to this book, he is not alone in having experienced a (generally unacknowledged) *volte face* on the subject of postmodern theory, moving from an initial and uncritical endorsement of the 'cultural turn' to reluctant critic – but only after others had drawn attention to its conservative political underpinnings.

35 This profusion of contradiction and theoretical inconsistency is, perhaps, nothing more than evidence for Žižek's contrarian approach to everything, a nihilism-licensing aporia conceded in an interview where he admitted both that 'It is also important not to say what everybody else is saying. It is boring...' and that 'I am utterly pessimistic about the future, about the possibility of an emancipated communist society'. See 'Slavoj Žižek: A Life in Writing', *The Guardian* (London), 16 July 2011. For similarly dismissive utterances about a future role for a specifically leftist emancipatory project, along the lines of 'Marxian Communism is an impossible fantasy', see Žižek (2014: 129, 146).

is too powerful to be opposed, let alone overturned, therefore, he then promotes the formation of yet more 'new social movements', along the lines that 'we will have to invent new forms of large-scale collective action'.[36] In a similar vein, arguing that blaming 'Eurocentric colonialism' is a taboo that should be discarded, Žižek proceeds to blame 'failed states' on precisely the same concept.[37] Advocating a reversion to a self-sufficient peasant economy, a mythical Golden Age image of pre-colonial societies as self-sufficient and isolated rural communities, Žižek reproduces a staple of the populist discourse he criticizes.[38] Moreover, he insists on labelling migrants uniformly as victims of what Žižek terms 'apartheid', which not only defines the issue as one of race – an interpretation he rightly criticizes – but also ignores a crucial distinction (the missing dimension of 'belongingness' that gives so much political and ideological power to the meaning of apartheid) between the identities of black workers oppressed by that system and those currently moving to other nations.[39] Again, like so many others, he calls now for the return of class and class struggle, yet denies the efficacy of core elements – such as false consciousness – structuring Marxist political economy.[40]

Current debate about immigration, Žižek proclaims, takes the form of answers to two questions: left-liberals advocate a European open-door policy, while in order to protect European culture populists want a closed-door one.

---

36 Žižek (2016: 5, 44–45).

37 Žižek (2016: 46–47, 101).

38 Žižek (2016: 44, 101). In keeping with this, Žižek (2014: 146ff., 151, 155) advocates a return to gift-exchange as a basis for an emancipatory, non-capitalist form of economic activity. As many anthropologists have pointed out, in non-capitalist societies gift exchange reproduces its own forms of hierarchy, inequality, subordination and control.

39 For the application of the term 'apartheid' to the exclusionary situation facing all those who migrate towards Europe, see Žižek (2016: 54). The distinction noted here concerns the different kinds of location in which obstacles to free movement and circulation operate. Clearly, apartheid refers historically to such processes *within* a specific national context – South Africa – that the black population rightly claimed as its own. This does not apply currently to the movement from one country in Europe to another, since – unlike the case of apartheid – there is no innate 'belongingness' that can be invoked by those who migrate. Bluntly put, what victims of apartheid are excluded from and thus laying claim to is their own nation, whereas migrants are seeking inclusion in a country already belonging to others.

40 Žižek (2016: 57–58, 60–61, 110). Symptomatically, Žižek (2014: 150) inverts Marx's negative characterization of religion as a form of false consciousness – a concept the efficacy of which Žižek anyway denies – and opts instead for a positive characterization, or religious belief as 'the foundation of a new form of actual social life in solidarity'. He also approves of Heidegger's dictum that 'only god can save us'.

Both answers are dismissed as 'the double blackmail', although he regards left-liberalism as the 'greatest hypocrisy', since its humanitarian 'display of virtuous altruism' merely attracts more refugees, thereby precluding the 'reconstruction of global society' regarded as necessary.[41] Although correctly noting that mass immigration fuels European populism, Žižek nevertheless fails to understand that the two answers he perceives as inadequate – the pro-migration attitude of left-liberals, the anti-migration one of populism – exclude another position, that advanced by Marxist political economy. The latter has maintained historically that, in order to curb labour market competition which benefits capital by dividing the working class and undermining its organization, immigration has to be controlled and regulated in the receiving nation.[42]

Despite tentatively recognizing this, Žižek tries – unsuccessfully – to combine it with a subjectivist view of the reasons for migration undertaken by an ethnically 'other' refugee, and thus misses the implications for any emancipatory project. Regarding migrants uniformly as Muslims, and the latter for the most part as bearers of or sympathetic to Islamic fundamentalism, Žižek uses this conflation in order to interrogate an East/West cultural antimony. He follows Badiou in dismissing the significance to Islamic fundamentalism of religious belief, adopting instead a psychologistic reading whereby invocation of this form of cultural 'otherness' is seen merely as a form of envy, a frustrated *desire* for that which is opposed.[43] By contrast, Marxist political economy interprets this same invocation of cultural 'otherness' as a populist *rejection* of what the West represents (capitalism, eventually socialism) and stands for (liberalism). Žižek perceives Islamic fundamentalism simply as nihilistic – as having neither project nor programme, which is clearly not the case.[44] While he is correct in identifying the presence of a discourse-against, Žižek is wrong to claim that it is unaccompanied by a discourse-for. Adherents of Islamic

---

41 Žižek (2016: 8–9).

42 Marxist theory about immigration as part of the industrial reserve army is considered in some detail elsewhere (Brass, 2014b, 2014c) and below in this volume (essay 19). Predictably, in an earlier text Žižek (2014: 21–22) denies the efficacy of the industrial reserve army, despite the fact that conceptually it is central to a Marxist understanding of the dynamic that is capital accumulation.

43 Žižek (2016: 74–75, 86). Not the least problematic aspect of this desire/opposition psychologistic duality is that it eliminates the possibility of socialism, insofar as the dichotomy posits merely a wish to be part of what is – namely, the capitalist system – while opposing it, rather than a wish systemically to transcend what is. In other words, a socialist transition is ruled out.

44 Žižek (2016: 88).

fundamentalism do not want to be part of Western capitalism, to which in the end they are implacably antagonistic: any desire that exists is directed by them towards an *alternative* to capitalism (a going-back to a more authentic past, governed by correspondingly pure forms of religious belief and cultural practice), not to Western capitalism itself.

All of these epistemological difficulties stem from the central fact that immigration-as-problem is seen principally in non-economic terms, largely as an ideological and political one. The latter is for Žižek a 'crisis of legitimation', deriving from the population in the receiving nation not being consulted about this, which leads him to reinstate the postmodern trope that ideologically 'we are constrained to cultural relativism'.[45] Oscillating nonchalantly between race and class as the defining characteristic of the immigrant subject, he advocates breaking the impasse of multiculturalism so as to be able to 'move beyond mere tolerance of others'.[46] This, argues Žižek, is to be done by offering migrants having a different cultural/ethnic/national identity the possibility of 'a common struggle', since we all face the same problems: what this proposal entails, therefore, is unity in order to realize 'a positive universal project' leading to an 'emancipatory *Leitkultur*'.[47] However, it is difficult to formulate, never mind realize, a common emancipatory project in furtherance of a 'common struggle', given that Žižek remains agnostic on the systemic dynamic of class and race, as a result of which he has nothing to say about socialism as a desirable outcome, and the capture of the state as a way of achieving this.[48] In short, his emancipatory project fails to move beyond the slippery domain of 'compromise', another way of saying 'tolerance', the very position Žižek maintains it is necessary to transcend.

---

45 Žižek (2016: 10–11, 70, 75, 77, 98–99).

46 Žižek (2016: 100).

47 When considering who will participate in this 'common struggle', and why, Žižek (2014: 96, 222–223) follows what is by now a familiar path: if the working class won't behave in the revolutionary manner allocated to it, then expand the category so as to include those elements not usually thought by Marxism to be part of a proletariat. Hence the inclusion of slum dwellers, members of the lumpenproletariat, etc., among those he signs up for his emancipatory project.

48 In line with his idealist endorsement of gift-exchange, Žižek (2014: 152) opposes the redistributive role of the State via taxation, and maintains instead that those who produce wealth – by which he means the rich – 'should be treated as the true givers whose contribution should be fully recognized...instead of taxing the rich excessively, one should give them the (legal) right to decide voluntarily what part of their wealth they will donate to common welfare.' At this point, it is necessary to confess, words failed me.

Agrarian Populism in Academia

Lest it be thought that such debates about identity are mere abstractions circulating as ivory tower controversies without material effect, three illustrations underline the extent to which political influence can be and is exercised both within and beyond academia by those whose views are supportive of the 'cultural turn'. One is the overlap between what Scott argues in support of his case for the existence in Asia of a space he calls Zomia, and what Gumilev maintains is the location of Eurasia, the context and history of which have become central to Russian nationalist discourse.[49] Another concerns the impact of postmodern notions of identity on immigration policy followed by New Labour.[50] And the third, outlined below, entails how and why a resurgent populism established itself in a social science journal. All highlight not just problems generated by the inability of those such as Žižek to break with the 'new' populist postmodernism, but also the reversals indicated by Luxemburg.

Controversy in academic debate over the issue of identity can be illustrated with reference to the way peasant economy/culture has been reconceptualized over the past three decades. The pre-war image of innate family farmers as embodiments of national identity, a populist discourse mobilized by the political right in Europe and Asia, was replaced by modernization theory during the post-war era.[51] The object was to promote economic development, thereby challenging populist images of unchanging and unchangeable rural 'otherness'. With the advent of neoliberalism in the 1980s, however, there has been an academic resurgence of agrarian populist interpretations, and a consequent return to pre-war concepts of peasant economy/culture.[52] Populism has now established itself in academic journals dealing specifically with agrarian issues, where advocates of pro-farmer and food-first concerns proclaim the virtues

49 See review essay 12.

50 See essay 19.

51 On this and the following point, see Brass (2014a: Ch. 3).

52 This academic re-essentialization of peasant economy/culture undermines a claim strongly made by Fortes (1945: 223 n2) that 'the curious myth that anthropologists want to "preserve" untouched native societies as "museum pieces" is so absurd that it hardly deserves comment. Those who put it about merely show their ignorance of modern anthropological research work, as well as a shocking lack of understanding of the historical processes of our times'. Whilst it is true that in the immediate post-war era, when development was on the agenda, there was indeed a move away from the study of the 'noble savage' as pristine object, what Fortes did not bargain with was that such de-essentialization in the name of modernity would be relatively short-lived, and subject to reversal (on which see review essay 12 and essay 18 in this volume).

of smallholding agriculture and rural mobilizations like the *Via Campesina*. This trajectory can be illustrated with reference to the way its components – discourse, politics – combine and alter over the recent history of one social science publication concerned specifically with these issues: *The Journal of Peasant Studies* (*JPS*).[53]

The degree to which the *JPS* has recently espoused a populist approach is evident from the way 'land grabbing' and 'food sovereignty' are privileged. The period following 2009 has been marked by the publication of many articles dealing sympathetically with these issues, and the reason for this emphasis is clear from the introduction to a Forum on the subjects.[54] The latter categorizes 'land grabbing' as a continuation of imperialism and colonialism, as such a threat to 'rural communities' where those with 'non-traditional land titles' are expelled from their holdings. To oppose this process, the journal editors announce a study agenda 'exploring practical and policy alternatives to current patterns of land deals', to be based on 'political ecology and political sociology…centred on food, biofuels, minerals, and conservation'. Its declared object is to incorporate and complement 'a range of policy-oriented donor and NGO-led reviews, as well as more activist political work', thereby championing on the one hand 'alternative visions' (= 'food sovereignty', 'land sovereignty') to corporate land appropriation, and on the other agency involving 'grabbing back' peasant holdings.

Among the ideas commended are those advocating 'the cause of small family farms…from a human rights perspective', and the agency of NGOs, transnational agrarian movements such as *La Via Campesina*. No mention is made of socialism, either as a desired objective or as a central emplacement of longstanding historical debate about agrarian change and the role in this of rural producers. The inference is simply that depeasantization is in itself bad, rather than part of a much wider dynamic licensing and leading to systemic transition. A token reference to the need to be aware of 'naïve populisms' notwithstanding, this recent *JPS* agenda is one that all exponents of agrarian populism – contemporary and historical – would recognize and approve.[55]

53 This political shift towards a populist agenda coincides largely with an editorial change effected by the publisher in 2008, and the installation of a new and very different editorial regime in 2009. The causes and political impact of this transformation are considered in more detail elsewhere (Brass, 2015).

54 Borras *et al.* (2011).

55 Borras *et al.* (2011: 211). By contrast, Trotsky – a strong critic of populism – insisted on the importance of permanent revolution because, unlike many others, he recognized the power of existing counter-revolutionary forces to block/subvert any/every initial working class mobilization. What is the point of stopping at a bourgeois democratic stage when

Together with calls for peasant 'autonomy', concepts such as 'land grabbing', 'land sovereignty' and 'food sovereignty' reinstate populist discourse about peasant = Nature = 'natural', to be contrasted as such against a category of 'others' which one populist categorizes as 'artificial people' covering all those who – unlike peasants – cannot be said to be 'natural'.[56]

Resurgent populist analyses encountered more recently in the *JPS* include those by Jan Douwe van der Ploeg and Henry Bernstein.[57] 'My own position', accepts Bernstein, 'is that small farmers today have to seen as studied as petty commodity producers'.[58] That he remains a populist sympathizer is evident from other admissions: 'In certain conditions populist movements can have progressive elements...[they] are an important reality of contemporary politics...One can identify more progressive tendencies that we can encourage... I have no problem with relatively small-scale farming as part of the future'.[59]

---

it is in the interests of the forces assembled to proceed straight to a socialist one? Here Trotsky had in mind the difficulty posed by peasants once they have land, a situation in which they – as proprietors – invariably part company with workers. He based his views on what happened in 1930s Spain, Germany, France and China, all places where capitalism had already established a firm foothold, and not – as Stalin and others argued – where it was still absent. His critique of agrarian populism, an argument persuasive in the 1930s, is today if anything even more compelling.

56 Patel (2009a: 165).

57 A book in which van der Ploeg (2009) advocates re-peasantization carries an endorsement by Bernstein, another agrarian populist (on which see review 4 and review essay 11 in this volume). Van der Ploeg thinks that the problems of food production and supply can be solved by returning to a form of subsistence-oriented peasant farming by self-sufficient smallholders. As many – very many – studies confirm, the idea of an egalitarian and pristine peasant economy shielded from the wider capitalist system is a fiction, a chimera that only populists think exists and will work ('The book demonstrates that such repeasantization is vital for the construction of a sustainable world'). Yet van der Ploeg appears to subscribe to this false dichotomy: 'the peasant mode of farming fundamentally differs from entrepreneurial and corporate ways of farming.' It doesn't: there are many peasant farmers whose economic logic – rent, wages, investment fund, profits – is indistinguishable from that of a capitalist enterprise. The majority of peasant farms invariably buy or sell labour-power, and are thus by no means self-sufficient. Nor are they all the same economically, appearances to the contrary notwithstanding. Also, where such farms coincide with kinship units, they are internally differentiated in terms of ownership of or separation from the means of production. This latter issue is one that has gender implications, since those excluded from inheritance/ownership of land are usually the females in the rural household. Because what he 'sees' (literally) is only a peasant farm, however, van der Ploeg subscribes to the myth that a different economic logic is at work. It isn't.

58 Bernstein (2013: 163).

59 Bernstein (2013: 170).

Another more recent *JPS* contributor, Raj Patel, similarly endorses a populist approach, and fails to address critiques of this.[60] Although he accepts that 'not all farmers are equal, and neither are their social organizations', therefore, Patel nevertheless evades its implications for his argument, observing that 'this isn't a book that can cover them.'[61] A result is his uncritical endorsement of the new farmers' movements in India simply because the object of their struggle is the State, an approach which ignores both the fact and the impact of class differences within such mobilizations (see below). A similarly evasive approach is evident in another recent *JPS* contribution, where from the outset the reader is informed that the 'class character of the peasantry [is] a discussion that is beyond the scope of this article'.[62]

The 'new' P(l)easantries?

The political difference between the earlier and current *JPS* can be illustrated with reference to the contrasting approaches to new social movements, many of which are represented in the umbrella organization *La Vía Campesina*. An earlier *JPS* analysis of new social movements in rural India underlined their class character and ideology, reflecting the economic interests of rich peasants and commercial farmers agitating for lower input prices and higher crop prices.[63] In the more recent *JPS*, however, this has been replaced by a more enthusiastic and less critical approach, one that endorses the *Via Campesina* as a politically-inclusive grassroots agency which, because it is anti-capitalist, must therefore be an authentically progressive mobilization.[64] Overlooked or downplayed is the fact that now such agrarian movements frequently involve

---

60 Contributions by him include pieces in *JPS* 36/3 (2009), 38/3 (2011) and 40/1 (2013).

61 Patel (2007: 16, 322 n.20).

62 Edelman and James (2011: 82). That Edelman has problems differentiating the peasantry in terms of class is evident from an article by Jansen and Roquas (2003) in a special issue published during the earlier period which was very critical of his own interpretation about the meaning of devil pact narratives in Central America. When considering the latter, Edelman missed the fact of class struggle, and instead misinterpreted it as a discourse uniting landowner and worker. According to Jansen and Roquas (2003: 275), therefore, Edelman regarded 'the devil pact entered into by the landlord not as a story that tells something about wage labour and class antagonism but rather as [supporting] the conclusion that rural people themselves identified with [the landlord] and his wealth, finding little problem in his riches besides common envy.'

63 See the contributions in Brass (1995).

64 For example, Patel (2009a: 119ff.).

a struggle between capitalist producers competing in a *laissez faire* global market. In this kind of conflict, not only is 'anti-capitalism' an ideological defence by small or medium commercial farmers against larger rival producers, but in furtherance of this terms like 'land grabbing', 'land sovereignty' and 'food sovereignty' form a crucial part of a populist discourse invoking an ancient and 'natural' sectional (rural-not-urban) identity.

Endorsing a claim advanced by 'new' populist postmodern theorists (Alvarez, Escobar), therefore, one recent contribution about the *Via Campesina* in the *JPS* maintains implausibly both that class differences 'are no longer the barrier they once were', and that '[t]he neoliberal model forced a restructuring of state – society relations, and it was in this space that new forms of social movements that are more autonomous, horizontal, and more based on collective identities rather than just social class began to flourish'.[65] Another and subsequent contribution on the same theme insists that what it terms 'a new correlation of forces' now pits big business against peasants, adding that new social movements are consequently 'cross-class'.[66] Significantly, among the member organizations of the *Via Campesina* are two Indian farmers' movements: the *Bharatiya Kisan Union* (BKU) from Uttar Pradesh, and the *Karnataka Rajya Ryota Sangha* (KRRS). Earlier analyses published in the *JPS* and elsewhere showed that each of these regionally-specific mobilizations was led by and reflected the interests of better-off components of the rural population.[67] Further, in the case of the BKU, that many of its supporters also voted for the Hindu chauvinist *Bharatiya Janata Party* (BJP).

That not much has changed in this regard is evident from the fact that the earlier demand by farmers' movements for better returns (= 'remunerative prices') continues into the present, albeit dressed-up in more acceptable language stressing eco-friendly 'sustainability', 'food security' and 'land sovereignty'. Hence the objectives pursued by *La Via Campesina* stipulate not just attracting investment, thereby 'strengthening the small-scale farm sector' by creating 'payment incentive programmes', but also establishing local/regional/global market conditions 'that meet the needs of small-scale farmers'.[68] The latter is to be achieved in turn both by providing 'Southern countries with preferential access to Northern markets', and by simultaneously implementing policies designed to 'minimise dislocations from trade liberalization'.

As before, what the farmers' movement objects to is not capitalism *per se*, but rather the market advantage currently enjoyed by large agribusiness

65 Mártinez-Torres and Rosset (2010: 150, 151).
66 Rosset (2013: 753, 772).
67 See Assadi (1995, 1997), Gill (1995), and Hasan (1995).
68 Patel (2009b: 693, 695).

enterprises.[69] Again, as before, this agenda reflects the economic interests of actual or aspiring small capitalist producers, rich peasants and commercial farmers. Not only is socialism as a desirable end wholly absent from this *Via Campesina* programme, therefore, but by asserting a right to individual property ownership so as to continue the cultivation/sale of food crops, in furtherance of which they are pursuing a realignment of market conditions in their favour, its members seek merely to establish for themselves a better competitive position within the existing capitalist system.

Where the earlier critical approach to 'new' social movements is concerned, the exclusionary pattern on the part of those connected to the more recent JPS is hard to disguise. Thus, for example, a JPS article on Chiapas by Calleros-Rodríguez makes no reference to the earlier special issue in the same journal on this very subject edited by Washbrook, where the question of class differences within the ranks of the EZLN movement was foregrounded.[70] References to the critical approach published earlier in the JPS to this kind of rural agency are similarly absent from two recent books about peasants. Despite a lengthy description in his book of the new farmers' movements in India, Bernstein makes no mention of the earlier JPS special issue on this subject.[71] References to the presence and effect of class differences within rural social movements generally are also missing from a book by Hall, another recent JPS contributor.[72] In effect, a previous and more radical history is either denied or dismissed as wanting by what is now a populist agenda.

Themes

This book is arranged into three sections, of which the first consists of short reviews covering a wide variety of topics, periods, and contexts. These extend from the 'impasse' debate about India; a couple of *festschrift* volumes; an

69 Similar demands were made by peasants and farmers who were members of the Green International, which emerged during the 1920s and was the precursor of the present-day *Via Campesina*.

70 Calleros-Rodríguez (2014). As shown in the contributions by Villafuerte and van der Haar to the earlier JPS special issue edited by Washbrook (2005), ethnic struggle in Chiapas generates not inter-class but intra-class conflict, since land occupied as a result of invasions by Zapatistas in the Montes Azules area is in fact that of another indigenous group, the Lacandón Indians.

71 On this, see review 4 in this volume.

72 Hall (2013: Ch. 6). That such an exclusionary pattern is not confined to the study of rural agency is evident from an analogous silence about prefiguring critical approaches to the capitalism/unfreedom link (Brass, 2014d).

analysis of rural change; an history of young low-paid workers in the United States; accounts of the Berlin/Deutscher episode in academia and the Occupy Wall Street movement; an important theoretical contribution to Marxist theory; to, finally, a dystopic novel about academic responses to Muslim politics in France and a film about Chinese cockle pickers in England. Like the next two sections, a theme pervading the first one concerns an inability to recognize three things: the acceptability to capital of unfree labour-power; that populism is the anti-capitalism of the political right, whereas Marxism is the anti-capitalism of the left; and the presence of long-standing debates about these issues.

The second section consists of review essays, and begins with a collection which refuses to recognize the presence of Marxist contributions to its subject. Review essay 10 argues that a number of essays in this book adhere to imperial or neoclassical economic historiographic traditions, both of which are not just problematic but also revisionist in their approach to the issue of pre- and post-emancipation forms of unfree labour. Privileging empiricism, and for the most part eschewing theory, revisionism attempts to depoliticize analysis of relations such as slavery, indenture and bonded labour in colonial contexts. Symptomatic examples of this revisionist argument – as applied to rural labour in South Africa, India and the Caribbean during the latter part of the nineteenth century – are examined, and the reasons for their shortcomings explored.

Over the past half century the theory, practice and politics informing development studies have followed contrasting trajectories, a tangled epistemological pattern displayed inadvertently by some of the contributions to three of the four books assessed in review essay 11. This inconsistency has resulted in confusion, not least where current Marxist approaches to the agrarian question are concerned. Unsurprisingly, therefore, misinterpretations of unfree labour plus the jettisoning of class analysis have led to the abandonment of socialism, and its replacement with nationalism and bourgeois democracy as desirable political objectives. By locating rural class formation and agrarian struggle in a global capitalist context, however, one of the four books demonstrates the continuing importance of socialist politics to the study of development.

Review essay 12 considers the case made by James Scott for the existence of Zomia, described by him as a large non-state region in Asia populated by self-governing, subsistence-oriented and egalitarian hill people. The latter he regards as empowered practitioners of 'state evasion', inhabitants who have chosen not to be part of valley society, characterized negatively by Scott as the locus of state rule, class hierarchy, inequality, and unfree labour, to be contrasted as such with highland Zomia, where these same characteristics are non-existent. Against this view, it is argued that Scott's interpretation of Zomia is consistent with a resurgent populist historiography, not only re-essentializing peasant society, but also idealizing socio-economic marginality by redefining rural poverty as a form of cultural empowerment. Now academically well entrenched, this conservative approach is in keeping with the *zeitgeist*, replacing as it has earlier political and social science theory which advocated economic development and modernization. A postscript adds a comparative dimension to this critique.

Review essay 13 looks at the implications both of the rejection by current global labour history of Marxist political economy, and of replacing its class analysis with a more inclusive concept of 'proletarian multiverse.' In keeping with similarly broad categories ('subaltern,' 'multitude') advocated by the 'new' populist postmodernism, among the key components regarded by global labour history as agents of a progressive anti-capitalist mobilization are undifferentiated peasants and the lumpenproletariat. However, since the latter categories are generally hostile not to capitalism but to socialism, their agency cannot be seen as progressive, let alone revolutionary.

The third section begins with essay 14, a personal account of detention, interrogation, imprisonment and, finally, expulsion from Peru in 1975. Whilst conducting anthropological fieldwork in an agrarian cooperative just outside Quillabamba, I was arrested and, in police custody, subsequently transferred by lorry across the Andes to Cusco, and then by plane flown under guard to the national capital, Lima. The episode marked a shift from the usual anthropological status of an observer to a rarer one of a participant, and the advantages/disadvantages of this change are outlined and assessed. A postscript considers further aspects of this episode, and charts (as well as commenting on) processes taking place behind the scenes (at the parental home, at Sussex university, at the Foreign and Commonwealth Office in London, and at the British Embassy in Lima) unbeknown to me at the time.

Given current interest in the agrarian cooperative as an egalitarian institutional form to counter the economic effects of neoliberalism, essay 15 considers how and why class divisions/distinctions operated inside one such unit in the 1970s. Of particular interest is the way idioms and forms of struggle used by bureaucrats, peasants and agricultural labourers in a Peruvian agrarian cooperative during that decade challenge one of the enduring myths of development theory. The latter invokes a familiar dichotomy to explain the failure of rural cooperatives: a powerful state bureaucracy imposing inappropriate policy on an undifferentiated and uniformly powerless peasantry. The case study presented here suggests that, on a number of crucial issues (privatization of co-owned means of production, the employment of labour-power that was unfree), it was much rather better-off peasants who overruled bureaucrats and imposed their own accumulation project.

Essay 16 looks at the way the link between capitalism and bonded labour has been interpreted and reinterpreted in the debate over the past half century about rural development in India. A number of those who initially equated debt bondage with a pre-capitalist production relation, and dismissed arguments that unfree labour and accumulation were compatible, changed their minds and espoused the interpretation they had previously opposed. Among the resulting errors perpetuated by more recent entrants to this debate is a misinterpretation of Marxist theory about both relational and systemic transition. The ensuing confusion has prevented them from understanding either the genesis of the debate about the role of unfreedom in advanced capitalism, or why – in the form of deproletarianization – bonded labour currently serves the ends of the agribusiness enterprise.

Considered in essay 17 is the same issue, but in terms of a more specific political outcome: namely, the link between unfree labour and a transition to socialism. Recent contributions to this important debate about political economy maintain that, because Marxist theory failed to understand the centrality of unfreedom to modern capitalism, a new explanation of this link is needed. It is argued here that, although many of these new characteristics are in fact no different from those identified earlier by Marxist theory, the latter has been shorn of its revolutionary content and outcome. Unlike Marxism, which allocates to the shift from unfree to free labour a central role in licensing a transition from capitalism to socialism, these recent contributions maintain that solutions to the problem of unfreedom can be found within capitalism itself, and thus possess no consequences for the continued process of accumulation.

Essay 18 considers the difficulty the capitalist university system has had historically with radical political dissent, and charts the uneasy presence within academia of socialists, socialist politics and socialist ideas, as a consequence of which Marxism was a theory and practice located outside academia. Throughout the twentieth century, and especially from the 1960s onwards, the expansion of higher education meant that Marxism shifted into the universities, and became increasingly part of academic discourse. The resulting entry of socialists into university teaching positions did indeed entail political compromises, but not on the part of bourgeois academic institutions, a process which it is argued led inevitably to the dilution and/or deradicalization of socialist theory. Searching for an alternative paradigm, a number of these erstwhile Marxists signed up uncritically to a populist/postmodern critique of neoliberalism, unaware of its reactionary roots and the fact that the political right also had an anti-capitalist discourse. In short, the search for socialist hegemony exercised from within what is a powerful capitalist institution – academia – has been and is misplaced, and the struggle for its realization must shift once more, onto the street and away from populism.

The final contribution, essay 19, examines the historical and current debate about immigration, and suggests that Marxism has always conceptualized this process negatively, as a method of expanding the industrial reserve army of labour, generating competition between workers, and thus to the advantage of employers. Support of or opposition to immigration reveals contrasting epistemologies: economic arguments for and against labour market regulation, deployed from different ends of the political spectrum by Marxist theory and capitalists, and broadly non-economic ones, based on considerations of justice, citizenship and humanitarian considerations. The latter, it is contended here, unwittingly support the economic arguments made by employers wishing to retain or expand their access to the industrial reserve army of labour.

PART 1

Reviews

∵

Old London Cries, I

CHAPTER 1

Reinventing India?*

This book by two authors based at Giddens' LSE (known locally as the University of the Third Way) consists in essence of large chunks of narrative interspersed with the occasional theoretical claim: the latter is either frequently tendentious or, more problematically, at odds (sometimes completely) with what each author has stated previously. The story the book tells is by now a very familiar one, and concerns the struggle between on the one hand a 'from above' attempt at 'the reinvention of India by Hindu nationalism' (= 'elite revolt') and on the other a process of 'from below' emergence onto the political stage by a mainly rural population (= 'subaltern mobilization') composed of Scheduled Castes and Scheduled Tribes. Among the more important bit-part players in this story are the various discourses contesting/supporting 'modernity', neo-liberalism and communal identity, and – most significantly – their role in the appearance of *hindutva*, or the reactionary project of the Indian political right. It is also a story that is chronicled these days by many of those who earlier failed to make this connection, but whether as an act of expiation or expediency it is frequently difficult to tell.

Misgivings about the adequacy of the presentation are not dispelled by an initial and contradictory set of statements that '[t]his is not a "theoretical" book, though we believe that it is sensibly informed by theory' (p. xix). It is perhaps because of this a-theoretical approach that rather too much explanatory significance in the early chapters is attached to the agency and/or historical role of political leaders (what Nehru, Gandhi, Bose, Patel, Prasad did or did not do) and not enough to what was happening – or not happening – at the rural grassroots. More importantly, downgrading theory in this manner cannot but undermine any subsequent attempt at historical explanation: how is it possible to address complex and much debated theoretical issues – such as the Gramscian notion of 'passive' revolution, the nature and determinants of rural class structure/formation/struggle, and the agrarian question itself – without at least indicating that they are contested and thus the subject of conflicting interpretation? Unsurprisingly, a failure to interrogate these concepts which are central to their analysis, results in a number of problems and confusions.

---

* The book reviewed is *Reinventing India: Liberalization, Hindu Nationalism and Popular Democracy*, by Stuart Corbridge and John Harriss (Oxford, Polity Press, 2000). An earlier version of this review appeared in *The Journal of Peasant Studies*, Vol. 29, No. 1 (2001).

Other theoretical difficulties stem from the fact that large parts of the book rest heavily on the work or ideas of a particular individual. Rather than developing their own views, therefore, Corbridge and Harriss (pp. 85ff., 104, 106, 117–119, 128, 178, 254–255 notes 2, 4, 12, 14 and 19, 264 note 9) rely mainly on the ideas about 'passive' revolution, peasant politics and political trends (and much else besides) contained in a collection of essays by Partha Chatterjee: this is ironic, since Chatterjee is a stalwart of the Subaltern Studies project the postmodernism/populism of which Corbridge and Harriss are now keen to distance themselves from (see below). The fact and implications for their argument of Chatterjee's Subalternism, and in particular his anti-modern/anti-rationalist epistemology as embodied in a search for 'traditional community', are raised for the first time only very late in the book (pp. 194ff.): predictably, the response of Corbridge and Harriss to this is perplexity and puzzlement (for more evidence of the latter, see Harriss, 1998).

Their discussion of the debate about the agrarian question in India (pp. 62–65, 80–81, 201) is similarly confined to Varshney's views on the subject, an approach which ignores both the rich and extensive literature on and disagreements about this complex issue. Equally problematic in this regard is their delinking of class and peasant differentiation. Characterizing the latter process as Leninist, and then dismissing its applicability to India, Corbridge and Harriss (p. 83) adopt instead the 'peasant pauperization' argument associated with the semi-feudal thesis: namely, that the rural workforce in India is composed not of agricultural labourers but of an impoverished smallholding peasantry. Not the least problematic aspect of this claim is that it is contradicted by what is stated earlier in the book: that by the mid-twentieth century rural households consisted of agricultural labourers, not peasants, albeit disguised as tenants or sharecroppers (p. 11). More importantly, Corbridge and Harriss forget two things. First, exponents of the semi-feudal thesis themselves invoke Lenin as a theoretical precursor. And second, Leninist theory about peasant differentiation is itself premised on the existence of an allotment-owning workforce, or agricultural labourers who have access to land. This, as Lenin pointed out, did not alter their *class* position, which was that of a rural proletariat and not a landowning peasantry.

In the first part of the book, which traces the discourse of 'modernity' in India, Corbridge and Harriss deploy the concept 'passive' revolution (pp. 21, 31, 38), which describes a process of 'from above' modernization. The assumption behind this approach is that capitalist development in some sense requires the emergence of civil society, and the absence of meaningful democratic reforms after 1947 is attributed by them to the 'weakness' of the Indian bourgeoisie (pp. 31, 38). The inference, that had it been 'strong' (or perhaps 'hegemonic') this class would have pushed through a real programme of democratic reforms, is one which Corbridge and Harriss again share with adherents of the semi-feudal thesis, for whom the absence or non-realization of a capitalist transition in India is similarly an effect of a 'weak' national bourgeoisie, that has also been unable to implement its democratic project.

Significantly, exactly the same kind of argument has been made by conservative historians to explain the political 'exceptionalism' of German development. Accordingly, the rise of fascism is linked not to the capitalist crisis of the 1930s but rather to the absence of a bourgeois revolution during the nineteenth century, the resulting 'weakness' of both an industrial capitalist class and a civil society in Germany leaving democracy to weak to resist the resort by its agrarian ruling class (Prussian *Junkers*) to Nazism. This is a comforting thesis, in that if fascism was indeed a pre-capitalist reaction against capitalism, then this breaks – very clearly – all links (economic, political, ideological) between capitalism as a system of production and the rise of fascism, a point Trotsky made repeatedly and powerfully throughout the 1930s (with regard to Spain as well as to Germany). An epistemological effect of this 'exceptionalist'/late-development argument (fascism = feudal reaction, therefore capitalism ≠ fascism) is to let capitalism off the hook, which is precisely why it was used in post-war West Germany to legitimize capitalist development there.

It is this kind of argument that has been deployed – in metropolitan capitalist and Third World contexts alike – in order to justify (disastrous a-) political alliances with what were (wrongly) deemed to be elements of the 'progressive national bourgeoisie'. As with exponents of Indian 'semi-feudalism' and German 'exceptionalism', therefore, for Corbridge and Harriss the problem appears to be the absence of a meaningful transition to bourgeois democracy, and not the presence of capitalism. The term 'appears to be' is used here because throughout the book it is unclear whether the 'weakness' of the Indian bourgeoisie, and the corresponding failure of a civil society to develop, made it possible in turn for the reactionary *hindutva* forces to emerge and consolidate, or much rather the latter was the outcome of a strong and emerging petty bourgeoisie (particularly in rural areas) opposed both to international capital and to an indigenous working class. Hindu reaction culminating in the BJP (*Bharatiya Janata Party*) conquest of power is linked to a middle class who are fearful both 'of the disorderly realm of democratic politics and…the threats which it poses to their privilege' and of 'the rising tide of Indian democracy', a grassroots mobilization signalling the entry of 'Backward Communities' into politics, a process that Corbridge and Harriss term 'empowerment from within' (pp. 192–193, 202, 212).

However, precisely what the causal link between these two processes – 'elite revolt' and 'subaltern mobilization' – is, remains unclear: at times the inference is that the 'from above' process was a response to the 'from below' one, while at others the opposite appears to be the case. Indeed, it is not clear from the book whether some of the elements involved in what Corbridge and Harriss term 'subaltern mobilization' ought more accurately to be categorized as part of the 'elite revolt'. This confusion derives from problems with the class identity of those who engage in grassroots agency, and consequently what the latter was designed to achieve. Hence the statement (pp. 75, 123) that a salient and increasingly important aspect of Indian political life from the 1970s onwards when 'traditional authority [was] no longer generally accepted' was the challenge-from-below, in the form of a threat 'from subaltern classes'. Although Corbridge and Harriss (pp. 97ff., 174) regard this subaltern/plebeian 'assertiveness' as resistance by low caste agricultural labourers increasingly aware of their political rights, it is nevertheless the case that in a significant number of instances such 'from below' agency in India has been that of a low caste petty bourgeoisie and not rural workers. The authors in fact hint at the latter point in passing (p. 257 note 8), but its implication for their argument escapes them.

At the heart of the book lies an unsolved mystery, and one that requires explanation. Why, precisely, have its authors not only abandoned earlier positions they held, and changed their minds about the analytical relevance of populism, postmodernism, neo-liberalism and class, but also remained silent about this *volte face*? It is important, therefore, to remind ourselves what each of these co-authors has argued previously, and how the position they held then not merely differs from the one they hold now, but – particularly where postmodernism, populism, romanticism, class and neo-liberalism are concerned – is in some instances diametrically opposed to this. Perhaps to disguise both the fact and the extent of this shift, Corbridge and Harriss (p. xx) now claim, rather surprisingly, that '[o]ur analysis is unashamedly unfashionable': on this point some reassurance is in order, since being unfashionable is certainly not among the many sins they stand accused of here. At a time when neo-liberalism and postmodernism, twin variants of a vehemently anti-Marxist theory, were colonizing development studies, both co-authors of the book under review were exponents of what was then termed the 'impasse' position (Booth, 1985, 1994; Corbridge, 1990, 1994; Harriss, 1994), a thinly-disguised postmodern endorsement of 'resistance'/'empowerment' inside the capitalist system, a process based on plural identities celebrating 'diversity', 'difference' and 'choice'. The book under review, however, makes no mention of the 'impasse' debate, let alone the contributions to this by Corbridge and Harriss, nor is any 'impasse' text (either by them or by others) listed in its bibliography. That their views have changed is clear, but the reasons for this are less so.

On the issues of postmodernism and populism, the extent of the *volte face* on the part of both Corbridge and Harriss is striking. When the postmodern onslaught on development theory was at its height, therefore, Corbridge sided with the attacking forces, to which he extended an unambiguous welcome. His contribution to a volume edited by Booth (1994) at that time, endorsing the 'impasse', was accordingly 'a positive assessment of the populist and post-modern turns [in the study of development]' in which he acknowledged 'the power of the postmodernist critique in regard to questions of difference and representation', concluding that '[t]here can be no gainsaying the strengths of the populist and postmodern/post-colonial challenge' (Corbridge, 1994: 91, 96). A not dissimilar view was taken by Harriss (1994: 193), who in a contribution to that same volume accepted that his insistence 'on the importance of understanding the ways in which class relationships are culturally constructed clearly owes something to the influence of postmodernist "deconstruction" of concepts such as class'. Although in the early 1990s Harriss had recognized the possibility that in India a 'dangerous populism' was emerging (Harriss, 1992: 213), this admonition was subsequently disregarded. By the mid-1990s, therefore, both co-authors of the book under review were endorsing the postmodern/populist approach of James Scott, and in particular his 'everyday forms of resistance' framework (see, for example, Corbridge 1994: 114 and Harriss, 1994: 181ff., 186ff.). Having espoused Scott's 'moral economy' framework, Harriss (1994: 186) then forcefully rejected a critique (made by this reviewer) that it was a backwards-looking and thus conservative form of romanticizing grass-roots agency in contemporary rural India.

For the co-authors of this book, it would seem, the past is indeed a foreign country where they did things differently. Not only is populism in India recast here in a negative mould and condemned as a 'dangerous game' and a 'populist-nationalism' that is 'inherently destabilizing [and an] authoritarian means for maintaining control' (pp. 67 note, 73, 86, 88, 132), but Corbridge and Harriss now maintain that '[w]e are drawn only in part to the claims of post-development, or to [the] suggestion that the class-based politics...are being replaced increasingly by the politics of issue-based social movements, and by mobilizations based on ethnicity...' (p. 238). The populism/postmodernism of Scott has undergone a similar process of reassessment (in this connection it should be emphasized that it is not Scott but rather Corbridge and Harriss who have changed their minds: the problematic nature of his framework notwithstanding, Scott has at least remained consistent in his views throughout the period in question). Objecting to the critique by Scott of 'high modernism', therefore, Corbridge and Harriss assert confidently that '[w]e have problems with an account of Indian politics which seems so relentlessly to celebrate "difference" or the "fragment"...' (pp. 32, 246–247 note 21). Ignoring their own earlier positive interpretation of 'moral economy', they (pp. 207–208) are now critical of its deployment by environmental movements in India in order to defend 'natural economy'.

Postmodernism itself is given short shrift (see also Corbridge 1998). In contrast to earlier to earlier endorsements of its stance on 'questions of difference and representation', Corbridge and Harriss (p. 174) now reject postmodernism and 'orientalist attitudes (whether held by outsiders or by Indians themselves) which treat the Indian "Other" as essentially different'. Postmodernism is roundly condemned in the book under review, both for the view that '"European modernity" has no place – or no roots – in Europe's Other, in "*Bharat*-India"', and for 'a refusal to accept "external" guidelines for political action or negotiation', a situation which 'leaves the armoury of anti-secularism bare when it comes to the adjudication of disputes between religious and ethnic groups' (pp. 39, 198–199). Again in contrast to previously expressed views, Corbridge and Harriss upbraid an anti-secularism influenced by postmodern/populist theory on the grounds that 'its agendas for change [stem both from] a romanticized account of religious faith or community [and from] ringing denunciations of the state and modernity', as a consequence of which the co-authors of this book are now 'prepared to raise the charge of complacency against the [postmodern and populist] protagonists of anti-secularism in India' (p. 199). To this latter sentiment one can only add, *sotto voce*, the words 'and not before time'.

The same is true of romanticism, particularly as this applies to idealized constructions of 'natural'/rural 'community'. Forgetting their own earlier adherence to romanticized views, and also their denial that such views constituted a romanticization, both authors are now highly critical of precisely these same forms of romanticization and correspondingly silent about their own earlier complicity with them. Now (at last) they recognize 'that the anti-state and pro-community logics of the anti-secularist position will prove to be less than robust in organizing a political opposition to the exclusionary projects of a militant Hinduism' (p. 199). In other words, and as some have argued for a long while now, the space for reactionary nationalism is created by, among other things, precisely the anti-state/anti-modern discourse of a backward-looking populism that emphasizes 'otherness'/'difference'. Observing, for example, that environmental activism 'is weakened by its romantic accounts of "community" or a "natural economy"', Corbridge and Harriss then proceed to invoke only their own very recent (= post-conversion) writings on the subject as evidence for their having correctly identified the prefiguring epistemology of such romanticism (pp. 208, 268 note 11). A further irony in this regard is that Paul Hirst, whose work Corbridge continues to invoke favourably, has himself advocated a return to yeoman farming, or precisely that kind of rural romanticization which both authors of the book under review now condemn.

Following in the footsteps of others, Corbridge and Harriss (pp. 127ff., 179ff.) now accept that the rise of Hindu revivalism was due in no small measure to the ability of the BJP to present itself as the defender of an authentic Indian culture (= the basis of the nation) against a combination of internal/external forces (non-national + international = anti-national) threatening it, amongst which were to be found not only Muslims (= internal 'other') but also global capital (= external 'other') and Congress, its internal ally. In asserting that the BJP is not opposed to modernization or economic liberalization, however, Corbridge and Harriss (p. 174) fail to spot the fact that the success of *hindutva* mobilization lies in its capacity to refocus political discourse – that is, precisely the ability to generate 'false consciousness', the efficacy of which Harriss (1994) earlier denied – by diverting public debate/gaze away from economic issues (which divide Hindus along class lines) and towards/onto the ideological domain of culture (which unites Hindus separated by class).

As with postmodernism, populism and romanticism, so with class and neo-liberalism. Earlier, therefore, Harriss (1994: 181, 186–187) was content to adopt a typically idealistic position, in which the concept 'class' was in effect dissolved into competing subjectivities, neither of which were verifiable ('[w]e have no reason for saying that one or other of these different and conflicting versions of class relations and of the idea of the community as a "moral economy" is "true" and the other "false". The statements have equivalent veracity as comments upon essentially contested constructions'), a symptomatically postmodern aporia that negated the concept altogether. This hostility to class analysis also pervaded a subsequent text (Harriss, 1997: 12, 13), where 1970s/1980s approaches to agrarian change in India based on class differentiation of the peasantry were dismissed by him in unambiguous terms, as 'sterile' and 'misleading'. The same approach informed his initial view about the support received by the farmers' movements: 'I do not believe', noted Harriss (1992: 214), 'that the "Farmers' Movements" are properly described as "rich peasant" or "kulak" movements... [t]he "Farmers' Movements" are not "rich peasant movements"'. In keeping with this approach, which eschews oppressive/exploitative perceptions of class, debt bondage has in the past been characterized by Harriss (1982a; 1992; 1994) in positive terms, as a benign non-capitalist relation based on patron-clientage, 'moral economy', and 'reciprocity', that provides agricultural labourers with a 'subsistence guarantee'. The same is true of Corbridge, who earlier advocated the redefinition of exploitation, and the replacement of a labour theory of value with vague and populist notions such as 'a sensitivity to the multiple sites of oppression and unfairness' and 'the needs and rights of [non-class-specific] strangers' (Corbridge, 1994).

Now, however, the concept 'class' has made something of a comeback. In contrast to their earlier hostile views on the subject of class, and their correspondingly favourable disposition towards a postmodern/post-Marxist/neo-liberal approach, therefore, Corbridge and Harriss (p. xx) now assure us that 'in a context in which the economic ideology of neo-liberalism remains influential, and in which "post-structuralist" and "post-colonial" ideas are pervasive', their present 'unfashionable' concerns remain 'with class formation and the dynamics of accumulation'. Notwithstanding the occasional contradictory slippage – for example, that current struggles 'cannot be resolved into conflicts between classes', an endorsement of the jibe about '"wooden Marxist political economy"', and a defence of religious essentialism (pp. 138, 160, 175ff.) – they aver that in India 'class-based politics continue to remain important', and in the concluding chapter of the book they reiterate that their commitment is 'to a tradition of scholarship which centrally concerned with class and the dynamics of capital accumulation' (pp. 235, 238). 'Difference', Corbridge and Harriss conclude (p. 229), 'is not always a blessing'. They now agree that (p. 202; see also p. 226) 'it is misleading to suppose that [populist/non-class] citizen's movements, NGOs and community organizations – for all their evident vibrancy in India – provide an alternative to the state', and further that what determines the effectiveness or ineffectiveness of such mobilizations is 'the balance of class power'. In what amounts to a complete rejection of positions to which each of them subscribed earlier, Corbridge and Harriss (p. 227) now question '[t]he cultural turn [= postmodernism] in development studies', adding that 'there is a danger in "post-development" studies [= postmodernism] that the state is seen as the embodiment of modernity in a disabling way.'

Their interpretation of bonded labour has also received a makeover, and is accordingly presented now in a very different light: as a cause of rural poverty and an oppressive/exploitative relationship designed by capitalist rich peasants who 'seek to re-establish forms of labour bondage against the assertiveness of labourers' in order to force indebted landless workers to 'sell their labour power even at rates below the "market" wage' (pp. 83–84, 257 note 15; see also p. 105). Adopting an unmistakably Marxist tone, they now note (pp. 167–168) that: 'The sheer supply of labour in India makes exploitation possible on the basis of absolute surplus value – that is, on the basis of sweated labour that is combined with new technologies'. Rather than a benign/'reciprocal' relation that is incompatible with the advanced productive forces of capitalism, therefore, the meaning of unfree labour has metamorphosed: such relations, the authors of this book confidently assert, are not only reproduced by capital in its struggle with labour but also compatible with new technology. This suggests that the authors' current position on this subject is not so different from the Marxist interpretation which regards unfree relations of production as the decommodification of free workers by capitalist employers (deproletarianization, in other words). Such a view, however, is not only wholly at odds with that espoused previously by Harriss; it is also one which he earlier dismissed as inapplicable to Tamil Nadu because of the over-supply of workers there (Harriss, 1992: 208; 1994: 189–190).

During the mid-1990s, both Corbridge and Harriss were among those in the academy who were drawn to varieties of neo-liberalism: that of Rawls and Roemer in the case of Corbridge (1994), and that of Douglass North in the case of Harriss (Harriss, Hunter and Lewis, 1995). On this point too, it seems, they have changed their minds, and now recognize the compatibility between the process of economic liberalization and Hindu nationalism (p. xix) as well as the fundamental problems raised by neo-liberal theory itself. Their current opposition to market capitalism is clear, for example, not just from their outright rejection of 'the economic arguments of neo-liberalism' (p. 194), but also from the dismissive aside about 'the more anodyne accounts of the state and politics...found in some neoliberal writings on liberalization' (p. 159) and from the categorical assertion in this book that '[w]e have no truck...with the triumphalism that informs Francis Fukayama's account of "the end of history"' (p. 238). Indeed, at times it almost appears to be the case that Corbridge and Harriss (pp. 161ff.) are intent on upholding the veracity of the traditionally more pessimistic views of Marxism about recent Indian development against more optimistic neo-liberal interpretations. This, however, is deceptive, since neither of them would claim to be a Marxist, not do they fully understand even now the theoretical parameters of a Marxist critique.

Both the completeness of this whole about-turn, and a corresponding forgetfulness about the opinions they themselves held previously, however, are evident from the views that Corbridge and Harriss now express about the 'new' farmers' movements and criticize others for not sharing (p. 105):

> Some have described them as being amongst the so-called 'new social movements', issue-based, standing outside regular party politics, capable of mobilizing large numbers of people, and organized to resist and to make demands upon the state rather than take it over. They point to the apparent success of the farmers' movements in mobilizing people from across different rural "classes" and argue that this demonstrates the redundancy

> of the conventional Marxian class sociology. Others, *to whose views we are ourselves inclined*, argue that these movements are vehicles and expressions of the interests of the richer and most commercially dependent cultivators, and that the participation by...poor peasants and landless labourers in actions taken by the farmers' movements has frequently depended upon coercion, and upon ways in which they have in which they have organized around ties of caste and kinship ... across north India, the farmers' movements helped to create conditions which were conducive to the communal...upsurge of the 1990s, and so have assisted in...the growth of Hindutva politics (emphasis added).

It is difficult to believe that the above passage could have been written by the same authors who earlier not only condemned Marxist theory and class analysis, and denied that the 'new' farmers' movements were rich peasant or kulak mobilizations, but also welcomed (and were criticized for endorsing) populist/postmodern concepts of 'difference'/'otherness' that were in many respects not so different from those deployed by Indian nationalism.

This about-face has to be set in turn against the claims now made by Corbridge and Harriss concerning both their own prescience and also the lack of foresight on the part of others. The latter point is made right at the start of the book (p. xviii), where the authors state that the fact that modernity and colonialism were opposed also by Hindu cultural nationalism has been erased or neglected by academic social scientists since, in the view of the co-authors, this kind of discourse 'did not fit well into the models and theorizing of mainstream social science'. Similar kinds of assertion are found at regular intervals throughout the book. Blaming others for 'complacency' (p. 198) in not recognizing the political implications of the underlying epistemology of arguments about the innateness of 'otherness'/'difference', Corbridge and Harriss insist that – unlike them – social science has neglected Hindu cultural nationalism, and thus romanticized natural economy and rural community (pp. 208, 268 note 11). Studies of Indian politics published in the 1990s, they aver, 'made little reference to the BJP or to Hindu nationalism' (p. 111), and '[t]he assertion of Hindu nationalism in the last decade, after a century of struggle in which it seemed for so long and to so many – not least political scientists – to be only of marginal influence' (p. 192). Moreover, the fact that 'the rise of the rich peasantry...has exercised a decisive influence over the development of India since independence' is, they claim, an argument only they – plus Varshney and Pranab Bardhan – have made (pp. 83, 103, 252 note 23). In a similar vein, Corbridge and Harriss insist they were among those who spotted the problematic nature of 'romantic accounts of "community" or a "natural economy"' (pp. 208, 268 note 11). To put it very mildly indeed, these are surprising claims.

The nearest Corbridge and Harriss come to an admission of different views held previously is when they accept that '[t]here is a confessed Whiggishness in our historiography, writing as we do after the success of the Bharatiya Janata Party in the 1998 and 1999 general elections...[t]o those writing on Indian politics in the later 1980s [the re-emergence of the Indian right did not seem] as important as [it does] to us writing ten years later' (p. 249 note 18). However, even this welcome *mea culpa* is limited in scope (confined as it is to the rise of *hindutva*), a fact which disguises the full extent of previous epistemological complicity with positions they now reject or criticize, and thus also of their paradigm shift. Furthermore, if the claim is that everyone writing about the Indian subcontinent missed the political significance of the BJP/rural connection, then clearly this is incorrect. Criticisms of post-structuralism, neo-liberalism, populism, the romanticization of peasant community, and the connection between them all and the rise of the 'new' farmers' movements (= rich peasantry), the ruralization of Indian politics, and the *hindutva* ideology of the BJP were made some time ago in *The Journal of Peasant Studies*, long before the 1998 and 1999 elections (see, for example, Vol. 21, Nos. 3 & 4, April/July 1994; Vol. 22, No. 3, April 1995; and Vol. 24, No. 4, July 1997).

That the authors have changed their minds on an even earlier occasion, in a similarly absolute fashion, about an equally important subject (the link between the Green Revolution and radical grassroots mobilization) is also hinted at, again in the endnotes towards the end of the volume (p. 251 note 4). Because he has tended to follow the prevailing orthodoxy rather to closely and uncritically, therefore, Harriss has shifted his viewpoint constantly and substantially over the years: from some vague form of Marxism initially in the 1970s, to an espousal in the 1990s of agrarian populism and neo-liberalism; now that the latter have been undermined, he appears on the evidence of this book to be drifting back towards something like his original standpoint. Attention is drawn to this fact in order to make a serious point that has application well beyond the book under review. Why should anyone accept an argument that is likely to be replaced as soon as a newer (not better) one gains ground? In short, a difficulty that stems not so much from a change of mind as from the causes of and reasons for this: namely, a willingness to accept ideas merely because they are 'new', without analysing them in any great depth, either epistemologically or politically. One can only hope that if they ever write another book, separately or together, this lesson – an absence of theoretical consistency leads inevitably to analytical contradictions and thus incoherent argument – is one that both Corbridge and Harriss will have taken to heart.

CHAPTER 2

Saints and Sinners*

Of the many and varied kinds of academic text, the festschrift is perhaps the nearest equivalent to a vanity publication. The gulf between on the one hand the public image of academic practice as the virtuous pusuit of knowledge, and on the other the private reality informing much academic practice – venality and opportunism, intellectual appropriation and suppression – is perhaps nowhere so much in evidence. All too often, the festschrift amounts to nothing more than the demonstration of fealty on the part of a group of clients rounded up by an institutionally powerful individual approaching retirement, who – to crown his career and simultaneously to show his peer group in the academy how politically efficacious he continues to be – insists on one last public outpouring of deference. Parallels with feudal power are compelling, not least in the symbolic aspect of ritual humiliation visited by a patron on his retainers (vassals, serfs). Not only are the latter required to abstain from criticism, therefore, but frequently in the course of composing a contribution to the festschrift they are also expected to identify new fields to be included in the many glorious conquests undertaken by their master, thereby not just conserving but extending his myth and its power.

The only really transparent approach to this kind of celebratory volume is that adopted some thirty years ago by Frank Manuel (1972: ix), Professor of History at New York University, who confessed unashamedly that: 'This is my sixtieth birthday; but since the temper of the times is not conducive to the gathering of an appropriate *Festschrift* by my students, I thought I would prepare one for myself'. This declaration of intent to blow his own trumpet, in the absence of others who would agree to blow it for him, is commendably forthright and somewhat rare in academic life. Mercifully, it is usually necessary to participate in such an exercise only once in a lifetime (patrons generally demand undivided loyalty), and in my experience the most revealing aspect of such an occasion can be the number (and identity) of those who decline to contribute, thereby risking the wrath of the dedicatee. One of the more

---

* Reviewed here are: *Thinking Social Science in India: Essays in Honour of Alice Thorner*, edited by Sujata Patel, Jasodhara Bagchi, and Krishna Raj (New Delhi: Sage, 2002), and *Development and Deprivation in Gujarat: In Honour of Jan Breman*, edited by Ghansham Shah, Mario Rutten, and Hein Streefkerk (New Delhi: Sage, 2002). An earlier version appeared in *The Journal of Peasant Studies*, Vol. 30, No. 2 (2003).

enduring clichés circulating in the academy is that – insofar as a festschrift has any meaning – most of those who get one do not deserve this, while many of those whose work actually merits this kind of recognition never receive such a volume.

None of the above considerations apply to Alice Thorner, who – as the contributors to her large and impressive festschrift rightly point out – has not only been an influential voice in the study of rural India but done this in a refreshingly self-effacing manner. In her case, there is actually no reason to be so modest, since together with Daniel Thorner she wrote what remains one of the most important analyses of agrarian transformation in India (Thorner and Thorner, 1962), a text on which all scholars of rural India continue to depend. She has also written what in my view is easily the most perceptive account of the mode of production debate in India (Thorner, 1982), for which all those conducting research on rural India are similarly in her debt. The respect accorded to the dedicatee, and the affection with which Alice Thorner is regarded, are clearly evident from the intellectual distinction of many contributors to the volume, which includes what might be termed a Who's Who of Indian studies (Amiya Kumar Bagchi, Uma Chakravarti, Leela Gulati, Christophe Jaffrelot, Claude Markovits, Joan Mencher, Ashok Mitra, Jaques Pouchepadass, Patricia Uberoi, and Elizabeth Whitcombe). It is perhaps significant that, the immensely useful nature of her scholarly work notwithstanding, she has never occupied high academic office, let alone been awarded a personal chair. This says more about academic life and institutions than it does about Alice Thorner, and her intellectual achievements are not merely not diminished but actually enhanced by virtue of having been done outside the academy.

In many ways, Jan Breman, the dedicatee of the second festschrift under review here, is all the things that Alice Thorner is not: he has held high academic office, he has been a professor, and he has conducted and published large amounts of research on rural India. Such is the extent of his institutional influence that it is possible to observe – with only a little exaggeration – that Gujarat, an area of Western India where he has undertaken most of his fieldwork, will in academic terms forever remain a part of the Dutch colonial empire. Amsterdam University, where he teaches, has been responsible for the production of no less than 11 doctorates on Gujerati society (p. 11). Yet the warmth that pervades the Alice Thorner festschrift is noticeably absent, and the contributors to her volume are far more numerous and distinguished than those contributing to his (only David Hardiman is of an equivalent scholarly rank). The reason for this is, I think, clear: appearances to the contrary notwithstanding, the work of Alice Thorner – an 'outsider' or 'sinner' – has made a greater impact on the study of rural India than the much larger oeuvre of Jan Breman.

It is undeniably the case that some of the research Breman has done borders on the useful. His historical account of the way in which coolie regime operated on the tobacco plantations in the Dutch colony of Sumatra during the second half of the nineteenth century is a courageous piece of work, and one that dispels many of the myths about the benign nature of these productive units (Breman, 1989). His more substantial ethnographic work on Gujarat from the early 1960s onwards, however, is far less valuable, not least because of its longditudinal character. It is this latter element that, ironically, has over time increasingly exposed the shortcomings of – and correspondingly undermined – the claims made by him periodically concerning the process of agrarian transformation taking place there.

The introduction, by Shah and Rutten, is not just embarrassingly uncritical, verging on the sycophantic, but also inaccurate. Language is also a problem. To begin with, the title itself appears incomplete, lacking the word 'essays', and constructions such as '[t]he worst victims were the toiling masses' (p. 10) could be better expressed as 'the victims worst affected were…'. A more serious deficiency, however, is the plethora of vague terms – such as 'toiling masses', 'the poor and labouring underclass', 'the down-and-out, oppressed strata of Gujaratis', etc. (pp. 10, 17, 33) – scattered throughout the contribution by Shah and Rutten. This imprecision is in a sense symptomatic, in that it merely reflects Breman's own lack of clarity concerning the sociological composition of the rural population of Gujarat and the relational forms structuring agricultural production there. Ironically, some of the contributions to the volume reflect, rather neatly and probably unwittingly, the theoretically eclectic nature of Breman's own approach. Thus, for example, the piece on the contradictions of economic growth by Hirway and Terhal (pp. 37–58) is a straightforwardly neo-classical endorsement of the market, albeit qualified by a call for state intervention. Its conclusion – 'Gujarat is at the crossroads today. It is about time that its leadership understood the linkages between economic progress and poverty reduction, and accordingly designed the roles of the market and the state in the development process' (p. 56) – is, unfortunately, essentially meaningless, and naïvely attributes to those who rule Gujarat a lack of understanding about the nature of the poverty/capitalism link. Like Breman himself, one might add.

No contributor to the volume edited by Shah, Rutten and Streefkerk refers to, let alone examines the political implications of, the many and rather obvious epistemological confusions informing Breman's work over the years. The absence of a critical approach to Breman's work – either as a result of not questioning his claims, or not pointing out that findings being presented contradict them – is due to a number of causes. A general decline in the importance attached to debate (see Brass, 2000b: 139–140, note 4), perhaps, plus the fact that few of those who cite his work (particularly that on unfree labour) actually read what he has written, whilst the work of those who have criticized it is not always published or – when published – read. For anyone who has actually studied his books and articles, these confusions and the contradiction to which they give rise are impossible to miss. Some of these confusions stem from theoretical eclecticism: the attempt, for example, to combine the 'dominant caste' framework – a major influence on Breman (pp. 22, 33–34 n3) – with the subsequent concerns informing Marxist development theory.

Others derive from unannounced changes of mind, a difficulty structuring his many contradictory post-1990 arguments about agrarian relations and capitalism in Gujarat. Initially, therefore, Breman insisted that capitalist development was accompanied by proletarianization and a corresponding decline in unfree labour, characterized by him as a feudal relation incompatible with economic growth. Prior to 1990, his view about the capitalism/unfreedom link was that the decrease in bonded labour amounted to a process of depatronization, which deprived workers of a subsistence guarantee, and was for them an undesirable development. The element of unfreedom inherent in patron/client relations was interpreted by him as something that commercially-minded employers attempted to discard but workers fought to retain. In all published writings after 1990, however, he maintains that what is termed 'neo-bondage' and 'the new bondage' is, after all, not just compatible with the accumulation process but actually central to agrarian capitalist growth in Gujarat. Shah and Rutten (pp. 20–21) are clearly unaware of all this when they state that 'Breman stripped the mask of "patronage" off the landowners' and, further, that 'his study of "agrestic serfdom" in the [Gujarat] villages...resulted in his (first) book on the bonded system called hali, and was to lead him to debate the shifting and changing forms of "bondage" that workers found themselves in'. This ignores the fact that Breman did not discuss shifting forms of bondage so much as discard his original position (unfreedom declines as capitalism develops) and replace it with a diametrically opposite one (capitalist producers prefer bonded labour). Precisely why he did this when he did, and so suddenly, has yet to be revealed.

Equally glaring is the contradiction between Breman's enthusiasm for an untheorized concept of empowering grassroots assertiveness, as this encompasses peasant agency in India, and his condemnation as disempowering those struggles based on caste and ethnic identity. That these two forms of grassroots agency might coincide escapes Breman, however, since – just as with the poverty/capitalism link – once again this obvious point seemingly takes him by surprise. Thus we are told by Shah and Rutten (p. 23) that 'Breman was stunned by the "anti-Muslim pogrom" that took place in the city of Surat immediately after the destruction of [the] Babri Masjid in Ayodhya'. Very clearly, in some instances – Gujarat being a case in point – there is an overlap between these two mobilizing discourses, grassroots assertiveness taking the form of caste/ethnic mobilization. As has been noted elsewhere (Brass, 1997; 2000b), this difficulty stems in turn from a failure on Breman's part to understand that grassroots assertiveness has to be differentiated politically. In short, it is necessary to distinguish between wage struggles and trade union organization on the one hand, and the lynching of workers and peasants belonging to a particular caste/ethnic group by workers and peasants from another caste/ethnic group. Both are 'from below' forms of agency, or assertiveness, but each is informed by a very different kind of politics. The inability to differentiate grassroots assertiveness politically suggests that it is incorrect to claim, as do Shah and Rutten (p. 23), that the 'fact that some of the worst perpetrators of violence against Muslims had been migrant workers' is an issue that Breman has 'faced…squarely'.

Nor is it correct to state, as do Shah and Rutten (pp. 22–23), that '[t]he impact of his writings [on debt bondage] have had…in raising the ire of the authorities have been salutary for researchers, activists, legal facilitators and policy makers alike'. Much rather the contrary, Breman's view of patronage as a benign form of 'subsistence guarantee' for the very poor has been invoked by those opposed to the abolition of bonded labour, a point made to me repeatedly during the 1980s by scholars, researchers and activists in India. Even after the 20-point programme, which outlawed unfree relations, therefore, government officials continued to deny the existence of debt bonded labour, on the grounds that workers attached by debt enjoyed better conditions that free wage labour in terms of assured food, employment, clothes, homestead land, and credit (Das, 1979: 8–9).

It comes as no surprise, therefore, that all the flaws which pervade Breman's own work on agrarian relations are found also in most of the contributions to this volume. Thus the examination by Uma Kothari (pp. 115–132) of the changing role of female agricultural labour in South Gujarat from the 1960s to the 1980s reproduces many of the problematic claims made by Breman himself. Among these are the conflation of labour assertiveness and proletarianization, that patronage in the past was 'based on mutual respect', and that agricultural workers regret the loss of 'guaranteed regular employment' associated with attached labour (pp. 122, 125). Because Halpati landless rural workers have rejected permanent employment based on debt bondage as servile, and are consequently no longer deferential to landowning Patidars, the latter have turned increasingly to other kinds of labour: seasonal and/or casual labour, composed of local women and migrants (pp. 116–117, 119–120). Like Breman, Kothari regards this as evidence for a process of worker emancipation and gender empowerment, arguing that local female labour employed on a casual basis is free since it is not now 'at the beck and call of employers' (p. 129). The difficulties posed for claims about emancipation/empowerment by the fact that women still work for long hours in the fields for low wages is explained away by reference to the presence of 'prevailing social customs' which prevent them from taking better-paid jobs available locally in growing industrial enterprises, plus the withdrawal of patronage (pp. 121, 124, 125). Not only are such 'explanations' unpersuasive, but the reasons for this are also clear.

As she differentiates employment in terms of duration only, and not free/unfree relations, Kothari (pp. 119–120) like Breman mistakenly assumes that only permanent labour is unfree, and that casual workers – both local and migrant – are by definition free. Again like Breman, she ascribes free labour to assertiveness on the part of rural workers who, she observes, 'no longer want to be tied [labour]' and 'do not feel bound to one farmer' (pp. 127, 128). What Kothari forgets, however, is that not wanting to be – or not feeling oneself to be – unfree is not the same as not actually being unfree. Nor does she consider that non-permanent categories of worker – local female and migrant – may also be unfree, as much research in India suggests they are. Indeed, she contradicts herself when noting that in some 'households all members may be "tied" to a particular landholding household whereby men work as daily agricultural labourers and women and children as domestic labourers,' and further that Halpati female workers 'have access to loans in times of need', an arrangement which hints at the continued presence of debt bondage (pp. 125, 127). Crucially, she ignores the fact that the bonding of workers is frequently a response to assertiveness on the part of agricultural labourers, unfreedom being the way in which employers reimpose control/discipline in the agrarian labour process.

Adopting a different strategy, Streefkerk (pp. 133–149) manages to chart the growth of workforce casualisation occuring in South Gujarat over the past three decades without mentioning that his analysis contradicts the claims made by Breman about the same process. Whereas in the recent past Breman (1999a: 297) has argued that the trend towards casualization *improved* the bargaining power and job security of permanent workers, Streefkerk (pp. 138ff.) by contrast shows the opposite to be the case. The latter argues that two thirds of the workforce is now composed of 'temperwali' or contract workers, and that capitalist enterprises employed temporary workers in order to *undermine* the bargaining power (and thus cheapen the cost) of unionized permanent workers. Furthermore, such labour is now increasing supplied to capitalist enterprises by contractors, who not only 'keep the difference between what they really pay the workers and the money reimbursed by the company' but also extend loans to their workers, over whom they 'maintain a powerful grip' (pp. 140–142). This finding confirms the accuracy of the claim (Brass, 2000b), denied by Breman, that what is occurring is not proletarianization so much as workforce restructuring involving deproletarianization. Instead of pointing this out, however, Streefkerk erroneously conveys the impression that his findings support Breman's argument.

We are informed constantly about Breman's concern at how badly off the rural poor are in the midst of an economically prosperous Gujarat, how much he cares about the poor, 'his commitment to the well-being of the downtrodden', and how he was 'shocked by [their] abject poverty and…wretched indigence' (pp. 11, 17, 20), sentiments which are undoubtedly true. Although no one can doubt the sincerity of Breman's concern, two unasked questions are nevertheless inescapable: should anyone who has conducted research in India really be surprised at the poverty/capitalism connection, and is well-meant concern by itself enough? The answer to both these questions is rather obviously no, not least because rural poverty and exploitation has after all followed on a fairly regular basis the spread of capitalism throughout the so-called Third World. In the end Breman's commendable indignation about the plight of the rural poor in Gujarat possesses little impact and less effect, and will remain so unless it is harnessed to a theoretically rigorous – and thus an equally powerful – analytical framework purged of eclecticism and contradiction. Simply to berate capitalism for being exploitative is to do nothing more than acknowledge the obvious.

CHAPTER 3

Seeing Ghosts*

That two hundred years have passed since the legislative abolition of the transatlantic slave trade by Parliament has been marked in the UK in a number of ways, some predictable, others less so. First, by a year-long celebration of this event as the outcome of a virtuous and selfless moral crusade conducted by a benign British ruling class (it wasn't). Second, by the belated recognition that unfree labour has not been eradicated, but still persists (it does). And third, by an unseemly rush on the part of some writers and academics to jump on the bandwagon, and claim in media articles or interviews that the contemporary presence of unfree labour was something they themselves had recognized all along (they haven't). Thus far, however, the most important, the most eloquent, and certainly the most relevant contribution to this anniversary is a depressing but tellingly brilliant film directed by Nick Broomfield, *Ghosts*.[1]

Although fictional, *Ghosts* is based on an episode that occurred in February 2004 on the northwestern coast of England: the death in Morecambe Bay of 23 illegal Chinese immigrants who were drowned on a single night by the incoming tide as they were picking cockles. The term 'ghosts' has a double meaning: the way in which Chinese immigrants describe non-Chinese 'otherness', it also refers to the fact the immigrants themselves are invisible, 'not-seen' and thus also 'other'. Following one of the illegal workers – played superbly by Ai Qin Lin – from her parental home in rural Fujian, China, to London, then Norfolk and finally Morecambe Bay, it is the portrayal on film of an episode confirming what the persistence of unfree labour actually entails. In this lies the achievement not just of its director, Nick Broomfield, but also of the actors (excellent, moving and utterly convincing performances from Ai Qin Lin, Zhe Wei and Zhan Yu) and the producers/distributors (Channel 4 and Tartan Films). *Ghosts* is firmly in the same political tradition as films like *Salt of the Earth* (1954), directed by Herbert Biberman, *Culloden* (1964) and *The War*

* Reviewed here is *Ghosts*, a film directed by Nick Broomfield; scripted by Jez Lewis and Nick Broomfield; with Ai Qin Lin, Zhe Wei and Zhan Yu. Produced/distributed by Channel 4 and Tartan Films, 2006. Running time: 96 minutes. An earlier version appeared in *The Journal of Peasant Studies*, Vol. 34, No. 2 (2007).

1 It was seen by the reviewer at the local arthouse cinema in Richmond-upon-Thames, where – encouragingly – the audience was larger than is usually the case for this kind of film.

Game (1965), both directed by Peter Watkin, and *In Search of Famine* (1982), directed by Mrinal Sen.[2] There can be no higher praise than that.

Not the least impressive aspect of the film is the way in which the Chinese immigrant workers are depicted. Ai Qin is forced to migrate in order to pay for the schooling of her young son; this she does reluctantly, in the knowledge that she will as a result miss much of his childhood. Migrants are portrayed as ordinary people, like us, who do the same kind of things as we do – cycling with a child in a seat on the back of the bike, joining in games with children in the school playground – and have the same kind of hopes and fears. It would have been easy to sentimentalise their story, by imbuing it with an heroic veneer, but this Broomfield does not do.[3] It is precisely by showing their 'ordinariness' that he succeeds in bridging the ideological gulf between the migrant-as-other and the selfhood of the film audience. If they are no different from us, we are forced to ask, why are they treated in this way? If they can be treated like this, moreover, can we not also be?

The systemic link between debt, coercion and control over labour-power is manifest throughout, a pervasive aspect of what is euphemistically termed 'the migrant experience'.[4] The latter is punctuated by violence inflicted on Chinese workers, from the beginning to the end of their story. When the immigrants arrive in London, therefore, they are beaten by the Snakeheads waiting for them. These are moneylending gangsters who have financed the six-month journey, and the workers as a result owe them large sums of money. Migrants are forcibly instructed to phone home and confirm their arrival, so that their families in China release the next tranche of debt repayment. Subsequently, a worker who cannot make a debt repayment that falls due is told that if it is not made members of his family will be killed. The house where the immigrants live is the object of a violent raid by the police, after which neighbours break into the house, daubing the wall with racist graffiti and emptying their rubbish bins

2 Like *Ghosts*, each of these films has addressed in a fictional manner a politically controversial issue: the struggle by Mexican Americans on strike; the battlefield slaughter of the Scots during the Jacobite uprising; the impact of martial law following a nuclear attack on the UK; and the 1943 Bengal famine.

3 Although the Chinese immigrants are clearly aware of the reasons for their exploitation, and also object to this, neither of these facts add up to the kind of 'empowering' quotidian agency that exponents of the 'everyday forms of resistance' framework insist is always present in such contexts.

4 Apart from the central episode at Morecambe Bay, many of the other events depicted in *Ghosts* are corroborated in a special report based on research by Hsiao-Hung Pai, 'Inside the grim world of the gangmasters', *The Guardian* (London), 27 March 2004. See also her 'Another Morecambe Bay is waiting to happen', *The Guardian* (London), 28 March 2006.

over the kitchen floor. Finally, when picking cockles, the Chinese immigrants are attacked by other cockle-pickers, locals on whose 'turf' the Chinese are working.

Those who recruit the immigrants in China promise good pay and conditions, telling them that they will earn £250 per week and showing prospective migrants photos of previous Chinese workers who made this journey now standing in front of large and new cars. Once in England, a familiar myth is continuously asserted: migrants are told by the gangmaster that they, too, will one day own a house and live comfortably. Needless to say, the reality is somewhat different: squalid living conditions in over-priced and over-crowded accommodation, coupled with poor working conditions for long hours and low pay.[5] Travelling from London to rural Norfolk, Ai Qin and the other Chinese immigrants work first in a meat processing factory, preparing chickens for supermarkets, and then in the fields, harvesting spring onions and apples, also destined for supermarkets.

The workers are routinely deceived, defrauded and misled by all those they encounter: personnel in labour exchanges have to be bribed in order to provide information about employment; the labour contractor cheats them, holding back large portions of his workers' pay; and the landlord is interested only in how many rent-paying immigrants he can cram into his house. Along with the other labourers in the gang, Ai Qin works 14 hour shifts for a weekly payment of only £100, it being claimed that 44% of her wage held back is deducted 'for tax'. When she complains, the gangmaster shouts back at her that 'you are nothing, an illegal'.[6] These are the conditions to which English politicians, capitalists

5 That the object of the gangmaster system is capitalist restructuring, or the replacement of free labour by unfree – and thus cheaper and more easily controlled – workers so as to enhance profitability, is finally being recognized. Hence the following: 'Ensuring the influx of foreign labour is not used to undercut the wages of domestic employees is another key challenge. The Low Pay Commission's last annual report expressed concerns that the growing use of migrant workers was being used by unscrupulous employers to circumvent the minimum wage'. See 'Immigration drives an economic revival', *The Guardian* (London), 21 March 2007. Even the normally conservative members of the Bank of England monetary policy committee now accept that resort by employers to such low wage unfree workers is 'limiting the bargaining power of labour' in other sectors of the economy – see 'wage claims kept low by fear of foreign workers, says MPC member', *The Guardian* (London), 31 May 2007 – which is precisely what capitalist restructuring is designed to do.

6 Even when official complaints *are* made, nothing happens. Despite some 45,000 investigations and 19,000 complaints from the public about employer non-compliance with UK minimum wage legislation, there has only been one criminal prosecution. According to the General Secretary of the Transport and General Workers Union, 'it is common knowledge

and central bankers refer when they aver proudly that migrant workers keep wages and interest rates low, thereby increasing the profitability of British manufacturing industry.[7]

Among the many images that stay in the memory long after the film has ended are three in particular, all at Morecambe. First, the immigrants travelling resignedly across the sands out to a distant and more dangerous area to gather cockles at night, where they have been forced to go by a combination of the low pay rates (they have to collect more cockles) and racist attacks by locals (preventing them from working in safer areas nearer the shore). Second, the ominous silence of the incoming tide: as darkness falls it rushes in, covering their implements of production – a bucket and rake – lying on the sand, as the tired Chinese workers rest in their van unaware of what is happening around them. And third, the final image of them alive: in the night and stranded on top of their van, now almost covered by the sea; the latter is visually and symbolically the darkest, and also the most distressing, of the whole film.

However, *Ghosts* is not without humour and irony. Thus the process of migration is depicted in the style of 1940s B movies, which illustrated international travel by means of a moving line traced across a map, a device recreated by Spielberg in the films *Raiders of the Lost Ark* (1981) and *Indiana Jones and the Last Crusade* (1989). This is a way of signalling travel-as-an-exciting-foreign-adventure, which in *Ghosts* it is, but not in quite the same benign way as presented by Spielberg. In a similar vein, the pastoral opening scenes in Fujian province, where migration starts, contrast absolutely with a grey and drab

that there are all too many employers who take advantage of the flexible-labour market to try and avoid paying the minimum wage. The lack of prosecutions suggests that they are getting away with it.' See 'Deluge of complaints on minimum wage abuse', *The Sunday Times Business Section*, 29 April, 2007.

7 See, for example, 'Migrants hold down inflation, says governor', *The Guardian* (London), 14 June 2005; and 'Migrants have lifted the economy, says study', *The Guardian* (London), 27 February 2007. According other accounts – 'The PR tycoon, a private dinner and PM's meeting with Euro lobby group', *The Observer* (London), 17 September 2006, and 'Shortage of pickers may hit strawberry crop', *The Guardian* (London), 28 May 2007 – businessmen and the National Farmers' Union are lobbying for open access by East European workers to UK markets, thereby providing capitalist producers with an expanding industrial reserve army of labour. Invoking *laissez faire* principles, the house journal of UK capitalism makes no secret of the fact that the object of expanding the reserve army of labour composed of (unfree) workers who are cheap is to enhance profits by depressing wages: '...it must be remembered that the case for free immigration is primarily one of liberty. Employers should be free to hire whom they want...[i]f a government doesn't respect these basic liberties, isn't it likely to violate investors' freedoms too?...[s]o it's clear that free immigration is a good thing for the economy and the stock market... Lower wages mean lower prices and lower interest rates...', etc., etc., *Investors Chronicle*, 27 April to 3 May, 2007.

England, where it ends, neatly reversing the myth which informs the migrant experience (fleeing poverty, hopelessness and oppression to a land of freedom, opportunity, riches and plenty). When Ai Qin and another Chinese worker go shopping for food in a local supermarket, they find that they cannot afford to purchase the expensively priced spring onions on sale there, the very same ones they had picked in the fields earlier.

The two criticisms which can be made of the film are minor, and do not detract from its quality and political importance. The first concerns a loose end not tied up, while the second is seemingly a concession to a redemptive conclusion. Thus a notable absence is the specifically English dimension of the gangmaster system portrayed in *Ghosts*.[8] The result is that those who purchase the cockles harvested by the Chinese immigrants, and who in a crucial sense profit from and ensure the reproduction of this form of exploitation, remain literally invisible (= 'ghosts'); they are thus not seen to be part of the problem.[9] That the main character, Ai Qin, is rescued from drowning, and as the only survivor manages to return to her family and child in China, also seems a partial concession to the necessity of a film – even about this kind of subject – having to have a 'happy ending'.

Although *Ghosts* is a masterpiece, a film that should be seen by everyone, and certainly anyone with an interest in the form taken by labour regimes in a twenty-first century capitalist agriculture, it should be seen especially by two categories of academic. One is composed of neoclassical economists, who insist – wrongly – that in a capitalist system all rural migration is not only freely chosen by its subject, but also non-coercive and empowering for workers involved. The other consists of exponents of the semi-feudal thesis, who insist similarly – and also wrongly – that unfree relations of production are incompatible with capitalism, and that where these are encountered, coercion is either an indicator of a non-capitalist labour process (when its coercive aspect is irrefutable) or not coercion at all, merely an incidental and unimportant dimension of what is in reality free wage labour. For those in each of these categories, a viewing of *Ghosts* should be made compulsory, perhaps even in the manner of Alex DeLarge in Kubrick's film *Clockwork Orange*.

---

8 On this, see House of Commons Environment, Food and Rural Affairs Committee (2003) and Brass (2004).

9 This omission may be due to the fact that, hitherto, English courts have convicted only 'foreign' gangmasters. See, for example, 'Gangmaster convicted over "slave" workers', *The Guardian* (London), 4 February 2005; 'Gangmaster denies he led cocklers', *The Guardian* (London), 20 September 2005; and 'I got calls from people in the sea. The tide was coming up', *The Guardian* (London), 25 March 2006. The gangmasters in question were Ukranian and Chinese nationals.

CHAPTER 4

Brief Encounters with Class*

In his first-ever monograph, Henry Bernstein attempts to trace and explain the world-wide history of agrarian change in just 123 pages (excluding glossary). The claims made for this book are not exactly modest. A 'state-of-the-art...small book on a big subject', it is said to be of 'world-class quality' that 'sets the tone and raises the bar' (pp. vii, xi–xii). Its object is no less than to indicate 'what are the current issues and debates [and] who are the key scholars/thinkers'. As is so often the case, there is an inverse proportion between such grandiloquence and the analysis which follows. Bernstein's problems are twofold: many issues/contexts/periods are covered far too briefly, and what he does manage to cover is invariably misinterpreted.

Allotted space is not used wisely, since a number of definitions that appear in the text are repeated twice, once at the end of a chapter and again in the glossary; in effect, appearing thrice. In a longish book this repetition need not necessarily be a problem; in a short one, it is. Constraints on space mean that, as the book proceeds, abbreviated lists of events/episodes (for example, land reforms on pp. 98–99) become the norm, a point Bernstein concedes (p. 84). Victims of this simplifying procedure include historical trajectories and conceptual elaborations.

A mini-history of European colonial expansion in the seventeenth and eighteenth centuries is followed swiftly by an equally truncated version of industrial capitalism and imperialism over the nineteenth and twentieth centuries (pp. 40–45). Yet another periodization of the same history emerges subsequently, which merely adds to the difficulty (pp. 87–88). In a similar vein, 'new' food regimes come and go with ever-increasing rapidity (pp. 66ff., 81ff.), their 'moments' and distinctiveness shrinking along with the reasons for their being categorized as such.

Much the same is true of theory. Qualification is piled upon qualification (see the discussion on class, Chapter 7), until little remains of the original concept. Thus the Table setting out patterns in colonial labour regimes descends into confusion as the accompanying text lists numerous exceptions to its categories (pp. 54–55), the unresolved problem being rounded off by what becomes a familiar refrain ('I come back to this later'). These problems arising

* Reviewed here is *Class Dynamics of Agrarian Change*, by Henry Bernstein (Halifax NS, Fernwood Publishing, 2010). An earlier version appeared in *Capital & Class*, Vol. 35, No. 2 (2011).

from space constraints are compounded by the misleading way issues covered are presented.

Bernstein misunderstands the dynamic and significance of unfree labour, because his interpretation of agrarian relations is indistinguishable from that of Banaji (pp. 32,ff., 50, 55, 119), Maintaining that there is no such thing as unfree labour, Banaji (2003) conceptualizes all historical working arrangements simply as 'disguised' wage-labour that is contractually free. This ignores the fact that unfree workers get paid and also appear in the labour market, but not as sellers of their own commodity. By abolishing the free/unfree labour distinction, therefore, Banaji aligns himself with anti-Marxist theory in general, and neoclassical economic historiography in particular (Brass, 2003a).

Banaji's views about what is and what is not Marxist theory should be treated with caution, but the book omits to do so. Instead, Bernstein (pp. 26–27) argues incorrectly that Marx regarded *all* social relations of production – capitalist and non-capitalist alike – as unfree, because the alternative to the free sale of labour-power is starvation (= no choice). However, the choice Marx had in mind was different: not between the free sale of labour-power and starvation, but the ability of a worker who is free to sell his/her commodity to the highest bidder. Choosing between better-paid and less-well-paid jobs, and thus between employers – and consequently the free/unfree distinction – is central to Marxist interpretations of class formation/struggle/ consciousness.

Difficulties conceptualizing class derive in turn from the fact that Bernstein's approach has been, and remains at heart, an agrarian populist one (see review essay 11, this volume). An unsuccessful attempt to reconcile Lenin's model of class differentiation of the peasantry (into rich, middle and poor strata) with his own view about petty commodity production as 'a contradictory unity of class places' (pp. 103ff.) cannot disguise the peasant essentialism underlying this approach. Bernstein seemingly wants to retain smallholding as a theoretical carapace, its class differences notwithstanding.

This enables him to include peasant family farmers within his all-inclusive sociological category ('classes of labour') of those uniformly exploited by and thus opposed to capital. What Bernstein overlooks is that equating peasant 'self-exploitation' advanced by the populist Chayanov with the Marxist 'peasant persistence' argument of Kautsky (p. 94) misses the point that the latter maintained rural subjects were exploited as *workers*, whilst the former – like Bernstein himself – insists they are exploited as *farmers*.

The book is also marred by curious silences. A decade ago Bernstein complained that a book synthesizing debate about peasants had failed to cite a single article from *The Journal of Peasant Studies*. Yet now he himself does precisely the same, making no reference to anything in that journal over the years

2000–2008, despite the fact that during that period it published important special issues on peasants in present-day Russia, Latin America, China and Mexico. Nor is there any reference by him to the special issue in that journal on the new farmers' movements in India, despite a lengthy description in Bernstein's own book of this very mobilization (pp. 121–122).

Similarly absent is any reference to the debate which has had the most far-reaching impact on the recent study of agrarian change: the postmodern 'cultural turn' that was greeted with enthusiasm by many of those writing about Third World development, the result being a stampede to replace Marxist theory and concepts such as class disempowerment with notions of subaltern empowerment. The irony is that Bernstein's 'classes of labour' (pp. 110ff.) includes *de facto* workers who – because they still have access to smallholdings – continue to regard themselves as peasant proprietors, or the cultural identity postmodernism depicts as empowering.

Not the least significant of these silences is the political void at the centre of Bernstein's narrative: a failure theoretically to link class formation/struggle and agrarian transition to a socialist outcome, a connection made historically (and currently) by all Marxist analyses. Since this absence is probably an effect of his agrarian populist approach, those wishing to understand the link between socialist politics, peasant differentiation and the dynamics of agrarian change should turn once again to the classic Marxist analyses of these issues, as outlined in the work of Lenin, Kautsky and Trotsky.

CHAPTER 5

Interns Interned*

Few these days need convincing as to just how 'feral' neoliberalism has become. Having first undermined the ability to oppose politically (anti-strike legislation, union busting, employment outsourcing, the fall of communism, the rise of 'New Labour') and ideologically (the promotion of vacuous 'celebrity', the 'cultural turn' displacing Marxist analysis), capital then proceeded to asset-strip entire nations (privatisation, economic crisis in the euro zone). Resources that would otherwise be available for investment in education, health, infrastructure, public-sector jobs or welfare programmes were accordingly diverted to off-shore tax havens. Any pretence at media objectivity about such developments has long-since vanished, as craven interviewers privilege the opinions of 'the markets' (bankers, oligarchs, hedge-fund managers, speculators and financiers), grovelling before multi-millionaire CEOs who advocate yet more deregulation and austerity.

A 'feral' aspect of this race to the bottom that is perhaps not as well known concerns the impact on capitalist social relations of production. That neoliberalism entails the rise of gender-specific part-time working is not disputed; less commonplace is information about other working arrangements (sweatshops, unfreedom) affecting different categories of labour (migrants, youth). For this reason alone, this empirically useful but theoretically flawed book by Ross Perlin is a welcome addition to our knowledge of the way capitalism is transforming its workforce.

Interns are temporary unpaid or low-paid young workers, mostly college students, who toil for long hours under coercive forms of control (pp. 16–17, 112, 141). Perlin charts the rise of internships, as capitalist enterprises in the US and Europe increasingly replace full-time employees (permanent, unionised, well-paid) with this kind of cheap, short-term contract labour. By insisting on academic credits gained through work experience, universities and colleges fuel the endless supply of student workers (pp. 83ff., 93). From paying for a placement via tuition fees, a student is now expected to have to bid against others to get one, as companies auction their internships (pp. 145ff.). Despite a rhetoric of empowerment (acquiring skills, exercising autonomy, a step

---

* Reviewed here is *Intern Nation: How to Earn Nothing and Learn Little in the Brave New Economy*, by Ross Perlin (London, Verso, 2011). An earlier version appeared in *Capital & Class*, Vol. 36, No. 2 (2012).

towards well-paid permanent employment), interns do no more than menial tasks, receive little or no payment, and rarely obtain full-time jobs (pp. 23–24, 29, 70, 91).

The weaknesses of the book are theoretical and political: the attempt by Perlin both to account for the rise of internship, and to suggest a solution. Although exploitation and cost-cutting are acknowledged, unpaid internship tends to be analysed economically in terms of psychologistic factors ('a lack of respect') or human capital (pp. 126–127, 129). Perlin sees internship as a deviation from the capitalist norm, and locates remedies within capitalism itself. Internship is described variously as a 'system that has gone off the rails', an 'explosion gone haywire', an 'unfair advantage [that] distorts markets', the result being a 'manipulated marketplace' (pp. xvi, 4, 62, 140). Because internships 'don't follow the normal dynamics of the rest of the job market', Perlin (p. 141) observes, nothing is 'less natural than patterns of supply and demand in the internship marketplace'.

Eschewing a class-struggle approach, Perlin is baffled by the fact that, despite its origins in academia, researchers and policy-makers remain silent about internship or look the other way (pp. xiii, 29), a view that overlooks a rather obvious cause: the long history of complicity by many senior academics with similarly exploitative working arrangements (= research assistants). His solution – 'to restore a fair, competitive system' by means of enforcing existing laws (pp. 63, 72, 78) – is based on the mistaken view that a benign capitalism can be recuperated.

Having noted that collective bargaining, healthcare and pensions were outcomes of full-time, well-paid jobs during the Keynesian era, Perlin then argues that 'the push for flexibility' – that is, part-time/temporary/casual employment – came from the workers themselves, part of the 1970s 'revolt against work' (pp. 37ff.). This is a somewhat idealised view: whilst it is true that benefits accrued from Keynesianism, the latter was itself a response to increased worker militancy after 1945. It was this process of from-below class struggle – unionisation, strikes, higher actual/social wage – that elicited the capitalist response: casual jobs, part-time employment, outsourcing, decentralisation and deregulation. Restructuring of the labour process, or the *de*composition of the existing workforce and its *re*composition – class struggle as waged from above, in short. *This* is the dynamic informing the 'explosion' not just in internships, which Perlin seeks to explain, but also in kindred relational forms (see Brass, 1999; 2011a).

Ironically, the importance of class struggle is clear from case studies Perlin himself documents. Thus the 1938 Fair Labour Standards Act, which outlawed child labour and established a minimum wage and overtime pay, was circumvented in 1947 by the exemption of trainees from its provisions (pp. 64ff.). This exemption was subsequently used by employers to justify not paying interns the minimum wage, or for over-time (p. 72). Similarly, during the 1980s, Disney World used cheap interns to replace well-paid full-time workers, in the process undermining trade union organisation established throughout Florida since the 1960s (pp. 10–11).

Late in 2011, this from-above class struggle was given a further impetus, as Newt Gingrich, a contender for the Republican presidential nomination in the USA, advocated repealing laws prohibiting the employment of child workers, thereby making available to capital the labour-power of children from poor families. This is not, as some imagine, travelling back to the 18th century, but rather travelling forwards: evidence for the maturity, not the backwardness, of 21st-century capitalism. Lip-service to the contrary notwithstanding, therefore, the capitalist state has no intention of doing much about internship, because it contributes to profitability.

The only way of eradicating such relations is to address the root cause of internship, since the latter is itself no more than the effect of increasing levels of class struggle and capitalist competition as globalisation spreads. One has to eliminate the reason why such work arrangements are reproduced in the first place (capitalism), an approach that in turn requires making clear what is to be put in its place (socialism). Legal enforcement, favoured by Perlin, derives from the possibility of a return to a steady-state 'benign'/'caring' capitalism, a golden age from which neoliberalism can be eternally banished. It can't, since the two are connected, and it is just a question of time before one turns into the other.

CHAPTER 6

Marxist Academics and Liberal Hypocrisy*

Although no socialist requires persuading as to the unhappy marriage between Marxism and academia, the details that emerge from this illuminating and important book are nevertheless truly shocking. The story Caute tells concerns an episode in the early 1960s, when Isaiah Berlin, a self-proclaimed liberal academic, not only blocked the appointment of Isaac Deutscher, a revolutionary Marxist intellectual, to a Chair at Sussex University, but then lied about this, telling everyone – including Tamara Deutscher (and others, see Essay 18 in this volume) – that he had done no such thing (pp. 275ff.).

Caute gives this episode its full and proper context (pp. 7–18, 19–35). The social, political and ideological differences between each protagonist could not have been greater. From a wealthy Russian family that fled the 1917 revolution, Berlin had a visceral hatred of communism; he occupied senior academic posts throughout his life, not only dabbling in university politics and gossip but also advising the great and the good on both sides of the Atlantic. Producing the occasional slim tome, Berlin was honoured by the British establishment, and lived comfortably to a ripe old age.

By contrast, Deutscher was a member of the outlawed Polish Communist Party, lost many family members in the Holocaust, and escaped the Nazis by fleeing to England, where he eked out a living as a journalist. The latter notwithstanding, Deutscher managed to write – among many other things – pathbreaking studies of Sino-Soviet politics, of Stalinism, and a brilliant trilogy on Trotskyism. A study of Leninism remained unfinished, due to his early death and the denial of an academic post that would have enabled him to complete it. As Caute (p. 34) notes, 'Deutscher's oeuvre was formidable: it is a remarkable record for a man working alone, without a university faculty to help him in his research and thinking'.

Significantly, the antipathy Berlin felt toward Deutscher was due not just to their political differences but also to the fact that the latter had critically reviewed a book by the former. According to Caute, 'without doubt this was the killer event in Berlin's attitude to Deutscher', the result being that Deutscher

---

* A review of *Isaac and Isaiah: The Covert Punishment of a Cold War Heretic*, by David Caute (New Haven: Yale University Press, 2013). An earlier version appeared in *Science & Society*, Vol. 78, No. 4 (2014). Appended here is a Postscript detailing aspects not recorded in the original review.

was excluded not just from the Sussex job but also from journals and conferences to which Berlin had a connection (pp. 64, 88). Having condemned Deutscher in a private and confidential letter to the Vice-Chancellor as 'the only man whose presence in the same academic community as myself I should find morally intolerable', Berlin then falsely told Tamara that 'it would have been a betrayal of every intellectual value in which I believe if I had allowed this to sway my judgment consciously in judging his fitness for an academic post' (pp. 285–286).

That academia has always been full of such hypocrisy is unsurprising, as is the fact that the main victims have been radicals. Among those who did not compromise politically, and consequently were denied posts in British universities over the second half of the twentieth century was George Rudé, like Deutscher a Marxist, excluded by Alfred Cobban who, like Berlin, was a scion of liberalism and an advocate of intellectual pluralism. These academic exclusions on political grounds, however, are only the best-known and most notorious instances of what was and remains a common practice. University disapproval of radical academics often takes more subtle forms, less absolute than exclusion but with palpable material outcomes for those affected. Cambridge did not send undergraduate students to be supervised by Maurice Dobb because he was a Marxist economist, and – his intellectual achievements and impressive publications record notwithstanding – he was promoted to a Readership much later than is usual in such cases, only when he was close to retirement.[1]

Other, not as well-known but none-the-less similar cases in different contexts involved scholars such as E.H. Carr, Daniel Thorner, David Abraham and Jack Stauder. My own case fits this pattern. Whilst teaching at Cambridge during the 1990s, I was told by the head of the department that my politics ran the risk of my being labelled a 'troublemaker' (his word) by others in the same faculty, which underlines the point being made here. Namely, that Marxists inside the academy who persist with their political views imperil thereby their employment prospects. Sure enough, in my case this is what happened, when I applied as an internal candidate for a tenured post at Cambridge, the teaching of which I had been undertaking proficiently for five years.

1 The introduction (Hobsbawm, 1969: 1, 8) to his festschrift observes both that the fact he held a university post at the same time as being a Marxist made Dobb a rare and 'virtually unique species in British academic life', and that '[t]here can be no doubt that his [academic] career has suffered from his long association both with Marxism and with the Communist Party.'

Encouraged to apply by a senior academic, I asked him to be my referee, which he agreed to do. My candidacy was rejected at the shortlisting stage, but it was not until later that I found out why. Just as Berlin had done in the case of Deutscher, so the reference written for me by the academic in question was an 'annihilatingly hostile' one, a straightforward attack on my politics, describing my work as 'aridly Marxist...with no space for culture'. Again like the Berlin/Deutscher episode, an exclusionary act effected simply on political grounds was something the referee himself had condemned earlier. And yet again like the Berlin/Deutscher affair, it was a self-professed liberal academic who, having expressed strong disapproval of exclusionary acts on the grounds of a different politics, proceeded to do this very thing.

Like most other ruling class institutions, universities survive by periodically announcing that they have changed fundamentally so as to bring them into line with current progressive objectives. However, as accounts that emanate periodically from those who have lectured within academia underline, such announcements are at best premature and at worst untrue. Among the progressive objectives frequently claimed to have been accomplished is that holding revolutionary socialist views is no longer a hindrance to academic employment or promotion. That such political tolerance and pluralism are now accepted – let alone practiced – within academia is an enduring and self-serving myth, a point demonstrated by the Berlin/Deutscher affair.

Academics generally have had an easy ride where public esteem and perception are concerned. They occupy a position on a spectrum at one end of which are positioned journalism and public relations, whose practitioners are widely recognized as purveyors of opinions favourable to the interests of press barons or corporations who pay their wages or salaries. Academics, by contrast, tend to be placed at the virtuous end of the same spectrum, and consequently are still regarded by many as engaged in searches for truth, a disinterested endeavour unconnected with pecuniary gain or institutional advancement.[2] For anyone who still thinks of the capitalist university as a politically neutral or even a benign institution, therefore, Caute's book serves as a cautionary tale; for those who know otherwise, it confirms them in their belief.

2 They are perceived as being, in the words of Conor Cruise O'Brien (1969: 1), 'historically the most deeply committed to liberal values, including the primacy of the unrestrained pursuit and promulgation of truth.' As Chomsky (1969) has argued, however, there is a long history showing the opposite to be the case: that in terms of venality and duplicity, the majority of academics are in fact no different from their journalistic and public relations counterparts.

Postscript

It is now possible to supply more of the background to the episode referred to briefly in the above review, about what happened when in 1993 I applied as an internal candidate for a tenured Development Studies post in the Social and Political Sciences Faculty at Cambridge. The senior academic who, as my referee, wrote that hostile reference attacking my politics, was the late Geoffrey Hawthorn, then a Reader in Sociology and Politics in the same Faculty, to whose course I had contributed substantially in terms of teaching and tutorials.[3] He not only encouraged me to apply for the post, but unambiguously undertook to support my application ('I can give you my word that were you to decide that you were on a hiding to nothing in continuing to do so much supervising for Paper 17, and to withdraw that work, it would not in any way affect any support...I would give you for a post here', letter to me dated 3/11/1992). In describing my ideas as having 'no space for culture', Hawthorn ignored the obvious fact that most, if not all, of my published work at that point was about culture.[4]

Most significantly, although my politics were not the same as his, he had not raised this political difference as 'a problem' before my application for the Development Studies post at Cambridge, much rather the contrary.[5] Again like the Berlin/Deutscher episode, Hawthorn had earlier condemned academic exclusion on political grounds, observing in a letter to me dated 21/6/1992 that '[i]n my long experience of examining for the Tripos...across a wide range of papers – including ones that are politically more charged than ours – I have never [encountered political bias]. One often reads scripts that are not, politically, to one's taste; but no examiner that I've known would mark anyone down

3 Revealing the identity of the person who wrote the hostile reference serves a twofold purpose. It not only confirms that others in the same Faculty were not responsible for what happened, but also underlines the disparity between what was done on this occasion by my referee and the efforts on my behalf undertaken by Bill Epstein (see the Postscript to essay 14 in this volume). Although neither Epstein nor Hawthorn shared my political views, their actions could not have been more different: Epstein said nothing publicly, but nevertheless worked tirelessly and successfully behind the scenes to secure the return of my fieldwork notebooks; Hawthorn by contrast professed support for my candidacy, and then strongly opposed this in the privacy of the selection committee.

4 What he meant by making this ludicrous claim was not that I ignored culture (I don't) but that my approach to it was far more critical than his own.

5 Following my unsuccessful application for the Cambridge post, my teaching on the Development Studies paper was taken away from me on the grounds (subsequently shown to be incorrect) that there were no longer any funds to pay for it. A while later, my connection to the Faculty itself ceased.

just for this. What matters always is that the case any candidate makes, *whatever* it is, is well made' (original emphasis).[6] In keeping with this endorsement of political openness, during a 2009 interview with Alan Macfarlane, Hawthorn stated 'it still seems to me that Cambridge flourishes because it tolerates intellectual heterogeneity'. Such public rhetoric about the existence of political and theoretical plurality, however, is deceptive.

It is clear, therefore, that such commitments in theory to 'intellectual heterogeneity' are not reflected in practice, and thus not worth the paper they are written on. Indeed, Hawthorn himself concedes this very point when in the same 2009 interview he confesses that 'I have become increasingly sceptical of the use of intellectual positions to deny other peoples lives; I have come to appreciate the radical cultural contingency of things, so that things that are done in the name of any belief I react against'.[7] That 'other people's lives' include not just those promoted by the 'new' populist postmodernism but also those of the rich and powerful, and that consequently the belief he reacts against is anything critical of these kinds of 'otherness', can be gleaned from the fact that the target of the 'counterfactual historiography' advocated by Hawthorn is Marxism.[8] Whereas socialists maintain there is an unfolding logic to historical development, albeit open to different emphases and interpretations, those who adhere to a 'counterfactual' approach deny the efficacy of systemic patterns *per se*, arguing much rather that all history is – and can only ever be – a random

6 That my teaching was consistent with this stipulation concerning quality ('[w]hat matters always is that the case…, *whatever* it is, is well made') was conceded earlier that same year, when Hawthorn wrote 'were it not for his efforts, I'd find it impossible to continue to teach the undergraduate paper here on Development with the success we now do…the fact that some of the highest marks within the paper are for answers to questions on the subjects that [Brass] himself teaches speaks for itself'.

7 Unsurprisingly, perhaps, this point went unmentioned in the overly respectful obituaries for Hawthorn. Contrary to what was stated there – that 'his intellectual trajectory was never predictable', and that '[h]e managed something very unusual: to be passionate without being doctrinaire' – which claimed erroneously that he didn't have a politics (the inference being that he was consequently incapable of acting in line with such views), he did.

8 His vehement opposition to Marxist theory is evident from, for example, the following statement (Hawthorn, 1978: 13): 'Marxist and neo-Marxist theories of development and underdevelopment are doubly deficient: they do not produce a satisfactory theory of the more strictly economic relations, and (which is their more distinctive ambition) they do not produce a satisfactory theory of more broadly social and political (or "political economic") relations either.' That similarly tendentious intellectual judgments made by Hawthorn have not gone unchallenged is evident from replies by Gillian Rose and John Thompson to his review of their books in 'Ideal Speech', *London Review of Books*, Vol. 3, No. 21, 19 November 1981.

process (= contingent).[9] Although Hawthorn perceived himself (and was seen by others) as being a progressive liberal academic committed to intellectual plurality, therefore, he was in fact anything but this; the hostile reference and his role as referee in the episode described here accordingly has to be seen precisely as what it was – that of a political conservative engaged in, to use his own words, 'reacting against'.

9 See Hawthorn (1991). Like postmodernism, which invokes aporia so as to dismiss the Enlightenment project, Hawthorn also objects to grand narratives and thus the possibility of a nomothetic framework in the social sciences, championing instead a 'counterfactual' approach that takes us back to the-length-of-Cleopatra's-nose school of history ('Cleopatra's nose, had it been shorter, the whole face of the world would have been changed'). The hidden agenda of this approach is one that has been dismissed – not just as conservative historiography but as bad history – by Evans (2014: 154), who among other things notes that '[t]he leap...from the absence of the Black Death in fourteenth-century France to a fall in the fertility in the eighteenth century that led to an acceleration of economic growth, as proposed in Geoffrey Hawthorn's volume, is unsupported either by the extremely unlikely starting point, or by convincing historical linkages that posit a consequence over three hundred years later in the development of industry'.

CHAPTER 7

Backing into the Limelight*

These two books are important, but not in the way meant by their author. Together they reveal as clearly as need be the seductions and pitfalls awaiting those who announce that s/he, finally, has the answers to hitherto elusive questions about revolutionary practice – the 2011 Occupy Wall Street (OWS) movement in Zuccotti Park – and the anarchist theory about debt and democracy informing this. 'In one year', declares Graeber (2013: 149), 'Occupy managed to both identify the problem – a system of class power that has effectively fused finance and government – and to propose a solution: the creation of a genuinely democratic culture'. These claims are unpersuasive, largely because of an approach which refuses to commit to a political and economic programme.

Graeber harks back to an era of industrial capitalism, seen by him as a golden age, and about which in terms of criticism he appears to have little to say. No longer able to regard themselves as middle class, equated by him (Graeber, 2013: xix, 66–67, 70, 142) with a perception of the police and credit providers as 'basically on your side', Americans 'from solidly middle-class families' support OWS because they are unable to repay loans to educate themselves, being either unemployed or in poorly-paid jobs. Graeber fails to note that while such mobilization is certainly radical, it is not necessarily leftist: in the 1930s opposition by 'solidly middle-class families' not to capitalism but to 'money power' (= 'financialization') generated support for the political right. Contrary to his belief that questioning the role of money automatically constitutes a 'challenge to the very nature of the economic system,' therefore, implicit in much grassroots bourgeois anger at finance and the power of money is the view that, once banks are reformed, a benign/kind capitalism can be recuperated. Indeed, data provided by Graeber (2013: 93) showing that 'a plurality still prefer capitalism' undermines his assumption that OWS support equals a desire to change the economic system.

Questioning whether neoliberal 'financialization' is actually still capitalism, Graeber (2013: 78–79) misunderstands the changes that have occurred in the

* Reviewed here are *Debt: The First 5,000 Years*, by David Graeber (New York: Melville House Publishing, 2011), and *The Democracy Project: A History, a Crisis, a Movement*, by David Graeber (London: Allen Lane, 2013). Under the title 'A Stroll in Zuccotti Park', an earlier version of this review appeared in *Capital & Class*, Vol. 38, No. 1 (2014).

world economy, as a result of which he interprets accumulation in national, not international terms. Like others (Hardt and Negri, 2001; Harvey, 2003), therefore, he seems to think that what we have now is no longer capitalism but some form of non-capitalist 'financialization'. Real industrial capitalism, Graeber maintains, is now located only in the BRIC economies (China, India, Brazil). In the United States, by contrast, what we have is akin to 'feudalism'.

This misinterpretation overlooks two things. First, and most importantly, that capitalism is now global: one cannot separate European and American deindustrialization from the BRIC economies, since the latter are where European and American multinational corporations outsource production. These businesses are still capitalist enterprises, and are still part of a capitalist system that is now global in scope, in which they extract surpluses in order to accumulate. And second, within Europe and the United States manufacturing still takes place, albeit in a different form. Production hasn't vanished so much as been decentralized and downsized: a lot of it takes place in smallscale units – sweatshops – that have replaced largescale factories. In other words, it too has been outsourced, only nationally, not internationally.

The analysis of debt – which according to Graeber (2011) informs OWS practice – is also full of inconsistencies, not least the claim to have spotted developments no one else was aware of. Claims about the novelty of the case being made structure the view (Graeber, 2011: 351), for example, that Marxists 'still tend to assume that free wage labor is the basis of capitalism...all those millions of slaves and serfs and coolies and debt peons disappear...we write them off as temporary bumps in the road'. No we don't, and some Marxists – this reviewer included – have been arguing against this orthodoxy for a very long time (in my case some three decades).

Similarly, Graeber's (2011: 231, 427 note 27) assertion that as a result of debt '[l]arge populations [in ancient society] did, in fact, sink to the rank of serfs and clients' is followed by the mistaken view that '[w]hat I am saying flies in the face of much of the conventional scholarly wisdom'. He also claims to have come up with the slogan 'we are the 99%' (Graeber, 2013: 40–41), yet exactly the same words are found in a 1940 war-time diary entry by Orwell (1968: 344). In a sense this is hardly surprising, since academia – rather like neoliberal capitalism itself – is currently witnessing the proliferation of claims to have discovered – yet again – an issue, concept or problem that has long been known about.

Interestingly, Graeber's view of debt recalls that advanced by Roman Catholicism during the 1930s economic crisis, with the difference that religion was seen as a bastion against the global spread of the same unholy trinity (finance capital, liberalism, and communism). Thus Belloc (1937) was able to promote Roman Catholic ideas on the grounds that historically the Church condemned liberalism and usury, a protection swept away by the Reformation. His argument was that, no longer held in check by the power of the Church, economic liberalism and usury generated the competition that destroys the virtuous small producer, and unleashes what he maintained were the three un-Godly forces of history – capitalism, the proletariat, and – ultimately – communism. The conservative and hierarchical character of the Church notwithstanding, this backwards-looking anti-capitalist discourse permits it to present itself plausibly as part of any solution to the crisis of capitalism.

The desire to create a genuinely democratic culture is equally problematic, since what Graeber describes is simply a process of 'people' coming together without, however, being able to agree on a programme. Notwithstanding its being no more than symbolic action, a form of non-violent moral protest, therefore, OWS is regarded by him (Graeber, 2013: 89, 98, 109) as 'a revolutionary movement' that is successful, not despite but – perversely – because it had neither programme nor demands. This lacuna stems in turn from the diverse social composition of OWS, which in effect precludes a politics beyond the tautology 'we don't like the present situation'. How to move forward, and on the basis of what, is accordingly not addressed.

Democracy, we are told (Graeber, 2013: 186) is no more than 'collective deliberation', thereby evading a number of crucial questions. Having asserted the primacy of democratic practice, encompassing not just a diverse social composition and ideology, but predicated on an undefined concept of 'economic justice', itself the result of absent programme and demands, only very late (Graeber, 2013: 170) is the prefiguring issue raised: that of *content*, which in turn structures or negates form. In short, it is necessary to ask what happens if there is no consensus because of a lack of agreement, especially concerning property relations and the division of labour?

Like Belloc, Graeber (2013: 178ff., 183–184) advocates a return to village community, the inhabitants of which are peasant smallholders cultivating and living in harmony outside capitalism. This is the agrarian myth, propagated by Russian populism in the late nineteenth century, and in the early twentieth shown by Marxists to be untrue. Village communities are neither egalitarian nor inherently democratic, and now – as for a long time past – are penetrated by capitalism and subject to class differentiation. Simply put, they are not external to but part of the capitalist system, as many anthropologists conducting fieldwork in rural contexts attest. Thus the panchayat system in village India is a form of class rule, not the least important aspect of which is the enforcement of bonded labour relations on indebted agricultural workers. Similarly, the South African apartheid government handed local administration to tribal authorities who could be relied on to exercise 'traditional' justice on those who stepped out of line, a policy in keeping with the apartheid system.

Critical of Marxism generally, and in particular because it advocates capturing the state, Graeber (2011: 448, note 83; 2013: 29, 182, 189, 190) endorses instead the 'state-avoidance' argument of James Scott (2009), which claims that Asian uplands were self-governing locations where people fleeing lowland oppression sought and found refuge and emancipation. This idealization of 'state-repelling zones of asylum' to which people voluntarily migrate is consistent with the 'new' populist postmodernism (see review essay 12, this volume), but not supported by ethnographic evidence. The latter suggests that populations neither choose to migrate to upland areas (but go because they are forced off valley land), nor – once there – are they beyond the reach of the lowland state. Consequently, they are anything but empowered and safe in such contexts.

In keeping with this idealization, Graeber (2013: 202, 206–207) thinks the state will dissolve of its own accord, and then all will be well, which takes no account of class differences and struggle. What he fails to consider is the fact that those with property, power and wealth who control the state will not willingly surrender this – much rather the opposite: they will fight tooth-and-nail to retain what they own. No amount of appeals to 'reasonableness' will change this, nor will any movement that adopts non-violence as its tactic.

All these difficulties have, to some degree, their origins in the academic institutionalization of anti-capitalist discourse, to the extent that it has become a practice without a theory, and thus without a programme. A large factor contributing to the dilution and/or deradicalization of leftist debate – certainly in the UK – has been the post-1968 entry into university jobs of many who thought of themselves as socialists. In the intervening years there has been a wholesale shedding of leftist political views in academia, once these ideas ceased to be fashionable. This unravelling of leftism from within is not how the issue is usually depicted, which tends to attribute it simply to an attack from without (which has certainly taken place), and not to a forgetting or an abandonment of principles by those within academia. An old and very depressing story, one that was familiar to the Bolsheviks who saw their revolutionary ideas taken up and watered down by academia, a corrupting effect on leftist theory and practice epitomized recently in the photo of Eric Hobsbawm kneeling to receive an establishment decoration from the Queen.

Marxists like Trotsky (1930), Serge (1963) and Guevara (1967), by contrast, all wrote about their experiences after having participated in major revolutionary upheavals; none of these struggles – in Russia, Spain and Cuba – was conducted with the safety-net of a well-paid university post to fall back on. Although Graeber (2013: 5) sees himself as victimized by academia for his political beliefs, it is a perception which sits awkwardly with his current position as Reader at London University. Other anthropologists are not as fortunate, having been excluded from academic jobs because of leftist political views and/or arrested/interrogated during fieldwork (see review 6 and essay 14, both in this volume). This is compounded by further contradiction.

Thus advocacy of a 'leaderless democracy' does not prevent Graeber from moving centre stage as a reluctant *jefe supremo*, a role evident not just from the blurb on the front cover – 'The single academic who has done the most to shape the [OWS] movement' – but also from the following observations in the book itself (Graeber, 2013: xii, 3, 8, 15, 38, 48, 84–85, 151): 'I'd already passed up two invitations to speak, but [another protester] was persistent'; a magazine editor 'asked me to write a column on the possibility of a revolutionary movement'; a friend 'invited me to see two of the founders' of the Egyptian youth movement; needing a lecturer to address a meeting 'after a moment's hesitation, I volunteered'; 'that summer I'd been giving almost constant interviews'; 'I ended up suggesting [changes which] improved the quality of our debate'; as 'I was on the scene and seemed to have some idea of what was going on…my [twitter] account had two thousand new followers'; 'in trying to understand the implications [a blogger] appealed to my own book on debt'; and so on and so forth. Unsurprisingly, he ends up comparing his own influence to that of Chomsky.

It is hard to avoid the baleful conclusion that Graeber risks becoming 'Mr Occupy,' much like an earlier 'revolutionary representative' who surfaced during the May 1968 student protests, and these days has a starring media role as 'Mr 1968,' reminiscing about a golden age of political activism and demonstrations. Backing into the 'revolutionary' limelight in this manner suggests a rather worrying tendency to want to lead, which in turn consecrates as radical what an individual thus lionized thinks. Is it any wonder, therefore, that from such a twofold process there emerges both a personality cult and a mistaken theory, a combination that, historically, has bedevilled much leftist politics?

CHAPTER 8

A Marxist Defence of Marxist Theory*

Any survey of academic discussion about how – and if – to oppose the onward global march of capital reveals a depressing picture. Opportunistic shapeshifting predominates, as political views are more often than not tailored to meet prevailing intellectual fashion, whatever this might be. Such as it is, current debate concludes with the oft-heard refrain 'neoliberalism is nasty', a truism from which these days hardly anyone dissents (there are films promoting this view, e.g., *Inside Job* and *Two Days, One Night*). Even conservatives accept this, whilst insisting that nothing can be done to buck the dominance of 'the market'. Where people disagree is what to do about this, and here what passes for leftism has not a lot to say (there are exceptions, but very few). Many erstwhile Marxists in academia have abandoned the idea of a socialist transition, and as a result are unable to contribute much beyond repeating that capitalism is not at all nice (which we all know).

It is refreshing, therefore, to encounter a book which departs from this depressing pattern. Its author, Raju Das, has undertaken fieldwork in rural Orissa, and not only knows his Marxism but has also made important theoretical contributions to the analysis of the capitalist State (Das, 1996; Das, 2005; Das, 2007). In what is a wide-ranging analysis, the book covers many subjects, extending from Marxist theory, Maoism, and the State, via agrarian transition, the global capitalist labour regime, and the political economy of India, to anti-capitalist political protest and the nature and object of critique itself. Asking 'what is *the point* of being critical?', 'what really *is* Marxism?', and '*why* does the Indian State do what it does?', Das (pp. 18, 25, 71) poses deceptively simple but crucial questions. Considered here will be his answers to just three of them: the purpose of criticism, the Marxism/post-Marxism debate, and the path followed by the global capitalist labour regime.

Das (2013) belongs to that all-too-small band of Marxists who regard as problematic the burgeoning contradiction between on the one hand the ubiquity of academic critique, which 'attracts much grant-money' and on the other the absence of 'rigorous theory' (pp. 4–24, 134ff.). This mismatch he attributes to the fact that the object of critique is not material conditions but language,

* Reviewed here is *A Contribution to the Critique of Contemporary Capitalism: Theoretical and International Perspectives*, by Raju Das (Nova Publishers: New York, 2014). An earlier version appeared in *Capital & Class*, Vol. 39, No. 2 (2015).

which is accorded the status of 'separate reality' and thus reified. Rightly, he (p. 14) observes that 'much intellectual work simply runs away from…class divisions and class struggles in society and from [their] implications'. Among those he regards as guilty of this idealization are many leftist academics, and indeed it could be said that these days they appear too busy collecting awards or having prizes named after themselves to bother advocating something as trivial as revolutionary socialism.

Whereas such academics imagine they are speaking truth to power, more usually they are doing the opposite: speaking power to truth. All too often, therefore, one hears of the receipt of yet another sizeable research grant the stated object of which is 'to understand why global poverty still exists', as if we didn't already know, and have done for some time now. This is accompanied by yet more postmodern celebration of ethnically 'other' culture as empowering, despite 'traditional' or 'authentic' identity frequently masking rural poverty. It could be argued that what currently passes for development studies programmes carried out in universities is akin to the collection of rent on the misery of impoverished others inhabiting the so-called Third World. A case in point is the approach of 'post-Marxist' theory, itself the target of a withering broadside from Das (pp. 55ff.).

Subordinating ever larger portions of the globe to the market, capitalism has triggered not a class politics but a populist reaction. Since many in academia have endorsed the latter epistemology in preference to class analysis, they are consequently unable to criticize such mobilization. This is one of the reasons why there has been a widespread reaffirmation of peasant essentialism, a populist approach to rural grassroots structure and agency rightly criticized by Das (pp. 15, 46–47 n. 117, 67, 85 n. 159, 87 n., 97–98, 101, 106, 161). Because many of those who regard themselves as leftists have forgotten what Marxist theory actually teaches, they have as a result espoused 'new' populist postmodern theoretical positions: not just peasant essentialism, but also the innateness of nationalism, the desirability of grassroots ethnic empowerment, and rural tradition as mobilizing discourse. Epistemologically, these views are no different from the identity politics advocated by conservatives.

Distinguishing between such external critiques of Marxist theory, which are non- or anti-Marxist, and internal critiques which remain Marxist, Das (pp. 25ff., 50 n.127, 57) reminds us that Marxism is about class formation/difference/struggle. Its object is to capture the State, enabling workers and poor peasants to put into practice an agenda that reflects *their* political and economic interests. The significance of this distinction emerges clearly from his analysis of current developments in the global labour regime. Das (pp. 79ff., 89ff.) defends but interrogates the Marxist concept deproletarianization, which reverses and challenges the earlier orthodoxy that, because unfree labour is an obstacle to accumulation, capitalism automatically replaces it with a workforce that is free. Much rather, introducing/reproducing unfree production relations is nowadays part of the way class struggle is waged 'from above'. Along with downsizing/outsourcing, deproletarianization is a method whereby employers restructure their labour process, cutting costs so as to maintain/enhance profitability. An expanding industrial reserve army makes this kind of restructuring not just possible but also necessary.

Nevertheless, asks Das, why resort to deproletarianization when capitalists have so much labour-power from which to choose? The response to this important question is that where accumulation is both international and operates in a *laissez faire* global market, if one business has access to the industrial reserve army then so does the competition. In such an environment, the additional capacity to use unfree labour-power gives any commercial employer a competitive edge. Unfreedom can be deployed in the class struggle as a capitalist weapon for different reasons: in some contexts it is introduced because workers' organization is strong (as a way of undermining this), while in others because such organization is weak or absent. That is to say, either on account of labour having too much bargaining power, or due to the fact it has too little. A workforce is accordingly never composed entirely of labour-power that is unfree, any more than it is of that which is free; the preponderance of one or other is determined by and in turn determines the existing balance of forces in the class struggle.

However, and understandably, Das is concerned that the focus of the development debate may now have shifted too far in the direction of the capitalism/unfreedom link. This can be explained (but not necessarily justified) in three ways. First, where unfreedom has been reintroduced into a labour process that is capitalist, political economy teaches that such a development corresponds historically to a regression. This is because so much – politically, ideologically and economically – hangs on whether or not worker emancipation has been achieved. Second, it must be remembered that, as announcements of a positive correlation between accumulation and unfree workforce continue to proliferate, accompanied more often than not by unwarranted claims to have 'discovered' it (on which see Brass, 2014d), this was not always so. Although at present the global incidence of unfreedom may indeed be trending in terms of investigation/explanation, as Das notes, this did not apply some three decades ago when the case about deproletarianization emerged. And third, the current emphasis on this aspect of economic development can also be attributed in part to the way academic fashion operates, a point he addresses when considering the role/object of criticism.

To conclude: the central theme of this important book, namely that by being a 'dialectical, historical and materialist way of knowing, Marxism is a form of explanatory critique of society with *a practical intent*' (p. 28, emphasis added), neatly sums up the tasks socialists face. By doing so, Das has contributed substantially to the defence of Marxist theory, a significant achievement in the present hostile intellectual climate.

CHAPTER 9

Houellebecq, Anthropologist?*

Despite the fact that it is neither an ethnography nor a theoretical analysis, but rather a work of fiction, the book reviewed here ought to interest anthropologists. Written by Michel Houellebecq, widely regarded as *l'enfant terrible* among French intellectuals, *Submission* is a dystopic novel addressing an important and topical political question: the emergence in France of a Muslim party, the subsequent election of its Presidential candidate, and the consequent Islamization of the nation. Its themes of de-secularization, along with political, ideological and female subordination (pp. 217, 247), are for Houellebecq no more than a confirmation of the historical insistence by Islamic religion on humanity's subjection to God, thereby reversing the Enlightenment project.

An author with a controversial political reputation, Houellebecq has been accused of both Islamophobia and racism, and is frequently vilified by the media for his views and writings. The question raised by *Submission* is not, as some tend to think, whether he is pro- or anti-Islam but rather what would an Islamic government in a European nation do, and what sort of policies would it adopt. To address this issue is not to commit oneself to a position on Islam, let alone to endorse Islamophobia, but rather to do what Muslim opinion itself says non-Muslims must do: take Islam seriously, and look at what it has to offer to different categories in non-Islamic nations. That is precisely what Houellebecq attempts to do, grounding his characterization in shifting (and perhaps shifty) attitudes of intellectuals, and the extent to which they are prepared to come to terms with any/every regime, so long as it offers them rewards.

However, it is hard to reconcile accusations of Islamophobia and racism levelled at Houellebecq with his expressed views (Houellebecq and Levy, 2011: 38, 56) both that the 'vast majority of immigrants of Muslim origin in Western Europe are peaceable people,' and that anti-semitism is a 'stupid idea'.[1] Rejecting the label 'new reactionary' attached to him by the French media, he (Houellebecq and Levy, 2011: 111, original emphasis) points out that a 'reactionary is someone who favours some previously existing social

* Reviewed here is *Submission*, by Michel Houellebecq (London: William Heinemann, 2015). An earlier version of this appeared in *Critique of Anthropology*, Vol. 36, No. 1 (2016).

1 He also makes common cause with Muslim feminists – such as Taslima Nasrin and Ayaan Hirsi Ali – who have criticized the teachings of Islam about the subordinate position of women in society.

configuration – something it is possible to return to – and someone who militates in favour of such a return. Whereas, if there is an idea, a single idea that goes through all of my novels, which goes so far as to haunt them, it is the *absolute irreversibility of all processes of decay* once they have begun.'

The appearance of the French edition of *Submission* coincided with the murderous attack on the satirical magazine Charlie Hebdo in January 2015, and Houellebecq has been in hiding and under police protection ever since.[2] Of interest is the contrast between on the one hand the sympathetic and supportive attitude on the part of broadly liberal opinion throughout Europe towards Salman Rushdie when his novel criticizing Islam elicited a *fatwā*, and on the other the condemnation by the equivalent segment of European opinion aimed at Houellebecq for doing much the same kind of thing. Part of the problem derives from his contradictory utterances, on occasion simultaneously endorsing antithetical views. Although he perceives himself as 'fundamentally atheist', he is nevertheless sympathetic towards Tibetan theocracy represented by the Dalai Lama (Houellebecq and Levy, 2011: 108–109, 140). In much the same vein, being critical of pastoral images of the French countryside (Houellebecq and Levy, 2011: 116, 117) does not prevent him from defending their veracity.

The central character in *Submission* is an academic based in Paris, François, who faces loss of his university post when the candidate of an Islamic party, the Muslim Brotherhood (MB), wins the 2022 French Presidential election and introduces Sharia law. Public officials are required to convert to Islam, women are expelled from the workforce (thereby 'solving' the male unemployment problem), and the education system is geared to religious teachings of Islam. These events leading to an 'other' and – in the context of a bourgeois secular democracy – less benign political culture uphold the dictum that the nearer to the present the future dystopia is, the more troubling the times we live in. Yet the book is not so much Islamophobic as – very subtly – Islamophile, in the sense that submission is presented as not merely inevitable but – for some – a beneficial outcome: a full range of economic and social rewards are seen to be on offer to certain categories by the MB. Chief amongst these are male academics.

---

2 Many of the issues raised by Houellebecq have become more, not less, important as a result of the Bataclan massacre in November 2015. I passed through Paris the day after that event, and could not but be aware of the wide-ranging discussion it generated, much of it of an intellectually thoughtful and sophisticated nature.

The main targets of Houellebecq's ire are academics in general and leftist academics in particular, the latter for having in effect helped to lay the intellectual ground for the conquest of power by the MB. Described as 'progressive mummified corpses' who were 'extinct in the wider world', the left is dismissed (p. 126) as 'paralysed by [the MB] multicultural background', as a result of which it 'had never been able to fight [them]'. A university lecturer who converted out of conviction 'reserved his bitterest scorn for his Islamo-leftist colleagues,' because (pp. 228–229) 'Islamo-leftism was a desperate attempt by mouldering, putrefying, brain-dead Marxists to hoist themselves out of the dustbin of history by latching on to the coat-tails of Islam.' Although the ostensible target of this critique is Marxism, such an indictment is more accurately directed at postmodernists, whose aporia has indeed privileged identity politics.

Academics who abandoned socialism and instead embraced postmodern identity politics are blamed by Houellebecq for creating an ideological space filled by the MB. In an important sense, this complicity is depicted as the equivalent of having deserted their posts in time of war. Hence the indictment by François of a fellow academic as 'his inner man of the left was fast asleep' (p. 21). When socialists are placed third in the first round of the election, after the National Front (NF) and the MB, and then enter into coalition with the latter to keep out the NF, François laments his colleagues' lack of concern about this outcome, observing that 'they seemed completely unworried, as if none of this had anything to do with them…university professors can't even imagine political developments having any effect on their careers' (p. 63). This culminates in what for Houellebecq is clearly an act of intellectual submission amounting to venality. In order to obtain, or retain, university posts, academics are required to convert to Islam and teach 'intelligent design' (= creationism), which many do, in the process not only receiving higher salaries (funded by Saudi Arabia) but also enabling them to 'get many wives' (pp. 150, 212, 221–222, 244–246).[3]

Houellebecq also indicts the political right, but for a different reason. Whereas leftist academics who embrace a postmodern end-of-Enlightenment-values *weltanschauung* are seen to be inconsistent, rightwing French nationalists who endorse Islam are by contrast shown to be entirely consistent. For its part, therefore, the political right, composed of nationalists (= 'Nativists') who are 'catholics, royalists, nostalgics, [and] romantics at heart' (p. 54), are soon won over by the MB. This is because, in common with Islam, French 'Nativists'

3 For a similar argument concerning the politically corrupting impact on leftist politics of the post-1968 entry into academic jobs by socialists, see Brass (2015).

oppose atheism, egalitarianism, communism, materialism, progress and modernity: for followers of Islam, 'the real enemy – the thing they fear – isn't Catholicism. It's secularism...[the MB] think of Catholics as fellow believers' (pp. 127, 230–231).[4]

Similarly acceptable to the French right are many of the economic policies adopted by the MB. Not only does the transfer of women away from paid jobs and into the family home result in falling unemployment, therefore, but shifting welfare provision from the State onto the family cuts public expenditure by some 85% (pp. 162, 174). In keeping with this approach, the new President endorses the distributist 'Third Way' discourse (= neither capitalism nor communism) of G.K. Chesterton and Hilaire Belloc, an ideology the beneficiaries of which are small family businesses, farmers and artisans – potential/actual capitalist producers, in short (pp. 166–167).

A central difficulty facing Houellebecq remains that the scenario presented in the book – the coming to power of a government espousing/promoting Islamic beliefs – is a subject so overlaid with knee-jerk reactions, that even the act of raising it as an issue meriting examination invariably and very quickly elicits accusations of Islamophobia, which emphatically it is not.[5] One advantage enjoyed by anthropology is that it is permitted critically to examine discourse that is deemed to be politically sensitive, and in this sense the fiction of Houellebecq discharges the same function as ethnography. His self-description (Houellebecq and Levy, 2011: 79) as 'to identify myself with the role of the recorder' could almost be that of an anthropologist. Confessing an admiration for 'the detached, composed light that sociology brings to bear when it succeeds in dissociating itself from immediate ideological issues' (Houellebecq and Levy, 2011: 278), the kinds of issues he raises are in essence no different from those that interest anthropology. That ethnography has long adopted a more nuanced position on the questions Houellebecq asks is evident from views expressed by, among others, Lévi-Strauss.[6]

---

4 This is a more persuasive argument than the one advanced by Todd (2015), who insists much rather that Charlie Hebdo protests represented anti-Muslim sentiment emanating from Catholic reaction. This contrasts with the view of Houellebecq, for whom the compatibility between Islam and Catholicism stems not just from advocacy of religious belief but also from a common antagonism towards secularism.

5 This kind of political 'forbidding' emanates, unfortunately, from some of those who regard themselves as leftists. However, socialists must beware of doing precisely what supporters of capitalism try to do to them; namely, forbid raising basic questions about proposed fundamental change to the existing system, the practice of closing down debate known as 'no platforming'.

6 Asked whether the hostility of one culture toward another was automatically racist, he (Lévi-Strauss and Eribon, 1991: 150) replied: 'Active hostility, yes... But that cultures, all the

By portraying the MB Presidential candidate as a personally congenial and politically accommodating individual, who successfully avoids alienating French non-Muslims, Houellebecq implicitly raises the same kinds of questions as those surrounding changes to the pattern of capitalist development itself. In the case of the latter, therefore, a system which starts out as seemingly benign (state capitalism, centrally planned and regulated accumulation, with welfare provision based on full or near-full employment) becomes over time nakedly oppressive (global spread of the market, deregulation, increased unemployment, outsourcing/downsizing, intensification of competition and exploitation, imperial conquest and war). So with Islam – and, indeed, all regimes informed by religious ideology – as theological precepts come to dominate, culminating in increasingly illiberal policies (on women, punishment, dissent).

It could be argued that, in this sense, each systemic form (capitalism, Islam) follows a similar trajectory, their differences notwithstanding. This potential transformation, as it affects Islam no less than capitalism, is something that no anthropologist would ignore. For this reason, it is difficult to share the optimism advanced by an earlier political assessment (Worsley, 1984: 230), to the effect that '[i]ndustrial class consciousness and militancy are thus perfectly compatible with older Islamic values and institutions, which supply wider meanings than those of purely materialist ideologies'. That radical Islam is adaptable to a secular European bourgeois democracy is therefore a problematic view, and one that Houellebecq sets out to interrogate, albeit in fictional mode.

Those who might think that what the MB does (or does not do) in Egypt ought to be central to any discussion of the book, miss the point entirely. The issue raised by Houellebecq is not the relevance or otherwise of an Islamic government in a country where it has a longstanding political and cultural presence, as in the case of Egypt, but rather what its impact might be on a European nation with an equally longstanding secular and bourgeois democratic tradition. As anthropologists would hasten to argue, France is not Egypt, any more than Egypt is France. Similarly, a description of the book as Islamophile is ironic, in that important characters (academics, public intellectuals) rapidly come to see virtue in a new government that, entirely coincidentally (of course), rewards them financially and socially.

This is a problem that historically has dogged French intellectuals, who have never shied away from engagement with contentious political issues

---

while respecting each other, can feel greater or less affinity with certain others, is a factual situation that has always existed. It is the normal course of human conduct. By condemning it as racist, one runs the risk of playing into the enemy's hand, for many naïve people will say, if that's racism, then I'm racist.'

(Dreyfus, Vichy). Implicitly the shadow of WWII collaboration with the invader – submission of another kind – also hangs over the book, and with it the familiar issue of the role of French intellectuals and their political complicity raised earlier in the writings of those such as Pierre Drieu La Rochelle (1958), Julien Benda (1928, 1958), and Paul Morand (2002).[7] In the words of Houellebecq (p. 226), the problem is that '[f]or the French, an intellectual didn't have to be *responsible*. That wasn't his job'. It is precisely this question of responsibility – and its political consequences – that *Submission* asks in relation to the link between Marxism and postmodernism.

Equating postmodern identity politics with Marxism is profoundly mistaken, since Marxism is emphatically not the same as identity politics – the two positions are in fact diametrically opposed and incompatible (as has been argued by this reviewer for three decades now). What is being said here is that there *are* Marxists who still think identity politics and Marxism are essentially the same, and these are the ones criticized. Although Houellebecq is not himself a Marxist, he has nevertheless spotted and made the same connection. He blames them not for the rise of an Islamic government (a ridiculous notion) but for not being Marxist enough in their criticisms of identity politics which in turn have made such a development possible.

The concluding words of the novel are put by Houellebecq into the mouth of a senior academic – one of the first to convert – who is promoted to high government office by the new regime. Upholding the view that 'the summit of human happiness resides in the most absolute submission' (p. 217), he commends Islam on the grounds that it 'accepts the world as such'. Regardless of whether or not the dystopia is plausible, for social scientists who read this book its interest lies elsewhere. Along the lines of be careful what you wish for, Houellebecq has painted a worrying picture of the kind of future licensed by public intellectuals and/or academics who subscribe to postmodern aporia. It is a view consistent with a position he has endorsed elsewhere: namely, that 'in everything, foresee the end' (Houellebecq and Levy, 2011: 112).

7 As has been argued elsewhere (Brass 2014a: Ch. 8), the defence by Morand of an elitist aesthetic image of Venice – one not available to the plebeian mass tourist who is not and can never become an 'initiate' – is linked in turn to his justification for having collaborated with the Vichy regime in 1940. Invoking the historical precedent of the 1797 Venetian government letting in Napoleon so as to preserve the city and its culture, so Vichy – insists Morand – collaborated with the invading Germans in order to preserve France and its culture.

PART 2

Review Essays

Old London Cries, II

CHAPTER 10

The Struggle of/(over) Post-emancipation Rural Labour

(*'At Their Perfect Command'?*)*

> Thus we are told, that the state of the slaves is one of blissful contentment; that they would not take freedom as a gift; that their family relations are only now and then invaded; ...that generally they are kindly treated, &c. ... It is a commentary on the contented state of the slave population that the writer finds two or three always, and often many more, in every one of hundreds of Southern papers examined.[1]
>
> An observation by HARRIET BEECHER STOWE about plantation slavery in the antebellum American south.

•••

It is all very well to say that a man is a man whether his skin is white or black; but it is certain that the vast majority of West Indian blacks – all but the very few really educated members of the class – are not men but children, great, strong, generally good-tempered children, but always fickle... It seems proved that it is *possible* to educate individuals of this class to the grown-up stage; but this does not alter the fact that the great mass of them remain children, in all but physique. The handling of these powerful children, since they form so large a part of the labourers of the Colony, is a matter the study of which is essential to the few supervisors of this labour; and an essential to success in the Colony is the power of keeping a perfectly just, strong, and kind hand over these people. The emancipation was essentially as would be the sudden freeing from all control of a party of school children; and the results were similar. For the moral effect on the character of the negroes of this too sudden step taken half a century ago, we still have, and shall long have, to suffer. Its more immediate effect was the temporary annihilation of

---

* Reviewed here is *After Slavery: Emancipation and its Discontents*, edited by Howard Temperley (London: Frank Cass Publishers, 2000). An earlier version of this review essay appeared in *The Journal of Peasant Studies*, Vol. 28, No. 3 (2001).

1 Beecher Stowe (1853:402).

> the labouring population of the Colony; for the freedmen recognized no need to work.[2]
>
> An observation about British Guiana made by SIR EVERARD IM THURN, a Colonial Governor and High Commissioner.

∴

This book is an anachronism, a collection that would have been regarded as intellectually unchallenging even in the 1950s.[3] Espousing either an imperial historiography redolent of Coupland, or a more recent neo-classical economic approach, most of its contributors display an evident distaste for theory and thus tend to privilege empiricism.[4] Where a theoretical framework is deployed, moreover, it is of an undeniably revisionist character which downplays the negative aspects of slavery and indenture.[5] All the contributions are written as though important current debates about unfree labour – for example, the reasons for its existence and continuation, its meaning, and the influence on the latter of Marxist or postmodern theory – had simply never taken place. When

2 Im Thurn (1892:8, original emphasis).

3 The second part of the title of this extended review is taken from an 1872 report entitled *On the Condition of the Freed Slaves in Native Cochin* [*India*], reproduced in Kusuman (1973: Document XXXIX), where it is stated that: 'The landed gentry are interested in maintaining on their estates a body of labourers at their perfect command. They do not believe that coolies will be available always when wanted or devoted to the work assigned…Hence they [the landed gentry] are unwilling to part with the freed slaves and by an understanding among them not to seduce or patronize each others labourers keep the slaves in a state of hopeless dependence on themselves.'

4 For the shortcomings of the imperial historiographical tradition associated with Coupland (1933), its impact on the study of the West Indies, and in particular its core argument that slave emancipation was the outcome of an humanitarian crusade, see the still important critique elaborated by Williams (1966:197ff.).

5 Among the revisionist contributions not examined in detail here, therefore, is one about slavery in Sub-Saharan Africa by Suzanne Miers (Temperley, 2000: 237–264), who in a previous text about Africa attempted to redefine slavery as a form of kinship (Miers and Kopytoff, 1977), a procedure which entailed purging unfreedom of its coercive and oppressive content in order to represent it as a variant or extension of kinship. Also – and inevitably – found among the contributors is the ubiquitous Stanley Engerman, who in a concluding overview purportedly about comparative analyses of post-emancipation labour (Temperley, 2000: 281–300) simply restates all the arguments presented in the volume without challenging any of their basic assumptions.

the systemic dynamic governing the reproduction of unfreedom is posed, this invariably takes the form of the 'vestiges' argument: namely, the assumption that unfree labour is a pre-capitalist relation, the reproduction of which is not merely unconnected with capitalism but an obstacle to the accumulation process, a view which ignores the existence of many examples to the contrary.

Even in a very general sense, the deployment of theory could be said to be crucial in determining the scope of a volume such as this: namely, in defining the boundaries both of the subject itself and of the period covered. In the case of the latter, for example, the concepts 'after slavery' and 'post-emancipation' might conceivably extend the analysis to include all forms of labour relation from the ending of slavery to those which exist in the present. This in turn would require a complex theoretical approach, capable of addressing and explaining the interrelation between a multiplicity of processes (the development of capitalism, the agrarian question, and the different forms taken by the class struggle, to mention but a few). Needless to say, no such exercise in definition is mooted, let alone attempted, the result being a lack of conceptual and temporal boundaries In the absence of the latter, the focus of this review will accordingly be on a twofold definitional struggle: by the ex-slaves themselves, against the attempt by their erstwhile owners to reconstitute them as unfree labour, and by the contending historiographies (Marxist, revisionist) interpreting this process, each of which disagrees over the coercive/non-coercive meaning of the post-emancipation production relations which emerged as a result of the first kind of struggle. Before examining some of the contributions, therefore, it is important to link the absence of theory and debate to a particular silence which pervades the book.

I

Marxist theory about unfree labour has a long history, extending from the work of Marx, Lenin and Kautsky, through that of C.L.R. James and the participants in the transition debate of the 1950s and 1960s, to interventions in more recent discussions.[6] The latter include, for example, discussions about slavery and other forms of unfreedom in not only in the ancient world, but also in the

6 The text by C.L.R. James (1938) on Toussaint L'Overture and the slave rebellion in the French colony of San Domingo during the late eighteenth century was – and remains – a seminal influence on Marxist interpretations of slavery. For the feudalism-to-capitalism transition debate of the 1950s and 1960s, see the collection edited by Hilton (1976). Theoretical problems raised by Marxist and non-Marxist analyses of slavery and slave society were also considered

Caribbean, in the post-bellum American south, in the South Pacific region, and in Africa.[7] Marxist theory also informed much of the 1970s debate about debt bondage and the mode of production in India and, more generally, about the unfree nature of the work regimes in South Africa under the apartheid system and on Asian plantations and Latin American estates during the nineteenth and twentieth centuries.[8]

Because Marxists regard chattel slavery, indenture and debt bondage as exploitative forms of surplus extraction which generate antagonistic relations between employer and worker, they also maintain that consequently the reproduction of these unfree relations necessarily entails coercion. For Marxists, therefore, the object of such unfree relations is to compel workers engaged in class struggle to agree to lower wages and worse conditions than they would otherwise accept. On the subject of unfree labour, as on other theoretical issues, disagreements certainly exist within Marxism itself; broadly speaking, however, there is a discernable theoretical gulf between Marxism on the one hand, and on the other those nominally distinct but epistemologically similar analyses of unfree labour categorized under the general rubric of revisionism.[9]

Influenced on the one hand by neoclassical economic historiography (with its view of unfreedom as an economically empowering form of 'subsistence guarantee' or 'patronage') and on the other by postmodernism (with its view of unfreedom as a culturally empowering manifestation of 'popular culture', and 'everyday forms of resistance'), revisionism wrongly argues that unfree labour

---

at this conjuncture in a survey issued by the History Group of the Communist Party of Great Britain (Browning, 1964).

7 For important Marxist interpretations of slavery and/or other forms of unfreedom, see the texts by de Ste Croix, (1981; 1984) about the ancient world, those by Moreno Fraginals (1976) and Rodney (1981) about the Caribbean, those by Angelo (1995) and Lichtenstein (1996) about the post-bellum American south, those by Graves (1993) and Panoff (1994/5) about the South Pacific region, those by Meillassoux (1975; 1991) and Munslow and Finch (1984) about Africa, and that by Wolf and Hansen (1972) about Latin America.

8 The Marxist contributions to the debate about the mode of production in India are contained in Rudra *et al.* (1978), Alavi *et al.* (1982), and Banerjee (1985), while the connection between unfree labour and the South African apartheid system is outlined in Marxist terms by, among many others, Wolpe (1972) and Legassick (1977). For an analysis of the work regimes on Asian and Latin American plantations during the nineteenth and twentieth centuries, see the collections edited by Daniel *et al.* (1992) and Florescano (1975).

9 On the subject of unfree labour, internal Marxist debates focus on a number of interrelated questions. These concern the compatibility (or otherwise) between unfreedom generally and advanced productive forces, the extent to which capitalism is defined by the presence of free labour, and whether or not a systemic transition to capitalism and/or a capitalist agriculture require a relational transformation involving the elimination of unfree labour.

is the outcome of worker consent/choice, and consequently evidence for the non-existence or decline of employer oppression/power.[10] Because they regard slavery, indenture and bondage more benignly as form of 'subsistence guarantee', neo-classical economic historians – unlike Marxists – maintain that unfree labourers are empowered by and thus choose to remain within such employment relations.[11]

---

10 The conceptualization of unfreedom as a form of 'subsistence guarantee' is perhaps the most frequently encountered revisionist argument, deployed by neoclassical economic historians and postmodernists alike, against the negative theorization of agrarian relations such as debt bondage. This enables revisionism to change the meaning of unfree labour: namely, by focussing on what is presented as a positive relational element, that of job security for the workers involved. This interpretation permits in turn such employment arrangements to be reconfigured as outcomes structured by consent. In an act of reciprocal exchange, therefore, labourers willingly forgo both economic mobility and the higher wages that accrue from this, in return for guaranteed work throughout the year, albeit at lower levels of remuneration. The difficulty with this interpretation is that in many parts of the so-called Third World, unfree production relations currently flourish in contexts where a capitalist agriculture has developed, and consequently where higher paid employment is on offer throughout the year. Accordingly, in these contexts bonded labour is designed to restrict the capacity of workers personally to commodify their own labour-power on a period-specific basis: not for the full year, but just for that portion of the agricultural cycle when demand for workers is at its peak. Such workers do not receive payment for those periods of the agricultural cycle when an employer has no work for them, and when as a result they are free to seek alternative jobs (if there are any): during the off-peak season, however, when a 'subsistence guarantee' is needed, none is forthcoming. Since it permits rural employers to obtain and retain labour-power for the duration of the peak season, at a price below the wage level that would otherwise be necessary to attract free wage labour at this point is the agricultural cycle, therefore, debt bondage benefits not the worker (≠ subsistence guarantee) but the employer. Other aspects/variants of the 'subsistence guarantee' argument are considered below.

11 Claims to the contrary notwithstanding, there is a discernible project to the pattern of revisionist arguments, as exemplified by the role of 'epidemiological' explanation in its discourse. The insistence by revisionism that slaves, indentured workers and bonded labourers were/are 'choice-making' subjects exercising subjective preferences, and hence the related claim about the lack of necessity for coercion, its general ineffectiveness, or its overall absence, are all confronted with the problem of evidence about slave oppression, as embodied in high mortality rates. Accordingly, revisionists seek to explain these kinds of empirical phenomena by invoking different causes. Faced with data confirming the high mortality rates of slaves and other forms of unfree labour, the existence of which threatens to undermine their argument, therefore, revisionists attribute these to 'natural' causes. In contrast to Marxists, who link the high incidence of mortality among unfree workers to malnutrition, maltreatment and/or overwork, and regard it as an effect of capitalism, as planters cut back on labour costs in order to maintain profitability during

Part of the difficulty faced by revisionists is that those who think like them no longer enjoy the unchallenged dominance they once did. Since the mid-1970s, when *Time on the Cross* was published, neo-classical economic historiographical views have tended to monopolize interpretations of past and present forms of unfree labour.[12] More recently, however, this situation has begun to change, and the neo-classical economic historiographical view of unfree labour is now increasingly challenged, especially by scholars who are Marxists.[13] Revisionism, however, continues to operate as a hermetic discourse,

---

periods of crisis, revisionists adopt an 'epidemiological' explanation, and contend that worker mortality was largely an effect of a lack of immunity on the part of newly-arrived workers. There is absolutely no mystery, however, as to why revisionists generally and neo-classical economic historiography in particular should be more comfortable with the view that workers died because of a lack of resistance to disease, rather than as a result of poor working and living conditions. Given its assumption that a 'well-working market' benefits all involved, neo-classical economic theory is supported by the former thesis (= incidence of disease/death separated from the immediate socio-economic context and is thus beyond the power of 'from above' agency to alter) but undermined by the latter (= not everyone benefits from the market, which suggests in turn the presence of antagonistic class relations and struggle). That this is the sub-text informing an 'epidemiological' explanation is evident from the following symptomatic neo-classical economic observation (Shlomowitz, Brennan, and McDonald, 1996: 13), about the reasons for the high mortality rates affecting unfree labour recruited from the Pacific islands for work on the plantations during the nineteenth century: 'Given the crowded living conditions on plantations and given that Pacific islanders were susceptible to new diseases, disease dissemination and high mortality were inevitable whatever government regulations were in force and however benevolent were employers'.

12 The seminal interpretation of slavery from a neo-classical economic historiographic view is that by Fogel and Engerman (1974). The creation of a 'usable history' has been one of the more significant political results to emerge from the combined impact of the *Time on the Cross* debate about chattel slavery in the antebellum American south on the one hand, and of the ubiquitous 'everyday-forms-of-resistance' framework structured by postmodernism on the other, each of which has reinforced attempts to revise the meaning of unfree labour in the United States, Latin America, India, and Australia.

13 It would be wrong to give the impression that all additions to the present debate about unfree labour fall into the Marxist or revisionist camp. There are, of course, recent texts about unfree labour that are neither Marxist nor revisionist, but which nevertheless represent a return to nineteenth century discourse in another form. One is the abolitionist strand exemplified by Bales (1999; 2000), whose journalistic approach combines the moral outrage of human rights discourse with the breathless air of travel reportage: for example, '[t]he 11-year old boy I met in India... [t]he recently freed 22-year-old woman I met in Paris...in Western Brazil I watched enslaved workers', etc., etc., etc. (Bales, 2000: 38, 39, 43). Although performing the useful role of popularizing views about the acceptability

and evidence of theoretical and/or methodological disagreements between it and Marxism is wholly absent from the volume under review. The reason for this is significant: not a single contributor to this collection is drawn from the ranks of Marxist scholars. Revisionists can, of course, argue that neo-classical economic historiography is right, and those who criticize it from a Marxist perspective are wrong. In order to do this, however, it is necessary to engage with the analysis of opponents, and this the book under review palpably fails to do. It simply ignores recent Marxist contributions to the debate about unfree labour.

As a glance at the bibliography of any current Marxist text about unfree labour would confirm, holders of this view are not afraid to engage with the interpretations advanced by those with whom they disagree: in contrast, Marxist analyses of unfree labour are simply ignored by most revisionists. The latter not only invoke texts by fellow revisionists in support of their own claims but also utilize the familiar procedure of dismissing-by-chronologizing, which entails categorizing an opposing view as chronologically 'old' (= not-new). Marxism is by inference constituted as a viewpoint that is not even worth addressing, which in turn permits those who adopt this procedure to ignore interpretations which challenge and frequently undermine their own. What revisionists fail to point out, however, is that their own views also have a long lineage in the debate about unfree labour. Possessing epistemological roots in conservative ideology, agrarian populism and nationalism, therefore, revisionist claims generally can also be said to be chronologically 'old'. As significant, perhaps, is that postmodern (or 'new') varieties of revisionism are now being used by the state and employers in many Third World contexts to support political arguments that unfree labour is nothing more than a specific form of cultural 'otherness', to condemn trade unions as inappropriate universals or Eurocentric impositions, and to justify current workforce restructuring.[14]

---

to capitalism of unfree labour that have been circulating in the academy since the mid-1980s, this journalistic approach fails to investigate the causes of and debates about this link, and consequently misrecognizes both the nature of the problem and thus also its solution. For exponents of abolitionist discourse, therefore, the difficulty lies not with the system – that is, capitalism itself – but with the non-enforcement of legislation. Devoid of theory and politics, this kind of approach accordingly displays an evident inability to comprehend the systemic reasons why unfree relations continue to exist in the late twentieth century.

14 Because neoclassical economic theory and postmodernism both decry moral judgement, each denies the possibility of objective value standards (dismissed by postmodernists as 'foundational'). Like postmodern theory about the social, therefore, neoclassical economics seeks to empty economic behaviour of value judgements, the only acceptable

II

The distaste for theory signals its presence and effects early on in the volume. Symptomatically, therefore, in his introduction to the collection Howard Temperley fails to go beyond stating the obvious, that forms of unfreedom continue to exist: why this is so, let alone what systemic conditions give rise to bonded labour in the late twentieth century, is a question he is unable to pose, let alone answer.[15] Much the same is true of Gad Heuman's essay about resistance to apprenticeship in the Caribbean, which is not only bereft of theory, and replete with platitude and error, but also presents nothing empirically that is not already well known.[16] In his case the issue of theoretical misunderstanding does not even arise, since he appears to be wholly unaware of the debate about 'everyday-forms-of-resistance', and thus also of its epistemological implications for his own particular case study.[17] The musty flavour of the volume as a whole, however, is best conveyed by the three contributions

criterion being the maximization of subjective utility: since the normative component of this utility is not posed, any/all forms of desire projected in this manner are consequently perceived as good, regardless of content.

15 Temperley (2000: 1–10).

16 Temperley (2000: 135–149).

17 Unsurprisingly, therefore, the essay by Heuman in the book under review does not go much beyond the conclusion to an earlier essay by him on the same subject (Heuman, 1988): namely, the staggeringly obvious – not to say banal – finding that running away was a form of slave resistance. One is tempted to ask when has running away not been, in a very general sense, an act of resistance? To leave the issue there, however, is of the same order of profundity as a conclusion that water is wet. The important questions raised by the all-embracing concept 'resistance' – such as what kind of systemic transformation did it presage (if any), was such 'resistance' in fact acceptable to planters because it corresponded to a safety valve mechanism which did not threaten the *status quo* – all seem to have escaped Heuman's grasp (as also that of another text on the same subject, by Bush, 2000). His simplistic assumption that running away corresponded to an empowering 'from-below' form of 'resistance' overlooks the degree to which, historically, colonial planters and other agrarian capitalists have often encouraged ethnic/tribal identity, and smallscale/individual acts of resistance based on this, precisely in order to discourage mass mobilization arising from class solidarity (the political and economic effects of which all rural employers feared). Because certain kinds of 'from below' agency enabled planters to divide and rule a much larger and ethnically heterogeneous workforce, therefore, far from being an unproblematically empowering manifestation of grassroots opposition, resistance on occasion corresponded to exactly the opposite process: a *disempowering* form of accommodation to the existing class structure, all the more so for being presented by those such as Heuman as empowering 'assertiveness' on the part of those-below.

examined in detail below: by Swaisland on South Africa, by Temperley on India, and by Emmer on the Caribbean.

In a vainglorious account of the early activity undertaken by the Aborigines' Protection Society, Charles Swaisland, who is described as an erstwhile colonial administrator in Nigeria, focuses on parliamentary debates about unfreedom.[18] His essay conveys the impression that this human rights organization was a force for good in South Africa throughout the nineteenth and early twentieth century, when its benign intervention took the form of opposition to the Boers and the provision of support to indigenous blacks struggling against oppression. Where South Africa is concerned, however, the role of the Aborigines' Protection Society has unfortunately been anything but progressive. As the newly-merged Anti-Slavery and Aborigines' Protection Society, therefore, it not only endorsed the promulgation of South African Natives' Land Act of 1913 – legislation excluding non-whites from landownership that formed the basis of the 'separate development' policy which underpinned the apartheid system – but prevented black political opinion from publicizing its opposition to this law.[19] His experience during this episode led Sol Plaatje, the first secretary of the African National Congress, to describe Sir John Harris, the Organizing Secretary of the Aborigines' Protection Society as 'the South African government's most sturdy defender'.[20] More recently, a member of the Society's governing body published a text defending the apartheid system in South Africa, a book that also carried an endorsing foreword by the joint President of the Society, all of which allegedly suggest that nothing much has changed in this regard.[21]

The large, theoretically complex, and much-discussed subject of unfree labour in Asia is addressed in a short and wholly inadequate essay by Howard

18 See Temperley (2000: 265–280). To reduce a discussion about the post-emancipation labour regime in rural South Africa to what was said about this in parliamentary debate or by NGOs is to evade the much larger and more complex question of the systemic role of unfree black labour in the economic development which occurred in that context during the late nineteenth century and most of the twentieth. Throughout this period, this debate has involved virtually the whole of the political spectrum in South African society. As in the case of India (see below), there is in the case of South Africa a vast and rich literature, both about the issue of unfree labour itself and also about the debates generated by this (for useful accounts of which, see Wilson and Thompson (1971), Lacey (1981), O'Meara (1983), and Saunders (1988)), none of which Swaisland appears to have consulted.

19 On this point, see Willan (1979).

20 See Willan (1984: 200). It comes as no surprise that the reasons given by Harris (1933) for the ending of slavery are no different from those of Coupland.

21 The text in question is by Sawyer (1986).

Temperley, about one historical episode: the delegalization of slavery in British India.[22] Much of the text in this narrowly-focussed contribution appears to be the same as a chapter in a book written by him some thirty years ago, and its author has not seen fit to acquaint himself with wide-ranging and important debates about unfree labour in India which have taken place since then.[23] Unsurprisingly, therefore, in the absence of any analysis much of this essay fails to move beyond the merely descriptive. Since he has knowledge neither of the theory concerning unfreedom in India nor longstanding and more recent debates about this, Temperley – like Swaisland – is reduced to reciting (yet again) the details of British Parliamentary debates over slavery, this time with reference to the Indian subcontinent.[24] In a breath-takingly complacent catalogue, all the claims which recent debates referred to above have shown to be false are reproduced once again, and presented here unchallenged as fact. Thus we are informed that Indian slavery was benign, that slaves were better-off than landless workers, that slavery was a form of 'subsistence guarantee', that it was part of an indigenous system of reciprocal rights and obligations, and that because unfreedom was structured by caste, it was acceptable to the slaves themselves.[25] According to Temperley, therefore, not only was there no slave discontent or rebellion in India, but slaves did not even aspire to freedom.

The claims that in India slavery was benign, that slaves were better-off than landless workers, and that consequently they had no cause for complaint (let alone rebellion) rest centrally on the assumption that unfreedom corresponded to a beneficial 'subsistence guarantee', a mutually advantageous material arrangement premissed on reciprocal exchange between worker and employer. For the worker concerned, therefore, the negative relational aspects of unfreedom (lack of bargaining power, low wages, etc.) were offset by the promise of landlord provision during the off-peak agricultural season (when no employment was available) or in periods of economic crisis (such as famine). Unfortunately for Temperley, evidence suggests not only that generally no such 'subsistence guarantee' existed, that in most instances there was no actual need for it, but also that where there *was* a need for a 'subsistence guarantee' it was the creation of landlords themselves, who then invariably failed to deliver.[26]

---

22 Temperley (2000: 169–187).

23 For the chapter in question, see Temperley (1972: 93ff.).

24 Temperley (2000: 169–173, 181–183).

25 Temperley (2000: 174, 175, 177, 179, 180).

26 This situation, whereby rural employers in India deprived their bonded labourers of a 'subsistence guarantee', continued into the post-Independence era. On this subject, therefore, Patel (1952: 77) observes: 'when the bonded labourer agrees to serve under a

About agrarian relations in early nineteenth century India, therefore, Hjejle remarks in a seminal text (of which Temperley is seemingly unaware): 'The idea, which I have come across several times, that the slaves at least were entitled to work and to a subsistence, did not hold good in Malabar, Trichinopoly and Tanjore, where their wages were either cut or stopped altogether when there was no employment'.[27] Both the absence of a need for a 'subsistence guarantee' during the working lifetime of unfree labourers in south India during the nineteenth century, together with the abandoning by landholders both of old or infirm slaves who were no longer able to work and of tied labour during periods of famine, is also confirmed by other sources.[28] Moreover, where no general condition of scarcity exists, but in which an employer to whom workers owe debts remunerates them at levels he himself fixes, poverty/starvation is a direct creation of producers themselves, so as to exercise more control over labour-power. This was true of Kerala in 1870s, where it was the landlord's hold over labour-power which generated the need by workers for a 'subsistence guarantee' in the first place.[29] In this particular instance, therefore, the requirement for a 'subsistence guarantee' did not precede and operate independently of landholder power.

When finally he considers the reasons why contemporary forms of unfreedom continue to exist in spite of earlier legislative abolition, Temperley unwittingly deploys claims associated with the theoretically problematic semi-feudal thesis: namely, that debt bondage is an effect of pauperization, and a form of worker dependency on landlords that is neither capitalist nor feudal (p.185).[30] Such a view ignores the fact that in India following the green

master, he has promised not to work for any other person. *But the master does not guarantee work for him for the whole year. When there is no work for him, he is given neither food nor grain allowance...This is also the time when there is hardly any farm work to be found in the neighbourhood*' (emphasis added).

27 See Hjejle (1967: 96).

28 These other sources include Saintsbury (1972), Saradamoni (1980), Manickam (1982), and Arnold (1984). As Degler (1976) and Tiwary (1985) point out, much the same is true of nineteenth century Brazil, where plantation slaves who became too old for work were manumitted by their 'generous' masters, and also of Bihar during the early 1980s, where creditor-employers encouraged older bonded labourers (whose usefulness as agricultural workers had ended) to free themselves, yet strongly resisted attempts at self-emancipation on the part of young bonded labourers.

29 For the generation by landlords of a need for a 'subsistence guarantee' in 1870s Kerala, see Kusuman (1973).

30 In contrast to those such as Dingwaney (1985), who maintain that the continuation of unfree labour in India after the legislative abolition of slavery in 1843 is evidence for the persistance in the agrarian sector of long-standing feudal relations, Mayer (1982:108) comments: 'The steady overseas demand for labour from industrial agriculture in Ceylon,

revolution era, bonded labour has been reproduced by capitalist rich peasants and not by landlords, and thus by the need of employers to lower costs and maintain control over labour-power and not by pauperization *per se*. Lacking a theoretical framework which enables him to understand this, Temperley's conclusion is predictably a motherhood-and-apple-pie cliché: 'in the present, as in the past', he opines, 'the principal task facing solutions to India's problems is finding ways of eliminating conditions...that encourage such practices [= unfree labour] to develop'.[31] The latter observation would normally form the starting point of, not the conclusion to, an analysis of the reasons for the continued existence of unfree relations.

The essay by Pieter C. Emmer, about indentured labour in the Caribbean during the period 1834–1917, is not merely inadequate and revisionist but comically so.[32] As in the case of Temperley, all the old, long-discredited canards are paraded by Emmer yet again (indenture = 'choice' = economic empowerment), joined on this occasion by some 'new' ones almost entirely of his own invention (the post-emancipation economic plight of Afro-Caribbean ex-slaves was psychologically determined and thus of their own making). Invoking 'modern archival research' (by whom and where published we are not informed), Emmer paints a rose-tinted picture of indentured labour on Caribbean plantations in

Malaya and elsewhere put pressure on the landowners to tie labour down, and it was this which produced the "debt bondage" which is so often interpreted, not as the modern form of labour relationship that it was, but as a form of traditional domination'. Like many of those who espouse a neo-classical economic historiographical framework, exponents of the semi-feudal thesis (Patnaik, 1985; Breman, 1974; 1985; Byres, 1996) maintain that capitalism and unfree labour are systemically antithetical, and that consequently where these exist unfree relations are archaic remnants destined to be eliminated by capital, which strives to replace such 'pre-capitalist' (or 'semi-feudal') forms with free wage labour. Again like their neo-classical economic counterparts, many exponents of the semi-feudal thesis insist that the main opposition to the elimination of unfree relations in India (and elsewhere) comes not from above, in the shape of employers generally and agrarian capitalists in particular (both of whom attempt unsuccessfully to eradicate unfreedom), but rather from below, in the form of rural workers who struggle to reproduce these linkages because they correspond to 'patronage' or a 'subsistence guarantee' extended by kind-hearted employers/masters. And again like neo-classical economic historians, those who endorse the semi-feudal thesis have as their theoretical (and thus political) objective the development not of socialism but of capitalism.

31 Temperley (2000: 186).

32 See Temperley (2000: 150–168). For other versions of the same kind of slavery/indenture-is-good-for-the-slaves/migrants argument, structured by the concept 'the History of European Expansion' and presented in the journal *Itinerario*, see Emmer (1997a; 1997b).

which Asian migration becomes an early form of package holiday tourism.[33] Thus we are told that nineteenth century Caribbean planters followed a policy of 'amelioration', as a result of which plantation workers enjoyed higher wages, better working/living conditions and a reduction in their workload.[34] Unsurprisingly, therefore, he also denies that those who migrated to or worked on the plantations were coerced/unfree/misled, and consequently insists that Asians went to and remained in the Caribbean voluntarily, because they were attracted by the good living/working conditions there. Planters, he avers, employed indentured migrants not because such workers were unfree but simply for organizational reasons, because employers 'required a special type of labour'.[35]

---

33 Claims unsupported by evidence are problems frequently encountered in articles written by Emmer. For example, in an earlier text (Emmer, 1987) comparing demographic rates of Indian and Javanese indentured labour in Surinam, one is suddenly confronted with the following assertion: noting that far fewer Indians than Javanese still worked on the plantations, this difference is 'explained' by Emmer in terms of a 'preference' on the part of Javanese communities in Surinam for continued plantation work. The inference is that, unlike Indians, indentured labourers from Java remained on the plantations because they wanted to, an argument in keeping with standard revisionist claim about 'choice-making' workers exercising subjective preferences. Unfortunately for Emmer, evidence contained in other texts (Kloosterboer, 1960: Ch.3) contradicts this, and suggests that Javanese indentured labourers were legally prohibited from commodifying their own labour-power (or exercising a preference about whether, and for whom, to work). Despite low wages and overseer brutality, therefore, they continued to work on plantations because of coercion and penal sanctions (fines, imprisonment).

34 That planters were in any sense benign is a myth that was effectively dispelled some time ago by, among others, Marvin Harris (1969). Similarly, all the central emplacements of the 'subsistence guarantee' as applied by Fogel and Engerman (1974) to the plantation economy of the antebellum American south – that in terms of infant mortality rates, life expectancy, housing, clothing, health care, and food, slaves were better off than free workers – have been shown to be unsustainable empirically (Sutch, 1975; Gutman, 1975; David *et al.*, 1976). Unfortunately, this has not prevented the periodic reappearance of both claims (benign masters, 'subsistence guarantee') in revisionist analyses of unfree labour.

35 These organizational reasons, Emmer infers, have to do with post-emancipation labour shortages on the plantations, and the argument as presented by him projects this as a technical issue: that is, simply in terms of the need on the part of planters to secure adequate and sufficient numbers of workers. As Emmer must surely be aware, the concept of labour shortage is itself problematic. Thus a shortage of workers may exist in absolute terms, where in the absence of free labour employers utilize unfree equivalents. The same concept, however, may also refer to a relative scarcity of labour, where this commodity is available for hire but not at a price which employers are willing to pay. In the latter case, it is the cost and not the availability of labour-power which is at issue. This distinction is

Having claimed that indentured migrants from India were not coerced or misled into working on the plantations, the second part of his argument concerns why they and not the Afro-Caribbean freedmen emerged as the economically successful group in the history of the West Indies. In this connection Emmer repeats and endorses the self-serving justification advanced by planters at the time: namely, that – unlike Asian migrants – Afro-Caribbean ex-slaves were impervious to the attraction of high wages on offer.[36] Accordingly,

---

expressed most clearly in a recent book (Shapiro, 1998: 51) about the reasons for the employment of unfree labour in the Tennessee coalfields during the late nineteenth century, where the following point is made: 'The public rhetoric of mine managers...masked their most important motivation in seeking the use of convict labourers. Attracting free workers to Tennessee's mines may have been a worry in their early years of operation; but as both blacks and whites flocked to and helped build coal towns in the 1880s and the early 1890s, problems of labor supply dissipated...These industrialists viewed the convict lease first and foremost as a means of cutting labor costs, both directly and by dampening the activity of mining unions'.

36 See Temperley (2000: 155, 158). It is clear from what he has written previously that, where 'doubt remains about whether the slaves were positioned to grasp the intricacies of the market', the problem for Emmer (1992: 35–36) concerns centrally 'the non-capitalist behaviour [= imperviousness to wage incentives] of the ex-slaves and their backward-bending labour supply curve', a view that brings him dangerously close to endorsing the myth of the 'lazy native'. A long-discredited emplacement of colonial discourse, the myth of the 'lazy native' is perhaps best captured in the following description, where it combines with and reinforces the concept of the 'benign master' as provider of a 'subsistence guarantee'. Writing about African slaves owned by Arabs, therefore, Orde Browne (1933: 14–15) invokes all the usual stereotypes: 'Thus the first experience that the African received of working regularly for another man was in the form of slavery; ... As always in the case of forced labour, the worker was most inefficient unless closely supervised, and this was not to the taste of his easy-going Oriental master; probably only a very moderate standard of performance was exacted... It was the master's part to provide food and all other requirements, and to care for the sick and aged, and the slave was thus freed from all responsibility or anxiety. Under a rule in the main kindly...he lived entirely in the present, without any incentive to industry, enterprise, or forethought. The system accorded well enough with African mentality. Sheltered from most misfortunes, except those occasioned by the master's wrath, he led a congenial, carefree life;... The greatest injury inflicted on him by it was the mental state which it produced; the very features which rendered it tolerable to him were those that demoralized his character. Sly evasion was his attitude towards a task in which he had no interest, and he received a prolonged education in reluctance to work; his weak points of irresponsibility and lack of forethought were cultivated, and there was little encouragement for the evolution of individuality or character. When, therefore, people who had acquired this mentality were confronted by the prospect of free labour for wages, they were certain to prove unsatisfactory; they had been taught to shirk, not to work, and found it very difficult to absorb the idea of labour for another combined with

ex-slaves 'were cutting…ties with the most expansive sector of the economy and thus forgoing considerable amounts of income [a situation] which prevented the freedmen from profiting from the readiness of the planters to pay a market wage'.[37] A result of what he identifies as innate psychologistic traits is that, unlike Asian immigrants, Afro-Caribbean ex-slaves were not educated 'for the market society…[they] were not prepared to face the ups and downs… in the market for labour'.[38] Any economic problems faced by freedmen during the post-emancipation era were thus their own fault, and not that of the planters, who attempted 'to create a labour force responsive to monetary incentives'.[39] The difficulty with Emmer's argument is that it is a farrago of nonsense from beginning to end.

Not a single rose-tinted claim made by Emmer and his 'new' research, either about the general process of post-1850s 'amelioration', the absence of coercion/unfreedom, the benign disposition of the planter class, the payment of high wages, or about the imperviousness of Afro-Caribbean ex-slaves to market forces, survives even a cursory examination. Moreover, his view is contradicted both by twentieth century (= new) and by nineteenth century (= old) sources.[40] Concerning the unfree nature of indenture, therefore, even

---

profit for oneself. The ex-slave is thus freqently incapable of providing even for his own requirements, and he forms a most discouraging type with which to have any dealings'. For the strong belief on the part of capitalist farmers in South Africa in the existence of a backward sloping labour supply, see Wilson and Thompson (1971: 120–123).

37 Temperley (2000: 161).

38 See Temperley (2000: 165). A conceptual outgrowth of the 'lazy native' argument, the view about the educative value of unfree labour posits that because the 'native' is 'lazy', it is necessary to compel him/her to commodify labour-power. The inference is that, left to themselves, Afro-Caribbean ex-slaves would not otherwise learn how to make their labour-power available to planters and other employers wishing to purchase this. The view about 'the effect of forced labour on primitive mentality' was dismissed as nonsense a long time ago by the ILO (International Labour Conference, 1929: 236) in the following uncompromising terms: 'It must be recognized that, although increasingly deprecated in authoritative circles, a stubborn opinion still exists that man's duty to work can best be inculcated upon a native by measures of compulsion'. Like the 'lazy native' argument, therefore, the view about the educative value of compulsion serves to disguise the fact that what is at issue is the price and not the availability of labour-power.

39 Temperley (2000: 158).

40 Ironically, among the many 'new' sources which contradict Emmer's present claim that Asian indentured labourers were aware of their destination and not coerced into migrating to the Caribbean are his own earlier articles. About the recruitment of Indian indentured labour for Surinam, therefore, he has written (Emmer, 1984: 95): 'In theory, the process of recruitment was regulated in such a way that it was distinctly different from

conservative texts are unambiguous, as evidenced by the opinions expressed on this subject by Sir George Campbell, a high-ranking colonial administrator with first-hand knowledge not only of tenure and famine conditions in India but also of the dynamics generating/governing late nineteenth century outmigration from the subcontinent to the Caribbean.[41]

Comparing plantation labour in the post-emancipation American South with that in British colonies, Campbell's description of the latter bears repeating: 'In order to obtain the means of carrying on the coolie emigration the [colonial] Government has been induced to sanction a system which would not be tolerated in the case of white labourers. [Indentured migrants from India] are bound down to labour for a term of years. They do not engage themselves to masters whom they know, or to any individual, but are engaged to serve in the colony, and on their arrival are assigned to a master. They are afterwards subject to be re-assigned and transferred from one master to another, and from one estate to another, during the term of their indenture, without their own consent or voice in the matter. In short, call it as we may, and justify it as on the

---

enslavement...In practice, however, there were several aspects which bear resemblance to the enslavement of Africans during the previous period.... In theory, all indentured labourers were recruited to go to one specific country... As in the slave trade, the British Indian migrants, like the Africans, had no idea where they were being taken'.

41 During the latter part of the nineteenth century, Sir George Campbell (1824–92) not only held important administrative/judicial posts in the colonial government of India, travelled widely and carried out comparative analyses of different land tenure systems, but he also formulated the Indian tenant right question (security of tenure for cultivators), produced the report issued by the Indian famine commission of the late 1860s, and conducted ethnographic research into the tribal populations of Bengal and the Central Provinces. Accordingly, the combination of on the one hand his work on the Indian land tenure system, his ethnographic studies and official investigations into famine conditions all licensed an understanding of the reasons for migration itself, while on the other Campbell's background in colonial administration/law provided a corresponding insight into both the actual process of outmigration and working/living standards at the Indian migrants' destination. His observations about the different stages of indentured migration are interesting precisely because they were informed by a Victorian ruling class colonial ideology at the high point of imperialism. The latter notwithstanding, Campbell regarded indentured migration from Asia as unfree, and employment/living conditions on Caribbean plantations as coercive/oppressive. He would undoubtedly have baulked at Emmer's current description of these same processes at that conjuncture as a tension-free and empowering transition by Asian indentured workers to a Caribbean rural idyll inhabited by benevolent planters and 'choice-making' Indian migrant labour.

whole beneficial, if we can, there can be no doubt that it is a temporary, modified, and supervised slavery, so long as the obligation to labour lasts'.[42]

In contrast to Emmer, who maintains that because of the delights of plantation work indentured labour voluntarily remained in the Caribbean after the contract ended, Campbell observes: 'What I have always insisted on is, that at any rate after the indenture has expired, the coolie is entitled to be treated as a free man...my great complaint has been that Colonial authorities, under the guise of vagrancy laws and the like, have curtailed that freedom and equality to the extent of making the emancipated coolie's life unendurable till he consents to re-indenture'.[43] On the question of better working/living conditions and a reduced workload, much the same is true: on Grenada in 1878, for example, 'persons in charge of the estates neither took care of the coolies nor paid them, nor provided for them when sick, and worked them to such a pitch that few would survive'.[44] Needless to say, all this is confirmed by other nineteenth century sources.

Thus the detailed report by the West India Royal Commission into the conditions on the plantations throughout the Caribbean during the early 1890s indicates that, rather than everyone benefiting from economic growth, as claimed by Emmer, increasing profitability was linked instead to wage reductions.[45] In the case of Trinidad and St Vincent, therefore, low wages persisted even when prices for plantation crops were high, and on the sugar plantations of Trinidad wage cuts varied between 5% and 60%. Low wages and the withholding of payment resulted in worker debt to plantation stores,

---

42 See Campbell (1879: 114–115), whose view of Asian indentured migrants as unfree is confirmed by virtually all those who have written about the plantation labour regime in the Caribbean (with the obvious exception of those defined as revisionists). For example, Williams (1970: 355–356) notes: 'Every immigrant was bound to reside on the plantation on which he was under indenture; he was thus attached to the soil. If found anywhere else, without a ticket of leave or a certificate showing exemption from labour, he could be stopped, without a warrant, by the Protector of Immigrants or any person authorized by him in writing, by a plantation policeman or by the employer or his manager, or overseer, and taken to the nearest police station; if convicted, the penalty was a maximum of seven days imprisonment, with or without hard labour. Absence without leave carried a maximum fine of two pounds for males, one pound for females. Absence for three days constituted desertion;... The penalty for the immigrant...was a maximum of five pounds and/or a maximum imprisonment of two months. If indentured labour was free, it was, to paraphrase Carlyle, freedom plus a constable'.

43 See Campbell (1879: 115–116).

44 See Campbell (1879: 118).

45 On this and the following points made in the paragraph, see West India Royal Commission (1897).

which gave rise in turn to the truck system, one of main causes of unfreedom. Similarly, the report reveals that far from being reduced, as claimed by Emmer, the workload was much rather augmented during the same decade. Not only were there no labour shortages on the plantations at this time, but the immigration of indentured Asians continued despite a local abundance and availability of free workers.

The reason for this apparent paradox is obvious to everyone, it seems, except Emmer. As is well documented, the situation faced by the late nineteenth century plantation economy in the Caribbean was one of crisis, as overproduction resulted from increased capitalist competition.[46] In order to maintain or enhance profitability, therefore, planters were neither ready nor willing to pay high wages to workers who were free, and thus able to bargain over the price of their labour-power. Why agrarian capitalists resorted to the employment of indentured migrants in such circumstances is not difficult to discern. Planters in Jamaica admitted that the object of indenture was to undermine the bargaining power of locals, while their counterparts in St Lucia candidly expressed a preference for unfree workers: 'asked why planters prefer coolie to native labour', a planter replied 'because the former is more reliable, *being compulsory*'.[47]

This divide-and-rule strategy is confirmed by what others said at that conjuncture.[48] Thus another planter observed tellingly: 'It is of great importance to us to endeavour to provide a portion of other labourers, whom we might use as a set-off, and, when the time comes, makes us, as far as possible, independent of our negro population; and it has occurred to us that a moderate number of Bengalese...might be very suitable for our purpose'. Similarly, an attorney who represented planter interests argued: 'I think the safety of whites

46 On this point see Albert and Graves (1984).

47 See West India Royal Commission (1897: 70, emphasis added).

48 This divide-and-rule strategy also operated in the antebellum American south, where one of the economic objectives behind the employment of unfree labour was to undermine the bargaining power of and thus keep down the wage levels for workers who were free. During the 1850s, therefore, Frederick Law Olmsted (1953: 90) noted that 'white labour cannot live in competition with slave-labour. In other words, the holder of slave-labour controls the local market for labour', while Harriet Beecher Stowe (1853: 427) observed similarly that 'the filling up of all branches of mechanics and agriculture with slave-labour necessarily depresses free labour'. Such views were confirmed by Frederick Douglass (1845), an ex-slave who regarded poor whites as victims of slavery; he attributed the racism he experienced to the fact that free workers were forced to compete with unfree labour, and thus found it difficult to secure improvements in wages and conditions of employment.

depends very much upon the want of union in the different races of labourers'.[49] *Pace* Emmer, not only did Caribbean planters prefer bonded labour, but the reason for this was not simply technical – because they 'required a special type of labour' – but rather in order to pre-empt/undermine rural working class organization/mobilization. The object of introducing labour that was unfree was, in short, to reduce the cost to planters of employing *all* forms of labour-power: not just that of the Asian migrants themselves, but also that of local Afro-Caribbean ex-slaves.[50]

Neither is there any support for Emmer's contention that Afro-Caribbean freedmen were psychologically impervious to monetary incentives, and that for this reason they missed out on the largesse distributed to all and sundry by a benign planter class. The truth of the matter is, of course, exactly the opposite: it was precisely because ex-slaves in British Guiana exhibited class consciousness and organized/operated as free workers during the latter part of the nineteenth century, by bargaining over wages, conditions, and duration of work, as well as withholding their labour-power and/or selling this to the highest bidder, that planters began to replace them with indentured migrants who – because they were unfree – were unable similarly to bargain about the

49 Both these quotations are cited in Mangru (1987: 40, 43).

50 This corresponded to the familiar process of workforce restructuring, a procedure whereby employers replaced free and more costly forms of labour-power with ones that were unfree and thus cheaper. The effects of the low wages which resulted from such divide-and-rule tactics adopted by planters were still in evidence some twenty years after the ending of indenture. Hence the negative impact of unfree labour on the working conditions of and wages received by local free workers – i.e., those Afro-Caribbean ex-slaves who themselves did not or could not migrate in search of higher wages elsewhere – outlined at that conjuncture by an economist based in the British West Indies (Shepherd, 1938: 247–248). He noted that 'The abundant supply of labour and the ease with which slaves, or later indentured immigrants, could be obtained prevented any pressure on employers for improvements in working conditions. Indentured immigration, it is true, was conducted under Government supervision, but *the minimum requirements of the immigration ordinance were very low and tended to become the standard for all other labourers…wages were extremely low.* Men and women received only 25 cents, or a shilling and a halfpenny, for each day actually worked during their five-year period of indenture. Indentured labourers could not leave the estate for employment elsewhere without the consent of the protector of Immigrants. They could be compelled to work as and when required by the employer and at any kind of work he cared to choose. *Other employees found it necessary to conform to these conditions in order to retain employment…*The annual earnings [in the late 1930s] still remain very low. Records of several hundred men showed an average of only a hundred dollars per annum. You cannot hit many high social spots with an income of only £20 a year' (emphasis added).

price of their labour-power, and sell it elsewhere or withdraw it when pay/conditions were not to their liking.[51] In other words, a labour market already existed, in that local workers were responsive to the 'pull' of wages and the 'push' of landlessness (or insufficient land). The necessity of having to bring a labour market into being, as embodied in Emmer's assertion about the imperviousness of Afro-Caribbean ex-slaves to monetary incentives, is not an issue: what is the issue is how much they – as owners of labour-power – were to receive for the sale of this commodity.[52]

Where economic mobility in the form of a capacity personally to commodify or recommodify labour-power was concerned, therefore, freedmen did not face the same problem as indentured migrants. Since wages were too low to attract them onto the plantations, Afro-Caribbean workers who were free to sell their labour-power sold it for higher payment elsewhere: accordingly, some 25,000 Jamaicans migrated to the Panama zone to work on the construction of the canal, others went to the banana plantations in Costa Rica, and yet others to work on railway construction in Puerto Rico.[53] *Pace* Emmer, those who resisted the formation/reproduction of a market in free labour were the planters and not the Afro-Caribbean ex-slaves: the former subjects did so because they wanted a cheap workforce 'at their perfect command', whereas the latter subjects by contrast struggled to commodify labour because – having ceased to be slaves – they sought higher wages and to this end were no longer prepared to accept either the low-paid work or the kind of unfreedom planters had traditionally imposed on them.

III

Part of the blame for the intellectually regressive and dismal theoretical quality of this volume lies with the journal where the collection first appeared as a special issue, *Slavery and Abolition*: the unrelenting empiricism of the latter is due to the apparent discomfort of its editors with anything resembling

51 See, for example, Rodney (1981) and Mangru (1987).

52 The view about the imperviousness of Afro-Caribbean ex-slaves to market forces is one that Emmer appears to have inherited from earlier works on the agrarian structure of the Dutch East Indies, by conservatives such as Furnivall (1944) and Boeke (1953), in which the backward-sloping supply curve was perceived as indicative of a profound and unbridgeable difference between Eastern and Western approaches to economic development (Arndt, 1987: 149–150).

53 See Beachey (1957).

theoretical debate, an outlook which explains (but does not excuse) the absence of anything approaching serious discussion and, consequently, the unchallenged presence in the book of so many erroneous (not to say laughable) claims/arguments.[54] This is to be regretted, not least because the systemic reasons for the historical and continued existence of unfree labour are important, as evidenced by the fact that these questions are now attracting renewed interest both in academic circles and also among organizations concerned with development issues.[55] In short, it is a subject which deserves better and more serious treatment than that provided by this volume.

54 It comes as no surprise to learn that elsewhere one of the editors of the journal in question endorses the 'subsistence guarantee' argument as applied to post-emancipation Caribbean plantations. 'Many of the former slaves no longer wanted to be associated with the plantations', he writes (Walvin, 1992: 326), '[b]ut their new-found freedom had its costs. *Whatever else the plantations had done, they had provided a modicum of paternalistic material protection.* They had, after a fashion, housed, clothed and fed their black labour force' (emphasis added).

55 Not only has a Nobel economics laureate (Sen, 1999) suddenly discovered – rather late in the day – that bonded labour has not vanished but continues to play an important role in the perpetuation of global poverty and underdevelopment, therefore, but unfree labour employed in the Export Processing Zones of the Third World has similarly been categorized as a key political issue for the twenty-first century by a popular journalistic text (Klein, 1999) influencing many of those currently participating in the anti-globalization movement (Seattle, Prague).

CHAPTER 11

Shifts and Stasis in Development Studies*

Throughout the 1980s and 1990s, decades that witnessed the rise of neoliberalism and the demise of actually existing socialism, those on the political left who wrote about development issues followed one of three paths. The first was straightforwardly to embrace positions hitherto considered incompatible with socialism, an apostasy that identified its adherents as belonging to the 'love your enemy' camp. Hence the stampede on the part of many in academia to jump on the twin bandwaggons of neoliberal economics and/or postmodern theory, and the myriad variants influenced by these frameworks.[1] Among the most common where the study of the peasantry was concerned was the 'new' postmodern populism, a theoretical approach that replaced political economy, the focus of which was on the disempowerment of class relations, with the analysis of identity politics as the form of rural grassroots empowerment.

Rather than being differentiated by class, as Marxists had long argued, peasants were re-essentialized by 'new' postmodern populists (= those in the 'love your enemy' camp) as undifferentiated smallholders and then reconstituted as the authentic embodiment/bearers of national/regional/local culture. In these analyses revolutionary action aimed at overturning the capitalist system by capturing the state gave way to resistance (preferably of the 'everyday' sort) designed to do no more than secure a systemically unspecific notion of democracy. No longer destined for the dustbin of history, an homogeneous peasantry

* Reviewed here are *System in Crisis: The Dynamics of Free Market Capitalism*, by James Petras and Henry Veltmeyer (London: Zed Books, 2003); *Agrarian Studies: Essays on Agrarian Relations in Less Developed Countries*, edited by V.K. Ramachandran and Madhura Swaminathan (London: Zed Books, 2003); *Reclaiming the Land: The Resurgence of Rural Movements in Africa, Asia and Latin America*, edited by Sam Moyo and Paris Yeros (London: Zed Books, 2005); *A Radical History of Development Studies: Individuals, Institutions and Ideologies*, edited by Uma Kothari (London: Zed Books, 2005). An earlier and much longer version of this review article, titled 'Weapons of the Week, Weakness of the Weapons: Shifts and Stasis in Development Theory', appeared in *The Journal of Peasant Studies*, Volume 34, No.1 (2007).

1 The impact on development studies of prevailing intellectual fashion is an issue that, for obvious reasons, still awaits a chronicler. When considered, the reason for a change of opinion is subject to a classic form of displacement: from the context of the viewer him/herself to that of the viewed. Its cause is invariably – and wrongly – attributed simply to exogenous factors, such as a new dynamic or a new set of circumstances operating in or affecting the area studied.

cropped up as the eternal 'other' of capitalist development in a variety of discourses about rural agency ('new social movements', 'the subaltern', ecofeminism, 'post-colonialism', 'post-Marxism', and 'post-capitalism').

The second or 'I told you so' path was followed by those who remained Marxists. The latter, although in a minority and sometimes outside the academy, continued to argue for socialism whilst simultaneously pointing out the conservative or reactionary epistemology and politics structuring the 'new' postmodern populism. Included among the criticisms made by 'I told you so' Marxism was that the postmodern reification of ethnic and peasant identities undertaken in the name of aporia and/or plurality amounted to a reconfiguration that underwrote the worldview of conservatives and those on the political right.[2] As these Marxist criticisms of the 'cultural turn' started to make an impact, a number of those in the 'love your enemy' camp began to reconsider their views, and return to positions they had abandoned earlier.

Changes of this kind were due invariably to an absence of knowledge about theory, and a consequent unawareness of the connection between the epistemological lineage of the political right and that of the 'new' postmodern populism. Timing is therefore a crucial indicator of a shift from the 'love your enemy' to the 'I told you so' camp. All 'critiques' of postmodernism by those who had been in the 'love your enemy' camp, and then realized the mistake of their albeit fashionable political allegiance, tend to date from the mid-to-late-1990s onwards, when the reactionary underpinnings of the 'new' postmodern populism had already been exposed by Marxist dissidents of the 'I told you so' variety.

Adherents of the third path followed a different line, one that combined avoidance (of debate) with reiteration (of the analytically implausible). Not part of the dissident camp, therefore, were yet others who, although (nominally) Marxists, engaged in defensive action in order to protect arguments that were theoretically increasingly unsustainable. They succeeded only in becoming full-time curators of a myth of their own devising. Neither shifting their views according to the tides of theory, nor however criticizing those who did, Marxists (or perhaps 'Marxists') of this particular variety were as a result unable to say 'I told you so'. For this reason, their contributions both to the defence of Marxism and more generally to the development debate unfolding throughout this period were correspondingly fruitless, and represent a form of theoretical stasis where the study of peasants is concerned.[3]

2 Three of these Marxist dissidents were Petras and Veltmeyer, on which see more below, and Brass (1991).

3 That followers of this third path were among the participants in a conference the objective of which, according to the editors of the *Agrarian Studies* volume (Ramachandran and

Without knowledge of this background, and how exponents of particular theoretical views either changed or did not change their minds, it is impossible accurately to evaluate any of the numerous histories of development currently in circulation. Since the four volumes under review here – all from the same publishing house, one that has specialised in development issues – aspire to make an impression on this already overcrowded field, it is important to provide some of the contributions they contain with this kind of context. Contrary to the impression frequently created by *post hoc* accounts of the development debate that took place over the latter part of the twentieth century, therefore, the intellectual itineraries of some of those who participated in this can best be described as circuitous.[4]

Only one of the books reviewed here – that by James Petras and Henry Veltmeyer – is by Marxists who initially took the second path (= the 'I told you so' variety). Although some of the other books – the volumes edited by Uma Kothari, by V.K. Ramachandran and Madhura Swaminathan, and by Sam Moyo and Paris Yeros – contain a few contributions by those who followed the same path, rather better represented than perhaps they should be are those who followed both the first (= 'love your enemy') and the third (= avoidance/reiteration) paths. The main focus of this review article is on the agrarian question, because of its centrality to development theory, to the debate about rural transformation, and to the rôle in them of peasants and agricultural workers.

I

Two of the books under review here, those edited by Kothari and by Moyo and Yeros, are in the main of a generally poor standard (= 'theory lite').[5] Neither volume bothers to interrogate, let alone define, what precisely is meant

---

Swaminathan, 2003: xi – emphasis added), 'was to provide a forum for discussion and debate on *new* theoretical and empirical research from a left perspective on agrarian relations in less-developed countries', is ironic indeed.

4 It is impossible to surmise from the confident assertion about how old and well-known are '[e]legiac accounts of the loss of rural ways of life, or of the despoliation and neglect of the countryside', that one of the authors (Corbridge and Jones, 2005: 1) is the same person – Corbridge – who a decade earlier missed precisely the longevity and pervasiveness of this very ideology when endorsing its latest manifestation, in the form of the 'new' postmodern populism.

5 Why two contributions to the volume edited by Moyo and Yeros (by Ampuero and Brittain, and by Veltmeyer) are regarded as the sole exceptions to this and the following criticisms is outlined below.

by the central rubric informing their respective collections.[6] Most of the contributors have little or nothing to say about the historical trajectory followed by development studies that has not been said before, at length and better, by others. What they do say is frequently confused and/or inaccurate, and in not a few instances amounts to no more than a list of those (wrongly) considered to be the 'great and the good' of development studies. Somewhat predictably, hyperbole is much in evidence. Contrary to the absurd claim that appears on the back cover, therefore, none of the contributors to the volume edited by Kothari are by any stretch of the imagination 'leading thinkers in Development Studies'.

Both volumes contain accounts of the debates about development over the latter part of the twentieth century that, most charitably, can only be described as misleading. This they manage to be in one of two ways, and frequently both. On the one hand, therefore, are acts of commission: inaccurate claims – made either by the contributors themselves, or on their behalf by other contributors – to have played a crucial part in spotting and then denouncing the emergence of a politically reactionary discourse (nationalism, populism, the 'cultural turn'). On the other are inadvertent acts of omission: that is, an equally misleading silence about important contributions that did have an impact on the development debate, but for some reason go unmentioned. The latter aspect in particular constitutes evidence of a below-par approach to the issues discussed, and indicates a worrying unfamiliarity with the literature about development. Such a lack of knowledge underlines yet again the presence of an unfortunate trend – dumbing down – across the social sciences.

---

6 To say, as does the editor of *A Radical History of Development Studies*, that the volume 'is a radical chronicle because it includes plural conceptions of development history and adopts a critical perspective towards, and engagement with, orthodoxies of development theory and practice' (Kothari, 2005: 1), is to say nothing, since stated thus the term remains politically meaningless. In short, it fails to differentiate between a 'critical perspective' of development that emanates from the political left and one that originates from the discourse of the political right. Both are covered by the spuriously progressive (and hence slippery) concept 'radical', and the volume simply repeats the same mistake as an earlier volume on the same subject (Horowitz, de Castro, and Gerassi, 1969), the difference being that now there is no longer any excuse for making this kind of error. That Kothari is wholly unaware of the different politics structuring this rubric is evident from her categorization as radical not just Marxist theory but also 'post-colonial and feminist perspectives and analyses', and the classification of them all as 'thinking from the "left"'. Unlike Marxism, both post-colonial and feminist essentialisms have strong roots in conservative discourse (on which see Brass 2000a; 2003b; 2006). An inability on the part of its editor to spot this difference augurs badly for the rest of *A Radical History of Development Studies*, a misgiving that is indeed borne out.

Evidence of this is scattered throughout both these volumes. Thus, for example, in their contribution to *A Radical History of Development Studies* about environmentalism, populism and development, Phil Woodhouse and Admos Chimhowu fail to mention – let alone consider – even fairly standard (let alone important) texts making this same connection.[7] The centrality of gender to populist discourse about ecology is ignored, notwithstanding the ideological potency of an epistemology that associates females with subsistence cultivation on smallholdings. This stems from (and in turn licenses the continuation of) a relay in statement equating women with nature, the latter with peasant family farming, and them all with a powerful form of national identity that is both agrarian and 'natural'. Woodhouse and Chimhowu also draw a naïf and theoretically spurious distinction between populism and what is termed 'political ecology'. All ecological discourse is *by definition* political, regardless of whether it identifies itself (and is identified by others) as such.

Like a number of other contributions to the volume edited by Kothari, the one by John Harriss is not only contentious, and silent about the deep roots of the development debate as well as more recent crucial interventions in this, but also tediously replete with autobiographical details.[8] Rather surprisingly, his historiographical account begins – after a brief genuflection to the 1940s and 1950s – in the mid-1960s, a short while before he himself 'entered the scene, as the first ever student of development studies'.[9] The subsequent forty year history of development studies is divided by him into four periods: a 'time of promise' (1965–80), 'hubris' (the 1980s), 'reinvention' (the 1990s), and

7 See Woodhouse and Chimhowu (2005: 180–199). Although their remit is populist discourse with particular reference to Africa, Woodhouse and Chimhowu somehow manage to overlook not just earlier texts on this subject (Kofi, 1978), but also the classic article on African populism by Saul (1969). Unsurprisingly, much of what is found in the latter analysis is encountered also in (but not transcended by) their own contribution. Similarly absent is another seminal text, published over a decade ago by Jackson (1993), dealing with environmentalism, gender and populism. That such lacunae occur in a volume the stated intention of which is 'to stimulate new thinking on where the discipline may be moving' is scarcely credible. It also invites a riposte that – on this evidence – development studies shows no sign of movement, never mind travelling with a particular destination in mind.

8 Harriss (2005: 17–46).

9 See Harriss (2005: 21). The claim to be 'the first ever student of development' accurately captures the flavour of this contribution. Its egocentric focus and narrow timeframe result in a corresponding failure to recognize that the study of socio-economic development, its causes and effects, has a very long lineage, stretching far back into history. To confine the study of development to the formally constituted academic rubric of development studies is rather like saying that the study of art and literature had no existence before the foundation of art colleges and university literature departments.

'post-development' from the year 2000 onwards, an era labelled one of 'recovery or decline'.[10]

Much of this account is devoted to the intellectual challenges from a small number of academic institutions/texts to the neo-liberal economic policies advocated by World Bank. The picture drawn by Harriss is of a few, beleaguered individuals bravely engaged in a war against the unthinking market-oriented barbarians dressed in sharp suits who descend from skyscrapers in New York to inflict neo-liberal ideas/programmes on unwilling academics and peasants alike. His concluding words are a call to arms: 'The challenge for development studies, therefore, lies not so much in resisting the critiques that derive from postmodernism, in "post-development" theorizing...as in renewing its relevance through improved historical understanding of development...This calls for a *critical* engagement on the part of development scholars with development policy-making rather than placing development studies at the service of fads...'.[11] One would not guess from this that Harriss has himself uncritically espoused a number of passing fads in development theory, including ones that were mutually irreconcilable epistemologically and politically. From time to time he has changed his view in a manner that can only be described as spectacular.

The portrayal by Harriss of a uniformly beleaguered group of development theorists within the academy conducting an heroic struggle against the forces of darkness outside (neo-liberalism, postmodernism, post-development, the World Bank) is a comforting image, but in every respect an erroneous one.[12]

10 Harriss (2005: 19ff.).

11 Harriss (2005: 39, original emphasis).

12 Much development theory of the kind Harriss currently favours assumes that the causes of underdevelopment and rural poverty are basically ones of knowledge. If only those in the state apparatus of capitalist nations really understood the true nature of the problem, this discourse proclaims, they would very quickly change policies for the better. Such a view is naïf, in that it overlooks or downplays the main reason why the capitalist state fails either to promulgate or – where promulgated – to implement plans/policies that actually are advantageous to poor peasants and agricultural labourers: namely, the political power in national or international contexts of those classes that own/control the means of production/distribution/exchange. For Harriss (2002b), therefore, the capitalist state remains a potentially disinterested – and thus benign – agent in the development process, capable/desirous of and indeed willing to engineer fundamental transformation. What adherents of this approach fail to realize is that without the expropriation of landowners and agribusiness enterprises on the one hand, and the capture of state power by workers and poor peasants on the other, fundamental transformation is either off the political agenda or stays only on paper. Much the same point has been made in an interesting article by Das (2005) on the state and social capital in India.

To begin with, since his account ignores the long history of development theory, he fails to comprehend that opposition to development is both political and recurring. A case in point is the 'new' populist postmodernism, which is mentioned by him only briefly and then dismissed as unimportant, thereby overlooking the fact that it is a conservative discourse that has strong roots stretching back at least to the 1890s.

What Harriss still does not appear to understand, therefore, is that once postmodern teleology is conceded, economic development itself goes out of the window, as – in the name of cultural 'otherness' – poverty is installed in its place. Part of the same difficulty is his naïf faith in the efficacy of piecemeal solutions (= 'engagement with development policy-making'), a micro-level reformist approach to development problems that capital quickly circumvents or subverts.[13] Moreover, because it takes no account of just how many development theorists were or became enthusiastic supporters of market 'solutions' to underdevelopment (poverty, unequal distribution of wealth), his rose-tinted 'us'/'them' polarity breaks down.[14]

Nor does Harriss have anything to say about how frequently he himself succumbed to the temptation of passing fads. His own trajectory over the period in question amounts to nothing so much as a political zig-zag, swerving from one analytical framework to another as each in turn hove into view and established itself as an academic orthodoxy. During the 1970s and into the 1980s,

13 This very point was made in critical observations published long ago (see Review 1 in this volume), and strangely is the only argument in that critique which Harriss chose not to heed. However, this same misplaced faith in the efficacy of piecemeal solutions has found a new champion. In his contribution to the volume edited by Kothari, it is Bernstein (2005: 111, original emphasis) who now advocates the importance to Development studies of '*applied* knowledge of practical benefit in the formulation and implementation of development policies and interventions'.

14 When considering the same issue elsewhere in the collection edited by Kothari – namely, why was it that the study of development 'has not only survived the current period of neo-liberal ascendancy...but has prospered in British universities' – Bernstein (2005: 115) also overlooks this simple explanation. Development studies thrived in part because of a willingness on the part of its practitioners to apply market 'solutions' to problems of underdevelopment. The extent to which this connection eludes Bernstein is evident from a subsequent observation that, although the 'wider intellectual, and political, understanding of development as a process of struggle and conflict' has been 'lost', 'such oppositional thinking thrives outside the institutional spheres and practices of development studies' (Bernstein, 2005: 119, 134 note 17). The unintended irony structuring this observation – that political dissent vanished from the academy only to reappear on the streets – underlines as precisely as possible the point being made here (the rightwards turn taken by development studies), and thus requires no further comment.

therefore, an era when development studies came under the sway of Marxism, he was a Marxist.[15] During the 1980s and into the 1990s, by contrast, when the academic influence of Marxism began to wane, as anti-Marxist critiques gained ground, Harriss threw his lot in with exponents of the anti-Marxist 'impasse'.[16] He switched his allegiance again in the early 1990s, when both marginalist economics and the 'new' populist postmodernism were in the course of becoming dominant paradigms in development studies, and decided that, after all, his sympathies lay with them.[17] After 1995, however, when a number of Marxists of the 'I told you so' variety had launched an effective counterattack against the 'new' populist postmodernism, yet another *volte face* took place.[18] The result was that, by the year 2000, Harriss had assumed yet another identity, and announced that he was now a long-standing critic of the selfsame 'new' populist postmodernism.

Harriss never ceases to astound by his ability constantly to reformulate a position on development theory. The pattern of different and contradictory

15 See, for example, Harriss (1982a; 1982b). At this period, therefore, one encounters the application by Harriss (1982: 204ff., 282ff.) to rural Tamil Nadu of a Marxist analytical framework. Elsewhere his view (Harriss, 1982b: 23) was that Marxism 'seems to be most appropriate for studies relating to rural development (both as policy and process) because it is inherently inter-disciplinary, and because of all the approaches that we have reviewed it is the one which is most centrally concerned with issues of distribution and with poverty.' In his contribution to the volume edited by Kothari under review here, Harriss (2005: 24) accepts that initially he subscribed to 'a self-conscious project of restoring the unity of social science, around a broadly Marxist perspective'.

16 Details about this particular shift are set out in a critical review of the 'impasse' position (Brass, 1995; see also review 1 in this book). Despite having contributed to a volume espousing the notion of a development 'impasse', and arguing strongly that the debate about agrarian change in India was indeed at an 'impasse', Harriss nevertheless felt able to write about the 'impasse' debate shortly thereafter (Harriss, 1998: 294–295) almost as though it had nothing to do with him.

17 This emerges most clearly in contributions by Harriss published in the early 1990s. 'The study of agrarian change,' he proclaimed (Harriss, 1994: 180–181) at that conjuncture, 'thus points to the limitations of conventional Marxian political economy because of the way in which, by its reduction of politics to economics, it consistently fails to account for politics.' As indicated in review 1 (this volume), he was then also supportive of 'everyday-forms-of-resistance' and the Subaltern Studies approach.

18 Those Marxists of the 'I told you so' variety who – against the grain – wrote critiques during the early 1990s of the 'new' populist postmodernism were Petras (1990) and Brass (1991; 1995). For the epistemological link between on the one hand postmodernism, and on the other the subaltern studies project, the new social movements framework and the 'everyday forms of resistance' theory associated with James Scott, see Review Essay 12 in this volume and also Brass (2000a).

views adhered to throughout a thirty-year period is impressive in terms of its consistent commitment to inconsistency, resembling as it does nothing so much as a frenetic roller-coaster ride from one theoretical framework to another. Perhaps he is just too easily swayed by a new idea. Alternatively, since Harriss unknowingly admits to eclecticism, and parades the fact that he has no sense of contradiction ('...by the time I went to India to begin my fieldwork at the end of 1972 I had a research plan...influenced by Lipton's theory of the optimizing peasant [and] also expecting to analyse the differentiation of the peasantry and the process of rural capital accumulation'), this trajectory may be no more than evidence of confusion on his part.[19] Whatever the reason, he is right about one thing: the importance for development studies of institutions.[20] The institutions in question, however, are not those Harriss thinks they are, those 'obstacles to change' located in the rural Third World; rather, they are academic ones situated in metropolitan capitalist countries, through which have swirled successive discourses about development.

II

Quantitatively, the largest input to the edited volumes is provided by Henry Bernstein, who contributes two lengthy articles to the books under review; one in *Reclaiming the Land*, and one in *A Radical History of Development Studies*.[21] Since between them these amount to some sixty pages, one might expect at the very least to encounter there a useful account of development theory plus numerous insights into the way this has emerged, and why. Unfortunately this is not the case.

In their lengthy introductory piece to *Reclaiming the Land*, the two editors Moyo and Yeros cite Bernstein on numerous occasions, allocating him a central rôle in almost every crucial debate that has taken place in development theory over the past twenty years.[22] No one else is cited by them as frequently, and certainly no other contributor to the volume is projected in such a heroic light. Time and again, the two editors of this book inform us, it was Bernstein who was the first to spot the theoretical significance of this or that wrong argument about development, and then to denounce such error to the world. So impressive a record naturally invites any reviewer to examine the claims.

19 Harriss (2005: 22).

20 Harriss (2005: 17).

21 Respectively, Bernstein (2005a: 67–101) and Bernstein (2005b: 111–137).

22 Moyo and Yeros (2005: 8–64).

Not only is Bernstein said by Moyo and Yeros to have contributed in a major fashion to our understanding of both the agrarian question and the history of post-1945 capitalist development, therefore, but he is also credited with the discovery that peasant economy is reproduced by agribusiness for its own purposes.[23] Further on in this same glowing litany we are informed that it is thanks to Bernstein that everyone now knows that peasants are not socio-economically homogeneous but divided along class lines, into a rich, middle and poor peasant stratum.[24] Described fulsomely as a '[l]eading analyst of agrarian change', he is then given a starring rôle in the formulation of Marxist theory about new social movements.[25] As drawn by the editors of *Reclaiming the Land*, the picture could not be more clear: it is thanks to Bernstein that we understand anything and everything worth knowing about development theory over the previous two decades.

This picture is, of course, not just one-sided, and thus profoundly misleading, but also in certain important details the opposite of what is actually the case.[26] Although Moyo and Yeros disclaim that '[e]rrors of fact and interpretation remain our own', they concede that it was Bernstein himself who provided them with 'insightful comments'.[27] Moyo and Yeros are culpable of not having examined more rigorously the lineages of the debates they discuss, and in particular where and by whom these were initiated. From this omission stem the many mistakes they make in assigning to this or that participant an heroic rôle in formulating the development theory of the past two decades. Not the least problematic aspect of their presentation is the misleading way contributions to *The Journal of Peasant Studies* do or do not feature.

Thus, for example, Marxist theory about new social movements and the 'new' populist postmodernism (= 'the cultural turn') was indeed formulated in that journal throughout the 1990s, but by a journal editor other than Bernstein.

23 Moyo and Yeros (2005: 14, 15, 18).

24 Moyo and Yeros (2005: 25).

25 Moyo and Yeros (2005: 35, 44).

26 *Pace* Moyo and Yeros, it is *not* the case that Bernstein argued – let alone initiated the argument – that agribusiness reproduced peasant economy for its own purposes. What he did claim was much rather the reverse: that petty commodity production was capable of reproducing itself, even where capitalism was already present. This, as all those who write about the peasantry ought by now to recognize, combines the theory about peasant family farming long associated with the work of Chayanov (1966) with the everyday-forms-of-peasant-resistance framework associated more recently with James Scott (1985). Both are exemplars of agrarian populism, as was Bernstein until his *volte face*.

27 Moyo and Yeros (2005: p. 56, note 1). An input from the same source to their other contribution in the same volume is also acknowledged by Moyo and Yeros (2005: 202, n1).

It is noticeable how thinly sourced are the accounts by him, both in *A Radical History of Development Studies* and elsewhere, of the 'cultural turn'. There are few signs of Bernstein having conducted any original research into populism, let alone the 'new' postmodern variety about which he now expounds so frequently. References to the latter are notable either by their recent publication (when critique of the 'new' postmodernist populism and the parameters of the debate had already long been established) or by their absence.[28] And yet Bernstein was an editor of the journal throughout the 1990s, a period when a number of articles and books based on them embodying precisely such a critique of the 'new' postmodern populism were published.[29] It cannot be possible, therefore, that he is unaware of these texts. Why then is there no mention of any of them in these volumes, either in his own contributions or those by others?

Similarly misplaced is the assertion by Moyo and Yeros that it was Bernstein who first drew attention to the internal differentiation of the peasantry, a claim that overlooks two things. First, the fact that class distinctions within the peasantry were mentioned by most contributors to that journal from 1973 onwards. And second, the one exception to this was Bernstein himself, whose analytical framework did not for a long time include the concept either of the agrarian question (on which see below) or of petty commodity producers internally differentiated by class. Rather than being ahead of the game where development theory was concerned, therefore, Bernstein has invariably been either behind this or wrong, and usually both.

This, perhaps, is the reason behind his many changes of mind, of which the most basic involved what started out (and for a long time remained) an agrarian populist analysis of petty commodity production. Gibbon and Neocosmos

---

28 Marxism, Bernstein (2005b: 127) informs us in *A Radical History of Development Studies* 'has been largely displaced by the various currents of post-structuralism, postmodernism and the like…[i]n relation to development studies, the effect of the postmodern(ist) "turn" is to deny the validity of any conception of development other than as for an imperializing (Northern) discourse imposed on the South.' These 'various currents' are described further as 'combinations of nationalist, populist and deconstructionist elements' (Bernstein, 2005b: 128), thereby reproducing precisely the case made against the 'new' populist postmodernism by this reviewer throughout the 1990s and published in Brass (2000a).

29 Articles criticizing the 'new' postmodern populism appeared in *The Journal of Peasant Studies* throughout the 1990s. Despite being significant critiques of the cultural turn – as suggested by, among many others, Chaturvedi (2000: vii–xix) – not one of them is cited by Bernstein in either of his contributions to the volumes edited by Kothari and by Moyo and Yeros.

demonstrate convincingly that during the 1970s and 1980s Bernstein's epistemology was not Marxist but much rather Chayanovian.[30] Among the many points they make in their devastating critique are that he not only adhered to 'a *peasantist* form of subjectivism' and an essentialist '*peasant* "logic of subsistence"', but also (and therefore) unknowingly reproduced what is the classic populist dichotomy between the State on the one hand an undifferentiated peasantry on the other.[31]

Now, however, Bernstein himself is not only critical of the '[populist] belief in the peasantry as "a class", and [the] aspiration to its "independence" as a class', a view to which he himself adhered earlier, but dismisses this approach confidently as one of the 'currently modish versions of populism that champion anti- or "post"-development'.[32] He goes on to say both that 'the post-developmentalist/neo-liberal conjuncture provides apparently favourable conditions for the revitalization (recycling) of the basic populist argument',

---

30 See the critique of Bernstein (1977; 1981; 1982) by Gibbon and Neocosmos (1985), the accuracy of which has been confirmed subsequently by Leys (1996: 12, 64) who identifies Bernstein as a fellow dependency theorist. Adherents of this view, as Leys (1996: 176) himself accepts, 'tended to focus on the relative limitations of Africa's capitalist classes and tended to ignore their growth paths over time...They tended (like the Russian populists a hundred years earlier) to see capitalism as something occurring only in the visible, formal sector of the economy and to overlook the ongoing gradual but crucial transformation of rural relations of production into increasingly commercial and finally capitalist relations...'. The Chayanovian theory informing Bernstein's arguments at that conjuncture has also been noted by Johnson (2004): 'What is definitive about the peasant form of production is that, regardless of ownership, the logic of production is subsistence. Building upon Alexander Chayanov's theory of a peasant mode of production, Henry Bernstein... argues [in 1979] that peasant production is distinguished from capitalism because there is no appropriation and realization of surplus value or accumulation of capital.'

31 See Gibbon and Neocosmos (1985: 162–163, 187, original emphasis). Although at the beginning of the 1990s Bernstein was keen to distance himself from the State/peasant dichotomy that marked his earlier position, he nevertheless continued to adhere to an essentialist concept of peasant economy located inside the wider capitalist system. Indeed, he himself comes close to admitting that he has retained this central element of the populist claim (Bernstein, 1990: 72): 'The starting-point must be to view peasants today as agrarian *petty commodity producers within capitalism*. This is also the position of more sophisticated populists...' (original emphasis). For more of the same, see Bernstein (1992: 30).

32 See Bernstein (2001: 9 note 19, 17, 18). The same is much in evidence in his contribution to the volume edited by Kothari, where one encounters many criticisms of populist approaches to development. For example, that 'NGO activity...the jargon of "participation", "empowerment", "stakeholders" and the like is most pervasive...[a]long with tendencies to celebrate the "local" and "indigenous"', etc., etc. (Bernstein, pp. 120, 134 note 19).

and that '[i]t is not difficult...for such neo-populism to insert itself in the discourses of "community" action (decentralization, civil society, and the like) currently favoured by neo-liberalism'. This particular change of mind – from supporter to critic of agrarian populism – is just one of the many things that elude Moyo and Yeros.[33]

As his contribution to the volume edited by Kothari demonstrates, Bernstein has regularly changed his mind on a wide variety of development issues, a characteristic he shares with Harriss, another contributor to the same collection. Not only did Bernstein metamorphose in the 1980s from a populist to a (self-proclaimed) Marxist, therefore, but throughout the 1990s and since his views have undergone further substantial shifts. Both the fact of and the extent of these changes are evident from the following example. On a number of previous occasions, Bernstein took part in and endorsed the importance for a socialist politics of debates about class 'impurities', and commended 'sophisticated analyses of class relations' that discuss the latter in terms of 'pure'/'impure' forms.[34] Now, however, he states in the volume edited by Kothari that 'analytical class "purism" remains a major obstacle to the renewal and development of Marxist investigation'.[35]

The kind of difficulty these theoretical shifts give rise to is nowhere more evident than in the confused manner in which Bernstein conceptualizes

---

33 Nor, it should be added, are they the only ones. In his contribution to the volume edited by Kothari, Harriss (2005: 34) refers to the exchange between Bernstein, Gibbon and Neocosmos, but makes no mention of the fact that both the latter are extremely critical of the former. An earlier reference by him (Harriss, 1997: 7–8) to the same exchange does mention the element of criticism. Elsewhere another text cites both Bernstein and Gibbon and Neocosmos in a misleading fashion not so different from that of Moya and Yeros, noting (Oya, 2004: 292, n.11) only that 'emphasis is given on the prevalence of "petty commodity production" (PCP), which combines class locations of capital and labour and within which concrete processes of differentiation occur in Africa'. Since no mention is made of the fact that Gibbon and Neocosmos are highly critical of Bernstein, this kind of conflation is rather like saying that Charles I and Cromwell both had views about kingship and republicanism, which undoubtedly they did – but ones that were inimical.

34 See Bernstein (1994: 64; 2000: 41, 44), where he states unequivocally that of central importance to an understanding of class formation and class struggle in a capitalist context is the fight 'against all forms of "tied" labour arrangements based in personal dependence, debt bondage, patronage, etc. – in short, "deproletarianization"....which denotes the denial or loss of the one positive "freedom" of the proletarian condition...namely workers' mobility within labour markets.'

35 Bernstein (2005b: 130).

the agrarian question.[36] In an attempt to re-invent, not to say improve upon, the classic Marxist analyses of Lenin and Kautsky, Bernstein maintains implausibly that there are not one but two agrarian questions: that of capital (= modernization), and that of what he terms 'labour'.[37] The latter concept is woolly in the extreme, and thus never properly defined, oscillating uneasily between 'labour'-as-(undifferentiated)-peasants, 'labour'-as-workers, and 'labour'-as-any/everyone-who-works-manually-on-the-land.[38] Having abandoned class analysis – or, as he terms it, 'analytical class "purism"' – what Bernstein appears to be serving up is a reheated version of a now familiar dish: the conceptually empty but very fashionable 'multitudes' of Hardt and Negri.[39]

Despite presenting his own interpretation of the agrarian question as a significant departure from the assumptions informing that of Byres, Bernstein follows the epistemology of the latter rather too closely and consequently a number of theoretically contentious issues/claims made by Byres

36 Difficulties arising from a misunderstanding of the agrarian question is a problem Bernstein has in common with Byres (see below). Hence the observation by Bernstein (2005b: 126) in the volume edited by Kothari – that '[i]t may well be that the questions...posed are not the right ones' – is not just the only statement encountered in his contribution with which it is not possible to disagree but also the one that accurately sums up his own analytical approach.

37 Written at the end of the nineteenth century, and still relevant today, the two main analyses by Marxists of the agrarian question are those of Lenin (1964a) and Kautsky (1988). Unsuccessful attempts to improve on them include not just Bernstein (1996/97; 2006) but also Byres (see below).

38 See especially Bernstein (2006: 4, 6). If all that Bernstein is saying is that those who purchase labour-power have different political interests from those who sell it, then this is self-evident and amounts to no more than a tautology. However, this political difference does not translate theoretically into a bifurcated agrarian question in the manner he proposes, not least because the political interests of those selling their labour-power are themselves not uniform. This is because the latter category is invariably composed of those whose class position is not the same, a point that Bernstein is unable to confront (let alone explain) now that he has jettisoned 'analytical class "purism"'.

39 Where this leads is unsurprising. Hence the banal conclusion to a presentation (Bernstein, 2006: 13) where we are told that we have 'to recognize and...to be able to analyze the contradictory sources and impulses – and typically multi-class character – of such struggles, in ways that can inform a realistic and politically responsible [*sic*] assessment of them.' This is World Bank speak: 'politically responsible' – politically responsible for whom? Even non-Marxists start, not end, with this kind of question, one that Marxists do not themselves pose. Those rural struggles that are – and have been – 'multi-class' (= 'multitude') do not resolve anything politically, nor can they. For an incisive critique of the pseudo-sociological notion of 'multitude' informing the currently fashionable postmodern nostrums of Hardt and Negri, see Petras (2002).

are permitted to slip by unchallenged.[40] Initially, Bernstein maintained that there was not one but three agrarian questions: the capture of political power by a peasant/worker alliance, the form taken by capitalist development in agriculture, and the transfer of agricultural surplus for industrialization. Termed 'the problematics of politics, production and accumulation', these three components of the agrarian question are attributed respectively to Engels, to Lenin and Kautsky, and to Preobrazhensky.[41] Subsequently the three components are consolidated into two: production and accumulation combine to become the agrarian question of capital, while politics – based on 'the methodology of class analysis' – is deemed henceforth to be the agrarian question of 'labour'.[42]

A very brief examination of the same six paths of agrarian transition as Byres (England, Prussia, the United States, France, Japan, and Taiwan/South Korea) leads Bernstein to two conclusions. First, that as accumulation in a context of a global imperialism is now no longer determined by the necessity of effecting a capitalist transition in agriculture, the agrarian question of capital is effectively at an end.[43] And second, that the agrarian question of 'labour', by contrast, remains on the agenda, a fact Bernstein links to the political efficacy of this issue where anti-colonial and national democratic movements are concerned. About this interpretation of the agrarian question, the way it is subdivided, and its compatibility with Marxist theory, one can make the following points.

---

40 Most notably the assertions made by Byres about the social relations of production (see below). Just how far Bernstein manages to distance himself from the analysis of Byres is evident from statements (Bernstein, 1996/97: 22, 51, 52) to the effect that his own analysis 'builds on the project of T.J. Byres' comparative political economy of agrarian transitions', that he himself has 'been privileged by the fruits of [Byres'] intellectual labour, and the agenda it has enriched', and that '[Byres] continues to be a beacon of light in our collective project' [*sic*].

41 See Bernstein (1996/97: 23ff.), where the references are to Engels (1990), Lenin (1964a), Kautsky (1988) and Preobrazhensky (1965).

42 On the centrality of 'the methodology of class analysis' to the agrarian question of labour, see Bernstein (1996/97: 25), where the specifically political component – that element which is retained as the agrarian question of labour – is described as involving 'struggles for democracy *and socialism*' (emphasis added). The significance of this last objective will become clear below.

43 Hence the observation (Bernstein, 1996/97: 43, 50) that 'a century of modern imperialism has extended the determinants of industrialization far beyond the prospects of agrarian transition in landscapes inhabited exclusively by classes of landed property and agrarian labour', a situation in which 'the end of the agrarian question *without its resolution* [amounts to] the elimination of any prospects of agrarian transition as a route to comprehensive industrialization in contemporary poor countries'.

To begin with, the compartmentalization of the agrarian question into three (politics, production and accumulation) or two (capital and 'labour') distinct components purports to identify separate problematics that in reality do not exist. Although the theoretical contributions of Lenin, Kautsky and Preobrazhensky are confined by Bernstein to the economic domain of production and accumulation, the latter were all firmly anchored in a discourse about the politics of the agrarian question, outside of which none of their contributions has any meaning. Thus, for example, during the 1880s and 1890s Kautsky opposed the attempt by German Social Democracy to seek the electoral support of peasant proprietors, by tailoring its political programme to suit them (price supports, debt write-offs). In much the same way, Preobrazhensky – like Trotsky – warned that policies such as price supports for foodstuffs in 1920s Russia would favour kulaks, and strengthen their political capacity to oppose the implementation of a socialist programme in the countryside.[44] In other words, the distinct problematics and the separate focus identified by Bernstein are not ones found in any of the classic Marxist texts on the agrarian question.

Rather than classic Marxist analyses, the theoretical and political affinity of Bernstein's interpretation of the agrarian question is with another and more recent work, by Alexander Gerschenkron.[45] Bernstein notes uncontentiously that in Germany economic crisis 'pushed the Junkers into mass politics for the first time,' where, with the support of the peasantry, they defeated the Weimar Republic and contributed to the rise of Hitler. Most controversially, however, Bernstein then seemingly follows Gerschenkron in characterizing this as an attack on capitalism and democracy by pre-capitalist social forces, of which Junkers were a part. According to Bernstein, therefore, 'Gerschenkron's analysis...was explicitly political in its concern with democracy'; what is not said is that this was not socialist but *bourgeois* democracy, which – together

44 For this argument, see Preobrazhensky (1980) and also Bukharin and Preobrazhensky (1922: 316ff.), where the centrality of this same case emerges clearly ('The rich peasant greeted the [Bolshevik] revolution inspired by the most rosy hopes and anticipations, but as a result of the revolution he found himself stripped of part of the land which he had owned before it occurred. As long as this class of rich peasants continues to exist, its members will inevitably prove to be irreconcilable enemies of the proletarian State and its agrarian policy... The petty-proprietor mentality of middle peasants...inclines them to form an alliance with the rich peasants,' etc.).

45 The text in question is Gerschenkron (1943), on the importance of which to his own analysis of the agrarian question see Bernstein (1996/97: 47ff., 52). Although Gerschenkron is invoked by Bernstein mainly with regard to agrarian transition in Prussia, it is nevertheless clear that the influence of the former extends to much of re-interpretation presented by the latter.

with an incipient capitalism – Gerschenkron maintained required defending from those on the far right in Germany.[46] In keeping with this approach, Bernstein questions the 'dominance of industry [and] the urban bourgeoisie', and goes on to cite endorsingly texts that categorize post-1871 Germany as a context where 'military-aristocratic' power was strong and a bourgeoisie, by contrast, was 'politically weak'.

The dual inference is that, insofar as they retained their 'distinctive feudal ancestry', therefore, the Junkers were in a fundamental way anti-capitalist and thus a complete transition to capitalism had yet to be effected.[47] About this two things need to be said. First, that these same Junkers were in the forefront of the struggle against the Weimar Republic, and contributed to the rise of Hitler is evidence of their political opposition not to capitalism but to the possibility of socialism.[48] And second, the characterization of Junkers as 'feudal' corresponds to the *Sonderweg* thesis, the central claim of which is that, because they were and remained an economically backward class, German fascism was

46 For the centrality of economic backwardness to his ideas not just about Germany but also about Russia, see Gerschenkron (1955; 1962). The latter is classified by Renton (2001: 146 note 3) as one of the exponents of the *Sonderweg* thesis, and according to Fishlow (2003) 'Gerschenkron's analysis is conspicuously anti-Marxian'.

47 See Bernstein (1996/97: 49). The inference that Junkers were in any way anti-capitalist is controversial, and some analyses (Tirrell, 1951: 12, 16) maintain that large landowners in Prussia took an active interest in agricultural production, and were already capitalist by 1800. Even if the latter conjuncture seems too early, it is clear from the United States Senate Commission (1913: 267ff.) appointed by President Wilson that on the eve of World War I the purpose of mortgage credit associations (*landschaften*) was to provide Prussian landowners with capital for agricultural improvements. Large proprietors were accordingly able to borrow for agricultural investment 'at lower rates and under more favourable conditions than would otherwise be possible', and in 1912 some two thirds of estates larger than a hundred hectares had availed themselves of such loans (United States Senate Commission, 1913: 381ff.). In purely economic terms, therefore, the existence of financial institutions specifically in order to provide Junkers with capital for agriculture, plus a 60% uptake of these credit facilities, is difficult to reconcile with the categorization of the Prussian landlord class as 'anti-capitalist'.

48 That socialism and not capitalism was the object of struggle conducted by Junkers is clear from many things, not least the fact that among the committees operated by the Chamber of Agriculture was one concerned with day labour on farms, the task of which was to give employers 'advice in case of breach of contract' (United States Senate Commission, 1913: 371). In other words, an institutional form of employer collusion in rural areas, so as to police and enforce unfree labour relations in agriculture, thereby attempting to pre-empt the emergence of conditions favouring the development of a working class consciousness.

an effect of bourgeois revolutions that failed. His theoretical affinity with Gerschenkron, therefore, means that Bernstein ends up sharing the same assumptions as the 'semi-feudal' thesis about the inherently non-capitalist nature of the landlord class, and (consequently) the substitution of bourgeois democracy for socialism as the main political objective. Ironically, this is not so different from the interpretation of the agrarian question held by Byres.[49]

Hence the importance of asking to what is the transition to be? Because of this adherence to the theoretical framework of Gerschenkron and not Marxism, socialism is off the political agenda of the agrarian question as (re-) interpreted by Bernstein.[50] What one is left with as the dual object of systemic transition in his framework, therefore, is an as yet unspecified form of capitalism in economic terms and bourgeois democracy in political terms. Not only is the latter goal one that Bernstein shares with the project of the 'new' postmodern populism, but the inability to conceptualize a systemic transcendence of capitalism is a resulting difficulty also common to both theoretical approaches. This difficulty is itself compounded, and the extent of an epistemology shared

49 See below. Among the more surprising claims made by Byres that Bernstein fails to interrogate is that capitalism and unfree labour are incompatible, as the employment of latter prevents the installation of developed productive forces. Accordingly, Byres' argument that in the antebellum US slavery 'effectively blocked the development of capitalism in the South' because slave resistance placed 'strong limits on the instruments of production that can be deployed' (i.e., unfree labour was less efficient than free workers) is accepted by Bernstein (1996/97: 30–31) unchallenged. Although Bernstein notes that 'Southern landowners did introduce technical change,' he nevertheless reiterates Byres' view that unfree labour was an obstacle to technical change. The problem with the claim that unfreedom is necessarily inefficient because slaves, serfs or bonded labourers do not fully apply themselves when working on behalf of an employer is clear. Not only could the same argument be applied to a capitalist factory, in that free workers similarly undertake acts of sabotage in order to slow down speed-ups or production schedules, but it fails to take into account the important role of coercion. The latter took the form of overseers who whipped slaves who did not maintain the desired level of work intensity, and the eviction of tenants who did not work efficiently on the feudal landlord demesne.

50 Nominally the political dimension of the agrarian question as interpreted by Bernstein (1996/97: 25, emphasis added) is about the politics of a transition 'to democracy *and socialism*'. That Bernstein no longer perceives socialism as part of the way in which the agrarian question is to be 'resolved' politically is clear from observations (Bernstein, 2006: 6) such as '[t]he most "virtuous" realization of the logic of the "classic" agrarian question, in transitions to both capitalism and (once) socialism...' Now that he has abandoned socialism as a political objective, the politics of transition can only be about some form of bourgeois democracy.

with the project of the 'new' postmodern populism underlined, when the fate of class is taken into account.

Two final points concern the extent to which the capital/'labour' bifurcation works, even within the framework as proposed by Bernstein. The first point, therefore, concerns the agrarian question of 'labour', and its continuing efficacy in the absence of class analysis and socialism as a political objective. Having split the agrarian question in two, into that of capital and that of 'labour', and announced further that of these two only the latter has contemporary relevance due 'to the methodology of class analysis', Bernstein has now written 'analytical class "purism"' out of the agrarian question. Utilising his own epistemology against him, how can there still be an agrarian question of 'labour' if he has jettisoned both socialism and class analysis?

The second concerns the agrarian question of capital: is it 'over,' as Bernstein claims? Here, too, the answer is no, in the sense that surplus extracted by agribusiness from agriculture is reinvested in industry elsewhere, not least through keeping wages for agricultural labour-power low (by means of unfree relations, among other things). In this way, additional surplus-labour can be extracted and redistributed throughout global circuits of capital. It is also realized in the form of lower food prices, which in turn permit the bundle of wage goods that register as costs of industrial accumulation in other contexts to be lower, thereby contributing to the process of capitalist development elsewhere. Ironically, this is what Bernstein himself accepts happened in the case of plantation agriculture in the Southern US which, insofar as it contributed to accumulation both in the Northern US and Britain, cannot therefore be regarded in a wider systemic (*not* relational) sense as being an obstacle to accumulation. If this is true historically, then why is it not also true now, when – as Bernstein himself argues – the circuits of agrarian and industrial capital are more than ever inextricably connected?

This point has been made by others previously, this reviewer included. That 'plantation slavery blocked industrialization in the American South...but contributed to industrialization both in Britain *and* in "the American road to capitalism"' is an argument conceded by Bernstein.[51] Once this premise has been accepted, any other claim about the 'completion' or 'ending' of what Bernstein categorizes as the agrarian question of capital is *ipso facto* redundant.[52]

51 See Bernstein (1996/97: 41, emphasis added).

52 The case is put thus (Bernstein, 1996/97: 43): 'In short, a century of modern imperialism has extended the determinants of industrialization far beyond the prospects of agrarian transition in landscapes inhabited exclusively by classes of landed property and agrarian labour.' If one were to state less categorically 'extended *but not closed off completely*

As will be seen below with regard to the way Byres misunderstands the agrarian question, this is true even where the crucial and historically important link between worker-as-producer-of-commodities and worker-as-consumer-of-commodities has been broken. In such circumstances, the accumulation project of capital (or, as Bernstein terms it, the process of modernization) continues independently of the purchasing power of a class of workers in a particular location. That such workers nevertheless continue to sell their labour-power to a capitalist producing commodities destined for markets elsewhere means that – for them – the agrarian question of 'labour' is still inextricably linked to the agrarian question of capital.

Where the agrarian question is concerned, therefore, it makes no sense to decouple the position and agency of 'labour' from those of capital. Without one, the other has no meaning: there can be no agrarian question *only* of capital, any more than there can be one *only* of 'labour', for a variety of reasons. Rather obviously, the political and economic interests/objectives of 'labour' do not operate in a vacuum but in relation to the social forces owning/controlling the means of production at any given historical conjuncture. Separating them in the manner indicated by Bernstein is not merely a-historical but suggests the possibility that what he terms 'labour' may possess interests/objectives that transcend history rather than being determined by it. This, of course, is what populism argues with regard to the peasantry, the characteristics of which are perceived as immanent and unchanging, regardless of the economic system (feudalism, capitalism, socialism) in which smallholders are located.

The suspicion remains, therefore, that notwithstanding his recent opposition to the 'new' populist postmodernism, lurking behind the term 'labour' purged of its 'analytical class "purism"' is actually peasant economy, and that the object of dividing the agrarian question in two is to retain within development discourse something akin to a Chayanovian model. This supposition is reinforced by his expulsion from the development agenda of both a socialist project and its subject, the working class.[53] Hence the insistence by Bernstein

---

the determinants of industrialization', his claims would be less problematic; but then the concept of an agrarian question of capital as having been accomplished – a core element in Bernstein's framework – would itself no longer hold.

53 That he has now joined the ranks of those for whom socialism is no longer part of the agenda of development studies is clear from what Bernstein (2005b: 127, 131) states in the volume edited by Kothari. Hence the observation that 'in the light of historical experience to date it may prove impossible to rethink notions of any feasible socialism(s), and of socialist development, that can be projected into a forseeable future...a viable Marxist political project – the future of socialism – in current and forseeable conditions remains as problematic as ever, and even more unanswerable'. As will be seen below, the

on the fact that 'the paramount role of the Leninist party and its sociological foundation, the "organized working class", is no longer viable.'[54] In its place, he then goes on to argue, grassroots agency must henceforth be that of 'anti-globalization movements' engaged in 'popular nationalist politics'.[55] Perhaps all this is no more than evidence of Bernstein's agrarian populist views reasserting themselves.

As important is the fact that delinking the constituent elements of the agrarian question creates a space for the continued relevance of a nationalist politics based on grassroots culture. The irony here is that, having at last recognized that nationalism poses a problem for any progressive notion of development, Bernstein has in effect reinstated the possibility of a 'from below' form of this specific kind of political identity by virtue of separating the agrarian question into one of capital and one of 'labour'. Decoupling them not only negates the Marxist claim that nationalism is a specifically bourgeois ideology but also (and thereby) cuts the ideological link between the 'from above' reproduction of this discourse and its 'from below' circulation. Henceforth it becomes possible to argue that nationalism is indeed virtuous and as such a legitimate aspect of the agrarian question of 'labour'. Indeed, this is precisely the claim made by two forms of (anti-Marxist) agrarian populist theory: by the revisionist Otto Baüer during the 1920s, and by many exponents of the subaltern studies project currently.

III

Of those who followed the third path, it might be said, somewhat uncharitably but nevertheless accurately, that they were facing the wrong way when

abandonment of socialism as a political objective is yet another position Bernstein shares with Byres.

54 Bernstein (2005b: 129).

55 Hence the claim (Bernstein, 1996/97: 52) that the continuing efficacy of petty commodity production is itself supported by 'the generalization of the "peasant path" in the discourses and programmes of anti-colonial and national democratic movements'. This view that the resolution of the agrarian question is in essence about the survival of peasant economy and the struggle for bourgeois democracy is once again a theoretical position that Bernstein shares with the exponents of the 'semi-feudal' thesis. For the latter, therefore, agrarian transition entails the replacement of landlord capitalism (= the Prussian path) with peasant capitalism (= the American path), a transformation in which one form of capitalism (unbenign, landlord, undemocratic) is followed not by socialism but by another 'pure' stage of capitalism (benign, peasant, democratic).

the (conservative) attack finally came. Rather than engaging with the reactionary epistemology of the postmodern onslaught, therefore, they continued to ponder over whether or not the agrarian sector of this or that nation in the so-called Third World was truly capitalist. Unfree labour was (mis-) interpreted by them as evidence for the non-existence of a capitalist agriculture. Having pronounced the latter absent, they proceeded to advocate a reformist politics based on the existence of a 'progressive national bourgeoisie' that would usher in capitalism, democracy and free labour. They were, of course, wrong on all counts.

Into this particular category comes the contribution to the *Agrarian Studies* volume by Terry Byres, a longstanding commentator on rural political economy.[56] His presentation of the agrarian question is essentially a restatement of the argument contained in his book, where a decade ago he elaborated a lengthy and sustained defence of the semi-feudal thesis.[57] A combination of silences, contradiction, and theoretical contortion, the contribution by him to the volume under review unfortunately reveals nothing more than the procrustean nature of such an exercise.[58] The source of his theoretical problem is not difficult to discern. In his book Byres restricted his analysis of the agrarian question, and its process of systemic transition, to individual nations, and consequently discounted the crucial rôle of the wider context in the development of capitalism. Any process of agrarian transition, and the way in which the agrarian question is or is not 'resolved', accordingly takes place within a national framework: capitalist development, surplus extraction, and its transfer

56 Byres (2003: 54–83).

57 See Byres (1996) and also Byres (1995: 565ff.). For yet earlier references to the feudal and/or semi-feudal character of the post-1947 Indian countryside, see Byres (1974: 223, 246, 247, 248, 251).

58 With some surprise one learns (Byres, 2003: 59 note 4) that this already redundant thesis is to be expounded yet further, in no less that three additional volumes, to appear at some point in the future. There may, however, be another and simpler explanation for the frequent presence in his writings of references to forthcoming – but never appearing – volumes by him and others (see, for example, Byres 2000: 240). It is noticeable that, whenever faced with a difficult or potentially contradictory point of theory, Byres states that the issue in question will either be the subject of a forthcoming book, or would need another book to address. Typical, perhaps, are the following two examples. First (Byres, 1996: 8): 'I stress that in this book no attempt is made at an exhaustive treatment of the criteria by which one might assess whether or not capitalist agriculture was developing. A separate, full-scale work would be necessary to do justice to such an undertaking.' And second (Byres; 1998: 220): 'I can only promise to address some of these issues in a future treatment.' The need to engage intellectually with an awkward piece of theory is thereby postponed *sine die*.

from agriculture to industry, are all said to occur within the confines of the same nation state.

This, Byres insists, is still the case today. Reproducing the postmodern conceptual emphasis on 'diversity', he rejects what he terms the 'determinism of global capital', and embarks on a grand taxonomic tour disappearing down ever-proliferating agrarian paths.[59] Taiwan and South Korea, for example, are in his view, 'unmistakable instances of successful agrarian transition', but in Japan a capitalist transition occurred without wage labour and neither landlords nor peasants there became capitalists.[60] The northwestern Indian states of Punjab, Haryana, and Uttar Pradesh, however, are in his opinion instances of a 'wage-based agriculture', that is, of capitalism, developed 'from below' by rich peasants.[61] Latin American countries, we are then told, are all going down the Prussian road of landlord capitalism; except, that is, for the American or farmer road followed by Mexico after 1934, Peru after 1969, and Chile in the 1967–73 period.[62] The paths of agrarian transition themselves become ever more tortuous, encompassing as they do not just the landlord and peasant road but also now a 'merchant road' and a 'contract-farming road'.[63]

Like a Victorian explorer who is lost and without maps, Byres is destined to continue on this fruitless and never-ending taxonomic journey. It is not hard to imagine him plunging yet further into the forested terrain of a distant land, announcing as he vanishes from view 'Another path! I have found yet another path of transition'. Nor is the reason for this difficult to understand: what the semi-feudal thesis cannot deal with, therefore, are instances of workforce decomposition/recomposition undertaken by agrarian capitalists in the course of their class struggle with rural labour.[64] This process amounts to

---

59 Byres (2003: 65).

60 See Byres (2003: 61, 66). Japan is accordingly categorized as 'a quite distinct capitalist agrarian transition'.

61 Byres (2003: 71).

62 See Byres (2003: 72–73). The prevalence in the article by Byres of references to texts about Latin America written in Spanish raises a difficult question – about sources cited in languages other than English – first encountered in his book (Byres, 1996). The latter exhibited a mismatch between on the one hand the citation by him of German texts, and on the other their contents. At least one of the texts contained arguments that were the opposite of those he attributed to it.

63 Byres (2003: 75–77).

64 The irony of Byres (1987) taking Chakravarty (1987) to task for excluding class struggle from his analysis of the contribution by Marxist political economy to an understanding of development theory, when this is precisely what Byres himself does with regard to the acceptability to capitalist producers of unfree labour, requires no further comment.

deproletarianization, and entails either the replacement of existing free labour with unfree equivalents, or the conversion of the former into the latter.

Rich peasants in each of the 'capitalism-from-below' case studies cited by Byres – Punjab and Haryana in northwestern India, the eastern lowlands of Peru after 1969 – employed bonded labour in order to lower costs and maintain discipline.[65] This suggests that where a class of rich peasant capitalists has emerged over the latter part of the twentieth century, a pattern corresponding to a supposedly more benign form of capitalism (= the American path), agricultural workers employed by them on a permanent, seasonal or temporary basis were not free, as Byres maintains. In other words, accumulation *did* occur in the agrarian sector, but the social relations of production linking landless workers and capitalist proprietors were *not* those characteristic of a rural proletariat.

This reviewer has maintained for almost three decades now that the Panglossian adherents of the 'semi-feudal' thesis are wholly mistaken. Their view is that, as capitalism develops, agribusiness will replace unfree labour (debt peonage, bonded labour) with a workforce that is free. Against this it has been argued strongly that there is no inherent tendency on the part of capital to replace unfree production relations with free equivalents, particularly when cost/control considerations – vital in the class struggle – favour the continued employment of labour that is unfree. What exponents of the semi-feudal thesis thought – and think – is that all social relations of production in Third World agriculture will gradually metamorphose into those that characterize agriculture in metropolitan capitalist countries. By contrast, I have shown that the exact opposite is the case: agrarian relations in advanced capitalism are increasingly coming to resemble those in Third World agriculture.[66]

Accordingly, the major weaknesses in – and thus objections to – Byres' view of agrarian transition are twofold. First, that it is restricted to an untenable notion of capitalist development as simply and everywhere an endogenous (= national) process. And second, that capitalism is itself defined untenably, as

65 Details about the unfree relations of production utilized by rich peasant capitalists in each of these case studies are presented in Brass (1999). That agrarian capitalists still prefer unfree workers to labour-power that is free, not just in the eastern lowlands of Peru but also in both the Santa Cruz region and the north Amazon of Bolivia, is clear from current research into the operation of the *enganche* system in these areas (Assies, 2002; Bedoya Garland and Bedoya Silva-Santisteban, 2005a; 2005b). For confirmation that in Haryana the incidence of unfree labour is as entrenched as ever, see Mukherji and Sahoo (1992), Chowdhry (1993) and Rawal (2004).

66 This point – about the resurgent role of gangmasters in British agriculture – has been made in Brass (2004).

existing only where free wage labour is also present. On the first point, therefore, the attempt to confine the agrarian question within the boundaries of contemporary nation states ignores the (really rather obvious) fact that nowadays surplus extracted from agriculture can fuel accumulation and industrialization in national contexts other than that where cultivation initially takes place. Indeed, this is norm throughout much of the so-called Third World, where the financial and investment strategies of agribusiness enterprises are international in scope. This is not, as Byres claims, a 'descent into a kind of "world system" determinism' – that is, determination by globalization – but rather determination by *capitalism*, as located within a global *system* that contains both national and international capital.[67] Accepting that 'transnational capital makes a powerful assault on poor countries', Byres nevertheless remains uncomfortable with the conceptualization of capital and capitalism at a level beyond the individual nation, and questions the efficacy of international capital.[68]

The resulting flaw in the framework linking accumulation to the agrarian question is clear. A lack of capitalist development is equated with a stagnant home market, itself an effect of the lack of purchasing power by impoverished workers whose low wages are due to the fact that they are unfree. Because he is operating with a model of a closed economy, defined by national boundaries, Byres misses the point that agribusiness enterprises in an international capitalist system break the link between consumption and production. Simply put, it does not matter to agrarian capitalists exporting commodities produced with unfree workers (composed of landless labourers and poor peasants who are bonded) if these are unable to consume, since the market where the output is sold is located elsewhere. Not dependent solely on its own home market, both national and international capital can as a result employ unfree labour, the presence of which would place limits on any economic growth predicated on the existence only of a domestic market. Capitalist development can and does take place where the rural workforce is unfree and thus impoverished, since both accumulation and profitability are determined not by the home market (which may be non-existent or negligible) but by an international one.

The same kind of difficulty faces Byres' inability to recognize the presence of endogenous capitalism within national contexts. Because they employ labour that is unfree, rich peasants cannot in his view be capitalist producers. Although within the ranks of the peasantry 'constrained tendencies towards capitalism might be dimly perceived', therefore, 'nowhere had a class of rich

67 For this claim, see Byres (2003: 58).

68 Byres (2003: 57, 58, 65, 76ff.).

peasants become a class of capitalist farmers'.[69] For this reason, rich peasants are for Byres always on the verge of becoming agrarian capitalists, but they never succeed in making a breakthrough into this category. As long as their workforce is unfree, capitalism is destined not merely to be late in spreading to the countryside but never actually to arrive there.[70] For exponents of the semi-feudal thesis such as Byres, therefore, peasants cannot, by definition, be or become capitalists as long as they employ unfree labour. Hence the possibility that capitalist producers might prefer workers who are unfree to free labour is excluded *ab initio*.

These theoretical shortcomings have deep roots. Since the object of the development debate that took off during the 1960s was simply to augment economic growth, there was no difference between on the one hand bourgeois economists pressing for capitalist development in the so-called Third World and on the other exponents of the semi-feudal thesis, like Byres. All sought the holy grail of increased agricultural productivity, and thus what they took to be the obstacles to this.[71] Common to the semi-feudal thesis and to neo-classical economics, therefore, was the extirpation of unfree relations of production (debt bondage, bonded labour) that each wrongly held was incompatible with the accumulation process in the countryside. When unfree workers were encountered where they should not be – employed in a labour process that was capitalist – one of two theoretical 'solutions' was adopted. Either the labour process in question was declared to be pre-capitalist, and awaiting a transition to capitalism, or the fact of accumulation was accepted and the workers employed there were relabelled as free labour.[72]

---

69 Byres (2003: 57).

70 This emerges clearly from a comparison of early texts by him with more recent ones. Hence the following assertion (Byres, 1974: 235): 'Rich peasants were not the "masters of the countryside" at Independence – the landlord class was still very much in command – and they were not to be clearly seen in all parts of India. They were a class of capitalist farmers in embryo, in the womb of the old order.' A quarter of a century on, nothing much has changed in this regard. 'Rich peasants,' we are told by Byres (2000: 266) in a much later text, 'constituted a class of proto-capitalists, that still bore the stigmata of a pre-capitalist order.'

71 For the centrality to his framework of the systemic conditions licensing increased agricultural productivity, see Byres (2000: 239). It is, in his words (Byres, 2003: 55), a question of 'what is it that has allowed the unleashing of capital accumulation, in both town and country, that has lain at the heart of capitalist transformation'.

72 For the view that unfree relations of production (= 'semi-feudal features') are incompatible with capital accumulation in agriculture, see Byres (1996: 29, 78). For the relabelling by him of bonded labour employed by capitalist producers as 'free wage labour', see Byres

The difficulty with this is obvious. At best, the assumption of bourgeois political economy was that economic growth would eventually lead to a more egalitarian redistribution of wealth. At worst, that it did not matter if such redistribution failed to occur, since the object of development theory was simply to promote accumulation. Once bourgeois political economy had succeeded in making industrial growth the centrepiece of the development agenda, its ideological task was accomplished. That of Marxism, however, was not, its object being to formulate theory about the next step: the link between capitalist development and a transition to socialism. This the exponents of the semi-feudal thesis notably failed to do.[73]

Having collaborated theoretically and ideologically with bourgeois political economy, by supporting the push for Third World accumulation, exponents of the semi-feudal thesis then continued to repeat the mantra that the agrarian sector of these countries was 'not yet capitalist' or 'not capitalist enough'. Its proponents still argue, even now, for the necessity of boosting agricultural performance in India, so that the ever elusive agrarian capitalist – the absent 'other' of the semi-feudal framework – may finally emerge onto the historical stage and begin to provide a surplus for what in their view is an as-yet insufficiently realized drive to industrialization. This, it seems, will continue to be their view as long as the production relations they regard as capitalist – 'pure' wage labour that is free, in other words – are not encountered in agriculture.[74]

(1996: 38). For examples of the same views – the attempt to redefine as free those unfree workers employed in capitalist agriculture – but this time held by neo-classical economic historians, see Fogel and Engerman (1974) and Steinfeld and Engerman (1997). Not the least of the many ironies about this epistemological overlap is that, over the years, Byres has always insisted that a vast theoretical gulf separated his own (semi-feudal) analytical framework from that of neo-classical economists such as Michael Lipton. This overlap has not escaped the notice of other contributors to the *Agrarian Studies* volume. In the subsequent discussion (Ramachandran and Swaminathan, 2003: 84ff.) of the papers by Byres and Keith Griffin – the latter dismissed by Byres (2003: 91) as a neo-classical economist – some present drew attention to the epistemological similarity between them (Ramachandran and Swaminathan, 2003: 84).

73 Socialism is not merely nowhere on the semi-feudal agenda, therefore, but never has actually been a part of this (see, for example, Byres 1982:136; 1991:3; 2005: 85).

74 The palpable fact of unfree labour employed by agrarian capitalists has led to an equally palpable discomfiture on the part of exponents of the semi-feudal thesis. An example is the way in which Byres (1999) attempts to sidestep the persistence of bonded labour in the highly commercialized agriculture of the most advanced regions in India. In the states of Haryana, Punjab, Uttar Pradesh, and Andhra Pradesh, therefore, he is unable to deny that the 'dominant classes' – for really rather obvious reasons, he cannot bring himself to write 'agrarian capitalists' – do indeed utilize 'various tied labour arrangements'.

Since in many parts of the so-called Third World unfree labour is the relation of choice where agrarian capital is concerned, this means in effect postponing opposition to capitalist development there until the Greek Calends.[75]

IV

Not all the news about the rural dimension of development studies is bad, however, and one of the three edited volumes under review – *Reclaiming the Land* – does contain two useful articles. These are by Henry Veltmeyer, examining land occupations in Latin America, and by Igor Ampuero and James J. Brittain, looking at the political economy of the armed struggle in rural Colombia.[76] The latter contribution traces the recent history of opposition to US intervention, and considers the agrarian programme of the peasant-based guerrilla movement, FARC-EP.[77] That by Veltmeyer is best considered in relation to the book he co-authors with Petras.

Together with Petras, Veltmeyer has studied the grassroots dynamics in rural Latin America, and the way these have been formed by and against US imperialism. Both of them can rightly claim in their different ways to have followed the second or 'I told you so' path. Over the years Petras has written a series of texts that have contributed substantially to the understanding both

However, he then goes on to describe as 'contradictions' in the emancipatory process (unfree → free) the fact that in Andhra Pradesh the incidence of female attached labour has increased, and qualifies it yet further by casting doubt on this being a widespread a phenomenon (Byres, 1999: 18–19). Symptomatically, therefore, he fails to question the extent to which such developments in the capitalist labour process (free → unfree) are typical, categorizing them as 'anomalies' (= 'contradictions') instead of asking whether in fact they *are* anomalies.

75 The extent of the current overlap between the semi-feudal thesis and neoclassical economic theory regarding the necessity of yet more capitalist development in the so-called Third World is evident from a comparison of Byres' epistemology with that informing the marginalist approach of Lal (2004). The latter, like Byres, argues both that economic growth *per se* is a desirable end and that it is capitalism that will deliver this throughout the Third World. Where such an argument leads is equally clear. Lal concludes that, as empires guarantee economic development, imperial conquests are 'natural', they result in mutual gains and have 'promoted peace and prosperity'. That a neoliberal economist holds this view about the continuing and benign rôle of the market as a solution to the problems of underdevelopment is unremarkable; that much the same kind of argument underpins the view of a self-proclaimed Marxist is, to put it mildly, surprising.

76 See Veltmeyer (2005: 285–316) and Ampuero and Brittain (2005: 359–382).

77 Ampuero and Brittain (2005: 372ff.). On this subject generally, see also Brittain (2005).

of development theory in general and especially of agrarian transformation in Latin America.[78] His early research, plus the articles based on this, was on the transformation of and land occupations in rural Chile during the 1960s.[79] Since then, Petras and Veltmeyer have built an impressive *oeuvre*, some of the more important examples of which have been published in this journal. The focus of much of their recent work (separately and together) has been on the impact of neoliberal economic policies on agriculture in Latin America generally.[80]

Petras has been conducting research on and writing about development issues for close to forty years, and Veltmeyer for almost as long. Both are rightly considered to be among the best informed commentators on Latin American political economy. Not only is the depth of their general background knowledge about agrarian reform, peasant movements, capitalist development and imperialism unrivalled, therefore, but their analyses have been and remain informed by a commitment to socialist politics.[81] The breadth of their approach is evident from the co-authored book under review, which amounts to a cogent analysis (and powerful indictment) of global capitalism, with particular reference to Latin America. Among the wide variety of issues covered are: capitalism and imperialism in the era of globalization; the economic crisis faced by Argentina as a result of neoliberal policies and the 'from below' response; and the ecological collapse of cod stocks off Newfoundland, a consequence of overfishing.[82]

As important are the criticisms they make of the deleterious impact on the study of rural Latin America of postmodernism, on which their claim to have

78 See Petras and Morley (1990) for contributions to and comprehensive examinations of debates about Latin American development. For an evaluation of the agrarian reform programmes in Latin America during the 'development decade', see especially Petras and LaPorte (1971).

79 These analyses – by Petras (1969), Petras and LaPorte (1971: 125ff., 233ff.), and Petras and Zemelman Merino (1972) – of rural Chile are based on an in-depth knowledge of the historical context combined with fieldwork research.

80 See Petras and Veltmeyer (1997; 2001b; 2003b; 2005), Petras (2003) and Veltmeyer (1997; 1999; 2000); also Petras, Veltmeyer and Vasapollo (2005) and Saxe-Fernandez, Petras, Nuñez, and Veltmeyer (2001).

81 Unlike many others on the left, Petras (2006b) has not been afraid to tackle politically difficult issues.

82 These issues are covered in Petras and Veltmeyer (2003c: 2–22, 23–40, 41–67, 68–110, 203–218, 132–153). For a critique of imperialism, and how this systemic form remains extant (claims by others to the contrary notwithstanding), see Petras (2002). On the link between capitalism and overfishing in Newfoundland, see also the useful analysis by Overton (2000) about its impact on the rural economy and the resulting debate, an approach which complements that of Petras and Veltmeyer.

followed the 'I told you so' path of Marxists writing about development theory rests.[83] Unlike the rose-tinted views of Harriss about intellectuals, therefore, Petras long ago saw that much self-proclaimed 'alternative' development theory – such as post-structuralism, post-development, redemocratization, and postmodernism – was in fact politically conservative. Generated and then reproduced within the academy, such discourses were (he argued) in keeping with the broad shifts taking place globally during the period from the 1960s to the 1980s, transferring political and economic power from labour to capital.[84] Veltmeyer, too, has produced trenchant critiques of the 'cultural turn', long before these became common.[85]

Quick to spot the nonsense propagated by the Latin American variant of the 'semi-feudal' thesis, Petras early on drew attention to the fact that the cause of rural poverty, inequality and underdevelopment was not – as claimed – 'feudalism' but capitalism.[86] In contrast to Byres' analytical approach, Petras and Veltmeyer point out that in Mexico at the beginning of the twentieth century, where agricultural production had been penetrated by foreign capital, 'brutal forms of torture and labour control [= debt peonage] were not part of an archaic (or "feudal") dynastic order exercising a benign form of authority over the Mexican countryside and its denizens, but the means of maximizing profits for modern capitalists in Europe, North America and Mexico City.'[87] Not only do they root their analysis of rural transformation in the political economy of class, therefore, but Petras and Veltmeyer have also retained within their framework the crucial element of class struggle.

---

83 See Petras and Veltmeyer (2003c: 18–19). Hence the validity of the observation (Petras and Veltmeyer, 2003c: 180) that: 'Much current non-Marxist – especially postmodern – analysis of the peasantry...either ignores the state altogether or recognizes its presence and impact but denies that its agency is based on class.'

84 This argument was made early on, in the now classic analysis by Petras (1990) and also in Petras and Morley (1990: 147ff.).

85 See for example Veltmeyer (1997).

86 'The major tactic of this approach,' he argued (Petras, 1970: 378, 379, 382), 'is to ascribe the problems of Latin American development and motivation to "feudalism," "traditionalism," or "Hispanic culture"... Latin landowners who pay low wages and exploit their workers for profits [exponents of this approach maintain,] are not like their counterparts in California or Texas – they are "feudalists" acting out the Spanish heritage.' Rightly, he aligned himself with the approach of Andre Gunder Frank, who 'effectively destroys the myth of the feudal past so often cited and exploited by U.S. scholars as a means of defending capitalist development as a "democratic alternative" to Latin American stagnation.' This critique remains as relevant today as it was then, with the difference that it no longer applies simply to US academics.

87 Petras and Veltmeyer (2003c: 171).

Their general approach to the issues raised by the agrarian question is thus infinitely superior – both empirically and theoretically – to the work of Bernstein and Byres on the same subject. If proof were needed that an agrarian question of 'labour' (= the political component) cannot exist independently of one of capital, then it is to be found in the work of Petras and Veltmeyer. Central to their analyses of mass mobilization in rural Latin America has been the rôle of the State.[88] In the name of economic efficiency – a concept no different from that which informs the agrarian question as interpreted by Byres – the neoliberal State has not only withdrawn crop subsidies and cut back on technical and other inputs to agriculture, but also dismantled tariff protection. The outcome is hardly surprising: the State is now seen by those at the rural grassroots as having created a space for cheap imports that undercut then ousted peasant cultivation, whilst at the same time depriving those engaged in the latter process of a capacity successfully to compete (= resist).

The political response on the part of agrarian movements (the MST in Brazil, the EZLN in Mexico) representing smallholders affected in this way has been twofold. First, to target US imperialism, international capitalism (= neoliberalism), and the nation State (= the handmaiden of neoliberalism and US imperialism).[89] And second, to shift the terms of the ideological debate, away from a non-specific concept of 'economic efficiency' and towards the notion of 'social ends'. Unlike discourse about landownership based on a non-specific notion of 'economic efficiency', which in a capitalist context invariably hands agribusiness a clear ideological advantage, the notion of property rights being structured mainly by social ends favours smallholding producers who – according to market criteria – have no place surviving.

The discussion about who should own land, and why, has thus been moved by peasants and agricultural workers who form the grassroots membership of these rural movements.[90] The latter have shifted their debate with the State about development from one simply about economics (which they feel they are bound to lose) to one about 'the social' (where they perceive their winning chances as better). Consequently, grassroots political consciousness is still tied

---

88 Petras and Veltmeyer (2003c: 156ff.). See also Petras and Veltmeyer (2003a), and Petras (2006a).

89 Brittain (2005) also notes that as capitalism has become a global relation, neo-liberal economic policies advocated by US imperialism have fuelled the grassroots resistance that sustains the powerful guerrilla movements in rural Colombia.

90 In this they have been aided by those theorists (Adolfo Gilly, Guillermo de la Peña in Mexico; Gail Omvedt in India) – for the most part 'new' populist postmodernists – whose ideas reflect the prevailing views about such movements.

to access to land, and individual smallholdings are perceived as the solution to the problem of landlessness. However, not only is this largely a defensive measure (= the need to meet immediate subsistence requirements) in the face of a hostile State and neoliberalism, but it is also combined with a variety of grassroots co-operative initiatives transcending individualism. The presence of some form of co-ownership by peasants of common property resources therefore amounts to an organizational type that might conceivably prefigure socialism. This, Petras and Veltmeyer maintain, is how the rise of the new wave of agrarian movements in Latin America should be understood.[91]

V

Both kinds of approaches to development theory considered here – those which changed and those that remained the same – illustrate as clearly as need be the main problem confronting those who still write about the peasantry from a Marxist viewpoint. The difficulty lies not with Marxism itself, as claimed by development theory hostile to socialism, but rather with what these days passes for Marxism. Of the books under review, only that by Petras and Veltmeyer is informed by a commitment to a socialist politics. Contributions by Bernstein and Byres to the volumes edited by by Kothari, by Ramachandran and Swaminathan, and by Moyo and Yeros, suggest that socialism is regarded by neither of them as a necessary and/or viable objective. Where

91 See also Petras (1998), and Petras and Veltmeyer (2001a). That the source of individualistic 'conservatism' – insofar as it can be regarded as such – is not innate to peasant farmers and agricultural workers, but rather lies outside them, in terms of the wider economic context in which they operate, necessarily gives rise to optimism about the political direction of future change. This was recognized a long time ago by Mann (1929: 80, original emphasis), who wrote: 'After long experience of Indian farmers in many parts of India, I think that this idea of innate conservatism among the rural classes is not correct, and possibly they are less averse to change than a very large proportion of the farmers of western countries. I have seen, again and again, within twenty years an old but less efficient implement replaced almost entirely, over large regions, by one more efficient, or an improved type of seed replace that in use for a hundred years, or the employment of artificial manure become general. And it would really seem to be true that readiness to adopt new methods is the characteristic of the Indian cultivators, provided they are *proved*, to their own satisfaction, to be of advantage, and provided they give a return which will warrant the borrowing of capital at high interest.' As a socialist option has been in effect banished from the approach to the agrarian question of Byres and Bernstein, neither of them retains a progressive politics capable of transcending capitalism.

Harriss is concerned, since he has changed his views so often it is no longer possible to say with confidence what politics underwrites his approach to the study of development.

Siren calls to rewrite Marxism 'for our times' have been heard often before, and then – as now – they amount to code for something else. What this meant in the past, and what it means currently, therefore, is not so much a rewriting as a writing out of Marxist theory, in an endeavour to clear Marxism off the development agenda. In the case of Bernstein, this is in effect a result of his attempt to reinterpret the agrarian question by artificially dividing it up, separating out its integral components (politics/production/accumulation; capital/'labour'), and then announcing that only the political element – the agrarian question of 'labour' – remains current. An obvious contradiction Bernstein ends up facing is that, having abandoned class analysis and socialism, how is it possible still to speak of (never mind define) an agrarian question of 'labour'?

This antinomy stems from earlier theoretical hybridity. Far from having initiated debates about the pattern of post-1945 rural development, the class differentiation of the peasantry, the agrarian question, the significance of new social movements, and the rise of the 'new' populist postmodern theory (the 'cultural turn'), Bernstein has been either wrong or silent about all these issues. Hence the understandable need on his part for a change of mind. The result of these epistemological shifts, plus the jettisoning of class analysis and consequently socialism, deprives his development theory of a political objective that transcends either capitalism, nationalism or bourgeois democracy. In this, the stasis informing Bernstein's framework is ultimately no different from the one structuring that of Byres.

In the course of a never-ending search for the answer to the agrarian question, Byres has managed to do no more than display an unrivalled misunderstanding of the historical patterns of systemic transition. Because of a failure to recognize that capitalist producers restructure the agrarian labour process, therefore, Byres cannot account for use by them of workers who are bonded in preference to ones that are free. Unfree labour is accordingly classified as a residual form, an anomalous 'pre-capitalist' relation that is incompatible with accumulation. Unsurprisingly, therefore, his attempt to theorize the agrarian question is structured by multiple confusion, about what precisely a process of transition entails, and thus when this can be said to have been accomplished. The outcome in terms of a political economy of development is simply stated.

Marxists who recognize the acceptability of unfree labour to capital, consequently argue that the transition is not to capitalism but rather to socialism. By contrast, since exponents of the semi-feudal thesis misinterpret bonded labour as a 'pre-capitalist' relation, they cannot but advocate yet more efficient capitalism. Confining the agrarian question to national contexts, exponents of the semi-feudal thesis also insist on economic growth as primary, a goal that not only allows capitalism off the hook, and banishes socialism from the political agenda, but also permits the old myth of a 'progressive national bourgeoisie' to flourish. These are objectives with which no bourgeois supporter of the capitalist system itself could quarrel.

Byres' difficulty is compounded by a refusal to recognize the impact on agriculture of an international capital that, because it delinks production and consumption, does not have to worry about demand in the locality where crops are grown. This is the reason that export agribusiness enterprises – whether national or international – can and do employ workers that are unfree. The great strength of the approach by Petras and Veltmeyer is that they never forget to situate their analysis of a Latin American country, its history, its agrarian struggles, and its State, in the wider context, one where United States imperialism enforces the economic interests of a capitalist class that is international in scope. The contrast between this broad comparative framework and the narrow focus of Byres is absolute.

Like Bernstein, Byres forgets that the agrarian question is linked indissolubly to *capitalism*, and thus also to its form(s) of class struggle. Insofar as this systemic mode continues to reproduce itself economically, therefore, not only is the agrarian question no longer connected simply to the fate of this or that national capital, but announcements of closure (= 'the *resolution* of the agrarian question') are necessarily premature. Although Bernstein accepts that capitalist development elsewhere occurs as a result of unfree labour employed in a context labelled 'pre-capitalist', neither he nor Byres consider that unfree labour might, after all, be compatible with accumulation within such contexts, and is thus not an 'obstacle' to capitalist development anywhere.

The theoretical dilemma facing Byres is reversed in Bernstein. In his interpretation of the agrarian question, Byres has to define production relations as 'free' so that Junkers can be categorized as capitalists and a transition declared accomplished. Although Bernstein also accepts Byres' contention that these production relations are 'free', he nevertheless comes close to defining Junkers as 'feudal' and pre-capitalist. Accordingly, both are found not in the Marxist camp but rather in that of its opponents, either on a temporary basis (where fundamental theoretical shifts in the analysis of petty commodity production are concerned) or on a permanent one (where the stasis of semi-feudal framework is concerned). With 'Marxists' like these, one might ask what need is there for a non-Marxist development theory?

CHAPTER 12

Zomia, or a Postmodern History of Nowhere*

These days there is a recognizable form of academic *folie de grandeur*, whereby as one gets older, an individual begins to regard him/herself as an all-purpose cultural commentator. Having started modestly, reporting the findings from a particular fieldwork location, the academic in question arrives finally at a stage where s/he feels able to redefine the whole theoretical approach to 'his/her' research area, perhaps even the wider discipline itself, or – as in the book reviewed here – to invent an entire region. Not the least satisfying aspect of this career progression, seen from the viewpoint of the academic concerned, is that it mimics all the acts of imperial conquest: a foreign territory is acquired, its resources looted and property seized, and clients are placed upon its throne.[1]

In the nineteenth century, imperialism renamed portions of the globe without reference to the wishes of the people who lived there. Having planted a flag on a piece of land that did not belong to them, imperialists declared that henceforth it would be known by a name of their own choosing. At the start of the twenty-first century, it can be argued that a similar kind renaming occurs, but this time by academics of portions of the globe they study, again without reference to those who occupy the spaces in question. From a campus usually located in a western capitalist nation, the identity of an existing Third World country is declared to be invalid, and its current designation henceforth to be replaced with a more 'authentic' one. In each instance, an overriding pronouncement either accompanies or amounts to an act of conquest: the earlier one a material colonization, the later one merely an intellectual occupation of an 'other' space.

---

* Reviewed here is *The Art of Not Being Governed: An Anarchist History of Southeast Asia*, by James C. Scott (London and New Haven, CT: Yale University Press, 2009). An earlier version, entitled 'Scott's Zomia, or a Populist Postmodern History of Nowhere', appeared in *The Journal of Contemporary Asia*, Vol. 42, No. 1 (2012).

1 It is possible to extend this simile further, in that the capacity to acquire intellectual territory depends also on command over manpower, a resource generally available only to senior academics. The list of research assistants whom Scott (p. xvii) acknowledges as having 'saved me many months of futile toil' is impressive. Indeed, at times the book appears to be the result of many hands, all working to different agendas. The reason for thinking this is the extent to which contradictory statements/claims surface periodically throughout the book, one argument in an early chapter being undermined – seemingly unknowingly – by what is said to be the case in a later chapter.

According to Scott, 'Zomia' is a new name for the 'largest remaining non-state space in the world' a vast area extending from northeastern India, via the Central Highlands of Vietnam, to the Chinese provinces of Yunnan, Guizhou, and Sichuan and western Guangxi.[2] Covering some 2.5 million square kilometres and home to a population of one hundred million, 'Zomia' consists of self-governing hill peoples who, Scott insists, must be seen not as remnants of socio-economically more advanced societies, but rather as empowered upland populations who chose not to be part of lowland contexts ruled by the State. Historically, hill communities have sought refuge in uplands precisely so as to avoid (= 'state evasion') what he terms 'state-making projects', involving slavery, taxation, and corvée labour.[3]

From this desire on the part of upland inhabitants 'to keep the state at arm's length' stem their egalitarian organizational, institutional and cultural forms (kinship structure, subsistence agriculture, cropping patterns, ethnic identities), all of which are consequently regarded by Scott 'as political choices'.[4] What we mistakenly categorize as marginality, impoverishment, illiteracy, and a backward culture, he maintains, are all perceived as 'chosen' by the subjects themselves, and thus empowering. Unlike lowland areas, where state power, class hierarchy and inequality prevail, highland communities are by contrast egalitarian, subsistence-oriented and non-state locations.[5] Those on the periphery choose to be there, in pursuit of which objective they resist-the-state, a form of grassroots agency designed to protect peasant economy.

As drawn by Scott, the socio-economic contrast between hill and valley contexts is stark, and involves the following oppositions (outlined in Table 1):

---

2 Scott (2009: 13).

3 'Zomia' is described by Scott (2009: 127, 178) both as 'an historical sanctuary for state-evading peoples', and as 'a pattern of settlement, agriculture, and social structure that is state-repelling'. Not the least ironic aspect of the book is that Scott (2009: 86) endorses the work of Reid (1983), who argues that slavery in Southeast Asia was mild and benign. If this was so, then why did upland inhabitants flee there in order to avoid it?

4 See Scott (2009: x–xi, 7–9, 157, 179, 183, 187).

5 See Scott (2009: 18–19, 135, 186). His view (Scott, 2009: 132, 157) that '[t]he Cossack frontier of Tsarist Russia was notable…for its egalitarian social structure' would come as news to most commentators on Russian history. Both the fact of Cossack landholding inequalities, together with the causes, are outlined by Blum (1961), who maintains further that communal lands were communal in name only. Peasant differentiation among rural Cossacks was also noted by Lenin (1964b: 33), who observed that 'they are a section of the population consisting of rich, small or medium landed proprietors…in one of those outlying regions of Russia that have retained many medieval traits in their way of life, their economy, and their customs. We can regard this as the socio-economic basis for a Russian Vendée.'

TABLE 1 *('Good') hills versus ('bad') valleys*

'Good'	'Bad'
hill zone ('Zomia')	valley zone
mountains	arable plains
periphery	centre
state avoidance (non-state space), a 'region of refuge' chosen by its inhabitants	state imposed on the population
sociologically/ideologically marginal 'other' domain	domain of sociological/ideological incorporation
anti-development, anti-progress, anti-modernization	development, progress, modernization
ethnically diverse	ethnically uniform
free/autonomous rural communities of independent farmers ('escape agriculture')	population unfree, slavery rife
politically self-governing, ungoverned	governed, oppressive
egalitarian (non-class, or 'escape social structure')	hierarchical social structure (class)
illiteracy/orality	literacy
healthy	diseased

It is argued here that what for Scott is a valley/'bad' versus hill/'good' paradigm, based as it is on a mutually exclusive set of oppositions, is not merely unsustainable, but is so on the basis of evidence provided throughout his book. Moreover, contrary to his claim, this approach is not in fact new. It is part of a resurgent populist historiography that has become academically entrenched over the past three decades, replacing earlier variants which advocated economic development and modernization, now virtually banished from the intellectual agenda.[6]

6 As is evident from other contributions to this volume (see Review 4; Review Essays 11 and 13; and Essay 18), Scott's views are entirely in keeping with a resurgent populism that, amongst other things, has colonized academic journals covering agrarian issues. This takes the form of a pro-farmer and food-first discourse which, on the one hand privileges smallholding

In an important sense this book signals just how far social science discourse has shifted politically since the 1960s development decade. At the latter conjuncture, the main concern of development theory (Marxist and non-Marxist alike) was to end rural socio-economic marginality in the so-called Third World, by bringing peasants and agricultural workers into the wider society. As participants both in the process of economic growth and the political system, the rural poor would then be able to secure better pay/conditions leading to increased living standards. Linked to existing poverty, illiteracy and oppression, therefore, rural marginality was perceived negatively, as an indicator of backwardness and underdevelopment, and thus as a problem to be solved.

From around the 1980s, this approach was not merely abandoned but actually reversed.[7] Henceforth marginality was recast as a form of empowerment, a revision that coincided with and was effected by the rise both of neoliberal economics and of the 'new' populist postmodernism. Peasant/ethnic identity was re-essentialized, and reaffirmed theoretically as an 'authentic' form of selfhood that was eternal due to its culturally indissoluble 'natural' character. Customs, traditions and practices as these already existed at the rural grassroots were now celebrated/endorsed by the 'new' populist postmodernism as forms of cultural 'difference', to be cherished as such.

To effect this reversal, the same revisionist discourse simultaneously challenged the theoretical approach linked to the 1960s development framework. Declaring the latter a tainted foundational/Eurocentric meta-narrative, the 'new' populist postmodernism dismissed concepts such as class, modernity,

---

agriculture and rural social movements, and on the other ignores or downgrades the importance of class differences transecting both peasant economy and agrarian mobilizations.

7 One of the very few on the left to anticipate this reversal was Baran (1957: 4): 'As long as reason and the lessons to be learned from history were manifestly on the side of the bourgeoisie in its struggle against the obscurantist ideologies and institutions of feudalism, both reason and history were confidently invoked as the supreme arbiters in the fateful contest. There are no more magnificent witnesses to this grand alliance of the ascending bourgeoisie with reason and historical thinking than the great Encyclopaedists of the eighteenth century, than the great realists of the nascent bourgeois literature. But when reason and the study of history began revealing the irrationality, the limitations, and the mere transitory nature of the capitalist order, bourgeois ideology as a whole and with it bourgeois economics began abandoning both reason and history. Whether this abandonment assumed the form of a rationalism driven to its own self-destruction and turning into the agnosticism of modern positivism, *or whether it appeared frankly in the form of some essentialist philosophy contemptuously rejecting all search for and all reliance upon a rational comprehension of history*, the result was that bourgeois thought (and economics as a part of it) turned ever more into a neatly packaged kit of assorted ideological gadgets required for the functioning and preservation of the existing social order.' (emphasis added).

development, and progress as inappropriate for an understanding of the rural Third World. Pivotal to this epistemological *volte face* was a specific form of agency, the object of which was no longer the revolutionary capture and control of the state. Just such a non-revolutionary mobilization was provided by Scott, in the form of his notion of 'everyday-forms-of-resistance', whereby quotidian/smallscale agency undertaken by peasants is said to block every attempt by the state to effect all its 'alien' policies/processes designed to transform the status quo.[8]

In this book the 'resistance' model is taken a step further, and is now imbued with a spatial dimension: rural populations are located in upland areas, protecting their autonomy from a malign lowland state. In short, it constitutes ecological determinism, a form of functionalism, one moreover attributed to subjects who, it is claimed, choose to be marginal.[9] Whereas the old functionalism maintained this was good for the wider society, the more recent populist postmodernism insists it is functional for the individuals concerned, who are empowered thereby.

Ostensibly, the populist historiography of Scott is consistent with anarchism, in that he peoples his Zomia with free inhabitants, self-sufficient cultivators exercising self-management (= 'autonomy') in egalitarian smallscale rural communities beyond the reach of the state. However, this is misleading. Despite advancing his resistance-to-the-state theory under the progressive label of an anarchist history, Scott's anti-state discourse has more in common with views of libertarian philosophers, anarcho-capitalist thinkers, and neoliberal economists.[10] For all the latter, as for Scott, opposition to the state as an institution remains absolute, and stems principally from its taxation policy, perceived by libertarians as an illegitimate appropriation, a view which overlooks the redistributive functions linked to this role.

Anarchist political theory opposed to the state as an institution not only does so mainly on the grounds that historically it has acted on behalf of the wealthy, in whose interests it has invariably suppressed grassroots movements opposed to the rich, but also sees virtue in the progressive attempts by the state committed to public works and welfare programmes, to regulate capital and rein in the market. This emphasis is very different from that of libertarians generally (and anarcho-capitalists in particular), who seek much rather to prevent

8 See Scott (1976; 1985; 1990).

9 Hence the relay-in-statement whereby 'geographical marginality' = 'cultural choice' = 'zone of resistance' (Scott, 2009: 157).

10 For these views, see Spencer (1884), Nock (1935), Nozick (1975), Rothbard (1982), Hayek (1960), and Friedman (1962).

such expenditure, so as to enable the rich to retain more of their wealth that would otherwise be taken from them by the state in the form of taxation.[11]

Broadly speaking, grassroots agency labelled by Scott as a process of 'resistance' against the state frequently entails attempts to get the state involved, and thus does not correspond to a wish to 'avoid' this institution. Much rather the opposite, in that agency by slum-dwellers and poor farmers on occasion is designed to make the state pro-active on their behalf, and put into practice its own policies or legislation enforcing minimum wage levels and land reform programmes. Accordingly, his unambiguously all-embracing concept of anti-state agency overlooks the presence of contrary instances.

By putting pressure on the state through class struggle, therefore, workers in urban contexts have managed to secure improvements in pay and conditions, not to mention the franchise, which enabled them to consolidate such gains. It was by *stripping away state intervention* – the very process Scott endorses – as has occurred in many parts of the world after 1980, that workers have lost this kind of protection, and been left at the mercy of the markets. This is the reason why Marxism has always argued for the capture (*not* the avoidance) of the state, and its subsequent use to implement a socialist programme. Resistance-to-the-state, in other words, also occurs in valley and urban contexts, but of a different kind, by a different subject, and with different objectives. So confining agency to hill populations, as Scott does, is incorrect.

Another contrary example concerns the Karen, an indigenous population who feature in the book as occupying 'hiding villages' so as to evade the state.[12] Describing the struggle between the Karen and the Burmese military, Scott outlines how the former flee in response to forced labour exactions by the latter. He calls this the technique of 'state evasion' typical of Zomia, and invokes the Karen response as evidence for an anti-state pattern of subsistence and social organization. The problem with this is twofold. To begin with, Scott bases his account simply on publications by the Karen Human Rights Group, which portrays the indigenous population simply in terms of ethnically 'other' victims.[13] More importantly, Scott omits to mention that in the late 1940s these tribals were fighting for a separate ethnically-specific Karen state, the political object of the Karen National Defence Organization (KNDO). Furthermore,

11 For the importance of the political distinction between these forms of libertarianism, see Walter (1969: 10), Carter (1971: 28ff.), and Marshall (1992: 559 ff.).

12 See Scott (2009: 179–182). He notes (Scott, 2009: 88) how the Karen undertook slave-raids, selling those captured to lowland traders, which further undermines the description of them simply as 'victims'.

13 See Scott (2009: 377).

this move towards Karen statehood was supported by conservative politicians in Britain, in order to undermine Burmese independence and retain access to mineral deposits in a future Karenistan.[14] Simply to portray all grassroots agency undertaken by the Karen as invariably endogenous and 'state-repelling' is therefore problematic.

Like all other 'new' populist postmodernists, Scott regards development, progress, and modernization as three historical evils, associated by him with 'state-making' in the lowlands.[15] Contrasting his own argument about 'state-evading migration' to 'an old view' allocating the state a central role in economic growth, he dismisses the latter as 'still part of the folk beliefs of valley people'.[16] The conceptual troika of development, progress, and modernization is in Scott's opinion based on the mistaken view that hill people can and should be integrated into the wider society, or – as he puts it – 'make the transition to a more civilized way of life'. By conflating an argument about ideology (hill communities = 'uncivilized') with one about economics (= growth), therefore, he deploys the former to cast doubt on the historical efficacy of the latter.

In short, what Scott opposes is any attempt not just to bring such marginal populations into the wider society but also to include them in its development project; namely, those who advocate that hill people and other marginals 'be made the object of development efforts to integrate them into the...economic life of the nation.' The targets of this populist critique are obvious: 1960s modernization theory and – more broadly – Marxism, since each approach endorses systemic change, their political differences notwithstanding.[17] Let the indigenous hill peoples remain as they are, he seems to be saying; indeed, they and their way of life must be protected from any development project generated by the state, a view that has a politically worrying antecedent.

A precursor of Scott's 'Zomia' model, therefore, was advanced eight decades ago with regard to Africa. This argument began, like that of Scott, by supporting the idea of 'tribal cohesiveness', presented as empowering for the indigenous population. From this it went on to propose the adoption of a system of 'separate parallel institutions', one set for Europeans who 'live in the same country'

---

14 In pursuit of this latter objective, foreign supporters of Karen statehood disguised themselves as a human rights organization, the Friends of the Burma Hill People.

15 Scott (2009: 4–5, 98ff., 119).

16 Scott (2009: 128).

17 Hence the complaint by Scott (2009: 187–188) that '[a]ny effort to examine the history of social structure and subsistence routines as part of a deliberate political choice runs smack against a powerful civilizational narrative. The narrative consists of a historical series arranged as an account of economic, social and cultural progress...this narrative is profoundly misleading'.

and another for the natives. Its author decried the 'old practice [which] mixed up black with white in the same institutions', presenting this as a form of self-criticism, blaming an over-powerful colonialism for its negative impact on the colonized ('after the native institutions and traditions had been carelessly or deliberately destroyed'). In what was a clever rhetorical device, separateness was presented as a virtuous act undertaken by whites, intent not merely on restoring but protecting traditional African culture the merits of which they had only just recognized.

This virtuous act, it was then revealed, would entail 'segregation' based on 'separate institutions for the two elements...living in their own separate areas'. Since 'institutional segregation carries with it territorial segregation', the policy advocated 'gives the native his own traditional institutions on land which is set aside for his exclusive occupation'. These holdings will be 'adequate' for tribal needs, both now and in the future, and those working in towns will also live apart, again in recognition of their cultural 'otherness'. Like the inhabitants of 'Zomia' in Southeast Asia, therefore, the African 'other' was to occupy his/her own physical space, a policy which would enable an innate historic identity, together with its cultural traditions/practices and local institutions, to flourish unhindered by the state. Formulated by Jan Christian Smuts for the whole of Africa, this theory of separate development as a benign way of empowering and protecting the native population underwrote the South African apartheid system.[18]

The point is that what was being proposed by Smuts in the 1930s (a policy culminating in the Bantustans), together with the reasons given for it – an empowerment of indigenous cultural 'otherness' in need of protection from an overweening state – are in essence little different conceptually from the defence by Scott of 'zones of refuge' and 'shatter zones' informing his analysis of 'Zomia'. Like Scott in the case of 'non-state' Southeast Asian indigenous hill peoples, moreover, the South African government justified the policy of separate development on the grounds that it was what the black population wanted. Each *chose* to live apart, an empowering decision which consequently

---

18 See Smuts (1930: 74–103). Fear of socialism was the reason for encouraging African institutions/culture and supporting existing tribal authority. Hence the view (Smuts, 1930: 86, 87) that, if 'the bonds of native tribal cohesion and authority are dissolved, the African governments will everywhere sit with vast hordes of detribalized natives on their hands, for whom the traditional restraints and the discipline of the chiefs and elders will have no force or effect.' If this 'despotic authority of the chiefs' broke down, he feared the emergence of Bolshevism.

meant that such a policy should not be seen (by outsiders) as an oppressive exclusionary measure imposed on them.

As Scott's claim unfolds, constructing 'Zomia' as some form of Southeast Asian utopia, it also unravels, its flaws becoming increasingly evident. Despite his claim that '[w]hat I have to say in these pages makes little sense for the period following [1945]', therefore, many of his arguments are illustrated with reference to episodes in the 1950s, 1960s, 1970s and 1980s.[19] Nor is it the case that 'Zomia' is confined to Southeast Asia, since according to Scott the model is geographically/historically ubiquitous, and consequently 'mini-Zomias' are found everywhere and at all times.[20] Other difficulties with 'Zomia' are equally obvious.

If, as Scott insists, non-state peoples are largely missing from the historical record, and they themselves leave few accounts of what they did and thought, how is it possible to be sure about these latter aspects? This is especially true where motive – institutional/organizational forms deemed 'refuges', 'empowering', and 'chosen' – is attributed to the population concerned. Here Scott is faced with a familiar methodological dilemma: the wish to construct a history of the 'other' depends in turn on information that is missing. As he himself accepts, its non-existence is precisely the reason for their absence from the historical record in the first place. Time and again, therefore, an initial caveat about data and/or sources for a particular claim being scarce or lacking is subsequently disregarded.[21]

Neither is it the case, as claimed by Scott, that such a narrative – about resistance by non-state people – is unjustly neglected, since tales concerning heroic grassroots struggle against a malign state power are a staple of foundation myths in almost every country.[22] Many aspects of this narrative informed the 1893 Turner thesis, which maintained that westwards settlement of the United States frontier was based on the individualism, self-reliance, hardiness, egalitarianism and indomitability of independent smallholding proprietors resisting appropriation/incorporation.[23] In a reversal of the paradigm advanced by Scott, this discourse insisted that the political nature of the

19 Scott (2009: xii, 150–151, 154, 157, 169, 172, 195).

20 See Scott (2009: 25, 167 ff.). Areas to which Scott applies his 'Zomia' model include not just the Roman Empire, ancient Egypt and Greece, but also Amazonia, Latin America, Africa, the Balkans, the Philippines, Pakistan, Russia, Europe, and the Middle East (Scott, 2009: 6, 8, 24–25, 123–124, 127, 131ff., 157, 189).

21 See, for example, Scott (2009: 137, 140, 141, 144, 162, 164, 197).

22 For this claim, see Scott (2009: x, 31).

23 Turner (1949).

American state was shaped historically by 'free farmer' democratic ideals generated on its frontier.[24] All of which suggests, *pace* Scott, that unilinear models of incorporation by the state (= antagonistic to the 'other' located on its periphery) are not wholly accurate.

Moreover, having originally claimed that his interpretation of Zomia as an empowering 'region of refuge' chosen by its inhabitants is 'a new way to think of area studies...', Scott later concedes that 'the perspective we propose for understanding Zomia is not novel'.[25] Much the same case, Scott accepts, was applied earlier to Latin America by Gonzalo Aguirre Beltrán, who argued that the indigenous population there sought refuge in areas beyond Spanish control.[26] Unlike Scott, however, Aguirre Beltrán pointed out that indigenous people did not choose to migrate in this fashion; rather, they were forced off the better valley land they already occupied, and subsequently went in search of alternative holdings in highland areas. This is a very different dynamic from the one advanced by Scott, who maintains that such migrations were voluntary.[27]

---

24 'This perennial rebirth,' comments Turner (1949: 2, 8), 'this fluidity of American life, this expansion westward with its new opportunities, *its continuous touch with the simplicity of primitive society*, furnish the forces dominating American character. The true point of view in the history of this nation is not the Atlantic coast, it is the Great West... From the time the mountains rose between the pioneer and the [Eastern] seaboard, a new order of Americanism arose' (emphasis added).

25 See Scott (2009: ix, 26, 130). He also agrees (Scott, 2009: 191) that the claim 'that the choice of shifting cultivation is preeminently a political choice', is one that 'hardly originates with me.'

26 Like his mentor, Ángel Palerm (who, in the same way as Scott, also described himself as an anarchist), Gonzalo Aguirre Beltrán was at the forefront of 1950s Mexican agrarian populist *indigenista* theory (Hewitt de Alcántara, 1984; Suárez, 1990). This was itself a continuation of peasant essentialist ideology encountered in Third World contexts during the first half of the century: not only the *indigenista* discourse of José Carlos Mariátegui, Hildebrando Castro Pozo, Haya de la Torre and Fausto Reinaga in Peru and Bolivia (Brass, 2003b), but also the populist nationalism of Ranga, Deva and Lohia in India (Brass, 1995). Common to them all was the view that, beneath the alien imposition of a foreign colonial state, an indigenous peasant culture and institutions – embodying what they regarded as an authentically national identity – survived intact, forming thereby a socio-economic blueprint for the future.

27 That inhabitants of upland Southeast Asia may not actually be there by choice either, also emerges subsequently when Scott (2009: 139–140) accepts that 'this geographical bastion against state expansion [is one to which] the population seeking to evade incorporation have been driven', a consequence of being forced off valley land and into the highlands. Later, however, he reverts once again to his initial argument, disputing the claim (Scott,

Another prefiguring model, also from Latin America and unmentioned by Scott, is the concept 'verticality', which – much like Scott in the case of Southeast Asia – argued for the existence of a specific Andean peasant economy based on the control of different ecological niches (capitalist valleys, peasant mountains).[28] However, as critiques long ago pointed out, this apparently ecologically distinct hill economy was in fact reproduced by valley capitalism.[29] To regard the former as a highland 'region of refuge', the systemic 'other' of the valley, was to reify both Andean peasant economy and the reproduction of its cultural/institutional forms. Spatial distinctiveness notwithstanding, this undermines claims about the degree to which such zones can ever be regarded as autonomous, to the extent of having an dynamic which operates independently of the wider socio-economic system.[30]

A similar difficulty arises with regard to chattel slavery and other forms of unfree labour (corvée, debt bondage, forced labour), depicted by Scott as distinctly lowland and state-imposed oppressions.[31] Indeed, people fleeing to the uplands so as to avoid becoming unfree workers in the lowlands is one of the main reasons why the uplands are described by him as areas of 'popular freedom'.[32] However, it transpires that not only was slave hunting/raiding common in hill areas, but also 'hill people and not a few hill societies as a whole became deeply implicated in the [slave] trade'.[33] Finally, he acknowledges that the state/unfreedom versus the non-state/free dichotomy does not hold,

---

2009: 172–173) that lowland peoples 'were driven into the hills, reluctantly, by virtue of force majeure.'

28 Murra (1975).

29 For these critiques, see Sánchez (1977, 1982) and Bradby (1982).

30 Objections to Murra's concept of verticality included the view that peasants in the Andean highlands are in fact members of the industrial reserve army of labour, physically drawn from 'regions of refuge' by capital in order to generate surplus-value and then returned to these locations when no longer required for the purpose of accumulation. As will be seen below, much the same kind of dynamic operated with regard to Scott's Zomia, where lowland economies appropriated unfree labour-power (slaves, debt peons) from the highlands.

31 See Scott (2009: 10, 23 ff., 33, 67 ff., 84 ff.).

32 Scott (2009: 19, 33).

33 See Scott (2009: 87–88). This concession has implications for his claim (Scott, 2009: 18–19) about egalitarianism, and particularly that women in hill regions enjoy an innately higher status. Evidence from Southeast Asia suggests otherwise. In the polynyandrous households of sub-Himalayan India, for example, indebted males sent female relatives into prostitution so as to pay off loans owed by males to moneylenders (Brass, 1999: 37). Similar instances of bonded female labour are reported for Eastern Nepal (Malamoud, 1983: 221).

lamenting that '[alas] the most important hill commodity for expansive valley states was its manpower...slaves became virtually the standard of value by which other goods were denominated', captured and supplied to the lowlands by trading partners in the highlands. Hence the central argument of his thesis – namely, highlands as 'regions of refuge' – breaks down at this point, since it turns out that upland communities were themselves divided between victims (from which slaves were taken) and predators (those who took/sold slaves).

The notion of hill societies being not just 'state-repelling' but also proof against slave-raiding expeditions and 'starving would-be pillagers of foodstuffs' is also contradicted by ethnography.[34] During the early 1920s, J.H. Hutton, a member of the Indian Civil Service and later Professor of Social Anthropology at Cambridge, undertook a tour of the Assam-Burma border region, part of what is now categorized by Scott as 'Zomia'. Combining ethnographic research among the Naga Hill tribes with a survey of the area, Hutton reveals a very different picture from the idealized image applied by Scott to such regions.[35] Contrary to the claim that the inhabitants of these stateless zones perceived the colonial state as the enemy, villages in the Naga Hills were perpetually at war with each another, in furtherance of which they frequently requested the assistance of the military escort accompanying Hutton – then a representative of the colonial state – in slaughtering and burning neighbouring settlements.[36] The dystopian picture that emerges from Hutton's findings, a Hobbesian one of a continuous war of all against all, scarcely accords with the conceptualization by Scott of these areas as 'state-repelling' regions of 'asylum' or 'zones of refuge'.

Unaware of the extent to which his claims about 'Zomia' are rooted in populist historiography, a long-standing discourse championing a rural 'other' opposed to and excluded from development/urbanization/modernization, Scott gives too much credence to the hill communities as 'regions of asylum/refuge', the economic autonomy enjoyed by their inhabitants, as well as to the innate desire on the part of this 'other' always to resist the state and its development project. Unless one is aware of the background to this historiography,

---

34 Scott (2009: 178ff.).

35 Hutton (1929).

36 See Hutton (1929: 21, 58–59), who recounts an incident whereby one Naga village hid its food in a neighboring settlement, fearing the colonial military escort accompanying Hutton's (1929: 34) survey team would steal this, 'feeling confident enough that we should not touch their contents there. And rightly, for we did not, but their [clan] friends did, for when [the villagers] got back, after we were well away, devil a basketful of rice did they find left...at all. Yet it is hard to tell what else they could have expected...[t]hey would certainly have done the same themselves.'

the absolute nature of the epistemological about-turn that has occurred in the study of development over the latter part of the twentieth century, the *volte face* is difficult to comprehend. Economic backwardness, criticized from the 1960s onwards on the grounds that it deprived rural populations of basic amenities and improved living standards, was from the 1980s onwards converted by adherents of the 'new' populist postmodernism – Scott among them – into a form of empowerment, actively chosen and defended by its subject.

However, to argue, as does Scott, that people in less-fertile upland areas choose to live and work there (and are consequently empowered by their situation) is rather like saying that hill farmers who scratch a precarious living from poor quality soil choose to do this, as do slum dwellers located on the poorly-resourced fringes of urban conurbations. Such conditions are not chosen by their subjects in preference to all other options; much rather, many of those belonging to marginal populations live/work there only because it is in such peripheral locations that land is available or cheap, rents are low, and they are unable afford the cost of living/working in better-resourced areas. That rural/urban inhabitants who are marginal make do and mend in these circumstances is self-evident (verging on the tautological), but this is emphatically not the same – as Scott appears to think – as their choosing to do so or being empowered thereby.

Insofar as it conveys a claim to be located on the radical end of the political spectrum, the label 'anarchist history' applied by Scott to his analysis is misleading, and serves merely to disguise its conservative underpinnings. Now that economic development, wealth redistribution, progress and modernity are more-or-less off the social scientific agenda, it is unsurprising that postmodern populist approaches like this one should surface and proclaim that what exists is a form of empowerment for 'those below'. Learn to accept what you are (= poor peasants and agricultural labourers) and enjoy what you already have (little land, low wages, bleak prospects) is the unspoken sub-text of the book. Verily, it is a tract in keeping with our neoliberal times.

Postscript

The above critique of Scott's Zomia seemingly goes against the grain, in that – contrary to the way his everyday-forms-of resistance framework is perceived by many in academia – it challenges the label anarchist historiography which the author attaches to his work, and instead argues that the analysis more correctly belongs on the right of the political spectrum. Among the reactions to my critique of Scott – comparing his defence of Zomia in terms of cultural 'otherness' specifically to the white South African regime justification of the apartheid system, and more generally to conservative discourse – was that it was simply too harsh.[37] Given what is known about the politics of Lev Gumilev (1912–1992) and Eurasianism, and their overlap with the way Scott interprets the area he defines as Zomia, it could be argued that, much rather, the case made by me then was not harsh enough.

Eurasianism was conceptualized in the 1920s by émigrés fleeing the 1917 Russian Revolution, and its anti-communist epistemology unsurprisingly reflected this origin. Its principal exponent was Gumilev, whose arguments promoting Eurasianism contained what is a familiar dichotomy, a discourse-against and a discourse-for. Central to his discourse-against was opposition to West European and its Enlightenment project, blamed for imposing a false political trajectory (democracy, liberalism) on Russia that culminated in the Bolshevik revolution. Instead, the true (= 'authentic') path as embodied in its discourse-for maintained that Russia should follow lay in the East, with the steppe peoples of inner Asia. To this end, the Eurasianist historiography of Gumilev not only privileged religious, national and ethnic identity, but drew on linguistic theory to validate its claims: namely, the structuralism of Trubetskoy and Jakobson, which decoupled meaning and language, thereby denying a connection between the latter and material conditions.[38]

---

37 For example, Grant (2013: 354) describes the critique as 'a bit extreme', and Delande (2013) regards it as being a 'very critical reading of Scott's book, which accuses the author of playing into the hands of conservative neoliberalism'. Whilst not agreeing with them, such reactions are nevertheless understandable, since encountering an unsettling comparative dimension must be something of a shock to holders of parochial views. Unfortunately, the same cannot be said of the attempt by Chandra (2015: 571, n1) to dismiss what is characterized by him as a 'scathing critique' because in his opinion it is 'not unproblematic'. Not only is there lacking any explanation as to why the critique of Scott is thought to be 'problematic', but the object of Chandra's article inadvertently betrays the reason for this. Claiming to identify 'emancipatory possibilities' which 'reinvigorate the study of resistance', Chandra seeks to rehabilitate the Subaltern Studies approach, which together with Scott's everyday-forms-of-resistance framework is now widely criticized, many analyses over the years having undermined both the theoretical case made by and evidence contained in these 'new' populist postmodern arguments (none of which are addressed). Nor is the principal claim made by Chandra – namely, the significance of resistance was simply that it happened (= 'assertiveness as empowerment') – novel, being as it is a patronizing trope long known about (on which see Brass, 1999: 230–231, 251 n81).

38 See Clover (2016: 55), who notes that 'the writings of Trubetskoy [and] Jakobson...sought to argue that cultures and civilizations have natural boundaries...characterized by an entire substratum of unconscious relationships between language sounds, music scales,

From their theory about language, structuralism laid the ground for the 'Eurasian Language Union', which referred to an area defined simply by linguistic affinities that were themselves governed by an inner logic.[39] This in turn led Trubetskoy, Jakobson and Gumilev to the view that Eurasia was an area defined additionally by cultural affinities, since what occurred within such contexts was determined internally, giving rise to a unity that persisted over time regardless of processes operating outside it.[40] Significantly, this model is in terms of epistemology and politics similar to three others.

First, Herder's view about how the closeness of the link between language and popular culture in effect precludes the incorporation of cultural traits/influences from other societies.[41] Second, Chayanov's theory of peasant economy, whereby the peasant family farm is subject only to an internal dynamic – the producer/consumer balance – and thus reproduces itself historically without reference to processes occurring in the wider economic system.[42] And third, postmodernism, which deprivileges class, class consciousness and

folk dress, art and even architecture which will naturally occur over a certain territory and end at common geographical frontiers of common culture'.

39 See Clover (2016: 51 ff.).

40 To illustrate this contention, Jakobson invokes the example of the Russian folk tale, about the specificity of which in terms of 'a deeper reality' he notes (Jakobson, 1970: 185, 191–192) 'there arises the not unimportant question as to why, in the land of its birth, the Russian spoken language and oral tradition, and in particular the Russian folk tale, remained so long unrecorded in writing. Here we are confronted with one of the most peculiar features of Russian cultural life, which sharply distinguishes it from that of the occidental world. [...] According to the experience of modern linguistics, language patterns exhibit a consistent regularity...at the base of all these types lie universal laws. This schematic and recurrent character of linguistic patterns finds its explanation first of all in the fact that language is a typical collective property. Similar phenomena of schematism and recurrence in the structure of folk tales throughout the world have long astonished and challenged investigators.' That the underlying ('deep') structure of the folk tale was not affected by the Bolshevik revolution and its ('Western') categories of class formation/struggle is clear from the assertion by Jokobson (1970: 194) that: 'intensive collecting in Soviet Russia indicates that the harvest among the Russian folk tale is not dwindling... [n]either in the *kolkhozes*, nor in the workers' settlements, nor in the Red Army, do the tales die out.'

41 Like postmodernism, Herder was antagonistic towards the Enlightenment because it challenged the innateness and validity of popular culture, which in his view emerged from and embodied the 'authenticity' of a specific location (Brass, 2014a: 268 ff.). Again like postmodernism, he was correspondingly hostile towards 'foundational'/Eurocentric/international concepts of identity (class, economic) that transcended particular territories.

42 For Chayanovian neo-populism, see Brass (2000a).

class struggle, all dismissed as forms of Enlightenment/Eurocentric 'foundationalism' which are consequently inapplicable to 'indigenous others', not just in the so-called Third World but also contexts such as Zomia and Eurasia.

During the 1970s Gumilev categorized as a 'universal phenomenon' his notion of 'ethnos' (= primordial/permanent form of 'national or ethnic self-identification'), theory of 'Ethnogenesis', a procedure and concept found also in Scott.[43] Like Gumilev's Eurasia, therefore, Scott's Zomia is not only characterized by 'pluriethnic inclusiveness', but also constitutes an '[e]cological niche' which is 'one distinction around which ethnogenisis can occur'.[44] Ethnogenesis is depicted by Gumilev as the 'other' of Marxism, an explicitly anti-Marxist theory about how steppe people 'dominated' Eurasia.[45] Its population, he argued, cohered over two millennia due to a shared language and culture, a process reinforced by a shared geography. The latter – exactly like Zomia – formed 'a unique geographical zone', the population of which grew 'more similar with time' and diverged 'from those outside this zone'.

Many of the characteristics that Gumilev attributes to Eurasia are in fact no different from those Scott identifies as present in Zomia. Indeed, superimpose a map of one territory on the other and, with the exception of the Russian landmass, the fit is more or less exact.[46] Just as Scott regards as mistaken the perception of Zomia as a marginal, impoverished and culturally backward area, so Gumilev similarly objects to the categorization of Eurasia as 'isolated, perpetually maligned, backward societies'.[47] Each perceives the margins as in reality the locus of an historically ancient and enduring social order, and thus a more 'authentic' cultural identity.

Scott also reproduces an explanation concerning 'passionate loyalty' akin to the 'passionarost' of Gumilev, conceptualized by the latter as 'an instinctual urge' amounting to 'a theory of the irrational in human history' determined by 'the biological impulse that drives men to irrational deeds'.[48] Unsurprisingly,

43 See Clover (2016: 125) and Scott (2009: Ch. 7).

44 Scott (2009: 242).

45 On these and the following views held by Gumilev, see Clover (2016: 134–135).

46 Compare the map of Zomia in Scott (2009: 17) with that of Eurasia in Clover (2016: x), which indicates the extent of an overlap.

47 Clover (2016: 11).

48 See Clover (2016: 2, 95, 100, 124) for the definition by Gumilev of 'passionarost'. For evidence of this conceptual overlap, see Scott (2009: 265): 'The point is that once created, an institutional identity acquires its own history. The longer and deeper this history is, the more it will resemble the mythmaking and forgetting of nationalism. Over time such an identity, however fabricated its origin, will take on essential features and may well inspire passionate loyalty'.

this instinctivism (= feeling, not reason) has political implications. Finally, therefore, the 'new' populist postmodernism of Scott shares with the Eurasianist historiography propounded by Gumilev the reason for their academic fashionability. Both were the result of a search for alternative, non-Marxist paradigms to explain development and grassroots mobilization following the end of 'actually existing socialism'. In the cased of Eurasianism, Gumilev's ideas rose to prominence during the 1990s since they formed a narrative that coincided with an upsurge in Russian nationalism. At this same conjuncture, moreover, both the latter (Gumilev's Eurasianism + Russian nationalism) fused with the ideas of far-right European theorists such as Evola, Guenon and de Benoist.[49] Currently, this same discourse is said to enjoy the support of those close to Putin.[50]

49 See Clover (2016: Ch. 8), who outlines how the reactionary bohemia of Moscow eclectically combined Eastern religion, mysticism, occultism, fascism and traditionalism. On the far-right views of Evola, Guenon and de Benoist, see Brass (2000a, 2014a).

50 Charles Clover, 'Lev Gumilev: Passion, Putin and Power', *The Financial Times* (London), 12–13 March 2016.

CHAPTER 13

The Populist Drift of Global Labour History*

For more than a century, Marxist theory has been continuously reformulated/ discarded in order, so it is claimed, to bring it into line with existing conditions. This has entailed two things. First, questioning the central tenets (class, labour theory of value), and in particular the accompanying process of class formation/consciousness/struggle. And second, attempting to find a replacement for the working class as the subject of the historical process. From Eduard Bernstein and von Vollmar to Fanon and Hall (third world), Marcuse and the New Left (students), to Guha (subaltern) and Hardt and Negri (multitude), this has entailed arguing that categories outside the working class – peasants, lumpenproletariat, artisans, petty bourgeoisie – should be recruited for the socialist cause, either because they were thought to be as – if not more – radical than the proletariat, or because they were actually part of the latter.

Broadly speaking, there have been two opposing ways of doing away with Marxist theory about class as a political and analytical concept. One that has been popular earlier was to claim that, as it was no longer a relevant aspect of a changed world, class as an analytical and political category should henceforth be discarded. A later one that has grown in popularity is to make class so inclusive (subaltern-as-worker) that, in effect, it ceases thereby to be relevant by virtue of nobody being outside it, yet everybody possessing an additional set of non-class values/interests/identities which end up overriding the fact of class relations. Where relevant, the chronological difference between these two approaches evokes the old cliché about history repeating itself, first as tragedy (class non-existent) and then as farce (class all-inclusive). The latter is the one followed by van der Linden and Roth, who have assembled a volume in order – yet again – to dispose of Marxist political economy. Because it falls into the category of a *symptomatic* approach to its subject, both the arguments presented and the reasons for their popularity require further scrutiny.

What van der Linden and Roth do, therefore, is to dismiss the Marxist critique of political economy on the epistemologically interrelated grounds that it is Eurocentric and methodologically nationalist, a consequence being that

---

* Reviewed here is *Beyond Marx: Theorising the Global Labour Relations of the Twenty-First Century*, edited by Marcel van der Linden and Karl Heinz Roth (Leiden: Brill, 2014). An earlier version of this extended review, titled 'Who These Days is Not a Subaltern? The Populist Drift of Global Labour History', appeared in *Science & Society*, Vol. 81, No. 1 (2017).

both its narrow conception of the proletariat and distinction between free and unfree labour no longer apply. Instead, they advocate the conceptual expansion of what is termed a 'proletarian multiverse' to include numerous other social categories and groups, whose agency will become the deciding factor in any struggle with capitalism. None of these arguments is new: dismissing Marxist political economy has a long lineage, as do attempts to extend class inclusiveness.

It is argued here that not only are all their objections wrong, based as they are on a misreading or non-reading of Marxist theory, but the inflated category of worker they suggest as an alternative is nothing other than the categories 'subaltern' or 'multitude' which underwrite the identity politics of the 'new' populist postmodernism. Since key components of this expanded 'proletarian multiverse' are hostile to socialism, not capitalism, their agency cannot be regarded as progressive, let alone revolutionary.

I

Politically and economically, the period from the late nineteenth century onwards has been marked by a never-ending process of improving-by-discarding central aspects of Marxist theory. In particular, this process has been applied to its arguments about the formation/composition of class, the accompanying process of consciousness/struggle, and how the latter are in turn connected to the transcendence of capitalism and a transition to socialism. The object of improving-by-discarding Marxism has been – and is – always the same: finding a 'new' historical subject to complement or replace the working class. It is a revisionist approach that shares an epistemology with not just with populism, but also with conservatism.

During the 1890s debates about the political direction to be followed by German Social Democracy, Kautsky and Leibknecht warned that attempts by Eduard Bernstein and von Vollmar to expand its electoral base by recruiting the support of the peasantry were based on a failure to distinguish between the two forms of anti-modernist anti-capitalism: on the one hand populism, which is antagonistic to the notion of class, and consequently is opposed only to financial/international capital, and therefore supportive of nationalism; and on the other Marxism, which is opposed to capitalism *per se*, and thus supportive of class identity and internationalism.[1] The same issue resurfaced in

1 On these points, see Gay (1952), Salvadori (1979), Hussain and Tribe (1984), and Tudor and Tudor (1988).

the 1960s with Marcuse, for whom students were the 'new' subject, and Fanon, for whom the same category was composed of peasant migrants to towns.[2] As will be seen below, this process has come up to date both with the identity politics of Hall, the Subaltern of Guha, the 'multitude' of Negri and Hardt, and now with the kind of labour historiography followed by van der Linden and Roth.

As deployed by van der Linden and Roth, therefore, the specific category of class is inflated so as to become the more general one of 'subaltern,' into which is decanted everyone-and-his/her-dog, all of whom are said to be actually or potentially in the ranks of those opposed to capitalism. Hence the expanded 'proletarian multiverse' consists of occupational categories wrongly subsumed by van der Linden and Roth under the rubric of 'proletariat'.[3] It contains not just components of the working class recognized as such by Marxist political economy (manufacturing labour, farmhands, seasonal agricultural labour, seamen) but also undifferentiated petty commodity producers characterized by a variety of different property relations (artisans, smallholding peasants, serfs, sharecroppers) and the lumpenproletariat (beggars, vagabonds, criminalized urban sub-proletarians). Historically and currently, none of those in each of the last two categories has struggled to achieve socialist objectives: much rather the opposite, in that the agency of petty commodity producers and lumpenproletarians has frequently been mobilized by capital against a working class on strike or engaged in revolutionary action.

This inflation of categories deemed to be progressive simply because of their opposition to capitalism, has generated claims that their collective action is designed to achieve systemic transcendence, a view which ignores a crucial distinction: populism is the anti-capitalism (such as it is) of the right, whereas Marxism is the anti-capitalism of the left. It is a difference overlooked by what claims be a new type of academic practice: 'global labour history' (hereafter GLH), 'new labour history' or simply 'labour history,' the *raison d'être* for which, van der Linden and Roth insist, is the need to discard Marxist political economy and thus to 'devise a new conceptualisation [and] a new theoretical narrative'.[4] These days, it seems, numerous arguments encountered in the social sciences are prefaced by similar declarations announcing the birth

2 See Marcuse (1970) and Fanon (1963).

3 See van der Linden and Roth (2014: 451).

4 See van der Linden and Roth (2014: 16). The focus here will be on van der Linden, due mainly to what can only be described as an institutional ubiquitousness. In the recent past there seems to have been no conference on the subject of labour historiography without his presence on the organizing committee, an ability to invite contributions that amounts in effect to an agenda-setting capacity.

of a 'new perspective,' an effect perhaps of having to lay claim to relevance in the economically unforgiving competitive environments that are neo-liberal academic institutions. Invariably, such claims about 'newness' turn out to be nothing more than resuscitated old paradigms.

Among the many accusations levelled against Marxist political economy in the name of GLH, therefore, is 'methodological nationalism'.[5] This ignores the fact that all Marxists conceptualize accumulation as an international process, and have always perceived capitalism as having a systemic dynamic possessing national/regional/local dimensions. Indeed, Marxist theory explicitly connects the necessity of working class mobilization, the ability of producers to restructure their labour process, and an expanding industrial reserve army to this internationalization of capital accumulation. It is an accusation, moreover, that is ironic, given that van der Linden – unlike Roth, who has produced valuable empirical work on the German working class – has never undertaken fieldwork in Third World contexts to which he now applies the term 'subaltern worker'.[6]

This may help to explain why van der Linden is unaware of the difficulties in grouping all the various categories – sharecropper, slave, debt peon – under a single 'subaltern'/'multitude' rubric.[7] It may also help to explain why his record in promoting analyses developed by others earlier is not encouraging: in the past, he has championed the views of Jan Breman and Jairus Banaji about rural labour relations, despite the fact that both are confused about theoretical categories/processes central to their interpretations.[8] Such a background renders problematic any challenge to Marxism in the name of what GLH now thinks it knows about 'large parts of Asia, Africa and Latin America'.[9]

II

Because in their opinion it amounts to 'exclusionary thinking' that is a nineteenth century residue, van der Linden and Roth make no secret of their

5 See van der Linden and Roth (2014: 445).
6 For this work on the German working class, see Roth (1997).
7 This kind of difficulty was in effected conceded by him some time ago. In a letter dated 30 December 1991 inviting me to join him and Jan Lucassen in formulating the programmatic agenda for a proposed conference on 'the transition from unfree to free labour', van der Linden stated it was because I had already written much about this topic, admitting that 'the problem is...that we [Lucassen and van der Linden] know much more about free than unfree labour'.
8 For these positive assessments of Breman and Banaji, see van der Linden (2003a: 249ff.; and 2010: xi–xv). Critiques of both the former are set out in Brass (2003a; Essay 16, this volume).
9 See van der Linden and Roth (2014: 16–17).

opposition to Marxist political economy. Hence the view that 'if one wants to remain a revolutionary, one needs to abandon Marxism,' insisting further that 'the Marxist theory of value is obsolete [and] the theory of revolution needs to be thoroughly reconceptualised.'[10] The reason for this antagonism to Marxist political economy is clear: 'if we assume that the Marxian "doubly-free" wage-workers are no longer the strategically privileged part of the global working class,' conclude van der Linden and Roth, 'then this has far-reaching consequences for the development of theory'.[11]

Objecting to the privileging by Marxism of 'the doubly free wage worker' – those who 'can dispose of their own labour-power...for sale' – seen by socialists as the hegemonic agent of historical transformation, van der Linden and Roth dismiss this role on two interrelated counts.[12] First, because historically – and in the Third World, currently – free wage labour has been numerically small, and conceptually the working class should henceforth include those categories (especially unfree labourers) not regarded by Marxist political economy as belonging to the proletariat. And second, because these 'impure elements' that Marxism excluded from the proletariat on the grounds that they were politically reactionary (small merchants, artisans, peasants, lumpens) participated in labour movements.

In order to reconfigure 'the subaltern and subordinate position of the working class within the analysis of the capitalist dynamic,' therefore, van der Linden and Roth maintain it is necessary to address 'labour-history's conceptualization within the Marxian critique of political economy,' noting that '[f]or obvious reasons, the dispute surrounding the model of "doubly-free wage-labour" is key to this'.[13] Dismissing this core element of Marxist theory, van der Linden and Roth then endorse the view that Marx was unaware of the conditions leading to 'the ongoing re-emergence of unfree labour,' adding that 'labour-history and the concept of labour within the Marxian system makes it seem quite doubtful whether that system can continue to serve as a reference-point for considerations on the development of a dynamic critique of the political economy of labour.'[14] However, as his analyses both of child and female workers in the UK and of the plantation system in the American South underline, Marx was indeed aware not just of the acceptability but of the importance to capital of unfree labour. This recognition stemmed in turn from the role he

10 Van der Linden and Roth (2014: 17, 453, 473).
11 See van der Linden and Roth (2014: 17).
12 Van der Linden and Roth (2014: 16, 17).
13 See van der Linden and Roth (2014: 445, 454).
14 Van der Linden and Roth (2014: 457, 475).

attached to the class struggle, and how it enabled capital to erode any/every gain – including freedom – made by workers as a class.[15]

In order to declare the free/unfree distinction redundant, thereby permitting a conceptual inflation of 'proletarian multiverse,' van der Linden and Roth attempt to replace what Marxism argues is the act of selling/purchasing labour-power with a transaction involving leaser and leasor.[16] By 'methodologically liquidating the false monopoly position of "doubly-free wage-labour"', therefore, many different kinds of work arrangement can be fitted inside the ranks of the working class. Accepting that the 'distinction between a lease and a sale may appear insignificant,' van der Linden and Roth in effect acknowledge the difficulty facing this argument.[17] The point made by Marx and Marxists is that when acquired and put to work in the labour process by the capitalist, the commodity labour-power creates more than its own value, surplus-value, which accrues to the employer who now owns and sells the commodity produced by this labour-power. This surplus-value is something which – when acquired by the capitalist – is not returned to the worker. Unlike labour-power, therefore, a house, when leased, does not itself create value.

Having discovered that capital can and does use labour-power that is unfree, van der Linden and Roth then extend this to argue that any/all unfree labour-power is both to be included as part of the proletariat and to be regarded as engaged in a struggle for systemic transcendence. Whereas capital does indeed use labour-power that is unfree, a fact that many Marxists and Marxism generally have long known about, this does *not* mean that such categories are either part of the proletariat or engaged in a class struggle to transcend capitalism.

III

These epistemological shifts by GLH must be seen as part of a much larger political and ideological transformation taking place over the second half of the twentieth century. Within industrial capitalist nations, the 1950s was characterized by the perception that workers were no longer as oppressed economically as before, an interpretation that fuelled the quest for another revolutionary subject, culminating in the rejection of core Marxist theory, the espousal of national/ethnic cultural 'otherness,' and the emergence of populist concepts such as 'subaltern' and 'multitude'. A case in point is Stuart Hall, viewed by

15 On this point, see Brass (2011a: Chapter 2).

16 Van der Linden and Roth (2014: 459).

17 Van der Linden and Roth (2014: 471).

many on the left as a scion of Marxism, despite his privileging of ethnicity over class. This is evident from many sources, not least an analysis which underlines the extent of his endorsement of the 'new' populist postmodernism, and how far he had moved away from Marxism.[18]

To begin with, Hall's focus is on 'identity', regarded by him as having come to the fore as a result of a fourfold 'decentring' in Western thought: three of these are associated with the work of Marx, Freud, and Saussure, characterized by him as 'the great figures of modernism'. These are very different from the 'fourth force of destabilization', which entails much rather to a challenge to the 'discourses of rationality' on the part of the Third World 'other', the outcome being the 'relativization of the Western World'. In other words, this fourth 'decentring' is none other than postmodernism, which Hall claims signals the end of the 'great social collective identities' linked to modernity, and in particular to class. In place of the latter, he argues, we are now left with – and have to accept – cultural identity, 'the surreptitious return of difference and otherness'. From this stems the following claim advanced by Hall: 'When I started to write about Thatcherism in the early [1970s], I thought it was largely an economic and political project. It is only more recently that I understood how profoundly it is rooted in a certain exclusive and essentialist conception of Englishness. Thatcherism is *in defence* of a certain definition of Englishness' (original emphasis).

Contrary to what Hall claims, however, Thatcherism *was* largely a political and economic project, amounting to class struggle waged 'from above' aimed at extending/consolidating *laissez faire*, which in turn depended on undermining/destroying working class organization/institutions. Part of this struggle was an embrace of cultural – *not* economic – nationalism, an ideological smokescreen the object of which was to divert attention from neoliberal policies. It is wrong, therefore, to maintain – as does Hall – that Thatcher was engaged simply or mainly in 'living all the great moments of the English past again' as a primary or *sui generis* political design. It was a means to an end, and not an end in itself.

Of particular significance is how this misinterpretation then leads Hall to champion postmodernism as a populist alternative to Marxism. Accordingly, he proceeds to celebrate the victory over pristine British culture of 'otherness', promoting the ethnic identity of the 'other' as a process of 'cultural recovery'. For Hall, therefore, positioning this 'other' ethnicity means 'the relation that peoples of the world now have to their own past', which is 'part of the discovery of their own ethnicity. They need to honour the hidden histories from which

18 See Hall (1989b: 9–20).

they come [and] understand and revalue the traditions and inheritances of cultural expression and creativity'. His conclusion is that '[t]here is no way...in which those elements of ethnicity that depend on...understanding one's roots, can be done without'.

In effect, Hall advocates the replacement of a forwards-looking class consciousness/struggle against capitalism with a backwards-looking cultural identity rooted in a pre- or non-capitalist Third World, which is precisely what the GLH considered here and those contributing to the subaltern studies project also advocate. This is what he means by 'cultural recovery', referred to by him as 'the enormous cultural relativization of the entire globe'. Rather than uniting along class lines in order to wage war against capitalism as a system, thereby putting a socialist transition on the political and economic agenda, Hall instead argues for fragmentation along and privileging of traditional non-class identities. In short, a non-material 'alternative' to Marxism that leaves the accumulation process intact.

In part, the origins of this misinterpretation are found in the New Left response to earlier debates, those about the prevalence and impact of 1950s economic affluence and political apathy. Thus the working class in Britain were perceived by Hall to have been co-opted politically by the welfare state, full employment, prosperity and the consumer boom of the immediate post-war era.[19] Describing 'working class prosperity' as a 'mixed affair', Hall nevertheless concedes that 'it is *there*: the fact has bitten deep into the experience of working people' by providing them with a 'sense of security'.[20] Mistakenly thinking that the welfare state, full employment, and better wages/conditions were here to stay, and thus signalled the end of economic conflict between capital and labour, Hall shifted his explanation. The focus, in short, turns to ideology and language, and with it the importance of establishing hegemony, which already carries with it hints of the 'cultural turn', in that discourse is separated from class and increasingly comes to be seen as autonomous.[21]

Against those who might perceive this as too negative an interpretation, therefore, it can be argued that Hall played a crucial role in laying the groundwork and thus prefiguring the 'new' populist postmodernism. A key aspect of this shift – from opposition to the endorsement of market individualism – was the mistaken view that, in order to defeat Thatcherism, it was necessary for those on the left to become more like her politically. This shift was embodied

19 Hall (1960).

20 See Hall (1960: 79, original emphasis).

21 For these views, see Hall (1977a, 1977b, 1989a).

in an analysis by Hall entitled 'Learning from Thatcherism'.[22] Although ostensibly the lesson was – unproblematically – about the importance of political commitment, actually – and most problematically – it concerned the desirability of taking over the same political agenda. Hence the tenor of the following recommendations: 'We [on the left] may have to acknowledge that there is often a rational core to Thatcherism's critique… Contestation, however, is not enough, because by itself it is too negative… To develop a more positive perspective means thematizing [the fiscal crisis of the state] around the "politics of choice" or the question of the market versus the state. The popular theme of "choice" has no "necessary belongingness" to Thatcherism…[it] is as much part of popular radicalism as it is of the populist radical right… The so-called "rediscovery of the market" is not a phenomenon exclusively of the right.'[23]

Arguing for 'the left "appropriation" of the market', Hall in effect advocated a complete about-turn, ending up on the same political ground as the Adam Smith Institute. Significantly, this view, which manifested itself in the New Labour project of Blair, was based on the mistaken perception of popular culture under neoliberalism as chosen by 'those below', and thus for them a form of empowerment. It comes as no surprise that many of the most enthusiastic contributions to Hall's festschrift were written not by Marxists but by 'new' postmodern populists (James Clifford, Néstor García Canclini, Judith Butler, Gayatri Chakravorty Spivak).[24]

IV

That Marxism and socialist internationalism are currently less popular than they used to be is obvious, and scarcely needs mentioning. What is of interest, however, is the way in which erstwhile adherents of this politics are now reinventing themselves. There seems to be a competition involving ex-Marxists to see who among them is able to denounce socialism in the most vehement terms. A not untypical example is Hardt and Negri, who resort to the well-tried but erroneous formula (socialism = fascism) so beloved of cold warriors of old.[25] The fact that what passed for socialism in many Eastern European nations was nothing of the sort, and thus the root of the difficulty to which Hardt and Negri allude has more to do with the deployment of non- or anti-socialist

22 Hall (1988: 271ff.).

23 See Hall (1988: 276, 278, 279).

24 For Hall's festschrift, see Gilroy, Grossberg and McRobbie (2000).

25 Hardt and Negri (2005: 255).

ideas/arguments under the guise of socialism, is something which neither of them address.

Prior to the 1939–45 war, most peasant parties throughout Europe and Asia were strongly nationalist, and agrarian populist organizations generated much rural grassroots support for right wing (as in the United States, India, Bulgaria and France) or fascist movements (as in Japan, Spain, Italy, Germany, Slovakia, Hungary, Croatia and Romania). Many of these European peasant parties were also members of the Green International, the forerunner of the present-day *Vía Campesina*, espousing a similar agrarian populist ideology and advocating much the same kind of political and economic policies.[26] This was because for populism a 'pure' (or middle) peasantry engaged in smallholding cultivation within the context of an equally 'pure' village community (that is, unsullied by an external capitalism or socialism) was presented as embodying all the culturally-specific attributes – timeless/sacred 'natural' and ancient bonds such as ethnicity, language, religion, customs, dress, songs, traditions – that were constitutive of a 'pure' national identity.

Populist discourse equating peasant with Nature and nation was not confined to Europe and Asia. During the pre-war era, an ideologically powerful form – conceptualizing the smallholder as ethnically/culturally/economically 'other' (*indigenismo*) – was applied to the Central and Latin American peasantry. Those living and working in rural Latin America were autochthonous, the 'noble savages' of myth whose organizational modalities were perceived by British and North American anthropology as innate and unchanging. Unaffected by class divisions (a characteristic, it was claimed, only of urban society), members of the indigenous community inhabited what has been described as an Andean ecosystem enabling them to reproduce themselves economically on a continuous basis as petty commodity producers.[27] Because of this, the epistemology characterizing *indigenismo* overlaps with a politically far more potent ideology: the foundation myth at the centre of nationalist ideology.

26 The antagonism between Communism and peasant parties affiliated to the Green International was set out by the latter's Vice-President, who attributed this to the fact that 'in all aspects [they] are diametrically opposed'. See Vlado Matchek, 'The International Peasant Union', *The Tablet*, 19 March 1949, pp. 180–181. Communism promoted internationalism, State planning and collectivization, but was antagonistic to private property, religion, and nationalist ideology. By contrast, peasant parties were nationalist and supportive of religion, but against both collectivization and the State, blamed by them for low output prices and high input costs. The latter were exactly the same complaints made by the new farmers' movements in 1980s India.

27 For this view, whereby the Andean ecosystem is interpreted as structured by 'verticality', see Murra (1972).

In this particular guise, *indigenismo* invokes 'the other' deployed over time in political and – more importantly – ideological battles waged not just against colonialism (of the Spanish and Portuguese), but also against neo-colonialism (of the United States) and imperialism (of international capitalism).

In an important sense the contributions to the volume by van der Linden and Roth signal just how far social science discourse has shifted politically, and returned once again to pre-1939 positions. The main concern of 1960s development theory (Marxist and non-Marxist alike) was to end rural socio-economic marginality in the so-called Third World, by bringing peasants and agricultural workers into the wider society. As participants both in the process of economic growth and the political system, the rural poor would then be able to secure better pay/conditions leading to increased living standards. Linked to existing poverty, illiteracy and oppression, therefore, rural marginality was perceived negatively, as an indicator of backwardness and underdevelopment, and thus as a problem to be solved.

During the latter part of the twentieth century, this approach was not merely abandoned but actually reversed. Henceforth marginality was recast as a form of empowerment, a revision that coincided with and was effected by the rise both of neoliberal economics and of the 'new' populist postmodernism.[28] Peasant/ethnic identity was re-essentialized, and reaffirmed theoretically as an 'authentic' form of selfhood that was eternal due to its culturally indissoluble 'natural' character. Customs, traditions and practices as these already existed at the rural grassroots were now celebrated/endorsed by the 'new' populist postmodernism as forms of cultural 'difference', to be cherished as such.

To effect this reversal, the same revisionist discourse simultaneously challenged the theoretical approach linked to the 1960s development framework. Declaring the latter a tainted foundational/Eurocentric meta-narrative, the 'new' populist postmodernism dismissed concepts such as class, modernity, development, and progress as inappropriate for an understanding of the rural Third World. Pivotal to this epistemological *volte face* was a specific form of agency, the object of which was no longer the revolutionary capture and control of the state. Just such a non-revolutionary mobilization was provided by 'everyday-forms-of-resistance', whereby quotidian/smallscale agency undertaken by peasants is said to block every attempt by the state to effect all its 'alien' policies/processes designed to transform the status quo.[29]

28 For the 'new' populist postmodernism, see Brass (2000a, 2014a).

29 See Review Essay 12 in this volume.

What has emerged, therefore, is an anti-capitalist ideology belonging to the same agrarian populist lineage as before the second world war, promoting a supposedly novel (= postmodern) demand by petty commodity producers and related categories of 'otherness' (smallholding peasants, artisans, women, tribals) for a return to traditional culture and community authority, and with it the recuperation of an eternal identity emblematic of an authentic process of 'belonging' as embodied in indigenous selfhood. Henceforth artisans, cultivators and tribals were to be discussed in terms of non-class agency, that undertaken by 'diverse' social groups composing a 'multitude' and designated as 'subaltern'. The latter, argued those holding such views, were no longer about the desirability of economic development leading to socialism, nor were they aimed at the capture and exercise of State power.[30]

V

That van der Linden and Roth endorse a postmodern agenda is clear not just from the accusation of eurocentrism levelled at Marxism, from privileging subjective perceptions of cultural identity over objective economic relations, but also from the extension of the latter to incorporate the 'diversity' of the former (the concept value being as a result shifted in an analogous manner). In order to arrive at an 'emancipatorily oriented conceptualization of the political economy of labour,' therefore, van der Linden and Roth maintain one has to understand its 'diversity' in terms of a social, economic, sexual, generational, ethnic and cultural heterogeneity, and the 'dynamic of resistance' and 'everyday conflicts' specific to each of these categories.[31] This entails in turn a labour-theory of value connected not to capitalist production – as Marxist political economy argues – but rather to what they term a 'fundamental right to existence' on the part of a 'broadened definition of the working class'.[32] The latter, according to van der Linden and Roth, 'constitutes itself not as a homogenous entity but as a multiverse of strata and social groups' structured in turn by 'families, communities, fraternities and sororities, benevolent societies and craft associations, secret societies and action groups,' all of which are formed by 'self-determined cultural norms.'

30 Among them were and are Guha (1982–89), Beverley, Aronna and Oviedo (1995), Beverley (1999) and Hardt and Negri (2005).

31 Van der Linden and Roth (2014: 446).

32 Van der Linden and Roth (2014: 447–448).

The resulting jumble of socio-economic groups and categories, where only cultural diversity reigns supreme, is an overarching identity elsewhere labelled by van der Linden as 'subaltern,' the composition and characteristics of which also coincide with what he terms 'multitude'.[33] To demonstrate the efficacy of such overlapping definitions, van der Linden and Roth invoke what they take to be the historical/geographical persistence and never-changing patterns of the peasant family farm. Hence their view that '[o]ne need think only of the persistence of the peasant-family economies in the redistributive communes of Tsarist Russia [and] the indigenous regions of Latin America [as well as] the continuity of the decision-making processes that have been playing out within these families for centuries.'[34] Along with slaves and indentured labour, therefore, the 'self-employed labour' of undifferentiated peasants are said by van der Linden and Roth to form a 'proletarian multiverse' or 'multitude'. Hence the relay-in-statement whereby 'proletarian multiverse' = subaltern = multitude = undifferentiated peasants.[35]

The expanded composition of 'proletarian multiverse' that characterizes the GLH of van der Linden and Roth is sociologically and politically similar to the 'subaltern' of Guha and the 'multitude' of Hardt and Negri. In the case of the Subaltern Studies approach, therefore, class difference is replaced by an opposition between on the one hand the 'elite' and its 'state', and the on the other the 'masses'/'popular masses'. Thus Guha's category of the 'subaltern' encompasses all forms of 'subordinate' who do not belong to the 'elite'; that is, all those 'of inferior rank... whether this is expressed in terms of class, caste, age, gender and office or in any other way'.[36] The politically and sociologically problematic nature of the 'subaltern' is evident from its all-embracing social composition: among its ranks, therefore, are to be found 'the lesser rural gentry, impoverished landlords, rich peasants and upper middle peasants'. The fact that it includes those whose *class* position and interest correspond to those of an agrarian petty-bourgeoisie, and as such are employers of and opposed to those of a rural proletariat, rightly identifies the 'subaltern' as an agrarian populist category. This is unsurprising, in that the Subaltern Studies project was essentially a *nationalist* discourse aimed at recovering an unheard grassroots voice silenced by British colonial historiography.

Much the same is true of Hardt and Negri, whose concept 'multitude' erases all economic and property relations linking the individual self to the world,

---

33 See van der Linden (2003b, 2008).

34 Van der Linden and Roth (2014: 448).

35 Van der Linden and Roth (2014: 449, 451).

36 Guha (1982: 8).

thereby making the struggle against neo-liberalism so inclusive that it is difficult to conceive of any category of 'selfhood' not wholly signed up by them to the defeat of a correspondingly externalized global capitalism. On this basis, only with some difficulty could one exclude bankers, oligarchs, hedge-fund managers, financiers, and speculators from such a broad-based form of anti-capitalist mobilization. The absence of class trapped between the exclusiveness of individual selfhood on the one hand, and the inclusiveness of being-in-the-world on the other, is evident from the observation that 'we are a multiplicity of singular forms of life and *at the same time* share a common global existence' (original emphasis).[37] For them, therefore, no distinction exists between a millionaire and an agricultural labourer, each of whom is simultaneously 'a singular form of life' and both of whom 'share a common global existence'. In other words, between the irreducibility of the self and the sameness of humanity at the global level there is nothing, and the space in which class relations are usually to be found is for Hardt and Negri empty of socio-economic content.

VI

Noting the presence of an alternative interpretation – the culturalist displacement of class categories in India by the Subaltern Studies project – van der Linden and Roth avoid engaging with this, observing merely 'the need to newly mediate economic and cultural categories.'[38] They accept that 'such alternative models are foreign to those who believe the Marxian paradigm can be developed further'.[39] In the absence of the insistence by Marxist political economy of the necessity for a transition to socialism, what kind of future is prefigured by an analytical approach based on 'subaltern'/'multitude', one that focuses on how 'peasant subsistence-economies...are integrated into the world-economy'?

Unsurprisingly, it turns out to be 'an autonomous world-society [where] the mass-poverty of the South has been overcome and the subsistence-economies have been restored and expanded.'[40] This is no different from the fictional one envisaged a century ago by the agrarian populist theoretician Chayanov, for whom an ideal type future would be a rural arcadia composed of rural petty

37 Hardt and Negri (2005: 127).
38 Van der Linden and Roth (2014: 453).
39 Van der Linden and Roth (2014: 475).
40 Van der Linden and Roth (2014: 480, 482).

commodity producers.[41] A result of smallholding opposition to socialism, a future Russian Peasant Republic would restore private property in the form of the peasant family farm, and be a place where collectives, industry, planning and state intervention were correspondingly absent.

This agrarian populism is a view shared not just by the Subaltern Studies project but also by Maria Mies, a contributor to the volume, for whom 'peasant subsistence-production in the Global South' amounts to the celebration of 'autonomous life,' a 'different economy and society, one congenial to women, nature and human beings.'[42] Her aim is to shift critique away from Marxist political economy and onto gender and the household, with the object simply of 'transforming everyday life.' Influenced by eco-feminism, which equates females with Nature and subsistence agriculture and romanticizes pre-capitalist societies, Mies argues that economic growth *per se* is inappropriate and hence disempowering for a variety of Third World 'others' (women, tribals, peasants).[43] Unsurprisingly, therefore, she advocates a reversion to subsistence agriculture, her perception of the future being a self-sufficient, autarchic peasant society.

Subscribing as it does to essentialist peasant/gender identities, such eco-feminist theory has been associated historically with the politics of populism/nationalism, and in India such idioms are particularly supportive of communal politics.[44] Notwithstanding this problem, van der Linden and Roth endorse the approach of Mies, observing that the 'feminist critique of Marx's model of the political economy of labour...is one that we owe much to,' not least because in their view Marx failed to appreciate the extent to which female workers generate surplus-value.[45] This, too, is wrong, since in his analysis of the way in which capitalists restructured the labour process, replacing more expensive male workers with cheaper female (and child) labour-power, he was indeed aware of the important economic role of gender- and age-specific labour components in the accumulation process.[46]

Nowhere are the problems confronting any attempt to promote agency of the 'subaltern' or 'multitude' based on an inclusive 'proletarian multiverse' revealed more clearly than when one considers the political and ideological

41 On Chayanov's fictional peasant utopia, see Kremnev (1977).

42 See van der Linden and Roth (2014: 474).

43 Mies and Shiva (1993).

44 For details about the politics of ecofeminism, see Staudenmaier and Biehl (1995) and Cochrane (2007).

45 Van der Linden and Roth (2014: 457ff.).

46 Marx (1976: 590); Marx and Engels (1976b: 491).

forms taken by such grassroots agency, which Marxist political economy interprets as a transition from class-in-itself to class-for-itself. This difficulty can be illustrated with regard to each of the main categories included by Roth and van der Linden in their all-embracing 'proletarian multiverse': an undifferentiated peasantry and the lumpenproletariat. Significantly, perhaps, neither editor of the volume on GLH has anything to say about how peasant economy featured in the debates between on the one hand Marxism and on the other populism, and especially its Chayanovian variant.[47]

VII

The difficulty with subscribing to what is in effect a Chayanovian model of peasant economy, as Roth and van der Linden do, is that it has been shown to be false. A supposed economic stability of petty commodity production, endorsed by populists during the late nineteenth century, by neo-populists during the early twentieth, and currently by adherents of the 'new' populist postmodernism, is part of the agrarian myth. Equally mistaken is the support for this invoked by van der Linden and Roth: as many accounts confirm, in Asia and Latin America peasants have long been differentiated along class lines.[48]

Numerous instances confirm that, in political terms, many peasant movements are not merely not progressive but conservative, and in some cases reactionary. This is evident not just from the historical examples of the Vendee in 1790s France, the Cristeros and the Sinarquistas in 1920s and 1930s Mexico, but also Peru and India in the 1960s, where rich peasants in turned against poor peasants and agricultural workers with whom they had previously been in alliance against a now-expropriated landlord class. More recently, regionally specific components of the new farmers' movements in 1980s India were led by and reflected the interests of better-off components of the rural population.[49] This agrarian mobilization included members who were themselves employers of unfree labour, and many of its supporters also voted for the Hindu chauvinist BJP (*Bharatiya Janata Party*).

---

47 The only references in the volume to Chayanov's model of peasant economy are uncritically endorsing ones by Henninger (2014: 290–292, 294, 301), who omits to mention any of the many critiques of this agrarian populist interpretation.

48 On peasant differentiation in Asia and Latin America, see the contributions to Brass (2003c) and Washbrook (2005).

49 For details about new farmers' movements in India, see Brass (1995a) and Assadi (1997).

Categories to which van der Linden and Roth affix their broader definition of working class membership ('proletarian multiverse'), with the object of promoting such agency as actually or potentially a progressive form of mobilization, include not just peasant smallholders, but also the lumpenproletariat. There is, however, much historical evidence to the effect that significant elements belonging to this category are more often to be found in the ranks of the counter-revolution. Employers also frequently turned to the lumpenproletariat for strike-breakers, using them to replace workers who had withdrawn their labour-power in support of higher wages and better conditions.

Before Marxism, members of the lumpenproletariat were criticized largely on moral grounds, for being 'dissolute,' 'improvident,' 'lazy' or 'uncivilized'.[50] The focus of Marxism, by contrast, has been mainly on the *political* role of the lumpenproletariat, and in particular the way it has been mobilized historically by reactionary elements opposed to class struggle waged by the proletariat. Furthermore, it is necessary to distinguish between those components of the lumpenproletariat who have previously been employed as wage labourers, and thus retain not just the effects of that experience but also a concept of class solidarity based on it, and those who lack this kind of background. These crucial distinctions are ones that GLH fails to make, thereby replicating the mistaken perception of unfree workers as part of these 'dangerous classes'. Recognizing the dangers posed by the reproduction or reintroduction of labour that was unfree, Marx argued that its 'other' – free, well-paid, permanent working arrangements – had to be fought for. In terms of a socialist transition, it was the latter, not the former, who composed the 'dangerous classes' feared by the bourgeoisie: that is, free workers in well-paid, permanent jobs, organized and confident, were the ones who were best placed not just to confront owners of the means of production but also to advocate a socialist transition.

That the role discharged by the lumpenproletariat during acute periods of class struggle is reactionary is clear from the similarity of its characterization by those at the opposite ends of the political spectrum. For Marx, therefore, the lumpenproletariat is not just 'a mass quite distinct from the industrial proletariat,' but during the 1848 revolution in France, when the 'emancipation of the workers...became intolerably dangerous for the republic...there remained only one way out: to set one section of the proletariat against the other.'[51] Echoing this assessment, the conservative Lamartine describes the same lumpenproletariat as 'partly dressed in rags [but] defending the State and property of a luxurious capital,' and celebrates its populist message which 'proclaimed

50 See, for example, Wright (1969: 359ff.).

51 See Marx (1973b: 52).

the fusion and concord of different classes.'[52] Marx's negative interpretation is complemented by what he and Engels wrote when criticizing Max Stirner for conflating the lumpenproletariat with the working class. In common with so many others then and now, Stirner also celebrated the lumpenproletariat as authentic rebels, a view derided by Marx and Engels on the grounds that it identified 'the proletariat with pauperism, whereas pauperism is the position only of the ruined proletariat, the lowest level to which the proletarian sinks who has become incapable of resisting the pressure of the bourgeoisie.'[53]

Taking issue with populists who accused Kautsky of 'driving from the ranks of the proletariat numerous genuine working people', including the lumpenproletariat, Lenin observed in 1906 that 'to date [populists] have produced nothing to show that tramps, handicraftsmen, and domestic servants have created a Social-Democratic movement'.[54] Three years later, he criticized optimistic advocacy of a revolutionary upswing involving the 'pauperised petty bourgeoisie', noting '[n]or does there appear to be any reason why the pauperised town petty bourgeoisie should be brought in just at this moment.' Why this was so, Lenin explained, was that '[l]umpenproletarians are *sometimes* distinguished for their sharp conflicts, and *sometimes* for their amazing instability and inability to fight' (original emphasis), dismissing as 'opportunism' such attempts to recruit these elements for socialism. About the latter Lenin concluded, in words that might apply equally to exponents of mobilization by the 'subaltern'/'multitude'/'proletarian multiverse', that they 'have not yet told us about the *object* of the struggle…but they make haste to tell us about the *means* of struggle in order to proclaim themselves "revolutionaries"'.

That in the course of anti-capitalist struggle the lumpenproletariat and the petty bourgeoisie are usually to be found in the ranks not of the working class but in those of its opponents is evident from many other examples. According to Volkov, therefore, the social composition of those who espoused popular anti-modernist ideology in Germany during the 1890s capitalist crisis included small independent artisans, traditional craftsmen, white-collar employees, lower officials, small retailers and peasant smallholders.[55] It was these very same elements who – together with lumpenproletarians – went on to support

52 See Lamartine (1849: 184–185).

53 Marx and Engels (1976a: 201–202).

54 See the English version of Lenin's *Collected Works*, volume 5 (p. 157). He recounted how in Switzerland during 1912 capitalists used elements of the lumpenproletariat to act as strikebreakers, and other similar references to its reactionary political role can be found in his *Collected Works*, volumes 15 (pp. 384–385), 18 (p. 161), and 26 (pp. 460, 468).

55 Volkov (1978).

the political right during the capitalist crisis of the late 1920s. In Germany and Italy they formed the core element both of the *Freikorps* and the *Squadristi*, and later of the Brownshirts (SA or *Sturmabteilung*). Similarly, van Onselen shows how at the same conjuncture urban gangs in Johannesburg composed of a depeasantized lumpenproletariat targeted black migrant workers, from whom they stole and by whom they were feared.[56]

What these examples underline is the over-optimistic nature of positive interpretations attached to the grassroots agency of peasants and the lumpenproletariat, two key elements regarded by GLH as part of the 'proletarian multiverse' on the 'dynamic of resistance' of which any future emancipatory politics depend. It is not the case that Marx and Marxist political economy have overlooked or ignored such agency, much rather the opposite: the contrast made by them between the working class on the one hand, and on the other the lumpenproletariat and an undifferentiated peasantry is made in order to draw attention to their politically-distinct interests. Thus the concept 'dangerous classes' has to be differentiated in terms of a potential/actual political threat. That posed by important components of what GLH defines as the 'proletarian multiverse' – the lumpenproletariat, undifferentiated peasants, and unfree labour – is aimed not at capitalism but at socialism. By contrast, the threat posed by the working class as conceptualized by Marxists is against capitalism, not socialism.

VIII

These days leftists are faced with a contrast that is historically all too familiar. On the one hand, therefore, there is a seemingly unstoppable *laissez faire* capitalism engaged in restructuring its labour process, outsourcing/relocating/downsizing employment. As the global industrial reserve army increases, so does casualization and impoverishment. On the other, the populist response is to advocate expanding the range of social forces from which support against capitalism is to be drawn. The difficulty with this is simple: history warns against these attempts conceptually to admit into the ranks of the proletariat elements whose class position (owners of means of production, buyers of labour-power), political ideology and cultural discourse (privileging religion, nationalism, ethnicity) are hostile to socialism. Hence the dilemma confronting the endorsement by global labour historiography of 'new' populist postmodern theory: how can struggle undertaken by such relationally distinct

56 van Onselen (1977).

components ever become that of a proletariat (class-in-itself) to realize itself as such (class-for-itself)?

This kind of populist approach is not new, similar ones having been advanced in the course of revisionist debates from the 1890s onwards. When in the 1950s capitalism appeared less powerful, and the class struggle in industrial nations seemed to diminish in intensity, some leftists shifted the political emphasis from class to cultural identity, a change that would have far-reaching implications. In keeping with this, the authentic revolutionary subjects in Third World were said to be depeasantized alienated migrants residing in urban slums, an heterogenous ensemble whose sole unifying characteristic was a shared element of cultural marginality where capitalism was concerned. The failure on the part of the 1960s development theory to question – and thus to settle ideological accounts with – the politics informing rural culture enabled its subsequent categorization by exponents of the 1980s 'cultural turn' as a progressive grassroots discourse, one that validated indigenous and other forms of nationalism.

None of the claims made currently by global labour historiography – that unfree labour is central to accumulation, that consequently such workers are members of the proletariat, and as such they and other 'marginals' must be regarded as committed to collective action designed to transcend capitalism – is in fact new. Nor is it the case that Marxist political economy ignored or has been wrong about such issues. Neither are they as politically radical as global labour historiography imagines, since the desire to recruit virtually everyone into a broad anti-capitalist movement ignores the fact that many of its components – small commercial farmers, simple commodity producers, lumpenproletarians, sharecroppers, petty traders and merchants – are either actual or aspiring capitalists, and as such are opposed only to certain forms of capitalism, and not to capitalism *per se*.

The latter notwithstanding, the global labour historiography considered here insists that this kind of grassroots mobilization – rights-based, non-Marxist – is both effective and (therefore) something the rural Third World 'other' does successfully. From around the 1980s, such forms of localised resistance by peasant farmers – identified as core elements of these 'new' social movements – became the focus of study by the 'new' postmodern populism, exponents of which claimed this to be the most progressive and potent kind of rural agency. Under a variety of labels ('the subaltern', 'the multitude,' 'proletarian multiverse'), the political desirability of such multi-class alliances reflecting the interests of a rural bourgeoisie or petty bourgeoisie that sought neither a transition to socialism, nor to transform capitalist property relations or capture/control the capitalist State, surfaced in an increasing number of non- or even anti-Marxist analytical frameworks.

The crucial political question global labour historiography fails to pose, therefore, is: who are the 'dangerous classes,' and whom do they threaten? Marxism argued that, as a result of struggle waged against capital, the working class was in a position to formulate a political consciousness which challenged the very nature of capitalism itself, a process which enabled its subjects to contemplate and effect an alternative: putting a socialist transition on the agenda. Marxism was adamant that this did *not* apply to the lumpenproletariat, elements of which were to be found, much rather, in the ranks of reaction, joining forces with those (royalists, nobility, landlords, capitalists) opposed to socialism. Subsequently, Marxists identified peasant proprietors – but not poor peasants – as belonging to the same political category. Because such elements perceived their interests as upholding private property (and smallscale accumulation), and although hostile to particular forms of capital (agribusiness, finance), they too were antagonistic towards socialism. From the viewpoint of capital, therefore, the 'dangerous classes' are not the lumpenproletariat or better-off peasants, neither of which seek nor are able to effect a socialist transition, but rather the working class, which does and can. It is precisely this contradiction that analyses promoting subaltern identity and agency overlook.

PART 3

Essays

∵

Old London Cries, III

CHAPTER 14

The Sabotage of Anthropology and the Anthropologist as Saboteur*

What follows is a brief account of arrest and imprisonment while carrying out fieldwork on a rural co-operative near the town of Quillabamba in the Province of La Convención, Peru. Between 1958 and 1962 this particular area in the Department of Cusco was in the view of one observer 'the scene of the most important peasant movement of that period in Peru, and probably in the whole of South America'.[1] At the time of fieldwork, therefore, it was a location where any research into peasant organization, trade unions, etc., was still regarded by the authorities as suspect and potentially subversive.

It must be emphasized, however, that the account in neither a cautionary tale nor a contribution to the literature of prison memoirs. Rather, it serves both to illustrate and to reinforce the truism that anthropologists engaged in fieldwork are not merely observers of class struggle but also part of the struggle itself, and it is precisely in exceptional circumstances such as those outlined below that the anthropologist-as-participant takes precedence in a dramatic manner over the anthropologist-as-observer.

I

At 4 in the afternoon of 22 March 1975, five students (two male, three female) from La Católica University in Lima, Luis Mamani (then Secretary-General of the Provincial Peasant Union Federation), Enrique Lara (a staff member of the state research organization CENCIRA) and the anthropologist were arrested in Quillabamba and taken to the *Guardia Civil* (hereafter GC) barracks, where statements were made and personal effects confiscated.[2] Although at this

* An earlier version appeared in the *Journal of the Anthropological Society of Oxford*, Vol. XIII, No. 2 (1982). Appended at the end for the first time is a Postscript, a commentary on the events outlined here in terms of both what went on then that I was unaware of and what is known now.

1 Hobsbawm (1969a: 31).

2 An additional arrest, of a US national, was made subsequently. All the names of the detainees have been changed, to protect their identities. Those of officials, authorities and the military, however, have not.

stage no specific charges were mentioned, from the intense police activity and the tone of their remarks ('we are checking with Lima where your friend *x* is known for political subversion', etc.) it was clear to us that a process was just beginning.

Our detention in the barracks (without food, drink or bedding) lasted until 3 am the following morning, when we were all transferred to an open army lorry which then set off for a destination still unknown to us. We were later informed by one of the four *Guardias* (armed with light machine-guns) positioned at each corner of the lorry that the destination was Cusco, the Departmental capital, a journey of some 280 kilometres up into the Sierra. During the day the lorry occasionally halted in a small village along the route so that we could buy food and drink. Here the local GC would congratulate the escort on their capture of the '*guerrilleros*', and the inhabitants would gather to look at us and comment among themselves.

That evening the lorry was met on the outskirts of Cusco by a further escort of armed *Guardias* commanded by very senior officers who (ominously) raised the canvas cover on the back of the lorry over us (to prevent recognition) and accompanied us down into the city to the GC HQ. The women in the group were taken away, and the men were shut in an empty stone cell with no light; later we were taken out individually for a body-search and to be photographed for the GC files. As in Quillabamba, no food, drink or bedding was provided, a deprivation compounded by the climatic difference between tropical lowland Quillabamba (3,400 feet above sea level) and highland Cusco (11,440 feet above sea level). The clothing we had was inadequate to withstand the very low temperatures of the Sierra winter, and that night the five male detainees had to share two sleeping bags (two per bag and one on top).

At 2.30 am in the early morning of 24 March I was woken by the GC on sentry duty and taken from the stone cell to the courtyard outside, where another GC put a red hood over my head. I was then guided (pushed) by these two up a wooden stairway and along a passage to a room on the second floor, where I was seated on a chair and left alone for half an hour. Later someone came into the room and took the hood off my head: the room itself was empty, except for the chair I occupied, in front of which were positioned two very bright reflector lamps focussed on my face; to one side stood a broad-shouldered 'heavy' in a mask revealing only his eyes, nose and mouth. The interrogator was in an adjacent room connected with mine by a microphone system, and the questioning followed explicitly political themes.

At 5 am I was taken to another GC barracks in the city and locked in a small single cell until 7 am that morning, when all the detainees (or political prisoners, as we had now been officially classified) were reunited in a larger cell, each one of us having experienced the same form of interrogation procedure the previous night. Later that morning we were taken across the city to the HQ of the PIP (*Policía de Investigaciones del Peru*, or the political police) for further investigation and interrogation.

Unlike the cell walls in the GC barracks, the walls of the cell in the PIP HQ were covered in graffiti containing messages and political testaments of past detainees, dates of arrest and torture, and references to political events unrecorded in the official Peruvian press. Here we remained without light or bedding and only small amounts of food (bought by the women in the group and passed to us on the rare visits they were allowed to make), awaiting the commencement of another round of interrogations. No outside contact was possible, a PIP officer informed us, until the investigation was complete; meanwhile we would stay incommunicado.

At 11 pm on the night of 25 March the interrogations began: now guilt of political activity on our part was assumed, merely to be confirmed. The object of interrogation had changed, since for the PIP the problem was no longer just one of identifying a political position but rather to establish the existence of concrete activity deriving from and in furtherance of this political position. To this end, the more sophisticated questioning of the PIP attempted to locate the inconsistencies and contradictions in the prisoners' chronological sequence of dates, times, persons and events, a tactically superior approach when compared with the narrowly political and less subtle questioning of the GC designed only to elicit political position and opinion. Where the GC interrogation method had attempted to instil terror, the method of the PIP was designed to create confusion: the menace of the GC was explicit (and therefore resistible), while that of the PIP was implicit (and unpredictable, making apostasy a certain resolution to an uncertain situation).

Two PIP officers would rapidly and simultaneously ask questions on different themes (sometimes related, sometimes not). To most of these questions no complete response was either required or permitted, since the method sought precisely to expose the incipient contradiction of the half-formed answer, the recognition of which by the prisoner reinforced his uncertainty and undermined his argument whilst instantly uniting his interrogators in common exploration/exploitation of this discovered theme. In short, the object of this method was to destroy the prisoner's concept of time, and its element of continuity. When each of us had been interrogated in this manner, we were returned to the cell below, from where it was now possible to hear the deliberations of the PIP upstairs concerning the various forms (the legal constructions) that might be taken by the political indictment. This related particularly to the acceptance by a military court of what in the current political context constituted anti-government activity.

Accordingly, at 11 am on 26 March we were taken to the offices of the military tribunal in Cusco. Here we were told that the charge was 'sabotage of the agrarian reform', a common holding charge employed against political opponents of the junta (Amnesty International, 1979: 6), and that we would be detained in prison until the tribunal was ready to hear the case against us. At mid-day we were handed over to the *Guardia Republicana* (the prison police) and taken by prison van to Quenkoru Gaol, where we were to remain for the next seven days.

Situated eight kilometres outside Cusco, Quenkoru Gaol consists of a single open-air compound surrounded by wire fencing and watchtowers. It contains two cell blocks, one for convicted prisoners (*culpables*) and the other for those awaiting trial (*inculpables*). We were incarcerated in the latter, in a special section reserved for political detainees, who at the time ranged from student leaders (who had been in detention for nine months) to twenty male villagers (*comuneros*) still untried for killing their landlord six years previously. The members of our group occupied themselves with political discussions and the organization of a legal defence, a process which entailed the hiring of politically sympathetic lawyers who offered to defend us for nominal fees.

After the others had been through a similar procedure, Enrique Lara, Luis Mamani and I were taken to the offices of the military tribunal on the morning of 3 April, where further statements were made and cross-examinations carried out. That evening, the officers composing the military tribunal arrived at the prison and presented us with their written judgments, in all cases a conditional discharge. This indicated that the detainees were to be released from custody, but nevertheless confined to the city of Cusco while the PIP continued with the investigations. As we collected our belongings from the cell block, other inmates told us that PIP personnel had been seen at the prison entrance, a warning ignored by us in the euphoria of imminent release. Accordingly, the *Guardia Republicana* escorted us to the prison gates and pushed us through the narrow exit into the street beyond, where we were instantly rearrested by the PIP, hustled into a van and driven back to their HQ.

During this second period of detention, the PIP were more openly hostile, threatening to use torture and confining us for long sessions in standing positions with hands behind our heads. The next day (4 April) we were taken to the offices of the Commandant of the XI Military Zone (the Departments of Madre de Dios, Cusco and Puno) and political boss of the whole region, General Luis

Montoya y Montoya, who in a lecture to us on the objectives and achievements of the Peruvian 'revolution' made explicit the reasons for our initial arrest and subsequent re-arrest: namely, the separation of dissident political thought (allowed) from dissident political action (disallowed). We were then returned to the custody of the PIP, where we remained for the next three days.

Renewed activity on the morning of 7 April indicated, we thought, that in the interim the PIP had formulated new charges, and we were as a result being taken once again to the offices of the military tribunal in the south of the city, the direction in which the PIP vans were travelling. Instead, the vans continued on towards the airport, finally coming to a stop on the side of the main runway to await transport to Lima. Amidst the now familiar security procedure we went aboard the plane, and were seated at the rear of the aircraft under heavy guard. Half an hour later we arrived in the national capital, and were loaded into police vans and taken to the State Security Section (*Seguridad del Estado*) in the Lima HQ of the PIP.

Although the questioning process continued as before, it was now more rigorous and coordinated; each detainee was simultaneously interrogated by a combination of PIP officers, two or three of us being questioned in this way at the same time. The walls of the interrogation rooms were covered in complex charts and diagrams which purported to trace connections between each detainee: after every interrogation the material content of these charts increased, but no new line of questioning was introduced nor charges made.[3] As the routine established itself once more, it became clear that the only development in my particular situation would be expulsion; the Peruvian nationals might still be handed over to military intelligence, the SIM.

On 16 April I was summoned to the office of Sardo, the chief of the Lima PIP, where I was informed that my case had been decided by the Minister of the Interior, General Richter Prada, and that I was required to leave Peru within forty-eight hours. It was made clear that the expulsion order precluded flying over Peruvian national territory, since if an aircraft in which I was travelling was compelled to land, the expulsion order would be technically infringed.[4]

3 A new charge of 'illegally attending a political meeting during the state of emergency' was subsequently formulated.

4 The element of farce, albeit tinged with menace, persisted right to the end. Accompanied by Embassy personnel, I arrived at Lima airport, only to be told by Peruvian officials there that I should be in prison, to where they intended to return me. Hasty phone calls were made to the Ministry of Interior, and eventually I was permitted to board the plane, just about ready to depart, my hand luggage being thrown after me through the now closing door of the aircraft.

II

Unlike the elaboration of an ethnographic text, where the guise of 'objectivity' mediates reality through the intervention of the anthropologist as its necessarily external interpreter, the events outlined above represent an antithesis to this customary attempt at objectification. An anthropologist is instead absorbed within, and becomes part of, the social process under examination. The distinction between the social components of a process observed, and the observer of that process, is the ideological product of the separation of the 'professional observer' from the 'subjects observed'. Given the concreteness of this ideological construct, the observer (in the capacity of anthropologist) possesses a guaranteed autonomy in relation to the activity of the subjects being studied.

During the period of the events, however, this element of externalised that-sidedness specific to anthropological practice was transformed into its opposite, the corollary of the subsequent internal this-sidedness being that the autonomy of the observer was guaranteed no longer. In the course of this transformation, the distinction between observer and observed was deprived of some of its more important constituents, the power of a new and hitherto unknowable situation erasing pre-existing ideas and attitudes, and in the process creating new alliances and possibilities (political, social).

This element of restructuring was both determined and necessarily preceded by the *de*structuring of distinct identities which gave rise to the observer/observed polarity. The synthesis entailed the development of significantly similar identities, a conflation resulting from the imperatives of the new political context (the state of emergency). Elimination of previously distinct identities was itself doubly determined, by mutually reinforcing processes. On the one hand, therefore, the establishment of a common political identity *for* the detainees (the object of interrogation), and on the other the construction of a common political identity *by* the detainees themselves (the effect of imprisonment). Both these processes were based on the eradication of originally significant political differences between the detainees and a corresponding emphasis on common elements (constructed during imprisonment). In other words, the creation of a new subject fulfilling the opposed requirements of the protagonists.

The two sites of this conflict/contradiction/transformation were: on the one hand, the interrogation room (the domain of the state and *its* definition of identities), where agents of the state sought either to mould the subject into a pre-given identity, or merely to confirm the pre-existence of this same identity; and on the other, the prison cell (the domain of the detainees and *their* definition of identities), where the process of displacement and political relocation of the subject was confirmed and reinforced. This transformation of the individual identity and its subsumption under a group identity did not, of course, affect each detainee in the same manner. For those already committed politically, the events served as confirmation of that commitment; for those not similarly committed, the events acted as a catalyst in the change of political consciousness.

An example of the latter was Luis Mamani, whose original reaction was hostility toward the students, identifying them as the principal cause of his own arrest: had the students not been present in Quillabamba and attracted the attention of the authorities, he himself would not have been arrested. During the course of the interrogations, however, Luis's analysis of the situation changed, as did his ideas about its political significance and determinants. The locus of blame for his arrest shifted from the students and their presence in Quillabamba to the reformist politics of the legal advisor to the Federation, Dr Augusto Medina. The latter was criticized by Luis for politically restraining and weakening the Federation, and consequently enabling the state to move against its leadership, an impossible act had the Federation possessed political strength.

Throughout the period of imprisonment, Luis contributed his knowledge of federation politics to general discussions of the agrarian reform programme, adopting the theoretical viewpoint of the group as a whole. For their part, the PIP encouraged this development, since the increasing similarity in views (evidenced in the course of interrogation) appeared to sustain the concept of a pre-existing conspiracy, thereby confirming the correctness of the PIP's action in re-arresting the members of the group.

The transformation of identity results in conflict within the subject(s) experiencing this. Hence the discarding of autonomy by an anthropologist shifts the latter into the realm of social activity usually occupied by the objects of anthropological practice, and the observer too becomes like the observed a subject materially constrained and oppressed by the same elements of legal/political coercion in general and state repression in particular.

This point has been noted elsewhere with respect to a similar set of circumstances:[5]

> ...the affair had positive aspects too. The workings of the structure of power [in the Brazilian sugar plantation] had been brought out much more clearly than would have been the case under normal circumstances.

5 de Kadt (1970: 288).

> I had been made to *feel*, rather than simply *understand*, something of the process of intimidation of workers and peasants, and something about the reasons for their passivity in the face of the powers that be (original emphasis).

Paradoxically, 'abnormal circumstances' uncover a potential contradiction not only at the level of the individual subject, but also within the nature of the repressive apparatus of the state: *in order to destroy the existing opposition to itself, the state necessarily creates and extends the conditions of the existence of this opposition.* The formation of a new consciousness in this manner is, in short, determined by the operation of the state repressive apparatus. It makes possible a situation in which a peasant union leader can be made aware by students of political events (and their significance, both in general and specific terms) beyond his immediate sphere, and can in turn make those same students aware of political events, conditions and activity that in other ('normal') circumstances would never be revealed to them.

Postscript

Forty years after the events recounted above, it is possible to provide a commentary on them in the light of what I have learned since, both about what was happening then unbeknownst to me, and what is now known to be the case. The main source of information about what was happening then derives from documents, many of them marked 'restricted', which indicate the way diplomats attached to the British Embassy in Lima and The Foreign and Commonwealth Office (FCO) in London perceived the situation.[6]

Where the latter institutions are concerned, these documents and other accounts suggest either views bordering on the farcical, or a wish to be rid of a 'problem' as quickly as possible. One exchange in particular illustrates the element of farce. In the course of their inquiries about the penalties I might incur, my parents spoke briefly on the phone with the British Consul at Arequipa, in Southern Peru. On being told that the charge was a political one, he replied in all seriousness 'I'm not entirely sure, but I don't think they shoot them for that'.

6 These documents surfaced in the course of legal action taken by the FCO in an attempt to recover from my parents the costs of a very expensive lawyer the British Embassy provided for me to answer the charges made by the Peruvian authorities. All the other detainees used local lawyers, who provided their services free of charge.

It is not difficult to imagine the effect this alarming yet ill-informed opinion as to the predicament I faced had on my parents.

That the object of action by the FCO and the Lima Embassy was to resolve the situation without becoming involved to any degree (to 'make it go away' as quickly as possible) emerges clearly from the documents. Hence complaints encountered in one, to the effect that 'this case...is proving to be both tiresome and difficult' and 'the trials and tribulations we [have] endured', referred not to FCO/Embassy dealings with the Peruvian authorities but rather to those with my parents and me. At the centre of this difference in approach was the issue of whether or not I would be permitted to continue with my fieldwork.

On the subject of my returning to Peru in order to conduct further research, an internal FCO communication, written by the First Secretary at the Lima Embassy and dated 27 November 1975, noted: 'As far as Brass coming back here is concerned, I told him before he left (when he asked me the same question) that I thought this would be unwise. Rightly or wrongly, he now has a "police record" in Peru and even if he could re-enter Peru there could be no guarantee that the authorities might decide once more to take notice of him. If this happened, and even if he were innocent, a second involvement with the authorities would be likely to be even more difficult for him than his first experience. I have therefore suggested to him that he should direct his social anthropology studies elsewhere.'

The same document continues in a more revealing vein: 'I see no good reason and possibly some danger in embarking with Brass on correspondence along these lines'. Quite why there was perceived to be a 'danger in embarking... on correspondence along these lines' is evident from the contrast between the resolution of my situation and that of another foreign detainee. Whereas advice from the Embassy and the FCO was that expulsion was the best possible outcome, and that media publicity about my case should be avoided lest it antagonize the Peruvian authorities, another detainee who was also a foreign national was permitted to continue with his work.[7] This was because influence was used on his behalf, and pressure exercised on both the Minister of Interior and the PIP not to prevent the detainee from remaining in the country.

Among those arrested, therefore, was a US national undertaking missionary work in the Cusco area. As revealed by a recent Wikileaks document, he was permitted to continue with this undertaking in Peru after the Bishop of Lima interceded on his behalf with the Minister of the Interior, who then instructed

7 The recommendation of the British Ambassador in Lima was 'that when talking to the parents [the FCO should] urge them as firmly as possible to say nothing to the press [because] any critical publicity...could risk causing adverse reaction and set matters back'.

the PIP 'not to hamper plans' of the person concerned.[8] Although the reason for this intervention and its acceptability to the Peruvian authorities can only be guessed at, what is not open to dispute is that intervention on behalf of a foreign national was made and worked. This contrasts with my case, where the opposite is true: not only was intervention perceived as impossible and counter-productive, but expulsion was consequently deemed to be the best and only option.[9]

The non-intervention policy followed by the FCO/Embassy approach to my case also differs strikingly from that of my thesis supervisor at Sussex University, Professor A.L. (Bill) Epstein (1924–99). Because of the political difficulties he himself experienced during fieldwork in the 1950s on the African copperbelt in what was then Northern Rhodesia – Bill Epstein quickly recognized the seriousness of the situation and promptly intervened on my behalf.[10] Although my fieldwork was nearing completion, most of my notebooks were left behind in the research area, and on my return to Sussex University I was faced with the distinct possibility of not having enough data to write up the doctoral thesis. Bill Epstein immediately marshalled his resources and networks to secure the return of my notebooks, and it was largely due to his efforts that these were sent back to me. It was not until much later, however, when I saw copies of the

8 The relevant Wikileaks document goes as follows: '[US] Embassy source report that Auxiliary Bishop of Lima Luis Bambaren (Catholic) has interceded with Interior Minister Richter Prada and Richter has ordered Peruvian police not to hamper plans of [the US national] to continue missionary work in Cuzco area. [The named person is] expected to return to Cuzco later this month.'

9 The Foreign and Commonwealth Office reported that 'the Ambassador's view is that Mr Brass's release with 48 hours to leave the country was the best that could be hoped for in the circumstances. It is true that throughout the second period of detention no charges were made against him, but under the present state of emergency the Peruvian authorities were fully within their legal rights in detaining him for further enquiries about his possible involvement in activities in the Cuzco area. There are those in the Peruvian Government who would like to claim that recent troubles in Cuzco are the result in part of a "foreign plot" [which] ruled out unconditional release... It is perhaps worth noting that the Honorary Consul in Cochabamba was worried about Mr Brass when he was in Bolivia and reported that he had troubles with the local authorities when he indoctrinated [*sic*] the peasants on class equality etc. The Honorary Consul, who says she lived in expectation of hearing that Mr Brass had been picked up by the Bolivian authorities, said she issued dire warnings for him to "keep his anthropology within the bounds of discretion"'.

10 Whilst conducting fieldwork, Epstein (1992) was asked to address a meeting so as to explain his research objectives to miners who were on strike in support of the African National Congress. A result was that the colonial authorities prevented him from continuing with his research there.

letters he sent on my behalf, that the true extent of his endeavours became apparent. My point is that he need not have done this (there were others who drew back from involvement), nor did he demand fealty from those he helped in this manner.

A final question, and one that remains impossible to answer, concerns the negative impact of this episode on my employment prospects in academia. Senior members alongside whom I taught courses in university departments showed a marked antipathy towards my politics, to the extent of blocking appointment to permanent posts when these became available. One such instance, referred to briefly elsewhere in this book, demonstrates this clearly. Given the antipathy expressed in the FCO/Embassy documents towards what were perceived (in some instances not merely wrong but farcically so) to be my political opinions and actions, along the lines that I had 'indoctrinated' peasants, it is not impossible that such judgments were made available to those in universities when I applied for jobs there. That the political identity established for me by a combination of the Peruvian authorities, the FCO and the British Embassy in Lima, may indeed have followed me around subsequently cannot therefore be ruled out.

CHAPTER 15

How Agrarian Cooperatives Fail

*Lessons from 1970s Peru**

> For the Bolsheviks, cooperation was only a stage in the socialist transformation of agriculture; for Chayanov, cooperation was the ideal compromise, combining the advantages of small peasant property with the technical advantages of large-scale farming.[1]
>
> An observation by BASILE KERBLAY in his introduction to Chayanov

∵

Among the numerous suggestions currently given credence by many development theorists and peasant leaders, and made now by those of them seeking a way of off-setting or preventing the continued depeasantisation effected by neoliberal capitalism, is a return to an earlier solution: agrarian cooperatives.[2] Producer or consumer cooperatives – the two classic forms – constituted a democratic space within capitalism, early advocates insisted, where a specifically plebeian consumer/producer might exercise what was thought to be a form of grassroots autonomy.[3] This entailed, among other things, the ability by

* An earlier version appeared in *The Journal of Peasant Studies*, Vol. 34, No. 2 (2007).

1 Chayanov (1966: lx).

2 The positive link between modernization, economic growth and agrarian cooperatives was a common theme in much of the development literature that emerged from the 1960s debate about the so-called Third World, especially that addressing issues of peasant farming and rural poverty: see, for example, Srivastava (1962), Weitz (1965), Schiller (1969), Griffin (1970), Worsley (1971), Galeski (1972), Dorner (1972), Baldwin (1972), Barraclough and Collarte (1973), Walinsky (1977), and the contributions to the volume edited by Nash, Dandler and Hopkins (1976). This link, and its desirability in terms of agrarian reform programmes in the Third World, had already been strongly recommended by the United Nations Department of Economic Affairs (1954: 233ff.) during the previous decade. For an examination of the different political meanings attached to the term 'cooperative', and the implications of this for its form of property relation and control over the forces of production, see Schiller (1969) and Warriner (1969: 56ff.).

3 On cooperatives as a form of 'democratic control', see Carr-Saunders, Florence and Peers (1940: Part 3). For a similar view expressed subsequently, that cooperatives 'involved attempts to transform capitalistically organized agriculture – the farms of North Africa and the haciendas of Latin America – into a more equitable and socialist institution', see Nash and Hopkins (1976: 7). For useful critiques of this approach, see Petras and LaPorte (1971) and Huizer (1983a).

members of a cooperative to control prices of commodities produced or consumed, thereby mitigating – if not circumventing – the impact on them of the wider accumulation process.[4] As important in terms of development criteria has been the eradication of rural poverty, thus extending social justice to the landless.[5] Historically, the main targets of this kind of organization have been family farms and peasant smallholders, either in underdeveloped countries or in areas of metropolitan capitalist nations untouched by the accumulation process.[6]

Reasons for the present enthusiasm for a return to peasant cooperatives as a form of socio-economic regeneration in rural areas of the so-called Third World is not difficult to discern.[7] By combining in larger units, so the argument

4 Accepting that 'so long as powerful interests of privately owned capital exert so strong an influence...it is impossible for the co-operative system to operate freely in its own way', Carr-Saunders, Florence and Peers (1940: 249–250) nevertheless adhere to the notion of cooperatives as the 'other' of capitalist enterprises, maintaining that 'within their limitations (they) give real experience of industrial democracy in action'.

5 On land reform as a method of eradicating rural poverty and inequality, thereby achieving social justice for the poorest peasants and landless workers, see Barraclough and Collarte (1973: 33) and the World Bank (1975a; 1975b; 1978).

6 A comprehensive overview of a wide range of agrarian cooperative arrangements in Europe before the 1914–18 war is found in the United States Senate Commission (1913) appointed by President Wilson. That the main target of such arrangements was usually smallholding agriculture is evident from the fact that in the Middle East (Keen, 1946: 35) '...ownership of the holding – or a suitable tenancy agreement – is a necessary prelude to the full development of co-operative societies'.

7 The current uncritical enthusiasm for peasant cooperatives as a solution to rural poverty is itself part of a much wider phenomenon: the forgetting of history generally, and that of Latin American development theory and practice in particular. As has been noted frequently in this journal, the latter form of amnesia is itself a process that is invariably coupled with an uncritical espousal of the 'new' postmodern populism, an aporetic relativism which anyway denies the importance of history. Where the study of rural Latin America is concerned, this combination – forgetting history plus endorsing the 'new' postmodern populism – is epitomized in two recent observations by Taylor (2005). First, that the argument that Latin American states co-opt the peasantry is not a 'novel claim'; and second, that the 'new' postmodern populism is 'an essential part of...micro-level politics [without which] no progress can be achieved'. It may well be the case, as Taylor claims, that the argument about the co-opting of the peasantry by Latin American states is not new. But it needs repeating precisely because converts from Marxism to postmodern populism – such as Taylor – have forgotten its political importance, and need to be reminded of this by those who have remained Marxists. Among the many things overlooked as a result of forgetting history is that the ethnicity and nationalism informing the 'new' postmodern populism feed directly into the discourse of the political right, a fact difficult to reconcile with any notion of progress. Significantly, perhaps, Taylor was one of those who pronounced the *enganche* relation – see below – an

goes, smallholders gain the benefits of economies of scale: not just access to more efficient productive forces but also to economically more rational input provision and marketing systems.[8] They also benefit from the delivery by the state of technical expertise, extension services, financial arrangements and credit facilities that would be denied them as small peasant farmers. This 'from above' discourse is matched by a 'from below' call – in the name of democracy and autonomy – by many indigenous movements and their supporters for a return to traditional institutional forms of community organization.[9]

---

empowering form of free labour. In this he joined not just other revisionists – for example, Bauer (1979) – but also neoclassical economists and postmodernists who similarly revised the meaning of debt bondage from a coercive/oppressive relation to an outcome of worker 'choice', a reinterpretation that has been shown to be wrong (Brass, 1999: 170, 190–192, 200, 202, 203, 206, 208–209, 214, 216). About these different theoretical approaches to rural Latin America, two final points can be made. First, given that Taylor has proved to be mistaken so often and on so many issues, the politically complacent remarks he makes in his review are in a sense encouraging. If he disagrees so strongly with Marxist criticisms of postmodernism and subaltern studies, then these criticisms must perforce be right. And second, his amnesia underlines the veracity of the old cliché that those who forget history are condemned to repeat the (analytical and political) mistakes it warns against.

8 For an earlier version of the argument about 'returns to scale', see Balogh (1966: 67), who notes that the 'organization of co-operatives would enable the rational use of land and water, and the carrying through of infrastructure and agricultural investment'. Also, Eckstein and Carroll (1976: 236ff.) and the view (Griffin, 1987: 226) that: 'Producers' cooperatives...manage to generate a small financial surplus and thus by this criterion perform better than the state farms... The peasant farms...do well by this criterion. The peasant producers have almost no capital with which to work, but their output per unit of capital is very high. Strictly in allocative terms there should be a redistribution of capital from state farms to the peasant sector...'.

9 See for example the Zapatistas in Chiapas, where Subcomandante Marcos (Duràn de Huerta and Higgins, 1999: 271) equates democracy with decentralization: 'We believe that the practice of direct democracy can achieve...recognition for certain aspects of the social life of the communities. When I say communities I'm not referring only to indigenous communities but also to villages, city neighbourhoods and agricultural collectives (*ejidos*). This is to suggest that people can discuss and take decisions about how to resolve their own problems, and to suggest that these decisions will be infinitely better than the decisions that are normally taken from the centre.' Producer cooperatives composed of small farmers in poor countries are also seen by many well-meaning but politically naïve non-government organizations as efficacious solutions to rural poverty. Such arrangements do not rely on the state for inputs, preferring instead to organize 'autonomously' at the grassroots. In these cases, positive views about this institutional form – the agrarian cooperative – underwrite prevailing wisdom about the desirability and possibility of 'fair trade' within the wider context of neoliberal capitalism, a development approach endorsed by NGOs which regard producer cooperatives as a feasible method of 'trading out of poverty'.

The inference is that, even where agriculture is capitalist, institutions like agrarian cooperatives are – as they were in the past – capable not just of protecting vulnerable petty commodity producers from the impact of accumulation, but also of providing them with an alternative way of earning a living, one that is secure and economically viable.[10]

Without class analysis, however, the struggle in such post-reform institutions is necessarily seen as being one between on the one hand a monolithic and powerful state, and on the other an undifferentiated and uniformly powerless peasantry.[11] Accordingly, much of the recent theory about peasant/

10 This continuing support for the cooperativization of smallholding agriculture on the part of those addressing development issues in the rural Third World is evident from a number of sources. See, for example, Pearse (1980), Baviskar (1980), Young, Sherman and Rose (1981), Lele (1981), Leons (1982), Apthorpe and Gasper (1982), Tendler (1988), Attwood and Baviskar (1988), Korovkin (1990), World Bank (1991), Barraclough (1991: 156ff.), Rodgers (1996), and some of the contributions to the volume edited by McMichael (1994). The World Bank has also organized a conference for 2007 entitled 'Cooperative Finance: Global Good Practices'. Current endorsement of agrarian cooperatives as the way forward in rural Latin America is also encountered in an USAID-funded study (Vásquez-León and Finan, 2007) that is part of a larger project conducted in collaboration with ACDI/VOCA (Agricultural Cooperative Development International and Volunteers in Overseas Cooperative Assistance): 'Smallholder rural producers in developing countries face multiple challenges and opportunities that arise from an increasingly globalized economy... Smallholder rural societies often represent values that center on place and community where the goal is not so much to maximize profit but to achieve a viable and stable livelihood in the community and on the land...producer cooperatives may play a fundamental role in allowing rural populations to achieve these goals.'.

11 It is striking just how far the element of class has vanished (or, more accurately, been banished) from current histories of and narratives about rural transformation, and the contrast with the equivalent kind of analyses being written in the 1960s and into the 1970s. At the latter conjuncture, even non-Marxists recognized the impossibility of examining agrarian reform units in Latin America (and elsewhere) without a reference to the impact on them of an only slightly modified pre-reform class structure. Hence a review of writings about rural transformation at that conjuncture by an agronomist working for the UN Food and Agriculture Organization (Domike, 1973: 64) drew attention to this very issue, noting of the Chilean agrarian reform programme the importance of 'internal conflict among the campesinos', and adding that: 'No politician, and only the naïvest social observer, believes that settling the overall campesino-landowner conflicts in favour of the former resolves the matter henceforth.' Much the same note of caution informed the conclusion written during the early 1960s by Thorner (1980: 185), another non-Marxist, in his perceptive analysis of cooperativization in rural India: 'Experience in many countries has shown that cooperatives can serve as a means by which peasant cultivators can help each other to improve their position. But the success of rural cooperatives presupposes

state relations has been informed by a familiar dichotomy: a strong and active state facing and unproblematically ordering in its own image the livelihood of a weak, hapless and passive peasantry. This is evident from, for example, a widely cited analysis of debates about rural transformation written at the same conjuncture as the case study outlined here, which maintained that in the Andean region of Latin America 'the state has used credit policies and political patronage to discriminate in favour of larger and more politically quiescent cooperatives'.[12]

There are a number of variations on this theme. One does not challenge the assumption that peasants are uniformly downtrodden, but nevertheless recasts them as unaccepting of their fate. Consequently, all peasants – regardless of class differences – are seen as engaged in heroic forms of agency, of the 'everyday forms of resistance' kind (waged against the state), for the same end.[13] Another recognizes that a contributory factor to the failure of agrarian cooperatives is to be found internally, but characterizes this in psychologistic terms: a grassroots disposition to peasant 'egoism' focused against an external 'other'.[14] The conclusion arrived at is, inevitably, that the state is

---

a modicum of social equality, political democracy, and economic viability among the villagers. These preconditions have not been present in village India and are still not present today. If the cooperative movement in India is to get anywhere, two things must happen... (1) the power of the village oligarchs...must be curtailed; and (2) the Government must become an instrument of the ordinary people, and must be considered as such by ordinary people.'

12 The text in question is Goodman and Redclift (1981: 123), where the following argument projecting the strong-state/weak-peasant dichotomy is also encountered: 'Political control of the new agricultural technologies...lies with the technical staff who decide which cooperatives should receive most help from the state, and whose close supervision of their accounts ensures that the surplus is appropriated on terms favourable to the state.' This echoes a similar conclusion arrived at earlier by Long (1977: 173), who observed of Peru that 'co-operatives often result in increased centralization and state control. They do not always entail greater peasant and worker participation at local or national level.'

13 This strong-state/weak-but-resisting-peasant is an ever-present theme in monographs by Scott (1976; 1990; 1998).

14 See, for example, McClintock (1981: 84), who maintains that in the case of Peru 'with the transformation of the hacienda into a self-managed cooperative in the early 1970s, the clientilistic orientations of peasants gave way to a new set of orientations most simply described as "peasant egoism". Collaborative and participatory attitudes emerged among peasants towards their fellows in the cooperatives; but...a sense of solidarity did not extend to peasants beyond the cooperative, or to the Peruvian nation and its government.' Because it ignores class divisions within the peasantry who are cooperative members, this idealized view is wrong: it cannot capture the fact that antagonism is directed as much

too powerful and too interventionist, and thus is somehow either largely or wholly responsible for the failure of agrarian cooperatives where and when this occurs.[15]

Fathers against Sons

As on so many other issues, differences of political interpretation – endorsement or criticism – of agrarian cooperatives in the development process can be traced to fundamental theoretical disagreements between populism and Marxism. Populists have been – and are – broadly supportive of agrarian cooperatives, and perceive in them a viable solution within (but not part of) capitalism to problems faced by family farms and peasant smallholders.[16] This was because, by taking marketing and distribution away from merchants and/or middlemen, petty commodity producers hoped not merely to retain a higher proportion of surplus generated but also to avoid debts to financial capital,

internally – against 'their fellows in the cooperatives' – as externally, against those outside production cooperatives.

15 This view about the undesirability of state intervention in Third World agrarian cooperatives was also one advocated in the 1960s by neoliberal economists. Opposing state resource provision and regulation as 'market distorting', one right-wing development theorist (Bauer, 1971: 365) argued at that conjuncture that '[t]here is no general case for subsidising cooperative societies [in Africa] rather than other forms of enterprise. If co-operatives are to be supported, this is appropriately carried out by the provision of advisory and supervisory services for a limited period [since otherwise] such organizations are subject neither to the commercial or competitive test of the market'. A decade later, in a political climate more favourable to his *laissez faire* views, the same neoliberal economist (Bauer, 1981: 176) felt able to categorize agrarian cooperatives receiving inputs from the state as 'quasi-totalitarian regimes'.

16 Ironically, this view finds echoes in the approach of some Soviet writers to Third World development in the 1970s: one such (Ivanov, 1979: 205) declared that production cooperatives in rural Africa constituted 'an alternative to capitalist development'. In a similar vein, another (Ulyanovsky, 1974: 449) maintained: 'It is planned that these agricultural supply and marketing co-operatives should in future be adapted as producer co-operatives... successful development of agricultural co-operation in the political conditions now obtaining in Burma could provide a basis for the gradual transition of rural Burma to a non-capitalist path of development.' For the centrality of cooperatives to agrarian populism generally, see Mitrany (1951) and Wiles (1969: 168); for their importance to Russian and North American populism, see respectively Maynard (1942: 61ff.) and Danilov (1988) and Buck (1920: 65ff.) and Canovan (1981: 26ff.).

and with it the possibility of depeasantization.[17] Because of these objectives – taking economic power away from ('Jewish') finance and giving it to the peasant farmer (= embodiment of the nation) – cooperatives also found support among those on the political right in 1920s and 1930s Europe.[18]

The main neo-populist advocate of rural cooperativization was Alexander Chayanov, a Russian theoretician of the 1920s whose ideas about rural development remain influential where the study of Third World agriculture is concerned.[19] By organizing themselves into cooperative units, he argued, peasant family farms would generate virtuous marketing and consumption linkages favouring their economic reproduction.[20] Accepting that rural cooperatives

---

17 Writing about the farmers' movement – the Grange – which took place in the United States during the late nineteenth century, Buck (1920: 65, 66, 67) observes: 'It was but natural, then, that the Granges should be drawn into all sorts of schemes to divert into the pockets of their members the streams of wealth which had previously flowed to the greedy middlemen. [...] The most common type of coöperative store was that in which the capital was provided by a stock company of Grange members and which sold goods to Patrons at very low prices. The profits, when there were any, were divided among the stockholders in proportion to the amount of stock they held, just as in any stock company...Farmers' agencies for the disposal of produce met with greater success. Coöperative creameries and elevators in several States are said to have saved Grange members thousands of dollars.'

18 Asked what was the attitude of Fascism towards cooperatives, the leader of the British Union of Fascists (Mosley, 1936: Question number 68) answered: 'The Co-operative Societies will play a greater not a lesser part in the Fascist State. They support the Fascist principle, which requires the widest possible diffusion and ownership of capital. They oppose both the Socialist principle of State ownership, and the capitalist principle of the concentration of capital in the hands of a few exploiters. Under Fascism...[t]hey will be genuine trading concerns serving the people.' For the role of rural cooperatives in Fascist Italy during the mid-1920s, see Schneider (1928: 163–164). This is not to say that agrarian cooperatives were or are in some sense 'fascistic' institutions; it is to say, however, that such units should not be regarded as innately (or, indeed, prefiguratively) socialist.

19 The view that rural cooperativization worked economically and socially, and could have continued to do so had the 1917 Bolshevik Revolution not intervened and dashed what was a viable democratic solution to the difficulties faced by peasant economy, is a position commonly taken by commentators on Russian political and/or rural development – such as Walkin (1963: 147ff.), Lewin (1968) and Volin (1970: 112ff.) – who were either critical of or hostile to Soviet agricultural policies and the post-1917 agrarian programme.

20 In his endorsing introduction to Chayanov's book on peasant cooperatives, Danilov (Chayanov, 1991: xii) accepts that the object of agrarian cooperatives was 'to rescue the peasant population of Russia from ruin and proletarianization', the object being to '"keep capitalism out" of the Russian countryside'. According to Chayanov (1991: 17–18) himself, 'peasant cooperatives in our opinion represent, in a highly perfected form, a variation of

'cannot be thought of in isolation from the social and economic foundations on which they are based', Chayanov nevertheless maintained that such units – like the peasant family farm itself – were located systemically outside capitalism, and in an important sense constituted an alternative to it in terms of economic organization.[21] His theory about the desirability of vertical integration involving petty commodity producers survives today in the form of a similarly enthusiastic approach by current populists to food commodity chains.[22]

Marxists by contrast have been – and are – opposed to this benign view.[23] At the beginning of the nineteenth century, Lenin pointed out that in Germany and Russia such organizational units did not solve but much rather embodied

---

peasant economy which enables the small-scale commodity producer to detach from his plan of organization those elements of the plan which a large-scale form has undoubted advantages over production on a small scale – and to do so without sacrificing his individuality.'

21 See Chayanov (1991: 17). In his opinion (Chayanov, 1966: lviii), therefore, 'horizontal concentration of production offered only limited advantages in agriculture....; on the other hand, vertical concentration allowed agriculture to achieve a revolution comparable to that of the steam engine in industry. The whole point of this vertical integration was to reconcile the maintenance of peasant farms in the biological processes of intensive cultivation and livestock breeding... [t]he agricultural cooperative was to be the instrument of that integration.' He concludes (Chayanov, 1966: 263): 'Sometimes this vertical concentration, in accord with the general economic situation, assumes not capitalist, but cooperative or mixed forms. In this case, control of the system of trade, elevator, irrigation, credit, and processing undertakings that concentrate and guide agricultural production in part or in whole belongs, not to the holders of capital, but to the organized small commodity producers who have contributed their own capital to these undertakings or have been able to create social capital.'

22 See, for example, the framework informing the analysis of food commodity chains by Bernstein (1996), whose continued adherence to a Chayanovian epistemology has been traced elsewhere (see extended review 11 in this book).

23 In the case of Russia at the beginning of the twentieth century, the reason for this is brought out succinctly by a contributor to a volume edited by Shanin (1988: 182–183): 'Whereas the majority of Marxist economists believed in the advantages of concentration because such is the tendency of the capitalist mode of production, Chayanov maintained that horizontal concentration of production offered only limited advatages in agriculture. In an area of extensive cultivation where 2,000–8,000 hectares of grain land can be farmed with appropriate machinery, the optimal dimensions of productive units will not be the same as they are in a region of sugar-beet cultivation where the more intensive use of machines makes transport costs grow disproportionately beyond an optimum of 200–250 hectares. In other words, natural conditions themselves impose certain limits on the possibilities of a horizontal concentration. These difficulties disappear, however, for vertical integration: small farms can benefit from all the advantages of scale by using

all the contradictions of capitalism.[24] Critical of the neo-populist endorsement of agrarian cooperatives, he warned against their being regarded as a political panacea for the economic problems of poor peasants under capitalism.[25] In a similar vein, Preobrazhensky argued that not only did agrarian cooperatives possess no innate trend towards the socialization of petty commodity production, but also that in a capitalist system rich peasants would assert their control over the dynamic and direction of such units.[26] Although Lenin softened

---

the formula of cooperatives. That is why the competitive power of peasant farms versus capitalist farms or collective farms was much greater.'

24 For the capitalist role of cooperatives in German agriculture, see Lenin (1961a: 205ff.). Comparing the populist agrarian programme of the Socialist Revolutionaries to the revisionist views of Eduard David in Germany, Lenin (1964d: 422, 433) observed: 'All sorts of societies (co-operatives) and the communal purchase of land will always benefit the rich peasants most… Two basic ideas, and, correspondingly, two main points in the programme, run through the pattern of David's "work". He glorifies agricultural co-operatives, expecting all possible blessings from them, demanding that the [German] Social democrats help develop them, and (just like our Socialist Revolutionaries) failing to see the bourgeois nature of these alliances between petty proprietors and agrarian capitalists, big and small. David demands the conversion of large farms into small ones, and waxes enthusiastic over the profitableness and efficiency [of the latter].' For the endorsement of peasant cooperatives by David (and others) in their debate with Kautsky during the 1890s, see Hussain and Tribe (1984).

25 'It is deception,' Lenin (1964c: 205, 207) said of the Socialist-Revolutionaries' programme, 'to assert that "co-operatives of every kind" play a revolutionary role in present-day society and prepare the way for collectivism rather than strengthen the rural bourgeoisie… [t]heir conception of the path leading to socialism is peerlessly characterised by their substitution of the development of co-operatives for the class struggle. In their estimation of the present stage in the agrarian evolution of Russia, they have forgotten a trifle: the remnants of serf-ownership, which weigh so heavily on our countryside.'

26 Of producer cooperatives under capitalism, and the struggle in these contexts between rich and poor peasants, Preobrazhensky (1965: 219, 222) wrote: 'Under capitalism…cooperatives can exist only if they adapt themselves to the law of value…Since cooperatives can exist in capitalist society without in any way threatening its existence, this shows quite plainly that cooperation in itself contains no active principle of transformation in the direction of socialized production relations. The Utopians of cooperation affirmed the contrary, but were beaten by the entire practical experience of capitalism and of cooperation itself. […] If we strike a balance of the struggle between these two ways of organizing labour [the collective way and the private capitalist way], exclusively in the field of agricultural production…then we shall have to recognize the following. The state farms have until recently *contracted* their area to the advantage of petty production [while] the area of kulak and semi-kulak holdings has increased more rapidly. The reason is that the kulak holding, which grows organically out of scattered petty commodity production, has hitherto provided more opportunities for the organization of labour in agriculture on

his line on peasant cooperatives in the 1920s, Kritsman found both that farm members of cooperatives in Russia at that conjuncture were better-off peasants, and that exploitative relationships continued within and between peasant households, but remained hidden.[27]

For their part, both Trotsky and Luxemburg cautioned against underestimating the ability of petty commodity producers – in whatever institutional form they were organized – to put obstacles in the path of the socialization of the agrarian labour process.[28] It was precisely because of the risk of peasant counter-revolution designed to maintain (or expand) individual property rights that Trotsky advocated permanent revolution, or an immediate transition to socialism.[29] This same point was echoed by Luxemburg, who opposed

capitalist or semi-capitalist lines than the state economy has provided for the organization of labour on its lines. The balance can be changed not by some socialist miracles on the territory of petty peasant production, taken by itself, but only by a more profound influence of large-scale urban industry on peasant farming.' This is confirmed at roughly the same conjuncture by an exchange reported in the United States Senate Commission (1913: 843), when Captain L.A. Bryan, committee member of the Irish Agricultural Organization Society, answered questions about the political direction of farmer cooperatives in the following manner: 'Q. Does cooperation tend to socialism? A. No. Socialism does not do for society what cooperation does. In 1868 and 1869 the individuals took up cooperation as an antidote for socialism. Some socialists, however, make exceedingly good cooperators, not for that reason, but because they are both. Among our leading agricultural cooperators we have no one who professes to be a socialist. One is a voluntary organization, the other is compulsory.'

27 For the softening of views about peasant cooperatives in 1920s Russia, see Lenin (1966: 467–471). This optimism has to be offset by the findings of Kritsman (1984: 109, 140), who noted, more generally, that '[u]sury and trading capital are also interlinked, in that trading operations are, to a growing extent in rural life, connected with credit. Frequently usury and manufacturing capital are similarly interlinked. The widely dispersed phenomenon of advances of grain is accompanied by the unpaid "working off" on the farm of the lender. This is in effect a form of interest on the loan, although they would claim they make no profit out of it. There is a lack of recording of trading and especially usury capital.' This description might well be applied to the agrarian cooperative in La Convención examined below, where bonded labour relations linking rich and poor peasants were similarly 'hidden' within the kinship and fictive kinship domain.

28 See Luxemburg (1961) and Trotsky (1967). The latter (Trotsky, 1967: 131) observed that such a threat to the socialization of agriculture should not be interpreted as evidence for the superiority of smallholding cultivation (or peasant economy) over largescale production. It hardly seems necessary to point out that many of those now writing about the agrarian question in Latin America and elsewhere continue to do just this.

29 On this Trotsky (1962: 235) observed: 'The programme of the equal distribution of land thus presupposes the expropriation of all land…If we bear in mind that this expropriation

land seizures by petty commodity producers on the grounds that this created a new and powerful stratum of proprietors who would – with greater success than a small group of landlords – block further attempts to socialize the means of production in agriculture.[30] Unlike populists, such an outcome was seen by Marxists as an inevitable effect of class struggle within an agrarian cooperative structure.

Because Chayanov interpreted the peasant family farm in terms of unit where the social relations were those of kinship, however, he tended to overlook the extent to which such links were also ones of class.[31] The different

---

would have to be one of the first acts of the new [socialist] regime, while commodity-capitalist relations were still completely dominant, then we shall see that the first "victims" of this expropriation would be (or rather, would feel themselves to be) the peasantry. If we bear in mind that the peasant, during several decades, has paid the redemption money which should have converted the allocated land into his private property; if we bear in mind that some of the more well-to-do of the peasants have acquired – undoubtedly by making considerable sacrifices, borne by a still-existing generation – large tracts of land as private property, then it will be easily imagined what a tremendous resistance would be aroused by the attempt to convert communal and small-scale privately owned lands into state property.'

30 The accuracy of this prognosis – the reinforcement at the rural grassroots of ideas about individual ownership (= proprietor consciousness) would in the end undermine policies based on the co-ownership of land – was borne out by the Latin American agrarian reform programmes of the 1960s. As Jacques Chonchol (1972: 110), the Minister of Agriculture in the Chilean government of Salvador Allende, accepted, '[a] much more serious problem [facing socialists] is that, in general, the [persistence of private property in an agrarian cooperative] tends to perpetuate the image of the traditional farm in the peasant's mind. An agrarian reform process is not just a question of redistributing land, but should involve an entirely new conception of the economic and social organization of agricultural enterprises'.

31 Like many anthropologists, Chayanov – although an economist – focussed on the kinship domain as this affected the economic reproduction of the peasant household. He maintained that the logic driving the latter was demographic, in that the economically active members of peasant family farms worked only as hard (= 'drudgery of labour') as was necessary to reach the subsistence level for themselves and the unproductive components of the household (the very young, the very old). The resultant equilibrium, called by him the 'labour/consumer balance', was the driving force behind the reproduction of peasant economy. It was this, in the form of cyclical demographic mobility affecting peasant household personnel – not the process of class differentiation into rich, middle and poor strata – that structured the economy of the Russian countryside. Left to themselves, he argued, such peasant family farms would continue to function unabated, regardless of the wider economic system (feudalism, capitalism, socialism). For examples of the application by anthropologists either of an implicitly kinship-not-class model, or of an explicitly

components within such units stand in relation of ownership of and separation from means of production belonging not just to their own household but also other ones.[32] The fact that members of a peasant family work for and sell their own labour-power both to their own household head and also to other similar units in the vicinity was for Chayanov nothing more than proof for the economic dynamism/adaptability/flexibility of peasant economy.[33] In an important sense, therefore, it is unsurprising that these kind of transactions should also operate within the context of an agrarian cooperative, where they would have been interpreted by him in the same benign way.[34]

Thus the purchase and sale of peasant family labour-power inside a cooperative structure was for populism evidence of the viability of smallholding agriculture, rather than – as for Marxism – an indication of the socio-economic differentiation of the peasantry.[35] As the case study presented here confirms,

---

Chayanovian framework, to the analysis of rural Peru, see Orlov and Custred (1980) and Seligmann (1995).

32 Although a similar process is outlined by Moberg (1983) in the case of peasant cooperatives operating in Nicaragua during the early 1980s, the era of the Sandinistas, he sees the element of class consciousness that emerged from this process as positive. This is due in part to a failure to differentiate the peasantry, and consequently to equate 'peasant' with 'class' – an epistemological approach adopted also by populists.

33 That his approach was essentialist is evident from the fact that, when drawing up his typology of peasant farms in 1920s Russia, Chayanov (1991: 27) accepts that it 'took no account of the work inside and outside their villages and households'.

34 It is incorrect to argue, as does Jasny (1972: 200), that Chayanov rejected 'the need for production co-operatives'. What Chayanov objected to was not production cooperatives *per se*, but rather collective farms. All property on the latter notionally belongs to the state, which plans and closely directs cropping patterns, production generally and distribution; those who work in such contexts are, in terms of ownership rights landless, and in effect the employees of the state. By contrast, agrarian cooperatives retain within their ambit private holdings owned and operated by peasant proprietors who – although they participate in and have access to some economic resources in common – nevertheless remain independent cultivators: insofar as this entailed the continuation of peasant family farms, it was an arrangement of which Chayanov approved.

35 A belief in the supposed viability of smallholding agriculture, and a simultaneous overlooking of peasant differentiation, are reasons why a number of those wrongly regarded as Latin American socialist or Marxist theorists should more accurately be considered populists. This is particularly true of Hildebrando Castro Pozo (1936; 1947) and José Carlos Maríategui (1968), whose 1930s *indigenismo* was structured by idealized concepts of pre-Hispanic rural community. Their nationalist politics were based on a familiar populist opposition: between on the one hand a virtuous and ancient indigenous peasant economy based on subsistence cultivation and embodying traditional cultural values/practices, and on the other a malign feudal tenure imposed at the Spanish Conquest by an alien

class divisions within the peasantry not only surfaced inside the cooperative structure, but also defined the accumulation project on this sector. The economic direction followed was accordingly determined in a large part by a struggle – involving peasants, the state and agricultural workers – for control over the labour-power of non-owning kinsfolk resident on peasant family farms. An ability to maintain control, by means of the debt bondage mechanism (the *enganche* system), played an important role in deciding the economic reproduction of the agrarian cooperative.[36]

Powerful Peasants, Broken Bureaucrats

Examples from many different contexts in the so-called Third World indicate that the state has been not so much unwilling but unable to impose its will at the rural grassroots.[37] In Chiapas, therefore, the 1994 Zapatista movement

---

colonialism. Accordingly, for Castro Pozo (1947: 14) the economic logic of the pre-Hispanic Andean community – consisting of *minifundios* – was a system of authentically socialist peasant cooperation that would automatically flourish once 'foreign' landlordism and its form of tenure – the *latifundio* on which tenants paid labour-rent – had ceased ('*Los yanaconas conservan sus antiguas prácticas comunales, ellos en el futuro organizarán las cooperativas de producción convenientes*'). Elsewhere, in a section entitled 'Cooperativa Agricola Inicial', Castro Pozo (1936: 274–275) outlined the virtuous (and in his view incipiently socialist) connection between rural community (*ayllu*) and traditional forms of exchange labour (*minga*), despite the fact that in La Convención during the 1970s such 'traditional forms' hid what were actually exchanges between rich peasants of the labour-power of their unfree workers.

36 That unfree labour would continue to play an important economic role within agrarian cooperatives, and have an impact on the accumulation project within such units, was not recognized at the time. One commentator who came near to this, however, was Solon Barraclough. Musing on the link between tenure relations and the formation of a domestic market for consumer goods, he (Barraclough and Collarte, 1973: 30, 302–304 note 17) observed in passing that in the American south a century earlier the low purchasing power of plantation slaves had posed difficulties for the expansion of a mass market for domestic manufacturing, concluding that the 'analogy with the present development problem in much of Latin America is obvious.' Since he assumed that labour-rent owed a landlord was carried out by the tenant in person, the fact that the unfreedom which continued in the post-agrarian reform era was that linking ex-sub-tenants and migrant workers to ex-tenants was not something he addressed.

37 It should be emphasized that this inability on the part of the state to impose policy at the rural grassroots was doubly determined: by opposition not just from domestic capitalists (better-off peasants) but also from international capitalism (particularly as mediated through US foreign policy). The importance of the latter has always been central to the

gathered support in a rural context where the Mexican state was historically weak, not strong. Because of the virtual *laissez faire* policy adopted towards them over the years by the Mexican state, indigenous peasant communities were in effect politically autonomous.[38] Powerful landowners or commercial farmers in the northeastern Indian state of Bihar have succeeded in having bureaucrats transferred when the latter raise questions about bonded labour.[39] Similarly, policy differences between the local and central state in Burma/ Myanmar, and the way in which petty commodity producers cultivating rice play these different administrative levels off one against the other, underlines the extent to which low ranking bureaucrats are sometimes at the mercy of more powerful class elements in the countryside.[40]

Counterposing an undifferentiated agrarian bureaucracy to a similarly homogeneous peasantry is therefore wrong. While low-level bureaucrats are clearly at an advantage when dealing with poor peasants and agricultural labourers, this is not the case when they deal with rich peasants, merchants and/or large commercial farmers.[41] Those belonging to the latter category are economically powerful in their own right, and thus capable of blocking policies or proposals that threaten their own interests, or engineering the transfer

analyses of more perceptive commentators (e.g., Petras and LaPorte, 1971) on the fate of agrarian reform in Latin America. By contrast, neoclassical economists have tended to overlook this international dimension in their never-ending search for 'perfect markets'. Hence the apposite observation by Domike (1973: 57–58) about one such: '[A] redistribution of land as profound as that visualised [by a neoclassical economist] could only take place in a vastly different environment from today's. There is already enough black humour in the selection of the topic, without being forced to believe that the reforms could occur in some hermetically sealed political environment. The economist's assumption that all markets and institutions would stay as they are makes almost no sense historically, even though it permits him to make his model work.'

38 See van der Haar (2007).

39 This is recounted by Das (1979: 27) in the following manner: 'What turned out to be even more embarrassing for the Government [of Bihar, which had denied the existence of bonded labour] was the fact that the Deputy Commissioner of Palamau [District], on whom the Bonded Labour Abolition Act, 1975, put the responsibility of freeing and rehabilitating bonded labourers in his district, discovering the cases of 581 bonded labourers, some of whom had been enslaved for years for paltry debts… The erring Deputy Commissioner was transferred.'

40 See Thawnghmung (2003).

41 That relations between state officials and peasants are far from straightforwardly ones of domination/subordination is evident, for example, from a recent study (Nuijten, 2004) of complex relations between officialdom and peasants in western Mexico.

and even the removal from post of low-level bureaucrats who oppose them. Even when they wished to do so, therefore, junior officials have been unable to prevent better-off peasants in agrarian co-operatives from appropriating co-owned resources (land, technical inputs) and employing poor peasants as hired workers.[42] There are numerous historical instances, in Latin America and elsewhere, of internal appropriation or employment of landless labour effected by better-off rural producers.

From the early 1950s onwards, *ejido* land in the Laguna region of Mexico was worked by hired labour composed of the landless kin of *ejidatarios*; the former worked not only for (or instead of) the latter, but also for local landowners and industries.[43] Similarly, rural cooperatives in India during the late 1950s were managed by rich farmers for their own benefit; moreover, on such units the manual labour was undertaken by hired workers rather than the co-operative members themselves.[44] Petty commodity producers who were beneficiaries of the far-reaching agrarian reform programme carried out in Chile by Salvador

---

42 Gender was an additional form of socio-economic inequality that persisted within new institutional forms that were organized by the state following agrarian reform programmes in the so-called Third World. For examples of the way in which women continued to experience discrimination in the agrarian labour process of rural cooperatives in Mexico and China, see Isaac (1995) and Li (2005).

43 See Wilkie (1971), whose findings in this regard challenge earlier and more optimistic views about the Mexican *ejido* system (Simpson, 1937; Whetten, 1948: 215ff.).

44 See Thorner (1964; 1980: 168ff.). As outlined by Catanach (1970), the cooperative movement as a source of rural credit has a long history in India. From the 1920s onwards, cooperativization was seen by colonial administrators (Calvert, 1922; Darling, 1925, 1930, 1934, 1949; Brayne, 1929;) and agronomists (Mann, 1967) in India as a way of breaking the hold moneylenders had traditionally exercised over the rural economy, particularly in the agriculturally important region of Punjab. The assumption was that by providing smallholding peasants with institutional credit for improving cultivation, they would no longer have to depend on – and owe high interest debts to – village moneylenders. The result would be increases not only in economic growth but also in the wellbeing of petty commodity producers, and a corresponding decrease in peasant alienation and unrest. As Thorner and others demonstrated, however, because it failed to address the issue of class the mere fact of cooperativization did not solve the problem of debt and dependence in rural India after Independence. Much rather the opposite, since better-off cultivators used the loans they obtained from cooperative (and other institutional) sources in order to tighten their control (via the debt bondage mechanism) over the poor peasants and agricultural workers they employed. The same kind of pattern operated in the case of the agrarian cooperative in 1970s La Convención (see below).

Allende in the early 1970s refused to admit the landless labourers they employed to cooperative membership.[45]

In the case of China after 1976 and Russia after 1989, appropriation of common property was carried out by better-off producers, who – so as to pre-empt a looming privatization – opportunistically took over resources (mainly land) hitherto owned by the state and operated by the members of the agrarian collective.[46] Much the same happened in Cuba, where post-1989 the extension/consolidation of private property in land generally, the consolidation of ownership rights within cooperatives, the hiring by the latter of wage labour without property rights, labour market competition with peasant proprietors for workers, and the expansion of the black market all indicated a trend towards the privatization of agriculture.[47]

What all these instances suggest is that – even under socialism of one kind or another (Russia in the 1920s, Chile in the early 1970s, Cuba in the 1980s) – peasant cooperatives cannot be said to be subject to the overarching power of the state and its agencies. Contrary to the picture drawn in much of the development literature of an all-powerful state apparatus imposing its dictat on uniformly disempowered peasants, therefore, the dichotomy is much rather the opposite: a powerful group of peasants, among whom the better-off strata feature prominently, confronting – and frustrating the economic and political designs of – state bureaucrats.[48] This pattern is confirmed by the case study presented here, which illustrates how this struggle was played out in 1970s

45 On this point de Vylder (1976: 187) notes: 'The [agrarian cooperative] system was, of course, very advantageous to those workers and former sharecroppers who became members and who, in general, were quite reluctant to let other sectors of the rural proletariat enter the cooperatives and share all the benefits. New privileges and large differences in economic status were thus inevitable consequences of this new social stratification introduced on all [agrarian cooperative] settlements.' For a similar kind of response in the case of rural cooperatives in post-independence Algeria, see Clegg (1971: 52ff.).

46 On this process of internal appropriation, see Chossudovsky (1986: 42ff.) and Allina-Pisano (2005).

47 See Deere, Pérez and Gonzales (1994).

48 This, it should be emphasized, is not a vindication of the 'everyday forms of peasant resistance' approach. The latter counterposes an homogenous peasantry, the political objectives of which are perceived as benign, positive and progressive, against a malign state apparatus, drawn in correspondingly dark hues. As the case study presented below outlines, such a simplistic peasants = good versus state = bad polarity cannot explain two things. First, the fact that grassroots resistance is by better-off elements not opposed to capitalism but rather in furtherance of an accumulation project more to their liking. And second, that the state was interested in bringing poor peasants and landless workers into the agrarian cooperative structure, an objective that ill accords with the label 'malign'.

Peru, and examines the reasons advanced by the protagonists in this conflict for holdings the views and taking the positions they do.

Unlike the usual way of theorizing peasant/bureaucrat relationships, the analysis presented here of the agrarian reform agency of the Peruvian state and its organizational role in the development of a post-reform cooperative structure in the eastern lowlands seems to cast the bureaucracy in an heroic mould and the peasantry in an unheroic mould.[49] Accordingly, two interconnected theoretical points should be made clear from the outset. First, the struggle inside the cooperative structure between the agrarian reform agency and the peasant membership is one that involves different fractions of capital. And second, the supremacy of one or other of these different fractions itself possesses implications for the accumulation project to be followed.

The economic and politico-ideological dimensions of the struggle between the different fractions of capital are as follows. On the one hand, therefore, the accumulation project pursued by agency personnel acting on behalf of the reformist military government might be categorized as progressive insofar as it requires co-ownership of the means of production, improved productive forces, and a hired workforce consisting of free wage labour in receipt of minimum wages and social benefits.[50] In this situation capitalist development is correspondingly dependent on raising the purchasing power of a rapidly expanding rural proletariat, a combination that contributes to the emergence of institutional forms that prefigure socialism. It was perhaps the latter, together with the view that the agrarian reform programme embodied notions of social justice as well as increased productivity, which attracted some of the political activists who had previously fought against the landlord class.[51]

49 It might be objected that the case made here, about the ability of better-off peasants to frustrate the policy of what is the circumstances was a weak state bureaucracy, and how this in turn undermined the agrarian cooperative system in 1970s Peru, is done with the benefit of hindsight. This, however, is not the case. Many of the issues structuring this process – the role within the cooperative structure of class and rich peasants in particular, the continuation of unfree labour, and the privatization of cooperative land – have all been the subject of previous analyses. What is new – and presented here for the first time – are the views about this as expressed by those involved: bureaucrats, cooperative members, and agricultural workers.

50 Sorj (1977) and Fitzgerald (1983: 67ff.) regard this variant as state capitalism. For useful accounts of the tensions generated in Peru generally by agrarian cooperatives operating in a capitalist market, see Caballero (1980; 1981).

51 For example, in the case of La Convención outlined below, the Regional Chief of the agrarian reform agency was a kinsman to and espoused some of the political views held by Vladimiro Valer and Hugo Blanco, two activists who belonged to the Revolutionary Left Front

On the other hand, the accumulation project undertaken by rich, middle, and better-off poor peasants may be categorised as regressive in the sense that it was based on individualistic tenure relations, rudimentary technology, and a low-paid workforce deprived of the social wage and composed for the most part of unfree labour.[52] Here capitalist accumulation is less rapid and does not require a corresponding expansion in living standards of the workforce; furthermore, as regards economic structure and politico-ideological consciousness, it entails not so much proletarianization as the deproletarianisation of the workforce, a transformation linked to the operation in La Convención of the debt bondage mechanism (*enganche*). In short, capitalism which blocks the emergence of those socio-economic and political forms that prefigure (and thus enable a transition to) socialism.[53]

I

From Estate to Agrarian Cooperative: La Convención, 1969–75

In political terms, the 1969 Peruvian agrarian reform programme enacted by the military government of General Juan Alvarado Velasco is widely regarded

(*Frente de Izquierda Revolucionario*) and were prominent in the peasant movement of 1958–62. Hector Béjar, another militant who participated in the guerrilla movement of the mid-1960s (see Béjar, 1970), subsequently held executive office in the government agency for social mobilization (SINAMOS or *Sistema Nacional de Apoyo a la Movilización Social*).

52 Unfree labour was of two kinds: poor peasants who resided locally, and had been subtenants before the agrarian reform; and smallholding migrants from neighbouring provinces, who were recruited by labour contractors (*enganchadores*) for seasonal work in La Convención. Both involved the debt bondage mechanism, and workers recruited in this fashion were employed (on a permanent or seasonal basis) by peasant proprietors on their private holdings; those of the latter who were also members of the agrarian cooperative also deployed such forms of unfree labour-power onto this sector. That unfree labour still flourishes in the eastern lowlands of Peru is evident from the analysis by Bedoya Garland and Bedoya Silva-Santisteban (2005b).

53 This interpretation challenges that advanced by exponents of the semi-feudal thesis, who maintain wrongly that peasant capitalists represent the bourgeois democratic – or progressive – way in which the agrarian question is resolved. It is only in cases where capitalist development follows the reactionary Prussian form of agrarian transition (whereby landlords expropriated peasants), exponents of semi-feudalism hold, that unfree labour persists. For an example of this incorrect argument – that in Peruvian agriculture peonage is a precapitalist relation – see Korovkin (1990: 3, 22, 159 note 2).

as one of the three most progressive land redistributions carried out in Latin America.[54] A decade after the reform process, forty percent of the land in Peru had been expropriated, and reallocated to 35 percent of all rural families, most of it in largescale cooperative units.[55] Economically, however, the agrarian reform was deemed to have been less successful: although total agricultural output increased, particularly after 1968, in relative terms production failed to keep pace with population growth.[56] The decline of the reform programme in the mid-1970s was due both to external factors (the increasing cost of imported fertilizers, competition from foreign agribusiness enterprises) and to internal ones (the fiscal crisis of the Peruvian State).[57] Here it is intended to examine the inability of the Peruvian state to regulate the accumulation model on the

---

54 The other two were the agrarian reforms carried out by Castro in Cuba during the early 1960s, when some 60 percent of agricultural land was allocated to the reformed sector, and by Allende in Chile during the early 1970s, with 36 percent of agricultural land in the reformed sector (McLintock, 1981: 61, Table II.1). The role of agrarian reform in generating Latin American development at that conjuncture was set out succinctly in Barraclough and Collarte (1973: 146): 'In the first stages of industrialization, national enterprises have an already existing market for their manufactured goods that initially were supplied by imports. Once these markets are saturated, however, the emerging industry has to look for new ones. It is generally very difficult for small and new industry to complete effectively in the foreign market, a situation which leaves few alternatives other than widening the markets of domestic consumption. Otherwise, the growth of the industrial sector will reach its apex once import substitution possibilities have been exhausted. It is therefore necessary to achieve an income distribution which will allow the expansion of internal demand for the goods and services of the new modern sectors, if development is to continue without serious interruptions...this expansion of internal demand for goods of the national industries would be much easier if the *campesino* masses had a constantly increasing buying power.'

55 The outcome is summed up by Crabtree (2003: 138): 'The agrarian reform implemented by the military government in the 1970s changed the structure of landholding through the expropriation of landed estates and the reorganization of these into cooperatives of varying types. By providing land to those who had previously been landless, it represented a major step towards greater equity in the countryside. It also established new channels of participation.... As output levels dwindled in the years after the reform, pressure built up to change the model. In the late 1970s and early 1980s, the agrarian reform was abandoned and the process of dividing up the cooperatives began.'

56 Over the 1950–76 period there was a 2.7 percent increase in the population of Peru and only a 2.2 percent increase in agricultural output (Caballero, 1986: 8). For agricultural production indices over this period, see Thorp and Bertram (1978: 279, 315, Tables 13.13 and 15.5). As Caballero rightly points out, agricultural growth was regionally variable: output remained generally stagnant in the highlands, but expanded in both the west coast and eastern lowland areas of the country.

57 On this, see Caballero (1986).

cooperative structure in the reformed agrarian sector and the corresponding dismantling of the reform process from within by the peasantry.[58]

La Convención the northernmost province in the Department of Cusco, is located on the semi-tropical eastern slope of the Peruvian Andes. Although its inaccessible geographical situation prevented extensive colonization and settlement until the early twentieth century, the province has since the sixteenth century formed part of the Andean rural estate system (*latifundia*) imposed at the Spanish Conquest.[59] The area is ideal for the cultivation of valuable cash crops such as sugar, cocoa, coca, tea, and particularly coffee.[60] Prior to the expropriation of the landlord class in the 1969 agrarian reform, La Convención was characterized by socio-economic differentiation of the estate peasantry, as rich tenants extended the sown area devoted to coffee.[61]

---

58 This suggests that it is incorrect to claim, as does Korovkin (1990), that the main changes in the cooperative structure were due to the economic crisis of the 1980s, when the Peruvian state ceased to provide financial and other inputs. The case of the agrarian cooperative in La Convención – an area not mentioned by her – considered below indicate that the weakness of the Peruvian state was as much to do with internal factors (an inability to impose its accumulation project on peasants) as with external conditions emanating from the wider international capitalist economy.

59 Prior to the 1969 agrarian reform, rural estates in La Convención were among the largest in the whole of Peru, and the landlord class in the province not only intermarried but also combined agricultural and industrial economic activities, owning property in urban as well as rural areas (Valderrama and Ludmann, 1979; Mörner, 1991: 110–111, Figure 4.2).

60 See Cuadros (1949) and Tupayachi (1959). During the early part of this century, owners of these latifundia leased uncultivated plots to peasant migrants from the southern highlands, who thereby became tenants (*arrendires*) contributing a contractually-stipulated number of days labour-service on the landlord enterprise as rental. Before the 1940s labour-rent payments were low, and as the world market price for coffee rose during the 1950s, estate tenants possessing large holdings began to cultivate this crop and accumulate capital through its sale to local merchants (*rescatistas*). Landlords responded by increasing the amount of labour-rent payable by tenants, and the latter in turn leased a portion of their holdings to one or more sub-tenants (*allegados*), who henceforth discharged the labour-service obligations owed to the landlord.

61 This period was also marked by an increasingly acute struggle between the latter and their landlords over the ownership and control of land and labour on the estate system, The conflict culminated in the peasant movement of 1958–62, as attempts by landlords to raise labour-rent or evict tenants was met with the growth of peasant unions, land invasions, a general strike throughout the province, the organization and repression of guerrilla activity, and finally the expropriation of the landlord class. For the details of this struggle, see MacLean y Estenós (1965), Villanueva (1967), Neira (1968), Craig (1969), Gott (1970), Blanco (1972), Fioravanti (1974) and Brass (1989a).

The antecedents of the conflict with the state agrarian reform agency (ONRA or *Oficina Nacional de Reforma Agraria*) are located in the events of the 1960s.[62] During this period agrarian reform agency functionaries occupied a contradictory position in the class struggle, and were thus the object of political opposition from both the landlords and peasants: the former accused ONRA of failing to prevent union organization, arguing that the state sought the political support of smallholders, while the latter accused ONRA of supporting the landlord class by failing to expropriate it, as well as not providing technical, financial, and other infrastructural inputs to peasant production.[63] In an important sense, therefore, the elimination of the landlord class at the end of the 1960s and the beginnings of the 1970s focussed union hostility solely on what was from the viewpoint of its peasant constituents the negative function of ONRA: the nonprovision by the latter of new means of production, and its attempt to exercise control over the existing productive forces on (and hence the accumulation project of) the cooperative sector in the ex-estate system in the province.[64]

In La Convención, as in many other areas of Peru, the 1969 agrarian reform merely conferred private property rights to existing holdings, and did not attempt a redistribution of land and other economic assets. The result was that erstwhile tenants with large holdings, *de facto* rich peasants in the pre-reform era, were confirmed as such by the agrarian reform programme. The same was true of middle and poor peasants, whose usufruct rights to tenancies and subtenancies were converted into ownership. By expropriating only the landlord class, therefore, the state left the rest of the pre-reform rural class structure

62 ONRA grew out of the Institute for Agrarian Reform and Settlement (IRAC or *Instituto de Reforma Agraria y Colonización*), which was itself set up by the Peruvian state in the early 1960s to oversee land reform in La Convención and provide the peasantry there with technical assistance.

63 See Neira (1968: 114ff.) and Alfaro and Ore (n.d.: 34–37, 108–113). The acceptability of agrarian cooperatives to those on the right of the political spectrum is evident from the fact that, in Peru during the mid-1940s, even an agronomist who advised the landlords' association – the *Sociedad Nacional Agraria* – endorsed them as a means of improving both the output by and the livelihood of petty commodity producers. See Klinge (1946: 346ff.). In his opinion (Klinge, 1946: 350), peasants cannot but benefit from agrarian cooperatives (*'En las condiciones modernas de la economía mundial las cooperativas son indispensables para la existencia del pequeño productor y para una distribución mas equitativa de la renta nacional…'*, etc.).

64 For evidence of widespread peasant opposition to ONRA in La Convención during this period, see Trias (1975: 18–28).

intact; the inequality that existed was in effect shifted forwards, and now operated within the new agrarian production cooperatives.

As elsewhere at that conjuncture, agricultural labourers were not among the beneficiaries of this process; together with poor peasants, it was assumed, they would gain from being incorporated into agrarian cooperatives formed from land and assets expropriated from the landlord class. In the latter context, it was argued by supporters of the agrarian reform, the most vulnerable family farmers (*minifundistas*) with insufficient private holdings – those with less than five hectares – would not only have access to additional land and resources of which they were henceforth co-owning members, but also retain the whole surplus product generated by the deployment on this common property sector of their personal labour-power.[65]

The irony is that, in the case of La Convención during the early 1970s, it was these peasants – especially those with privately owned plots under 1.5 hectares in size – that were precisely the first ones to be expelled from cooperative membership for non-fulfilment of the statutory labour requirement.[66] A failure to meet the latter was due partly to the fact that their personal labour-power – which it was assumed such poor peasants would freely deploy onto the cooperative sector – had in fact been acquired by rich and middle peasants through the debt bondage mechanism. Some of these poor peasants did work on the cooperative land, but as unfree labourers deployed there by rich and middle peasant kinsfolk who employed them as substitute workers on the agrarian cooperative.

The agrarian cooperative in question was situated two kilometres outside the provincial capital Quillabamba, and covered an area of 946 hectares divided between two distinct but interrelated sectors of production.[67]

65 On this, see MacLean y Estenós (1965: 77).

66 This suggests that it is incorrect to argue, as does Caballero (1980: 93, note 19), that due to an excess membership, coupled with an unwillingness of members to expel one another, agrarian cooperatives in Peru at this conjuncture were unprofitable.

67 Although the case study presented here refers to one particular agrarian cooperative in the province during the early 1970s, the analysis is backed up by evidence from sources (Kapsoli *et al.*, 1974; Huizer, 1983b) which suggest that it applies equally to other agrarian cooperatives in La Convención at that conjuncture. Hence the description by Huizer of the impact of a differentiated peasant membership on the cooperative structure confirms the argument made here. '[A] serious problem within the [agrarian cooperatives]', he says (Huizer, 1983b: 29), 'was the internal differentiation between rich, middle and a majority of poor farmers, and the fact that the leadership of these [cooperatives] was generally in the hands of the rich or the middle farmers or those poor ones who aspired to become so. This differentiation considerably interfered with the cooperative spirit which is needed

The landlord (later the cooperative) sector, which consisted not only of 54 hectares of best irrigated flat land (*pampa* or *playa*) on the estate, but also of extensive infrastructural development (irrigation canals, two estate houses, milking and cattle sheds, storage facilities), livestock and machinery. Work on this sector, under the supervision of an overseer in the pre-reform era and a peasant member in the 1970s, is illustrated in Figure 1.

The peasant sector consisted of the remaining 717 hectares of hilly and less fertile land (*terreno accidentado*), on which was located the many plots of differing sizes sublet by the landlord to peasant smallholders who, as tenants or sub-tenants, paid various forms and amounts of rent in the period before the agrarian reforms of the 1960s. After the peasant movement of the late 1950s, tenants and sub-tenants on this particular estate, like those on the estates throughout the rest of La Convencion, became owners of their individual

FIGURE 1 *Working on the landlord sector, La Convención (Peru), c. 1950*
© TOM BRASS.

to make [such units] a success.' Earlier still, Petras and LaPorte (1971: 111) made much the same point about agrarian cooperatives in the province, observing that 'while the great landowners have been eliminated, the cooperatives have run into the problem of a defective social structure based on the old inequalities with respect to [tenants and sub-tenants], who were employed by the [tenants] to do some of their work. This pattern of social stratification has not only caused new social tensions but these conflicts have been interjected into the operation of the [peasant] trade unions and the cooperatives.'

FIGURE 2 *Drying Coca leaves on the peasant sector, La Convención (Peru), c. 1975*
© TOM BRASS.

landholdings. The work of drying the harvest of coca leaves in the courtyard of a peasant holding on this sector is illustrated in Figure 2.

In 1972 the landlord sector on this estate was expropriated and converted into a production cooperative (*comité de producción*). Of the 150 proprietors who had previously been tenants or sub-tenants, and who now owned land varying between 0.l2 of a hectare and 36 hectares in size, one third became members (*socios*) of the cooperative. These not only owned individual holdings on the peasant sector of the ex-estate but also henceforth co-owned means of production on the cooperative itself. In exchange for these co-ownership rights, however, each peasant member was contractually obliged to fulfil the statutory labour requirement (*aportación*): that is, to contribute personally two working days of labour per week on the cooperative, failure to do so – referred to as being *incumplimiento* – resulting in expulsion from the membership. In order to avoid this sanction, and also to profit from the inter-sectoral wage difference, many peasant members began to employ substitute labour.[68]

68 The ability of peasants belonging to the membership to appropriate a portion of the wage paid to agricultural workers on the cooperative stemmed from the wage difference between the peasant and the cooperative sector. Hence peasant members redeployed labourers from their own private landholdings, where daily payment was less than half that

Accordingly, the 1973–5 period was characterized by conflict within a membership composed of rich, middle, and poor peasant members for access to and control over labour-power, since this meant a corresponding ability to fulfil work conditions owed to the agrarian cooperative, the reproduction of member status, and thus continuing enjoyment of the economic resources conferred by the latter.[69] It was a struggle that involved the enforcement by rich and middle peasants of debt servicing labour obligations incurred by subordinate actual/fictive kinsfolk, a process effected through the invocation of the ties and obligations of co-parenthood (*compadrazgo*).[70] Converted from free to unfree labour by the debt bondage mechanism, poor peasants and landless workers who constituted these actual/fictive kin were as a result either prevented from seeking, or availing themselves of, higher wages available on the cooperative sector.[71] This was a struggle in which ONRA bureaucrats played a crucial part.

II

Peasants against Bureaucrats: The Theory

Much of the writing on relations between peasants and bureaucrats in post-reform Peruvian agriculture in general and the cooperative structure in particular operates – either explicitly or implicitly – with a model based on the dichotomy powerful-bureaucrats/weak-peasants in which the former

---

received on the cooperative sector, onto the latter context. When payment for every unit of labour-power supplied by each peasant member was made at the end of the year, those who had redeployed their own workers (or actual/fictive kinsfolk) in this manner reaped the benefit of this inter-sectoral wage difference.

69 Each proprietor on the ex-estate was classified as a rich, middle, or poor peasant on the basis of ex-tenant or ex-sub-tenant status together with the quantity, quality, and productivity of land owned. This last element was significant in differentiating the peasantry because of its crucial rôle in the cultivation of coffee, the most profitable cash crop grown on the peasant enterprise in the province.

70 The details of this process, and an explanation as to why such politico-ideological authority was so effective, are outlined in Brass (1986b).

71 As already noted, when the labour-power of these poor peasants and landless workers did appear on the cooperative sector, it was as a result of being deployed there by rich and middle peasant members. In short, because it was unfree, this labour-power was commodified by someone other than its owner.

are uniformly active ('those-who-do-things') and dominant while the latter are uniformly passive ('those-to-whom-things-are-done') and subordinate.[72] This simple polarity has been criticized by Long, who identifies three different approaches to the issue of state intervention in Latin American agrarian development: the capital-logic/commoditization model, the incorporation model, and the actor-oriented model.[73]

There are, however, two basic problems with this framework. First, there is essentially no difference between the capital-logic and incorporation models, insofar as commodification requires some degree of institutional incorporation, and vice versa. Moreover, both models adhere to the same top-downwards approach in which an adamantine state apparatus confronts (and limits the autonomy of) rural smallholders, a methodology which in turn reproduces the powerful-bureaucrats/weak-peasants dichotomy.[74] And second, the actor-oriented model favoured by Long himself is intrinsically a methodological approach to, rather than a theory about, relations between peasants and bureaucrats.[75]

In contrast to the other models, therefore, its bottom-upwards approach as embodied in decision-making and network analysis (subject ↔ state) tends to over-emphasize the determinacy of human agency, and thus runs the risk of voluntarism. Although he is correct to observe that macro-level agrarian

---

72 See, for example, MacLean y Estenós (1965), Isbell (1978), Guillet (1981), Shoemaker (1981), Valderamma (1982: 242ff.), and Figueroa (1984). The following assessment (Skar, 1982: 61) of cooperative assemblies in rural Peru is perhaps typical: 'The idea of democracy by vote…is a fairly new concept for the Indians. Voting procedures in the cooperative are criticized as simply being complicated devices by which the administrator or the government can attain their own goals. In many instances this is a fairly accurate interpretation of the situation.'

73 See Long (1988).

74 See, for example, Arce and Long (1993) in the case of peasant/bureaucrat linkages in Mexico. As is clear from the list of interviewees contained in the Appendix, this is also largely true of the methodological approach to peasant/bureaucrat relations in Peru utilized by Cleaves and Scurrah (1980: 291–297). They adopt a tripartite variant of the incorporation model (centralist/corporatist/liberal), which focuses principally on the character of the bureaucratic goals as regards the agrarian reform process (Cleaves and Scurrah, 1980: Chapter 7).

75 This point is conceded by Long (1989: 2), where he accepts that on the subject of peasant/bureaucrat relations '[i]nterface analysis…is essentially a methodological device for studying linkage structures and processes'. For a similarly atheoretical methodological approach to peasant/bureaucrat relations in a Peruvian agrarian cooperative at this conjuncture, see Alderson-Smith (1976). For an example of the same kind of populist 'farmer-knowledge-is-best' methodological approach, which ignores the fact that not all peasant farmers are the same in socio-economic terms, see Richards (2004).

policies are transformed at the micro-level, no reference is made to the way in which class formation and struggle influence and structure peasant/bureaucrat exchanges at the grassroots (subject ↔ class ↔ state).[76] Notwithstanding the useful points made by Long, therefore, his framework still lacks a theoretical as distinct from a methodological synthesis.

The difficulty with the powerful-bureaucrats/weak-peasants view is that it overlooks significant differences within both the peasantry and the bureaucracy. In the case of the latter, for example important institutional and locational distinctions exist which enable better-off peasants to express antagonism against those ONRA functionaries operating at the point of production in the cooperative labour process, who are not only the most subordinate but also the most immediately accessible agents of the state.[77]

By contrast, some anthropologists tend to regard this exposed position on the part of subordinate ONRA personnel at the point of production as a source not of vulnerability but rather of strength. Hence the following view:[78]

> The [ONRA] expert has control of rationality and so controls decisions within the participation process...Thus participation creates a more subtle form of dependence in which peasants are given the forms of power – rubber-stamping bureaucratic decisions – without the instruments.

A further observation from the same source informs that

> it was noticeable throughout *the short course* that peasants were only allowed to participate in any true sense when the decisions to be made were of a trivial nature – such as choosing the name of the Cooperative. When it had come earlier to a decision of such an important nature as

76 Because he excludes class from peasant/bureaucrat relations, Long (1988: 122) misrecognizes the reason for bureaucratic inactivity when confronted with privatization of collective land. Instead of wishing to oppose this, yet being powerless to do so, Mexican government officials are assumed to 'turn a blind eye' in such circumstances, and thus to condone this form of peasant appropriation.

77 The existence and political importance of intra-institutional differences is recognized by Long (1988: 117) but ignored by Cleaves and Scurrah (1980: 220ff.). In the case study presented below, functionaries such as the Sub-Director of the ONRA Departmental office in Cusco and the Chief of the ONRA Regional Office in Quillabamba were classified as high ranking bureaucrats. In terms of the area under his control and subordinate position to these two officials, the Coordinator of the local ONRA District office constituted a middle ranking functionary, while the Area Technician corresponded to the most junior position in the ONRA hierarchy.

78 See Conlin (1974: 31, 32, 33).

> whether or not a Cooperative should be formed at all from the various estates, pressure was applied by [ONRA] to bring about the desired decision (emphasis added).[79]

Superficially, the relationship between ONRA bureaucrats and the co-owning peasant membership of the cooperative in La Convención is similar, as the following three incidents (appear to) confirm.

Three Episodes

The first episode concerns events which took place during a drinking session at the old estate house on the evening of 6 November 1974 to celebrate a qualification awarded to the ONRA Area Technician (*sectorista*) attached to the cooperative.[80] When in the course of this prolonged drinking session, a peasant member 'insulted' the ONRA Area Technician by questioning his newly acquired title, the latter subject squared up to the former and challenged him to state that he (the peasant) was 'superior' (*¿Es usted mas hombre que yo? ¡Dimelo en frente!*).[81] A fight was narrowly avoided by the intervention of

79 Based on 1970s fieldwork in an agrarian cooperative just outside the city of Cusco in the Peruvian highlands, the study by Conlin (1974) is concerned with the way in which participation in the decision-making process by ONRA functionaries and peasants results in the dominance of the latter by the former. His approach, however, is structured by a twofold misrecognition that is common (see, for example, van den Berghe and Primov, 1977). Thus Conlin's presentation is structured by a concept of difference based not on class but ethnicity. ONRA functionaries are categorized simply in terms of mixed descent (*mestizos*) and peasants as indigenous (*indios*). The 'dominance' of ONRA functionaries in an *ethnic* hierarchy is transformed unproblematically into a corresponding position of *political* dominance. A second misrecognition stems from Conlin's synchronic method, the focus of which is on decontextualized incidents. When events that appear to support the notion of ONRA domination are located in a much larger process of struggle, the political relation that emerges is as likely to be one of political dominance over – rather than by – ONRA (see below).

80 The examination of the politico-ideological aspects of peasant/bureaucrat relations presented below is based on two sources in particular. First, materials compiled from data contained in the agrarian cooperative assembly meeting minute book (*libro de actas*) for 1972–75. And second, information obtained in the course of fieldwork itself. The presentation involves the theoretical dissection of verbal exchanges occurring within specific incidents/events at which the writer was present combined with a consideration of the discourse structuring particular issues over an extended period.

81 For the significance in La Convención at this conjuncture of beer drinking groups as *loci* where political discussions took place, and where decisions were taken about important aspects of policy affecting the operation of the agrarian cooperative, see Brass (1989b).

another peasant member, who both restrained and extracted a public retraction from the offender.

The second episode took the form of a public celebration in December the same year, on the occasion of the second anniversary of the formation of the cooperative, an event attended by the chief of the regional office of ONRA, an important and powerful local bureaucrat. After the formal ceremony of swearing-in (*juramentación*) officeholders recently elected to posts on the executive council of the cooperative, the participants sat down to the midday meal. The Regional Chief of ONRA occupied the seat of honour among the principal officeholders of the cooperative at the top table, and was served first. During the meal itself, he announced (to much applause) that he would sponsor the forthcoming football match by awarding a crate of beer to the winning team, and at the end of the meal both the ONRA personnel and the assembled peasant membership toasted each other in champagne purchased especially for the occasion.[82]

Watched by a crowd of spectators in the midst of whom was the ONRA Regional Chief, the football match between teams of peasants and workers who resided in different areas of the ex-estate took place shortly after the meal had finished.[83] When the match ended, drinking and dancing continued inside the courtyard of the new estate house until late at night. Called upon frequently to dance with the women present, an increasingly inebriated ONRA Regional

82 After undertaking to sponsor the football match, the ONRA Regional Chief immediately informed those at his table that this would be more expensive than the cost of purchasing a similar meal. By indicating that in providing a crate of beer he would outspend what he had consumed (and what had been provided for him by the hosts), the ONRA Regional Chief specified the material basis of the exchange, thereby emphasizing his own – or ONRA's – contribution and simultaneously devaluing that of the peasant membership.

83 Although this episode is presented here to illustrate the concept of ONRA 'domination', it is nevertheless the case that one particular aspect reveals the opposite tendency (ONRA domination by peasant members). Despite the fact that his skill at football was considerably less than that of the other players on both teams, the ONRA Area Technician – the most junior of the bureaucrats at the anniversary celebration – was the only possessor of a complete football kit (shirt, socks, shorts, and most importantly boots). Many peasant members of the agrarian cooperative who were among the spectators shouted loud critical comments, contrasting the professional footballing appearance of the ONRA functionary with his poor footballing performance. Significantly, much of this criticism was aimed not at the hapless ONRA Area Technician playing in the match but at the watching ONRA Regional Chief. This very public display of antagonism on the part of the peasant membership present operated as a metaphor for the contrast between the *appearance* of ONRA bureaucrats as 'professional' agronomists and the lack of agricultural skills when it came to their *performance* in the fields of the cooperative (about which more below).

Chief protested loudly (i.e. publicly) that this was only because he was a bourgeois (*porque soy burgués, nomas*) and announced finally that it was necessary for him to depart because he would have to be at work early next day.

The final episode concerns an unannounced visit to the cooperative by the same ONRA Regional Chief, who had come to congratulate the peasant members on the successful formation and operation of an enterprise to market their crops. On this occasion, the sudden and unexpected appearance of a high rankng ONRA bureaucrat (the affective nature of his mission notwithstanding) had a perceptibly unsettling effect on those taking part in a drinking group during the early afternoon (when they should have been working), and on two people in particular: a rich peasant member and the ONRA Area Technician.

The departure of the ONRA Regional Chief after a brief stay signalled an intensive round of self-justification on the part of the drinking group participants. The rich peasant asserted that, although he ought to have been in the fields of the cooperative supervising the labourers, it was necessary for him to undertake the sale/purchase of coca in the adjacent store because another peasant who should have been doing this had not turned up. In a similar vein the ONRA Area Technician pointed out to the other participants that as he was on vacation he had a right to be drinking at this time, adding that 'the Coordinator of the district office [his immediate superior] will soon be promoted due to my hard work.'

At first glance these three incidents seem to support the concept of ONRA 'domination' over the peasant membership of the agrarian cooperative, albeit in a double form: an explicitly coercive element of power in the first and last episodes, and a more diffuse (but nonetheless real) form of control exercised over the celebration proceedings in the second. Moreover, the latter also appears to support the notion of a politico-ideological hierarchy composed of a dominant ONRA and a dominated peasantry, a discursive opposition embodied in the self-identification by the ONRA Regional Chief as 'bourgeois', which implies that peasant members at the anniversary celebrations are correspondingly 'non-bourgeois'. There are, however, a number of discrepancies in this all-embracing polarity between dominant ONRA bureaucrats on the one hand and a subordinate peasantry on the other

The first concerns the sponsorship of the football match by the ONRA Regional Chief. If ONRA personnel are indeed dominant and politically all-powerful in the agrarian cooperative, then why is it necessary for a senior bureaucrat not merely to undertake this kind of sponsorship but also to ensure that peasant members are made aware of its materially non-reciprocal basis?[84]

---

84 It could of course be argued that, insofar as it corresponds to a show of power, sponsorship is itself part of the domination exerted by ONRA over the peasant membership.

As confirmed by the financial costs and politico-ideological objectives of religious officeholding in the *fiesta* system of La Convención, sponsorship undertaken by ONRA functionaries and other 'outsiders' (e.g., merchants) can only be understood as part a more general attempt to secure either the political or economic support of the peasant membership.[85] In the case of ONRA, sponsorship constitutes an attempt to obtain membership backing in the conflict with the peasant union while at the same time engaged in struggle with the former for control over the accumulation project on the cooperative.

The second discrepancy takes the form of the subordinate (or dominated) position of the ONRA Area Technician in two of the three episodes: in relation to the membership/spectators in the second, and to the sudden appearance of a high ranking ONRA bureaucrat in the third. Both the latter point to the existence of differences within ONRA, which in turn suggest that the fissures which transect formal institutional alignments are at least as important in determining the modalities of politico-ideological struggle as the conflict deriving from the ONRA/peasantry distinction.[86]

III

Peasants against Bureaucrats: The Practice

These discrepancies indicate that, while in the course of numerous day-to-day individual interactions/confrontation ONRA might indeed be described as exercising dominance over peasant members of the agrarian cooperative, the

---

In this particular context, however, sponsorship is not so much a display of strength (which neither seeks nor requires any response except recognition) as an endeavour to incur an obligation which must be returned at a later date. The explicit reference by the ONRA Regional Chief not just to the monetary value of his sponsorship of the football match but – more importantly – to the fact that it cost him more than the meal he received in exchange constituted an attempt on his part to establish just such a debt.

85 For the costs of *fiesta* sponsorship in La Convención during the pre- and post-reform era, plus the reasons for and impact of the changes that occurred, see Brass (1986a). The main religious officeholder during the 1975 *fiesta* celebrations in the agrarian cooperative was a middle ranking ONRA functionary, the Coordinator for the local district.

86 This point was confirmed by the ONRA Area Technician, who noted that high ranking bureaucrats in the same organization blamed middle and low ranking functionaries (such as himself) when planning schedules and targets on the agrarian cooperative were not adhered to or fulfilled.

totality of the relationship (in temporal terms the process) as distinct from the parts (or moments) suggests the opposite: a *process* whereby peasants exercise dominance over ONRA.

Since the view of ONRA dominance structured by a methodological approach which focuses on individual actions of decontextualized subjects is clearly inadequate, it is necessary to consider the balance of political power which emerges not from isolated instances but rather from a process of struggle (linking its different and sometimes contradictory moments) between ONRA and the peasant membership for control over the means of production on and the economic direction of the cooperative. This involves looking at conflict over three issues in particular: the forces of production (the loan for the purchase of new livestock and a tractor); the social division of labour (the non-fulfilment of the statutory labour requirement and the question of competence/non-competence in the labour process); and the production relation on this sector of the ex-estate (the payment of the agrarian debt, privatization/cooperativization).

The Loan for the Purchase of Livestock and a Tractor

During the meeting of the cooperative general assembly on 24 April 1973, peasant members agreed to request a loan of 1.4 million *Soles* from the state so as to renovate the infrastructure and purchase new means of production.[87] Both the Regional Chief and District Coordinator of ONRA attended the subsequent meeting on 3 August and responded favourably to this request, indicating that as ONRA now had funds at its disposal credit would be extended to the cooperative. In the course of another assembly meeting on 18 August, however, the District Coordinator adopted a less encouraging position, and withdrew the earlier undertaking by ONRA regarding the availability of the loan.

He pointed out that it had been delayed because inquorate assemblies due to non-attending members had prevented the Ministry of Agriculture from considering the request. When questioned about the same issue at a subsequent meeting on 9 January 1974, the ONRA District Coordinator replied: 'I have only just returned from my holidays. We are carrying out a feasibility study in relation to the loan, and this is not easy where livestock are concerned. We still know nothing.' (*yo recien llegue de mis vacaciones. El préstamo agropecuario estamos haciendo un studio, y no es fácil sobre el ganado. Nada todavía sabemos*). In the meeting of 6 March he was questioned again about the non-appearance of the loan, and answered in a similar fashion.

87 All prices are expressed in terms of 1975 Peruvian Soles (S/.). At the time of fieldwork, the exchange rate was approximately S/.100 = £1 Sterling.

By June the same year, two incidents revealed the extent to which the respective positions on this issue had been transformed. The first occurred during the general assembly meeting of 11 June, when the ONRA District Coordinator advised the agrarian cooperative to purchase new high-quality livestock from the agricultural fair in Huancaro; the peasant membership rejected this on the grounds that external (or ONRA) funds were unavailable and that there was insufficient internally-generated (or cooperative) capital. The second incident took place shortly afterwards, when in the course of the following general assembly meeting on 18 June a middle peasant member launched a fierce verbal attack on ONRA for the way in which it had mishandled the loan. He not only accused ONRA of 'deceiving' the membership over this issue, but also stated that the Regional Chief was 'spreading lies' about the cooperative to the Provincial Federation of Peasant Unions.[88]

Non-fulfilment of the Statutory Labour Requirement

Frequent references were made by ONRA bureaucrats of all ranks to another important issue: the non-fulfilment by peasant members of the agrarian cooperative of the statutory labour requirement. This was raised by the ONRA Sub-Director for the Department of Cusco during his address to the general assembly meeting of 3 August 1973, when he observed that to officials like himself it appeared that peasants seemed unwilling to work the estates which had been expropriated specially for their benefit (*los campesinos no querian trabajar después que sea expropiada los fundos*). The same issue was referred to in the following meeting on 18 August by the ONRA District Coordinator, albeit in a different form: inquorate assemblies as a consequence of non-attendance. He returned to this theme in the meeting of 5 March 1974, when the same ONRA functionary suggested that the labour deficit resulting from the non-completion of the statutory labour requirement should be made

88 The antagonism felt by members of the agrarian cooperative towards ONRA in general and its Regional Chief in particular over this issue was doubly structured. First, because of the 'deceit' practiced by ONRA in reneging on an original undertaking to provide the loan. And second, because when a high ranking ONRA bureaucrat then reported this about-turn to the Provincial federation of Peasant Unions, blame for the policy reversal was transferred from ONRA to the peasant membership of the agrarian cooperative. In the eyes of the cooperative members, therefore, the duplicity over the loan was thereby compounded: not only by shifting the blame in this manner, but also by seeking to gain support for this policy reversal from what was regarded by them – many peasants belonging to the cooperative were or had been union members/delegates/militants – as their own organization.

up in the form of workers brought in from outside the cooperative specifically to meet the shortfall.

The most acrimonious intervention by ONRA on this issue, however, took place in the course of the general assembly meeting convened on 21 May, when both a high ranking ONRA bureaucrat visiting from Lima and the Regional Chief directed critical remarks at the cooperative membership. The former pointed out that work was not being done, that the cooperative land which was irrigated and of good quality had been handed over to be worked, that if the peasant membership did not wish to work it they should say so, and (finally) did the membership wish to see the return of the landlord class. In a similar vein, the ONRA Regional Chief commented that as members were unwilling to descend from their private landholdings to carry out their statutory labour requirement on the cooperative sector, work in the latter context was 'mounting up'. He concluded by asking how, if cooperative members did not complete their work schedules, 'is [the instalment of the agrarian debt] going to be paid annually each June?' (*¿con que se va a pagar del interes del terreno en Junio annualmente?*).[89]

Given its centrality to member status, it is unsurprising that competition for and control over labour-power of actual and fictive kinsfolk, with which to meet the statutory labour requirement, was itself a source of enduring antagonism. Accordingly, expressions of hostility over access to workers were a constant feature of verbal exchanges between poor and rich peasant members. Thus one poor peasant member publicly teased two cooperative members – a middle and rich peasant – about over the debt bonded kinsfolk they employed as workers, describing the latter as 'slaves' (*esclavos*). This hostility came to a head when in December 1974 the same poor peasant member resigned from his cooperative post, citing as a reason the fact that 'I have no labourers nor do I wish to exploit' ('*no tengo peones ni quiero explotar*'). This view was expressed by him in a letter sent to a rich peasant, a member of the cooperative who employed unfree workers not just on his private holdings but also as substitute labour on the cooperative sector.[90]

---

89 Expulsion from membership of the agrarian cooperative of peasants who failed to meet their labour requirement was not of itself determined by these interventions. On both these occasions the issue of expulsion was already on the agenda for consideration – hence the presence of ONRA bureaucrats in the first place – and was therefore not introduced by the latter. They nevertheless commented on the relatedness of expulsion from the agrarian cooperative and the non-completion of the statutory labour requirement when this particular agenda item was discussed.

90 Although an attempt had been made by its author to erase the final part of this letter ('... nor do I wish to exploit'), it remained legible. The inference was not lost on its recipient, the rich peasant, who expressed anger at its content.

Competence/Non-competence in the Agrarian Labour Process

The issue of competence/non-competence in the agrarian labour process of the cooperative sector, and the allocation of blame for crop failures and livestock deaths, by its very nature involved conflict between the peasant membership and Area Technicians. The latter not only constituted the most subordinate functionaries in the ONRA hierarchy but – unlike middle and high ranking bureaucrats – also operated on a more-or-less continuous basis at the point of production, and could therefore be depicted by the peasant membership as directly responsible for any shortcomings that occurred.

The contradictory position of the ONRA Area Technician as regards this particular issue can be illustrated by two points raised in the course of the general assembly meeting on 5 March 1974. Whereas the first concerned absence, the second involved presence. On the first point, therefore, peasant members complained that their own cooperative sector was adversely affected because the Area Technician was in charge of other local agrarian cooperatives as well. As regards the second, when the peasant who held the post of Secretary on the political executive of the cooperative requested roomspace in order to carry out his official duties, he was instructed by the membership to share the room in the new estate house currently allocated to the ONRA Area Technician.

During the meeting of 20 July, however, this political officeholder informed the peasant members that he was being prevented from discharging his duties by the ONRA Area Technician who had told him 'we cannot both work in a single room' (*no podemos trabajar los dos en una sola habitación*). Accordingly, it was agreed by a majority vote that the Area Technician who 'gets on with his paperwork and doesn't concern himself with the work of the cooperative' (*el técnico hace sus papeles i no se preocupa del trabajo del comité*) should vacate the room and hand it over to the officeholding peasant.

On this same occasion another peasant officeholder was strongly critical of the ONRA Area Technician, blaming him for the 'forsaken' condition of the livestock and the lack of general economic progress on the cooperative sector (*el comité esta abandonado, los trabajos y los ganados a falta de dirección técnica, que el técnico no controla como debe ser*). The peasant officeholder then praised the good work of the previous ONRA Area Technician, under whose guidance a fine tomato crop had been produced, since he showed cooperative members how to fumigate and fertilize this crop (*el técnico anterior que controlaba bién en el campo i por esa razón se sacó buenos tomates en su periodo i ademas enseñaba a fumigar i preparar los abonamientos a los socios personalmente*), comparing this favourably with the ('bad') work of the present Area Technician who only showed one specific poor peasant member how to do these tasks.

(ONRA) *Theory versus (Peasant) Experience*

These three incidents, which illustrate the nature of conflict unfolding in the context of general assembly meetings on the agrarian cooperative, challenge the view which holds that, on questions of planning and control over agricultural production, ONRA bureaucrats exercised (unproblematic) dominance over the peasantry. As these episodes suggest, the situation was altogether more complex, and requires consideration of the contradictory elements structuring this particular struggle.

Rather than the possession *per se* of specialist knowledge about specific kinds of production technique (crop rotation, fumigation, etc.), the ONRA Area Technician can be characterized more accurately as disposing of this 'expertise', which is in fact transmitted by him to the peasant membership of the cooperative. Specialist production skills are not the private property of the individual ONRA functionary, nor (in the act/process of diffusion) may the latter subject be considered the sole repository of this knowledge.

Accordingly, it is precisely the *withholding* of this specialist knowledge by an ONRA Area Technician which constitutes a threefold threat to – and thus generates conflict with – the membership of the agrarian cooperative: it denies the latter a concomitant control over the labour process on the cooperative sector; control over the capacity to accumulate capital in this context; and, ultimately, and ability to control the reproduction of social relations of production both as co-owners of the cooperative and as individual proprietors on the peasant sector.

Politico-ideological struggle over this process takes a familiar form of claim and counter-claim. On the one hand, the attitude of the peasant members towards this specialist knowledge/technique is itself ambiguous. If they accept the transmission of ONRA 'expertise', they are themselves solely responsible for crop failures and livestock losses. To accusations from high and middle ranking ONRA functionaries about negligence in the labour process, therefore, the membership reply by blaming subordinate ONRA bureaucrats. However, this form of displacement requires in turn a process of distancing from ONRA-derived specialist knowledge and its reassociation with (low ranking) ONRA personnel on the cooperative sector, precisely in order to transfer the blame onto the latter for any production shortcomings/failures.

This process of distancing entails the reaffirmation by the membership of two things: the intellectual/manual distinction in the division of labour, and simultaneously the specificity of their own specialist knowledge (or agricultural expertise rooted in their experience as peasant proprietors). Hence the view expressed in the general assembly meeting of 20 July that by engaging in paperwork the ONRA Area technician neglected the work on the cooperative sector embodied not only a politico-ideological opposition between the intellectual labour of ONRA and the manual labour of the peasantry but also the irrelevance of the former when compared to the latter.

Both the ambiguity with regard to (the necessity of/distancing from/irrelevance of) ONRA 'expertise', and the struggle between bureaucrats and peasants for its control, are evident from the following opinion about ONRA functionaries:

> They are inexperienced. It is necessary to teach [Area Technicians], it is necessary to teach them wherever you may be because they are ignorant. They come here to teach [us] one thing after another. They make you fumigate cabbages: 'this is not the right kind of cabbage', they may tell you, 'you must therefore plant this sort'. They make you plant the wrong kind instead of the right sort. Little by little they learn through experience. Sometimes they are right, sometimes not, because they are all theory and no practice, they just pass on pure theory taught them in their studies. For example, if you argue on the basis of theory and I on the basis of experience, then disagreement follows, doesn't it. It may even result in a fight.[91]

At the same time, peasant members protest that Area Technicians are either absent from the agrarian cooperative or else show no interest in giving them technical guidance, while on the other ONRA functionaries respond that as peasant members devote most of their time to the cultivation of their privately owned landholdings, they are never present on the cooperative sector in order to avail themselves of ONRA skills/knowledge. Significantly, these interventions also contain oblique references to the class position of those involved. Thus peasant members regard the low ranking ONRA Area Technician as an employee: that is, a non-owning administrator discharging managerial/supervisory function at the behest and in the interests of the co-owning membership.[92] They also view with suspicion the attempt by such bureaucrats

91 *'Frescos son. A ellos hay que enseñar, en cualquier lugar a ellos hay que enseñar, porque ellos no saben. Ellos vienen a enseñar una cosa por otra cosa. Te hace fumigar el repollo; te pueden decir "esta clase de repollo no es tal cosa, entonces esto debes poner". Te hacen poner el malo, asi es que en vez de poner el bien. Poco a poco basandose apprenden. A veces le dicen tambien la verdad, a veces no pués, porque es que no son prácticos pués, pura teoría pués. Pura teoría te dicen, lo que ha estudiado en cursos. Por ejemplo, usted discute por la teoría y yo por la práctica, asi es que hay una discusión, no es cierto. Asi es hasta pelear pueden entrar.'*

92 As Montoya (1974: 99) notes, the fact that in many instances the pre-reform rôle of ONRA personnel was the administration of the landlord enterprise on behalf of (and frequently

to impart specialist skills to an ex-labourer who had only recently acquired member status, since it raised the spectre of an alliance between different categories of non-owning subjects (ONRA, labourers) against the co-owning peasant membership.

IV

'Somos Distintos': Class Consciousness on the Cooperative

The ONRA District Coordinator was particularly unpopular with the peasant members in this respect, for two reasons in particular. First, because he had attempted (unsuccessfully) to prohibit them from employing bonded labour on the cooperative sector, rather than working personally. Peasants who used substitute labour in this manner rationalized it thus: 'one has to make sacrifices to pay labourers [to work in our stead on the cooperative sector], and if we don't give them employment, ONRA won't'. And second, because this same ONRA bureaucrat had warned them that if the non-completion of the statutory labour requirement stayed at its present high level, he would arrange for co-ownership rights to be extended to workers on a neighbouring agrarian cooperative who had little land (and who would therefore be prepared to work personally).

For suggesting that outsiders who were also landless labourers be included as members of their cooperative, he was branded a 'traitor' by peasant members; this underlines the centrality of property relations, both to the peasant/worker distinction and to the element of class consciousness. The concept of politico-ideological difference dividing peasants who were members of the agrarian cooperative from labourers they employed was defined by them in terms of landownership and division of labour. In other words, that 'difference' plus the antagonism and conflict it generates was in the final instance an effect of the social relations of production on the cooperative was a point recognized by the respective protagonists themselves. This element of 'difference' was described thus by one permanent worker who was landless: 'Since I do not own land, I am unable to remain here [on the ex-estate]; not owning a holding means one cannot stay' (*no puedo estar en mi lugar como no tengo chacra; como no tengo arriendo, no puedes permanacer*).

---

employed by) the landowner of the estate facilitated an ideological shift whereby the ONRA Area Technician came to be seen as an employee administering the same (cooperative) sector, but now on behalf of its new owners.

Denied a wage increase, the permanent workers employed on the agrarian cooperative asked the members for small plots of land – between 0.25 and 0.50 of an hectare in size – on which to grow staple crops. A permanent worker who made this request emphasized the hard work contributed by labourers to the economic reproduction of the agrarian cooperative:

> Because we are now fulfilling [our production targets], we are working as labourers and from where are we going to obtain money? We earn very little, fifty Soles [a day] is very little, and with this [land] they [the membership] are going to help us because with our very strength we are helping the cooperative; if it wasn't for us workers, the cooperative would fail.[93]

The subsequent rejection of this request by the peasant members served, however, to underline the importance of the property relation as constitutive of the politico-ideological difference between peasants and labourers.

When asked whether peasants who were members of the agrarian cooperative worked as hard as labourers, one of the latter responded:

> There are some members who work, who expend their own energy in the cooperative, and there are some who just send labourers. For example, if you were a member you would have labourers on your peasant holding, you might have between ten and fifteen labourers, so you don't have to work, not even touch a blade of grass, not a thing, then you are a boss. Well, you have to come along to the cooperative to work, and you turn up at the last moment to collect your pay; taking everything from workers who have laboured all the year you reprimand these same workers saying 'they are not worth anything'...[members] send labourers rather than working personally. There are arguments because [members] do not wish to carry out the same kind of work [as us], there are a number of idlers among them.[94]

---

93 *'Porque estamos cumpliendo ya, estamos trabajando como obreros y de donde recaudamos plata? Estamos ganando poco pues, es muy poquito cincuenta Soles, y co eso nos va a ayudar porque nosotros con nuestro esfuerzo mismo estamos ayudando al comité; sino seriamos nosotros estos obreros, el comité fracasap's.'*

94 *'Hay unos socios que trabajan, que sueltan su propio esfuerzo en el comité y hay unos que mandan puro. Usted seria socio, en tu chacra tienes tus obreros, puedes tener hasta diez, quince obreros, asi es que usted no trabaja, no atoca ni una hierba, nada pues, usted es patron. Bueno, usted tiene que entrar al comité a trabajar y a la ultima hora nomasya usted vuelve a recibir su salario; de los obreros que han trabajajo al fin del año tomas todo,*

On all these issues, views expressed by the landholding members of the agrarian cooperative in La Convención were the mirror image of those held by their workers. In a letter to a rich peasant concerning who should and who should not be admitted as new member of the agrarian cooperative, therefore, one peasant proprietor noted:

> ...and in case there is going to be a new intake, that those who are enrolled must be landholders, and labourers ought not to be accepted as members because...it is not in our interest to enroll them.[95]

The same peasant member made this distinction when, on a subsequent occasion, he spoke in a general assembly meeting. Then he observed that, as a result of the non-completion of the statutory labour requirement, the membership were faced with a situation where 'we have sunk to the level of labourers' (*hasta a los obreros hemos caido*).

This notion of 'otherness' based on class also surfaced in the course of an acrimonious exchange between the President of the agrarian cooperative and the labourers working on this sector. On this occasion a group of the latter had complained to the member supervising work about the fact that they were toiling in the fields harvesting tomatoes – a hard task – while the President was permitted to remain indoors, sorting vanilla pods – an easy task. A labourer pointed out that, rather than shirk hard work, the President ought to set an example in this respect.[96] When he got to hear of this, the President stated

---

reprochas estos obreros "no valen nada" dices...mandan en vez de venir personalmente. Discutos hay, no quieren hacer igual, hay unos cuantos holgazones.'

95 *'i si en caso va haber nueva inscripción, que se inscriban los que tienen su chacra, no acepten a los obreros como socios por que...si van a participar ellos como socios no conviene asociarlos.'*

96 On the cooperative sector – as indeed elsewhere on the ex-estate – work activity was differentated by peasants and workers alike in terms of hard tasks (*trabajos duros*) and easy ones (*trabajos suavecitos* or *trabajos gauchitos*). The latter was a label applied to administrative or supervisory tasks, usually carried out by peasant members, while the former description referred to heavy manual work invariably allocated to landless labourers on the cooperative sector. One agricultural worker outlined the difference in the social division of labour: 'Here on the cooperative sector [the members] do not work, they seek out light and easy tasks. They like to take the produce to market, to sell it, to return, to supervise and to take charge of the accounts; this and nothing more is what they aim to do, easy work is what they seek. And to the labourers [the members say:] "you have to go and do such-and-such work". This is a problem we [labourers] forcefully bring to the attention of the President [of the cooperative]: "You, sir, as President your place is in the fields from where you should not be absent...as President you should be present here [working] in

angrily that he was an officeholder and 'no fucking worker tells me what to do – we are different' (*soy dirigente y carajo ningun obrero me diga que hacer – somos distintos*).[97]

V

Full Cooperativization or Privatization?

Finally, the political weakness of ONRA in its conflict with the peasant membership for control over production relations on the agrarian cooperative in 1970s La Convención may be illustrated by reference to two important processes of struggle. Payment/non-payment of the agrarian debt, and how this in turn was linked to divergent patterns of accumulation: full cooperativization or privatisation of co-owned land.

Payment/Non-payment of the Agrarian Debt

Compensation paid by the Peruvian state to the landlord class for expropriated means of production necessitated further appropriation from the agrarian reform beneficiaries themselves, in the shape of the amortization of the

the first furrow."' (*'aqui en el comité no trabajan, buscan trabajos suavecitos, gauchitos no mas. Quieren acomodarse en llevar al mercado el producto, vender, regresar, mirar, revisar; apintan eso no mas pues. Y a los obreros no mas pues, "tienes que ir tal, tal a trabajar". Eso es el problema porque al president a la fuerza lo estamos obligando: "usted, señor, como el presidente usted tiene que estar en la pampa, usted no debe ir...usted aca como presidente tiene que estar en el primer wachu."'*).

97 The labourer who had protested about inequalities in the social division of labour was subsequently threatened with dismissal as a result of this incident. Significantly, however, his cause was taken up by the one member of the cooperative who had himself been a landless worker. The latter observed that one less labourer would result in more work for those that remained, especially since peasant members failed to complete the statutory labour requirement; he added that, while it was one thing for peasants to order around labourers employed on their private holdings, this ought not to happen on the cooperative sector because 'here we are all equal' (*en la pampa todos somos iguales*). On an earlier occasion, before he became a cooperative member, this same landless labourer had together with another worker been condemned by a peasant member for writing on the schoolroom blackboard the words 'Exploitative Time and Official Time' (*comitieron un horror de escribir en la pizarra 'Hora Explotada y Hora Oficial'*). Both labourers were summoned to the cooperative meeting and compelled to explain this defiance to their employers. The members agreed that, since this was a first offence, no further action would be taken, but any similar occurrences in the future would result in instant dismissal.

agrarian debt. The extraction by the state of the resulting interest payments from the new co-owning peasant members on the agrarian cooperative would accordingly be one of the the more important (and sensitive) political tasks of the reform process. A primary objective of ONRA was thus to guarantee that the annual repayment schedule to the state was in fact met by the cooperative membership. From the outset, therefore, ONRA personnel constantly emphasized the interrelatedness of recently acquired co-ownership rights to means of production on the cooperative sector and the payment of the agrarian debt.

This issue was first raised by ONRA bureaucrats at the general assembly meeting of 28 August 1973, when both the District Coordinator and the Area Technician not only went through the title deed for the agrarian cooperative clause by clause, but also stressed that it was in fact a deed of *sale* which committed the peasant membership to fulfilling a specific set of conditions, the most crucial one being the payment of the agrarian debt.[98] The same point was made again subsequently by ONRA functionaries during the meetings of 6 March and 21 May 1974, when the District Coordinator and the Regional Chief reminded those present of the interest payment due in the month of June. It was on this occasion, moreover, that the ONRA Regional Chief questioned the ability of the co-owning peasant membership to meet the annual interest payment of 38,000 *Soles* in view of the extensive non-completion of the statutory labour requirement.[99]

Significantly, posing the problem in this manner was seen by peasant members as an oblique threat to their co-ownership rights. This was because it licensed a relay in statement, whereby the act of non-payment is inserted into a process, at the end of which lies the dissolution of the cooperative

98 The undertaking by the whole membership to pay the agrarian debt was embodied legally in clause 7(e) of the title deed to the cooperative sector and its means of production, a document signed by each member.

99 The agrarian debt was the compensation paid by the Peruvian state to the expropriated landlord class. The land, standing crops, constructions/installations, and livestock owned by the ex-landlord of this particular estate were valued by ONRA at S/.1,336,373, while interest on this sum came to a further S/.947,269. Repayable over a twenty-five year period (1974–99), the agrarian debt owed to the Peruvian state by the combined peasant membership of this cooperative amounted to a total of S/.2,283,642. During the initial 1974–78 period, when no interest was payable, the yearly instalment of this debt was only S/.37,890; over the next twenty years (1979–99), however, the annual repayment would have increased to S/.104,710. Zaldivar (1974: 63) has argued that the agrarian debt represented nothing other than a continuation of the absolute rent appropriated by the ex-landlord class from those ex-tenants and ex-sub-tenants who were now the co-owners of the cooperative sector. In 1979 the agrarian debt was finally written off by the Peruvian state.

production relation itself. Hence the following: non-fulfilment of the statutory labour requirement → expulsion from membership → non-payment of agrarian debt → separation from means of production on cooperative sector. Following this intervention by ONRA, and after abandoning planned expenditure on the purchase of high quality livestock for the expansion/improvement of the dairy herd, the peasant membership approved *in principle* during the general assembly meeting of 11 June to pay the interest owed to the state.

In the subsequent meeting, held on the 18 June, it was agreed further that the annual instalment of the agrarian debt would be met by revenue generated from the sale of cooperative livestock. However, when the President of the cooperative informed the meeting on 3 August that the annual instalment of interest on the agrarian debt was now due, the membership voted unanimously to withhold payment, thereby *in practice* reversing the decision taken two months earlier.

Privatisation of Cooperative Means of Production

As used here, the concept 'privatisation' refers to a specific mode of appropriation effected by peasant members of this particular agrarian cooperative during the early 1970s. It encompasses not only the individual/group appropriation/consumption of livestock, milk, seeds and agricultural implements, all of which belong to the cooperative as a whole, but also the parcellation of cooperative land itself, either for (private) agricultural production or for a (private) dwelling. The latter corresponded to a process whereby rich, middle and better-off poor peasant members divided portions of the cooperative land among themselves at the expense of the less-well-off poor peasant members.[100] As will become clear below, private appropriation of means of production on the cooperative sector was strongly opposed by ONRA bureaucrats.

When in the course of a general assembly meeting on 21 May 1974 a poor peasant member denounced a rich peasant member for having built a (private) dwelling on cooperative land, therefore, the ONRA Regional Chief intervened to ask whether permission for this had been sought or granted (*¿Quién lo dió ordenes para que se haga?*). The rich peasant replied that he had in fact informed the membership, and although undertaking to vacate this illegal dwelling he nevertheless claimed compensation from the cooperative membership

100 During 1974–5 the privatised area divided into individual plots amounted to 14 percent of the total pasture, fallow, and cropland on the cooperative sector of this particular ex-estate. According to Gonzales and Torre (1985: 7), more than 65 percent of the agrarian cooperatives on the west coast of Peru had already been sub-divided into individual holdings by 1985. Melmed-Sanjak and Carter (1991: 192) report that 16 of the 22 non-sugar producing agrarian cooperatives had also been divided up in a similar fashion by 1986.

as a whole for the cost of its construction (*yo le he hecho saber a la asamblea, y que me lo devuelva de mi construcción*). However, just as peasant members continued with their illegal occupation of private plots on the cooperative sector (judicial eviction by ONRA notwithstanding), so the rich peasant member continued to inhabit his illegal dwelling.[101]

Full Cooperativization?

The issue of full cooperativization was raised in general assemblies which took place on 13 and 21 May 1974. In the first of these two meetings, the membership voted unanimously to transform the production committee into a full production cooperative, after an ONRA bureaucrat had outlined the economic advantages and legal preconditions of such a transition.[102] When in the course of the subsequent meeting one week later the membership membership expressed a willingness to effect this transition immediately, the ONRA Regional Chief stated that full cooperativization remain impossible until such a time as the statutory labour requirement was completed by all the peasant members. A middle peasant responded by pointing out that 'we want to form a [full] cooperative since we are told that without this we cannot obtain loans' (*nosotros queremos cooperativizar porque nos dijó que por eso motivo no se puede sacar préstamos*).[103]

Conclusion

These latter episodes demonstrate the inherent paradox of political power (seemingly) exercised by ONRA bureaucrats during the early 1970s over three important and interconnected relational forms on this agrarian cooperative

101 When asked by this writer about the reason for ONRA opposition to privatisation, the Area Technician replied that the settlement area should be reserved for the exclusive use of poor peasants (*deficitarios*) who lived in the higher reaches of the ex-estate. This would enable them to come down to the cooperative sector more frequently and fulfil their statutory labour requirement. He was critical not only of the rich peasant for 'monopolizing' (*acaparando*) existing settlement land but also of another middle peasant member for converting the old school house into a similarly illegal private dwelling.

102 The agrarian cooperative was intended eventually to become fully cooperativized as part of the Integral Rural Settlement Project or PIAR (*Proyecto Integral de Asentamiento Rural*) for the province as a whole. As such, it would then be able to export produce directly, cutting out any intermediaries and thus retaining a higher proportion of the profits.

103 As the Area Technician informed this writer, ONRA also possessed a long-term objective linked to full cooperativization. A corollary of the latter was that all those resident (and owning land) on the peasant sector of the ex-estate would be faced with the choice of either becoming members of the (full) cooperative or being evicted from their holdings.

in La Convención, and yet a lack of effective control over the process of their reproduction/dissolution. First, the (external) production relation linking ex-tenants and ex-sub-tenants (now the peasant membership) to the ex-landlord, a relation mediated through the Peruvian state (and thus ONRA) in the form of the agrarian debt. Second, the (internal) production relation on the cooperative relation itself, in the form of the divergent paths of accumulation: privatization as against full cooperativization. And third, the link between peasant members and the agricultural labourers they employed on the cooperative sector, and the fear on the part of the former that the latter would – with the help of ONRA – replace them as co-owners of the agrarian cooperative.

In order to understand the contradictory nature (synchronically potent, diachronically ineffective) of these interventions by ONRA, it is necessary to locate them within mutually exclusive but indissolubly linked dynamics. Unable to obtain loans from the state in order to purchase additional means of production for the cooperative sector, the peasant membership adopted another economic strategy: this not only constituted the mirror image of that desired by ONRA, but also involved the privatization of existing means of production on the cooperative that had implications for the profitability in the latter context. Accordingly, the struggle between ONRA and the peasant membership during the early 1970s for control over the forces and relations of production on the cooperative sector corresponds to nothing less than a conflict over the political object, the direction, and the form taken by the accumulation process itself.

This was a struggle which, at that conjuncture, could be resolved in one of two different ways. On the one hand, therefore, fulfilment of the statutory labour requirement, increased output on the cooperative sector, payment of the agrarian debt, and quorate assembly meetings all constituted prerequisites of the ONRA accumulation project based on a transition to full cooperativization. Loans for the purchase of additional productive forces would in turn license further accumulation in (and profitability of) production in the cooperative labour process. On the other hand, non-fulfilment of the statutory labour requirement, non-payment of the agrarian debt, and inquorate assembly meetings determine (by contrast) a pattern of accumulation based largely on privatization in its variant forms: parcellation of cooperative land, slaughter and consumption of livestock. This involved the transfer of capital resources from the cooperative sector co-owned by the membership as a whole to (and thus accumulation in) the peasant sector where members owned individual holdings.

Instead of the usual dichotomy that locates struggle between peasant and state, which is the way that populism has interpreted – and continues to interpret – much rural conflict, the struggle in La Convención during the immediate post reform era was about class and rival patterns of accumulation. This conflict involved not two parties – peasant and state – but three: peasants who were members of the agrarian cooperative, the agricultural workers they employed, and ONRA. At the root of this struggle was the fear on the part of the membership that a failure to fulfil the statutory labour requirement would generate an alliance between ONRA and landless labourers, leading ultimately to the loss of co-ownership rights. These ONRA had threatened to take away from the existing peasant membership, and reallocate to agricultural workers.

Rather than wait for ONRA to deprive them of co-ownership rights and award these to labourers who were landless, however, peasant members embarked on the privatization of cooperative land. This appropriation by peasant proprietors of land and other resources on the cooperative sector of the ex-estate anticipated the kind of asset-stripping now practised by many capitalist enterprises operating in the current neoliberal global economy. The distinction is that, whereas in 1970s La Convención the agrarian reform agency attempted to prevent this from happening, nowadays the state in many different national contexts actively encourages this by means of deregulation and privatisation.

These two opposed paths – accumulation either on the cooperative or the peasant sector – are not only mapped out in terms of coherent economic ojectives but also embodied long-term politico-ideological implications. Whereas the accumulation project of ONRA envisaged full cooperativization not merely in institutional terms (production cooperative → service cooperative) but also – and perhaps more importantly – with regard to those peasants on the ex-estate who still remained outside the cooperative structure. The political incorporation of the latter – for the most part, the poorest segment of the poor peasantry – would be facilitated by the economic attractiveness of full cooperativization. However, the accumulation project followed by the existing membership not only impeded full cooperativization but also ensured that the labour-power of these same poorest peasants – those who might benefit from cooperative membership – remained anchored on the peasant enterprise as a result of the debt bondage mechanism.

The lessons taught by this case study from 1970s Peru are simple, and concern the role within agrarian reform units of the state and class. Contrary to received wisdom, therefore, the state is not as strong as much of the development literature claims; neither are its attempts at intervention and regulation as effective nor as malign as usually depicted. Equally clear is the reason behind much of the ineffectiveness of the state: the continued and unchecked process at the rural grassroots of class formation and struggle arising from this. Thus the problem of the state can be said to lie not so much with unwarranted regulation as with the imposition of agrarian reform units on an unreformed class structure in the countryside.

Such lessons challenge the prevailing wisdom, propagated by *laissez faire* theory but evident also in the views of NGOs and others that are opposed to neoliberalism, that where rural development is concerned, it is the strength of and intervention by the state and its bureaucracy that is the problem. This has generated and helped to sustain the main shibboleths – decentralization (= small-is-beautiful) and deregulation – that inform much current development theory and practice. It remains a truism, therefore, that any and all attempts to eliminate the causes of rural poverty and inequality without addressing the crucial issue of class, and how its formation and consciousness determine the implementation of policy, planning and regulation by the state and its bureaucracy at the rural grassroots, will of necessity fail.

CHAPTER 16

Capitalism Bonded Labour in India: Reinterpreting Recent (Re-) Interpretations*

> Were one to take the history of the ideological struggle over a period of a quarter-century, cut it into little pieces, mix them in a mortar, and command a blind man to stick the pieces together again, a greater theoretical and historical jumble of nonsense could hardly result than the one with which the epigones feed their readers and hearers.
>
> An observation made in 1929 by TROTSKY about discussions surrounding the theory of permanent revolution.[1]

•••

> **Circumlocution**, n. A literary trick whereby the writer who has nothing to say breaks it gently to the reader.
>
> An observation by AMBROSE BIERCE.[2]

∴

Introduction

Given the high rate of economic growth – around eight per cent annually – in India during recent times, it comes as no surprise that the nation is held up as an exemplar not just of a successful transition to but a dynamic instance of capitalist development.[3] The implementation by the Indian state of neoliberal

* An earlier and much longer version appeared in *The Journal of Peasant Studies*, Vol. 35, No. 2 (2008). The latter contained many footnotes that, for reasons of space, are not included here.

1 Trotsky (1962: 14).

2 Bierce (1967: 40).

3 See, among others, Bhagwati (1993), International Monetary Fund (1998), Ahluwalia and Little (1998), Kohli (2001), Panchamukhi (2002), Kapila and Kapila (2002), Amsden (2003), Ariff (2005), Stern (2006), Nayar (2007), Chakravorty and Lall (2007), Dossani (2008), Nayak (2008), Panagaria (2008), and Mahbubani (2008). The tone of these kinds of analysis is unmistakably celebratory, the focus being on economic growth with little or no consideration as to the role

economic policy, however, raises many questions about its beneficiaries, not least the impact on agricultural workers and poor peasants. Among these questions is one about the kind of capitalist labour regime emerging in the Indian countryside.

Did this transition require, as many in the past have argued, the eradication of bonded labour, or has economic development resulted much rather in the reinforcement of such relations? Were those who categorized debt bondage as a pre-capitalist relational form correct to do so, and has unfree labour consequently vanished from the countryside in India, as they maintained it would? In short, was unfree labour an obstacle to accumulation, again as many have argued previously, or has it turned out to be compatible with agrarian capitalist development in India?

That capitalism thrives on the employment of unfree workers is finally being recognized, as the many books and articles now being published about the subject confirm. It is a situation that vindicates those – such as this writer – who have made this connection all along. Not among the latter group, unfortunately, are three longstanding commentators on Indian agrarian change: Jan Breman, a Dutch anthropologist who writes about rural labour relations in Western India; and two development economists, Amartya Sen and Barbara Harriss-White, whose focus is on the causes of rural poverty. Not so long ago, they were among the many commentators who disavowed a connection between unfree labour and capitalist development. In what ways have their views changed, and with what effect on the long-term coherence of their arguments and those made by others subsequently?

Bonded Labour and the Development Debate

Over the past half century, unfree labour has re-emerged as a central issue in the debate about rural development in India and elsewhere. In the years following the end of the 1939–45 war, a central political concern of the then-dominant Keynesian theory was unsurprisingly not just economic reconstruction (mainly in Europe and Asia) but also development planning (in the Third World). A crucial aspect of the ensuing debate concerned the extent to which different relational forms constituted obstacles to capitalist development, and why. Central to these discussions was the link between capitalist development and modern forms of unfree labour (peonage, debt bondage, indenture, chattel slavery). Within the domain of political economy, it is a debate that has a very long historical lineage, and – accurately presented – never went away.

in this of outsourcing consequent on low pay and poor working conditions in India itself, bonded labour being but one aspect of this.

In the course of this fifty-year period, the prevailing orthodoxy about the meaning, the incidence, and the systemic role of unfree labour have undergone a dramatic shift. This can be divided into roughly four distinct stages. The first coincided with the 1960s and 1970s, when discussions centred on the implications of unfree social relations of production in Third World agriculture.[4] In the case of the mode of production debate, mainly about agrarian transition in India, bonded labour was regarded as incompatible with capitalist accumulation, and thus an obstacle to economic growth, an interpretation advanced by exponents of the then-dominant semi-feudal thesis.[5]

The second stage corresponds to the end of the 1970s and into the 1980s, when an opposing view gained ground: unfree production relations, it was argued, were not just acceptable to rural capital but in certain situations were its preferred form.[6] From the late 1970s onwards, therefore, another and very different view about the capitalism/unfreedom link was emerging in the sphere of development studies. As a result of fieldwork conducted in Latin America and India, articles published in this journal and elsewhere appeared throughout the 1980s and into the 1990s, challenging the then prevailing orthodoxy that capitalist transformation of the agrarian sector led to the replacement of unfree workers with free equivalents.[7] Much rather the opposite was the

4 Some analyses of agriculture in Third World countries – for example, Wharton (1970) and Shanin (1971) – made little or no attempt to address the nature of a connection between capitalist development and bonded labour.

5 On the mode of production debate, see Rudra, *et al.*, (1978) and Thorner (1982), which indicate both the extent of the influence exercised by the semi-feudal thesis, and the notable exceptions to this: Daniel Thorner and Ashok Rudra. Symptomatic of the dumbing down process affecting much current debate about the capitalism/unfreedom link is the dismissal by Lerche (2007: 15, note 20) of the earlier approach to bonded labour in India by Daniel and Alice Thorner (1962: 21ff.). Not only was their understanding of what constituted an unfree production relation far superior to that of Lerche, but – again unlike him – the theoretical approach of the Thorners (1962: 173ff.) was methodologically sound. Before pronouncing on what relations are or are not unfree, and why, Lerche could with profit have studied and learnt from what Daniel and Alice Thorner wrote about bonded labour in a theoretical and methodological analysis that remains as relevant today as it did when it first appeared.

6 Amongst whom were Mundle (1979), Desai (1984), and some of the contributions to the volume edited by Brass and van der Linden (1997).

7 Journal articles on unfree-labour-as-deproletarianization written during the 1980s were collected in a subsequent volume (Brass, 1999). Breman was aware of these texts: not only was he on the editorial board of this journal, in which a number of them originally appeared, but he also referred to their contents disparagingly throughout the 1990s (Breman, 1993: 301; 1996: 168; 1999a: 255–256; 1999b: 465–468; 1999c: 423), dismissing as nonsense ('implausible', 'an extreme position' amounting to 'doctrinal zeal', etc., etc.) the argument about deproletarianization (= the acceptability to capital of unfree labour).

case, it was argued, in that evidence from Latin America and India suggested agribusiness enterprises, commercial farmers and rich peasants reproduced, introduced or reintroduced unfree relations.

Labelled deproletarianization, this was a process of workforce decomposition/recomposition frequently resorted to by employers in their struggle with rural labour.[8] The object was to discipline and cheapen labour-power, an undeniable economic advantage in a global context where agricultural producers had to become increasingly cost-conscious in order to remain competitive. This reinterpretation effectively wrong-footed all those who had argued hitherto that agrarian capitalists replaced – not retained, let alone actively sought out – production relations that were unfree.

Flight of the Phoenix

Accordingly, there followed a third stage, consisting of what might be described as a decade of readjustment. Throughout the 1990s and into the new millennium, therefore, many of those who in the 1970s and 1980s equated bonded labour with a pre-capitalist production relation, and dismissed arguments that unfree labour and accumulation were compatible, changed their minds and espoused the interpretation they had previously opposed. Their analyses of bonded labour in India have as a result taken on a procrustean aspect, as later pronouncements clash with and are contradicted by earlier ones.

Broadly speaking, the response to being wrong footed was threefold: some continued to insist that unfree labour was incompatible with accumulation; others accepted the new interpretation, acknowledging that their earlier analyses were incorrect; yet others maintained, implausibly, that the reinterpretation was no different from what they had argued all along. Into this last category come Breman, Amartya Sen and Harriss-White. Without being aware

8 In this connection it is important to remind oneself what Breman wrote a decade ago about my argument that unfreedom was spreading in the Indian countryside as capitalism developed. Then he wrote (Breman, 1999c: 423, emphasis added) that 'Brass also opines that workers in a debt-dependency relationship have lost their proletarian status. By the "deproletarianization" process that he considers to be in progress, he understands "replacing free workers with unfree equivalents or by converting the former into the latter"... *Such reasoning implies that a process of capitalist transformation is in progress in the Indian countryside in which free labour is disappearing to make place for a regime of unfreedom. In fact the trend is the reverse.*' His position could not be more clear: my argument that unfree labour was reproduced by agrarian capitalists was in Breman's opinion wrong, since his view was much rather the opposite: namely, that such commercial producers were in fact replacing unfree workers with free labour. This is not what he says now (Breman, 2002), which is that unfree labour is 'pivotal to a capitalist mode of production'.

of this background, and the contradictions to which it gives rise, it is impossible to comprehend what the present debate is about, and why it takes the form it does.

The fourth and most recent stage is characterized by the entry into the debate of other, more junior researchers (de Neve, Jodhka, Rawal and Lerche), who also write about changes in the rural labour regime and how this affects the process of capitalist transformation in India. However, they remain unaware of the twists and turns informing the discussion, and in particular how the interpretation of unfree relations has shifted from being seen as incompatible with accumulation to being regarded a central aspect of the latter process.[9]

Seemingly oblivious to many contradictory statements made by Breman, Amartya Sen and Harriss-White over the years concerning the way production relations in the agrarian sector have altered, and why, these recent analyses permit their claims to slip by unexamined and thus unchallenged. Consequently, many of the errors perpetrated by them are reproduced in these newer contributions to the debate about bonded labour in India, necessitating similar changes of mind.

Perhaps all this is merely an indication of two things. First, that the political lessons about over-optimistic pronouncements about the efficacy of 'every-day-forms' of resistance and emancipation from bonded labour relations are finally being learned, although given the constant shifts in ideas one can never be too sure. And second, if earlier pronouncements on an issue turn out to be wrong, it has been difficult to avoid the impression that in some instances the response has been simply to incorporate the more accurate version.

There is, of course, no intrinsic problem with changing one's mind about an issue so as to bring an earlier and mistaken position into line with current thinking offering a more correct interpretation. Simultaneously to misrepresent those responsible for developing current thinking, and in effect to present the latter as though it had nothing to do with them, however, does raise serious questions about the nature and object of debate. Not the least of the many ironies is that, when made by an earlier analytical framework (deproletarianization) the claim about the acceptability to agrarian capitalists of unfree

9 Symptomatic of an unfortunate dumbing down of the debate over this issue is the purported identification by Lerche (2007: 10, note 13) of what turns out to be a non-existent theoretical difference. Noting that Jairus Banaji accuses me of arguing at the level of individual capital, and further that I have rebutted this accusation, arguing as I do at the level of social as well as individual capital, Lerche then pointlessly observes that 'Banaji's analysis nevertheless gains from having made this distinction explicit'. In other words, Lerche attempts to locate disagreement in a theoretical issue that he accepts is one which is in fact non-contentious.

labour is deemed wrong, but correct when made subsequently ('neo-bondage') by Breman.

Tracing the twists and turns in the interpretation of bonded labour in India, this presentation is divided into six parts. The origin of the problem, in the work of Breman, is examined in the first two sections, while the third looks at how many of the same difficulties surface in the approach of Amartya Sen and Harriss-White to this same issue. Sections four and five then consider the way in which these problems inform the debate about unfree labour as presented more recently by de Neve, Jodhka, Rawal and Lerche. The sixth section outlines the reason why, in a neoliberal global economy, agrarian capitalist producers can and do resort to deproletarianization, as well as the political implications of repositioning bonded labour in relation to accumulation.

I

On the Damascus Road

The attempt by Breman to sustain the claim that he has not in fact changed his mind about the acceptability to agrarian capitalists of unfree labour and the reasons for this forms the subtext to his most recent book.[10] Over the years he and I have debated this issue in many different books and journals, including this one. His claim is that no difference exists between the position he held in the 1970s and early 1980s and his views about the capitalism/unfreedom link that emerged around the late 1980s and the early 1990s.[11] Mine, by contrast, is that the evidence points unambiguously to the fact that he has indeed changed his mind, something moreover he has done without saying either that this is what has happened, or why.[12]

Let us remind ourselves of what Breman wrote earlier on this subject, since he himself seems to have forgotten. Initially, therefore, he insisted that capitalist development was accompanied by proletarianization and a corresponding decline in unfree labour, characterized by him as a feudal relation incompatible with economic growth. Prior to 1990, his view about the capitalism/unfreedom link was

10 See Breman (2007), a volume on which much of the following argument will focus.

11 His initial view was expounded during the 1970s and early 1980s, and is found in Breman (1974; 1985). The opposite view about the capitalism/unfreedom link emerged around the 1990s, and is encountered in Breman (1990: 527ff.; 1993: 300; 1996: 169; 1999a: 254–256; 1999b: 463–469).

12 For this case, plus evidence, see Brass (1997a; 1999: 217ff, 230ff.; 2000b).

that the decrease in bonded labour amounted to a process of 'depatronization', which deprived workers of a subsistence guarantee, and was for them an undesirable development. The element of unfreedom inherent in patron/client relations was interpreted by him as something that commercially-minded employers attempted to discard but workers fought to retain.

Thesis

Because his 1960s fieldwork coincided with the start of the development decade, he conceptualized the debt bondage of the *hali* system in terms that then prevailed. In keeping with the views of the semi-feudal thesis and neo-classical economic historiography, during the 1970s and into the 1980s, Breman argued that bonded labour was a non-capitalist relation; that it would be eliminated and replaced by a proletariat as capitalism spread throughout the countryside; and that consequently there were no forms of unfree relations – new or otherwise – in his western India fieldwork area.[13]

At that time bonded labour in rural Gujarat was interpreted by him as a *jajmani* arrangement licensing a patron client relationship which, Breman insisted, was seen by unfree workers as a desirable form of 'subsistence guarantee': its loss as capitalism developed was accordingly interpreted by him as 'depatronization'. Not surprisingly, since unfree relations were associated with 'patronage' and the *hali* relation, Breman interpreted the erosion of the latter as evidence for a decline in unfreedom itself.[14]

Accordingly, Breman dismissed the views of those who argued that unfree labour continued to exist in rural Gujarat, adding that 'there is no longer any question of labour bondage'.[15] Although casual workers received loans,

---

13 For these arguments, see Breman (1974; 1985). As noted previously (Brass, 1997a: 346ff.), before his change of mind in the late 1980s or early 1990s, Breman insisted that what was happening in rural Gujarat as capitalism spread there was a corresponding emergence of free labour, or a proletariat. That in 1985 Breman adhered to this view has been noticed by others. A decade ago, for example, Ashok Rudra observed (*Development and Change*, 18/1, January 1987, pp. 175–176) that 'the general trend is as identified by him (= Breman), i.e. of labour becoming more and more free.' To this Rudra appends the following comment: 'It is, however, a pity that he asserts "freeness" of labour without discussing what constitutes that quality for him.'

14 'My own study, at the start of the 1960s,' he accepts (Breman, 2003: 107), 'charted the erosion of the system of bonded labour, a process of change driven by a combination of economic and political factors. The institution of *halipratha* (labour bondage) had fallen in to disuse.' This is confirmed by what Breman (2003: 233) writes subsequently, that '(t)he trend towards technological modernization facilitated the escape of the rural underclass from the system of agrarian bondage that characterized the *ancien regime*.'

15 For this view, see Breman (1985: 307–308).

therefore, his view categorically was that 'their situation does not constitute an unfree working relationship', since in his opinion 'it is unsound to deduce from this [the existence of debt] that unfree labour continues in either the same form *or a new one*...[t]he binding which accompanies this cannot...be equated with unfree labour' (emphasis added).[16] Lest there remained any doubt about his view, he concluded emphatically that 'I shall regard as unfree only that form of debt-labour which is rooted in non-economic coercion...*this relationship has nothing to do with the essence of present-day control over agricultural labour*' (emphasis added).[17]

Antithesis

In all published writings after 1990, however, he maintains that what is henceforth termed 'neo-bondage' and 'the new bondage' is, after all, not just compatible with the accumulation process but actually central to agrarian capitalist growth in Gujarat.[18] Now, therefore, one encounters the following kind of statement: 'The *new bondage* that has emerged is not necessarily in conflict with the development of a capitalist mode of production. In other words, it is possible that labour becomes mobile but without being able to exercise free choice over the terms and conditions of work' (emphasis added).[19] Indeed, Breman has no compunction in taking to task others for not recognizing that '[u]nfree labour thus became pivotal to a capitalist mode of production'.[20]

So there we have it: the juxtaposition of two conflicting statements. In 1985, Breman asserts, capitalist development in the agrarian sector of Gujarat did not – *and could not* – involve bonded labour ('there is no longer any question of labour bondage'), let alone a form that was new ('it is unsound to deduce ... that unfree labour continues in either the same form *or a new one*'). Around 1990, suddenly, the opposite is declared to be the case: capitalism *does* entail bondage, and a *new* form of it. Then his view was that unfree labour was unconnected with accumulation ('this relationship has nothing to do with the essence of present-day control over agricultural labour'), and as such does not continue 'in either the same form or a new one'; now, by contrast, his view is

16 This argument is found in Breman (1985: 311).

17 See Breman (1985: 443–444).

18 That his views have changed is evident from what is contained not just in his latest book but also in his post-1990 publications. Despite the fact that the resulting inconsistency is clear for all to see, Breman has yet to explain why 'neo-bondage' emerged when it did.

19 See Breman (2003: 42).

20 This criticism is made by Breman (2002) of Houben and Lindblad (1999; 2002).

that a 'new bondage' compatible with capitalism has indeed 'emerged', and is 'pivotal to a capitalist mode of production'.

Despite the fact that the contradiction between these statements published five years apart is absolute and unequivocal, their author continues to claim – with ever decreasing persuasiveness – that his views on the capitalism/unfreedom link have not changed. Although no mention is made by Breman in his most recent book of my published work on unfree labour, it is difficult to disguise the fact that much of what he writes there is an attempt by him to answer my criticisms, and in particular how his views about the capitalism/unfreedom link have altered so completely.[21] Indeed, the justifications of positions held make the book sound at times like an extended reply to the many criticisms made by me previously of his work.[22] Breman even cites the same quotation from Patel as I did, makes exactly the same point about its significance, only to cast doubt on its applicability to Gujarat.[23]

Patronage, Coercion and Closed Villages

Insofar as a difference exists between the argument made by me throughout the 1980s that agrarian capitalists employed unfree labour-power, and the presentation by Breman from the 1990s onwards of same view, it concerns a materialist as distinct from a non-materialist emphasis.[24] My case about deproletarianization is based on unfreedom as this structures relations of production: attachment has shifted from permanent to casual and migrant workers, and debt bondage applies increasingly to landless labourers who are no longer

21 Between 1985 and 1990, when Breman's view about the connection between capitalism and bonded labour underwent a reversal, a number of articles by me appeared criticizing his claim that unfreedom was on the decline and being replaced by free labour, and pointing out that unfree relations were much rather acceptable to agrarian capitalists. These articles are listed in Brass (1999: 308).

22 Thus, for example, Breman (2007: 165, 188ff.) goes to some length to claim an affinity between his interpretation of bonded labour and that of the Thorners in their pathbreaking and valuable research on rural India, a claim that has been challenged by me earlier (Brass, 2000b: 127).

23 See Breman (2007: 59). For the initial reference to the work of Patel, see Brass (1999: 242, note 29).

24 Apart from this materialist/non-materialist emphasis, one might ask in what way, precisely, are the characteristics attributed by Breman to what surfaced around 1990 as 'neo-' or the 'new' bondage different from those attributed by me during the 1980s to deproletarianization? Both refer to the same pattern of rural change, whereby commercial enterprises in the agrarian sector reproduce social relations of production that are unfree in a labour process that is capitalist.

unfree throughout the whole agricultural cycle or on an intergenerational basis. By contrast, the main difference between past and present forms of unfreedom according to Breman is one of perception: whereas in the past bonded labourers regarded unfreedom as a form of 'patronage', now they no longer do so.

From this non-materialist concept of 'new' bondage stem many of the epistemological problems encountered in his interpretation, not least the way in which confusion persists regarding what 'patronage' actually entails, and whether its reproduction was voluntary or coerced.[25] Bonded labour is described by Breman as a form of 'patronage' because of landlords' desire 'to sustain the leisurely lifestyle they, as patrons, were accustomed to lead', and, further, that 'as clients [bonded labourers] enjoyed their [that is, landlords'] protection and support'.[26] In furtherance of his view that, because it corresponded to 'patronage', bonded labour was 'voluntary', Breman argues that neither the colonial authorities nor postmodernists such as Prakash regard the relation as coercive.[27]

---

25 This difficulty is highlighted in the less than clear attempts by Breman (2007: 189–190) at damage limitation, such as following: 'I emphasized the central importance of patronage in encouraging the master to employ servants on the basis of bonded servitude. In my view, the subsequent disintegration of halipratha (= patronage) is clearly the result of the gradual introduction of a capitalist mode of production... But this does not mean that the work regime that replaced halipratha did not contain elements reminiscent of the former system of bonded labour.... My concerns relate...to the claim that after the disappearance of the halipratha system, the halis were free to hire out their labour at the higher possible price. Although this freedom was restricted, I do not see this as detracting from the capitalist character of the agrarian economy.'

26 See Breman (2007: 37, 40, 66–67). That he still endorses a positive view of 'patronage' is evident from his observation (Breman, 2007: 67) that the '*hali* remained bonded to his master, but the element of patronage that had been so important in the past faded away. Little was left of the protection and support which the *hali* could depend on in difficult times.'

27 See Breman (2007: 36, 37, 44, 46, 55–56). That such a claim is debateable, he then says (Breman, 2007: 71, note 1), was pointed out only in 2004 by Neeladri Bhattacharya. Breman forgets that this was pointed out much earlier: precisely this criticism – his underestimation of coercion – was made by me in articles about unfree labour that appeared during the 1980s and 1990s. A decade after the postmodern interpretation by Prakash (1990) of debt bondage as non-coercive was the object of a sustained critique (Brass, 1999: Chapter 8), Breman too takes issue with this approach in his most recent book (Breman, 2007: 46ff.). The critical stance towards postmodernism of Breman now contrasts somewhat with the more favourable view taken by him earlier of Prakash (Breman, 1993: 298). That Prakash (1992: 38) reciprocated the earlier view by endorsing Breman's interpretation of the hali system is, perhaps, no more than evidence of the recognition by the former of the latter as a kindred spirit.

The difficulty here is simply stated: his argument that, since bonded labour was a form of 'patronage' it was also 'voluntary' and thus not based on coercion, is contradicted by much of what is said by him elsewhere in his most recent book. Hence this positive interpretation of debt bondage is no different from that criticized subsequently, where Breman notes that 'the Dublas themselves were blamed for their status as bonded servants,' adding that what this 'boiled down to was that they were halis because they wanted to be.'[28] This, he concludes rightly, 'is the well-worn argument that slaves become slaves because they lack the resolve to live and work in freedom,' the only problem being that – under the rubric of bonded labour = 'patronage' – it is an argument that he himself has advanced for four decades.[29]

Breman talks of 'disloyalty' and servants wanting/wishing to leave, while their masters were keen to keep them on as tied labour.[30] This, however, not merely contradicts but reverses his earlier claim, which was that masters wanted to discard their *hali* workers, whereas the latter wanted to stay in this kind of relation because they benefited from what Breman originally termed 'patronage'. It also contradicts what is said earlier in his most recent book, where he states that it was 'the economic security the relationship offered [which] explains why the Dublas preferred to bond themselves to a master... [a] perspective that bonded labourers must be envied rather than pitied.'[31] Neither party, he avers, 'strove to terminate the [bonded labour] relationship into which they had entered, nor were they eager to clear the "debt" on which it was based.'[32]

Given that earlier he associated unfree relations with 'patronage', and the erosion of the latter ('depatronization') as evidence for a corresponding decline in unfreedom, his concluding observation in his most recent book about the economic/non-economic function of the bonded labour relation in colonial Gujarat is a mass of contradictions. A landlord, we are told helpfully,

28 See Breman (2007: 106).

29 Lest one forgets, the core of the argument advanced by Breman throughout this period is that, as long as 'patronage' had a material reality – constituted a 'subsistence guarantee', in other words – agricultural workers not merely entered but sought out a bonded labour relationship voluntarily because they benefited from it. In a 1988 lecture, republished subsequently (Breman, 2003: 33), he makes this very point: 'As I have explained in an earlier publication, elements of patronage were inherent to this form [= hali] of voluntary servitude.'

30 See Breman (2007: 67ff.).

31 See Breman (2007: 37).

32 See Breman (2007: 47).

employed *halis* mainly for non-economic reasons, yet also principally for economic ones.[33] Once again, the reader is left wondering what, precisely, the situation actually was, let alone why. Much the same is true of the way the village economy and coercion are depicted in his most recent book.

Both the efficacy and the material benefits of 'patronage', and consequently its 'voluntary' and non-coercive nature, were – and are – attributed by Breman in turn to two interrelated causes: the lack of other economic jobs, and the closed nature of the village economy. His view that the lack of alternative employment opportunities was the reason why an agricultural worker entered a bonded labour relation for the 'subsistence guarantee' it provided was another of the claims I criticized.[34] A closed village society, I argued, was a stereotype that Breman himself has dismissed as a myth.

Despite accepting that 'I have in a number of other publications criticized the view of a closed village', he nevertheless contradicts this by maintaining that 'the economic activity under the *ancien regime* had indeed a limited scope – it was largely restricted to the locality and its immediate surroundings, and there was only a small quantity of money in circulation'.[35] This is in turn contradicted by another statement earlier in the most recent book, where Breman writes just as categorically that '[m]y conclusion contradicts the assumption

33 Hence the following (Breman, 2007: 47, 48): 'My view of halipratha in the early colonial economy of south Gujarat is the same as in the account on my first fieldwork study [in 1974]: in spite of the prominence I attribute to the patron-client aspect of the relationship, I still believe that the tie between master and servant was primarily driven by economic motives – for the master, it was the need for additional labour... Without the halis, the cultivation of sugarcane, an important commodity in the early colonial economy, would have been impossible.'

34 See Brass (2000b: 135–136, 143 note 54) for this particular criticism. Despite his emphasis on the lack of alternatives as being the driving force behind the acceptance by agricultural workers of bonded labour arrangements, Breman (2007: 29) reveals inadvertently that just such an alternative did exist. Hence the fact of what he terms 'land flight', whereby in the 1830s '[f]ields were left fallow [since land] flight, a classic weapon in the arsenal of peasants' resistance, remained a possibility because there was still plenty of waste land in the neighbouring principality of Baroda.' Indeed, Breman (2007: 67) cites with approval an official report from the 1920s which points out that 'labourers run away not because they get better terms elsewhere but because the treatment given to them is not at all sympathetic.' So even where alternatives in the form of employment or landholding elsewhere were not available, workers still 'absconded', which suggests that – *pace* Breman – coercion was an important reason why those who remained in bonded labour relations did so.

35 See Breman (2007: 59). Predictably, this notion of a closed village is contradicted by information contained elsewhere in the same book, where he (Breman, 2007: 28) notes that during the second half of the nineteenth century 'the construction of roads and of bridges across the larger rivers put an end to local isolation.'

that the village economy was a closed circuit that functioned solely to meet the needs of the inhabitants. No matter how important this was, monetary transactions played an important role in contacts with the outside world.'[36] As contradiction follows upon contradiction, the reader is once again left wondering what, precisely, it is possible to believe.

This applies also to the related issue of migration, and how unfree relations were intensified by commercial producers specifically as a response to alternative employment opportunities.[37] Having asserted that there was no 'evidence of an exodus of labour from agriculture...which forced the landowners to use coercion to ensure that there were sufficient labourers for tilling the land', Breman then immediately contradicts himself by stating on the same page that '[l]andless Dublas seized the opportunities outside agriculture to escape from the clutches of the landowners'.[38] In other words, coercion *was* necessary to retain labour-power in the agrarian sector, a fact conceded later in his most recent book when referring to 'landlords who used violent means to force runaway servants to return to the village.'[39]

II

Avoiding Theory (and Its Advantages)

As has been noted in previous critiques, a major part of the problem is that, in a field of study where some knowledge of theory is crucial, Breman has little

36 See Breman (2007: 28).

37 This link is part of my case about the economic dynamics structuring deproletarianization.

38 See Breman (2007: 63). The same point is made subsequently, where Breman (2007: 64) states that there 'was no mass exodus of labour from agriculture in the nineteenth and the first half of the twentieth centuries.' He seems to imply that, because outmigration from agriculture was seasonal and not permanent, this in some way supports a claim that the village in Gujarat remained more-or-less a closed economy, which is clearly not the case. The mere fact of this outmigration undermines his assertion both that 'there was only a small quantity of money in circulation', and that no coercion was necessary to retain workers. That the latter returned to the village, and were consequently vulnerable to pressures exercised in this context by or on kinsfolk, merely underlines how effective coercion would have been in these circumstances.

39 See Breman (2007: 185). In arguing that unfreedom was enforced both by masters collectively (refusing to employ runaways) and by coercion that took many forms – for example, pressure on or through kinship networks – Breman (2007: 54–55) now accepts a central part of my argument about coercion.

understanding of theory, not least because he uses concepts in a muddled fashion, often without defining them.[40] The result is that in each successive article or book by him one encounters what are in effect backtracking statements – along the lines of 'what I actually meant by this was…' – which merely adds to the confusion. This constant process of revision is itself a difficulty signalled by the frequent appearance of modifying terms such as 'new thoughts', 're-examined' and 'revisited' in article and/or chapter titles.[41] Whereas most authors deploy these terms to announce a reappraisal of the work of others, Breman generally uses them to amend views found in his own previous publications.

That he still misunderstands theory is evident, for example, from the following contradiction. Having finally taken on board the argument that capital thrives on unfree labour, as embodied in his use of terms such as 'the new bondage' and 'neo-bondage', Breman nevertheless asserts that I am wrong in arguing that bonded labour is displacing free workers.[42] In a similar vein, and notwithstanding his endorsement of the view that capitalism will not automatically replaced bonded labour with workers that are free, he talks of Dublas 'selling their labour', unaware that a capacity on the part of a worker personally to commodify and recommodify his/her own labour-power is a characteristic of production relations that are free.[43]

---

40 Others have noticed this difficulty. In the course of reviewing a book by Breman, Ashok Rudra makes the following apposite comments (*Development and Change*, 18/1, January 1987, pp. 175–176): '[The book is characterized by] extremely careless use of technical terms belonging to Marxian political economy. The most glaring example is his use of the term "social formation".… Now Breman uses the term in such combinations as "Social Formation within Agrarian production" (which is the heading for a chapter dealing with agrarian classes) and "Social Formation in South Gujarat"… Quite clearly, what he means by this term is something quite different from its meaning in Marxism. As the term does not occur outside Marxism, it is impossible to guess what meaning he attaches to it. … he [also] makes extensive [use] of the term "class", but does not stop anywhere to clarify how he defines it. This is all the more deplorable, given the vast body of literature [about] the concept of class. His tendency to use technical terms loosely is even more glaringly revealed in his uses of such phrases as "feudal formation" [,] "feudal pattern" [,] "feudal elite" [,] and even "seigneurial kind of Anavil Brahmins" [,] and of course "feudal mode".' Without irony, Breman (2003: 33) has observed subsequently about the hali relation that '[t]his type of servitude has been linked to easily with a…feudal lifestyle of dominant landowners', as though he himself had not made precisely this connection.

41 Not just the second chapter in his most recent book (see Breman (2007: 35) – 'The System of Bonded Labour Revisited'), but also in earlier books (see Breman (1993: Ch. 16) – 'Bondage and Dependency Re-examined').

42 For this assertion, see Breman (1999c: 423).

43 See Breman (2007: 36).

Empirically there are also problems, epitomized by the presence of howlers: earlier, for example, Breman confused the work of Epstein on Karnataka with that of Harriss on Tamil Nadu.[44] Breman's capacity to misinterpret issues or contradict himself is, unfortunately, seemingly endless. When considering the role of unfree labour in debates taking place within the Indian National Congress during the 1920s, for example, he maintains implausibly that '[t]he system of unfree labour inevitably came to light as knowledge about the agrarian structure and landscape increased, in and through the programme of agitation.'[45] This, as Breman must surely be aware, is incorrect: knowledge about the presence of the bonded labour system preceded the 1920s debates by a very long time, as numerous reports by the colonial authorities testify.[46]

There is also a methodological issue relating to historical sources for the frequent assertions made about views held by bonded labourers themselves. Thus, for example, Breman builds his case about the erosion of the hali system on a change in the perception of both parties as to its meaning. Noting the opinion of one researcher who during the early 1930s had 'failed to observe any signs of disappearance of the system', Breman counters this with the comment that '[t]his does not change the fact, however, that the relationship between master and servant was perceived very differently from the start of the twentieth century than at the beginning of the colonial era.'[47] How does he – how *can* he – know this, when those to whom such a general view is attributed – bonded labourers in nineteenth and early twentieth century Gujarat, in other words – left no first-hand written evidence as to what they thought about this relation?[48]

44 For details of this mistake, see Brass (2000b: 128).

45 See Breman (2007: 76).

46 The alternative is that Breman (2007: 86) really believes that '[c]learly, the Congress movement lacked sufficient insight into the fabric of rural society', which is naïve. That the latter is the case cannot be discounted, since there are other instances of this. Hence his touching faith in official commitments to redistribute land to the rural poor (Breman, 2007: 167): 'This review of the land reforms in post-colonial India leads me to conclude that they were designed and implemented in such a way that social classes like the Halpatis were systematically denied access to agrarian landownership.'

47 See Breman (2007: 69–70).

48 As Breman presumably knows, collecting information about what agricultural workers do or do not think on the subject of their employment conditions is difficult, not least because masters are rightly suspicious of what may be divulged in the course of a fieldwork interview. Whilst it is possible to obtain such information from bonded labourers when actually conducting fieldwork – and many Indian researchers have done this, despite the risks both to themselves and to their informants – retrieving the equivalent

Faced with views that undermine claims he makes concerning the efficacy of 'everyday-forms-of-resistance', Breman is compelled to fall back on assertions that his opinion about the situation is the correct one.[49] The methodological problem informing his approach is recognized – albeit reluctantly – only with regard to the impact of democracy introduced after 1947. This, he rightly observes, should have worked in favour of agricultural workers, by enabling them through the vote to exert pressure on those who held power to meet their specific interests. Despite the fact that this has not happened, and he himself has seen little evidence to support the view that the ruling class has changed in response to democratic pressure from below, Breman insists this was the one area – the franchise – in which 'the landless benefit considerably'.[50]

---

grassroots voice from the past raises special problems of accessibility. Even when opinions are attributed to bonded labourers by third parties in reports about working conditions in a distant era, how do we know whose voice we are hearing? Given this methodological difficulty, to make categorical statements about what bonded labourers in nineteenth century India 'perceived' is – to put it no more strongly – problematic in the extreme. By observing that when in 1947 a commission by the government of Bombay conducted research into bonded labour in south Gujarat, '[i]t was the first time that the Halpatis had been the subject of an empirical study and had been asked...about the nature of their employment, their wages, and their way of life', that Breman unknowingly concedes the point about an absent 'voice-from-below', which makes all talk of what bonded labourers thought or did not think – what they 'perceived' – before that conjuncture redundant.

49 Noting the presence of an interpretation that does not coincide with his, Breman (2007: 159) simply asserts that he is right: 'Does this observation that little changed in the balance of rural power suggest that the relations of domination and subordination continued as before? Not in my opinion. Certainly, there was little scope for manoeuvre, but to suggest that the situation stayed the same as it always had been ignores *the fact* that the landlords had lost some of their legitimacy and the landless mass had started to express impatience at their exclusion' (emphasis added), This underlines once again the methodological difficulty at the centre of his argument: namely, to impute motive and perception for which the necessary evidence is flimsy or non-existent.

50 'Only in one area', notes Breman (2007:187, emphasis added), 'did the landless benefit considerably, a change that had far-reaching consequences for Indian society: the introduction of the universal franchise. A great mass of people who had been largely invisible and had no voice had the opportunity after decolonization to express their views and bring them to the attention of their political leaders. ...those leaders responded to that mandate with carelessness and conceit. *This does not change the fact, however, that the introduction of democracy, without restrictions founded on wealth or schooling, had a profound emancipatory impact. If, as is often the case, I have difficulty in finding concrete evidence of this sea change,* I need only think of the frustration and powerless rage which it invoked among the high-caste landowners.' This illustrates as clearly as need be the problem faced

And as before, the language and concepts used by Breman are, to put it at its most charitable, very odd indeed. Too often one encounters in the pages of his latest book an assertion by Breman to the effect that 'I agree' or 'I disagree' with a particular text/argument, as if an utterance of this kind was by itself sufficient to resolve the issue in question. Undefined terms such as 'underclass', 'subaltern masses' and 'subaltern position' crop up periodically throughout the latest book, no effort being made to explain what these concepts mean, or who is included under their rubric and why.[51] Hence we are informed that 'the master-servant relationship was more a matter of lifestyle than social identity': one can only guess at what is meant here, and the extent to which it is ever possible epistemologically to separate 'social identity' from 'lifestyle'.[52]

An inescapable conclusion is that, as regards theory, Breman has been influenced by what was written during the 1980s about deproletarianization.[53] There is nothing wrong with this, since revising long-held views in the light of new interpretations is standard procedure in scholarly work. The problem lies elsewhere: an implausible insistence that he has not changed his mind, in the process attempting to claim a non-existent theoretical link between what he wrote earlier about bonded labour in Gujarat, and what he writes now. Ironically, when he eschews theory, and thus also the confusion this generates, Breman does have things of interest to say.

---

by Breman: the absence of evidence required for such prognoses notwithstanding, an over-optimistic assessment about emancipation of one form or another generates in turn misleading interpretations as to the nature of rural transformation.

51 For similarly undefined references to 'subaltern class', see Breman (2003: 3). At times it appears as if Breman simply plucks terms from the ether, and applies them to a particular situation or group without too much thought as to the result. Hence the statement (Breman, 2007: 159) that in the 1930s 'this refusal [by landlords] to grant the rural poor their human right to a dignified existence' combines the language of 1990s international legislative ordinances ('human rights') with an essentially meaningless sentimentality ('dignified existence'), neither of which contribute to an understanding of the situation described. Somewhat naïvely, it also assumes that a landlord really ought to have taken more notice of the 'rights' and 'dignity' of his bonded labourers, a view that could be advanced seriously only by someone who also thinks that 'patronage' actually benefited such workers.

52 See Breman (2007: 42).

53 Even the same language pops up in subsequent analyses. Thus, for example, the concluding observation about deproletarianization (Brass, 1999: 303) that '[j]ust as the formation of a rural proletariat can be the product of class struggle, so the latter process can also lead to its unmaking (= disempowerment)' finds an echo in the very title of a book (Breman, 2004) published shortly afterwards.

His work on the late nineteenth century plantation system in Sumatra, for example, is not merely courageous but important, and will continue – rightly – to define what others think and publish about the colonial regime there.[54] Based on the Rhemrev Report and archival research, the result is – in contrast to his work on Gujarat – an exemplary descriptive account by Breman that does make a notable contribution to agrarian historiography. Significantly, the value of the text about colonial Sumatra is due in no small part to the general absence of theory: in the best ethnographic tradition, Breman's account of the plantation regime there is mainly a narrative one, and thus largely free of the difficulties that characterize his muddled and conflicting interpretations of rural Gujarat.

III

Structural Adjustments

Breman is not the only one to have misinterpreted the link between bonded labour and agrarian capitalism in India, and then changed his views about the connection between them. Among those who have also done this are two neo-classical economists who have written extensively about development issues as these apply to rural India: Amartya Sen and Barbara Harriss-White. Both the latter – like Breman – have misunderstood not just the free/unfree labour distinction, but also and therefore its connection to the accumulation process, and thus the theoretical significance of this relational difference for the debate about agrarian transformation and economic development.

If one is writing about rural labour relations in India, an inability to understand not just the difference but also the significance of the distinction between free and unfree labour is rather obviously a serious shortcoming. Again like Breman, both Amartya Sen and Harriss-White have changed their mind subsequently about this issue, and in precisely the same way. Having initially declared bonded labour a residual and/or pre-capitalist social form, destined to vanish as Indian agriculture is transformed by capitalism, each now accepts

54 The text in question is Breman (1989), an interesting ethnography about plantation agriculture under Dutch colonialism. Among the many useful insights it provides are that the debt owed by an absconding worker was then allocated to others in his gang, an effective method of internal policing to prevent desertion (Breman, 1989: 156). Similarly effective in terms of deterrent were the practices of capital and other forms of punishment inflicted publicly in the workplace (Breman, 1989: 159).

that such production relations are much rather central to the accumulation project in the Indian countryside.

The contradictions inherent in bourgeois development economic theory about unfree labour, and also the extent of the assumptions it shares with the semi-feudal thesis to which Breman and others initially adhered, can be illustrated with reference to the case of Amartya Sen. Accordingly, the latter endorses not only the revisionist 'findings' by neo-classical economic historiography concerning the economically advantageous material conditions enjoyed by plantation slaves in the antebellum American south, but also the semi-feudal view of bonded labour as a pre-capitalist relation.[55]

Until very recently, Sen has ignored the implications for development theory and agrarian transition of the continued existence in the agrarian sector of the Third World of unfree labour.[56] This absence is in one sense surprising, since the theory of exchange entitlements which informed his views about famine was based on the notion of choice-making individuals, freely exchanging their commodities in the market, which is central to the neoclassical economic paradigm.[57] Now, however, unfree relations of production suddenly loom large in his analysis of development problems.[58]

---

55 The weight of evidence to the contrary notwithstanding, Sen (1999: 28–29) accepts at face value the much-criticized 'findings' by Fogel and Engerman (1974) that slaves on the antebellum plantation in the American south enjoyed a higher living standard of living than free workers in the industrial north.

56 In his initial work on famine and entitlements (Sen, 1980; 1981), for example, there was no mention of bonded labour as the outcome of famine in India. It was only much later that the existence of this link was even acknowledged, and then only in passing (Drèze and Sen, 1989: 74 note 21). Consequently, there has been no attempt by Sen to investigate the well-established and important historical connection, both in India and elsewhere, between starvation, destitution, and the resulting absence of entitlements on the one hand, and the entry by those affected by hunger into unfree relations of production on the other, in particular as this takes the form of the enforced sale of children by impoverished poor peasant households.

57 For Sen, therefore, famine episodes involved an exchange of equivalents between equals, a view which failed to take into account the degree to which the price of some of the assets exchanged (e.g., labour-power) declined in the course of famine, while that of others increased (e.g., food).

58 Hence the view (Sen, 1999: 3, 7) that 'development requires the removal of major sources of unfreedom: poverty as well as tyranny, poor economic opportunities as well as systematic social deprivation, neglect of public facilities as well as intolerance or overactivity of repressive states', and 'the battle against the unfreedom of bound labour is important in many third world countries today for some of the same reasons the American Civil War was momentous. The freedom to enter markets can itself be a significant contribution

Having identified in the concept 'market' both an 'economic' and a 'moral' dimension, whereby the latter corresponds to the right of an individual to transact freely, while the former involves a mechanism which delivers economic efficiency, Sen maintains that the current predominance of the 'economic' dimension – the emphasis on economic efficiency – obscures the existence and importance of the 'moral' dimension.[59] It is this second aspect, which he categorizes as the 'old heritage', that Sen now wants to reclaim.[60]

Even if the market does succeed in delivering economic efficiency, Sen argues, it may do so by depriving people of 'free choice' over 'where to work, what to produce, what to consume…'.[61] It is clear from the latter, however, that the absence of free labour is being used by Sen to criticize not capitalism but socialism, thereby emphasizing the real concern behind his attempt at rescuing the 'market'. Not only does he invoke the anti-socialist view ('the road to

---

to development,…'. However, although Sen notes the existence of a connection between rural poverty and unfree labour, he evades the fundamental issue of determination. Economic unfreedom is simply equated with 'extreme poverty' (Sen, 1999: 8), therefore, without addressing the crucial question of causality: that is, whether unfreedom gives rise to poverty, or whether poverty gives rise to unfreedom. To say, as he does, that the poor are unfree because they poor, is tautological – not to say banal.

59 Thus the claim by Sen (1999: 27–28) that '[t]he shift in the focus of attention of pro-market economics from freedom to utility has been achieved at some cost: the neglect of the central value of freedom itself.' 'This point', he continues, 'may look somewhat esoteric in the context of economic development in view of the priority that the development literature tends to give to generating high incomes, a bigger basket of consumer goods and other culmination results (= outcomes). But it is far from esoteric. One of the biggest changes in the process of development in many economies involves the replacement of bonded labour and forced work, which characterize parts of many traditional agricultures, with a system of free labour contract and unrestrained physical movement. A freedom-based perspective on development picks up this issue immediately in a way that an evaluative system that focuses only on culmination outcomes may not.'

60 See Sen (1999: 25). If the inference (for example, in the assertion that bonded labour constitutes an 'often neglected consideration') is that prior to it being raised by him (Sen, 1999: 7, 113) no one else had noticed either the significant presence and economic role of unfree labour in developing countries, or the connection between unfreedom and economic development, or indeed the morality versus efficiency argument, then clearly this is wrong. Similarly incorrect is his claim (Sen, 1999: 29) that bonded labour is 'in fact… one of the cases in which Marxian analysis has tended to have an affinity with libertarian concentration on freedom as opposed to utility'. This very point is addressed and then dismissed (Brass, 1997b: 22–23) in the introduction to a book (Brass and van der Linden, 1997) which Sen himself cites and which, one presumes, he has read.

61 See Sen (1999: 27).

serfdom') of neo-liberal cold warriors such as Hayek, therefore, but by castigating socialism for denying the free commodification of labour-power, Sen also appears to forget that such an outcome is in fact central to the process of Socialist planning.[62]

This highly problematic maneouvre – inculpating socialism but not capitalism for unfree labour – enables Sen to argue that the 'market' is a virtuous institution, and thus aids his attempt to rescue neoclassical economic theory from political bankruptcy where development theory and debt bondage are concerned. Rather like the arguments of Fogel and Engerman, the twofold subtext to his analysis is that the market is not responsible for unfreedom and, moreover, 'the market *cares*, so stay with it'.

Since it relates to the problem of a transition to free labour, therefore, the Sen has finally accepted what others recognized long ago: namely, both the centrality to bourgeois development theory of the presence/absence of bonded labour, and the common occurrence throughout rural areas in developing countries of unfree relations.[63] Like Breman intially, and other exponents of the semi-feudal thesis currently, however, Sen continues to regard bonded labour as a non- or pre-capitalist relation. Hence the contrast between 'developed capitalist economies', and contexts where 'these values [= the freedom to transact] are not yet developed'.[64] Similarly, not only does he speak of the 'unfreedom of pre-capitalist labour arrangements', and of the fact that '[t]he

---

62 Hence the view (Sen, 1999: 114) that 'the failure of bureaucratic Socialism in Eastern Europe and the Soviet Union' must linked to 'the more immediate issue of the denial of freedom in a system where markets were simply ruled out in many fields...people could be disallowed from using the markets even when they existed...they could be barred from seeking employment in an ongoing recruitment process'.

63 Hence the contrast between his current view, that 'the crucial challenges of development in many developing countries today include the need for the freeing of labour from explicit or implicit bondage that denies access to the open labour market', that 'this issue of market-based freedom is quite central to the analysis of bonded labour – common in many developing countries', that 'the absence of the freedom to transact can be a major issue in many contexts', that 'this freedom is critically important right now in many parts of the world', and further that 'labour bondage can be found in many countries in Asia and Africa' (Sen, 1999: 7, 29, 113), and earlier pronouncements about the same issue. Like so many others, therefore, a quarter of a century ago Sen regarded unfree labour as a residual form, and consequently maintained that bonded labour 'systems were common until quite recently, and still survive in some areas today' (Sen, 1975: 60). An earlier monograph (Sen, 1992) which addressed the subject of inequality made no mention of unfree labour and its role in the development process.

64 See Sen (1999: 112–113).

linked presence of labour bondage with indebtedness yields a particularly tenacious form of unfreedom in many pre-capitalist agricultures', therefore, but the continued existence of unfree labour is also linked by him only to 'traditional bosses'.[65]

Most problematic in this regard, and a clear indicator of confusion, is the fact that in support of his view that bonded labour is a pre-capitalist relation, Sen invokes the study of debt bondage in Bihar by Mundle.[66] What Sen appears to have forgotten, or perhaps does not know, is that Mundle holds exactly the opposite view: namely, that in Palamau district, Bihar, debt bondage relations were the form in which labour was subordinated to capital.[67]

Sheep in Wolf's Clothing (*1*)

Although broadly speaking Harriss-White adheres to a neoclassical economic framework, her approach is in theoretical terms an eclectic one. In her investigations of nutrition, food systems, welfare programmes and anti-poverty policies in India, and seemingly unaware of the contradictions involved, she combines marginalist and Marxist concepts with an unrelenting empiricism.[68] Like Breman and Sen, Harriss-White has changed her mind about bonded labour, and the acceptability to capital of coercion, debt bondage and unfreedom.

Initially, the main focus of analyses by Harriss-White was on markets and trade, and thus also on merchant capital, which she reified as autonomous and confined epistemologically to the sphere of circulation. Consequently, moneylending was seen by her as largely separate from – and thus unconnected to – the accumulation process. Not surprisingly, therefore, she associated debt bondage with economic backwardness ('imperfect markets'), and hence perceived it as an obstacle to development. The latter in turn was seen as awaiting

65 See Sen (1999: 29–30, 113–114).

66 Having identified bonded labour as 'a particularly tenacious form of unfreedom in many pre-capitalist agricultures', therefore, Sen (1999: 30 note 27) proceeds to note that '(a)n important empirical study of this aspect of bondage and unfreedom…can be found in Sudipto Mundle, *Backwardness and Bondage*'. The study in question is Mundle (1979).

67 In fact, Mundle has been criticized by exponents of the semi-feudal thesis (Chopra, 1985: 180–181; Tiwary, 1985: 212 note 40) for holding this very view.

68 Different books and articles by her exhibit either one approach or the other. Many of the texts that appeared throughout the 1980s and into the 1990s were informed by a neoclassical economic framework (Harriss-White, 1984; 1991; 1992; 1996), notwithstanding the occasional foray into what purported to be an attempt at Marxist analysis (Harriss-White, 1981). As is noted below, the latter – or rather, the eclectic deployment of Marxist concepts ('class struggle') – became more prevalent at the turn of the millennium.

the emergence of its two pristine agents: industrial capital and a proletariat composed of workers who are free.

At this conjuncture, therefore, her views about coercion, unfree labour and capitalism in India were no different from those originally held by Breman. Citing the early work of the latter, Harriss-White maintained in texts that appeared during the 1980s that, although the presence of debt 'constrains the economic mobility of labour', in her opinion workers nevertheless accepted this imposition, a situation she ascribed to the fact that these were pre-capitalist relations amounting to a benign and advantageous patronage.[69]

A decade later, her view remained that bonded labour relations were benign, non-coercive arrangements, from which debtors benefit and the reproduction of which is desired by them.[70] That Harriss-White continued to regard these production relations as pre-capitalist is evident from her characterization of them as evidence for 'imperfect markets' or 'market distortions', the inference being that employers would automatically replace unfree working arrangements with ones that were free as capitalism spread throughout the Indian countryside.[71] By the late 1990s, however, she was clearly uncomfortable

69 For the view that debts owed by a worker to his/her employer were the result of patronage, notwithstanding the fact that this entailed 'constraint' on the economic mobility of the labourer concerned, see Harriss-White (1981: 128). Endorsing the 1970s publications by Breman where he interpreted bonded labour both as 'patronage' and as a pre-capitalist relation, she (Harriss-White, 1981: 118, 127, 129) – like him – assumes that 'the wage labour market is compartmentalized and imperfect, and that vertical and particularistic ties of patronage...characteristic of precapitalist enterprise, are more important than [class in] the relationship to the means of production'.

70 Writing about smallholdholding peasants who borrow from merchants in North Arcot District, Harriss-White (1992: 69–70) accepts that 'moneylending merchants often receive more of a crop than is formally required to cancel a debt,' but attributes this to 'the inertia of the debtor, who anticipates future contractual favours as a reward for faithfulness.' She makes equally clear her opinion about the absence of coercion being due to 'ties of caste, which exist in an estimated half of all transactions, make it difficult to engage in coercive behaviour. And most important, agricultural production is simply less profitable than marketing and moneylending.' That her idealised view about patronage as a benign relational form remained the same in the 1990s is evident from a subsequent observation (Harriss-White, 1996: 253) that 'patronage is used to tie labour...[a] more overt form of labour tying is via debt, which effectively bonds the debtor, but which may also be offered on relatively advantageous terms and conditions.' For more of the same, see Harriss-White (1996: 255–256, 257, 258).

71 For Harriss-White (1990: 90), therefore, the presence of debt bondage is attributed to the view that 'labour markets are only partially and imperfectly developed'. On how such

with this analysis, perhaps because Breman had already revised his interpretation of bonded labour.

Harriss-White was clearly baffled by the co-existence of a capitalist development in Indian agriculture and agrarian relations she had categorized hitherto as 'backward' and thus obstacles to accumulation.[72] She then provided a clue for the presence of this apparent contradiction: capitalist restructuring of the labour process, involving the reintroduction of unfree relations.[73] Without quite realizing it, Harriss-White had in fact described workforce decomposition/recomposition undertaken by capitalist producers, a transformation that corresponds to deproletarianization.[74] The irony is that the latter concept is one she was subsequently to dismiss as inapplicable to changes taking place in the Indian countryside.

After the turn of the millennium, there is a discernible change in the framework Harriss-White uses to analyse the Indian countryside. Not only does her focus shift from trade and markets to labour regimes, but unfreedom metamorphoses from a pre-capitalist relation to one that is now acceptable to capital.[75] Gone are references to the continued employment by rural agribusiness

---

'market distortions' constitute obstacles to the formation of capitalist 'market perfection', see Harriss-White (1996: 255).

72 'In Coimbatore district', she observes (Harriss-White, 1996: 261) with some puzzlement, 'relatively advanced agrarian production relations, relatively advanced financial relations in trading and the consolidation of local as well as long-distance commerce seem to have made little difference to the backward ways in which labour is organised in commerce.'

73 Her confusion is evident from, for example, the juxtaposition of the following statements (Harriss-White, 1996: 248, 250–251): 'We have evidence of a retreat from wage labour... "Labour markets", however, are still very far from completely formed... Economic devices to retain [workers include] "sticks" (forms of tying and unfreedom [consisting of] debt bondage or contracts of long-term attachment....)' She misinterprets the shift from what is at this conjuncture interpreted as a 'retreat' from wage labour, the *sine qua non* of capitalism, which cannot as a result accumulate without a proletariat freely selling its labour-power in a 'perfect market'.

74 Hence the view (Harriss-White, 1996: 264, 265) both that the 'labour force in agricultural markets is far from the "freedom" ascribed to the capitalist proletariat, indeed the lack of freedom not to undertake wage labour in these firms is a defining feature of agrocommercial capitalist development', and that attempts 'to cut costs are leading to reversion to unpaid labour of various sorts [a tactic that] involves bonding or attaching labour so as to work in the firm, farm or domestic space and thereby to increase its exploitation by multiple use.'

75 This changed emphasis, from trade and markets to labour regimes, is evident in texts such as Harriss-White and Gooptu (2000) and Harriss-White (2003a). Although the market has

of bonded labour as an anomaly, and the latter relation is no longer seen as a pre-capitalist relation one, soon to be replaced with workers who are free. Instead, there are now more references to the politics of class, capital and labour, and even class struggle.[76] This is also accompanied by an almost imperceptible conceptual transformation in the meaning of bonded labour itself, from a benign form of patronage to a non-benign form of unfreedom.[77] Not surprisingly, such theoretical shifts give rise to contradiction and confusion when a comparison is made, juxtaposing earlier interpretations with subsequent ones.

Aware perhaps that she has been talking about deproletarianization without realizing it, Harriss-White nevertheless attempts to deflect potential criticism on this point. Conceding that the object of unfreedom is indeed to 'buttress accumulation by holding down the price of labour, controlling its movement, forcing debt', she then maintains implausibly that '[r]ather than deproletarianization, these practices can be seen as the tactics of a savage form of proletarianization, since wage labour is never free.'[78] The irony is unmistakeable: despite adopting Marxist language and concepts to examine agrarian relations in India, she simultaneously rejects a central tenet of this theoretical approach – that a proletariat is composed of labour-power that is free.

---

not vanished from her agenda, it is now examined in a rather more critical way (Harriss-White, 2003b), and the earlier notion of 'market perfection' is nowhere to be seen.

76 'It is hard for the economist,' Harriss-White (2003b: 492) now recognizes, 'to evade the proposition that markets are social and political constructs whose performance is affected and continually changed by relations of authority'.

77 See, for example, negative depictions such as 'the formation of private armies to coerce labour through brutal suppression', and workers being 'mired in debt-bondage' (Harriss-White and Gooptu, 2000: 96, 98). In a similar vein, elsewhere she observes (Harriss-White, 2003b: 489) that in 'developing countries, under conditions of non-voluntaristic (*sic*) commercialization (induced by the need to repay debts…)… market exchange is better understood not in terms of allocative efficiency but rather as a mechanism of extraction of surplus by one class from another.' In one particular respect, however, Harriss-White remains consistent: she continues to cite Breman in support of her arguments about bonded labour, but with a single notable difference. Just as earlier she endorsed his initial views about debt bondage as a benign form of 'patronage' and a pre-capitalist relation incompatible with accumulation (see above), so now she endorses the opposite view (Harriss-White and Gooptu, 2000: 94–95, 114) made by him post-1990, that 'neo-bondage' is compatible with capitalist production in the Indian countryside.

78 See Harriss-White (2003a: 24, note 37).

What Harriss-White forgets, therefore, is that in Marxist theory a proletariat consists of workers who must be able personally to commodify and recommodify their own labour-power. That is, free to sell to the highest bidder what for the majority of workers is their only commodity: labour-power. By maintaining, incorrectly, that a worker unable to do this ('wage labour is never free') nevertheless corresponds to a member of the proletariat, she eliminates the specificity of workers who retain – and take advantage of – the ability to commodify/recommodify their own labour-power.

The irony lies in the fact that earlier she seemed to recognize the importance of this condition: the unfreedom inherent in debt bondage relations was, she accepted, 'an attempt to link the labour and the money markets in order to deprive the employee of a choice of employer.'[79] As presented by Harriss-White now, however, the inference is that no difference exists between wage labour that is free and other relational forms (chattel slavery, indenture, debt peonage, sharecropping). This error is compounded by the fact that, as used by her, 'a savage form of proletarianization' is a sociologically meaningless description that could just as easily apply to slaves who were landless.

Moreover, the claim that bonded labour is nothing more than 'a savage form of proletarianization' reveals the bourgeois politics linked to the neo-classical economic framework that still informs the assumptions of Harriss-White. By eradicating this 'savage' kind of work arrangement, so the argument goes, a 'benign' and 'natural' form of capitalism will once again be restored, and reign supreme. As has been noted above, this is the same epistemology adhered to by Sen.

In short, once a 'savage form of proletarianization' no longer exists, a 'perfect' market and with it an harmonious employer/worker relationship can be resumed.[80] The underlying assumption, to which neoclassical economic theory subscribes, is that a 'steady state' (= 'benign') capitalism exists and can be recuperated.[81] By contrast, Marxism argues that 'savage' capitalism is the logical – and indeed necessary – outcome of the accumulation process, the coda to the capitalist system itself.

---

79 See Harriss-White (1996: 253).

80 Uncharitably, it could be said that with this conceptual dualism based on something akin to a 'naughty' (= 'savage') and – inferentially – a 'nice' (= 'benign') form of capitalism, one has finally entered the realm of a theoretically rigorous political economy.

81 Elsewhere (Brass, 1999: Chapter 5; 2003a) it has been argued that this has long been a project of neoclassical economic historiography about unfreedom: namely, the desire to purge capitalism of its tainted aspects, exorcising the ghost of unfree labour, thereby sanitizing the accumulation process so as to be able to declare capitalism 'nice'.

IV

The Way Forward?

The real mystery is not that Breman, Sen and Harriss-White have all changed their minds without saying that this is what they have done, but that others who also write about production relations in rural India are seemingly unaware of this *volte face*. Although Breman himself has ceased personally to debate these issues with me, this role has now been taken by a number of others who have recently entered the debate, in the process criticizing my interpretation of the link between accumulation and unfree production relations whilst endorsing the current view of Breman on the subject of bonded labour in India. Among those in this category are Geert de Neve, Surinder Jodhka, Vikas Rawal and a geographer called Jens Lerche.

All but one of the latter endorse the claim advanced by Breman after 1990, that Indian agriculture was characterized by a rising incidence of 'neo-bondage', a form of unfree labour acceptable to capitalist producers.[82] Thus, for example, Lerche reproduces unquestioningly the shift from what Breman has now classified as 'classical' bonded labour – in reality, a reference to unfree relations that are of permanent duration – to 'hard-nosed modern economic relations...often involving migrant labour'.[83] No mention is made of the fact that originally Breman described this transformation as one from a pre-capitalist workforce that was unfree to a capitalist proletariat, nor is reference

82 The sole exception is Rawal (2004). Although he makes the same argument – that the expansion of commercial agricultural production in western Haryana after the turn of the millennium has not eradicated but reproduced unfree labour – no mention is made by him of the fact that it has been made before, and is thus not new. Despite the fact that the focus of his analysis is on female workers in Haryana, no mention is made either of the earlier and important work by Chowdhry (1994) on gender relations in the same context.

83 See Lerche (2007: 13–14, 15). Having dismissed the entry into debt bondage by workers as being due to 'extra-economic compulsion', Lerche reiterates the 'subsistence guarantee' argument ('this is the best option available to them') advanced by Breman, without realizing that it is a now discredited explanation (Brass, 1999: 226–230). This is in keeping with his earlier idealization of unfree labour. Initially, therefore, Lerche (1995: 494) presented debt as a benefit (= 'patronage') arising from employer/attached labour relations, rather than a way of controlling workers. Thus the ability of an attached labourer to borrow at a monthly interest rate of five per cent instead of ten per cent was depicted by him in a positive light, instead of asking why borrowing was necessary in the first place. The latter has been attributed by me to the fact that low wages are inadequate, due in turn to the manipulation by employers of the credit cycle so as to ensure worker indebtedness, an explanation that Lerche (2007: 14) now accepts is correct.

made to the critiques by me of the way Breman conceptualized 'transition', pointing out its inconsistencies and contradictions.[84]

Seemingly unaware of the change of mind, and the analytical problems to which this has given rise, Lerche ends up recommending the post-1990 position of Breman as the way in which unfree labour and its causes should henceforth be studied ('The development away from classical bonded labour relations has been charted most thoroughly by Breman [who] is probably the foremost scholar on bonded labour and related issues in India... Breman argues convincingly...', etc., etc., etc.).[85] Because his views about bonded labour are based so closely on an uncritical endorsement of Breman, Lerche unsurprisingly reproduces many of the same errors and mistakes.

This is a difficulty that also informs the approach of Jodhka to the issue of unfree labour.[86] Criticizing me recently for questioning the efficacy of grassroots 'assertiveness' in undermining debt bondage, Jodhka endorsed the claim about the effectiveness of resistance by bonded labourers made by Breman, whose views on this issue he said he shared.[87] Now, however, Jodhka is critical of Breman for holding precisely the same view, in the process endorsing the point initially made by me against the resistance framework: namely, that its prognosis about the emancipation of bonded labour was over-optimistic.[88]

---

84 Not the least of the many ironies is that Lerche fails to note the extent to which the current argument made by Breman – that unfree labour is perfectly acceptable to agrarian capitalists – is no different from the position argued all along by me, a point he actually recognized a decade ago (see below). This would have become clear had the relevant exchanges (Brass, 1997a, 2000b; Breman, 1999a, 1999b, 1999c) been consulted, but unfortunately none of these texts is cited by Lerche. The latter also manages to refer both to the fact of and the substance contained in contributions by Banaji (2003) and Jodhka (1994; 1995; 1996) in their exchanges with me over the meaning of unfree labour. For some reason, however, Lerche omits to mention that responses to them all were published (Brass, 1995c; 1996a; 1996b), let alone anything said by me in those responses. The same is true of de Neve and Jodhka, neither of whom takes up in any detail the points contained in my critical analyses of Breman. A reader of their accounts of these exchanges could be forgiven for thinking as a result that no reply was forthcoming, whereas in each case the arguments or claims advanced by Breman, Jodhka and Banaji were effectively rebutted.

85 For these uncritical endorsements of Breman's views about bonded labour, seemingly made in ignorance of the contradictions involved, see Lerche (2007: 13).

86 The extent of the misunderstandings permeating Jodhka's notion of unfreedom is outlined elsewhere (Brass, 1995c; 1996a; 1996b).

87 For this endorsement of Breman, made amidst a more general criticism of my views, see Jodhka (2004: 467).

88 Currently his view takes the following form (Jodhka, 2007: 3928): 'However, the nature of much of the resistance that Breman [mentions] seems to resemble what James Scott

In much the same vein, de Neve also endorses the approach of Breman to the study of labour in India, noting that 'the influential work of Breman has given a new impetus to sociological research of labour in India and has pinpointed many fields of investigation which have for too long been neglected in anthropological studies of labour'.[89] What escapes de Neve is that, rather than departing from the main assumptions structuring research by anthropologists and sociologists in rural India, Breman instead reproduced them.

This is evident from the espousal by Breman of the two main social scientific orthodoxies prevailing at the time. On the one hand, the interpretation of bonded labour as a form of caste 'patronage/clientage' based on *jajmani*, a view associated with the then dominant approach of Srinivas and Dumont.[90] And on the other, the view that unfreedom was a non-capitalist relation destined to vanish as capitalism penetrated agriculture, a shibboleth generated by the then equally ascendant semi-feudal thesis. His subsequent change of mind – unnoticed by de Neve – was a result of a 'new impetus to research' that originated elsewhere.

Misinterpretations I

When it comes to misinterpreting issues to do with unfree labour, Lerche, de Neve and Rawal unfortunately exhibit the same tendency as Breman to get things wrong.[91] Like Breman, Lerche and Rawal each subscribe to unfreedom as a 'subsistence guarantee' argument, the latter maintaining that in Haryana agricultural labour 'felt that accepting bondage was better than going hungry'.[92] Both the origins of and the opposition to the view that unfree labour is acceptable to agrarian capitalists are among the things which Lerche fails to recognize. Thus he maintains wrongly that it 'is commonly accepted that, in India since the 1950s, there has been a move away from traditional debt

describes as "everyday forms of resistance"... As has been pointed out by the critiques of Scott, the political effects of such resistance are not of much consequence and rarely lead to empowerment of the poor, or any kind of social and economic transformation... something that seems quite obvious in the context Breman is located in. Yet he often seems to romanticize such instances of resistance'. This is precisely the criticism that I have levelled against Breman in the past (Brass, 1999: 231ff.).

89 See de Neve (2005: 26).

90 See Dumont (1970) and the essays collected in Srinivas (1987).

91 The tendency on the part of Lerche to misinterpret what has been said about bonded labour relations in India has not escaped the notice of others (e.g., Venkateshwarlu and da Corta, 2001: 32–33, note 5).

92 For the 'subsistence guarantee' argument, see Rawal (2004: 13) and Lerche below.

bondage, while new types of bondage, consistent with the capitalist economy have emerged.'[93] This assertion is quite simply incorrect.

Until the 1980s, therefore, the most common argument made with regard to agrarian transformation in India was that of the semi-feudal thesis, exponents of which – like Breman, Byres, and Patnaik – insisted that capitalists would replace unfree labour with free workers, a view that still informs much of the discussion about rural transition and the agrarian question.[94] Equally wrong is the assumption by de Neve that 'bringing back politics into the study of class in India' was something that happened only in the late 1990s.[95] Such a claim overlooks the fact that the political dimension of class was recognized not only by most contributors to the mode of production debate during the late 1960s and early 1970s, but also by those who conducted research on issues such as the new farmers' movements from the 1980s onwards. In short, the politics of class never actually went away.

A failure to understand the link between class and debt also leads Rawal to misinterpret the cause and enforcement of bonded labour in Haryana.[96] Maintaining that entry into debt relations is the way agricultural workers secure access to credit, he depicts unfreedom as being to the interests of employers and workers alike.[97] What he forgets is the crucial distinction between productive

---

93 See Lerche (2007: 13).

94 On the persistence of the semi-feudal thesis, see Brass (1994; 1995a; 1999: 154ff.; 2002; and review essay 11, this volume). It is – or should be – clear from the hostile responses not just to my theory about deproletarianization (Patnaik, 1995) but also to Mundle (1979) and Marla (1981) concerning the unfreedom/capitalism link just how 'controversial' and thus unacceptable have been analyses putting forward the view that agrarian capitalists continue to employ unfree labour because they find it meets their economic needs.

95 That 'bringing back politics into the study of class in India' is attributed by de Neve (2005: 21, note 4) to texts published only in the late 1990s by those such as Chandavarkar and Harriss-White suggests a worrying unfamiliarity on his part with the voluminous literature that appeared throughout the preceding decades dealing with class and politics as well as the relationship between them. This concern is underlined by the pronouncement (de Neve, 2005: 22) that 'class identities are themselves constituted by the modalities of caste, kinship and gender', a tautology with which nobody would disagree.

96 In criticizing Jodhka for maintaining that bonded labour in Haryana was on the decline, Rawal (2004: 12) omits to mention the fact that this very criticism had been made earlier (Brass, 1995c; 1996a; 1996b).

97 Hence the following view (Rawal, 2004; 10): 'Given the harshness of the terms of the *siri* contracts and extra-economic coercion faced by the *siris*, a natural question that we asked the *siris* was as to why they became *siris* in the first place. The two most commonly cited reasons for becoming *siris* were: [the] need for credit and high unemployment among casual workers.'

and unproductive loans that underlies the way credit differs from bondage also signals divergent causes and outcomes of borrowing in terms of class.[98]

Credit is a method of setting in motion the means of production, usually with the object of accumulating capital, out of the profits of which such borrowing is repaid. It is a productive loan that generally does not lead to economic losses on the part of the borrower. Debt, by contrast, is the method whereby an agrarian capitalist separates a smallholder from the means of production or a worker from the ability personally to commodify/recommodify his/her own labour-power. As such, it corresponds to an unproductive loan that does indeed result in economic losses for the smallholder and/or worker concerned.[99]

Rawal also misunderstands how and why the structure of enforcement has changed. A perception of credit as benign stems in part from his view that debt is a way in which labouring households gain access to fodder for cattle. This overlooks the fact that in Haryana those who have access to fodder are better-off elements among the workforce, and are thus also those who for this reason contribute to the pressure exercised on propertyless workers to fulfil their debt-servicing labour obligations.[100]

Misinterpretations II

Again like Breman, Lerche attributes to me views that I do not hold. I did not say present forms of coercion were impossible to access methodologically. What I did say is that they were *hidden*, and for this reason their presence was either not asked about (by the researcher) or not revealed (by the informant).[101] Either way, my point was that during fieldwork investigations

---

98 For this, see Brass (1999: 1, 16, 32, 192, 201, 204, 219, 224, 245, 250).

99 It is also the way in which producers acquire and retain control over the labour-power of the family members of the indebted worker, and thus a method of cheapening and disciplining agricultural labour.

100 See Brass (1990a: 54).

101 One reason why bonded labour has not been asked about is methodological: a belief widely held among those conducting research that such relations no longer existed, and there was thus no need to enquire as to their presence. This is a methodological difficulty from which, unfortunately, Lerche himself has not been immune. Almost a decade ago he maintained that in Uttar Pradesh debt bondage had diminished in importance as a form of control exercised by creditor-employers over rural labour, and that as a consequence emancipatory trends were in evidence. (This, it should be noted in passing, is not what he says now) In his opinion (Lerche, 1999: 184) this resulted in a situation where 'rural labourers have experienced a number of positive changes...and are increasingly able to assert what they now perceive to be their rights...the position of labourers has improved.' However, the case Lerche built about the wholesale relational change and emancipatory

conducted by researchers coercion *should* be asked about, and insofar as these days this is done more often than it has been in the past, as illustrated by the ILO research project, this object has to some degree been met.[102]

Moreover, the accusation levelled by Lerche at the ILO – that focussing on unfree production relations lets capitalism off the hook, since it diverts attention from the issue of free labour – is misplaced for three reasons in particular.[103] First, although he is critical of ILO as an advocacy organization, Lerche forgets that the latest publication by Breman has been done with financial assistance from just such an organization, one with a politics that is far more problematic than the ILO.[104] Second, the charge of diverting attention from free workers is one that could more accurately be made against Harriss-White, whose analysis Lerche endorses.[105] And third, he overlooks the impact eliminating bonded labour would have both on free labour and on capitalism.

Thus a focus on unfree production relations does not deflect attention from capitalist exploitation of workers that are free, much rather the opposite. Criticism of bonded labour leading to its elimination would in effect knock away the bottom rungs of the ladder that is the labour regime. This it would do by making costlier to employ the reserve army of labour on which agrarian capitalist profitability and competitiveness depends, as unfree workers were

trends was based on what happened to the Chamars, local labourers who, it turned out, accounted for less than one third of the workforce. Migrants, who were then in the process of becoming increasingly important components of the workforce, were not – he asserted – bonded labour, despite evidence to the contrary (withholding wages) together with the fact that, by his own admission, he was unable to interview any of them.

102 As noted in my earlier publications, a problem does exist with regard to past forms of unfreedom, where the subject of an agrarian relation is no longer around to be asked what his/her views about this were. In these situations, it is necessary to rely on descriptions of what the relation entailed. What does remain lost to the historical record, however, is what the subjects themselves though about these relations, or the very dimension (= perception) that Breman privileges in his interpretation of the way in which 'patronage' changed.

103 His objections are levelled specifically at two recent reports published by the ILO (International Labour Organization, 2001, 2005).

104 The organization in question is Anti-Slavery International, from which Breman (2007: x) acknowledges the receipt of a grant. No blame attaches to him for this, for clearly he was unaware of the background. As the Anti-Slavery Society, that same organization – in the person of its joint President – some two decades ago endorsed a book written by a member of its General Committee (Sawyer, 1986) containing a sympathetic portrayal of the apartheid system then still in force in South Africa.

105 For his endorsement of Harriss-White, see Lerche (2007: 18, 19).

converted (or reconverted) into free equivalents. Once this relational and price differential was eliminated, it would be easier for workers of different ethnic/regional/national identities to unite, organize and fight *as a proletariat* in the Marxist sense of the term. As is well established historically, this is the kind of outcome which capital everywhere has always feared. Similarly incorrect is the assertion by Lerche that the eradication of bonded labour is for governments an easy option, a problem that can be solved materially without too much difficulty, which is why this issue has in his opinion moved up the agenda of international agencies such as the ILO.[106] Much rather the opposite is the case, however, in that governments have shown a marked reluctance to do anything concrete about bonded labour.[107] What does happen is that slavery and other forms of unfreedom are *pronounced* illegal, and the problem deemed 'solved' thereby.

The stock response by governments faced with accusations that unfree labour continues within their jurisdiction has been – and remains – one of denial. When confronted with evidence of its continued presence, the answer given by a representative of the State challenged in this manner is that as such relations are illegal, they could not possibly exist.[108] Declared abolished simply

106 Hence the view (Lerche, 2007: 7) that this 'cocooning of the forced labour issue makes it relatively safe for governments and organizations to deal with.' Neither is it the case, as Lerche infers, that what the ILO has done is to 'ghettoize' the issue of unfree labour, thereby forcing debate about labour standards into a cul-de-sac. Again, the situation is much rather the opposite: the ILO has helped to bring this work relation out of ghetto, and thus to underline the extent to which exploitative relations many of those in the development debate said would vanish, are still with us. Not the least valuable contribution of the ILO to the discussion is to indicate the extent to which hired workers in agriculture are also unfree. This is a much more fruitful approach than that of Banaji (2003), who makes an artificial distinction between labour-power that is paid a wage and that which is unfree, and insists – wrongly – on them being mutually exclusive categories: all rural workers in receipt of payment are according to him hired workers who are 'free'.

107 The reason for this is simple. To do so would entail challenging the economic interests of rural capitalist producers – rich peasants, commercial farmers and agribusiness enterprises – whose increasing political power in post-1947 India is a matter of record (Chattopadhyay, Sharma and Ray, 1987; Brass, 1995).

108 Typical, perhaps, was the official response by the Indian government when asked in the mid-1960s by the UN Special Rapporteur on Slavery (Awad, 1966: 166) if 'slavery or any institution or practice similar to slavery, as defined above [including bonded labour] exist in the country?' The Indian Constitution, he was informed (Awad, 1966: 169–170), 'prohibits all forms of slavery including forced labour and consequently the existence of slavery or any institution does not arise.' The official reply noted that 'a practice in the form of "bonded labour" had been in existence in some parts of India,' adding both that

as a result of being outlawed, bonded labour in effect vanishes from the political agenda. Not only is there no reason for any further action on this issue, but those who attempt to enforce such legislation themselves become the target of State action.

If bonded labour is disappearing because agrarian capitalists seek to replace unfree relations with ones that are free, as neoclassical economists and advocates of the semi-feudal thesis claim, then in an important sense this relational form is indeed 'on the way out' and as such 'not worth bothering about'. According to this prognosis, bonded labour will vanish of its own accord as economic development takes place, and intervention by the ILO is effectively redundant.

However, if the opposite is the case and – as I have argued – bonded labour is in particular circumstances for rural capital the preferred relational form, then it will increase as economic development occurs. According to *this* prognosis, bonded labour is *ipso facto* part of the problem of capitalism. Unfree relations have therefore to be addressed politically as an aspect of the way in which the capitalist system functions and reproduces itself. To do so is not a distraction from but rather part of the wider struggle against the accumulation process and its labour regime.[109]

Misinterpretations III

Much like Breman himself, Jodhka, de Neve, Rawal and Lerche also experience difficulty in grasping theory, and thus display a similar tendency to

'[a]nyway this practice is dying out,' and that '[t]he State Governments concerned have taken recourse to legislative executive measures to abolish the system [of unfree labour] wherever in existence.'

109 This was the position taken by Marx (1985: 189), who commented as follows during the course of the Geneva Congress of the First International in 1866: '...the more enlightened part of the working class fully understands that the future of its class, and, therefore, of mankind, altogether depends upon the formation of the rising working generation. They know that, before everything else, the children and juvenile workers must be saved from the crushing effects of the present system. This can only be effected by converting social reason into social force, and, under given circumstances, there exists no other method of doing so, than through general laws, enforced by the power of the state. In enforcing such laws, the working class do not fortify governmental power. On the contrary, they transform that power, now used against them, into their own agency.' This kind of mobilization, undertaken by workers as a class, has to be distinguished from contemporary forms of non-class agency, directed by bourgeois NGOs designed to mobilize 'the poor' along ethnic, gender or national lines.

self-contradiction. Despite confirming that casual workers employed in the agrarian sector of Haryana are 'tied labour', Jodhka refuses to categorize these production relations as unfree.[110] Because 'such debt obligations of casual labourers were of a temporary nature', he states, 'describing [them as] "bondage"...would be an overstatement.' Not only does Jodhka make the common error in assuming that non-permanent work arrangements are *ipso facto* free, but he also omits to mention that in Haryana debt-servicing labour obligations incurred by casual workers are heritable and enforced by fellow caste members.[111]

Having said that I am wrong to argue that employers bond workers by means of cash advances, de Neve then contradicts this by observing that, in order to ensure a supply of workers and to prevent them from organizing as such, capitalists do indeed reintroduce unfree labour relations.[112] Such inconsistency is to some degree attributable to problematic methods: de Neve accepts unchallenged the benign account given him by a labour contractor regarding cash advanced to workers.[113]

That de Neve misunderstands theory about unfree labour is evident also from his claim both that it is employers not workers who are bonded and

110 See Jodhka (1998: 236).

111 That in Haryana even production relations of a temporary or seasonal duration result in the loss of a capacity on the part of an indebted worker personally to commodify labour-power is evident from Brass (1999: 87ff.). When debts incurred by these workers remain unpaid, they are passed on to their kinfolk and those belonging to the same caste enforce compliance with outstanding labour obligations. Among those who accept that such arrangements correspond to unfree labour is Rao (1999a; 1999b).

112 Compare the denial by de Neve (2005: 200) of labour as unfree, and his criticism of me for arguing not only that it is but also that employers use debt bondage to curtail or preempt the growth of a specifically working class consciousness, with his (de Neve, 2005: 312) subsequent admission that capitalist 'development in the informal economy might increasingly inhibit workers' ability to unite, while reintroducing forms of labour bondage in an attempt to obtain a stable workforce for expanding (export) markets.'

113 See, for example, de Neve (2005: 191–192), where a *maistry* recruiting labour states that in 'the past, the labourers were working seriously, but now, because of [cash advances] they started to take things easier. They know that the owner is bonded to them because they hold his money as an advance.' This idealised account is accepted at face-value by de Neve, despite the fact that in cases where 'a labourer does not turn up [for work] in the morning, the manager might go to his house and call him to the factory', and further, that 'the owner himself might go to the house of his workers to "drag" them to the looms [and] as I observed on several occasions, the managers did not hesitate to abuse the workers' (de Neve, 2005: 192).

disempowered by virtue of cash advances made ('reverse bondage'), and that the transfer by a worker of debt and bondage from one employer to another in some sense undermines the efficacy of unfree production relations.[114] Observing that 'having left or escaped one employer, the worker cannot but enter new bonds of debt and dependency with another employer', however, de Neve then accepts this is a situation in which workers 'fail to escape structures of subordination that keep them tied to the employers as a group'.[115] In other words, a result of cash advances made by employers or labour contractors is that workers are and remain unfree.

Much the same is true of Rawal. He criticizes my view of unfreedom, arguing that 'the recent evidence suggests that [in parts of Haryana] the relationship of casual workers with their employers impose substantial restrictions on the workers', unaware that the latter point is precisely one made by me.[116] Furthermore, maintaining that 'it is analytically inaccurate to confuse all indebtedness with bondage', Rawal nevertheless accepts both that '[i]t is true that indebtedness often imposes restrictions on the freedom of workers to sell their labour power' and that 'the *siris* in Birdhana faced severe forms of restrictions on their freedom to work for employers of their choice'.[117]

Where theory about why unfree labour is acceptable to agrarian capitalists is concerned, however, the most problematic claims are those made by Lerche. Unaware that Breman has had a change of mind, Lerche also reproduces many of the contradictions and much of the confusion that structures the theoretical approach of the former. Because of this, the framework used by me

114 The practice of cash advances made to workers is interpreted by de Neve as evidence for the bondage and disempowerment not of labour but rather of the employer. Not only is this a revisionist view he shares with neoclassical economic historians, but it also overlooks the capacity of employers to enforce repayment of such advances. Why 'reverse bondage' is no different from other forms of unfreedom in terms of outcome for the workers concerned is outlined in Brass (1999: 34, 182, 188, 189–190, 201, 207, 296).

115 See de Neve (2005: 200). For more of the same, see de Neve (1999).

116 See Rawal (2004: 13).

117 See Rawal (2004: 13). The closeness of the link between debt and bondage in Haryana is evident from the following (Rawal, 2004: 9–10): 'The *siri* system imposed severe restrictions on the freedom of the *siri* and his family to use their labour power and many *siris* worked under conditions of bondage. They were indebted to [employers] and were usually not allowed to quit working for [an employer] until their debts were cleared... The *siri* contract typically involved restrictions on the freedom of the *siri*, and sometimes even on other workers from his family, to work for any other employer.'

(= deproletarianization) is condemned, only then to be attributed mistakenly – and under a different name – to Breman (= 'neo-bondage'). Given the extent of the misunderstanding involved, the claims made by Lerche require a more detailed examination.[118]

V

Disinventing/Reinventing the Wheel

Objecting to my view that unfree labour is compatible with capitalism, Lerche insists that for three reasons deproletarianization is not a theory that 'provide[s] much by way of analytical clarity or insight.'[119] First, it is inconsistent with a Marxist framework that equates accumulation with free labour, or 'the generalised commodification of labour power'.[120] Second, that production relations based on advance payment (= worker debt) do not require coercion to secure loan repayment. And third, that because I do not provide 'an explanation of actually occurring phenomena' I cannot place 'the theory [about deproletarianization] into the historical context.'

118 The misinterpretations and errors made by Lerche are merely a symptomatic manifestation of what is unfortunately a wider difficulty. Like other recent entrants to the debate about unfree labour and capitalist development in India, he not only displays little knowledge of Marxist and non-Marxist interpretations but also is apparently unaware of background ethnographic material. In the case of rural India, there is an extensive and rich historical literature (e.g., Wiser, 1936; Beidelman, 1959; Hjelje, 1967), none of which seems to have been consulted, an omission that is especially problematic when an attempt is being made to differentiate capitalist from pre-capitalist relational forms. There is accordingly an inverse relation between on the one hand categorical pronouncements about what is and what is not bonded labour, what is and what is not Marxist theory, and on the other a familiarity with relevant theoretical/empirical analyses necessary to make such pronouncements credible, let alone authoritative.

119 For this and the following objections, see Lerche (2007: 8–9, 11–12, 21–22).

120 This claim was one made initially by Byres a decade ago, when he asserted – wrongly – that 'Marx clearly argues that free wage labour (free in the double sense) is crucial to a fully functioning capitalism' (personal communication, 11 September, 1998). It is a claim repeated verbatim by Lerche. When asked why a currently 'fully functioning' capitalism seems to manage quite adequately with production relations that are not free, exponents of semi-feudalism answer that what exists is not – or is not yet – a capitalism that is 'fully functioning'. We are all, it seems, destined to wait forever until capitalism is pronounced by them to be 'fully functioning'.

He concludes that 'without such a grounding the theory does not contribute to an understanding of the development of unfree labour in specific historical contexts, such as, for example, neo-liberal globalization.' Consequently, there is in his opinion 'a need to build a fully-fledged historically specific analysis of unfree labour relations and their relation to neo-liberal globalization', one moreover 'building on the work of those such as Breman who have already contributed towards such an analysis in an Indian context.'[121] Criticizing me – wrongly – for my supposed 'deviation' from Marxism, Lerche then ignores the fact that this accusation is one that applies more accurately to those such as Banaji, Harriss-White and Breman, whose palpably non-Marxist approaches to unfree labour he endorses. About such claims it is possible to make a number of observations.

Sheep in Wolf's Clothing (2)

To begin with, Lerche adopts what is now a familiar procedure: the arguments he presents against me are actually ones that I hold, having been made by me previously on numerous occasions in many earlier publications.[122] The second part of his analysis in effect contradicts all the claims about unfree labour and capitalism made in the first part, and he ends up unwittingly repeating the very case made by me.[123] This extends from the acceptance that bonded

121 See Lerche (2007: 22). Curiously, this is not what he said a decade ago, his interpretation having undergone something of a reversal in the intervening years. Lerche appears to have forgotten what he wrote on this subject earlier, when comparing my approach to unfree labour in India with that of Breman (Kapadia and Lerche, 1999: 4). Then he noted – correctly – that Breman was optimistic about the changes taking place in Gujarat on account of 'the rise of free relations' leading to a process of emancipation where bonded labour was concerned. This, Lerche pointed out – equally correctly – contrasted with my view, one that argued 'against the celebration of empowerment as it is often a substitute for analysing the class perspective', since for me 'the landed classes are succeeding in increasingly imposing unfree labour relations on rural labourers, in order to counter any class struggle from below.' In other words, the very view he attributed to me then he now attributes to Breman; this despite observing accurately at the time that what the latter perceived was the spread of free labour, relational emancipation and a corresponding decline in unfreedom.

122 This was the procedure followed earlier by Banaji (2003), on the details of which see Brass (2003a: 103, 122 note 7).

123 However, the assertion that I am wrong to hold a particular view, which Lerche subsequently accepts is right, clears the way for re-presenting the argument about bonded labour I have made all along, but now as though it had not been made by me.

labour is actually an unfree relation, to outlining the reasons for its current resurgence (class struggle leading to capitalist restructuring of the agrarian labour process).[124]

Having initially denied that debt bondage is unfree, therefore, Lerche then accepts that unfree labour is a widespread phenomenon.[125] Indeed, as the analysis proceeds, production relations involving debt are increasingly described as a form of unfreedom.[126] Thus he agrees that cash advances made to workers during the lean season and repaid in the form of cheap labour in the peak season do after all constitute debt bondage, thereby endorsing the way I explain this transaction.[127] By conceding that enforcement of bonded labour relations depends on employer collusion, and that labour contractors can

---

124 By accepting 'that while disagreements exist regarding whether or not in the long run capitalism may lead to "canonical" capitalism across the world, the empirical evidence is that this is not on the cards in the forseeable future, or at least as long as neo-liberal globalization rules', Lerche (2007: 21) in effect concedes the case I have made for the better part of three decades about the resurgent systemic role of unfree labour.

125 For the claim that bonded labour is free, see Lerche (2007: 9); for the opposite view, that bonded labour is unfree, see Lerche (2007: 11).

126 For references to production relations as unfree, see Lerche (2007: 14, 17). Realizing, perhaps, that what he is saying now – that debt bondage *is* an unfree production relation – both confirms what I have said all along and contradicts the claims he himself made earlier (that bonded labour was not unfree), Lerche (2007: 18) states lamely and unpersuasively that 'the analysis would lose its nuances if these relations were collapsed into one undifferentiated category, be it "unfree labour" or "unequal labour relations"'.

127 Initially, the claim was that cash advances did not entail unfreedom (Lerche, 2007: 9). Subsequently, however, one encounters the admission by Lerche (2007: 14) that debt bondage 'involves the tying in of prospective labourers through loans/advances given during the lean season before the start of the (mainly) seasonal employment relation. During the employment period against which the labourer has pledged his/her labour power, the labourer may only be paid a minimum allowance, while the overall payment is settled at the end of the seasonal employment.' This, he then agrees, 'compels the labourer to stay in the employment relation after the advance has been paid off…the labourer may in fact leave with little pay, or, maybe, with a debt that needs to be repaid through next year's seasonal work.' As Lerche accepts, this is a view no different from the one made by me in all my publications about unfree labour. Cash advances made during the lean season are repaid in the form of work at the time of peak demand, but at a lower wage rate, when through the sale of their labour-power on the market such workers might otherwise expect to earn premium wages (but are unable to do so, because they are unfree). References to this kind of procedure, the withholding of wages amounting to reverse bondage, are found in Brass (1999: 11–12, 34, 182, 188, 189–190, 201, 207, 296).

and do exercise coercion over long distances – precisely because the migrant workers they recruit are linked to them additionally by kinship, locality and/or family ties – Lerche once again not only contradicts what he said earlier but reproduces exactly the point made by me over the years.[128]

Turning to the reason why there is currently an increased incidence of bonded labour in a neoliberal capitalist context – a case he claims repeatedly has not been made and that I in particular have not addressed – Lerche then offers an explanation for this development. He attributes this resurgence of unfreedom to the fact that, from the mid-1970s onwards, 'Indian employers and governments have been on the offensive in their attempts to discipline the labourers and restructure production to achieve the maximum of flexibility and a docile and cheap workforce'.[129] It is impossible to read this without a sense of *déjà vu*.

The reason is that the explanation offered by Lerche is precisely the same as my argument about the centrality of class struggle to the reproduction of unfree labour, even down to the conjuncture itself.[130] In the course of restructuring the agrarian labour process, therefore, I have insisted *ad nauseam* that

---

128 By accepting that 'family bondage is common', that 'a degree of collusion' is necessary for unfreedom to be effective, and that kinship/locality/family ties enable labour contractors to exert pressure on migrants to fulfil debt-servicing work obligations, Lerche (2007: 14, 15, 16, 17) merely echoes long-standing arguments (Brass, 1999: 21ff., 23–24, 218–219) about the central role of kinship and/or collusion in the enforcement of production relations that are unfree.

129 See Lerche (2007: 18). This point is not merely reiterated subsequently – 'The anti-labour activities of Indian capital, and government, from the mid-1970s onwards, are best seen as part of the new international labour-unfriendly [*sic*] regime, or neo-liberal globalization' (Lerche, 2007: 21) – but recommended as a model for other contexts ('The Indian case provides pointers towards an analysis of the specific relationship between neo-liberal globalization and unfree labour in Latin America…'). Inexplicably, Lerche omits to mention the fact that just such a comparative approach has already been undertaken (Brass, 1999: 47ff., 80ff., 110ff., 182ff., 217ff.).

130 In a section entitled 'Unfreedom and Post-War Capitalist Development' (Brass, 1999: 272–273), the following point is made: 'From the mid-1970s onwards, a decline in transport and communication costs has resulted in a corresponding decentralization and fragmentation of the industrial labour process, as capital has has relocated production both within and between social formations. Accordingly, restructuring has occurred both in metropolitan capitalist countries and also in so-called Third World contexts, where the response of employers to increased levels of unionization has been a similar process of workforce decomposition and recomposition. Under an accumulation project geared largely to export led economic growth, therefore, the historical link between the expansion of a home market and capitalist development has been broken.'

capitalist producers replace more expensive free labour-power with cheaper and more easily controlled workers that are unfree.[131] Contrary to the unwarranted assertion by Lerche that deproletarianization remains a theory without a material referent, it is difficult to think of a context to which it has not been applied.[132] At this point, his 'critique' of deproletarianization collapses, as does the claim that I present no evidence in support of this theory.

Misinterpreting Marxism

The attempt by Lerche to decouple Marxist theory about the capitalism/unfreedom link from my argument concerning deproletarianization fares no

131 Compare the reasons advanced by Lerche for the existence of unfree labour ('discipline labourers...restructure production...a docile and cheap workforce') with the following definition of unfreedom plus the reasons for its existence: '(it is a process of) workforce restructuring by means of introducing or reintroducing unfree relations, a process of class composition/recomposition which accompanies the struggle between capital and labour. In contexts/periods where/when further accumulation is blocked by overproduction, economic crisis may force capital to *restructure its labour process* either by replacing free workers with unfree equivalents or by converting the former into the latter...such restructuring enables rural employers first to lower the cost of local workers by importing unfree, *more easily regulated, and thus cheaper outside labour*...' (emphasis added) Subsequently the same point is made with specific reference to India: 'It is (argued that) the existence of (long- or short-term) attached labour cannot be understood without regard to the class decomposition/recomposition (or *restructuring*) that accompanies class struggle in the Indian countryside, the object of which is to *discipline* (not habituate), control and *cheapen* labour-power...' (emphasis added) These quotations are both the definition and the cause of deproletarianization provided by me in my analyses of unfree labour (Brass, 1999: 13, 217; 2004). Moreover, it is a definition that Lerche manages to reproduce almost verbatim, notwithstanding his rejection of deproletarianization as an explanation for the connection between capitalism and unfree labour; and – despite claiming to have read the book – insisting that the reason for this link is one that I have yet to provide.

132 The claim made by Lerche (2007: 9) that 'there is no placing of the theory [about deproletarianization] into the historical context...[it] operates at a high level of abstraction...it is a model of what could happen under capitalism, but is not an explanation of actually occurring phenomena' is not merely nonsense but quite simply nonsense on stilts. The geographical contexts to which my argument about the capitalism/unfreedom link has been applied over the years cover a very wide range indeed, extending from Latin America (especially Peru), the Caribbean (especially Puerto Rico), India (especially Punjab, Haryana, and Bihar), Australasia (especially Queensland) to the USA and the UK. The full extent of this coverage is a fact that could be verified by anyone bothering to check either the Index to my book or the content of my publications. The only geographical context to which deproletarianization has not been applied by me is Africa (with the obvious exception of South Africa): this, however, has been done by Manzo (2005).

better. If the notion of free labour-power being crucial to a 'fully-functioning' capitalism is so central to Marxist theory, as he claims, why then do so many Marxists maintain the opposite?[133] Why do not just Marx, Engels, Lenin and Trotsky but also Mandel, Dobb, Kuczynski and Guérin all accept that accumulation does not necessarily require free labour-power, and can indeed do without this?[134] And why currently do 'fully-functioning' capitalists in so many different global contexts accumulate quite adequately using workers that are unfree?

Unfortunately, the endeavour by Lerche to interpret what is and what is not Marxist theory about unfree labour and capitalism does no more than underline the perils of his following Breman onto what for them both is unfamiliar epistemological terrain. Contrary to what Lerche asserts, therefore, the resort by capital to production relations that are unfree does find support in the views of Marx, both about the specific historical instances – child labour in Britain and plantation slavery in the antebellum American South – and more generally about the centrality to the accumulation process of class struggle.[135] Since other Marxists have made much the same point about the antebellum plantation economy, it is hard to see quite in what way this view can still be considered 'non-Marxist'. Hence the argument that unfree labour was perfectly acceptable to producers who were capitalist is not inconsistent with the theoretical framework of Marx himself. This is especially so when the dynamic role of conflict is considered, and how the relative economic importance of free and unfree labour is structured by the dialectic.

Semifeudalism/Marginalism Redux

The main exception to such Marxist views is Stalin, and those today – such as Lerche and Byres – who still adhere to his theory about semi-feudalism. That the acceptability to capital of unfree labour is incompatible with Marxist theory is accordingly a view held only by those who examine the current accumulation

---

133 It is simply incorrect to infer (Lerche, 2007: 10) that I claim free labour doesn't exist anywhere. To say this would be patently absurd, as is any impression that this is what I mean. What I have said – and do say – is that the incidence of unfree labour is not just much greater than generally supposed but may be increasing, a view confirmed by the detailed findings of the ILO studies. This is not the same as claiming that free labour is non-existent.

134 For details about these Marxist arguments, see Brass (2011a: Ch. 2).

135 Not the least of the many ironies is that the approach of Marx to the role of child labour in the capitalist economy of Britain during the nineteenth century is very similar to that used by organizations such as the UN and the ILO in their critiques of child labour in India and other developing countries, and whose views Lerche dismisses.

process through the lens of the semi-feudal thesis. Not only am I criticized by Lerche for questioning the semi-feudal thesis, but he then defends the view that 'in a mature capitalism free labour will have replaced unfree labour. In the long run, capitalism and unfree labour are not compatible. Existence of unfree relations means coexistence between capitalism and pre-capitalist modes of production…'.[136] It is perhaps no more than a measure of his confusion that, having endorsed the semi-feudal thesis (which decouples unfree labour and accumulation), Lerche then subscribes to the opposite approach (which links unfree labour centrally to accumulation).

The same kind of confusion informs the way he misinterprets the theoretical approach of Jairus Banaji to bonded labour in India. Thus for example, Lerche categorizes Banaji as a Marxist, despite citing an article which makes it clear that, on the subject of unfree labour, the theoretical affinity of Banaji is not with Marxist theory but rather with the neo-classical economic approach of Steinfeld and Engerman.[137] What Lerche forgets is that his endorsement of Banaji's notion of contract amounts to a *de facto* approval of neoclassical economic theory about unfreedom, and in effect negates the definition adopted by Marx for distinguishing that is free from that which is unfree: the capacity of its owner personally to commodify/recommodify his/her own labour-power.[138]

In this connection, it is also significant that Lerche claims – again incorrectly – that the double definition of unfreedom (an inability to retain the capacity not just to enter but also to exit freely from a work relation) is commonplace.[139] Not only is this not true of Banaji, but it also does not apply to neoclassical economists, who still operate with only the 'entry into' condition

136 See Lerche (2007: 9–10).

137 Banaji (2003) is described erroneously by Lerche (2007: 7) as someone who 'locates [his] work in relation to Marx, and distances [himself] from liberal views that argue that labour relations such as bonded labour are free and equal, since they are freely entered, contractual relations.' That the exact opposite is the case underlines the extent to which Lerche has misread the theoretical position of Banaji. In contrast to Marx, neo-classical economic historians such as Fogel and Engerman insist that the plantation was a modern capitalist enterprise because in their opinion its benign work regime, which involved incentives and rewards, was based on market 'choice'. That is, plantation slaves were to all intents and purposes no different from free labour, a position shared by Banaji. For the epistemological details of neo-classical economic historiography, see Brass (1999: Ch. 5).

138 The argument (Lerche, 2007: 9) that in a capitalist context a contract is anyway a 'normal' relation, and thus inferentially non-problematic, reproduces the old canard advanced by revisionists such as Bauer, and disposed of some time ago (Brass, 1990a).

139 Hence the view (Lerche, 2007: 15) that '[m]ost observers and agencies…now only focus on the exit clause, or accept that extra-economic coercion at either end of the labour relation makes it unfree.'

as the criterion of unfreedom. Where entry is 'voluntary', the relation is accordingly categorized as free.[140] Because he adheres to a neo-classical economic concept of contract as freely chosen by its subject, therefore, Banaji eschews the way Marxism conceptualizes unfreedom, the focus of which is on the inability to exit from a production relation.

Accordingly, Lerche follows Banaji and Byres in maintaining – wrongly – that, restrictions on the capacity of a worker personally to commodify or recommodify his/her own labour-power notwithstanding, contract is simply another form of free labour.[141] Equally misplaced is the assertion by Lerche that Banaji's 'argument gains strength [from the view] that capitalism means by definition, generalized free labour'.[142] What Lerche fails to notice is that for Banaji *all* production relations are free – capitalist and non-capitalist alike.[143]

140 In contrast to Marxism, therefore, whether or not a worker can exit from a contract 'chosen' by him/her is for neo-classical economics and Banaji alike immaterial to its characterization by them both as a 'free' relational form. This underlines yet again the mistaken nature of the assertion by Lerche that 'exit from' a work arrangement is a commonplace way of defining a production relation as free or unfree.

141 The presence of non-economic coercion, insists Lerche (2007: 9), does not make debt bondage unfree, because '[s]uch a relation would be free if the labourer were free to leave the relation after the end of the contract…[r]egardless of whether this would happen after one season or several years, this would be a free labour relation.' He forgets two things. First, that for a worker to conform to the Marxist definition of free labour, s/he must have and retain permanently the capacity to commodify or recommodify his/her own labour-power. Where such workers are unable personally and unconditionally to sell their only commodity, labour-power, the social relations of production are not (and cannot be considered to be) free. That migrant workers from northeastern India employed on a seasonal basis in the Green Revolution agriculture of northwestern India were deproletarianized is clear from the trajectory of their employment history. In their home villages, therefore, such workers are initially a proletariat, in that they offered their labour-power for sale. Once they have migrated to Haryana or Punjab, however, such workers are no longer permitted to offer their labour-power for sale to the highest bidder, and in fact are specifically prevented from doing so. In short, these workers have been deproletarianized: they were free but have become unfree. And second, he also forgets that classifying as free a production relation where restriction on the sale of labour-power is seemingly without limit ('season or several years') brings within the definition of 'free' labour not just debt bondage but also chattel slavery itself.

142 See Lerche (2007: 10).

143 This is obvious from the case made in Brass (2003a), a text Lerche cites and – presumably – has read. Oblivious to the fact that Banaji's argument about bonded labour is no different from that made by neo-classical economists, Lerche asserts that '[c]ompared to Brass's position, Banaji's understanding of forced labour succeeds better in theoretically contextualizing forced labour within capitalism, not least because it deals head-on with the

This, of course, is once again a view that Banaji shares with neo-classical economists, not least because marginalists regard capital as an ever-present (and thus 'natural') category, a pan-historical form that underlies all known working relations/arrangements, every variant of which is 'chosen' and therefore 'free'.[144]

Significantly, both the semi-feudal thesis and neoclassical economics eschew the role of class struggle in determining the presence/absence of bonded labour.[145] Exponents of the semi-feudal thesis abandon class struggle for socialism in favour of class collaboration to defend bourgeois democracy (= 'peaceful co-existence'). Since the semi-feudal thesis is based on the idea of class collaboration, from which all trace of class struggle has been purged, it is hardly surprising that – like Byres – Lerche misunderstands the important role of class struggle in determining production relations. No wonder neither of them are able to comprehend the role of unfreedom in advanced capitalism, and why it might serve the ends of the agribusiness enterprise.

It is on the face of it hard to think of a single claim made by Lerche regarding the debate about the connection between capitalism and bonded labour in India that is both his and correct. His analysis is as a consequence replete with epistemological inconsistency, empirically inaccurate claims and theoretical confusion. Either as a result of misrecognizing what is and what is not Marxist theory, or because he is unfamiliar with the relevant literature, Lerche ends up subscribing to contradictory positions in the debate about the systemic role of

---

contradictions involved.' Much rather the contrary, in that Banaji *avoids* the issue of capitalist unfree labour, by defining all production relations as free.

144 The sole criticism Lerche (2007: 10) levels at Banaji, that his framework is 'a-historical', is no different from the one initially encountered in Brass (2003a, 2005). In the latter texts the conclusion about Banaji was that (Brass, 2005: 119) his 'approach led in turn to a reductionist view, whereby all systemically-specific relational forms were henceforth collapsed into a single a-historical variant, characterized by him as hired labour that was "free"'.

145 There are also other points of convergence. As Byres (1996: 280, note 51) accepts, both his own (semi-feudal) approach and neoclassical economic historiography subscribe to the 'slavery retardation' thesis, or the view that the presence of low-paid unfree labour prevents the growth of consumer demand, and thus slows or prevents the process of market expansion on which the development of capitalism depends. However, such an interpretation operates only in cases where commodities produced by capital are destined for a mass market composed of workers who are unfree. Where this is not so, as in the case of export-oriented agricultural production sold in international markets elsewhere, then the constraint posed by unfree labour – limited purchasing power in a particular national context – no longer holds. It is the latter that applies to the current pattern of accumulation: neoliberal capitalism on a global scale.

bonded labour in India. On the one hand, therefore, Lerche criticizes the deproletarianization approach as unMarxist, yet reproduces much of this framework in a supportive way and mistakenly attributes it to Breman. On the other he endorses both the semi-feudal thesis and the contractual approach of Banaji, without at the same time realizing that the latter is based on neoclassical economic theory, and that each of these two frameworks decouples unfree labour and accumulation, or the very connection Lerche is as such pains to establish.

VI

Unfree Relations and Systemic Transition

It is a truism that capitalism shapes not only the labour process but also its worker in a way that is suitable for the prevailing conditions of production. Previous relational forms are not reproduced exactly, but aspects of such relations conducive not just to accumulation but also to competition and profitability can be and are adapted by capital to meet existing requirements. This is especially true currently, in a capitalist system that is global in extent and operates according to *laissez faire* principles.

Peasants – or Workers?

Hence the difference between historical and existing forms of bonded labour in India. In terms of categories of worker affected (permanent/non-permanent), their usufruct rights (access to or separation from property), and other crucial dimensions of the bonded labour relation (duration, heritability, coercion and enforcement), current unfree relations of production do indeed differ from past variants. Contrary to the claims examined above, it is precisely this difference that is addressed by and embodied in the concept deproletarianization.

Not only has attachment shifted from permanent to casual and/or migrant labour, and the debt bondage relation involve what are increasingly landless agricultural labourers, therefore, but the latter are no longer unfree throughout the whole agricultural cycle or on an inter-generational basis.[146] Furthermore,

146 These shifts have to some degree eroded the usual epistemological distinctions cited by Marxism as separating free labour from slavery. Among the more significant is the conceptualization of the free worker as someone whose labour 'must confront capital as *pure use value*, which is offered as a commodity by its owner himself' (Marx, 1986: 218, original emphasis). The labour of debt bonded workers who are either migrants employed on a seasonal basis or locals hired as casuals, and in receipt of wages, do indeed confront

such workers may under specific conditions (and only with the consent of their creditor) transfer their labour-power and indebtedness to another employer.[147] Both the nature of coercion and the enforcement of debt-servicing labour obligations have also undergone change.[148] All these points have been and are central to the case about deproletarianization.

A further distinction concerns both the political effect of deproletarianization, and the implications of this for the way in which systemic (not relational) transition is interpreted. Rather obviously, this issue is not one considered by exponents of the semi-feudal thesis or neo-classical economics, and those who confuse such views with Marxism. Within some Marxist theory, however, unfree labour has been interpreted specifically with regard to cultivators and smallholders: that is to say, coercion designed to affix producers to land on a permanent basis.

Although still important in some places, this objective is not – or is no longer – central to the process of deproletarianization. The latter concept has extended the debate about unfreedom in two ways: first, to those who are no longer cultivators, but who rely on the sale of labour-power for their livelihood; and second, to categories of worker (migrants, seasonal and temporary) that are

---

agrarian capitalists as 'pure use value'. Once acquired by the employer, however, labour-power 'offered as a commodity by its owner himself' is then prevented from being recommodified, and as such ceases to be relationally free.

147 This phenomenon, known as 'changing masters', is examined by me elsewhere (Brass, 1999: 23), where it was argued that the transfer of debts between masters 'constitutes a precise relocation of unfreedom in terms of the rural labour process. This transformation corresponds to a shift in the immobilizing function of debt from a continuous and intergenerational basis to a more period- and context-specific basis. Its operationalization is as a result confined to the months of peak demand in the agricultural cycle, when sellers of labour-power would otherwise command high prices for their commodity. Whereas the traditional form of bondage is unprofitable (requiring payment for time when labour-power is not engaged in productive activity), the modern form is not (and is akin to the kind of control exercised by a plantation over the seasonal labour-power of poor peasant households that reproduce their own subsistence during the off-peak in villages on its periphery.)' That such a phenomenon continues in Haryana is evident from the words of a bonded labourer there, who is reported as saying (Rawal, 2004: 12): 'We can leave the [employer] only after repaying all the loans taken from him. That can be done only by taking a loan from another [employer] and accepting to become his *siri*. So you can free yourself of one only by becoming bonded to another'.

148 Coercion to enforce debt-servicing labour obligations is exercised not 'from above', by a landlord, but rather 'from below', by fellow caste members and/or members of the worker's family/kin group.

not permanent or local. This it has done by focussing both on the conditions impeding the commodification of labour-power by its owner, and by highlighting that unfree relations are reproduced as the result of class struggle waged 'from above'. These were all considerations that Marx and a number of other Marxists regarded as central to an understanding of capitalism and the relational forms acceptable to it.

Where agricultural workers, who earlier have personally commodified their own labour-power, subsequently become unfree (their labour-power either ceasing to be a commodity, or being recommodified by someone other than themselves), what has occurred currently in a neoliberal capitalist context is a relational transformation that corresponds to *de*proletarianization.[149] Such workers are still landless; they still work for someone else on a permanent, seasonal or casual basis; they can still be employed in conjunction with advanced productive forces; they still receive cash wages; they may be migrants or work locally; and (under the control of a contractor, or in the form of changing masters) their labour-power can still circulate in the labour market; *but* – and this is the crux of the matter – they are no longer able personally to sell their own labour-power.

In short, because they do not meet the second of the two criteria laid down by Marxist political economy as necessary for the existence of free labour – freedom from the means of labour and also freedom personally to sell their own labour-power – they are now unfree workers who have been deproletarianized. Unsurprisingly, the difference between the latter and historical forms of bonded labour in India has economic and political implications. Not just for the role of bonded labour in the accumulation process, but also for the nature both of class struggle in the countryside and – consequently – of systemic transition itself.

Capitalism – or Socialism?

The distinction between peasant-as-debt-bonded and worker-as-debt-bonded is accordingly significant in another way: the characterization of unfree labour as acceptable or unacceptable to capitalism affects in turn what kind of systemic transition is on the political agenda. Historically, the concern expressed by British colonial administrators in India about the parasitic role of debt and moneylending derived from its negative impact on agricultural production,

149 This would include the rebonding of workers who, having previously been unfree, then managed to emancipate themselves, only to re-enter bondage subsequently, a process widely reported throughout India. On this point see Brass (1999).

and thus also on land revenue.[150] Currently, however, it could be argued that a noticeable shift has taken place in the way the economic role of debt is perceived.

Debt bondage in rural India was seen historically as a relation affecting mainly smallholding peasant farmers, not as sellers of labour-power but rather in their capacity as cultivators. In the colonial era, therefore, unfreedom occasioned by indebtedness was viewed as a problem that threatened the economic independence of the peasant cultivator in rural India, where in the words of an influential observer there was a 'perennial shortness and extreme expensiveness of working capital so as to get the best result in production from the land.'[151] Even those opposed to British colonialism held this view. Borrowing from landlords or village moneylenders involved high-interest repayment on loans, which prevented peasant farmers from investing in – and thus improving – their own agrarian labour process. The resulting appropriation of surplus from indebted smallholders was regarded by the colonial authorities as an obstacle to their productive capacity. The assumption was that by legislating against debt bondage, smallholding peasants who no longer had to repay high interest loans to village moneylenders would as a result possess sufficient funds for improving cultivation. This would then generate increases in economic growth on holdings operated by petty commodity producers.[152]

Significantly, on the issue of moneylending as an economic obstacle to a flourishing peasant economy there was little difference between the colonial authorities and those opposed to colonialism: each regarded indebted poor peasants essentially as sellers not of labour-power but of the product of their labour. That is, producers who – in the absence of high interest repayment necessitated by borrowing – would be able to increase output on their holdings. For colonialism, opposition to smallholder debt stemmed from concerns about agricultural production: a desire to increase output of foodgrains for domestic consumption, and simultaneously to ensure the payment of land revenue. The problem was accordingly one of economic efficiency, and debt

---

150 As numerous historical studies underline, the connection between peasant indebtedness and agricultural productivity in India was a constant *theme* informing the work of colonial administrators. The main concern of, for example, Darling (1925, 1930, 1934) and Trevaskis (1928, 1931–32), was to break the hold moneylenders had traditionally exercised over the rural economy, particularly in the agriculturally important region of Punjab.

151 See Mann (1929: 73–74).

152 Hence the kind of tenure that, as a result of eliminating debt bondage relations, either would be reproduced or came into being was *individual* peasant proprietorship, against which virtually all Marxists have argued (for many different reasons: political, economic, ideological).

bondage was characterized as an obstacle to the transformation of these smallholders into commercially viable producers.

The theoretical focus and political effect of a case based on the concept deproletarianization is somewhat different. It is no longer concerned simply with the unfreedom of smallholders *qua* cultivators, or about the desirability of establishing – or reproducing – an efficient peasant economy. Rather, it is about class struggle involving labour and capital, and thus a transition not to capitalism but to socialism. As interpreted by deproletarianization, therefore, unfreedom linked to the rising incidence of rural indebtedness in India (and elsewhere) concerns the viability of the subject as landless (or land poor) *worker*, not cultivator.

The political implications of this epistemological shift are twofold. First, it is no longer the case, as argued by semi-feudalism, that still on the political agenda are nationalism, bourgeois democracy, and political alliances with a 'progressive' bourgeoisie: the latter become, much rather, the target of class struggle. And second, debt bondage – which enhances control by rural employers over their workers – is now seen by the capitalist state not as an obstacle but much rather as a contribution to the economic efficiency of agriculture. Since it facilitates accumulation by lowering the cost of labour-power and also disciplining it, unfreedom can no longer be regarded as having a negative impact on agricultural production.

Because of this, the form taken by opposition to the existence of debt bondage has shifted, also in two distinct ways. Those who are not socialists can only invoke a moral discourse, one about the infringement of human rights. In a neoliberal global capitalist system this kind of opposition is fruitless, and destined to fail precisely because unfree labour is now such a crucial part of the accumulation process. By contrast, those who are socialists locate bonded labour within the wider dynamic of present-day class struggle, and argue that it is a relation that will – like the accumulation process itself – cease only with the transcendence of capitalism as a system of production. Accordingly, opposition to debt bondage – in India and elsewhere – necessarily entails opposition to capitalism itself, apart from which it has no – and now cannot have – meaning.

VII

Conclusion

Claims made here about the acceptability to capitalist producers of bonded labour – an unfree production relation that is prevalent in the agrarian sector of many countries, not just those in the so-called Third World – are grounded in Marxist theory, arguments to the contrary notwithstanding. This concerns in particular Marxist views about the interrelationship between the separation of the direct producer from his/her means of labour, the reproduction of the industrial reserve army, the process of workforce restructuring, and – most importantly – the conflict between labour and capital. Only in the undialectical framework used both by neoclassical economists and by adherents of the semi-feudal thesis (a species of Whig historiography) is there a failure to recognize such a dynamic.

As has been noted on many previous occasions, adherents of the semi-feudal thesis share with neoclassical economists a touching faith in the emergence and continued reproduction of a benign (= 'kind', 'caring') form of capitalism, one that will voluntarily do away with oppressive and exploitative relations such as unfree labour. Only then will there be a 'fully functioning' accumulation process, under the benevolent eye of selfless capitalists who are gentle, sweet and good. Not only was this never going to happen, but the developments in the world economy from the 1980s onwards, when capitalism went global and competition and class struggle became correspondingly more acute and international in scope, have effectively rebutted this conservative – not to say naïve – interpretation.

Unlike the semi-feudal thesis and neoclassical economics, most Marxist theory accepts that gains made in the course of class struggle can just as easily be reversed, the 'from below' relational emancipation (plus the advantages this confers) unravelling as a consequence of class struggle waged 'from above'. This is especially true of the way global capitalist regimes have been transformed over the past quarter of a century, a period dominated by *laissez faire* development policies. In such circumstances, economic and ideological benefits secured by workers and poor peasants in the course of conflict with employers and the capitalist state can be – and have been – watered down or cancelled by the reintroduction of unfreedom.

The resulting decomposition/recomposition of the labour process in rural India (and elsewhere) is a relational (not systemic) change that involves either the replacement of free labour by unfree equivalents, or the conversion of the former into the latter. This kind of agrarian transformation is (as I have argued for almost three decades) a form of capitalist restructuring that corresponds to deproletarianization, a concept which refers not just to permanent and/or local debt bondage relations but also to ones that extend to include migrant, seasonal and casual workers. In the course of restructuring the labour process, therefore, capitalist producers have not only replaced permanent labour with temporary workers but also shifted the element of unfreedom, from long-term employment to casual/migrant jobs.

That such a relational (not systemic) transition was occurring in many parts of rural India, particularly areas where accumulation had led to the emergence of an agrarian capitalist class, unfortunately escaped many commentators – among them Breman, Amartya Sen and Harriss-White – who were as a result wrong footed epistemologically. Because their focus was still on the coming of capitalism, their analyses originally interpreted unfreedom as an obstacle to capitalist development.

Accordingly, they missed the fact that unfreedom was being used in the class struggle – and increasingly so – not by feudal landlords in a context where capitalism had yet to develop but by agrarian capitalists (agribusiness enterprises, commercial farmers, rich peasants) in situations where capitalism had already developed. Unsurprisingly, this has generated substantial contradiction and confusion in subsequent interpretations by them about the presence, absence, meaning and economic role in Indian agriculture of unfreedom.

What seems to have occurred, therefore, is that a current interpretation of bonded labour as an economically important and/or capitalist relationship has in each case risen as a phoenix from the ashes of a previous and very different analytical framework. For this reason it is crucial to determine not just whether the present approach of Breman, Amartya Sen and Harriss-White is consistent with their earlier one, but also, if not, what then has been the resulting impact on the overall coherence both of their own arguments and of those made by others subsequently.

Why Breman is at such pains to establish a difference between bonded labour in Western India during the colonial and/or pre-capitalist era, and that which flourishes in the capitalist agriculture there currently, is not difficult to discern. The dilemma he faced is all too understandable. Initially, therefore, no such distinction was made by him for the simple reason that it was unnecessary to do so. During the mode of production debate of the late 1960s and early 1970s, Breman sided with (or did not dissent from) those who maintained that bonded labour was a pre-capitalist (feudal/semi-feudal) relation, and would accordingly vanish as capitalism spread to the countryside, and set about replacing unfree workers with free equivalents.

Throughout the 1980s, however, two things became clear. First, this was not happening: capitalist penetration of the Indian agrarian sector entailed much rather the reproduction of bonded labour plus an increase in its incidence, unfree relations being the working arrangement of choice where commercial producers were concerned. And second, others were arguing that unfree labour was a central part of the accumulation process.

One can only sympathise with the discomfort experienced by Breman, given that he had already committed himself epistemologically by asserting categorically that a new form of bonded labour neither existed nor could exist in an agrarian sector that was capitalist. His way of resolving this dilemma was simply to change his mind, and argue that a 'new' form of bonded labour ('neo-bondage') was indeed present in capitalist agriculture of Western India, notwithstanding the fact that this contradicted all earlier pronouncements by him on the subject.

A similar dilemma confronted Amartya Sen and Harriss-White, development economists who have analysed rural India through a marginalist lens. Because each of them did so initially either without a concept of class struggle, or else a misrecognition of this, neither has as a result been able to understand the significance of the free/unfree connection. As in the case of Breman, therefore, they too overlooked the presence – and consequently missed the significance – of bonded labour in the accumulation process, dismissed by them as a pre-capitalist anomaly, or idealised as a form of benign 'patronage'. Now that finally they recognize the centrality of debt bondage to agrarian capitalist production in India merely compounds the epistemological confusions informing their neo-classical economic framework.

As worrying in terms of its implications for the study of the way production relations have been transformed in rural India is the fact that this change of mind by Breman, Amartya Sen and Harriss-White has escaped the notice of others currently writing about the same subject. Without realizing it, de Neve, Jodhka, Rawal and Lerche reproduce the argument about deproletarianization, all the while presenting this as though it had not been made earlier. Among the many ironies, the following is perhaps the most striking. When made by me, therefore, the claim that unfree labour is acceptable to agrarian capitalists is deemed to be wrong. When Breman now makes the very same claim, however, it is deemed to be the way forward. With this kind of 'logic' it is quite simply impossible to argue.

CHAPTER 17

The Unsaying of Marxism: Capitalist Accumulation and Unfreedom*

Contrary to the expectations of much bourgeois economic theory, there is a rising incidence globally of unfree labour, which in turn puts on the agenda once again its role in the development process. For Marxist and non-Marxist political economy, the characterization of labour-power as free or unfree has been, and remains, a decisive factor driving historical change, involving as it does the form taken by class formation, class struggle, and class consciousness and thus also the possibility of a transition to socialism. Currently, however, Marxist theory about unfree labour is faced with an attempt to reproduce much of its analysis, but shorn of its revolutionary content and outcome. Any change for the better is accordingly confined to the capitalist system itself, beyond which there is *ipso facto* no need to go.

Addressing the link between unfree labour and neoliberal capitalism, a recent symposium in *The Journal of Development Studies* contains a number of claims about the current state of this debate, its epistemological shortcomings and the implications of this for the study of and prospects for economic development.[1] These focus mainly on the proposition that, because hitherto liberal and Marxist theory has failed to understand not just the acceptability but the centrality to capitalist accumulation of unfree labour, new analyses of this dynamic are now required. The latter are precisely what the symposium contributions intend to provide.

Challenging these claims, it is argued here that the way debate about the capitalism/unfreedom link is presented in the symposium is exclusionary, and thus misleading. This problem is compounded by the fact that claims made by the symposium are not confined to it: an analogous case, concerning the need for a new interpretation of the capitalism/unfreedom link, due to its neglect by the same two culpable paradigms (liberalism, Marxism), is now being made elsewhere.[2]

---

* Another version appeared in *Science & Society* Vol. 78, No. 3 (2014).

1 The contributions to the symposium are by Barrientos, Kothari and Phillips (2013), Frantz (2013), Kothari (2013), Barrientos (2013) and Berlan (2013).

2 Much the same case is made by Graeber (2011), Phillips (2011), Guérin (2013), and LeBaron and Ayers (2013).

For this reason, what amounts to a wider and symptomatic reading of the issue will also be examined.

A twofold feature common to these recent interpretations goes as follows. First, what is announced as a new explanation is declared to have replaced a previous Marxist analysis of the capitalism/unfreedom link. And second, when revealed, it transpires that many of the characteristics of this 'new' explanation are identical to those of the previous one they are supposed to have replaced. Since the characteristics that are different invariably turn out to be ones that the previous Marxist analysis had earlier shown to be false or flawed, these are not new either.

Of the five sections which follow, the first demonstrates that there are in fact two Marxist approaches to unfree labour; one decoupling it from and the other recoupling it to capitalist development. The second examines this Marxist divergence in terms of its implications for a socialist transition. Recent analyses which dismiss Marxist theory are considered in the third section, and their suggested alternatives in the fourth. That many of these latter explanations turn out to be little different from Marxist ones they dismiss, lacking a socialist transition as the desired outcome, is outlined in the fifth.

Obstacle or Aid to Capitalist Development?

Unfree labour re-emerged as an issue in the debate about rural development during the years following the end of the 1939–45 war, when a political concern of Keynesian theory was not just economic reconstruction (mainly in Europe and Asia) but also planning (in the Third World). A crucial aspect of the ensuing discussion concerned the extent to which different relational forms constituted obstacles to capitalist development, and why. Central to these deliberations was the link between capitalist development and modern forms of unfree labour (peonage, debt bondage, indenture, chattel slavery). In a welcome break with the prevailing 'whips and chains' concept – whereby the presence/absence of unfreedom was associated simply with visual images of physical oppression – Marxist contributions to the debate restored the sale/purchase of labour-power to definitions of work arrangements that were not free.

This they did during the 1960s and 1970s, when discussions focused on the implications of unfree social relations of production in Third World agriculture. In the case of the mode of production debate, mainly about agrarian transition in India, bonded labour was regarded as incompatible with capitalist accumulation, and thus an obstacle to economic growth, an interpretation advanced by exponents of the then-dominant semi-feudal thesis.[3] According to the latter, unfree labour was a pre-capitalist relation, destined to be replaced by a workforce that was free as capitalism spread throughout the agrarian sector of Third World nations. Like much non-Marxist theory, this variant of Marxism saw unfree labour as incompatible not just with capitalism but also with advanced productive forces, economic efficiency, skilled workers, and market expansion. The corollary of the inefficiency argument is that capital is seen as opposed to using unfree labour, and in contexts where the latter relational form is found, invariably strives to replace it with free labour-power.

From the 1980s onwards, however, another and very different Marxist view about the capitalism/unfreedom link was emerging in the sphere of development studies. Labelled deproletarianization, it challenged the then prevailing orthodoxy that capitalist transformation of the agrarian sector led to the replacement of unfree workers with free equivalents.[4] Much rather the opposite was the case, it was argued, in that evidence from Latin America and India suggested agribusiness enterprises, commercial farmers and rich peasants reproduced, introduced or reintroduced unfree relations. According to this alternative Marxist interpretation, unfree labour was not merely compatible with modern capitalism but in particular circumstances its relation of choice.

This was because deproletarianization of the rural workforce is a crucial part of the class struggle involving capital and labour. As such it enables capitalist producers to depoliticize, cheapen, or discipline their workforce. Where agricultural workers, who earlier have personally commodified their own labour-power, subsequently become unfree (their labour-power either ceasing to be a commodity, or being recommodified by someone other than themselves), what has occurred is a relational transformation that corresponds to *de*proletarianization.

This is a form of capitalist restructuring that corresponds to decomposition/recomposition of the labour process. It is a relational change that involves either the replacement of free labour by unfree equivalents, or the conversion of the former into the latter. Such workers do not meet the second of the two criteria laid down by Marxist and much non-Marxist political economy as necessary for the existence of free labour. Namely, freedom from the means of labour and also freedom personally to sell their own labour-power. These workers are

---

3 On the mode of production debate, see Rudra, *et al.*, (1978) and Thorner (1982), which indicate the extent of the influence exercised by the semi-feudal thesis, exponents of which include Patnaik and Dingwaney (1985) and Byres (1996).

4 Journal articles conceptualizing unfree labour as deproletarianization written from the 1980s onwards have been collected in two subsequent volumes (Brass, 1999, 2011a).

still landless; they still work for someone else on a permanent, seasonal or casual basis; they can still be employed in conjunction with advanced productive forces; they still receive cash wages; they may be migrants or work locally; and, under the control of a contractor, their labour-power can still circulate in the labour market; *but* – and this is the crux of the matter – they are no longer able personally to sell their own labour-power.

At issue is whether or not socialism should be postponed until after a 'pure' capitalist stage has been ushered in, by an equally 'pure' democratic bourgeoisie using correspondingly 'pure' relations of production. According to the semi-feudal thesis, landlords who employ unfree labour will be replaced in a bourgeois democratic stage by 'pure' agrarian capitalists who employ nothing but free wage labour, a stage in which peasant proprietorship reigns supreme. In other words, the abolition of landlord capitalism (= the Prussian path) will lead to peasant capitalism (= the American path), in the process realizing the classic two stages theory of agrarian transformation whereby one form of capitalism (unbenign, landlord, undemocratic) is replaced not by socialism but by another 'pure' form of capitalism (benign, peasant, democratic). In such a two stages pattern of transformation the duty of socialists is to press not for socialism but rather to support elements of the 'progressive' national bourgeoisie and to argue for the redistribution of land on an individual basis to smallholders (= 'repeasantization').

The theoretical focus and political effect of a case based on the concept deproletarianization is somewhat different. It is no longer concerned simply with the unfreedom of smallholders *qua* cultivators, or about the desirability of establishing – or reproducing – an efficient peasant economy. Rather, it is about class struggle involving labour and capital, and thus a transition not to capitalism but to socialism. As interpreted by deproletarianization, therefore, unfreedom linked to the rising incidence of rural indebtedness in India (and elsewhere) concerns the viability of the subject as landless (or land poor) *worker*, not cultivator. For this reason, opposition to debt bondage necessarily entails opposition to capitalism itself, apart from which it has no – and now cannot have – meaning.

Since those who write from within the semi-feudal framework are unable to recognize the central and important role of unfree labour in class struggle generated by the process of capitalist development, the outcome for their analyses in terms of theory is in both cases the same. Epistemologically unable to make this capitalism/unfreedom connection, they mistakenly conclude that, as the countryside in Third World nations is still characterized by archaic relational forms, agriculture continues to be in a pre-capitalist stage. In part, this misinterpretation stems from confining this analysis of capitalist development and markets to national economies, rather than locating them both in an international context. A corollary is that for them capitalism is still a progressive force, to be promoted economically and supported politically. The implications of this, both for development theory and for political practice, are profound.

Because their problematic is restricted to the coming of capitalism, therefore, exponents of the semi-feudal thesis have tended to focus on unfreedom simply as an obstacle to capitalist development. By its very nature, such an approach postpones a consideration of socialism, and thus precludes the necessity of having to examine conditions favourable or antagonistic to *its* development. Accordingly, the semi-feudal thesis also misrecognizes the fact that the role of unfreedom in the class struggle has undergone a dramatic change: in so-called Third World countries, it is now used not by semi-feudal landlords in a context where capitalism has yet to develop but increasingly by agrarian capitalists (farmers, rich peasants) in situations where capitalism has already developed, in order to pre-empt/prevent conditions that are favourable to a socialist transition.

Advocating Socialism

Following its theoretical elaboration not just by Marx but also by Adam Smith and Hegel, unfreedom is regarded here as part of specific ontological progression. Labour is identified first as the source of value, then as labour-power which is the property of its subject, and finally as a commodity which its owner is able to sell on a time-specific basis to a capitalist producer. Such an interpretation permits the loss of this capacity to be conceptualized as deproletarianization. The latter also recognizes that the object of unfreedom in a 'fully functioning' capitalism is no longer to affix a smallholder to land or simply to separate the latter from his/her means of production, but rather to deprive the subject of owning/controlling his/her own labour-power.

For this reason, the outcome of emancipation is different: the subject is reconstituted not as a peasant in a benign capitalism but rather as a worker engaged in struggle to transcend this. Of the two Marxist approaches to unfree labour, therefore, the semi-feudal thesis advocates completion of the capitalist project whilst deproletarianization links abolition to systemic transcendence. Emancipation from unfreedom premised on the identity of the subject as a worker points to a socialist transition, whereas any eradication of unfreedom based on peasant identity still puts a 'fully-functioning' capitalism on the political agenda.

In terms of development theory, the alternative Marxist interpretation arguing for deproletarianization broke not just with the semi-feudal thesis but also with a number of other influential paradigms featuring unfree labour: neo-classical economics, the 'disguised' hired workers approach, human rights discourse, and dependency theory. Conceptually, therefore, deproletarianization challenged neo-classical economic approaches to unfreedom, since these questioned the coercive nature of debt bondage and indenture, arguing that such working arrangements are the outcome of harmonious market exchanges in which choice-making individual labourers express subjective preferences.[5] For much the same reason, the alternative Marxist approach also challenged the argument by Banaji that all working arrangements are nothing more than variants of 'disguised' wage-labour, conceptualized as 'contract'.[6] By abolishing the free/unfree distinction, and maintaining instead that all rural workers – in late antiquity no less than in present-day capitalist India – are simply hired labourers who are contractually free, his approach is indistinguishable from neo-classical economic historiography.

Similarly, deproletarianization took issue with human rights discourse which puts its faith in what is perceived as disinterested state intervention to eradicate unfree labour.[7] Such a view disregards the fact that, since it enhances control by rural employers over their workers, unfree labour is now seen by the capitalist state not as an obstacle but much rather as a contribution to the economic efficiency of agriculture. The alternative Marxist interpretation also dissents from dependency theory, which maintained that free labour was found

5 See Fogel and Engerman (1974) and Steinfeld (2001) for neo-classical economic interpretetions of unfree labour.

6 See Banaji (2010). For marginalist economists, whose legalistic definition of contract Banaji endorses, freedom of contract means quite simply the ability of workers to enter working arrangements: that they are subsequently unable to withdraw from them without the consent of their employer does not affect his meaning. Banaji thereby unwittingly imbibes from neo-classical economic theory the view that a work arrangement is defined simply by the act of recruitment ('entry into'). This contrasts with Marxist theory, for which a work arrangement is defined by a process: the reproduction of the relational form ('entry into' + 'exit from'), as embodied in the ability of a worker personally to commodify and recommodify his/her own labour-power. Further details about this issue are contained in Brass (2003a).

7 See Brass (2011a: Chapter 8) for a critique of human rights discourse which looks to state agency as solution to the problem of unfree labour. Many NGOs committed to emancipation seek to effect this simply by establishing citizenship and civil society as a result of redemocratization. However, this is to be achieved without affecting existing property relations which give rise to and/or reproduce unfreedom in the first place.

in the centre (i.e., metropolitan capitalism), whilst unfreedom was reproduced on the non-capitalist periphery.[8]

This was in keeping with the epistemological dualism of the time, one that informed much of the debate about the mode of production and the transition to capitalism in Third World nations. The focus of the deproletarianization argument was on a different dynamic: not the centre/periphery dichotomy, a geographical model, but rather on class formation and class struggle. Because it was the latter that accounted for the presence of unfree labour, such relations were increasingly found where advanced capitalism was located; namely, the centre which dependency theory thought was the preserve of free labour.

Unsaying Marxism

The recognition, finally, that unfree labour has not gone away, and that it is a relational form perfectly compatible with capitalist production, has in turn spawned a mini-industry of what purport to be alternative interpretations as to why this link continues.[9] Among the current explanations, therefore, one encounters a multiplicity of epistemologically vague frameworks: the presence of unfree labour, we are told, is due to 'vulnerability', to 'non-standard work', or to 'precarious work'; it is, we are also told, simply a form variously of 'un-decent labour relations', of 'adverse incorporation into the global economy', 'of social reproduction', and of 'neoliberal governance'.

---

8 The dichotomy at the heart of dependency theory – free labour is found at the core, whilst unfreedom is reproduced on the periphery – is elaborated by Wallerstein (1979). Much the same difficulty faces Patnaik in her attempt to explain class and class struggle. Perceiving class through nationalist lens, she claims that workers in the capitalist heartland remained free at the expense of their counterparts on the periphery, where unfree production relations were imposed. This not only overlooks the presence of the latter in core areas (which continues), but also implies free workers were somehow complicit participants in the exploitation of unfree labour in the colonies. It also reproduces the dichotomy between developed core = capitalism = free labour-power, and underdeveloped periphery = non-capitalist = unfreedom.

9 A noticeable feature of these recent approaches, and an inevitable outcome of ignoring the long history of debate about the capital/unfreedom link, is their mutual interdependence in terms of citation, whereby each publication invokes the authority of every other contributor to the same discourse. Thus, for example, LeBaron and Ayers (2013: 890 notes 13 and 28) cite approvingly texts by Phillips and by Lerche, who is himself cited extensively by Guérin (2013). LeBaron and Lerche are cited endorsingly in turn by Phillips (2011: 11, 16, 20, 22, note 3) and Barrientos, Kothari and Phillips (2013: 1038).

On one point these recent explanations are unanimous: all declare Marxist interpretations of the capitalism/unfreedom link either to be absent or – at best – lacking in persuasiveness, for which reason a new interpretation is necessary. Phillips characterizes Marxist theory about unfree labour as unvarying, a twofold result being that such relations are located 'outside capitalism', and consequently 'rarely brought into consideration in these debates'.[10] Because it is confined within Marxism, existing debate about unfree labour is described by her as 'insular' and dismissed for its failure to engage 'with wider debates in political economy around questions of global production and trade, and the global dynamics of poverty and inequality.' She also objects to the free/unfree distinction of Marxism because in her view it privileges free labour – 'a different ethical and moral order' – thereby letting capital off the hook.[11]

Analogous criticisms of Marxist theory are made by Guérin, who like Phillips wants to do away with the free/unfree dichotomy, because these categories are in her view 'too rigid,' they 'limit the debate,' and diverge from 'empirical reality'.[12] Castigating Marxist debate for its 'very abstract' nature, Guérin invokes as her preferred model 'fine grained empirical studies' which avoid situating unfree labour in a particular economic system, whether feudal or capitalist.[13] However, this does not prevent her from arguing – again like Phillips – that 'unfree labour can go hand in hand with capitalism, and that it can be perpetuated and sustained by capital itself in order to accumulate surplus value.'

In keeping with these critiques, LeBaron and Ayers lament not just the absence of attempts to define unfree labour, but also the exclusion from this category of child workers.[14] Equally dismissive of Marxist approaches to unfree labour, Graeber similarly claims to have spotted developments of which Marxism was unaware.[15] Hence the view that Marxists 'still tend to assume that free wage labor is the basis of capitalism...all those millions of slaves and serfs and coolies and debt peons disappear...we write them off as temporary bumps in the road'.[16]

On the consequent need for 'fresh perspectives', there is also unanimity. According to LeBaron and Ayers, therefore, '[s]cholarly evaluation of this

10 Phillips (2011: 5, 10, 18–19).

11 See Phillips (2011: 6). This argument was disposed of previously in an article she does not cite (reproduced as essay 16, this volume).

12 Guérin (2013: 406, 411).

13 Guérin (2013: 410).

14 LeBaron and Ayers (2013: 877).

15 Graeber (2011).

16 Graeber (2011: 351).

resurgence of unfree labour is urgently required…explanations as to how and why unfree labour has proliferated remain inchoate' because the 'systemic factors that have underpinned the growth of this phenomenon…are stated but rarely explained or analysed.'[17] Barrientos, Kothari and Phillips concur, announcing their intention 'to make a fresh contribution to these ongoing debates by focusing on [forms of unfree labour] which have been widely neglected in this context.'[18] It is a claim reiterated just as strongly in the conclusion, where they assert that their 2013 symposium 'thus provides new insights into the persistence of unfree labour, a much over-looked issue in contemporary global development discourse.'[19]

Claiming that 'the reality' of unfree labour is missing from academic writing, an absence due to 'the near silence of critical political economy on the resurgence of unfree forms of labour exploitation,' the declared intention of LeBaron and Ayers is 'to refocus scholarly attention towards the broader political and economic significance of unfree labour.'[20] In criticizing the human rights approach, LeBaron and Ayers maintain that '[r]ather than a constituent element of capital accumulation's social relations, unfree labour appears as an individual relationship of domination that can be eliminated through state enforcement.'[21] Along with human rights discourse, Marxist theory is accused by them of failing 'to situate unfree labour's acceleration within broader processes of labour market restructuring,' invoking in support of this view the critique by Brass of the semi-feudal thesis.[22]

As to what should fill the gap left by Marxism, there is once again near agreement among the recent entrants to the debate. The object, according to Barrientos, Kothari and Phillips, is 'a global economy characterised by "decent work" for its labour force,' located on a 'continuum' at the opposite end of which are 'the very worst forms of "dirty, dangerous and degrading" work.'[23] In keeping with this approach, Guérin proposes an alternative framework whereby labour relations are placed on 'a continuum' spanning mild to harsh forms, ranging from 'fully unfree relations' to 'working conditions that are decent.'[24]

17 LeBaron and Ayers (2013: 874).
18 Barrientos, Kothari and Phillips (2013: 1037, 1038).
19 Barrientos, Kothari and Phillips (2013: 1040).
20 LeBaron and Ayers (2013: 875–876).
21 LeBaron and Ayers (2013: 876).
22 See LeBaron and Ayers (2013: 877, 890 note 20) and Brass (1999). No mention is made by the former, however, of the elaboration in the latter text of a different Marxist interpretation, linking unfree labour to capitalist restructuring.
23 Barrientos, Kothari and Phillips (2013: 1037).
24 Guérin (2013, 413–415, 418).

Having dismissed Marxism, Phillips then argues that 'fresh perspectives' are needed, since unfree labour should not be seen 'as a pre-capitalist form or a consequence of the absence of functioning markets'. Insisting that 'it is time to move the debate beyond these increasingly restrictive parameters...locating particular relations on one side or another of the dividing line', Phillips instead proposes 'three key points of distinction' between current and traditional forms of unfreedom.[25] Unlike the latter, therefore, much present-day unfree labour is not permanent but of short-term duration only; it is defined not by involuntary entry into the production relation but rather by an inability to exit from it; and in contrast to earlier times, these days unfree workers are paid. All these characteristics, Phillips assures us, 'are clearly evident in Brazilian agriculture and Indian garment manufacturing.'[26]

Endorsing the notion of a 'continuum,' and similarly indicting Marxist theory about deproletarianization, Barrientos, Kothari and Phillips dispute the free/unfree polarity since 'such rigid distinctions increasingly obstruct the task of understanding the nature and dynamics of unfree labour.'[27] They conclude that it is impossible to position 'contemporary labour relations...on one side or other of a clear dividing line between "free" and "unfree" labour.' LeBaron and Ayers also object to 'the rigid binary between "free" and "unfree" labour,' dismissed by them as 'simplistic binaries' which are 'completely untenable'.[28] Transcending this 'rigid binary' entails locating 'diverse modalities of labour exploitation [on] a spectrum or continuum.' Hence the connection between these relations should be 'approached dialectically,' as part of 'a single spectrum' arising from the need of capital for more efficient forms of control and exploitation.

A Debate Going Backwards

Not the least difficulty confronting those who search for new interpretations is the inadvertent recuperation of flawed arguments. Reinstating explanations that earlier analyses – Marxist and non-Marxist alike – showed to be mistaken, and the consequent rolling back of debate about the capitalism/unfreedom link, is due to a number of factors. These include uncertainty as to what

25 Phillips (2011: 11).

26 Phillips (2011: 13).

27 Barrientos, Kothari and Phillips (2013: 1038).

28 See LeBaron and Ayers (2013: 874, 877, 879). This theme about the rigidity of the free/unfree categorization is to be pursued elsewhere (LeBaron, forthcoming).

unfreedom itself and its proposed gradations actually involve. Hence the attempt to replace the free/unfree dichotomy, based as it is on the sale/purchase of labour-power, with a continuum ranging from 'harsh' to 'decent' employment, reinstates discourse about 'whips and chains'. This is an old and controversial argument, as is the equation of bonded labour with a benign form of 'subsistence guarantee', and an idealized notion of kinship as a relation unconnected with unfree labour.

One indicator of rolling back the debate is the conceptual reintroduction of unfree labour simply as an effect of physical coercion. This takes the form of replacing the free/unfree dichotomy with a 'continuum', whereby labour relations are graded from harsh or 'un-decent' treatment to ones considered 'decent' or mild. The latter model is a return to the 'whips and chains' argument, where unfreedom was associated largely with greater or less physical oppression.[29] It is a flawed interpretation disposed of long ago, both by Brass and by Sutch who, arguing against floggings on the antebellum Southern plantation as a barometer of the extent (or otherwise) of coercion, noted rightly that '[t]he frequency with which a punishment is administered is a poor measure of its effectiveness…it is the *fear* of eventual punishment which motivates behaviour…a slave need never to have felt the lash to know the consequences of disobedience.'[30] In other words, supposed gradations as evidence for greater or less unfreedom are meaningless.

Although all want to replace the free/unfree binary with a 'continuum,' therefore, confusion exists as to what precisely this entails. Thus, for example, LeBaron and Ayers endorse not just a 'continuum' to replace what they term 'rigid binaries' but also a dialectical approach to them. These processes, however, are antithetical. A 'continuum' projects a linear methodology, extending from at one end work conditions interpreted as 'very nasty indeed,' proceeding through a variety of 'more/less nasty' gradations, and so on up to employment conditions at the other end, categorized as 'quite nice' and perhaps even 'very nice.' Involving as they do assessments of degree, such multiple labels are necessarily subjective.

By contrast, the dialectic is applied to production relations that are distinct: in other words, precisely to the 'rigid binary' that is to be transcended. Moreover, here the process is different, in that the dialectic focuses on the interplay between the two components of a single free/unfree binary that is said – by LeBaron and Ayers, and others – not to exist. An illustration of dialectical

29 The point about bad working conditions is that they are an effect of unfreedom, not an indicator of its greater or less oppressiveness.

30 See Brass (1999, 20–21, 35 note 27) and Sutch (1975, 342, original emphasis).

materialism at work is where the initial presence of casual labour that is free (= thesis) is then transformed by 'from above' class struggle (= antithesis) into a workforce of casuals who are now unfree (= synthesis). This is precisely the Marxist approach informing the deproletarianization concept.

Ironically, therefore, in arguing for an approach to the link between free and unfree as a dialectical one between these two relational forms, an interpretation which in their view is missing from Marxist theory, LeBaron and Ayers manage to overlook the fact that the deproletarianization framework is built on just such an analysis.[31] Similarly incorrect is their claim that child workers are omitted from analyses of unfree labour, since this is a connection made not just by current Marxist theory but also by Marx himself.[32] The complaint that much debate about unfree labour is conducted without defining its characteristics does not prevent LeBaron and Ayers themselves from doing the same. A twofold result is, more broadly, the conflation of unfreedom with violence and repression – a staple of the 'whips and chains' argument favoured by the human rights discourse they criticize – and more specifically uncertainty as to whether it operates at the level of production or circulation.[33] Their insistence that conceptualizing present-day forms of unfreedom as 'new' slavery is a-historic is doubly misplaced. First, it overlooks the presence not just of a shared characteristic, but one that is central to the reproduction of each form:

---

31 Clearly set out at the very beginning of Brass (1999: 3, original emphasis), therefore, is the view that 'political economy also reinstates an epistemologically crucial historical dimension missing from culturalist and other approaches. As presented here, the link between free and unfree labour is a dialectical one based on struggle...between capital and labour, whereby free workers become unfree and vice versa. The objection to most texts about agrarian change in India, Latin America and elsewhere is that they subscribe to what is palpably an untenable concept of unilinear and irreversible *relational* (*not* systemic) transition.' Much the same can be found a decade later, in the conclusion to Brass (2011a: 271): 'Labour-power is neither always and everywhere free, nor is it always and everywhere unfree. What has to be understood is that historically there is a dynamic interaction between labour-power that is free and forms which are unfree, a dialectic informed by class struggle. Hence the latter process cannot but structure the prevalence in the trend of each form, the kind of social relation dominant at a given conjuncture being determined by the respective power – economic, political and ideological – exercised by those who either own or are separated from the means of production.' Although they make no reference to the later text, LeBaron and Ayers do cite the earlier one. Somehow the presence there of the very argument prefiguring that advocated by them as an alternative to Marxism was overlooked.

32 For the categorization of child workers as unfree, both by current Marxist theory and by Marx himself, see Brass (1999; 2011a: 51ff.).

33 LeBaron and Ayers (2013: 888).

in terms of production relations, both work arrangements are unfree. And second, it also ignores the fact that, where unfreedom has been reintroduced into a labour process that is capitalist, political economy teaches that such a development corresponds historically to a regression. This is because, as is argued here, so much – politically, ideologically and economically – hangs on whether or not worker emancipation has been achieved.

Barrientos, Kothari and Phillips are similarly keen to identify a break with what they term 'traditional understandings' of slavery and bondage, which defined working arrangements as unfree only where entry into the relation was involuntary.[34] Claimed as a novel finding by the contributions to their symposium, therefore, is the fact that contemporary forms of unfreedom arise from an inability to exit from employment relations. Unfreedom, they argue, must be seen as a constraint exercised at the point of exit from, not entry to, a work arrangement. What they overlook, however, is that even this point was raised initially by Marxist theory, in the course of an exchange between the deproletarianization and 'disguised' wage labour frameworks.[35]

Another indicator of the rolling back of debate about unfree labour is the retreat into empiricism. Hence the antagonism towards Marxism takes the familiar form of accusing such interpretations of an excessive reliance on theory. This, too, does not accord with reality, since Marxist analyses of the capitalism/unfreedom link combine theory with precisely the 'fine grained empirical studies' commended by Guérin.[36] Ironically, when the non-Marxist approaches she endorses – by Breman, Lerche and Jodhka – attempt the same combination, they encounter difficulties in analysing their findings precisely because they misunderstand theory.[37]

A further and relevant consideration in the rolling back of the debate is that, as many of these recent analyses are funded by organizations linked in one way or another to the State (the Department for International Development, the Economic and Social Research Council), the agenda in effect precludes systemic transcendence as a political resolution of socio-economic problems. Instead of class formation/struggle leading to a socialist transition, therefore, the dynamic centres on poverty and its amelioration within the existing

34 Barrientos, Kothari and Phillips (2013: 1038–1039).

35 The rival Marxist positions in this exchange, which originally took place during 2003, are set out in Banaji (2010: Chapter 5) and Brass (2011a: Chapter 4).

36 Conceptually, Marxist theory about deproletarianization was elaborated on the basis of fieldwork studies conducted in Latin America and India over a period spanning the mid-1970s to the early 1990s.

37 See essay 16, this volume.

capitalist framework. Given this political divergence, it is unsurprising that Marxist analyses of the free/unfree labour distinction are declared redundant, and alternatives to capitalism not posed.

Hence the analysis by Phillips links the issue of unfree labour to that of poverty, an approach which attempts to find solutions within a capitalist framework.[38] Similarly, the focus of Guérin's research is on micro-credit, and consequently her approach is guided by the concept of bonded labour as a form of 'subsistence guarantee'.[39] Among the reasons advanced by Guérin for the existence of unfree labour is a positive one, initiated not by employers but by the workers themselves: a desire to 'consume', her view being that 'the debates on bondage have neglected the role of consumption [which] must be considered...as an additional factor for wage advances.' According to Guérin, therefore, bonded labour can be a benign form of 'patronage' and 'job security' that corresponds to 'protection against extreme marginalization.'

About this claim a number of observations are in order. To begin with, it is not the case that debt incurred by the consumption needs of workers is a neglected aspect of the debate, as Guérin states. Indeed, the term 'consumption loan' which features prominently in the literature about debt bondage in India attests to the presence of this link in explaining the reproduction of unfree labour.[40] More important, however, is that by endorsing the element of consumption as a factor mitigating unfree relations, Guérin reinstates yet again another old and contentious interpretation.[41] Namely, the assumption that unfreedom corresponds to a beneficial 'subsistence guarantee', a mutually advantagous arrangement premised on reciprocal exchange between worker and employer. For the labourer, therefore, the negative relational aspects of unfreedom (lack of bargaining power, low wages, etc.) were offset by the promise of employer provision during the off-peak agricultural season (when no work was available). Evidence suggests, however, not only that historically no such

38 Phillips (2011: 9).

39 See Guérin, Bhukuth, Marius-Gnanou, Servet and Venkatasubramanian (2004), and Guérin, Roesch, Venkatasubramanian, and D'Espallier (2012). The second and most recent of these two analyses was a contribution to a journal special issue on the subject of *Poverty, Financial Inclusion and Livelihood Strategies*.

40 The many entries for 'borrowing, reasons for, consumption' listed in the Index of Brass (1999: 341) point to its centrality in Marxist analysis of unfree labour.

41 The 'subsistence guarantee' argument was advanced by Breman (1974, 1985) in all his earlier interpretations of debt bondage as a positive/benign form of 'patronage' which employers attempted to discard and workers struggled to retain. It was a view he abandoned after the unfreedom-as-'patronage' approach was subject to critical analysis (Brass, 1997a, 2000b).

'subsistence guarantee' existed, that in most instances there was no actual need for it, but also that when there *was* a need for 'subsistence guarantee' it was the creation of landowners themselves, who then invariably failed to deliver.[42]

In this connection, an additional problem arises from the epistemology whereby mistaken claims about the material reality of a 'subsistence guarantee' give rise to a similarly inaccurate concept of employer or landlord 'patronage.' As in the case of 'consumption' linked to a 'subsistence guarantee,' therefore, 'patronage' licenses benign interpretations of work relations that are unfree, and this is what Guérin does.[43] Arguing that the element of 'patronage' has shifted from the employer to the labour contractor, she views this as a positive development: since workers and contractors now belong to the same community, '[l]abour thus remains embedded within wider relationships.' The inference, that such relations are consequently egalitarian and devoid of coercion, ignores long-standing evidence to the contrary revealed by Marxist studies. The latter have demonstrated that, where bonded labour relations coincide with kinship networks, it is class differences and not the benign idiom of kinship or quasi-kinship 'reciprocity' that determine the reproduction of work arrangements that are unfree.[44]

Unaware of this, Berlan reasserts as valid the inaccurate view that kinship has nothing to do with unfree labour, which consequently does not – and cannot – operate within such a context.[45] The problematic nature of this claim is evident when she maintains – also wrongly – that '[i]n most of the literature, there is very limited reference, if any, to the household context of unfree labour relations'. Insisting that historically labour practices in Ghana were 'better' than elsewhere, Berlan reproduces a twofold idealization. Not only is the blame for present-day employment of children in commercial agriculture shifted from multinational corporations wanting cheap and easily controlled workers onto social problems occurring within peasant families, but she then argues that even in the latter contexts such labour-power is not unfree.[46] It comes as no surprise, therefore, that for Berlan the solution to bonded labour is to be found within capitalism.[47]

42 On this point see, among many others, Hjejle (1967: 96), Patel (1952: 77), Kusuman (1973) and Brass (1999).

43 Guérin (2013: 419).

44 See Brass (1999: Chapter 2).

45 Berlan (2013: 1091, 1093–1094).

46 Observing that 'child labour is very much embedded in the socio-local [*sic*] dynamics of Ghanaian society', Berlan (2013: 1098) decries what she regards as 'a tendency to pathologize child labour and focus on its negative and harmful consequences.'

47 Berlan (2013: 1097–1098).

Unsaying Marxism?

An additional difficulty facing those who search for new interpretations concerns the extent to which their suggestions are in fact novel. All too often, therefore, interpretations/arguments recently declared to be new or discoveries turn out to have been not just known about for a long time but also discussed at length.[48] The irony is unmissable. On the one hand, these new interpretations dismiss the relevance of Marxism in general, and the deproletarianization framework in particular. On the other, all of them reproduce not just the claim that unfree labour is in fact compatible with accumulation, exactly the case made earlier within the deproletarianization framework, but also the latter's critique of both neo-classical economics and the semi-feudal thesis.

Repeating the untenable proposition that every form of Marxism equates capitalism with free labour-power, many of these recent interventions fail to investigate what Marxists have actually said about this issue. Hence the claim by Graeber that the acceptability to capital of unfree labour is a connection that Marxism has failed to spot is quite simply wrong. Some Marxists – including this writer – have been arguing against this orthodoxy for a very long time. Earlier analyses by Marxists have shown very clearly that in many different contexts, at different historical conjunctures, capital can, does, and will use labour-power that is unfree.[49]

Claims that Marxist theory/debate about unfree labour is 'insular', and therefore fails both to engage with political economy, and to recognize the centrality of debt bondage in capitalist accumulation are quite simply wrong. The idea that, in some sense, Marxist theory about this issue operates in an

---

48 That debts are now owed not to employers but to contractors (who consequently possess the economic leverage to enforce bondage), plus an inability to change jobs without at the same time transferring the debt to the next employer, are among the findings claimed as 'new insights' by Barrientos, Kothari and Phillips (2013: 1040). However, loans taken from labour contractors and inter-employer debt transfers are phenomena that have long been known about in the literature about bonded labour, and are well-documented, as is clear from the relevant entries in the subject index of Brass (1999: 343, 344).

49 That unfree labour-power is compatible with accumulation is a view held by numerous Marxists, extending from Marx himself, through Lenin and Trotsky, Eugen Varga, Jürgen Kuczynski, Maurice Dobb, Ernest Mandel, to – more recently – James Petras, Alex Lichtenstein, José de Souza Martins, Karl Heinz Roth and Yann Moulier-Boutang. It is also a view held earlier by non-Marxist development theorists such as Daniel and Alice Thorner, and Ashok Rudra. For details about these different contributions to the debate, see Brass and van der Linden (1997) and Brass (2011a: Chapter 2).

epistemological vacuum is not correct. Far from being 'insular', therefore, deproletarianization is a concept formulated in part as a result of engagement not just with the neo-classical economic historiography (Fogel, Engerman, Steinfeld, Shlomowitz) but also with much non-Marxist theory (Adam Smith, John Stuart Mill, Hegel).[50] Nor is it the case that privileging free labour over unfree equivalents, as Marx himself and Marxist political economy does, benefits capital, much rather the opposite. In the context of class formation/struggle, workers who are free possess economic, ideological and political advantages that unfree counterparts do not have. These include the capacity to bargain over issues such as the sale and price of their labour-power, and the conditions and duration of work. Indeed, how else is one to explain the acceptability to employers of unfree labour.

Eradicating unfree production relations would in effect knock away the bottom rungs of the ladder that is the capitalist labour regime. This it would do by making it costlier to employ the reserve army of labour on which profitability and competitiveness depend, as unfree workers were converted (or reconverted) into free equivalents. Once this relational and price differential was eliminated, it would be easier for workers to unite, organize and fight as a proletariat, in the Marxist sense of the term. As is well established historically, this is the kind of outcome which capital everywhere has always feared. The free/unfree distinction, therefore, is crucially about conditions enabling or preventing the transcendence of capitalism. As such, it concerns wider issues that have been and are central to political economy, and is not – as Phillips maintains – simply the application of a 'different ethical and moral order' to labour-power that is free.

In describing 'adverse incorporation' as the exploitation and the extraction of surplus-value by capital from labour that is unfree, with the object of increasing profitability, a process made possible moreover by the global expansion in the reserve army of labour, Phillips reproduces both the characteristics of deproletarianization and also its *raison d'être*.[51] Similarly, each of the three key distinctions between past and present forms of unfreedom claimed by her as 'fresh perspectives' are in fact no different from those informing deproletarianization; that is, made by Marxist theory she rejects as inadequate. Thus the short-term duration of unfree relations, so as to save costs of employing labour when there is no work to be done, is exactly the point made by

50 This Marxist engagement with past and present non-Marxist positions is contained in Brass (1999; 2011a; 2011b).

51 Phillips (2011: 9–10).

Brass.[52] The same is true of the second distinction, about coercive exit as the defining aspect of present-day unfree relations, made in the course of an 'insular' debate with Jairus Banaji.[53] There, too, is found also the third point, about the fact that contemporary unfree labour is paid. Once again, the irony is unmissible.

The critique by LeBaron and Ayers of the view that unfreedom can be eliminated by state enforcement as unrealistic is also prefigured in Marxist theory. Exactly this point was made earlier by the deproletarianization approach, where it was argued that the meaning of unfree labour had changed, from being seen as an obstacle to accumulation (by advocates of the semi-feudal thesis) to a contributory element in generating higher productivity, and therefore economic growth. The role of the state shifted accordingly, from a negative perception requiring the elimination of unfreedom, to a neutral or even a positive one. The latter amounts in effect to ignoring unfree labour, since these kinds of working arrangements are now perceived as enhancing profitability.[54]

Agreeing that unfree labour exists, Guérin nevertheless asserts that 'what counts is not necessarily debt as an indicator,' and that 'bonded labour is not always the preferred working arrangement for capitalism,' views attributed to Brass.[55] This is then contradicted by numerous observations which follow: not just her suggestion 'that bonded labourers are those whose freedom, wages and bargaining power are significantly restricted by debt,' but also that '[m]aximizing or sustaining profit is, of course, the ultimate objective [of capital], and the main purpose of bonding labour through debt is to control, cheapen and discipline labour power.' In admitting that '[e]xit options do exist [but] workers [first] have to have paid off their debt', that 'debt is a central element of the labour relationship', and that '[f]or employers, the main advantage of shackling labour with debt is to ensure the continuous presence of a cheap and docile labour force', Guérin underlines the centrality of debt to unfreedom.[56]

52 See Brass (1999: 23). There it is argued that this 'transformation corresponds to a shift in the immobilizing function of debt from a continuous and inter-generational basis to a more period- and context-specific basis...whereas the traditional form of bondage is unprofitable (requiring payment for time when labour-power is not engaged in productive activity), the modern form is not...' Phillips ought to be aware of this, since it is contained in a book she actually cites (Phillips *et al.*, 2011: 6).

53 Again, since she cites the article (Brass, 2003a) where this case is made, Phillips (2011: 10, 32) ought to be aware of this fact.

54 This argument is found in Brass (2010; 2011c).

55 Guérin (2013: 411), Brass (1990b).

56 Guérin (2013, 414–415).

Given that most of her preceding analysis is indistinguishable from the Marxist case about deproletarianization she (and others) had questioned earlier, therefore, unsurprisingly in her conclusion Guérin in effect concedes its validity.[57] As of January 2013, she accepts, 'the gap between [cash] advances and wages is continuing to increase, which reduces exit options [= enhances unfreedom]…[d]ebt is still, however, used to cheapen wages, to impose hard working conditions and to restrict exit options.' A more concise endorsement of Marxist theory about deproletarianization is difficult to imagine. Insofar as the old cliché about imitation being the sincerest form of flattery has any truth, then Marxist development theory concerning the acceptability to modern capital of unfree labour-power stands vindicated, its dismissal by recent analyses notwithstanding.

Conclusion

It is suggested here that those currently seeking to replace the free/unfree relational distinction informing political economy with a notion of an intra-relational 'continuum' based on subjective assessments of employment conditions as 'nice'/'nasty', thereby not only reinstate the earlier 'whips-and-chains' descriptions of unfreedom but also reintroduce amelioration inside capitalism as an alternative to socialist transition. In effect, the latter outcome is removed from the political agenda. Although recent entrants to the debate implicitly accept the causes of bonded labour as defined by Marxist theory about deproletarianization, therefore, both the characterization of unfreedom and its solutions tend to be different.

Not the least significant consequence of arguing for an intra-relational 'continuum' is that the way the free/unfree dichotomy features in political economy is lost. Simply put, labour-power as the property of the worker plus its sale/purchase ceases to be the pivotal component leading to systemic transformation. Lost also are the outcomes of such alienation (separating the worker from value s/he produces): becoming/being/acting as a proletariat in the full sense of the term, and with it both the possibility and desirability of a transition to socialism. The dynamic of this process, as interpreted by the deproletarianization approach, is class struggle: not between a nascent bourgeoisie and feudal landlords, as in the semi-feudal thesis, but now between capital and its workforce moving from a class-in-itself to a class-for-itself.

The impression conveyed by recent interpretations of the capitalism/unfreedom link that there is a single Marxist approach to this issue, and

57 Guérin (2013, 419–420).

because it wrongly decouples accumulation and bonded labour fresh perspectives are required. These, it is then claimed, establish comprehensively what Marxist theory failed to notice: that unfree labour is demonstrably acceptable to capital. Having dismissed Marxist contributions to the debate about the presence and causes of unfree labour, recent analyses considered here then advocated interpretations that were either longstanding but flawed, or originally advanced by Marxist theory itself: neither of these is new.

What these recent analyses overlook, however, is that Marxist theory about deproletarianization not only identified a positive association between unfree labour and modern capitalist accumulation, but in doing so broke with the semi-feudal thesis, the 'disguised' wage labour argument and world systems framework. Issues such as the extent to which unfree labour is compatible with neoliberal accumulation, and whether or not coercive inception is the defining characteristic of such production relations, were all questions first raised by 'insular' Marxism, the very theory declared irrelevant by those who have subsequently incorporated many of its findings into what are termed 'fresh perspectives' on the problem.

Among the reasons for this difficulty is that neither Marxism nor those with whom it engages on this issue, and why, are examined in much detail. The contrast, between on the one hand confident assertion as to what is or is not the case with regard to the free/unfree distinction and its significance for political economy, and on the other what different variants of Marxism have or have not had to say about these issues currently and historically, could not be more stark. An inevitable consequence of dismissing all forms of Marxism is – and cannot be anything other than – theoretically debilitating. It is scarcely necessary to emphasize that this is a serious difficulty where claims are being advanced concerning new interpretations of an important debate.

The resulting contradiction is inescapable: is it feasible to dismiss Marxist theory about unfree labour, yet simultaneously reproduce its entire argument, shorn of the radical political outcome (a socialist transition)? One possible explanation for this antinomy concerns the locus of debate: that academia increasingly mimics all the shortcomings of neoliberal capitalism, including the competitive rush to assert property rights over long-established ideas. Other possible answers include unfamiliarity with longstanding debates about unfree labour, a decline in knowledge about Marxism, its currently unfashionable status within academia, and the unacceptability to powerful funding institutions of its revolutionary socialist politics. Whatever the explanation, it is clear that Marxist theory continues to exercise a profound influence on debate about unfree labour, its characteristics and dynamics.

CHAPTER 18

Academia as Mode of Seduction, or the Elephant in the Socialist Room*

'In the mid-twentieth century the dons regarded themselves with marked self-satisfaction.'

A Panglossian observation by ANNAN in what is a complacent defence of Oxbridge privilege.[1]

•••

Principle, *n*. A thing which too many people confound with interest.

A humorous observation by AMBROSE BIERCE on the interlinked economic and non-economic meanings of these terms.[2]

•••

Muhammad Tughlak has been defended by modern Indian historians. Power has never lacked eulogists, and historians, who are professionally obsessed with it, can explain anything, either by the *times* (disguising their adulation as scholarship), or by *necessity*, which, in their hands, can assume any and every shape. We must expect the same thing to happen in the case of rulers who are nearer to us than Muhammad Tughlak.

An observation by ELIAS CANETTI.[3]

∴

---

* This is a shortened version of a paper presented at a workshop on *Socialism at Issue*, held at St. Mary's University, Halifax, NS, Canada, on 23 October 2009.

1 Annan (1999: 278).

2 Bierce (1967: 228).

3 Canetti (1962: 434, original emphasis).

Introduction

It is a truism nowadays that a political critique of accumulation premised on systemic transcendence – that is, a break with capitalism *tout court* – has all but vanished from the social sciences in general, and especially from the agenda of development studies. The reason for this, however, is still the subject of discussion, by no means confined to those on the political left.

According to one interpretation, the capitalist system continues to reproduce itself because some of those at the grassroots (better-off peasants) benefit from this process, and thus deny support to political parties and/or mobilization advocating a transition to socialism. Others attribute this to widespread delusion arising from the end of actually existing socialism in 1989. Yet others insist that such delusion amounts to false consciousness which has its roots, partly, in the widespread academic challenges to socialism over the past quarter of a century.

Although there is a grain of truth in the first two explanations, of particular interest is the third one, not least because received wisdom currently discounts the political efficacy and/or role of academics.[4] What is commonly referred to as a crisis of Marxism, a consequence it is usually said of an inability on the

4 As embodied in the frequently heard lamentations about the lack of importance given nowadays to what intellectuals have to say about public affairs in Britain, a variation on an historical theme of 'absent intellectuals' (Collini, 2006). In some instances – for example, Ignatieff (1998), Geras (1998), Rowbotham (1999), and Furedi (2004) – this is depicted almost as a dereliction of duty on the part of those who, knowing better, should pro-actively communicate such fruits to the wider public. In this connection, it is difficult not to agree with the humorous observation made by Mark Twain (1875: 264) nearly one and a half centuries ago, about the wounded *amour-propre* of a self-important and indignant clerk: 'I have resigned. The Government appears to go on much the same, but there is a spoke out of its wheel, nevertheless. I was clerk of the Senate Committee on Conchology, and I have thrown up the position. I could see the plainest disposition on the part of the other members of the Government to debar me from having any voice in the counsels of the nation, and so I could no longer hold office and retain my self-respect. If I were to detail all the outrages that were heaped upon me during the six days that I was connected with the Government in an official capacity, the narrative would fill a volume. They appointed me clerk of that Committee on Conchology, and then allowed me no amanuensis to play billiards with. I would have borne that, lonesome as it was, if I had met with that courtesy from the other members of the Cabinet which was my due. But I did not. Whenever I observed that the head of a department was pursuing a wrong course, I laid down everything and went and tried to set him right, as it was my duty to do; and I never was thanked for it in a single instance.'

part of this theoretical framework to explain current development adequately, has – it is argued here – more to do with those who profess to be socialists. Hence the significance of the role taken by intellectuals in advocating and pursuing a transition to socialism: as Lenin pointed out long ago, without a revolutionary theory, there can be no revolutionary practice.[5]

Appearances to the contrary notwithstanding, the attack on Marxist theory of development has been as much an internal as an external phenomenon. Over the past three decades, therefore, this decline has to a large extent been a result of the abandonment by many socialists of the basic tenets of Marxism. This in turn has given rise to a related process: the belated realization of their inability any longer to address the crisis of capitalism has necessitated at least some of the subsequent changes of mind on the part of those in academia who ditched Marxism for more fashionable intellectual paradigms.

Significantly, the effect of this attack on Marxist theory has not been confined to Marxism: it has had a deleterious impact on the social sciences generally, and on theory about Third World development in particular. Hence the unravelling has not merely undermined socialism as a desirable objective of the development process, but also contributed to a wider disillusion with the very concept of development itself. Of crucial importance, therefore, is to understand not that but why Marxist theory has been discarded, and with it both the desirability and the practice of transcending capitalism leading to socialism.[6]

It is argued here that, once inside the academy, Marxist theory and practice were subject to two kinds of pressure that, in effect, resulted in its negation. Entry into or promotion within the university system frequently entailed discarding a commitment to Marxist theory/practice. By contrast, those who

5 The justly famous observation, which nowadays has the status of cliché, goes as follows (Lenin, 1961b: 369): 'Without revolutionary theory there can be no revolutionary movement. This idea cannot be insisted upon too strongly at a time when the fashionable preaching of opportunism goes hand in hand with an infatuation for the narrowest forms of practical activity.' In making this criticism, Lenin might almost have had in mind the forms of theory and practice now dominant: the 'new' postmodern populism and NGO agency. On the important role of intellectuals in a revolutionary movement, see also the 1919 essay by Lukács (1972: 12–18).

6 The search for internal causes (= betrayals) following defeat is, of course a common procedure. In the case of what happened to Marxism over the latter part of the twentieth century, and how its demise both as an intellectually acceptable method of explaining capitalism as a system of production, and as a method of dealing with this, is of sufficient importance and concern to warrant such an inward gaze.

remained socialists encountered political obstacles blocking entry into or promotion within the university system.[7] Either way, the result was the same: as a revolutionary theory/practice, Marxism has been – and continues to be – denied a place in academia.

Since the implications of this for socialism are not always acknowledged, let alone faced, it is proposed to do both here. The analysis which follows is divided into five sections. The first traces the political hostility of early Marxists to academics in capitalist institutions, a hostility reciprocated by bourgeois academia. For this reason, over the first half of the twentieth century the teaching of socialist ideas occurred mainly outside the university system, a situation reversed during the second half.

The second section examines the twofold result of this leftist 'entryism', whereby socialist politics were either affirmed at a cost of progress up the academic hierarchy, or discarded in order to ensure this. Examined in the third section is one of the contradictory epistemological outcomes of this apostasy: the academic dominance of the 'new' postmodern populism, due in part to the jettisoning of Marxist analyses, and the subsequent advocacy of 'bringing class back in'.

This is related in turn to the antinomy between socialist ideas and university 'collegiality', which – together with the consequent domestication of Marxism – is looked at in section five. The conclusion suggests that, in order to prosper, revolutionary socialist theory and practice have to return to the streets once more, there to confront and displace currently fashionable variants of the 'new' postmodern populism.

Liveried Footmen of the Bourgeoisie

In a sense, it is – or should be – unsurprising that the academy as a bourgeois ideological institution should be the prime target of Marxist critiques. Historically, those against whom Marxists have argued most strongly have been academics, seen rightly as the ideological defenders of the existing social order.[8]

---

7 There are, of course, notable exceptions: a case in point is James Petras, who has survived in academia without compromising his revolutionary socialist politics. Such instances are unfortunately somewhat rare, and his is the case that proves the rule.

8 That, historically, academia and academics have generally been defenders of the ideological status quo was recognized long ago by, among others, Newman (1899: 33), who in 1838 noted that 'Oxford never shows so well as when resisting innovation and rallying round an ancient principle'.

For this reason, the most common arguments deployed by Marxism against those in the academy have been twofold. First, that they are part of a university system which – in a capitalist context – is innately hostile to socialist ideas and practice. Second, even where socialists are employed by the academy, they are necessarily subject to institutional pressures that prevent or pre-empt a genuine commitment to revolution and/or systemic transformation.

Among most European socialists in the late nineteenth and early twentieth century – not just Marx himself but also Engels, Lenin, Trotsky, Luxemburg, Bukharin and Preobrazhensky – there was a deep suspicion of combined with uniform hostility towards academia in general.[9] This antagonism derived principally from the deleterious impact on revolutionary theory and practice of the reformism advocated by socialists holding senior teaching posts in the bourgeois university system at that conjuncture, a political group belonging to what was identified as *katheder*-socialism.

In the late 1870s, therefore, Marx expressed strong opposition to the increasing influence on leftist politics in Germany of *katheder*-socialism, describing its exponents (Adolph Wagner, Gustav Schmoller, Werner Sombart and Eduard Bernstein, among others) as 'counter-revolutionary windbags' composed of 'nonentities in theory and useless in practice [who] want to draw the teeth of socialism (which they have fixed up in accordance with the university recipes)' in order to 'make the [Social Democratic] Party respectable in the eyes of the petty bourgeoisie.'[10] Engels took a similarly critical approach, noting that during the mid-1880s universities in France and England were increasingly appointing *katheder*-socialists in an attempt to rescue capitalism from its contradictions, notwithstanding the 'rubbish' propagated by such academic 'socialists'.[11]

---

9 It must be stressed that such hostility on the part of early Marxists was most emphatically *not* to the fact of intellectual practice, but rather to its confinement to and control by academia. This view does not constitute anti-intellectualism, which objects to intellectual activity per se, and is a form of ideological 'primitivism' that has been the historical preserve of those on the political right.

10 These critical views about *katheder*-socialism, expressed by Marx in his correspondence, are cited approvingly by Lenin (1962: 366–367).

11 In a letter to August Bebel, written from London on 20 January 1886, Engels observes that the 'crumbling of German liberals in the economic field corresponds exactly to what is happening to English radicals. The old Manchester men à la John Bright are dying out and the younger generation, exactly like the Berliners, is doing patchwork social reforms... It is a splendid sign that the bourgeois must already sacrifice their own classical economic theory, partly for political considerations, but partly because they themselves have been compelled by the practical consequences of this theory to have doubts about it. The same

Lenin, too, was critical of the deleterious influence exercised on the working class movement by the reformist line advocated by *katheder*-socialism, dismissed by him as 'professorial socialism'.[12] When considering 'the turn of progressive public opinion towards Marxism' in Russia at the end of the nineteenth century, moreover, Lenin clearly delineates the element of opportunism – 'jumping on the bandwaggon' – at work among the exponents of *katheder*-socialism.[13] He was not for a minute taken in by this political 'conversion', however, accurately identifying its objective as being to dilute the element of struggle, turning thereby 'the nascent working class movement into an appendage of the liberals'.[14]

A deep suspicion of academia generally, and in particular of the true commitment of *katheder*-socialism to the transcendence of a socio-economic

---

is proved by the growth of *katheder*-socialism which in one form or another is more and more dislodging classical economics from the university chairs both here and in France. The actual contradictions created by the [capitalist] mode of production have become so glaring that they cannot be glossed over by any theory, unless it is the *katheder*-socialist hodgepodge which is no longer a theory but rubbish.'

12 See Lenin (1964e: 177). Elsewhere he takes issue (Lenin, 1961b: 357) with advocates of 'freedom of criticism' on the grounds that 'it is precisely the extensive participation of an "academic" stratum in the socialist movement in recent years that has promoted such a rapid spread of Bernsteinism' – that is to say, *katheder*-socialism. The latter is then described by him (Lenin, 1961b: 360) as being composed of 'opportunists [who] have long ago come out under a separate flag [and] have ignored theory', with the result that they engage simply in 'talking with the aim of saying nothing'.

13 Hence the view (Lenin, 1961b: 36): 'Meanwhile, Marxist books were published one after another, Marxist journals and newspapers were founded, nearly everyone became a Marxist, Marxists were flattered, Marxists were courted, and book publishers rejoiced at the extraordinary, ready sale of Marxist literature. It was quite natural, therefore, that among the Marxian neophytes who were caught up in this atmosphere, there should be more than one "author who got a swelled head…"'.

14 Taking issue with the attempts by *katheder*-socialism to find common ground – and thus form political alliances – with the bourgeoisie, Lenin (1961b: 362–363) observed: 'But an essential condition for such an alliance must be the full opportunity for the socialists to reveal to the working class that its interests are diametrically opposed to the interests of the bourgeoisie. However, the Bernsteinian and "critical" trend, to which the majority of the legal Marxists turned, deprived the socialists of this opportunity and demoralised the socialist consciousness by vulgarizing Marxism, by advocating the theory of the blunting of social contradictions, by declaring the idea of the social revolution and of the dictatorship of the proletariat to be absurd, by reducing the working class movement and the class struggle to narrow trade unionism and to a "realistic" struggle for petty, gradual reforms… in practice it meant a striving to convert the nascent working class movement into an appendage of the liberals.'

order at the apex of which they themselves were positioned, also informed most of what Trotsky said about those for and against Marxist theory/practice. In his survey of the pre-revolutionary social forces in Russia during 1905, for example, he presciently noted that intellectuals were only fair-weather friends who at the first sign of crisis would reveal their authentic political allegiance.[15] That is, not to the transcendence of capitalism, let alone to its revolutionary overthrow, but rather to the preservation of the existing socio-economic order.

This opinion did not change, as is clear from the view about Austro-Marxism he took when looking back on his life once in exile. Categorizing academic Marxists in 1907 Vienna 'as far from revolutionary dialectics as the most conservative Egyptian pharaoh', Trotsky continued: 'The psychological type of Marxist can develop only in an epoch of social cataclysms, of a revolutionary break with traditions and habits; whereas an Austrian Marxist too often revealed himself a philistine who had learned certain parts of Marx's theory as one might study law, and had lived on the interest that *Das Kapital* yielded him. In the old imperial, hierarchic, vain and futile Vienna, the academic Marxists would refer to each other with a sort of sensuous delight as "Herr Doktor." Workers often called the academicians, "Genosse Herr Doktor."'[16]

The same theme informs the criticisms Trotsky made about what passed for leftist politics in Britain during the mid-1920s. Hence the dismissal by him both

---

15 'The *democratic intellectual*,' wrote Trotsky (1972: 53, original emphasis), 'devoid of class force, trotted after the liberal bourgeoisie as after an older sister. It acted merely as its political tail. It abandoned it at moments of crisis. It revealed only its own impotence. It was confused by its contradictions – which had not yet fully ripened – and it carried this confusion with it wherever it went.'

16 See Trotsky (1930: 180–181). Noting that '[i]t was Hilferding who [in 1907] first introduced me to his friends in Vienna, Otto Bauer, Max Adler, and Karl Renner,' Trotsky (1930: 179–180) writes: 'They were well-educated people whose knowledge of various subjects was superior to mine. I listened with intense and, one might almost say, respectful interest to their conversation in the "Central" café. But very soon I grew puzzled. *These people were not revolutionaries*. Moreover, *they represented the type that was farthest from that of the revolutionary. This expressed itself in everything – in their approach to subjects, in their political remarks and psychological appreciations, in their self-satisfaction – not self-assurance, but self-satisfaction*. I even thought I sensed philistinism in the quality of their voices. I was surprised to find that these educated Marxists were absolutely incapable of applying Marx's method as soon as they came to the big problems of politics, especially its revolutionary turns. I first became convinced of this with regard to Renner… We had no common ground for continuing our conversation. I saw clearly that the man was as far from revolutionary dialectics as the most conservative Egyptian pharaoh.' (emphasis added).

of the universities as part of an institutional matrix supportive of conservatism and the bourgeois social order, and of academics themselves as 'complacent pedants', 'prattling eclectics' and 'sentimental careerists' who in his view were the 'liveried footmen of the bourgeoisie.'[17] Enmeshed as they were in the ideological apparatus of the existing system, such elements would and could only ever be part of the problem of capitalism, and not its solution.[18]

In much the same vein, and at roughly the same conjuncture, Luxemburg attacked the views of German 'bourgeois professors' entrenched in the academy who denied the economic significance of the international exchange of commodities, adhering instead to an intellectually untenable notion of 'national economy'.[19] Among those she criticized were Bücher and Sombart, dismissing the views of the latter as 'glittering tomfoolery'.[20] Most significantly, she – like

---

17 Along with 'Conservative clubs', 'the higher Anglican clergy' and 'priestly institutions', therefore, Trotsky (1973: 80) categorized Oxford University as being an establishment which for socialists were those of 'our enemies, and the revolutionary movement of the proletariat will inevitably break down their walls.' Further on he (Trotsky, 1973: 81) described Fabianism – supporters of which included academics – as 'complacent pedants, prattling eclectics, sentimental careerists [who were] liveried footmen of the bourgeoisie.'

18 Trotsky's suspicion of and antipathy towards bourgeois intellectuals is also evident from what he wrote about their role in pre-revolutionary Russia. 'Nor does the reactionary stupidity of the professional intelligentsia need to be proven after our experience of the Russian Revolution,' he notes (Trotsky, 1925: 19, 20), because a 'whole generation of Russian intelligentsia was formed (or rather deformed) by the efforts to conciliate monarchy, nobility and bourgeoisie, which filled the inter-revolutionary period (between the first Revolution of 1905 and that of 1917). Social determinism does not necessarily mean conscious self-interest, but the intelligentsia and the ruling class that keeps it are like connecting vessels, and the law of levels is equally applicable here.' This deep suspicion of the political and ideological role of the intelligentsia under capitalism is also found elsewhere in his writings (Trotsky, 1959; 1965: 251).

19 For the concept of 'national economy', see Bücher (1907: 83ff.). The critique of the latter was formulated by Luxemburg (1954) when teaching at the German Social Democratic Party School in the early years of the twentieth century. A similarly excoriating condemnation of academics – 'Professor Wagner' is described as autocratic, someone who 'addresses himself solely to his learned colleagues', whilst 'Professor Diehl [corrected a mistake] without a word to say when and by whom he had been thus enlightened' – is found in a long footnote written by her elsewhere (Luxemburg, 1951: 267, note 1).

20 On this, see Luxemburg (1954: 12, 14), where the following dichotomy is criticized: 'over here: industrial country; over there: agrarian state – that is the rigid pattern of world economic relations, as conceived by Professor Bücher and most of his colleagues.' It comes as no surprise that this discredited polarity still survives today in the economic analyses by adherents of the semi-feudal thesis.

Trotsky and Lenin – attributed bad theory to the fact that, being part of an establishment institution, academics engaged in 'intellectual flunkeyism': that is, a tendency to take a rose-tinted view of the ruling class as inherently progressive and reform-oriented, and thus to see its institutions as potentially/actually 'benign'.[21]

These kinds of criticism were echoed in the work of Bukharin and Preobrazhensky, both of whom noted in the 1920s that after the revolution 'even today we can be perfectly sure that the [Russian] universities in their present form, with their present professorial staffs, have ceased to be serviceable institutions.'[22] The reason for this, they added, was that 'these universities may be reformed by leavening the professorial staffs through the addition of persons who may not [be] the "learned specialists of bourgeois society" but who will be fully competent to effect the necessary revolution in the teaching of the social sciences, and will be able to expel bourgeois culture from its last stage.'[23]

The Things behind the Scenes

The operation of exclusionary practices on political grounds, plus the sensitivity of the academic establishment to suggestions of political bias when making appointments – substantial evidence to the contrary notwithstanding – can be illustrated by two episodes, both from the 1920s. Each demonstrates two things, both licensing the same conclusion. That such institutions are invariably hostile to socialists, who as a result find it hard to secure employment – let

21 Hence the following observation (Luxemburg, 1954: 42): 'Here we have the prettiest flowering of that intellectual flunkeyism which we have noted previously of German professors. According to professor Schmoller, the science of economics came into being at the command of enlightened absolutism. According to Professor Bücher the entire capitalist mode of production itself is but an achievement of the sovereign decision and the heaven-storming plans of absolutist sovereigns.'

22 See Bukharin and Preobrazhensky (1922: 239).

23 Bukharin and Preobrazhensky (1922: 243, emphasis added) continue: 'These favourable conditions, however, by no means suffice to overcome the difficulties of the proletarian State as far as concerns the provision of genuinely communist educational workers. The number of communists among teachers, as among specialists in general, is but an insignificant minority. *Most teachers are opposed to communism. The majority of them, however, are persons with an official type of mind, who are ready to serve any government* and to work any schedule, but who have a special fondness for a programme which was familiar to their fathers and their grandfathers.'

alone survive – in them, at the same time as remaining socialists, is hardly surprising.

Historically, therefore, it is not just Marxists who have been affected by such exclusionary practices, the existence of which underline the lengths to which the academic establishment has been prepared to go in order to suppress political heterodoxy.[24] Within the university system there has been longstanding opposition to views that may jeopardise it in one of two ways. Either financially, in terms of internal provision by the State or external subvention by foreign governments/organizations. Or by advocating opinions that challenge the very logic of academia as formulating/reproducing ideology favourable to (or, at least, not threatening to) the continued existence of capitalism.

The first episode involves a conflict during the early 1920s between two sets of (mainly academic) protagonist.[25] On the one hand, Arnold Toynbee, the

---

24 This kind of gate-keeping is reflected in the fact that, when making appointments to membership of their institutions, academics select those whose views do not conflict with their own, a tendency of 'like chooses like' that has a long history. Mark Pattison, whose memoirs are an important account by an insider of the way nineteenth century academia functioned, recognized this tendency when describing those deemed suitable for election to College fellowships in Oxford. 'Each fellow had a vote,' he writes (Pattison, 1885: 74–75), 'and many gave it irresponsibly. Like chose like. A drinking society chose a boon companion. Even those societies which had preserved self-respect enough not to sink into the condition of sots and topers preferred a "companionable" man to any acquirements or talents. The public opinion of the University approved this principle of selection, and had come to regard a college as a club, into which you should get only clubbable men.'

25 The seminal account of this episode is by Clogg (1986), on whom the following analysis draws. Among the many issues it raises, two are of particular interest. The first is methodological, about which Clogg (1986: vii) makes a crucial point, worth quoting in full. 'It is possible to document this extraordinary story in considerable detail, for a number of collections of papers, reflecting the views of all the major protagonists in the controversy, survive. Moreover, these records are sufficiently detailed to enable much of what the Greeks term the *paraskinia*, the things behind the scenes, to be reconstructed. One of the reasons for this would appear to lie in the fact that whereas telephones obviously existed in the early 1920s (King's College at that time had all of two lines) they were clearly not yet used for the transaction of academic business, and the conduct of academic intrigue, in the way that they would be now. [Consequently,] the historian has cause to be grateful for the fact that there is certainly no shortage of documentation.' The second is a political dimension that, as the author correctly surmises, was – and is – becoming more important. 'Toynbee's experiences during his tenure of the Koraes Chair,' notes Clogg (1986: viii), 'have a certain contemporary relevance in that they highlight some of the dangers inherent in the tendency manifest in recent years for British universities to look to external sources of funding when faced with financial stringency.'

original incumbent of the Koraes Chair of Modern Greek and Byzantine History at King's College, London; and on the other, the Greek subscribers who endowed the post, plus other academics at King's.[26] The cause was the criticism published in 1922 by Toynbee of atrocities committed by the Greek army in Asia Minor against Muslims, subsequent pressure from the donors resulting in his enforced resignation from the Chair in 1924.

Although the conflict was framed ideologically as one essentially between rival nationalisms (British, Greek), it is perhaps significant that the counterattack against Toynbee's critique of Greek atrocities equated his position with Bolshevism.[27] The inference was that someone holding the latter view should not be employed as an academic, an outlook shared – but for different reasons – by other senior members of London University hierarchy. Those in the latter also sought the dismissal of Toynbee from the Koraes Chair, since this in their opinion was the only way the endowment could be saved.[28] Revised conditions for the Koraes Chair, accepted by London University, amounted to a donor veto over the appointment, a situation that lasted until 1961.[29]

---

26 Not the least revealing aspect of the appointment to the Koraes Chair are the characteristics regarded as suitable for a candidate at this conjuncture. These demonstrate the class background required of those perceived as acceptable to academia. The characteristics are outlined in two quotations made by those on the appointment committee (Clogg, 1986: 26, 30). First, 'a gentleman by birth and education. From an old Devonshire family, he acted "the young squire" during the vacations.' And second, someone who should 'mix a little with educated Greeks as well as peasants [because] a foreigner who had no knowledge of England except from the conversation of farm labourers or navvies would get a rather one-sided view of things.'

27 Opinion in Britain supportive of Toynbee was clearly nationalist in sentiment (Clogg, 1986: 85), along the lines of 'those foreigners [= Greeks] have no right to dictate to us conditions governing the Koraes Chair'. For the accusation of Bolshevism levelled at Toynbee, see Clogg (1986: 58).

28 As Clogg (1986: 76–77, 89, 91) makes clear, pressure to get rid of Toynbee was put on King's College London by senior academics elsewhere in the university, led by R.W. Seton-Watson. Others who supported this move were Bernard Pares (Professor of Russian History and Head of the School of Slavonic Studies) and A.P. Newton (Rhodes Professor of Imperial History). Their fear was that university subsidies from other governments – Czech, Serbian, Polish and Romanian – for the study of these societies would be threatened as a result. In the words of Seton-Watson, the worry was that the episode would 'obviously raise the whole issue of foreign donors, and the consideration due to their rights, wishes or say prejudices'. For this reason, they voiced objections to Toynbee giving his side of the story (Clogg, 1986: 86ff., 90), thereby confirming their sensitivity to counter-accusations of political bias.

29 According to Clogg (1986: 91, 114), these conditions stipulated two things. First, that the university would prevent future holders from 'Professor Toynbee's scandalous behaviour'

The second example concerns the Professorship of Social Anthropology at Cambridge University, where in the mid-1920s an erstwhile pupil of W.H.R. Rivers was passed over in favour of a less-qualified applicant. A claim that the decision was politically motivated has been dismissed vehemently by Edmund Leach, a more recent holder of this Chair and himself a member of the academic establishment.[30] Although this episode has been framed in terms of rival theoretical positions *within* anthropology (evolutionists versus diffusionists), and the need on the part of British imperialism to see the department at Cambridge as a training ground for administrators maintaining British colonial power in India, there is another factor that is rarely mentioned.[31]

Of significance in this connection, therefore, is that Rivers himself had an interest in socialist politics, at this conjuncture a position which would have been an anathema to other senior academics – many of whom were conservative in outlook – in an ancient university.[32] Equally significant is the fact that

(= criticizing atrocities by the Greek army). And second, 'that Toynbee's own candidature when the Chair was once again advertised would be eliminated'.

30 The claim about political bias governing this appointment, made by Langham (1981: 179–180), was challenged by Leach (1984: 3), who disputed the view of the former that 'the succession of Hodson to Haddon was an imperialist plot with little academic justification.' Leach's own views about the benign nature of academic hierarchy are instructive. 'Let me be explicit', he has written (Leach, 1988: 11), 'I cannot really imagine a social system in which there was no social class hierarchy; but social classes based on academic attainment, which are soft at the edges are to be preferred to those of race in which, in theory, the edges are very hard.'

31 In view of the strong historical connection between anthropology and colonial rule in India (on which see Owen, 1973, and Kuper, 1973: 123ff.), the attempt by Leach to disavow a connection between the Cambridge appointment and the political objectives of British imperialism is somewhat disingenuous. Stauder (1974: 52) makes the following relevant point: 'A survey of the 27 Presidential Addresses to the Royal Anthropological Institute from 1893 to 1919 shows that in over half the President raised claims regarding the practical uses to which anthropology could be put in serving the Empire.' As Leach (1984: 6–7) himself admits, '[c]learly the events in question were important in the "history" of Cambridge anthropology for Hodson [the successful candidate] was later to become the first William Wyse Professor of Social Anthropology and, since he was already a close friend of his own successor, J.H. Hutton, who had similar interests, his appointment as the successor to Haddon served to set the tone of Cambridge anthropology for the next 25 years.'

32 For the interest of Rivers in not just in socialism but also in politics and the labour movement, see Slobodin (1978: 2, 69, 79–82, 185–186). The antagonism on the part of university authorities towards anything progressive, let alone connected to socialism, is evident from another episode at this conjuncture. The evidence, in the form of a letter (alternately patronizing and threatening), merits quoting in full (Ashley and Saunders, 1933: 37): 'In October, 1921, Miss Hardy, Secretary of the Oxford University Labour Club, wrote to the Vice-Chancellor asking for permission for the Club to hold a public meeting, at which

he was thinking of standing as a Parliamentary candidate for the Labour Party, a move which elicited strong criticism from fellow anthropologists.[33] Little wonder, then, that someone whom he had taught should be deemed unacceptable as a candidate for a senior academic post at Cambridge.

Academic Entryism and Exclusion

Throughout the nineteenth century the formation and consolidation of an urban industrial working class in Britain was accompanied by a fear on the part

Bertrand Russell was to speak. (His subject was "China", but the Vice-Chancellor did not know this.) She received the following reply: "Dear Miss Hardy – My reply to your request must be an unconditional refusal. I object to your Club, which you call the 'Oxford University Labour Club', holding any public meeting at all. Apart from the question whether Mr. Bertrand Russell is a desirable person to address Oxford undergraduates on problems that involve social morality, it is against the law of the university for undergraduate members to take part in meetings of an agitating tendency. It is still more objectionable that they should organize them. We also object to their assuming the name of Oxford University for a party union of a class-dividing tendency. If your Club wishes to exist, it must keep itself entirely private, both in respect of meetings and publications; otherwise we shall have to take steps. Your organizers ought to have asked my opinion before venturing to take such a name. I will now speak a few words to you more in *loco parentis*, as you are an undergraduate member of the University and newly admitted. I earnestly advise you to concentrate on the purpose for which you have come here, which is the increase of knowledge through honest study. It is premature for you to be taking violent sides in violent political controversies. What you want to do is to think and to know more. These public meetings do not make for the increase of knowledge or for greater clearness of thought obtained by fair and careful argument on both sides. You will be more fit to deal with social problems later, if you concentrate your mind and time on the more abstract studies that you have chosen to pursue. This advice applies equally to our women as to our men students. Yours faithfully (Signed), Lewis R. Farnell, Vice-Chancellor."'

33 It goes without saying that at this conjuncture – just before the 1926 General Strike – both the Labour Party and the labour movement (despite being reformist even then) were more radical politically than is the case now. According to Slobodin (1978: 79–80): 'It had been noted that Rivers knew some Labour Party intellectuals. He had also made acquaintances in trade union educational circles: at the time of his death [in 1922] he was planning two courses, one in anthropology one in psychology, to be given…at the Manchester school of the Workers' Educational Trade Union Committee…his decision to stand for Parliament was no joke to Rivers, nor to many of his colleagues who were dismayed… One suspects that it was the Labour Party affiliation that "furiously annoyed" some professional colleagues; it is likely that some Fellows of the Royal Anthropological Institute were less than happy at their president's decision to campaign under the banner of socialism.'

of capitalist producers lest this process lead to the emergence of a socialist consciousness.[34] For this reason, employers unsurprisingly concerned themselves with the political content of any education – formal or informal – on offer to or received by their manual labourers.[35] Calls for the reform of public education at this conjuncture rarely failed to mention its potential role as a way of counter-acting the spread of socialist ideas.[36] Not only did such concerns not diminish in the century that followed, but they were extended to cover those teaching and learning in higher education.

---

34 Because these are symptomatic pronouncements on the subject, the views of Sir James Kay-Shuttleworth are of interest. He was an influential advocate of educational reform, a result of investigations conducted in the working class areas of Manchester. This early work by him (Kay, 1969) was cited approvingly by Engels (1975: 350, 362, 364–366, 390, 467).

35 Hence the following observation by Kay (1969: 95, 97, 99): 'The preservation of *internal peace*, not less than the improvement of our national institutions, depends on the education of the working class... The ascertained truths of political science should be early taught to the labouring classes, and *correct* political information should be constantly and industriously disseminated amongst them... The relation between the capitalist and those in his employ, might prove a fruitful source of the most beneficial comments. The misery which the working classes have brought upon themselves, by their mistaken notions on this subject, is incalculable, not to mention the injury which has accrued to the capitalists, and to the trade of this country.' (original emphases) Warning against allowing associations of workmen from focusing their discontents on capital, he (Kay, 1969: 111) goes on to state that the 'radical remedy for these evils [trade unions, strikes] is such an education as shall teach the people in what consists their true happiness, and how their interests may be best promoted.' Some four decades later, his warnings have become even stronger (Kay-Shuttleworth, 1973: 24–25): 'These unions exert a domination over their members like that of any army, and are capable of sustained action... Regarded as political and social phenomena, such results may be a most potent means of attaining any object which the manual labour class may have a strong conviction would be for their common interests. Any statesman who fails to recognize the existence of the formidable tendencies of such a power, and *to provide for its right direction by a universal and obligatory provision for public education*...cannot long govern this country.' (emphasis added)

36 Such concerns arose from the fear of 'the mob in the streets', or as one influential educational reformer (Kay, 1969: 42–43) put it, 'a turbulent population, which, rendered reckless by dissipation and want, misled by the secret intrigues, and excited by the inflammatory harangues of demagogues' would engage in 'frantic violence of an ignorant and deluded rabble'. What is being said here is that, if employers fail to persuade the working class that they (the employers) are not to blame for the poor conditions in the workplace, by ensuring that labourers are educated to this end, the latter will fall prey to 'agitators' who counsel revolution, the result of which will be an attack on property. Thus education of workers is seen explicitly as a way of deradicalizing them, thereby preventing a 'mob in the streets' from becoming a threat to the 'stability' of the capitalist order.

During the first half of the twentieth century, when Marxist theory had an impact on the grassroots even in Britain, this occurred – significantly – outside the university system.[37] Not only was Marxism taught in courses attended by workers at the Central Labour College, and by the Plebs Movement, but it featured in study courses devoted specifically to political economy and its connection with working class history.[38] Despite a recent and methodologically flawed attempt to downplay the importance of socialist literature in patterns of working class reading, it is nevertheless the case that leftist outcomes structured most grassroots political alternatives to capitalism formulated at this conjuncture.[39]

Because academics were regarded by many on the left as hostile to a labour movement objective of socialism, therefore, workers' education was perceived

37 That an impetus to learn more about socialist theory not only originated at the grassroots but arose because of unhappiness with the kind of economic explanations in circulation at this conjuncture is evident from many accounts. Thus, for example, Beer (1948: 352–353) writes: 'As far back as May, 1905… I noticed a certain dissatisfaction among some [working class] students with the economic teaching of the [Ruskin] College professors. The students desired to be taught economics from Marx's *Capital*, particularly the labour theory of value, instead of the Jevonian theory of marginal utility. After the election of 1906, with the sudden surging of social problems, the dissatisfaction ripened into a conflict. The dissatisfied students formed a separate organization called the Plebs League and finally seceded in 1909. They established an institution of their own, the Central Labour College [where teaching was] to be based upon the recognition of the antagonism of interests between Capital and Labour.'

38 On the teaching of Marxism outside the university system during the 1920s and 1930s, see Ruskin History Workshop Students (1981) and the collection in Marxist Study Courses (1932–33). According to the Ruskin History Workshop Students (1981: 15), '[t]he main feature of the history inside the Central Labour College was its "totality". History was seen as an explanation of the political, social and economic conditions of mankind at that time. But, it was thought, only Marxism could do this satisfactorily.'

39 The text in question is Rose (2001), the findings of which about the reading habits of workers are based mainly on the pattern of library books borrowed. Among the claims is that even radical books borrowed from workers' libraries showed little sign of having been read. There are two reasons in particular for questioning this. First, many of my copies of classic Marxist texts published during the first three decades of last century, purchased by me from second-hand bookshops during the 1970s, earlier belonged to those who had been students at the Central Labour College. These books were all heavily underlined and annotated in the margins by their initial owners, which suggests claims that such texts remained unread are unfounded. And second, it fails to take into account the oral transmission of socialist ideas, whereby those who read Marxist texts communicated their content in discussions with those who had not.

as correspondingly incompatible with a capitalist university system. In the words of the General Secretary of the National Council of Labour Colleges, written around 1947, 'just as the labour movement found it necessary to be first industrially and later politically independent of the capitalist class, so in its educational work it needs to be educationally independent.' The reason for this, the same source continues, was because the 'pioneers of the Labour College Movement saw that the education that had grown up in the capitalist system was naturally biased against any new ideas that threatened that system.'[40]

Over the latter part of the twentieth century, however, orthodox leftist views about the role of academic institutions underwent something of a reversal. Rather than being seen as bastions of bourgeois thought the main objective of which was to defend capitalism, universities were perceived as places from which to mount an ideological attack on the capitalist system. This development has to be linked to a wider process, the cultural struggle during the cold war era between Stalinism and US imperialism, the object of which was to garner support among – and thus obtain legitimization from – Western European intellectuals.[41]

In an important sense, the expansion of higher education in the 1960s channelled this process into the university system, by creating additional (and salaried) employment opportunities for intellectuals who would otherwise have remained outside academia.[42] Once socialists were installed as professors, so the argument went, the teaching and thus the influence of universities would

40 For this view, see Millar (c.1947: 2–3). The latter elaborates on why a working class education should be located outside academia: 'The labour movement's object has been to improve the living conditions of the workers. Hard experience has taught it that to achieve a permanent improvement it is necessary to create a new social order. Do we find that in the struggle to build up the labour movement and to establish a new social order the educated classes and the universities, for example, acted as pioneers? On the contrary... The explanation of this is very simple. The education of any social order reflects the needs and interests of that social order. In consequence, the education provided in the capitalist social order was designed to buttress that social order and serve its purposes. The result was that the educated naturally looked at things through capitalist eyes even although many of them were not themselves capitalists.'

41 On this *kulturkampf* see Stonor Saunders (1999). According to the latter account (Stonor Saunders, 1999: 27), in 1947 'Zhadanov called upon the intelligentsia of the world to rattle their pens under the banner of Communism, and to hurl their ink against the American imperium.'

42 According to Collini (2006: 188), the number of students in British higher education doubled from fifty thousand in 1939 to one hundred thousand in 1960, and increased to nearly six hundred thousand in 1988 and one million in the year 2000.

undergo a radical transformation.[43] What actually happened was predictably different: in order to become part of the academy, and once inside to rise up its hierarchy, socialists were required to water down or discard their political principles, which is what a number of socialist academics did.[44]

In short, socialists who became professors ceased to be socialists, while those who remained socialists were frequently barred from university appointments. This is consistent with a wider pattern of non-revolutionary (= reformist/collaborationist) practice, the aim of which was to establish a leftist hegemony. Rather than challenge the nature and structure of a bourgeois institution, the object of this kind of reformist approach was much rather to convert to a Marxist viewpoint those 'progressive' elements of the bourgeoisie employed in the academy.[45]

---

43 Undoubtedly an aspect of this was a desire on the part of those on the political left to confer academic respectability on Marxist theory as a position that could legitimately take its rightful place in intellectual discourse, an objective that generated much optimism. 'Over a decade ago,' writes Shalin (1980: 362), 'the prospects for the academic legitimation of Marxism seemed negligible to its proponents... In the [1970s] the academic legitimation of Marxism in the United States proceeded at an accelerated pace: Marxist sociology departments appeared in the universities; radical and humanist sociologists consolidated their efforts organizationally; a Marxist section was established under the auspices of the ASA; dissertations fostering Marxist tradition were successfully defended; some thirty journals devoted to the Marxist cause were available to scholars in the United States by the end of the 1970s.' Whilst an admirable objective in the abstract, insofar as it represents an attempt to establish intellectual hegemony, in practice the search for academic respectability overlooks the institutional difficulties. Namely, the incompatibility between on the one hand the historical and continuing resistance by those in the academic hierarchy to Marxist theory/practice, and on the other the historical and continuing pursuit by socialists of promotion and advancement once inside the university system.

44 Claims to the contrary notwithstanding, it is nevertheless the case that advancement within academia has to some extent always been linked closely to two things. A willingness to refrain from criticizing those occupying senior positions in its hierarchy combined with a propensity to flatter them. On this kind of process, Trollope (1971: 10) long ago observed: 'Is it not singular how some men continue to obtain the reputation of popular authorship without adding a word to the literature of their country worthy of note? It is accomplished by unflagging assiduity in the system of puffing. To puff and to get one's self puffed have become different branches of a new profession.'

45 Such 'conversions' which did take place, it could be argued, had more to do with a desire to be seen as in step with modern fashion than with a genuine espousal of and commitment to socialist principles. Where the British working class movement is concerned, there is a long history of such political accommodation on the part of the bourgeois liberal intelligentsia. As Mirsky (1935: 211–212) notes of an earlier conjuncture: 'But in their "own" working class their "own" fellow countrymen of the proletariat, these

Just as Marxists who moved up the British academic hierarchy were transformed politically, therefore, so CPGB members who joined the Labour Party in order to change it in a leftist direction were instead themselves changed in a rightwards direction, as was CPGB policy which sought out alliances with a misnamed 'progressive' bourgeoisie. This was a common outcome of a misplaced and over-optimistic tactic of 'entryism', in its academic institutional variant as much as in its party political and class collaborationist forms.[46]

This academic 'entryism' has in turn given rise to contradictory but related phenomena. First, socialists who became professors, and ceased thereby to be socialists, were henceforth charged with gate-keeping duties, the object of which was to ensure that those who remained socialists did not gain entry into or prosper within the university teaching system.[47] And second, socialists who became professors but ceased to be socialists were nevertheless

intellectuals of the twenties were interested practically exclusively as raw material out of which to make their own careers. The growth of the labour party and the decline of the liberal party made it advantageous to such persons to make up to the "labour movement"... Thus in those years one saw ambitious young fellows from the aristocracy, the upper ranks of the middle class, and the bourgeois intelligentsia just stroll straight across into parliament as "labour men", while a crowd of young men from Oxford and Cambridge went straight into the labour party executive... or else, as lecturers on history or sociology or political economy, dabbled with "socialistic" ideas'.

46 Symptomatic of this process was the endorsement by many of the self-styled 'Marxists' connected with *Marxism Today* of the 'third way' – market individualism, privatization and capitalist consumption – in the (mistaken) belief that it was a 'social democratic alternative' to neo-liberalism. That such a belief was misplaced was obvious to not just to Marxists but indeed also to others right from the outset.

47 This kind of gate-keeping has a long history in academia, and its operation in England during the mid-nineteenth century was the subject of a satire by Thackeray. One such character, Crump, who came from a plebeian background (Thackeray, 1855: 50–51), 'is since advanced to be President of the College. He was formerly, and is now, a rich specimen of a University snob... To do Crump justice, he does not cringe now to great people. He rather patronises them than otherwise; and, in London, speaks quite affably to a Duke who has been brought up at his college, or holds out a finger to a Marquis. He does not disguise his own origin, but brags of it with considerable self-gratulation: – "I was a Charity-boy," says he; "see what I am now; the greatest Greek scholar of the greatest College of the greatest University of the greatest Empire in the world." The argument being, that this is a capital world for beggars, because he, being a beggar, has managed to get on horseback.' We see many present-day equivalents of Crump occupying senior positions in the Western academy. That is to say, those who proclaimed they were Marxists when Marxism was in vogue; who quickly transferred their allegiance to the non-Marxist or anti-Marxist paradigms that rose to prominence subsequently. Having come from an heterodox background (= 'I was a Charity-boy'), they now look kindly and less critically on a system that

required to display anti-capitalist credentials, which made them in a sense dependent on the research ideas formulated by those they had excluded from the academy.

Since in the social sciences it is – broadly speaking – still necessary to be seen to be a critic of capitalism, those who rise up the academic hierarchy have from time to time to renew/reinvent their credentials in this regard.[48] In a neat reversal of the cold war slogan, the means did indeed justify the end, but it was anti-capitalist ideas that were the means and an academic career that was the end. This is particularly important when a critical stance has itself been jettisoned in order to proceed smoothly up the hierarchy. The significance of this lies in its wider social impact. Politics comes to be seen as one more way in which to advance a career, an ephemeral commitment to be taken up and discarded at will, influenced by no more than intellectual and/or institutional fashion. Such expediency undermines confidence not just in politics *per se*, but more importantly in socialist politics, and reinforces the belief that those who advocate socialism lack principle, and whose insincerity is ultimately no different from those who espouse other kinds of politics.[49] As many of the

---

has recognized and rewarded their own merit, and thus appears to them to be egalitarian (= 'this is a capital world for beggars').

48 Needless to say, this phenomenon is confined neither to the social sciences nor to academia. Within and outside the latter context, however, the most notorious instances arose as a consequence of collaboration with reactionary politics during the 1930s. Numerous cases not only of the endorsement of rightwing ideas on the part of sociologists but also of their subsequent denials of having entered such allegiances are outlined in Turner and Kasler (1992). This pattern was repeated outside the academy, as exemplified by the case of the German composer Carl Orff. A recent documentary film, *O Fortuna* (2008), directed by Tony Palmer, reveals that Orff refused to intercede with the German authorities on behalf of his librettist, the jewish academic Kurt Huber, arrested by the Gestapo in February 1943. Well-placed with the Nazi regime, Orff possessed the kind of influence enabling him to intervene successfully, but chose not to so as not to jeopardise his career, leaving Huber to be tortured and executed. This moral cowardice was compounded when, after the war, Orff claimed falsely to have been a member (like Huber) of the White Rose resistance movement.

49 This is a crucial issue, one that has always played directly into the hands of conservatives, who have not been slow in using it to discredit political opponents. A case in point is Thomas Chandler Haliburton, an influential writer of popular fiction during the nineteenth century. Amongst the 'common sense' arguments put forward by an 'everyman' character Samuel Slick (Anonymous, 1838: 110–111, 113–114) was that every worthy cause – in this case slave emancipation – inevitably attracts the support of those who see it as a vehicle for the advancement of their own careers.

early Marxists pointed out, a refusal to compromise is an essential component of socialist politics.[50]

'Crude class analysis'

Among those Marxists who did not compromise politically, and consequently were denied posts in British universities over the second half of the twentieth century were Isaac Deutscher and George Rudé, whose cases are outlined elsewhere in this volume (review 6).[51] As demonstrated by Terry Eagleton in his bland review of a published volume of Isaiah Berlin's letters, there is still a

50 In the words of Trotsky (1936: 141, original emphasis): 'It was not flexibility that served (nor should it serve today) as the basic trait of Bolshevism but rather *granite hardness*. It was precisely of this quality, for which its enemies and opponents reproached it, that Bolshevism was always justly proud.'

51 In what amounted to a tacit sign of guilt, blocking appointment on political grounds was on occasion compounded by a subsequent denial of ever having done so. 'Many years later', writes Hitchens (2000: 141), 'I mentioned [in a book review] the old story of Berlin acting as an academic gatekeeper, and barring the appointment of Isaac Deutscher to a Chair at Sussex University. This denial had the sad effect of forcing Deutscher – who had once given Berlin a highly scornful review in the *Observer* [newspaper] – to churn out Kremlinology for a living; as a result of which he never finished his triad or troika of Stalin, Trotsky and Lenin biographies. In the next post came a letter from Berlin, stating with some anguish that while he didn't much approve of Deutscher, his opinion had not been the deciding one. I telephoned Tamara Deutscher and others, asking if they had definite proof that Berlin had administered the bare bodkin, and was told, well, no, not definite proof. So I published a retraction. Then came a post card from Berlin, thanking me handsomely, saying that the allegation had always worried and upset him... And now I read in Ignatieff's book [*Isaiah Berlin: A Life*], that it was an annihilatingly hostile letter from Berlin to the Vice-Chancellor of Sussex University which "put paid to Deutscher's chances"'. That the practice of self-styled liberal academics rarely accords with the ideological plurality their theory proclaims has long been recognized. Hence the observation some three decades ago by Conor Cruise O'Brien (1969: 2) pointing to the contradiction involving those 'who set out to "defend" liberal values, but whose methods of defense – which have included cases of deliberate and later-exposed deception – are incompatible with the values they purport to defend.' Significantly, in his complacent celebration of Oxbridge dons, Annan (1999: 228–229) also considers the Berlin/Deutscher episode, but justifies blocking the appointment on political grounds by Berlin, and instead criticizes Hitchens for publicizing and condemning this exclusionary act. This is a common reaction, as is evident from what happened when Caute resigned from All Souls, Oxford, in the mid-1960s over a matter of political principle, and proceeded to criticize college policy. Noting that 'knives were sharpened,' he continues (Caute, 1974: 41, original emphasis) that '[e]ven in those colleges where hostility towards All Souls was endemic, wise men closed ranks and condemned the *public* exposure.'

tendency on the part of socialists to pass over in silence political acts resulting in academic exclusion, and to treat the conservatism of a 'liberal' perpetrator as a harmless form of eccentricity that is 'not worth bothering about'.[52]

However, the academic exclusion on political grounds of Deutscher by Berlin and of Rudé by Alfred Cobban are only the best-known and most notorious instances of what was and remains a common practice.[53] Others similarly affected included scholars such as E.H. Carr, Daniel Thorner, David Abraham and Jack Stauder.[54] The challenge thrown down by the last named to

52 The review by Eagleton of the volume in question (Berlin, 2009) not only fails to mention the Deutscher episode but also lets Berlin off lightly, calling him 'a remarkably good-natured soul', and adding that '[n]ot even his sternest critic could fail to be impressed by his exuberance and vivacity.' See 'Urbane sprawl', *The Guardian* (London), 27 June 2009.

53 A Professor of French History at University College London, Cobban, who blocked the academic appointment of Rudé, was a vehement anti-Marxist whose revisionist interpretation of the 1789 French Revolution (Cobban, 1964) prefigured that of François Furet (on which see Comninel (1987)). It was this anti-Marxism that attracted commendation from one observer of academia (Annan, 1999: 248–249), who comments approvingly that Cobban, among others, was responsible for having 'finally demolished the Marxist interpretation of the French Revolution [as] a result [of which] the causes of the French Revolution dropped out of the category of problems that the academic élite found interesting.' Rarely can the political agenda behind exclusionary academic practices have been revealed more clearly: the expulsion from the arena of study of what for conservatives and reactionaries in the university system has been a troublesome process – revolution.

54 For the cases of E.H. Carr, Daniel Thorner, David Abraham and Jack Stauder, see respectively Haslam (2000), Thorner (1982a), Wiener (1991: 63–70; 2005: 94ff.) and Nader (1997: 107–146). Because of his refusal to condemn socialism, and despite not being a Marxist, E.H. Carr was denied a fellowship at Cambridge during the early 1950s, mainly as a result of an intervention by Noel Annan (Haslam, 2000: 165–167). Although – like Carr – Daniel Thorner was not a socialist, his critical stance on issues to do with economic development in India made him a target of McCarthyite witchhunts in the US, as a result of which he was unable to find an academic post there. The political reasons for and outcome of academic exclusion are evident from the following account (Nader, 1997: 115): 'The disturbing question repeatedly asked by younger anthropology professors like Jack Stauder at Harvard was: "To whom has anthropological work been relevant?"... Controversy over firing was fierce. Jack Stauder, an anthropologist who had degrees from Harvard, and from Cambridge University, and who had completed original work in Ethiopia on subsistence and environment, was fired, then rehired by Harvard, then finally his contract was not renewed. He was banned from teaching the fall semester after the student strike in spring 1969, and suffered the loss of salary in these transitions. The fact that his contract was not renewed was undoubtedly related to difficulties in finding employment during a time when the university had become the object of CIA activity. Stauder became an activist

the academic establishment is clear from the following: 'It is my opinion that, in the absence of revolutionary changes in the wider society, anthropology as a whole and as an institutional activity cannot be radically changed or reformed so as not to serve imperialism.'[55]

The largescale dismissal of leftist academics in the United States at the start of the Cold War, as a result of the witch-hunt conducted by the House Committee on Un-American Activities, is well known.[56] University teachers were forced from their jobs on political grounds over the period between the late 1940s and early 1950s, and many never again found employment in academic institutions.[57] Equally well known is the abandonment at this conjuncture by some on the left of their political beliefs, a process that culminated in a rightwards shift.[58]

In England, too, there were calls in the name of 'scholarly integrity' during the early 1950s for 'the dismissal of Communists from the British Universities'.[59] This confirms the central point being made here: that in cases where socialists employed in the university system have maintained a principled adherence to leftist views, their survival as academics has been put in jeopardy. In other words, the basic incompatibility between the values/ideology of the bourgeois academy and Marxist theory/practice.

Sociology and/as Socialism

In Britain during the first half of the twentieth century those Marxists who survived or prospered as academics were mainly historians – such as John Saville,

---

lost to scholarship because he analyzed the meaning of anthropology under imperialism, a contribution later generations of anthropologists too easily forgot.'

55 See Stauder (1974: 69) who continues: 'As long as we live within an imperialist system the same forces which now shape and utilize anthropology will continue to operate and will continue their institutional domination over the practice of anthropology.'

56 The standard account of this process is by Caute (1978: 407ff.).

57 According to Caute (1978: 552), '[r]eplies to professor Paul Tillett's questionnaire to 140 academics who had been dismissed on account of their political beliefs, indicated that the majority had subsequently been compelled to change careers and undergo extensive retraining.'

58 Among those following a political trajectory from left to right at this conjuncture was Irving Kristol, who shifted from Trotskyism to becoming an influential neo-conservative.

59 On this, see Rothstein (1953: 69, 74). The call for the expulsion of communists from teaching and/or research posts in British universities was made by the editor of the *Times Literary Supplement*. As Rothstein (1953: 74, original emphasis) notes rightly, '[i]t is quite apparent indeed that the writer of the editorial is least of all concerned with real scholarly integrity. What he is concerned about is political...*conformity*'.

E.P. Thompson, Eric Hobsbawm, and Rodney Hilton – or natural scientists such as J.D. Bernal.[60] This was due in part to the fact that historians are concerned mainly with the past, and as such they are perceived as less threatening than social scientists who talk about the present, and whose views may affect the future. Insofar as the main concern of natural scientists – even those on the political left – was to promote better and more efficient forms of economic growth, this was an argument that capitalism could (and later would) use to its own advantage.[61]

Accordingly, social science constituted a special case, in the sense that *notionally* it represented more of a threat to the existing class structure than other disciplines. This is because, unlike history, for example, social scientific

60 When they engaged with current events, some of these historians were either found wanting politically, or politically conservative. Although E.P. Thompson (1982: 1–33) demonstrated a courageous personal commitment in the struggle for peace and against the nuclear arms race (= 'exterminism'), this intrinsically laudable stance was nevertheless consistent with the single issue campaigns that characterized the 'new social movements' populism of that era. Moreover, it was a stance in keeping with his role as an historian, since he was responsible in part for laying the epistemological foundations of the 'moral economy' approach (Thompson, 1991: 185ff., 259ff.), which was taken up with such enthusiasm by the 'new' populist postmodernism. Less praiseworthy was the role discharged by another historian, E.J. Hobsbawm, whose position in academic life was less marginal than he frequently claims: unlike Thompson – who really was marginal – Hobsbawm was not just mainstream but rather well rewarded by the establishment – he is a member of the Reform Club and a Companion of Honour. From the safe refuge of a professorial chair at London University, Hobsbawm insisted that the only way forward for the British left was to abandon class in favour of a 'people's party'. In his view (Hobsbawm, 1981: 179), therefore, parties that have succeeded are 'people's parties with which the majority of the nation interested in progressive reform and change can identify: as spokesman for the nation in time of crisis.' This is the familiar territory of multi-class alliances based on the erroneous idea of a 'progressive' national bourgeoisie, a concept which underwrote the Stalinist Popular Front policies of the 1930s. That he was now travelling in a non-socialist direction is something Hobsbawm (1991: 322) accepts when he writes that: 'You may say that all this is an argument not for socialism but for a humanized mixed economy…I won't say no.' In England such populist nationalism was realized with the coming to power in 1997 of 'New Labour' under Tony Blair, who completed the anti- working-class neoliberal project begun by Thatcherism. Unsurprisingly, Hobsbawm (2009) has recently come out of the political closet, and declared that there is no longer any alternative to some form of capitalism.

61 Thus, for example, the idea of scientific planning in the 1960s favoured capitalism as much as (if not more than) socialism, and much of the expansion in higher education during that decade was premised on the need to provide accumulation with the kind of skills that foster economic growth.

theory and data – about property rights, tenure structure, land reform, planning and public spending – refer to the present.[62] As such, they could form the basis for alternatives not just to current socio-economic transformation, but also to a different set of actual/potential beneficiaries.

That the social sciences failed to do this is evident from Britain, where in the 1960s Anderson maintained that the lack of a 'from below' revolutionary tradition was due to a lack of an authentically indigenous sociological theory capable of challenging this dominant cultural inheritance.[63] In a discourse (doubly patronizing, to native and immigrant alike) the backwardness of English national culture was attributed by him simply – and wrongly – to the influx of 'foreigners' who provided the intellectual components of a national culture that the natives themselves had somehow been unwilling or unable to supply. The 'foreigner' is, in short, inculpated with the conservatism of national culture in Britain.[64]

Because he was unfamiliar with the distinction between populism and Marxism, Anderson failed to note that those on the 'left' have been equally at fault in this regard, a point borne out by the subsequent promotion/endorsement of the 'new' populist postmodernism – mistaking it for Marxism – by the journal he himself edited. Moreover, the indigenous sociology that *did* emerge – one has only to think of Giddens – reinforced the very political (not cultural) conservatism to which Anderson objected.[65] The problem lies not

62 Given its politically radical implications, the study of class relationships have always proved worrying to those in the bourgeois academy. In the latter context establishment historians have from time to time warned against this trend. Thus, for example, a recent biography (Cannadine, 1992: 225, 236) of one such endorses the utterances in this regard made by its subject, noting that 'Trevelyan's final warning, in his [1955] speech on the presentation of his festschrift, *against the excesses of crude class analysis*, has increasingly been taken to heart in recent years' (emphasis added).

63 Hence the view (Anderson, 1968: 4): 'A political science capable of guiding the working-class movement to final victory will only be born within a general intellectual matrix which challenges bourgeois ideology in every sector of thought and represents a decisive, hegemonic alternative to the cultural status quo.' The same text continues: 'It is enough to say this, to be reminded that in Britain, at present, there is virtually no organized combat of this kind, anywhere along the front.'

64 Anderson (1968: 56) claimed that historically English society has been a case of 'arrested development' due to the fact that a 'White emigration rolled across the flat expanse of English intellectual life, capturing sector after sector, until this traditionally insular culture became dominated by expatriates, of heterogeneous calibre'.

65 Anderson was not the only one whose optimism was misplaced. The same criticism applies to Sayers, who regards this period as one marking the Marxist coming of age in academia. He writes (Sayers, 2006: 2): 'By the end of the 1960s, Marxism could no longer be

with the presence or absence of sociological theory, as Anderson maintains, but rather with its politics: in short, not the fact of sociological 'totality' *per se*, but rather the kind of dynamic informing its structure and reproduction.[66]

The potential efficacy of social science emerged briefly in France during May 1968, when among the issues raised by students who took to the streets in Paris and elsewhere was the kind of sociology taught in university departments.[67] The fact that students' protest at that conjuncture included the conservative nature of the social science they were taught, and a corresponding wish to radicalize sociological theory, would of course have generated official anxiety as to the results of a meeting between students and revolutionary socialist theory/practice.[68] Not surprisingly, such a possibility both alerted and simultaneously underlined to the capitalist State and bourgeois authorities in

---

dismissed by academics in the west as only the ideology of the Soviets and their allies, it had become an influential component of a wider intellectual life. A new generation of young teachers, who had been radicalized as students in the 1960s and who came into academic life in the early 1970s, fought to have Marxist and other left ideas included in the curriculum in philosophy and other subjects. Their influence was soon evident not only in philosophy and political theory, but in every area of the humanities and social sciences. Marxism had become a component of the mainstream of British intellectual life. The tide of Marxism in Britain had reached a high point.'

66 This somewhat idealised view about the necessarily subversive role of a sociology which addressed the question of a total structure is stated thus (Anderson, 1968: 47): 'British culture never produced a classical sociology largely because British society was never challenged as a whole from within: the dominant class and its intellectuals consequently had no interest in forging a theory of its total structure; for it would necessarily have been an "answer" to a question which to their ideological advantage remained unposed.'

67 A common misapprehension, still pervasive today, is that in 1968 students rebelled because of what they had been taught by *Marxist* academics. The latter were accordingly blamed by many for the fact of student protests, the assumption being that had students not been radicalized in this manner they would not have taken to the streets. The situation was much rather the reverse: in 1968 students rebelled in part because of what they had been taught by *non-Marxist* academics. Among the latter was Alain Touraine, an enthusiast of new social movements whose ideas were dismissed (Cohn-Bendit and Cohn-Bendit, 1968: 40) as 'so much hot air'. In short, students wanted a more radical curriculum than that currently on offer: one that was much more critical of the way the capitalist system functioned.

68 Significantly, a principal target of student protest was the reformism advocated by orthodox communist parties. About the non-revolutionary politics espoused by the latter, Cohn-Bendit and Cohn-Bendit (1968: 168) commented: '[D]uring the months of May and June, the [French] Communist Party...played the game of the State and the bourgeoisie in theory no less than in practice.' The communism to which students objected was that of Stalin, regarded as too conservative, and accurately described (Cohn-Bendit and

the university system the dangers of permitting revolutionary Marxists to gain employment as lecturers in academia.[69]

This is a problem staring us in the face, literally so – but an uncomfortable one that few of us care to acknowledge. One of the reasons why bourgeois commentators are no longer as terrified as they used to be of what might happen if socialism and socialists gained a foothold in academic institutions – an apprehension that informed much writing from the late nineteenth century onwards – is accordingly not difficult to discern.[70] It is that, when to some degree

---

Cohn-Bendit, 1968: 147) as 'combining Leninist ideological phrases with electoral and reformist practices.'

69 A cynic might point out that neither the capitalist State nor bourgeois university authorities in France (and elsewhere in Europe) need have worried unduly about Marxists gaining employment in academia. What emerged as a result was not revolutionary Marxism but rather the a-historical structuralism of Althusser and Poulantzas that licensed the 'cultural turn' of 1980s postmodernism. Nor can the rightwards political movement of a whole generation of erstwhile socialist theorists – such as Lucio Colletti, Rudolph Bahro and Roger Garaudy – be accidental. Bahro and Colletti went on to become, respectively, an admirer of Hitler and a supporter of Berlusconi, while Garaudy underwent religious conversion, first to Roman Catholicism and then to Islam. Like Garaudy in France, the British philosopher Alasdair MacIntyre underwent a similar transition from being a socialist to religious conversion, in his case Roman Catholicism.

70 Among those on the right of the political spectrum whose attack on intellectuals was based in part on the fear lest socialist academics and socialist theory became established in the university system were Hayek (1954), Aron (1957), Cox and Dyson (1969–77), Nisbet (1971), Bauer (1971), Scruton (1985; 1987), Gould (1977), and Johnson (1996). Such attacks followed a common line, the main target being Marxism, albeit disguised frequently by critical references to non-Marxist thinkers. The concern of those on the political right about the influence of leftwing intellectuals on debate over capitalism is evident in the titles of the contributions to the volume edited by Hayek (1954: 33ff., 64ff., 93ff.): 'The Treatment of Capitalism by Historians', 'The Anticapitalist Bias of American Historians', and 'The Treatment of Capitalism by Continental Intellectuals'. In the case of Aron (1957: Chapters I–III), for example, the attack begins in familiar fashion by dismissing as political myths all the elements underpinning socialist theory: the left, the revolution, and the proletariat are all declared chimeras. It continues (Aron, 1957: Chapters IV–VI) by categorizing socialism as a religion, Marxists as the modern equivalents of medieval churchmen, and socialists as 'the faithful' who – as unthinking 'fanatics' – defy history that confounds determinism and counsels plurality. In a variation on an infamous historical utterance ('let them eat cake'), Bauer (1971: 317, 320) similarly decries the influence of Marxism, but with reference to development issues in the so-called Third World, noting that '[t]he dominant political influence in development economics has been exclusively meliorist in character,' and further that '[t]he influence of meliorism in development economics has been reinforced by that of Marxism, itself an especially powerful species

this eventually happened – in the 1960s – it was easily defeated.[71] Socialists who gained entry to the academic profession were either co-opted (ceasing to be socialists) or excluded (if they remained socialists).[72] This outcome has

of meliorism.' More recently, Johnson (1996: 52–53) insists that Marxism has been 'implanted in the public doctrine of the states his followers founded, so that it colours the teaching of all subjects in their schools and universities.' He continues: 'This has spilled over into the non-Marxist world, for intellectuals, especially academics, are fascinated by power, and the identification of Marxism with massive physical authority has tempted many teachers to admit Marxist "science" to their own disciplines, especially such inexact or quasi-exact [*sic*] subjects as economics, sociology, history and geography.' Concerns about ideological 'contamination' transmitted via the university system was expressed clearly by Scruton (1987: 56–57) in 1983: 'But it is far more useful to control the universities and the professional societies – for these channels, while narrow, are more firmly connected to the instruments of power. Ideas which gain currency among professors, lawyers, doctors and literati soon gain currency in parliament.' These kinds of cold war tract constitute the anti-intellectualism of reactionary populist discourse, and as such must be differentiated from the more subtle analyses of the social and ideological role of intellectuals by, for example, Benda (1928; 1929) and Gouldner (1979).

71 This defeat would have come as no surprise to old Bolsheviks, who – as has been seen above – regarded academia and socialist politics as incompatible. Although written about the Futurists, the description in the early 1920s by Trotsky of the way in which token opposition could easily be co-opted applies equally to 'radical' academics. 'As is known,' he noted (Trotsky, 1925: 128), 'nothing cataclysmic followed these rebellious protests of the long hair or the red vest of romanticism, and bourgeois public opinion safely adopted these gentlemen romantics and canonized them in their school textbooks.'

72 Examples are too numerous to list. Symptomatic of the naïveté exhibited by some on the left about this kind of political transformation and its implications is what Alex Callinicos, a socialist, writes in his obituary for the political philosopher G.A. Cohen (1941–2009). Accepting that Cohen tried 'to marry Marx to "rational-choice" theory,' that '[n]ot surprisingly, very little of Marx survived processing by rational-choice theory', and further that his 'later work was closer to more mainstream philosophy', Callinicos nevertheless asserts that 'Cohen's commitment to socialism remained much more than theoretical'. This is a bizarre judgement to make, especially since Callinicos accurately identifies the reason for this political shift – 'Jerry was Chichele Professor of Social and Political Theory at Oxford University until his retirement...and sometimes he seemed a little too comfortable with Oxford's peculiarly privileged life'. See Alex Callinicos, 'Remembering Jerry Cohen', *Socialist Worker*, 15 August 2009. This kind of leftist naïveté is by no means confined to the academy. Commenting on his contacts with a prominent member of the new left (then still editor of the *New Left Review*), the influential theatre critic and cultural commentator Kenneth Tynan – a self-indulgent bon viveur who moved in privileged circles and equated socialism simply with hedonistic individualism – noted in a diary entry for 1974 (Lahr, 2002: 189) that 'I can't take Robin Blackburn seriously: he takes me too seriously'. Unlike

lessons for two kinds of people: not just conservatives, who thought such 'entryism' would be successful, but also socialists who shared this belief.[73] Both were mistaken.

Capitalist Academia and/as Socialist Exile

In terms of the dynamic informing capitalist academia on the one hand and a socialist political movement on the other, a number of crucial distinctions exist.[74] Unlike participants in a mobilization with socialism already established as its objective, academics have continuously to find or subscribe to new analytical frameworks and interpretations of the way society is ordered, so as to justify their existence (and funding). In the social sciences generally, and especially in the area of development studies, this could be regarded almost as its raison d'être. Those in the academy who remained Marxists were frequently accused of being 'old believers' and of 'not moving with the times'.[75]

Blackburn, who thought that Tynan really was a socialist, Tynan himself knew this claim to be untrue.

73 Socialists themselves have on occasion been guilty of naïveté where the leftist credentials attached to institutions of higher education are concerned. A case in point is the Institute of Development Studies (IDS) at Sussex University, which in the period after the 'development decade' of the 1960s enjoyed an undeserved reputation as a hotbed of Marxism. A review (Bradby, 1975) of a book by Sahlins (1972) which appeared in a Marxist journal commented in a puzzled manner that 'I propose to pass over...the succeeding essay on "the sociology of primitive exchange", since the last chapter in the book, on Exchange Value and Primitive trade, while using marxist terminology, is so preposterously bourgeois that it should not go unnoticed, especially since this book is getting fashionable around the IDS.' On the margin of my copy (purchased second-hand) an earlier owner – clearly a Marxist wit – had written in green ink the following comment: 'IDS is preposterously bourgeois as well, therefore no contradiction.'

74 Similarities, of course, exist, particularly in the form of compromise, which afflicts socialist political movements as much as academia (on which see Widgery, 1976). Whilst not seeking to idealize socialism and socialists, therefore, it *is* important to recognize that a different dynamic – advocacy and achievement of socialist objectives – is not merely present but is also one that in a capitalist system distinguishes it from academia.

75 On occasion the accusation can be more sinister, as was my experience when teaching in the Anthropology Department at Durham University during 1981. At the time the 'Troubles' in Northern Ireland were at their height, and the British State and its army were engaged in a fierce military campaign against the Irish Republican Army. One of the courses I taught was about the historical and ethnographic background to the struggles in the six counties, and unbeknownst to me among those attending my lectures were serving

By contrast, socialists outside the academy are not required to keep their names in front of the public in quite this manner, not least because – unlike academics – they do not have to compete for diminishing research funds.[76] Socialists instead operate with a political theory and a related practice each of which already exists, and neither of which has to be constantly reinvented. For this reason, revolutionary socialists are not under the same kind of pressure as an academic: rather than continuously seeking innovative or new frameworks, therefore, their task is to put into practice *existing* theory.

Flight from and (shamefaced) Return to Class

The difference between these two dynamics, and its implications for the epistemological shifts occurring inside the academy, may be illustrated with reference to the analytical volatility structuring perceptions of the 'cultural turn'.[77]

---

officers in the British army. After a heated tutorial discussion about the Northern Ireland situation, I received a letter from one participant, a serving officer who had recently returned from a tour of duty with his regiment in Belfast. In the letter, which was addressed to me as 'Comrade Brass', he observed that '[i]t is unfortunate that I am not free to discuss the issue as to whether the IRA is fighting a war,' adding more ominously that '[y]ou still remain, I fear, a "security risk," and all the more "dangerous" for the fact that you are far more perceptive than I had hitherto given you credit for.' The implied threat was unmistakeable, not least because anyone suspected of being sympathetic towards Irish Republicanism was then – as is now the case with other 'enemies' – open to the accusation of being a 'terrorist'.

76 Unsurprisingly, having to keep ones name in front of the public is not the only trait academia shares with bourgeois celebrity culture. Just as the latter involves actors and rock stars evincing concern about any/every high profile contemporary political issue (global warming, world poverty, famine, etc.), so frequently interventions in fashionable debates by 'celebrity' academics succeed in revealing nothing but their ignorance about the issues in question. A recent attempt by Collini (2006: 473ff.) to assess the impact of celebrity culture on intellectual authority fails to analyse this in terms of politics, and thus reaches an anodyne conclusion. Hence the view (Collini, 2006: 495–496, original emphasis) that 'intellectuals can make use of existing media to reach those publics who, being neither as doped up nor as dumbed down as fashionable commentary suggests, *do* want to see issues of common interest [that are] more reflective or more analytical, better informed or better expressed.' While the latter point is accurate, the capacity and/or the willingness either of those who control the capitalist media to permit this, or of bourgeois academics in pursuit of media celebrity to provide this, is doubtful.

77 Not the least revealing impact of the cultural turn has been the response of those who initially endorsed the reactionary 'new' populist postmodernism. Responses to having been wrong footed in this manner usually take one of two forms. One has been self-reinvention, or the straightforward adoption of arguments and/or theoretical positions that were condemned earlier, a transformation that in effect negates the argument/

Initially, therefore, the 'new' populist postmodernism was greeted with enthusiasm by many of those writing about Third World development, the result being a stampede to replace Marxist theory and concepts such as class disempowerment with notions of subaltern empowerment.

This can be linked in turn to a number of things. First, to an intellectual failure to differentiate the 'new' postmodern populism from its 'other', Marxist theory. Second, to a consequent inability to formulate appropriate ideas about effective opposition to and mobilization against a newly resurgent global imperialism. And third, to an institutional pressure which requires infinitely elastic views that are always in line with academic fashion, whatever this might be.

What was at stake, therefore, was not just the form to be taken by economic growth in rural areas of the so-called Third World, but the very fact of development itself. Accordingly, the debate about petty commodity production was to some extent sidetracked down a *cul-de-sac*, where the focus of what remained an economic argument was one about whether or not peasant economy was an obstacle to the development of a capitalist agriculture. In doing so, many in the academy overlooked both the fact and the political significance of an emerging – or re-emerging – discourse in defence of the peasantry, the focus of which was not on its economic viability, but rather on smallholding as a form of cultural empowerment.

Nowhere was this more evident than in the epistemological recuperation by the 'new' populist postmodernism of a specifically cultural dimension of 'peasant-ness'. This was a discourse associated most powerfully with the Subaltern Studies project, formulated initially in the context of Asian historiography and latterly with regard to Latin American history. Reinstatement of the peasant voice as an undifferentiated/pristine subaltern 'other', untainted either by class, by economic development or by the wider capitalist system, was licensed by the dematerialization of discourse, itself an effect of postmodern deconstruction. The many ironies informing this analytical re-essentialization of peasant culture are difficult to miss.

At the root of the 'cultural turn' was the privileging by postmodern theory of language, and a corresponding deprivileging of socialism, materialism and class as illegitimate Enlightenment/Eurocentric forms of 'foundationalism' inapplicable to the Third World. Symptomatically, for postmodernism the central epistemological problem is to construct a model that subsumes all kinds/forms of narrative, a framework that accounts merely for the fact of narrative,

---

position held previously. A second response, and one that differs little from the first, has been seamlessly to elide what are two contradictory analytical frameworks, again in the hope that no one would notice this, or – when noticed – point it out.

not its purpose.[78] No significance is attached to the link between language and the material conditions that give rise to or sustain a particular narrative. Indeed, it is a link the very existence – let alone the efficacy – of which postmodern theory denies.[79]

That the purpose of postmodern deconstruction is nothing other than a decoupling of language and meaning – a project entailing the negation of concepts such as class, class consciousness and class struggle – was made clear early on by its practitioners (de Man, Derrida, *et al.*,) in what amounted to a manifesto.[80] However, this objective, together with its implications for Marxist theory/practice, was overlooked by many erstwhile leftist academics engaged in the study of Third World development who rapidly jumped on the postmodern bandwaggon. Consequently, they were unknowingly lured onto the epistemological terrain of the political right, little realizing that the re-essentialization of the peasantry found in the 'new' populism strongly influenced by postmodern theory that colonized development studies throughout the 1980s and 1990s was prefigured in 1930s reactionary conservatism.[81] The latter subscribed to the agrarian myth, which in turn informs both the 'old' and 'new' versions of populism.

Those in the academy who were wrong footed in this manner, and initially subscribed to the highly fashionable variants of the 'new' populist

78 See, for example, Barthes (1977: 79ff.).

79 In short, narrative is decentred, and thereby delinked from a concept of material reality, not least since for postmodern theory language and only language is 'the real'. Hence the view (Barthes, 1977: 123–124, original emphasis) that '[c]laims concerning the "realism" of narrative are therefore to be discounted… "What takes place" in a narrative is from the referential (reality) point of view literally *nothing*; "what happens" is language alone, the adventure of language, the unceasing celebration of its coming.'

80 Accepting that what it is proposing constitutes 'a move towards a theory of commentary,' an early collection of texts by leading postmodernists (Bloom, de Man, Derrida, Hartman, Hillis Miller, 1979: vii–viii) continues: 'Deconstruction…refuses to identify the force of literature with any concept of embodied meaning and shows how deeply such logocentric or incarnationist perspectives have influenced the way we think about art. We assume that, by the miracle of art, the "presence of the word" is equivalent to the presence of meaning. But the opposite can also be urged, that the word carries with it a certain absence or indeterminacy of meaning. Literary language foregrounds language itself as something not reducible to meaning…'

81 As Marxism has long argued, at the heart of 1930s reactionary discourse – in Germany, Italy and Japan – lay the essentialized concept of peasant as bearer/defender of a similarly innate ethnic or national identity. For those on the political right, therefore, an attack on one necessarily involved an assault on the other.

postmodernism, quickly rejected the latter once Marxist critiques made by others exposed the reactionary politics underpinning this discourse. The *volte face* on the part of those wrong footed is nowadays usually announced with the phrase 'bringing class back in', one that acknowledges the expulsion of this Marxist concept without however indicating their own role in its absence.[82]

Mutually Agreed Enslavement?

The dynamic that is an academic endeavour to 'move with the times', can be understood with reference to the ideology within higher education of what is referred to as 'collegiality'.[83] The notion of collegiality has different meanings

82 Among those engaged in the study of Third World development who have recently rediscovered the importance of class are David Lehmann, Barbara Harriss-White, John Harriss, and Henry Bernstein. In each case an initial endorsement of Marxist theory, and with it recognition of the analytical centrality of class, was followed subsequently by the abandonment of either Marxism or class, and in some cases both. This gave way to – or coincided with – an enthusiastic reception of the 'new' populist postmodern approach (Harriss, Lehmann), variants of neoliberal economic theory (Harriss, Harriss-White), or a return to agrarian populism (Bernstein). Details of these epistemological trajectories have been provided by me elsewhere (see review essay 11 and essay 16, this volume). Currently, however, one hears from them calls for the return of class, with no hint of the fact that it was they who were responsible for the departure of this concept in the first place. Thus, for example, Harriss (2009) decries the intellectual hegemony of the very same postmodern approach to which he himself switched earlier, noting that '[c]lass relationships...used to be seen as the motors of change in society. Now, they are often regarded as being much less significant than struggles over identity or nature. Analyses...of class relations have been swept aside by the ascendancy in the social sciences of approaches based on the idea of individual rational choice and post-modernist thinking.' Without a trace of irony, this self-description continues: 'Going against these current modes of thinking [his essays] develop the view that class relations continue to explain a great deal of what happens in societies.' Similarly, Harriss-White endorses a volume (Herring and Agarwala, 2008) making the same case, to which Harriss also contributes, in the following manner: 'The willful [*sic*] ignoring or destruction of class analysis obscures our understanding of the complex class and non-class dynamics of capitalism. [The contributors to the book] are to be congratulated for bringing class back in.' The same is true of Bernstein (in press), who now also calls for a return of that which he himself earlier questioned.

83 The seemingly more benign term collegiality can be regarded as the counterpart of sterner term 'professionalism'. Both invoke a hidden set of rules governing what it is and what it is not permitted to do, to think and to say, in academic institutions. Hence an infringement of this unspoken code (= 'rocking the boat') invites sanctions which are usually justified with reference to 'a lack of professionalism' on the part of the offender. Such an informal code exists apart from the formal rules stipulating behaviour and conduct an institution expects of its academics.

inside and outside academia. In the latter context, it frequently entails refraining from criticizing the work or views of senior academics, particularly if promotion is being sought.[84] Adherence to this notion of collegiality also facilitates being influenced by the work of colleagues who might be engaged in formulating or advocating anti-Marxist views.[85]

A willingness to conduct arduous research on behalf of a senior colleague, or allow the latter to take credit for work he/she has not done, is also seen as part of collegiality, and correspondingly helpful in terms of career prospects.[86] Such arrangements form part of a wider phenomenon that for obvious reasons is rarely addressed.[87] Namely, the university division of labour whereby those in

84 It is not difficult to spot the evidence of this process at work, since it usually takes a common form. Not only are critical observations conspicuously absent, therefore, but deferential platitudes jostle with the ritual stroking of 'big names', to whom are attributed important discoveries/arguments made not by them but by others.

85 This particular consideration played an important role in the dilution of Austro-Marxist theory, and its emergence as reformist *katheder*-socialism. Bottomore and Goode (1978: 11–12) point out that among the more significant intellectual currents in Vienna at that conjuncture was the Austrian marginal utility school, whose leading members were Carl Menger, Eugen Böhm-Bawerk and Friedrich von Wieser, all employed as academics at Vienna University. 'Not only did the Austrian school formulate a theoretical system that was quite incompatible with Marxist economics,' therefore (Bottomore and Goode, 1978: 12), 'but two of its members, Menger and Böhm-Bawerk were particularly hostile to socialism, and the latter published in 1896 a major criticism of Marxist economic theory which had some influence upon the views of of the revisionists...' The point is not that views hostile to socialism existed, but that to criticize those who advocated these views was difficult when they were in the same academic department or university.

86 Amongst other things, the notion of 'collegiality' validates and disguises patronage relationships within academia. The latter have a long history in the university system, albeit involving different subjects. During the nineteenth century, such relations involved members of the nobility as patrons and poorer undergraduates as clients. The search for influential and/or wealthy patronage among the student body was termed 'preferment-hunting' (Pattison, 1885: 202) or 'tuft-hunting', a quest described by Taine (1872: 241) as follows: 'I dined recently in the great hall of Trinity College, Cambridge. Three hundred persons were at table – everything was served on silver. There was a small side table for the undergraduates, who are noblemen, who wear a distinctive costume. At the universities...the young nobles are surrounded by tuft-hunters, students of low birth, who strive by their services and their servility to make their fortunes. A nobleman has always a living or a situation in his gift, and this he afterwards presents to his toady as a piece of charity.'

87 When addressed, such practices are for rather obvious reasons confined to the realm of fiction. Issues such as the unequal division of labour within the academy are an

non-tenured temporary posts are required to shoulder large teaching loads so that a more senior academic can devote time to other career-enhancing activities (e.g., writing for publication).[88] When this kind of production relation is found elsewhere in the capitalist labour process, there is generally no ambiguity regarding who is exploiting whom, and why.[89] In academia, however, there

---

enduring and prominent feature in the campus novel genre (e.g., Holbrook, 1994; Hynes, 2001). There are a few exceptions, in that the same forms of academic inequality are on occasion acknowledged as being central to the reproduction of the university as an institution: however, such accounts (van den Berghe, 1970) tend to depict these practices as 'natural', and fail to link them to a wider capitalist dynamic.

88 An exception is a recent fictional portrayal (Hynes, 2001: 63) of academic life in the American Midwest, where the division of labour in a university literature department is accurately described as follows. 'He passed through the steel doorway into a vast, white room of plasterboard cubicles, where the muffled rumble of the ventilators and the constant fluorescent buzz gave the place the feel of a sweatshop. Above the industrial hum rose the steady murmur of lonely women in their thirties and forties, their cubicles lined up like sewing machines in a shirtwaist factory... In each cubicle a thin woman in thrift shop couture looked up...with the hollow-eyed, pitiless gaze of the damned. A few composition teachers lived in hope: faculty wives making a little extra money, the department's own recent PhDs teaching a year of comp as they played the job market... But most of the comp teachers were divorced moms and single women with cats who taught eight classes a year and earned a thousand dollars per class, who clung to their semester-to-semester contracts with the desperate devotion of anchoresses. They combined the bitter esprit de corps of assembly-line workers with the literate wit of the overeducated: They were the steerage of the English Department, the first to drown if the budget sprang a leak. They were the Morlocks to the Eloi of the eighth floor. *Pace* Wallerstein, they were the colonial periphery, harvesting for pennies a day the department's raw material – undergraduates – and shipping these processed students farther up the hierarchy, thus creating leisure for the professors at the imperial center to pursue their interests in feminist theory and postcolonial literature.' Rather less sympathetic is the depiction by Holbrook (1994: 19–20) of the same kind of division of labour in an ancient British university, where a member of the reserve army of academic labour is described as 'one of those struggling hangers-on in the Cambridge scene, teaching on the fringe, a hack, really...[who] was critical of the Cambridge establishment, but there was a lot of that among the crammers who did supervisions for a pittance, and whom the University exploited.'

89 Once they rise up the university hierarchy, even socialist academics very soon begin to act in ways that are indistinguishable from CEOs in multinational corporations. Wiener (2005: 13–30) recounts the case of Elizabeth Fox-Genovese, initially a Marxist historian who, as she was promoted to more senior positions in the university system, became not only more conservative politically but also more tyrannical towards subordinates and/or junior staff in the same institutions. Among the tasks Fox-Genovese required of them were 'picking up her laundry, hosting parties for her, cleaning her house, and walking

is a tendency to see it simply as a mutually beneficial arrangement, a benign way in which actual/prospective junior staff acquire teaching experience.

Not surprisingly, collegiality also has implications for political debate, and the tenor in which this is conducted.[90] Whilst discussion *per se* is not discouraged, therefore, sustained academic debate premissed on strongly held political principle is frowned upon as 'rocking the boat'.[91] Symptomatically, this disapproval usually remains covert, and is generally not expressed directly. It does surface, however, in those arenas where institutional power is exercised, reproduced and consolidated. For example, in the references written on behalf of an individual being considered for a university appointment, or for tenure.

---

her dog'. A failure to comply with these and other tasks ('pay for lunches, teach classes for her without pay') resulted in threats that she could and would destroy their careers. As Wiener (2005: 14, 17) notes, she 'treated her assistant with "abuse", "verbal tirades", and "a loud, threatening and personally demeaning voice and manner" that was "deliberate, wilful and malicious"...a relationship that she herself was said to call "mutually agreed enslavement"'. The fact many of us, on reading this description, will think to ourselves that we, too, know of instances like this, confirms the very point being made here: how the structure and dynamics of academic life under capitalism are incompatible with socialist principles/practice.

90 That sustained academic debate – usually identified as such by the pejorative term 'polemical' (meaning the strong expression of views with which one happens to disagree) – is deemed unseemly emerges clearly from the description by Cannadine of the reason why one historian (Trevelyan) – a landowning member of the academic/political establishment – disapproved of another colleague (Namier) who belonged neither to the landowning class nor to the British establishment. Trevelyan, we learn (Cannadine, 1992: 207), 'certainly disliked his [Namier's] adversarial method of history writing and his incorrigible vindictiveness as a reviewer.' Later on the same page Cannadine opines that Trevelyan's 'doubts about Namier seem to have been well borne out...his [Namier's] gifts were more forensic and polemical than creative or expositional.' This constitutes an instance where a biographer of a fellow historian commends his subject for sharing his own view: 'rocking the boat' as an undesirable activity. This is unsurprising, in that the biography is written by one establishment historian in an attempt unsuccessfully to rescue another from deserved obscurity.

91 That a reputation for 'rocking the boat' may undermine employment prospects is clear from the following example. Writing about All Souls College, Oxford, during the early 1960s, an erstwhile fellow (Caute, 1974: 17) relates that 'several years ago, a minority of one third actually blackballed a scholar known to be one of the leading figures in his field anywhere in the world, and who was unanimously agreed to outstrip the other contenders as regards academic distinction. His crime – and I do not exaggerate – was to be a foreigner who did not suffer fools gladly.'

Another context where the element of collegiality operates is in peer group opinion sought when assessing a manuscript submitted to be considered for publication in journal or book form.[92] This is a particularly effective arena of academic gate-keeping power. Academic publishers are not only complicit with this flawed procedure, based as it is on a spurious notion of 'scientific objectivity', but pander to prevailing orthodoxy, since this delivers them a paying readership. When socialism was academically fashionable, as it has been in the past, commercial publishers were more than willing to produce texts embodying such views. As soon as these views cease to be fashionable, however, and are replaced with others, publishers quickly follow suit.

Those who continue to adhere to unorthodox political opinions, amongst whom revolutionary socialists tend to feature prominently, are in such circumstances either marginalized or – in the few cases where they actually exercise a gate-keeping function – have such a role taken from them. Unsurprisingly, the issue of gate-keeping applies with particular force to leftist journals. This is because where the latter sell out (in both senses of the term) to large publishers, *de facto* control passes from editors for whom socialist politics is a paramount concern, to a corporation where the main (or only) criterion is commercial success.[93] Once again, this underlines a central difference between the dynamic

92 Of all the practices conducted in academia in the name of 'objectivity', perhaps the most nonsensical consists of sending a journal submission or book manuscript to another academic for an opinion as to its suitability. This obviously flawed procedure frequently puts an argument or text into the hands either of a rival in the same field or a political opponent, with predictable results. Reviewing (= judging suitability) raises in a particularly acute form the issue of conflict of interest, not least when a submission in a given field, especially if it is a critique of existing interpretations on the subject in question, is sent to one of those criticized. This is because the temptation faced by such a reviewer – to reject what was in effect a rival paradigm – would be great. This is particularly the case where institutionally powerful university members are criticized; in these instances, important new work runs the risk of remaining unpublished simply because it takes a critical position *vis-à-vis* senior components of the academic hierarchy.

93 This trend has been strengthened as a result of the introduction by publishers of a spurious form of 'scientificity': namely, the impact factor. Asked why a purportedly leftist journal should be so concerned with securing an impact factor metric, a publishing initiative which many socialists find problematic, its editor replied that 'one of the main priorities of [the journal] was to gain inclusion in the ISI citation index [since] changes in the overall academy to a degree have forced our hand and many think it has become a necessity...[i]n terms of indexing, a large proportion of our contributors are working (not retired) academics and as a result do not have the luxury of publishing in journals which opt out of the indexing problem. One of the main attractions of the journal was

structuring academia and what happens in a socialist movement, where ideas about the political desirability of a basic set of principles are not subject to the same commercial pressure and/or whim of fashion.

We are the Problem

For two reasons, the position of socialists who secured academic posts in the social sciences became more precarious from the 1980s onwards. First, leftist theory came increasingly under attack as conservative and neo-liberal views gained ascendancy.[94] And second, the casualization of employment within the university system meant that pressure on those in temporary posts who continued to advocate Marxist theory/practice became even more pronounced. Many in senior positions who had earlier abandoned socialist politics now jumped on the twin bandwaggons of academic fashion, and adopted either a postmodern or a neoliberal economic framework. Yet others remained mired in politically bankrupt reformist paradigms, such as the semi-feudal thesis.

Part of the problem of this political retreat and non-engagement (except in a pointless, reformist way), therefore, was the espousal by adherents of the semi-feudal thesis of a nationalist politics during and after the 1960s 'development

---

always its ability to publish work from non-elite (Oxbridge/Ivy League) colleges and *increasingly it has become more and more essential (in terms of job security) for journals to gain admittance to such indexes.*' (emphasis added) Inadvertently, therefore, the point is conceded that even for leftist journals it is no longer only the pursuit of a socialist politics but rather career-boosting criteria that are now the main publication objective. Such hankering after a marketing device introduced by publishers not only entails being drawn into the logic of capitalist competition, but also carries the risk of discriminating against 'unpopular' views/interpretations that, in commercial terms, fail to attract a sufficiently large readership.

94 Among the very few who have recognized not just the fact of this process but also – and more importantly – its political effect is Petras. Long ago, he pointed out in a seminal article (Petras, 1990) that many intellectuals in Latin America were being seduced by institutional blandishments provided mainly by the United States. The dual object was on the one hand to promote ideas favourable to global capitalism and imperial expansion (the unchallengable nature of the market, the desirability of neoliberalism, the explanatory power of postmodernism), and on the other to dissuade/discourage advocacy of the main theoretical opposition to such a project: a revolutionary Marxist theory/practice.

decade'.[95] The ascent to political dominance throughout the Third World of a bourgeoisie meant the *de facto* realization of a nationalist project in these contexts, outside metropolitan capitalism. Its corollary was that academic reformists of the semi-feudal kind had nowhere else to go intellectually, and the politically bankrupt character of their arguments now became evident for all to see.

Turning to the political implications of postmodernism for Marxist theory/practice in the academy, these are not difficult to discern. To begin with, many on the left who abandoned Marxism for the 'new' populist postmodernism ended up fighting the wrong battle: for ethnic 'otherness' and national culture, rather than for class and internationalism. Consequently, populism become the theoretically dominant framework in the social sciences, and its counterpart – 'resistance' by individuals or by 'new' social movements – replaced revolution as the radical practice of choice.

Hence the depoliticization of political discourse within the university system as a result of what might be termed the institutional 'domestication' of Marxist theory and practice. Because the debate about what does and does not constitute Marxism now takes place largely within the academy, the faux-genteel manners of the bourgeois salon have in effect required that such 'debate' be bland, in the process depoliticizing it. This debilitating objection to critical debate has in turn facilitated a dilution and thus an undermining of Marxist theory. The resulting focus on non-class identities (age, gender, religion, sexuality, ethnicity, nationality) as 'subversive' *foci* of resistance by 'new' social movements overlooks two crucial points. Where these contribute to the accumulation process, both resistance and empowerment based on identities other than class have been and are encouraged by capital. Consequently, in

95 For critiques of the semi-feudal thesis, see Brass (2002; 2008). Significantly, perhaps, the central premiss of the 'semi-feudal' thesis – that capitalism seeks to replace workers who are unfree with free equivalents – is not merely wrong, but as tellingly no different in its (mis-) interpretation of Marx from the view usually advanced by apologists and/or defenders of capitalism. According to one such apologist for capitalism (Johnson, 1996: 68), therefore, Marx's 'thesis was that capitalism produces ever-worsening conditions; the more capital employed, the more badly the workers had to be treated to secure adequate returns. The evidence he quotes at length to justify it comes almost entirely from small, inefficient, under-capitalized firms in archaic industries which in most cases were pre-capitalist... In effect, Marx is dealing with pre-capitalist conditions, and ignoring the truth which stared him in the face: the more capital, the less suffering.' This is a variant of the whig interpretation of history: everything will get better and better.

most instances empowerment/emancipation linked to non-class identity can be achieved as much under capitalism as under socialism. As has been pointed out on many previous occasions, gender (and other non-class forms of) ideology circulating at the rural grassroots (= 'popular culture') in India and Latin America is not necessarily progressive in political terms.

One important outcome of discouraging critical debate, therefore, has been that many so-called 'Marxists' in academia have been permitted (uncomprehendingly) to smuggle what in some instances is anti-Marxist theory into Marxism, and passing off the former as part of the latter. Where theory that is epistemologically and politically incompatible with a Marxist approach is presented (and accepted) as being part of the latter, Marxism is undermined by a process of depoliticization. It is a problem which might be termed 'sailing under false colours', when non- and anti-Marxist positions are passed off as Marxist theory. Unless checked, therefore, the outcome is that Marxist political economy increasingly comes to resemble its 'other' until all difference between them is finally eroded.[96]

Another outcome, as important, was that the institutional dominance of populist postmodernism fuelled the practice of academic exclusion on political grounds, a difficulty that from the 1980s onwards applied with particular force to advocates of socialist theory/practice. Although this exclusionary practice has always been a feature of academia, the one crucial difference is that in the past this was done to revolutionary Marxists by conservatives and liberals. Currently such exclusionary practice is still applied to revolutionary Marxists, but now by postmodernists.

Against Populism, for Socialism

It is important to make absolutely clear what aspect of the university system is being criticized here. Not open to a negative judgement is the desirability of a higher education, self-evidently a positive element where socialists are concerned. Nor is it the case that criticism is aimed at those engaged in what might be termed workers' educational institutions. The object of censure

96 As noted above, this development escapes those – such as Sayers (2006) – who insist on seeing within the academy and elsewhere a resurgent interest in Marxist theory/practice. Hence the over-optimistic claim (Sayers, 2006: 4, 5) that because a 'number of movements kept the left alive during these difficult times,' and consequently there 'is every sign that they are now growing in strength and confidence, and this is leading to a slow but steady and unmistakable revival of the left... A revival of Marxist work in the area of philosophy is now also unmistakably under way.'

is much rather what happens to socialists who then seek a career in higher education, and specifically the price that must be paid by those following this course. Namely, a choice that frequently boils down to having to abandon either socialist beliefs/principles or university employment/promotion prospects.[97]

Linked to this is the need to emphasize – perhaps more strongly than usual – what is not being said here. There is no suggestion, therefore, that an alternative, raw intellectualism exists out on the streets, which our task as socialists is in some sense to rediscover. Much rather the opposite, in that a major part of the difficulty stems from the willingness of the academy to incorporate precisely such populist discourse unqualified and undiluted from the streets, and make this its own (= postmodernism) in an attempt to display its democratic credentials.

Accordingly, those who remain socialists are today caught between what is politically a case of Scylla and Charibdis. On the one hand, supposedly 'a-political' academic institutions which have always been and remain antagonistic to genuine Marxist theory/practice, and on the other purportedly 'a-political' anti-capitalist grassroots movements, similarly unsympathetic to genuine Marxist theory/practice. Ironically, in each case – the street and the academy – socialists are faced with the presence of the same kind of conservative mobilizing discourse: that of the 'new' populism, either in its 'everyday form of resistance' variant at the rural grassroots, or in its postmodern variant in the university system.

Conclusion: Back to the Street, as Socialists

Looking back over what I've written during the past three decades, a common theme begins to emerge, albeit taking the form of asides in footnotes. It is not merely that, historically and currently, academia is hostile to the teaching/expression of revolutionary Marxist theory/practice, but – more worryingly – socialist ideas have been espoused when institutionally fashionable, and discarded when institutionally unpopular. At best, this meant that many academics embracing socialist ideas were fair-weather friends.

97 It could be argued that, insofar as I myself taught at Cambridge during the 1980s and 1990s, this criticism applies equally to me. Throughout my time in academia, however, I refused to compromise on the issue of socialist politics, either in what I taught or published, and, indeed, ultimately paid the price for this (see Review 6, this volume).

Once socialists operate within academia, therefore, a different logic takes over. To begin with, political 'militancy' (even when restricted to theoretical interpretation) is frowned upon by senior elements in the academic hierarchy as 'unobjective'. More importantly, Marxism was henceforth subject to the shifts in intellectual fashion, and as such something to be discarded as soon as it became an obstacle to employment/promotion.

When a commitment to revolutionary Marxist theory/practice came into conflict with entry into or promotion within academia, as they always would, it was invariably the former that was discarded. For this reason, there is no one so forgetful about his/her own past as an ex-Marxist on joining and/or being feted by the academic establishment. In a variation of an old adage, it could be argued that Marxists never prosper, for when they prosper none do call themselves Marxists.

Affixing blame for this demise on an internal cause leads inexorably to a consideration of the fate of socialism and socialists within academia. At the beginning of the twentieth century, Marxism was by and large a theory and practice located outside the academy. Throughout the twentieth century, and especially from the 1960s onwards, however, this situation changed. The expansion of higher education at that conjuncture meant, among other things, that Marxist theory shifted into the universities and became increasingly a part of academic discourse. This transformation is, in the words of a current cliché, the elephant in the room: a problem which many of us are aware of, but are unwilling to confront.

Simply put, the very people who should be advocating a specifically *socialist* politics, defending a specifically *socialist* theory, and engaged in a specifically *socialist* practice, are in the context of academia subject to one of two kinds of pressure. Either they persist in their advocacy of socialist theory/practice, and are as a result excluded or blocked from further advancement. Or they are quickly seduced by the blandishments on offer, and co-opted by the system to which they had originally been opposed, in the process ceasing to be socialists. As a result of being drawn into and accepted by a major capitalist institution, therefore, it is easy to persuade oneself that there is indeed a 'benign' capitalism, a form that can be recuperated to the benefit of all. What is being argued, therefore, is the following: protestations to the contrary notwithstanding, the academy as a bourgeois institution is – like it always has been and under capitalism will always be – necessarily hostile to genuinely socialist thought. The entry of socialists into university teaching positions does indeed entail compromises and changes in attitude, but not on the part of the academic institution concerned.

It is socialists who are required to change, and this is a mass phenomenon which we have witnessed over the latter part of the twentieth century. The academic dominance of neoliberalism and the 'new' populist postmodernism were outcomes of just such a shift. Not the least important outcome is its deleterious effect on two specific processes. First, on the advocacy of revolutionary theory, without which – as Lenin once noted – there was (and could be) no revolutionary practice. And second, on the acceptability of socialism to those outside the academy, the potential/actual constituency for revolutionary Marxist ideas. Like Caesar's wife, socialists have to be above suspicion. Bluntly put, why should anyone take seriously the advocacy of socialism by an academic who shortly might just as easily shift his/her allegiance elsewhere, as fashion dictates? This is a heavy price, one moreover that is paid not by those who engage in a periodic *volte face*, but rather by those who remain socialists.

The corollary is inescapable: there being no real acceptance within academia of revolutionary Marxist theory/practice, the latter should henceforth cease to attempt to find a place there. It is not enough that struggle should move from the academy to the street; that, in a sense, has already happened. The struggle itself must also change, and be one *for* not just *against* something. That is, it must change from being simply an anti-capitalist movement redolent of populism to being a mobilization aimed at bringing about socialism.

In short, the search for socialist hegemony exercised from within what is a powerful capitalist institution – academia – has been and is misplaced. Those of us who espouse socialist politics should instead operate a self-denying ordinance where university posts are concerned, and return once more to the street, there to argue the case against populism and for a twenty-first century socialism. Not only is this the context where such a politics have operated most effectively in the past, but it is the only place where Marx and other Marxists insisted socialist views should be located.

CHAPTER 19

The Industrial Reserve Army: What's Not to Like?*

Among the issues many of those who participated in debates about Third World development over the second half of the twentieth century failed to spot are two in particular. Thus any gains made in metropolitan capitalist nations by workers in the course of the class struggle could just as easily be reversed (a process evident from the 1980s onwards), as could the historical movement of labour from economically advanced countries in Europe to less developed ones (the more usual pattern of imperial colonial settlement).[1] The focus here is on the latter process: that is, the general pattern of migration – not just from Eastern European countries, previously part of the USSR and now members of the EU – and its implications for more advanced capitalist nations in Northern Europe.

Needless to say, the question addressed below is a sensitive one, involving an issue that is both controversial for those on the political left and also feeds into most debates currently taking place in the UK and throughout Europe. Not only does it feature centrally in disagreements over EU membership – about whether or not to leave – but it is the main reason for the rise of populist and/or far right parties, as well as structuring policy formulated by business interests and their representatives in centrist and/or conservative organizations/groups. Contributions to this debate from those currently seen to be close to or actually on the political left, by contrast, are for the most part either absent or

* Details about the publication history of this essay are outlined in the Introduction to the volume. With few exceptions, no attempt has been made to update the analysis since it was written towards the end of 2015, not least because instances of the issues covered – such as calls by employer organizations for an open door policy and warnings by international agencies and others about the perils of leaving the EU – have simply multiplied.

1 For details about earlier migration patterns, see among others Phelps Brown (1962: 77ff.) and Erickson (1994). There is a noticeable contradiction here, one that is difficult to avoid. On the one hand, therefore, European colonization of other lands throughout history elicits strong condemnation from the populations affected, a view progressive opinion in the colonizing nations was and is rightly expected to share. On the other hand even questioning what is in effect a reverse movement, currently involving competition from those in what used to be colonies for jobs existing in erstwhile colonizing nations, is generally shrouded in opprobrium, and thus discouraged for fear of being labelled racist. Despite the fact that each has a deleterious impact on local livelihoods in their respective contexts, only the former tends to be perceived negatively.

contradictory: the latter – perhaps because of a well-meaning desire to simply to help – frequently end up supporting arguments that are no different from those advanced by employer discourse.[2]

Who Supports, Who Opposes

The question concerns the impact that an expanding industrial reserve army, in the form of immigration, has on the capitalist labour market, and thus also on an existing working class. Discussion of the issue, both by those supporting and those opposed to a deregulated labour market, involves two kinds of discourse: one principally about culture, the other mainly about political economy. In the late nineteenth century, therefore, the argument deployed against immigration tended to take a non-economic form (along the lines of 'these people coming here can't do the work properly, because it requires the kind of skills only we have'). That is to say, it was a discourse which focused mainly on the supposed cultural 'backwardness' of the migrant.

Now, by contrast, those categorized as 'these people coming here' either possess the necessary skills, acquired as a result of economic development in the country of origin, or don't actually need such skills, because production requires only or largely deskilled workers. Either way, immigration as an issue has been transformed, from one about the culture and 'backwardness' of the migrant him/herself to one about political economy, and the advantages/disadvantages of a potential/actual over-supply of labour-power in market of the receiving nation. This shift notwithstanding, the approach of much journalistic, NGO and academic discourse to the immigration debate adheres to non-economic and migrant-centric arguments, informed by concepts like justice, citizenship and human rights.

That something is amiss with these non-economic (= cultural) representations of immigration ought to be obvious from the current alignment of

---

2 One generally looks in vain through publications such as *Capital & Class* for a considered Marxist analysis of the connection between recent capital accumulation and the rising incidence of immigration. Ignoring what Marxist political economy has said about the role of the industrial reserve army in the class struggle, progressives – not just socialists but those on the centre-left and liberals – refuse to regard criticism of immigration as anything but racist. As will be seen below, such a position leads inexorably to support for unplanned labour market policies advocated by capitalists themselves. Exponents of these views rely for the most part on a cultural defence of migration, the only non-cultural arguments invoked being those made by neoclassical economic theory which perceives immigration as a positive contribution to capitalist development.

different class interests in the debate about this issue. On the one side therefore, tend to be many members of the working class, significant elements of which oppose the expansion of the industrial reserve army of labour and vote for populist parties; on the other are ranged capitalists and their political and ideological representatives, most employer opinion insisting on the economic benefits of immigration and consequently the necessity of an open door policy. If nothing else, this divergence on this one issue should alert socialists to the presence of a political difficulty in advocating humanitarian and/or culturalist arguments supporting what is in effect the continuing expansion within the capitalist system of the industrial reserve army of labour. Simply to forbid discussion about its impact on the existing workforce (that is to say, on all of its components: male, female, different ethnicities) so as not to incur accusations of racism inadvertently feeds into (and is thus supportive of) employer discourse.

A rather obvious problem with the case made here – the negative aspects of mass immigration when interpreted within a political economy framework as an expansion in the industrial reserve army of labour – is that it is invariably dismissed merely as racist.[3] What such a response demonstrates, unfortunately, is nothing more than the extent to which many leftists remain unable to differentiate arguments based on the materialism of Marxist political economy from culturalist ones linked to postmodern identity politics.[4] In part, the reason for this kind of reaction and the consequent privileging of a discourse about human rights, justice, culture and citizenship, is the Syrian crisis, which

3 The dismissal by Dummett (2001: 67) illustrates this point: 'Many other arguments are used by advocates of tight immigration controls. There seems little reason to consider them all in detail, since all are fallacious: they are expressions of racist attitudes or general hostility to foreigners rather than the product of serious assessment'. More often than not, forbidding discussion in this manner is heard from those who not only regard themselves as being on the left but also subscribe to arguments promoting an open-door policy. At odds with workers, yet in line with employers, such positions are held by those who mistakenly believe they are doing workers a favour by supporting unregulated migration.

4 It is important to be quite clear as to where blame for any charge of racism actually lies. If such accusations are to be made, then these should be levelled not at Marxists who interpret migration in terms of political economy (systemic transformation, class formation/struggle, labour market dynamics, relations of production, surplus appropriation, etc.), but rather at those who – in order to depict migration as empowering for its subject – insist on confining all discussion about immigration to the issue of culture. The latter results in a discourse which focuses on nothing more than the ethnic/national identity of the migrant him/herself. Not the least of the many ironies is the fact that on offer from those who stridently dismiss Marxist theory as 'economic reductionism' is an idealist form amounting to cultural reductionism.

has licensed the conflation of migrant and refugee identity. The result is that all forms of immigration now tend to be recast ideologically by NGOs, Church organizations, postmodern academics and liberal journalism simply in non-economic terms, and consequently viewed not as a labour market issue – which is how Marxists and capitalists interpret it – but as a humanitarian one.

The following analysis consists of six sections, the first three of which consider the economic case made by capitalists and Marxists for and against immigration, while the last three look at non-economic arguments by NGOs, journalists, academics and others supporting immigration on humanitarian/cultural grounds.

Class Struggle and the Industrial Reserve Army

There are numerous historical instances underlying the centrality to political concerns expressed by workers' organizations of the actual/potential economic impact the industrial reserve army might have on their struggle to defend/improve pay and conditions, especially in cases where employers restructure the labour process. Hence the role of immigration became an issue during the late 1850s when capitalists in the United States recruited migrants from Europe as replacements for unionized labourers who went on strike in response to wage reductions.[5] Much the same happened in 1890s Austria when employers there turned to Czech migrants so as to displace unionized German labour, undermining working class solidarity and fuelling the rise of nationalism.[6]

Current forms and pace of deskilling make possible the activation of hitherto unutilized elements belonging to the industrial reserve army of labour.[7]

5 See Powderly (1967: 210ff.).

6 See Whiteside (1962, 1975), who outlines why an expanding capitalist market in 1890s Austria, which pitted workers and migrants of different ethnicities against one another, led to the addition of the word 'national' to the term 'socialism'. Rapid capitalist development generated labour market competition and intense antagonism between Germans and Czechs, relatively well-paid local and cheaper migrant components of the same industrial workforce, a situation benefiting – and taken advantage of by – employers. Internationalism, social democracy, working class solidarity, trade unions, leftist political parties and socialism itself were all undermined as a result. That the same kind of process can be seen happening in Europe today, where the continuing expansion of *laissez-faire* capitalism and an industrial reserve army fuel the rise both of nationalism and of far right political parties, is too obvious to merit further comment.

7 About the perception by bourgeois economists of the connection between the reserve army of labour and capitalism, Marx (1976: 786) noted: 'Modern industry's whole form of motion

Although the latter encompasses those thrown out of work as a result of mechanization and technification, members of the reserve army can be incorporated by capital into its labour process for two distinct reasons. The first refers to a reserve to be drawn on when market demand expands, and capitalists need further amounts of labour-power. By contrast, the second refers to those who – as a mass of unemployed also part of the reserve army – are drawn on by capitalists not so much to increase production but rather as a weapon in their struggle against those still in work.[8]

In this second role, members of the reserve army are no longer used simply in addition to an existing workforce but now instead of the latter.[9] Replacing skilled, more costly and/or better organized workers already established

therefore depends on the constant transformation of a part of the working population into unemployed or semi-employed "hands". The superficiality of political economy shows itself in the fact that it views the expansion and contraction of credit as the cause of periodic alternations in the industrial cycle, whereas it is a mere symptom of them... When this periodicity has once become consolidated, even political economy sees that the production of a relative surplus population – i.e. a population surplus in relation to capital's average requirements for valorization – is a necessary condition for modern industry.' Against the tendency of bourgeois economics to interpret declining wages and living standards in a national context as an effect simply of demographic growth, he commented (Marx, 1976: 788, 790): 'Capitalist production can by no means content itself with the quantity of disposable labour-power which the natural increase of population yields. It requires for its unrestricted activity an industrial reserve army which is independent of these natural limits. [...] Taking them as a whole, the general movements of wages are exclusively regulated by the expansion and contraction of the industrial reserve army, and this in turn corresponds to the periodic alternations of the industrial cycle. They are not therefore determined by the variations of the absolute numbers of the working population, but by the varying proportions in which the working class is divided into an active army and a reserve army, by the increase or diminution in the relative amount of the surplus population, by the extent to which it is alternately absorbed and set free... It would be utterly absurd, in place of this, to lay down a law according to which the movement of capital depended simply on the movement of the population. Yet this is the dogma of economists.'

8 Sweezy (1946: 99, emphasis added) recognized the importance of this distinction, observing that 'the increasing use of machinery, which in itself means a higher organic composition of capital, sets free workers and thus creates "relative overpopulation" or the reserve army. Marx stresses the point that the existence of unemployed labourers is conducive to the setting up of new industries with a relatively low organic composition of capital and hence a relatively high rate of profit... *It would seem, however, that a more important effect of the reserve army is...through competition on the labour market with the active labour force, to depress the rate of wages and in this way to elevate the rate of surplus value.*'

9 The assumption that those expelled from the labour force by the application of machinery and technology would – after a brief sojourn in the reserve army – find alternative employment, is both pervasive and misplaced. It is linked to the notion that such workers would be

in the capitalist labour process with less skilled, cheaper, and/or unorganized ones, enables producers to exert a downward pressure on the pay, conditions and living standards of the proletariat generally, not just in particular national contexts. As is now very clear, such restructuring, based on an enhanced ability to draw on what is a *de facto* global reserve army in order to decompose/recompose the capitalist labour process worldwide, has followed the implementation in the Third World of the Green Revolution programme during the 1960s and *laissez faire* policies in the 1980s.[10]

For all these reasons, Marxist theory distinguishes between two dissimilar kinds of migration: labour bought in *to supplement* the existing workforce, because the latter is insufficient to meet the needs of production. The second form possesses a very different dynamic: migrants are recruited in order *to displace* the existing workforce, because the latter subjects either won't work for the low pay and poor conditions on offer, or – if in post – are deemed too costly to employ, the object being to replace them with cheaper foreign labour. It is the latter that historically and currently generates huge antagonism within the ranks of the working class affected, an hostility that frequently resorts to

---

employed as a result of investment in new enterprises by capitalists whose enhanced profits derived from the original labour-displacing strategy. This view is problematic, since it applies only when capital and labour are national in scope, and not international. Where the latter is the case, capital is able to do two things: either to invest elsewhere, in contexts where labour-power is available and even cheaper; or to employ (perhaps even to import) migrants who meet the same requirements. Whichever the instance, the outcome is the same: any new jobs created do not necessarily go to those expelled from the labour process because of technification/mechanization of production. The obviousness of this outcome notwithstanding, it is unfortunately still possible to hear – even from some on the left – the mantra that workers displaced in this manner will automatically find employment in new industries created by capital.

10 Most of those contributing to the development debate over the latter half of the twentieth century, it could be argued, were hoist by their own petard, in that they failed to anticipate one particular outcome licensed by the policies advocated: namely, generating increased skill levels in so-called underdeveloped contexts without at the same time providing well-paid/secure local employment for those with these skills, creates the very conditions that give rise to migration in search of such jobs elsewhere. All that was lacking at that conjuncture were the right political circumstances: in the shape of neoliberal policies (deregulation, outsourcing, downsizing) adopted in metropolitan capitalist nations, these circumstances emerged during the 1980s, and from the turn of the millennium the process of migration gathered pace. Rather than stay and fight for better pay/conditions locally, therefore, which is what much radical development theory imagined would happen, inhabitants of ex-socialist and/or Third World nations opted for a different outcome: the search for employment with better pay/conditions that already existed in other countries.

discourse about ethnic, national or gender 'otherness'.[11] The combination of the global spread of capitalist development, the internationalization of the industrial reserve army, and the restructuring of the labour process, has been accompanied by the second form (displacement). One result has been a resurgence of unfree labour-power of locals as well as migrants, a process of deproletarianization involving workforce decomposition/recomposition, whereby in the course of class struggle employers replace free labourers with (or convert them into) unfree equivalents.[12]

However, decomposition/recomposition of the labour process does not prevent employers from continuing to insist that they recruit migrants only because no locals are available or willing to do the work (see below), a thinly disguised attempt to represent merely as supplementing what is actually its 'other' – displacing the existing workforce. For many types of economic activity, however, members of the existing workforce do possess the requisite skills, or have acquired them, only to find that they are currently undercut in the labour market by migrants. What is at issue, therefore, is not so much skill and a lack thereof, but rather the cost of labour-power. Workers used to a standard of living established through a long process of 'from below' struggle', which itself depends on improving – or at least maintaining – existing income levels, understandably resist demands by the accumulation process to toil harder for lower wages. Migrants can and do undertake such work, due to conflicting reasons (unfree production relations, higher wages here than there, not belonging to trade unions). This, and not skills *per se*, is the real point of contention.

Clearly, then, it is the displacing form that drives capitalist restructuring, given the importance of cost considerations where accumulation occurs in a

11 It is somewhat curious that missing from the two most popular critiques of the current economic crisis, each by an author with a reputation as a radical scholar opposed to capitalism and sympathetic to Marxist interpretations, is a perception of the link between immigration and the industrial reserve army. Thus Piketty (2016: 164ff.) is supportive of further immigration as a positive contribution to what he terms an 'Open Europe', while Varoufakis (2016: 207) observes rightly that 'racism and a whiff of evil are spreading throughout the [European] continent', but then laments that 'freedom of movement for ordinary people' is 'severely circumscribed'.

12 Contributions to the debate about capitalism and unfree labour invariably omit to differentiate Marxist interpretations of unfree labour, between those which see it as an *obstacle* to capitalist development (the semi-feudal thesis), as a *useful* but not necessary part of capitalism (dependency theory), and as an *integral* aspect of the accumulation process itself (deproletarianization). Both the existence and the importance of a connection between on the one hand deploying labour-power that is unfree, and the processes of deskilling, trade unionization, reproducing the reserve army, capitalist restructuring and the profitability of accumulation are made clear by Marx (1976: 788, 793, 795).

global *laissez-faire* environment. Unsurprisingly, therefore, when asked why they prefer a migrant workforce, capitalists deploy the politically less contentious 'addition to' version rather than the 'instead of' form. This is a distinction recognized by workers themselves, as the case of recent strike action on a UK energy construction site indicates. When contractors recruited only migrants for work, locals displaced in this manner withdrew their labour, emphasizing their quarrel was not with foreign workers *per se* but rather with the companies and contractors involved. Although the latter attempted to justify this displacement by claiming no locals were available for recruitment, trade unions regarded the procedure as a thinly disguised attempt to lower costs by resorting to migrants.[13]

To Regulate...

The free market means an uncontrolled labour supply, always taken advantage of by capital as a way not just of undermining the bargaining power of existing workers, but also of rolling back any gains they have made (wages, conditions) in the course of the class struggle. This is precisely why socialists have always argued for state intervention/planning, to prevent this downward pressure on pay/conditions from continuing. Any attempt to circumvent or deny this, by for example downgrading or ignoring political economy and privileging non-class identity as a form of migrant self-empowerment, plays directly into the hands of capital. Although on the left (and centre-left) current discussion about the impact of the industrial reserve army on the existing workforce still tends to be dismissed as inherently racist, this was not always so. A century ago, socialism contemplated halting immigration so as to safeguard present and future gains made in the course of the class struggle.[14]

---

13 See 'Sympathy strikes for sacked workers likely to spread after oil refinery talks collapse', *The Guardian* (London), 20 June 2009. One local worker who had been displaced made clear where in his opinion the blame lay, stating: 'We've no grievance with foreign workers as such but we feel that they should supplement what we can't provide, and at the moment there are that many unemployed construction workers throughout the UK that are not given the chance to get these jobs. That's the grievance.' Confirming this, another local worker pointed out that: 'This all started because of cheap foreign labour. There are plenty of skilled local men but they can't get jobs because they are bringing the foreigners in. Their skills aren't as good but they cost less.'

14 Noting that 'Social-Democrats have always stoutly upheld the banner of Internationalism in the matter of alien immigration, [and that we] should be the last to champion any hard, abstract treatment of a great principle,' Belfort Bax (1895) proceeded to indicate when in his view it was legitimate to breach this principle. 'If it could be shown that the

The crucial role of the industrial reserve army in the accumulation process has long been recognized by Marxism, from Marx and Engels themselves to Rosa Luxemburg, Leon Trotsky, Maurice Dobb and Ernest Mandel. From statements such as 'a reserve army of workers...greatly increases the power of capital', and further that the 'constant artificial production of a surplus population, which disappears only in times of feverish prosperity, is one of the necessary conditions of production of modern industry', it is clear that Marx himself regarded an expanding industrial reserve army as the *sine qua non* of accumulation.[15] According to him, the reserve army comes into its own once the early stage of capitalism – that generally associated with primitive accumulation – has been left behind.[16] The threat an increasing reserve army posed not just to

---

admission of so-called destitute aliens was really serving merely as a safety-valve for Continental capitalism to get rid of an inconvenient encumbrance by extruding from their native country unemployed elements left stranded by the great industry at home; and if it could be shown that the introduction of these elements necessarily had the effect of lowering wages and the standard of living of British workmen, then, distasteful as it would be to us, we might admit the necessity of a law discouraging, or even prohibiting, the migration of such for a time.' The crux of the matter was expressed thus: 'We might do so [prohibit immigration] on the ground that even from a "labour," much more from a socialistic point of view, it were better for their own and for our sake that these [workers] should stay at home and organize industrially and politically for the emancipation of their class rather than perpetuate and extend misery by destroying the livelihood of their brother-slaves further west. We say at least that this is a standpoint which might be taken.'

15 See Marx (1969: 554, 560). Elsewhere he elaborates in an account that has an unmistakably contemporary ring to it (Marx, 1975: 285): 'In a society which is becoming increasingly prosperous, only the very richest can continue to live from the interest on money... competition for workers hardly exists any longer, and because the number of workers has increased, the competition among them has become all the more considerable, unnatural and violent. Hence a section of the working class is reduced to beggary or starvation...'.

16 Marx (1976: 784–785) emphasizes thus the central economic role played by the industrial reserve army in the capitalist mode of production: 'But if a surplus population of workers is a necessary product of accumulation or of the development of wealth on a capitalist basis, this surplus population also becomes, conversely, the lever of capitalist accumulation, indeed becomes a condition for the existence of the capitalist mode of production. It forms a disposable industrial reserve army, which belongs to capital just as absolutely as if the latter had bred it at its own cost. Independently of the limits of the actual increase of population, it creates a mass of human material always ready for exploitation by capital in the interests of capital's own changing valorization requirements. With accumulation, and the development of the productivity of labour that accompanies it, capital's power of sudden expansion also grows;... The path characteristically described by modern industry, which takes the form of a decennial cycle (interrupted by smaller oscillations) of periods of average activity, production at high pressure, crisis, and stagnation, depends on

hard-won wage levels and employment conditions but also to the protection of these gains – by means of solidarity among and capacity of an existing workforce to organize – was such that Marx gave serious consideration to opposing further immigration.[17]

In ways that anticipate current argument about withdrawal from EU membership so as to stem competition from the industrial reserve army, a century and a half ago Marx advocated severing the link with Ireland precisely in order to prevent migrants from competing with and undercutting English workers.[18] He insisted that working class emancipation in England depended ultimately on Ireland following its own path of capitalist development, and to this end international solidarity would take the form of support from English workers for Irish equivalents in their struggle for economic and political independence, as distinct from migrating to where this had already occurred.

Examining the formation and function of the industrial reserve army in Poland during the late nineteenth century, therefore, Luxemburg noted that

---

the constant formation, the greater or less absorption, and the re-formation of the industrial reserve army or surplus population.' Of particular interest is what he says next (Marx, 1976: 785): 'This particular cycle of modern industry, which occurs in no earlier period of human history, was also impossible when capitalist production was in its infancy.'

17 Among those who recognized this was Engels, who in a letter to Schlüter, dated 30 March 1892, observed (Marx and Engels, 1934: 496–497): 'Your great obstacle in America, it seems to me, lies in the exceptional position of the native workers. Up to 1848 one could only speak of a permanent native working class as an exception: the small beginnings of it in the cities in the East always had still the hope of becoming farmers or bourgeois. Now a working class has developed and has also to a great extent organized itself on trade union lines... [However,] immigrants are divided into different nationalities and understand neither one another nor, for the most part, the language of the country. And your bourgeoisie knows much better even than the Austrian Government how to play off one nationality against the other: Jews, Italians, Bohemians, etc., against Germans and Irish, and each one against the other, so that differences in the standard of life of different workers exist, I believe, in New York to an extent unheard of elsewhere. And added to this is the total indifference of a society which has grown up on a purely capitalist basis...towards the human lives which succumb in the competitive struggle: "there will be plenty more, and more than we want, of these damned Dutchmen, Irishmen, Italians, Jews and Hungarians;" and beyond them in the background stands John Chinaman, who far surpasses them all in his ability to live on dirt.'

18 For details, see Marx and Engels (1934: 289–290). Observing that '[t]he average English worker hates the Irish working man as a competitor who lowers his wage and his standard of life', Marx (Collins and Abramsky, 1965: 170) argued that the Irish Question was central to the interests of the labour movement in England, adding that 'to forward the social revolution in England...the decisive blow must be struck in Ireland'.

capital would always oppose any attempts to abolish it. This was because the presence of an industrial reserve army increased competition between not just those already in work but also those without jobs, enabling capitalists to reduce wages so as to maintain or raise profitability.[19] In support of Marx's view that the only thing regulating wage levels was class struggle, Luxemburg pointed to the crucial role played by the industrial reserve army in preventing or undermining the effectiveness of trade union organization and action designed to improve wages and conditions of work.

Much the same argument was made in 1939 by Trotsky.[20] Noting the hostility to the concept, he outlined how industrial reserve army was at that conjuncture formed by 'a whole generation of young people who have never had a job and have no hope of getting one', as a result of which they are 'forced to live at the expense of society'. It was this as much as anything that gave rise to the view that the final historical stage of the accumulation process would take the form of what Trotsky labelled a 'civil war against the proletariat'.[21] Part of this 'civil war' would involve turning workers against one another in their attempts to secure employment, a common tactic in a *laissez faire* economic context where capital has unfettered access to the industrial reserve army.

In the era following the end of the Second World War, when capitalism appeared less powerful, and the class struggle in industrial nations seemed to diminish in intensity, one Marxist who anticipated that capitalist accumulation worldwide depended on an expanding industrial reserve army of labour was Maurice Dobb. Presciently, amidst the end-of-ideology triumphalism during the 1950s accompanying claims that Keynesianism had solved the problem of capitalist crises, he cautioned against the illusion that accumulation was compatible with full employment ('a situation where the sack had lost a good deal of its sting as a disciplinary weapon, with the virtual disappearance of the industrial reserve army'). Sooner or later, Dobb warned, capitalist profitability would require the restoration of unemployment.[22]

---

19 See Luxemburg (2013: 15, 277–279, 288–293), where she notes that it 'is quite wrong in depicting capitalist wage relationships to focus only on the wages actually paid to industrial workers in employment, a habit of the bourgeoisie and its paid writers that has unfortunately been generally adopted even by the workers themselves. The entire reserve army of unemployed, from the occasionally unemployed skilled workers down to the deepest poverty and official pauperism, is a necessary factor in determining wage relationships.'

20 See Trotsky (1970: 20–21).

21 See Trotsky (1975: 268).

22 See Dobb (1955: 215–225). From the other side of the political spectrum, much the same point was made – albeit using different terminology – by Fisher (1946), Scitovsky (1958) and Robbins (1976).

Another Marxist who emphasized the dependency of accumulation process on the industrial reserve army was Mandel, who pointed to the historical connection between profitability, the long waves of capitalist expansion, and the availability of migrant labour.[23] Hence addressing the related issues of an unregulated expansion in the industrial reserve army and who benefits from this is a first step, after which – in a capitalist context – a government representing all workers (of whatever ethnicity and gender) can then proceed to implement regulation of wages and conditions. The alternative, as Trotsky pointed out, is a drift to the right on the part of the proletariat – fascism being a punishment visited by history on politicians of the left for abandoning the transition to socialism.

In his detailed investigation of the epistemology and structure of *Capital*, Rosdolsky outlines how Marx disagreed with Malthus for failing not just to historicize overpopulation and its causes but also to understand that surplus population and its economic role as an industrial reserve army was the effect of the accumulation process.[24] In his concluding observations about this issue, however, Rosdolsky argues that this role is cancelled by contemporary trade union activity.[25] Clearly, his optimistic prognosis about the ability of trade unions to prevent the impact of the industrial reserve – he was writing in the late 1960s – makes no account either of their diminished influence from the 1980s onwards, nor of capitalist outsourcing to take advantage of surplus labour abroad and mass immigration enlarging the reserve army at home. Things have changed for the worse, in other words, and Rosdolsky cannot be blamed for not having foreseen that.

...or Not to Regulate

There can be no doubt that employer discourse supporting continued high levels of immigration does so for economic reasons, emphasizing benefits to the

23 See Mandel (1980: 26–27).

24 See Rosdolsky (1977: 250–255), who goes on to note that: 'During periods of economic stagnation and at the beginning of upswings', therefore, the industrial reserve army (Rosdolsky, 1977: 298) 'presses down on the "active army of workers", by not allowing them to push their wage demands too high: and in periods of crisis it often prevents them from making use of their right to strike, to defend themselves against capital's offensive against their living standards'. The current resonance of this description is too obvious to merit further discussion.

25 See Rosdolsky (1977: 300).

nation.[26] Unsurprisingly, the focus has been and remains on issues connected to the supply, cost and control of labour-power. Hence opposition to caps on immigration has been framed by the British Chamber of Commerce as a constraint on the capacity of business to recruit sufficient workers, which in turn would impede economic growth, a position shared both by the accounting industry (Ernst & Young, KPMG, PwC, Deloitte) and by Japanese car manufacturing corporations based in the UK.[27] The same case is made by UK agribusiness corporations, arguing that now, as in the past, farm sector productivity relies on overseas workers.[28] An analogous point is made by the chief economic advisor to Lloyds Bank, who has argued similarly that migrants are necessary in order to provide care for an ageing population, while the head of an asset management enterprise has warned that curbs on migration would damage London as a financial centre.[29] Echoing this, the Bank of England Governor has defended continued UK membership of the EU by invoking the economic benefits to be gained by business from the contributions made by a migrant workforce to flexible labour markets.[30]

---

26 That a migrant workforce necessarily contributes to economic growth, as business interests frequently insist, is a problematic claim, since in terms of additional public spending on housing, transport, education and health services, not to mention state subsidies in one form or another (tax credits) to supplement low wages paid by employers, plus the fact that many such workers do not earn enough to generate tax revenues, immigration is not resource-neutral. This disparity is compounded by the fact that, where cheap migrant workers generate higher profits for capital, employers themselves avoid paying tax, thereby depriving the exchequer of even this revenue source arising from immigration.

27 See 'The cap on immigration cannot hold', *The Observer* (London), 22 August 2010; 'Immigration cap "threat to job creation"', *Financial Times* (London), 11–12 September, 2010; 'Immigration cap which will not fit', *Financial Times* (London), 6 October 2010; 'E&Y urges coalition to kill cap on migrants', *Financial Times* (London), 6 October 2010; 'UK carmakers attack cap on immigration', *The Guardian* (London), 28 October 2010; 'Economy "could suffer if migrant squeeze goes on"', *The International Independent*, 5 September 2011.

28 See 'Overseas seasonal workers are essential to agriculture', *Financial Times* (London), 5–6 September 2015. For an earlier version of the same discourse, see 'Farmers fear shortage of workers could hit fruit and veg supplies', *The Guardian* (London), 22 April 2008.

29 See 'Ageing UK needs 7m immigrants to survive', *The Observer* (London), 13 May 2007; and 'Cable backed by CBI in row over migrant curbs', *Financial Times* (London), 18–19 September 2010.

30 See 'EU supporters have nothing to disagree with', and 'Carney backs EU membership saying UK is "leading beneficiary"', *Financial Times* (London), 22 October 2015.

Such arguments stressing the link between migration and national prosperity ignore the phenomenon of 'jobless growth'. The latter refers to accumulation that does not benefit the domestic workforce, because labour is either employed abroad or comes from there. Economic growth does take place, as does profitability, but the advantages that capital – when justifying its own project – says this confers on the existing workforce are negligible or non-existent. This is compounded by two related claims from the same source: that economic growth benefits the wider society by generating jobs, which in turn generate purchasing power, thereby enhancing consumption and with it demand; and by generating tax revenue for the State to invest elsewhere. As noted above, neither of these arguments withstand scrutiny, since poorly paid jobs generate little consuming power and/or no tax revenues, and these days tax avoidance by capital means that revenues which would otherwise accrue to the State are instead located off-shore in tax havens.[31]

31 Relevant here is a communication published on the letters page of *The Guardian* (London) on 19 February 2016 under the title 'Divisions on the left over the benefits of staying in the EU', which merits quoting at length: 'Your pro-EU stance seems to suggest that leaving the EU is a preoccupation of the Tory right and all voters of the centre-left should be pro-EU because it somehow represents progressive politics and is a force for good. But this is a huge betrayal of the sections of society you purport to speak for. I live in Mansfield, the former mining mecca of the north Nottinghamshire coalfield. It is one of the poorest places in the country, with one of the highest indices of deprivation. Just under ten years ago a large industrial estate was built with EU money to regenerate the area in one of the satellite villages, Shirebrook. Mike Ashley decided to set up the Sports Direct HQ there, but instead of recruiting locally, he drafted in almost the entire workforce from elsewhere in the EU. Workers are on zero-hours contracts and the conditions are notoriously bad. So has the presence of such a large enterprise stimulated the local economy? According to a recently published report, Mansfield now ranks as the fourth poorest town in the country because of the absurdly low wages. But it is near the top of the chart for benefit dependency, poor health and low educational attainment. The town centre is still full of empty shops – the only growth has been the increase in the number of pound shops. As for migrants' disposable income, much of it goes abroad and is playing a large part in consumer spending in Poland and other countries. All this is clearly evidenced nationally by the fact that employment levels are rising, but productivity and wages are not… Quite clearly an unlimited supply of low-skilled labour…makes it ever easier for employers to offer zero-hours or insecure employment, both for migrants and for British low-paid. This is benefiting only business owners not known for their public-mindedness or even paying any tax. How can anyone on the left be in favour of a system that perpetuates this? Any improvements to workers' rights the EU may have secured have been and will continue to be fundamentally undermined by this, and arguing that we can change this from within is pie in the sky…'

Ironically, conservatism is aware of the potential/actual difficulty posed for its nationalist ideology by such open support on the part of capital for expanding rather than controlling the size of the industrial reserve army.[32] It is clear from the warning by the UK government that business organizations should play down what was termed their 'counterproductive' public statements in favour of EU membership.[33] Significantly, perhaps, in those cases where conservative politicians have either urged companies to recruit young workers already available in the UK labour market, or advocated immigration controls, they too have met with criticisms from capitalists.[34] A case in point is the hostile reception to the speech at the 2015 Conservative Party conference by the Home Secretary, questioning the benefits of mass immigration.[35] Combining the more usual cultural issue – concern that mass immigration would destabilize social

---

32 This contradiction between the requirements of employers as a class, whatever these might be, and those of the nation surfaced in the immediate post-1945 era, when capital was more on the defensive than now, and its advocates recognized the potential danger. Hence the view expressed by one of the latter (Goyder, 1951: 41–42): 'When Government by "interference" cuts across industry's conception of profitability, it vitiates the basis upon which private industry is at present organized. The industrialist cannot be blamed for looking primarily to the interests of his shareholders. He is playing the game according to the rules. But unless the rules of the game of industry can be made roughly to correspond with the needs of the nation, active co-operation between industry and Government will be in danger of breaking down.'

33 See 'Do not speak out in favour of EU, Cameron urges business leaders', *Financial Times* (London), 7 September 2015.

34 See 'British job plea fails to impress', *Financial Times* (London), 2–3 July 2011; 'Employers protest as minister says they should give Britons priority in the job market', *The Guardian* (London), 2 July 2011.

35 See 'May: the era of mass migration to UK must end', *The Guardian* (London), 6 October 2015; 'Migration "harming society"', *The Daily Telegraph* (London), 6 October 2015. Lest it be thought this was a progressive intervention on behalf of UK workers, it should be emphasized that the speech was designed to attract back to her party the political support that had shifted to UKIP. The same kind of strategy was used earlier by conservative politicians. During the late 1960s, for example, Enoch Powell (1969: 219, 231) maintained that immigration into the UK was unnecessary because it was not connected to the accumulation process. Consequently, it was for him an issue linked solely to questions of culture (in his words, 'racial and religious differences') standing in the way of social integration. Eschewing questions raised by the industrial reserve army, his view was that labour shortages in a developed economy would be solved not by migration but rather by more capital investment and 'better organization'. For Powell, therefore, economic arguments deployed to justify recruiting additional quantities of migrant labour from abroad were mere 'excuses' to legitimize the immigration that had already occurred.

cohesion – with economic issues (its negative impact on the wages and employment conditions of existing workers), her views were attacked by business representatives solely on economic grounds.

Opposing the criticisms of immigration expressed by the Home Secretary, therefore, a representative of the *laissez-faire* think-tank the Institute of Economic Affairs (IEA) asserted that it was 'not our role to intervene in decisions made by many millions of migrants and businesses who want to employ them.'[36] Both the Confederation of British Industry (CBI) and The Institute of Directors categorized such views as beyond the pale, the latter organization maintaining it was 'astonished by the home secretary's irresponsible rhetoric', accusing her of 'helping our competitor economies instead of our own', and describing as nonsense the 'myth of the job-stealing immigrant'.[37] For its part, the CBI reiterated claims both that migration had been positive for the UK economy, and that consequently no curbs or targets were necessary. More recently, the IMF has made the same point with regard to the EU as a whole, whilst accepting that in Germany 'migrants tend to earn 20 per cent less than domestic employees with similar characteristics.'[38]

That employers recruit migrant workers in preference to locals, and consequently that 'job-stealing' may not be the myth business organizations claim it is, emerges clearly from the employment practices followed by capitalist producers.[39] Hence the acceptance in a report by the Ernst & Young ITEM Club, which assesses the economic situation for business organizations, that cheaper foreign labour has indeed had a negative impact on wages, as well as displaced local workers.[40] Prominent capitalists such as George Soros and

---

36 For other examples of IEA advocacy of open door policy where immigration is concerned, see Bhagwati (1995), Stelzer (2001) and Becker (2011).

37 See 'Business rejects claims that jobs are lost to foreigners', *The Daily Telegraph* (London), 7 October 2015, and 'Business hits back at May over migrants', *Financial Times* (London), 7 October 2015. The sole concession made by pro-business discourse about the negative impact of immigration is the oft-heard refrain that the resulting downward pressure on wages affects only unskilled workers at the bottom end of the labour hierarchy. This logic passes without comment, despite being akin to an argument that, insofar as its effects are limited to the poorest elements of society, murder is acceptable.

38 See 'IMF stresses benefits of newcomers', *Financial Times* (London), 21 January 2016.

39 See, for example, 'Higher figures for foreign workers undermine ministers' claims', *The Guardian* (London), 11 December 2007; 'Firms hiring more migrants as UK workers struggle', *The Guardian* (London), 12 August 2009; and 'Demand for migrant workers greater than ever as firms reject unskilled school leavers', *The Guardian* (London), 24 August 2011.

40 See 'Migrant workers curb wages and keep interest rates low to boost economic growth', *The Guardian* (London), 18 December 2007. It notes both that 'the influx of foreign labour

Martin Sorrell have publicly declared their support for an open door policy on migrant labour.[41] Even the house magazine of British capitalism accepts that the presence of an industrial reserve (albeit not theorized as such) has a negative impact on wage rates.[42]

Significantly, the role of immigration in keeping down UK wage levels is confirmed by the most recent official data which suggests that in 2016 average pay growth for workers will remain at 2%, due to 'the ready availability of migrant workers [making] it easy for employers to fill vacancies'.[43] Non-nationals in the workforce have increased from 3.7 percent in 1997 to more than 10% currently, a situation which explains why '[w]age growth has repeatedly been weaker than forecasters have expected over recent years, despite the rapid rate of jobs growth which would usually be expected to lead to upward pressure on pay'. It is perhaps in response to this development that a conservative minister advised as the only remedy that UK workers must henceforth be prepared to toil as hard and as long as their equivalents in Asian economies, and – one might add – eventually for the same kinds of wage rates.[44]

---

had helped [keep down] growth in wages', and that 'young British-born workers were one group that appeared to have lost out in the jobs market over the past decade since they have felt the impact of the most recent wave of immigrants'.

41 An open door policy is advocated by the financier George Soros through his Open Society Foundation and its International Migration Initiative, as does Martin Sorrell, the CEO of WPP, through a variety of public pronouncements. See 'Immigration could be a solution to talent shortage, says Martin Sorrell', *Campaign*, 16 September 2015, and 'Immigration is a Lifeblood, Let's Not Cut It Off', 3 September 2013, at https://www.linkedin.com/pulse/20130903.

42 According to 'Economic Outlook: Wage Woes', *Investors Chronicle*, 20–26 November 2015, p. 14, therefore, 'workers' bargaining power is not as strong as you might infer from the fact that the unemployment rate, at 5.3 per cent, is at its lowest since early 2008. This is because the official unemployment rate greatly underestimates the excess supply of labour. As well as the 1.75 m unemployed, there are almost 2.3 m who would like a job but are classified by the ONS as "economically inactive"...[a]nd "inactivity" is a misnomer...541,000 "inactive" people moved into work. That's 23.3 per cent of all the "inactive" who wanted a job. This means that the "inactive" are almost as likely to move into work as the unemployed...'.

43 See 'Pay growth predicted to stall at 2% as number of skilled workers rises', *The Guardian* (London), 30 December 2015. According to the CIPD chief economist, 'With record levels of net migration into the UK increasing the supply of labour, it doesn't look like we're going to see a skills crunch any time soon'.

44 See 'Hunt: Britons must work like the Chinese', *The Guardian* (London), 6 October 2015, and 'Work like the Chinese', *The Independent* (London), 6 October 2015. The Trade Union response to this was that the minister 'was encouraging sweatshop labour in Britain'.

Non-regulation on Principle

Turning to non-economic reasons, these tend to be advanced mainly by those who advocate maintaining immigration either on the grounds of justice, or for humanitarian considerations, an objective to be realized by extending citizenship in the receiving nation. Such arguments emanate not just from development NGOs (Oxfam, Amnesty International, Save the Children) and Church organizations (Christan Aid, Cafod) but also from academia and journalism.[45] Thus, for example, a number of cultural and/or political commentators on, contributors to, and leaders in *The Guardian*, a liberal newspaper associated historically with progressive causes, have recently followed this line, and currently do so still.[46]

One such is Zoe Williams, a political journalist who objects to discussing the negative impact on the UK of migration, dismissing this as innately racist ('bigotry'). Even tentative attempts by the Labour Party to raise the issue not of halting but merely of regulating immigration elicits her condemnation.[47] The same humanitarian approach is endorsed by Natalie Nougayrède, who also frames the issue in terms of cultural diversity.[48] Noting the 'heartwarming mobilisation of volunteers, NGOs and human rights organizations' assisting

45 See 'Britain must do far more to help, charities tell PM', *The Guardian* (London), 4 January 2016.

46 Hence the antagonism in opinion piece contributions in this newspaper to reports and/or public statements questioning the economic benefits that immigration has conferred on the UK. See, for example, 'Plagued by imbalance' and 'Populism and prosperity', *The Guardian* (London), 2 April 2008; 'Do May's claims on immigration stand up to scrutiny?' and 'Theresa May turns the clock back to the nasty party', *The Guardian* (London), 7 October 2015. For an exception which considers the negative impact of migration not on the UK but rather on sending countries, see 'Britain's gain is East Europe's brain drain', *The Guardian* (London), 24 March 2015. Such commentaries on the news must be differentiated from reportage, which merely conveys information about data and/or events and episodes.

47 See 'Immigration: the big issue that the left just can't get right', *The Guardian* (London), 31 March 2015, and 'There's plenty more space for humanity on this "tiny" island', *The Guardian* (London), 2 November 2015. When challenged about Labour's open door policy on immigration whilst in power, Ed Miliband replied that 'employers undercutting wages – rather than immigration – was the cause of the problem.' See 'Labour leader barracked on immigration as he reaches out to voters', *The Guardian* (London), 30 April 2013.

48 See 'Diversity could be the making of Europe', *The Guardian* (London), 5 January 2016. For a similar view expressed by Nesrine Malik in another opinion piece, the focus of which is on culture, see 'The rampant migrant bogeyman is back', *The Guardian* (London), 14 January 2016.

migrants, her focus is simply on how national identity is to be defined/redefined and integration to be achieved. To effect this, therefore, '[n]ow is the time to launch a pan-European citizens' debate on [cultural] diversity'. Neither Williams nor Nougayrède address questions of political economy, much rather disavowing or downplaying the importance of any economic connection between an expanding industrial reserve army and the capacity of employers to impose declining wages/conditions on those already in work or seeking employment.

Much the same kind of approach and assumptions inform the advocacy of mass migration by Mohsin Hamid, another contributor to *The Guardian* whose humanitarian/culturalist perception of immigration ends up being indistinguishable from *laissez-faire* economic theory. Since in his view it offends against cultural pluralism, Hamid objects to the term 'civilization', which misses the fact that the same term encompasses also a non-cultural dimension.[49] Like Williams and Nougayrède, he limits migration conceptually to a question of culture, which is false. To equate opposition to immigration with a defence of Western 'civilization' misunderstands that the problem linked to the former is not so much cultural as *economic*. An increase in the supply of labour cannot but undermine the standard of living gained as a result of class struggle waged by workers over generations, to obtain and then protect not just wage levels and working conditions but also things like welfare provision, housing, education, and health care.[50] Ignoring all this, he asserts merely that 'civilizations are illusions', which wrongly overlooks the material aspect of this term.

By framing the question of 'civilization' simply in terms of culture, Hamid plays straight into the hands of capital, no less than the South African apartheid regime, which similarly confined this issue to one of culture, and its defence. His view about British society, and the prevalence/innateness of what Hamid takes to be its positive aspects – including the mistaken perception of the media as 'open to dissenting voices' – highlights one of the more important, but least mentioned, attributes of migration that makes it so attractive to capital.[51] Namely, the idealization of the socio-economic character of the receiving nation as benign, and consequently the less likely the emergence of

---

49 See Hamid (2014: xvi).

50 Significantly, a century ago Lenin used the term in precisely this way, noting that migrants from rural areas arriving in cities would be exposed to what he regarded as positive influences associated with historical progress ('civilization'), among which was the development of a consciousness of class, and solidarity with other workers engaged in a struggle with capital.

51 See Hamid (2014: 28, 40–41).

or political support for a systemic challenge from this source, when compared with existing workers who have long experienced austerity/oppression.[52] In short, the 'post-civilization' world desired by Hamid seems to be a place where international capitalism reigns supreme, as a result of a global reserve army exercising a continuous and unrelenting downwards pressure on wages, work conditions, and livelihoods, constantly adjusting them to the lowest common denominator.[53]

In order to uphold his idealist perception of neoliberalism as enabling everyone to choose to be whatever they want, Hamid invokes literature, a realm of make-believe where in his opinion reality asserts itself.[54] Avoiding the issue of what actually exists and is reproduced materially, therefore, he follows postmodernism in arguing that because an aspiration is declared by literature to exist, in reality it does indeed exist. Rather than restricting the issues raised by mass immigration to culture in general and literature in particular, and considering them instead within a political economy framework, Hamid justifies what is in effect a neoliberal position on the industrial reserve army in terms of a 'common humanity'.[55] In support of this view, he now categorizes migration as a 'human right', arguing that inhabitants of western nations should not oppose but welcome mass immigration and that anyway such movement is unstoppable and the pattern of the future ('The scale of migration we will see in the coming centuries is likely to dwarf what has come before').[56]

---

52 It is, of course, the case that throughout history a workforce composed of migrants has over time become class conscious, and thus open to mobilization/organization by trade unions and leftist political parties. However, as the example of the United States underlines, once this occurs, employers and the capitalist state quickly resort to new sources of 'green' labour in order once again to repeat the same process. All that happens, therefore, is that the cycle based on displacing radicalized workers with malleable equivalents continues unabated, a pattern that controlling/regulating immigration would make difficult, if not impossible.

53 Among the processes which Hamid (2014: 102, 112) regards as desirable are rapid capitalist accumulation, privately-owned media, and 'a soaring stock market'. His endorsement of an unthreatening agenda where capitalism is concerned ('mutual respect, greater engagement and more openness') is one with which few employers would disagree.

54 See Hamid (2014: xi–xii, 87ff.).

55 See Hamid (2014: 22–23).

56 See Mohsin Hamid, 'Why Migration is a Fundamental Human Right', *The Guardian* (London), 21 November 2014, and his contribution to a discussion on BBC Radio 4, *The World Tonight*, 12 November 2015. Much the same point has been made by Chibundu Onuzu, in another contribution to the same paper. Her cousin, she argues, 'wished to live in Europe simply because he wanted a better life...we want what you want...[w]e all want a better job', concluding in the same vein as Hamid that '[t]here are no fences high enough to stop

Confronted with this possibility, a socialist response would be to advocate more not less control over the labour market, by means of extending the regulation of labour-power and economic planning on a global scale, not – as Hamid and others suggest – simply to adopt a *laissez-faire* policy in the name of 'a common humanity'. Admitting that his approach to this issue is migrant-centric (preferring 'the terms migrant and migration to immigrant and immigration [because] the latter two seem to privilege the country of arrival'), Hamid makes no mention of the deleterious impact such a process would have in receiving countries, in terms of either wages/conditions/livelihoods of existing workers, or of the advantages such a process confers on employers and far right politics in these contexts.

Avoiding the (Economic) Issue

Each of the two benchmark analyses of migration, by Thomas and Znaniecki and by Berger and Mohr, was migrant-centric and – insofar as the topic was addressed – adhered to the 'as well as' or labour shortage interpretation of this process.[57] At the start of the twentieth century, therefore, the object of the influential study by Thomas and Znaniecki was to identify obstacles to social cohesion, and thus the reasons for 'the decay of communal solidarity'. Their concern was the problems generated by cultural erosion resulting from migration to the receiving country. Published just after the development decade, the focus of another important analysis, by Berger and Mohr, was mainly on the negative impact that migration had on the sending country. Since migration was regarded as a temporary work arrangement, migrants were conceptualized as essentially peasants, and migration as a 'disruption' of rural society in southern Europe. At that conjuncture, the principal concern was that migration would perpetuate underdevelopment in the European periphery.

Because at these different periods, half a century apart, the assumption was that the role of migration was simply to supplement an existing workforce, little or no attention was given to its economic impact on the receiving country. Instead, anxiety in each case was about either the process of adapting to

humans from aspiring.' See 'Migrants only want what you want. Why is that so frightening?' *The Guardian* (London), 26 June 2015. Bereft of any conception of the economic impact on workers in receiving nations, what such migrant-centric appeals to common human aspirations or identity do is merely to mimic *laissez-faire* discourse about the 'naturalness' of individualistic competition in the labour market.

57 See Thomas and Znaniecki (1958) and Berger and Mohr (1975).

a new life, or what was seen as the continuing viability of traditional peasant society in the village community migrants left behind. Just as the search by these earlier studies of migration was for social cohesion represented by idealized forms of community, so current approaches undertake a similar quest, only now for the attainment by migrants of bourgeois citizenship within the receiving social formation.

These themes surface in similar non-economic arguments made by others, this time in academia, searching for political solutions within the capitalist system. Invoking the desirability of justice and human rights from what are claimed to be progressive and/or centre-left positions, the same kind of approach combines support for the market with advocacy of citizenship and the continuation of immigration. Declaring that 'market institutions and policies that provide the right framework in which migrants and natives can find work can only enhance the potential benefits of migration', such idealised and over-optimistic analyses rely on a non-systemically specific state to ensure 'care and protection of its citizens'.[58] Because the State is perceived as benign, almost above the fray, it is an approach which merely seeks legislative interventions designed to achieve an 'appropriate balancing' between migrant and local worker.[59] This despite the fact that currently the State is not merely a capitalist but a neoliberal institution, the agency of which is to formulate/implement legislation favouring the accumulation process.

Reproducing the same argument as Hamid about immigration being a human right, Mezzadra looks at the problem simply from the viewpoint of a non-class-specific migrant (= 'the right to escape', 'the autonomy of migration'), not the migrating worker, nor the worker in the country of destination.[60] Such an approach makes it impossible to make common cause with labourers in the latter context when one is effectively in competition with them for the same jobs, the getting of which by the 'escaping' migrant at the expense of an actual/potential worker in another country is the only thing that seems to be seen as a legitimate political objective.

Accepting that his interpretation breaks with Marxist theory, Mezzadra advocates severing the conceptual link between the wage labour relation and labour-power, so that a 'heterogeneity of labour relations' composed of numerous other social categories and groups (undifferentiated migrants, petty traders, smallholding peasants, family farmers, sharecroppers, lumpen-proletarians) can be included among those whose agency will become the

58 For examples, see Giddens (2003), Anderson (2014) and Anderson and Hughes (2015).

59 See Freedland and Costello (2014).

60 Mezzadra (2006).

deciding factor in any struggle with capitalism.[61] However, since key components of these very broad categories – labelled by him 'subaltern' or 'multitude' – occupy not just different but antagonistic class positions, and thus are generally hostile not to capitalism but to socialism, their agency cannot be seen as progressive.[62]

In keeping with the non-economic epistemology of the 'new' populist postmodernism, justice and citizenship are conceptualized not in objective but subjective terms: rather than being defined by the receiving country, therefore, citizenship is said to derive simply from grassroots culture of the migrant him/herself.[63] Although misleadingly labelled by Mezzadra an 'alternative modernity', this notion of citizenship, rooted as it is in a misplaced Thirdworldism, licenses an uncritical acceptance of ideological forms in the sending nation, thereby leaving intact structures advantageous to capitalism. Among the latter are kinship and quasi-kinship relations, the hierarchy and authority of which can be – and have been – used to enforce bonded labour arrangements on migrants.[64]

---

61 Mezzadra (2011a).

62 For a critique of this broad view, held among others by advocates of global labour history, see review essay 13, this volume. The difficulty faced by trade unions – especially in their currently diminished role – in uniting local and migrant labour to form a common front against capital was underlined in the course of a 14 May 2014 interview on the BBC Radio 4. When asked why employers were recruiting workers like him in preference to locals, a recently-arrived migrant replied that he was prepared to do the same job for less pay. Asked, further, what he thought the impact of this would be on those currently in employment, he disavowed any sympathy for – let alone solidarity with – them, saying they would have to learn to live with such competition for jobs, and lower their wage expectations in keeping with the changed circumstances. (Predictably, this interview was followed by a discussion in which politicians from the mainstream parties dismissed any connection between immigration and cheap labour undercutting existing wages.) Also relevant is the following consideration: how likely is it that those who previously lived under Stalinist conditions in Eastern Europe would support any move, institution or political party designed to bring about socialism in the capitalist nation to which they had just migrated? In other words, to reproduce in the country of destination what might be interpreted by such migrants as the same kind of economic system as had previously existed in their original location. If – as is argued here – the reply is not at all likely, then this merely underlines the extent of the difficulty an expanding industrial reserve army with this kind of history poses for trade unions in the host country.

63 See, for example, Mezzadra (2011b), Balibar, Mezzadra and Samaddar (2012), and Mezzadra and Neilson (2013).

64 For the use of kinship and quasi-kinship authority to enforce bonded labour relations, see Brass (1999: 57ff., 125ff.).

The negative impact of the 'cultural turn' on the debate about the connection between migrant labour and accumulation, and more specifically on political economy approaches to and materialist interpretations of this link, should not be underestimated.[65] Although not an absolute distinction, opposition to immigration by those on the political right – for example, Enoch Powell – has tended to be on cultural grounds, stemming from its supposed dilution of a pristine ethnic and/or national identity, whereas that by leftists has been on economic grounds, the focus of which has been on the undermining of working class organization/solidarity.[66] Part of the difficulty is that many on the left replaced Marxist ideas with postmodern ones, in the process abandoning a materialist political economy and moving instead onto the epistemological terrain of conservatism. Having dismissed class and socialism as Eurocentric foundationalism, an academically dominant postmodern theory has essentialized non-class identities (ethnicity, nationalism) as innate and empowering.

Weaponizing Postmodernism

It would be wrong, moreover, to think that the influence of postmodern theory privileging non-class identity is merely a form of ivory tower discourse confined to academia, and thus has no purchase on government policy. A case in point is COMPAS, an academic think-tank that was a source of many of the ideas behind the *laissez faire* open door policy adopted by 'New Labour' at the turn of the millennium.[67] In pursuit of its two objectives – migrant integration

65 A broadly similar point has been made by Piketty (2014: 655, n. 2) who observes: 'When one reads philosophers such as Jean-Paul Sartre, Louis Althusser and Alan Badiou on their Marxist and/or communist commitments, one sometimes has the impression that questions of capital and class inequality are of only moderate interest to them and serve mainly as a pretext for jousts of a different nature entirely.'

66 See Powell (1969: 213ff.) and Fielding (1981). However, a caveat is necessary, since grassroots support for a populist party like UKIP expressed in terms of culture (a defence of 'Britishness' against the 'foreigner') may actually disguise underlying concerns about economic issues, such as labour market competition (Ford and Goodwin, 2014; Goodwin and Milazzo, 2015).

67 On the influence of those at COMPAS on the formation of 'New Labour' immigration policy, see Bowyer (2016: 172–176), according to whom '[COMPAS] was saying the kinds of things ["New Labour"] wanted to hear'. The idealist perception on the part of COMPAS of immigration simply as a cultural issue is set out in an analysis by one of its personnel (Spencer, 2007). Clearly, although not all research undertaken by COMPAS can be said

and citizenship – the declared brief of COMPAS was and remains one of 'informing policy-making and public debate', to which end it stresses the positive economic aspects of immigration ('growth in migrant labour was bringing benefits to the UK labour market [and] that fears about the impact on wages and unemployment were proving unfounded') and promotes the efficacy of non-class identity within the existing socio-economic system.[68] In the opinion of COMPAS, Blair ought to be commended because he 'showed a courage in opening up the UK's labour market... He leaves Britain on the map as a country which is firmly open to labour migration in a way that seemed inconceivable only a decade ago'.[69] As astonishing is the triumphalist endorsement of a *laissez-faire* approach informing its conclusion: 'That view [the economic benefits of migration] is now mainstream, and in a global economy it is unlikely that openness to labour migration...will be reversed. The job of government is no longer simply to control and exclude'.

Sensing, perhaps, that not all working class Labour supporters shared this positive assessment of 'New Labour' open door policy, this commendation is followed by the lament that, despite widespread grassroots opposition to a *laissez-faire* labour market, 'Blair made little attempt...to convince the public of the rationale for this new approach.'[70] For COMPAS, therefore, the main problem appears to be not the negative impact of an expanding industrial reserve army, but rather a failure on the part of 'New Labour' to persuade everyone as to the unalloyed economic benefits of mass immigration and increased competition for a declining number of jobs. In short, ignoring the Marxist case about immigration as a method by employers of expanding the industrial reserve army, COMPAS focuses instead on ways of integrating migrants once they have arrived (= extending citizenship), which in political terms is a way of avoiding engagement with the negative economic role played by migrant labour in the class struggle under present-day capitalism.

---

to subscribe to this view, this institution has nevertheless been influential in setting the terms of debate as interpreted by 'New Labour' politicians.

68 In an interview with Bowyer (2016: 172), a COMPAS associate insisted that 'immigration and [cultural diversity/"otherness"] brought positive good'. In keeping with this, Anderson (2015: 68–82) – another COMPAS associate – maintains that debates about immigration are centrally about 'worth', 'honour' and 'good citizenship', and less about 'economic impacts'. Unsurprisingly, this privileging of non-economic issues, together with her view that '[t]he logic of job competition that underpins labour migration policy should not be taken at face value [*sic*]', downgrades the importance of class struggle.

69 These views are expressed by Spencer (2007: 358).

70 For these views, see Spencer (2007: 348–349, 359).

It is difficult to escape the conclusion that such non-economic discourse about immigration, stressing the humanitarian aspects, frequently amounts to a situation whereby bourgeois media commentators and/or academics, for the most part well-paid and in secure employment, talk up the necessity of yet more labour market competition to be endured by those currently in poorly-paid short-term working class jobs. It is not hard to gauge the kind of 'from below' response to such advocacy that workers submit themselves to what amounts to a Dutch auction for jobs, when they see members of the bourgeoisie putting the jobs of others (= workers) up for tender, and then handing such employment to those willing to accept the lowest wages and poorest conditions.[71]

Little wonder therefore, when these advocates claim that what they are doing is making the case for a progressive – and perhaps even a socialist – programme, that any form of progressive (let alone socialist) politics has found it hard to attract working class support (now shifting in large numbers to populist parties). Although UKIP emerged during the early 1990s, its support increased from 2009 onwards, when it became clear that 'New Labour' had betrayed its own traditional grassroots by encouraging unregulated immigration. Accordingly, it is possible to trace a direct link from on the one hand the postmodern colonization of academic debate in the form of the 'cultural turn', the influence exercised by the latter on academics promoting an open-door policy on migration, to on the other the acceptance by 'New Labour' of such policy advice, and the subsequent rise of populist party like UKIP.

Insofar as it privileges cultural identity as empowering, therefore, postmodern theory is complicit with the kind of nationalist ideology represented by the far right. Eurosceptic populism thus corresponds to the reaffirmation by disadvantaged workers of British citizenship, thereby underlining the direction in which citizenship in a capitalist nation may ultimately lead.[72] Ominously, just as many on the left of the political spectrum moved rightwards, abandoning core beliefs (socialism, class) and espousing postmodern notions

71 What, one wonders, would be the reaction of these same bourgeois were a labourer in his/her turn to advocate not just more competition for their own media and/or academic posts, but also an intention to hand such employment to the candidate willing to accept the lowest payment and poorest conditions?

72 Although for conservative business interests it is the 'restrictive' (i.e. unwarranted) regulation emanating from Brussels that vexes, ironically it is the opposite that generates most hostility among working class UKIP supporters: an absence of European regulation over the labour market that licenses an expanding industrial reserve army. Accordingly, workers are not opposed to immigration because they are Eurosceptic, but are Eurosceptic because they are opposed to immigration.

of non-class identity as innate/empowering, so the far right has in turn moved onto the political ground they vacated, incorporating class identity into its own ideology. To the postmodern argument emphasizing the cultural identity of the migrant-as-'other'-nationality, the far right counterposes an argument similarly emphasizing cultural identity, only this time the nationality of the non-migrant worker (= British selfhood).

In the absence of socialist ideas/practice, and as capitalism spreads across the globe, this form of nationalist discourse can be deployed effectively by populists who claim it is the only way to safeguard/retain workers' jobs and living standards. Unless, and until, leftists succeed both in putting socialism/class back on the political agenda, and in decoupling an expanding industrial reserve army as a cultural issue simply about non-class identity from analysis examining the same process within a political economy framework, immigration will continue to pose questions without leftist answers. Worse still, the longer this remains the case, the more likely it is that under the present *laissez-faire* regime, immigration as a *class* issue will increasingly be absorbed into and consolidated within a populist agenda.

These difficulties have in turn rendered problematic any attempt to question assertions that privilege as empowering the non-class identity of the migrant. They have also added credence to the criticism levelled at Marxist theory concerning the negative impact of immigration on worker organization/solidarity, Marx's own views on the subject being dismissed as no more than an unfortunate residue of late Victorian racist ideology. Some think that immigration even divides Marxism off from non- or anti-Marxist theory, and perhaps no other issue has caused as much disagreement between socialists who see no wrong in an expanding availability of immigrant labour and local workers who oppose this. Yet Marx himself opposed restructuring, and warned that where this entailed pitting workers of different nationalities or ethnicities against one another, the resulting intense market competition for jobs encouraged by capital would undermine any material gains as well as hinder future advances made by labour.[73]

---

73 The realization of this particular effect – the deployment of the reserve army in the class struggle between labour and capital – was linked by Marx (1976: 786, note) in turn to the internationalization of the market. He did not, as some insist, confine the impact of the reserve army to national contexts and economies. It goes without saying that, insofar as the reserve army becomes global in scope, such a development licenses racist ideology among the proletariat in a given country, thereby splitting workers along national/ethnic lines. Equally unsurprising is that capital not only benefits from this but also encourages this kind of consciousness, in the process shifting the latter from the sameness of class to the difference of cultural 'otherness'.

Conclusion

Socialists have long argued that the industrial reserve army is one of the most powerful weapons in the economic armoury at the disposal of capital in its struggle with the working class. An expanding industrial reserve army, generated as a result of globalization, enables capital to adopt a divide-and-rule policy, and with it to give additional momentum to the 'race to the bottom' in pay and conditions. The case made here is not that Marxism was wrong about immigration, but much rather that it was right. The problem has been and remains that too few of those who imagine they are adhering to a progressive analysis omit to base their views on this approach, conflating humanitarian concern or postmodern identity politics with a materialist framework.

That trade unions oppose this 'race to the bottom', and attempt to organize migrant labour, is obvious and not open to dispute. The problem lies elsewhere, in that migrants coming from ex-socialist countries are understandably reluctant to sign up to anything that smacks of socialism. Those who claim that it is not immigration but austerity which is responsible for any decline in wages/conditions overlook the link between immigration, crises and austerity. As long as employers have access to an expanding industrial reserve army, they can attempt to solve their own economic difficulties and that of capitalism generally by maintaining or increasing profitability and competitiveness. It is only by depriving them of this escape route (= an expanding industrial reserve) that puts the transcendence of capitalism (= socialist transition) on the agenda.

The debate about immigration currently divides into epistemologically distinct arguments: economic and non-economic ones. Economic reasons for opposing or supporting immigration are deployed by those at either end of the political spectrum: by Marxists as well as capitalists, all of whom see it as a labour market issue. Thus employer opinion concerning the need for migrant workers is in effect the mirror image of Marxist theory about the industrial reserve army: each regards the latter as the driving force of the accumulation process. Like Marxism, employer opinion frames this requirement in economic terms, central to which are labour market issues; unlike Marxism, employer discourse stresses the economic advantage to the nation as a whole of a migrant workforce.

Influenced by the 'cultural turn', a similarly positive view is based on non-economic reasons. Having dismissed class and socialism as Eurocentric foundationalism, an academically dominant postmodern theory has instead essentialized non-class identities (ethnicity, nationalism) as innate and empowering. Hence the support for continued immigration which derives from non-economic reasons is based on justice, citizenship or humanitarian considerations. Their assumption is that, even in a *laissez-faire* environment, it is still possible to protect the rights of migrants and locals, whereas employers attempt to enhance competitiveness/profitability by playing one off against the other.

Under a neoliberal capitalist labour regime, therefore, the State will not seek to disadvantage producers striving for economic growth by protecting the rights of their migrant and local workers, much rather the opposite: any rights labour has managed to gain over the years will be stripped away. Hence the fatuity of a search for 'appropriate balancing,' an objective that amounts to no more than legislative tampering within a rampant market system. Unlike Marxism, such non-economic approaches fail to distinguish between the supplementing/displacing function of migrant labour, and thus miss its implications for political economy and the industrial reserve army.

Opposing any regulation of labour market access in the manner suggested by employer and non-economic discourse could set a precedent in the form of challenging the right of a future government following a socialist programme to undertake state planning by, for example, allocating labour-power on a regional basis, in accord with a national economic plan. The twofold socialist objective has to be: first, to defend the existing workforce, and migrants who are already part of this; but second, to oppose strongly any attempts by capital to add to their number. Although the position taken here is different from the one usually adopted by those on the left – that any/all opposition to migration should be opposed on the grounds that it is necessarily and automatically racist – the argument is consistent with the Marxist view that any/all attempts by employers to undermine and/or roll back gains made by workers should be opposed politically.

There is no mystery as to why Marxist theory opposes an expanding industrial reserve army in the shape of deregulated immigration. If jobs are taken by migrants at existing low pay levels and poor conditions, then employer incentive to pay more and improve working conditions so as to attract non-migrants vanishes. In short, the potential/actual displacement of existing workers as distinct from supplementing them very much determines labour migration policy in *laissez-faire* contexts, as pro-business governments have conceded. It is a difficulty that the mere extension of citizenship fails to address. As a solution to what is a wider systemic process, therefore, citizenship limits the response to the political and ideological domain, leaving intact a capitalist economy that generates and reproduces such problems in the first place. By shifting the emphasis from the economic role performed for capital by an expanding industrial reserve army to the attainment by the migrant of citizenship in the receiving nation, such an approach downgrades the importance of class struggle.

When the industrial reserve army is global in scope, as it is now, the element of struggle is correspondingly more acute. This is especially true of contexts where migrants are many and jobs are few, and competition in the labour market is particularly intense. In such circumstances, it is an issue which surfaces among the working class and their representatives as one of ethnic/national identity only so long as the continued reproduction of the system which gives rise to the industrial reserve army and its effects (low wages, fierce competition for jobs, and unemployment) is not addressed. In a capitalist context, therefore, socialists have on occasion argued that controlling the level of the industrial reserve army precedes and enables regulation. It diminishes competition in the labour market, thereby permitting workers and their representatives to begin to settle accounts with employers from a position of strength.

This is in keeping with the international solidarity required of socialists, in that wherever such a conflict occurred – *class* opposition to capital as it manifests itself and operates in *any* context – it would be supported, as would the accompanying struggle for a transition to socialism. This is the form that leftist internationalism should take: namely, establishing working class unity *within* nations, prior to extending the resulting solidarity *across* nations, thereby generating a common and wider struggle against global market expansion. What such a struggle should most certainly not include is action designed to do exactly the opposite: that is, reinforce the power of capital in any particular context, thereby contributing precisely to the global domination of *laissez faire*.

Bibliography[1]

Ahluwalia, Isher Judge, and I.M.D. Little (eds.), 1998, *India's Economic Reforms and Development: Essays for Manmohan Singh*, Oxford: Oxford University Press.

Alavi, Hamza, P.L. Burns, G.R. Knight, P.B. Mayer and Doug McEachern, 1982, *Capitalism and Colonial Production*, London & Canberra: Croom Helm.

Albert, Bill, and Adrian Graves (eds.), 1984, *Crisis and Change in the International Sugar Economy, 1860–1914*, Norwich and Edinburgh: ISC Press.

Alderson-Smith, Gavin, 1976, 'Peasant Response to Cooperativization under Agrarian Reform in the Communities of the Peruvian Sierra', in June Nash, Jorge Dandler and Nicolas Hopkins (ed.), *Popular Participation in Social Change: Cooperatives, Collectives and Nationalized Industry*, The Hague and Chicago, IL: Mouton and Aldine Press.

Alfaro, Julio, and Teresa Ore, n.d. [c.1974], *El desarrollo del capitalismo en la Convención y los nuevos movimientos políticos de campesinos con tierra 1963–73*, Lima: Universidad Cátolica del Peru.

Allina-Pisano, Jessica, 2005, 'Land Reform and the Social Origins of Private Farmers in Russia and the Ukraine', in Stephen K. Wegren (ed.), *Rural Adaptation in Russia*, London and New York: Routledge.

Amnesty International, 1979, *Briefing Paper No. 15: Peru*, London: Amnesty International.

Ampuero, Igor, and James J. Brittain, 2005, 'The Agrarian Question and the Armed Struggle in Colombia', in Sam Moyo and Paris Yeros (eds.), *Reclaiming the Land: The Resurgence of Rural Movements in Africa, Asia and Latin America*, London: Zed Books [see Review Essay 11].

Amsden, Alice H., 2003, *The Rise of the Rest: Challenges to the West from Late-Industrializing Economies*, New York: Oxford University Press.

Anderson, Bridget, 2014, 'Precarious Pasts, Precarious Futures', in Cathryn Costello and Mark Freedland (eds.), *Migrants at Work: Immigration and Vulnerability in Labour Law*, Oxford: Oxford University Press.

Anderson, Bridget, 2015, 'Precarious work, immigration and governance', in Carl-Ulrick Schierup *et al.*, (eds.) *Migration, Precarity and Global Governance*, Oxford: Oxford University Press.

Anderson, Bridget, and V. Hughes (eds.), 2015, *Citizenship and its Others*, Basingstoke: Palgrave.

Anderson, Perry, 1968, 'Components of the National Culture,' *New Left Review*, 50.

Angelo, Larian, 1995, 'Wage Labour Deferred: The Recreation of Unfree Labour in the US South', *The Journal of Peasant Studies*, Vol. 22, No. 4.

Annan, Noel, 1999, *The Dons: Mentors, Eccentrics and Geniuses*, London: HarperCollins.

1 Books that are the subject of a review or a review essay are identified as such.

Anonymous [Thomas Chandler Haliburton], 1838, *The Clockmaker, or the Sayings and Doings of Samuel Slick of Slicksville*, London: Richard Bentley, New Burlington Street.

Apthorpe, Raymond, and Desmond Gasper, 1982, 'Policy Evaluation and Meta-evaluation: The Case of Rural Co-operatives', *World Development*, Vol. 10, No. 8.

Arce, Albert, and Norman Long, 1993, 'Bridging two worlds: An ethnography of bureaucrat-peasant relations in western Mexico', in Mark Hobart (ed.), *An Anthropological Critique of Development*, London: Routledge.

Archer, Leonie (ed.), 1988, *Slavery and Other Forms of Unfreedom*, London: Routledge.

Ariff, Mohamed, 2005, *Liberalization and Growth in Asia: 21st Century Challenges*, Cheltenham: Edward Elgar Publishing.

Arndt, H.W., 1987, *Economic Development: The History of an Idea*, London and Chicago, IL: University of Chicago Press.

Arnold, David, 1984, 'Famine in Peasant Consciousness and Peasant Action: Madras, 1876–8', in Ranajit Guha (ed.), *Subaltern Studies III*, Delhi: Oxford University Press.

Aron, Raymond, 1957, *The Opium of the Intellectuals*, London: Secker and Warburg.

Ashley, M.P., and C.T. Saunders, 1933, *Red Oxford: A History of Socialism in the University of Oxford*, Oxford: The Oxford University Labour Club.

Assadi, Muzaffar H., 1995, '"Khadi Curtain", "Weak Capitalism" and "Operation Ryot": Some Ambiguities in Farmers' Discourse, Karnataka and Maharashtra 1980–93', in Tom Brass (ed.) *New Farmers' Movements in India*, London: Frank Cass Publishers (a special issue of *The Journal of Peasant Studies*).

Assadi, Muzaffar H., 1997, *Peasant Movement in Karnataka, 1980–94*, Delhi: Shipra Publications.

Assies, Willem, 2002, 'From Rubber Estate to Simple Commodity Production: Agrarian Struggles in the Northern Bolivian Amazon', *The Journal of Peasant Studies*, Vol. 29, Nos. 3–4.

Attwood, D.W., and B.S. Baviskar (eds.), 1988, *Who Shares? Co-operatives and Rural Development*, Delhi: Oxford University Press.

Awad, Mohamed, 1966, *Report on Slavery*, New York: United Nations.

Baldwin, Elaine, 1972, *Differentiation and Co-operation in an Israeli Veteran Moshav*, Manchester: Manchester University Press.

Bales, Kevin, 1999, *Disposable People: New Slavery in the Global Economy*, Berkeley, CA: University of California Press.

Bales, Kevin, 2000, 'The New Slavery', *Index on Censorship*, Vol. 29, No.1.

Balibar, E., S. Mezzadra, and R. Samaddar (eds.), 2012, *The Borders of Justice*, Philadelphia: Temple University Press.

Balogh, Thomas, 1966, 'Agricultural and Economic Development' [1961], in *The Economics of Poverty*, London: Weidenfeld and Nicolson.

Banaji, Jairus, 2003, 'The Fictions of Free Labour, Contract, Coercion, and So-Called Unfree Labour', *Historical Materialism*, Vol. 11, No. 3.

Banaji, Jairus, 2010, *Theory as History: Essays on Modes of Production and Exploitation*, Leiden: Brill.

Banerjee, Diptendra (ed.), 1985, *Marxian Theory and the Third World*, New Delhi: Sage Publications.

Baran, P., 1957, *The Political Economy of Growth*, New York: Monthly Review Press.

Barraclough, Solon L., 1991, *An End to Hunger? The Social Origins of Food Strategies*, London/New Jersey and Geneva: Zed Books and UNRISD.

Barraclough, Solon L., and Juan Carlos Collarte (eds.), 1973, *Agrarian Structure in Latin America: A Resume of the CIDA Land Tenure Studies*, Lexington, MA: D.C. Heath and Company.

Barrientos, Stephanie, 2013, '"Labour Chains": Analysing the Role of Labour Contractors in Global Production Networks,' *The Journal of Development Studies*, Vol. 49, No. 8.

Barrientos, Stephanie, Uma Kothari, and Nicola Phillips, 2013, 'Dynamics of Unfree Labour in the Contemporary Global Economy,' *The Journal of Development Studies*, Vol. 49, No. 8.

Barthes, Roland, 1977, *Image, Music, Text*, London: Fontana.

Bauer, Arnold J., 1979, 'Rural Workers in Spanish America: Problems of Peonage and Oppression', *Hispanic American Historical Review*, Vol. 59, No. 1.

Bauer, P.T., 1971, *Dissent on Development: Studies and Debates in Development Economics*, London: Weidenfeld and Nicolson.

Bauer, P.T., 1981, *Equality, the Third World and Economic Delusion*, Cambridge, MA: Harvard University Press.

Baviskar, B.S., 1980, *The Politics of Development: Sugar Co-operatives in Rural Maharashtra*, Delhi: Oxford University Press.

Beachey, R.W., 1957, *The British West Indies Sugar Industry in the Late Nineteenth Century*, Oxford: Basil Blackwell.

Becker, G.S., 2011, *The Challenge of Immigration*, London: IEA.

Bedoya Garland, Eduardo, and Alvaro Bedoya Silva-Santisteban, 2005a, *Enganche y Servidumbre por Deudas en Bolivia*, Geneva: International Labour Organization.

Bedoya Garland, Eduardo, and Alvaro Bedoya Silva-Santisteban, 2005b, *Trabajo Forsozo en la Extracción de la Madera en la Amazonia Peruana*, Geneva: International Labour Organization.

Beer, M., 1948, *A History of British Socialism*, London: George Allen & Unwin.

Beidelman, T.O., 1959, *A Comparative Analysis of the Jajmani System*, New York: J.J. Augustin Inc.

Béjar, Hector, 1970, *Peru 1965: Notes on a Guerrilla Experience*, New York: Monthly Review Press.

Belfort Bax, E., 1895, *Aliens*, http://www.marxists.org/archive/bax/1895/12/aliens.htm.

Belloc, Hilaire, 1937, *The Crisis of Our Civilization*, London: Cassell and Company, Ltd.

Belloc, Hilaire, 1941, *The Silence of the Sea and Other Essays*, London: Cassell and Company, Ltd.

Benda, Julien, 1928, *The Great Betrayal* (*La Trahison des Clercs*), London: George Routledge & Sons Ltd.

Benda, Julien, 1929, *Belphégor*, London: Faber & Faber Limited.

Benda, Julien, 1958 [1938], 'The Bourgeois Democracies and Germany', in Justin O'Brien (ed.) *From the Nouvelle Revue Français*. New York: Farrar, Straus and Cudahy.

Berger, J., and J. Mohr (1975) *A Seventh Man: The story of a migrant worker in Europe*. London: Penguin Books.

Berlan, Amanda, 2013, 'Social Sustainability in Agriculture: An Anthropological Perspective on Child Labour in Cocoa Production in Ghana,' *The Journal of Development Studies*, Vol. 49, No. 8.

Berlin, Isaiah, 2009, *Enlightening: Letters 1946–60* (ed. Henry Hardy and Jennifer Holmes), London: Chatto & Windus.

Bernstein, Henry, 1977, 'Notes on Capital and Peasantry', *Review of African Political Economy*, No. 10.

Bernstein, Henry, 1981, 'Notes on State and Peasantry in Tanzania', *Review of African Political Economy*, No. 21.

Bernstein, Henry, 1982, 'Industrialization, Development, and Dependence', in Hamza Alavi and Teodor Shanin (eds.), *Introduction to the Sociology of 'Developing Societies'*, London: Macmillan.

Bernstein, Henry, 1990, 'Taking the Part of Peasants?' in Henry Bernstein, Ben Crow, Maureen Mackintosh and Charlotte Martin (eds.), *The Food Question*, London: Earthscan Publications, Ltd.

Bernstein, Henry, 1992, 'The Origins of Rural Poverty', in Henry Bernstein, Ben Crow and Hazel Johnston (eds.), *Rural Livelihoods: Crises and Responses*, Oxford: Oxford University Press.

Bernstein, Henry, 1994, 'Agrarian Classes in Capitalist Development', in Leslie Sklair (ed.), *Capitalism and Development*, London: Routledge.

Bernstein, Henry, 1996, 'The Political Economy of the Maize Filière', *The Journal of Peasant Studies*, Vol. 23, Nos. 2–3.

Bernstein, Henry, 1996/97, 'Agrarian Questions Then and Now', *The Journal of Peasant Studies*, Vol. 24, Nos. 1–2.

Bernstein, Henry, 2000, '"The Peasantry" in Global Capitalism: Who, Where and Why?' in Leo Panich and Colin Leys (eds.), *Socialist Register 2001*, London: The Merlin Press.

Bernstein, Henry, 2001, '"Agrarian Reform" after Developmentalism?' paper presented at the Development Studies Association Annual Conference, University of Manchester, September.

Bernstein, Henry, 2005a, 'Rural Land and Land Conflicts in Sub-Saharan Africa', in Sam Moyo and Paris Yeros (eds.), *Reclaiming the Land: The Resurgence of Rural Movements in Africa, Asia and Latin America*, London: Zed Books [see Review Essay 11].

Bernstein, Henry, 2005b, 'Development studies and the Marxists', in Uma Kothari (ed.), *A Radical History of Development Studies: Individuals, Institutions and Ideologies*, London: Zed Books [see Review Essay 11].

Bernstein, Henry, 2006, 'Is There an Agrarian Question in the 21st Century?' paper presented at CASID Congress, Toronto, June 1–3.

Bernstein, Henry, 2010, *Class Dynamics of Agrarian Change*, Halifax NS: Fernwood Publishing [see Review 4].

Bernstein, Henry, 2013, 'Interview: Agriculture, class and capitalism', *International Socialism*, No. 138.

Bernstein, Henry, in press, 'Rural Livelihoods and Agrarian Change: Bringing Class Back In', in Norman Long and Ye Jingzhong (eds.), *Rural Transformations and policy Interventions in the Twenty First Century*, London: Edward Elgar.

Beverley, John, 1999, *Subalternity and Representation: Arguments in Cultural Theory*, Durham, NC: Duke University Press.

Beverley, John, Michael Aronna and José Oviedo (eds.), 1995, *The Postmodernism Debate in Latin America*, Durham, NC: Duke University Press.

Bhagwati, Jagadish, 1993, *India in Transition: Freeing the Economy*, Oxford: The Clarendon Press.

Bhagwati, Jagadish, 1995, *Free Trade, 'Fairness' and the New Protectionism*, London: Institute of Economic Affairs (Occasional Paper 96).

Bierce, Ambrose, 1967, *The Enlarged Devil's Dictionary*, London: Victor Gollancz Ltd.

Blanco, Hugo, 1972, *Land or Death: The Peasant Struggle in Peru*, New York: Pathfinder Press, Inc.

Bloom, Harold, Paul de Man, Jacques Derrida, Geoffrey Hartman, and J. Hillis Miller, 1979, *Deconstruction and Criticism*, London: Routledge & Kegan Paul.

Blum, J., 1961, *Lord and Peasant in Russia from the Ninth to the Nineteenth Century*, Princeton, NJ: Princeton University Press.

Boeke, J.H., 1953, *Economics and Economic Policy in Dual Societies*, New York: Institute of Pacific Relations.

Booth, David 1985 'Marxism and Development Sociology: Interpreting the Impasse', *World Development*, Vol. 13, No. 7.

Booth, David (ed.), 1994, *Rethinking Social Development: Theory, Research and Practice*, Harlow, Essex: Longman Scientific & Technical.

Borras, S.M., Ruth Hall, Ian Scoones, Ben White and Wendy Wolford, 2011, 'Towards a better understanding of global land grabbing: an editorial introduction', *The Journal of Peasant Studies*, Vol. 38, No. 2.

Bottomore, Tom, and Patrick Goode (eds.), 1978, *Austro-Marxism*, Oxford: Clarendon Press.

Bower, Tom, 2016, *Broken Vows: Tony Blair – The Tragedy of Power*, London: Faber & Faber.

Bradby, Barbara, 1975, 'Review of *Stone Age Economics* by Marshall Sahlins', *Bulletin of the Conference of Socialist Economists*, Vol. IV, Nos. 5–6.

Bradby, Barbara, 1982, '"Resistance to capitalism" in the Peruvian Andes', in A.D. Lehmann (ed.), *Ecology and Exchange in the Andes*, Cambridge: Cambridge University Press.

Bragg, Billy. 2006. *Progressive Patriot*. London: Bantam Press.

Brass, Tom, 1983, 'Agrarian Reform and the Struggle for Labour-power: A Peruvian Case Study', *The Journal of Development Studies*, Vol. 19, No. 3.

Brass, Tom, 1986a, '*Cargos* and Conflict: The Fiesta System and Capitalist Development in Eastern Peru', *The Journal of Peasant Studies*, Vol. 13, No. 3.

Brass, Tom, 1986b, 'The Elementary Strictures of Kinship: Unfree Relations and the Production of Commodities', *Social Analysis*, No. 20.

Brass, Tom, 1989a, 'Trotskyism, Hugo Blanco and the Ideology of a Peruvian Peasant Movement', *The Journal of Peasant Studies*, Vol. 16, No. 2.

Brass, Tom, 1989b, 'Beer Drinking Groups in a Peruvian Agrarian Cooperative', *Bulletin of Latin American Research*, Vol. 8, No. 2.

Brass, Tom, 1990a, 'The Latin American *Enganche* System: Some Revisionist Reinterpretations Revisited', *Slavery and Abolition*, Vol. 11, No.1.

Brass, Tom, 1990b, 'Class Struggle and the Deproletarianization of Agricultural Labour in Haryana (India)', *The Journal of Peasant Studies*, Vol. 18, No. 1.

Brass, Tom, 1991, 'Moral Economists, Subalterns, New Social Movements and the (Re-) Emergence of a (Post-) Modernized Middle Peasant', *The Journal of Peasant Studies*, Vol. 18, No. 2.

Brass, Tom, 1994, 'Some Observations on Unfree Labour, Capitalist Restructuring, and Deproletarianization', *International Review of Social History*, Vol. 39, Part 2.

Brass, Tom (ed.), 1995, *New Farmers' Movements in India*, London: Frank Cass Publishers.

Brass, Tom, 1995a, 'Reply to Utsa Patnaik: If the Cap Fits...', *International Review of Social History*, Vol. 40, Part 1.

Brass, Tom, 1995b, 'Old Conservatism in "New" Clothes', *The Journal of Peasant Studies*, Vol. 22, No. 3.

Brass, Tom, 1995c, 'Unfree Labour and Agrarian Change: A Different View', *Economic and Political Weekly*, Vol. XXX, No. 13.

Brass, Tom, 1996a, 'Yet More on Agrarian Change and Unfree Labour', *Economic and Political Weekly*, Vol. XXXI, No. 4.

Brass, Tom, 1996b, 'Misinterpreting Unfree Labour in Contemporary Haryana', *Economic and Political Weekly*, Vol. XXXI, No. 33.

Brass, Tom, 1997a, 'Immobilized Workers, Footloose Theory', *The Journal of Peasant Studies*, Vol. 24, No. 4.

Brass, Tom, 1997b, 'Introduction: Free and Unfree Labour – The Debate Continues', in Tom Brass and Marcel van der Linden (eds.), *Free and Unfree Labour: The Debate Continues*, Bern: Peter Lang, AG.

Brass, Tom, 1999, *Towards a Comparative Political Economy of Unfree Labour: Case Studies and Debates*, London and Portland, OR: Frank Cass Publishers.

Brass, Tom, 2000a, *Peasants, Populism and Postmodernism*, London: Frank Cass Publishers.

Brass, Tom, 2000b, 'Labour in Post-Colonial India: A Response to Jan Breman', *The Journal of Peasant Studies*, Vol. 28, No. 1.

Brass, Tom, 2002, 'Rural Labour in Agrarian Transitions: The Semi-Feudal Thesis Revisited', *Journal of Contemporary Asia*, Vol. 32, No. 4.

Brass, Tom, 2003a, 'Why Unfree Labour is Not "So-Called": The Fictions of Jairus Banaji', *The Journal of Peasant Studies*, Vol. 31, No. 1.

Brass, Tom, 2003b, 'On Which Side of What Barricade? Subaltern Resistance in Latin America and Elsewhere', in Tom Brass (ed.), *Latin American Peasants*, London and Portland, OR: Frank Cass Publishers.

Brass, Tom (ed.), 2003c, *Latin American Peasants*, London and Portland, OR: Frank Cass Publishers.

Brass, Tom, 2004, '"Medieval Working Practices"? British Agriculture and the Return of the Gangmaster', *The Journal of Peasant Studies*, Vol. 31, No. 2.

Brass, Tom, 2005, 'Late Antiquity as Early Capitalism?' *The Journal of Peasant Studies*, Vol. 32, No. 1.

Brass, Tom, 2006, 'Subaltern Resistance and the ("Bad") Politics of Culture: A Response to John Beverley', *The Journal of Peasant Studies*, Vol. 33, No. 2.

Brass, Tom, 2010, 'Capitalism, Primitive Accumulation and Unfree Labour,' in H. Veltmeyer (ed.), *Imperialism, Crisis and Class Struggle: The Enduring Verities of Capitalism – Essays Presented to James Petras*, Leiden: Brill.

Brass, Tom, 2011a, *Labour Regime Change in the 21st Century: Unfreedom, Capitalism and Primitive Accumulation*, Leiden: Brill.

Brass, Tom, 2011b, 'Primitive Accumulation, Capitalist Development and Socialist Transition: Still Waiting for Godot?' *Journal of Contemporary Asia*, Vol. 41, No. 1.

Brass, Tom, 2014a, *Class, Culture and the Agrarian Myth*, Leiden and Boston, MA: Brill.

Brass, Tom, 2014b, 'Is the industrial reserve army a racist concept?' *Capital & Class*, Vol. 38, No. 3.

Brass, Tom, 2014c, 'Taking Liberties', *Capital & Class*, Vol. 39, No. 3.

Brass, Tom, 2014d, Debating Capitalist Dynamics and Unfree Labour: A Missing Link? *The Journal of Development Studies*, Vol. 50, No. 4.

Brass, Tom, 2015, 'Peasants, academics, populists: Forward to the past?' *Critique of Anthropology*, Vol. 35, No. 2.

Brass, Tom, and Marcel van der Linden (eds.), 1997, *Free and Unfree Labour: The Debate Continues*, Bern: Peter Lang, AG.

Brayne, F.L., 1929, *The Remaking of Village India*, London: Oxford University Press.

Breman, Jan, 1974, *Patronage and Exploitation: Changing Agrarian Relations in South Gujarat, India*, Berkeley, CA: University of California Press.

Breman, Jan, 1985, *Of Peasants, Migrants and Paupers: Rural Labour Circulation in capitalist Production in West India*, Delhi: Oxford University Press.

Breman, Jan, 1989, *Taming the Coolie Beast: Plantation Society and the Colonial Order in Southeast Asia*, Delhi: Oxford University Press.

Breman, Jan, 1990, '"Even Dogs are Better Off": The Ongoing Battle between Capital and Labour in the Cane-Fields of Gujarat', *The Journal of Peasant Studies*, Vol. 17, No. 4.

Breman, Jan, 1993, *Beyond Patronage and Exploitation: Changing Agrarian Relations in South Gujarat*, Delhi: Oxford University Press.

Breman, Jan, 1996, *Footloose Labour*, Cambridge: Cambridge University Press.

Breman, Jan, 1999a, 'Industrial Labour in Post-Colonial India – I: Industrializing the Economy and Formalizing Labour', *International Review of Social History*, Vol. 44, Part 2.

Breman, Jan, 1999b, 'Industrial Labour in Post-Colonial India – II: Employment in the Informal Sector Economy', *International Review of Social History*, Vol. 44, Part 3.

Breman, Jan, 1999c, 'The study of industrial labour in post-colonial India – The informal sector: A concluding review', in Jonathan Parry, *et al.*, (eds.), *The Worlds of Indian Industrial Labour*, London and New Delhi: Sage Publications.

Breman, Jan, 2002, 'New Thoughts on Colonial Labour in Indonesia', *Journal of Southeast Asian Studies*, Vol. 33, No. 2.

Breman, Jan, 2003, *The Labouring Poor in India: Patterns of Exploitation, Subordination, and Exclusion*, New Delhi: Oxford University Press.

Breman, Jan 2004, *The Making and Unmaking of an Industrial Working Class: Sliding Down the Labour Hierarchy in Ahmedabad, Gujarat*, Delhi: Oxford University Press.

Breman, Jan, 2007, *Labour Bondage in West India: From Past to Present*, New Delhi: Oxford University Press.

Brittain, James J., 2005, 'A Theory of Accelerating Rural Violence: Lauchlin Currie's Role in Underdeveloping Colombia', *The Journal of Peasant Studies*, Vol. 32, No. 2.

Broomfield, Nick (director), (2006), *Ghosts*, a film scripted by Jez Lewis and Nick Broomfield (with Ai Qin Lin, Zhe Wei and Zhan Yu). Produced/distributed by Channel 4 and Tartan Films [see Review 3].

Browning, R., 1964, *Slave Society: Some Problems*, London: CPGB.

Bücher, Carl, 1907, *Industrial Evolution* (translated from the third German edition by S. Morley Wickett), New York: Henry Holt and Company.

Buck, Solon J., 1920, *The Agrarian Crusade: A Chronicle of the Farmer in Politics*, New Haven, CT: Yale University Press.

Bukharin, N., and E. Preobrazhensky, 1922, *The ABC of Communism* (Translated by Eden and Cedar Paul), London: The Communist Party of Great Britain.

Bush, M.L., 2000, *Servitude in Modern Times*, Cambridge: Polity.

Byres, Terence J., 1974, 'Land Reform, Industrialization and the Marketed Surplus in India: An Essay on the Power of Rural Bias', in A.D. Lehmann (ed.), *Agrarian Reform and Agrarian Reformism*, London: Faber and Faber.

Byres, Terence J., 1982, 'The Political Economy of Technological Innovation in Indian Agriculture', in R.S. Anderson, P.R. Brass, E. Levy, and B.R. Morrison (eds.), *Science, Politics and the Agricultural Revolution in Asia*, Boulder, CO: Westview Press.

Byres, Terence J., 1987, 'Sukhamoy Chakravarty on Marxist Economics and Contemporary Developing Economies: Some Comments,' *Cambridge Journal of Economics*, Vol. 11, No. 2.

Byres, Terence J., 1991, 'The Agrarian Question and Differing Forms of Capitalist Agrarian Transition: An Essay with reference to Asia', in Jan Breman and Sudipto Mundle (eds.), *Rural Transformation in Asia*, Delhi: Oxford University Press.

Byres, Terence J., 1995, 'Political Economy, the Agrarian Question and the Comparative Method', *The Journal of Peasant Studies*, Vol. 22, No. 4.

Byres, Terence J., 1996, *Capitalism from Above and Capitalism from Below*, London: Macmillan.

Byres, Terence J., 1998, 'The Need for the Comparative Method in the Social Sciences: An Essay with the Agrarian Question in India in Mind,' in Deepak Nayyar (ed.), *Economics as Ideology and Experience*, London and Portland, OR: Frank Cass Publishers.

Byres, Terence J., 1999, 'Rural Labour Relations in India: Persistent Themes, Common Processes and Differential Outcomes', *The Journal of Peasant Studies*, Vol. 26, Nos. 2–3.

Byres, Terence J., 2000, 'Pre-capitalist Economic Formations and Differential Agricultural Productivity: A Tentative Hypothesis', in K.N. Panikkar, Terence J. Byres, and Utsa Patnaik (eds.), *The Making of History: Essays presented to Irfan Habib*, New Delhi: Tulika.

Byres, Terence J., 2003, 'Paths of Capitalist Agrarian Transition in the Past and in the Contemporary World', in V.K. Ramachandran and Madhura Swaminathan (eds.), *Agrarian Studies: Essays on Agrarian Relations in Less Developed Countries*, London: Zed Books [see Review Essay 11].

Byres, Terence J., 2005, 'Neoliberalism and Primitive Accumulation in Less Developed Countries', in A. Saad Filho and D. Johnston (eds.), *Neoliberalism: A Critical Reader*, London: Pluto Press.

Caballero, José María, 1980, *Agricultura, reforma agraria y pobreza campesina*, Lima: Instituto de Estudios Peruanos.

Caballero, José María, 1981, *From Belaunde to Belaunde: Peru's Military Experiment in Third-Roadism*, Cambridge: Centre of Latin American Studies, Working paper No. 36.

Caballero, José María, 1986, 'Agriculture and the Peasantry under Industrialization Pressures: Lessons from the Peruvian Experience', *Latin American Research Review*, Vol. 19, No. 2.

Calleros-Rodríguez, Hector, 2014, 'Land, conflict, and political process: the case of the Lacandon Community, Chiapas, Mexico (1972–2012)', *The Journal of Peasant Studies*, Vol. 41, Nos. 1–2.

Calvert, H., 1922, *The Wealth and Welfare of the Punjab: Being Some Studies in Punjab Rural Economics*, Lahore: Civil and Military Gazette Press.

Campbell, Sir George, 1879, *White and Black*, London: Chatto & Windus.

Canetti, Elias, 1962, *Crowds and Power* (translated from the German by Carol Stewart), London: Victor Gollancz Ltd.

Cannadine, David, 1992, *G.M. Trevelyan: A Life in History*, London: HarperCollins.

Canovan, Margaret, 1981, *Populism*, London: Junction Books.

Carey, John, 1987, *Original Copy: Selected Reviews and Journalism 1969–86*, London: Faber and Faber.

Carr-Saunders, A.M., P. Sargant Florence, and Robert Peers, 1940, *Consumers' Co-operation in Great Britain: An Examination of the British Co-operative Movement*, London: George Allen & Unwin, Ltd.

Carter, A., 1971, *The Political Theory of Anarchism*, London: Routledge & Kegan Paul, Ltd.

Castro Pozo, Hildebrando, 1936, *Del Ayllu al cooperativismo socialista*, Lima: Biblioteca de la revista de Economia y Finanzas.

Castro Pozo, Hildebrando, 1947, *El Yanaconaje en las Haciendas Piuranas*, Lima: Compañía de Impresiones y Publicidad.

Catanach, I.J., 1970, *Rural Credit in Western India: Rural Credit and the Co-operative Movement in the Bombay Presidency, 1875–1930*, Berkeley, CA: University of California Press.

Caute, David, 1974, *Collisions: Essays and Reviews*, London: Quartet Books.

Caute, David, 1978, *The Great Fear: The Anti-Communist Purge Under Truman and Eisenhower*, London: Secker and Warburg.

Caute, David, 2013, *Isaac and Isaiah: The Covert Punishment of a Cold War Heretic*, New Haven, CT: Yale University Press [see Review 6].

Chakravarty, Sukhamoy, 1987, 'Marxist Economics and Contemporary Developing Economies', *Cambridge Journal of Economics*, Vol. 11, No. 1.

Chakravorty, Sanjoy, and Somik V. Lall, 2007, *Made in India: The Economic Geography and Political Economy of Industrialization*, New Delhi: Oxford University Press.

Chandra, Uday, 2015, 'Rethinking Subaltern Resistance', *The Journal of Contemporary Asia*, Vol. 45, No. 4.

Chattopadhyay, Boudhayan, S.C. Sharma and Aswini K. Ray, 1987, 'Rural/Urban Terms of Trade, Primary Accumulation and the Increasing Strength of the Indian Farm Lobby', in Boudhayan Chattopadhyay and Pierre Spitz (eds.), *Food Systems and Society in Eastern India*, Geneva: UNRISD.

Chaturvedi, Vinayak, 2000, 'Introduction', in Vinayak Chaturvedi (ed.), *Mapping Subaltern Studies and the Postcolonial*, London: Verso.

Chayanov, A.V., 1966, *The Theory of Peasant Economy* (edited by Daniel Thorner, Basile Kerblay and R.E.F. Smith), Homewood, IL: The American Economic Association.

Chayanov, A.V., 1991, *The Theory of Peasant Co-operatives* (translated by David Wedgwood Benn, introduction by Viktor Danilov), London and New York: I.B. Tauris & Co., Ltd.

Chomsky, Noam, 1969, 'Objectivity and Liberal Scholarship', in Conor Cruise O'Brien and William Dean Vanech (eds.), *Power and Consciousness*, London and New York: New York University Press.

Chonchol, Jacques, 1973, 'The Agrarian Policy of the Popular Government', in J. Ann Zammit (ed.), *The Chilean Road to Socialism*, Brighton: The Institute of Development Studies at the University of Sussex.

Chopra, Suneet, 1985, 'Bondage in a Green Revolution Area: A Study of Brick Kiln Workers in Muzaffarnagar District', in U. Patnaik and M. Dingwaney (eds.), *Chains of Servitude: Bondage and Slavery in India*, Madras: Sangham Books.

Chossudovsky, Michel, 1986, *Towards Capitalist Restoration? Chinese Socialism after Mao*, London: Macmillan.

Chowdhry, Prem, 1993, 'High Participation, Low Evaluation: Women and Work in Rural Haryana', *Economic and Political Weekly*, Vol. 28, No. 52.

Chowdhry, Prem, 1994, *The Veiled Woman: Shifting Gender Equations in Rural Haryana, 1880–1990*, Delhi: Oxford University Press.

Cleaves, Peter S., and Martin J. Scurrah, 1980, *Agriculture, Bureaucracy, and Military Government in Peru*, Ithaca, NY: Cornell University Press.

Clegg, Ian, 1971, *Workers' Self-Management in Algeria*, London: Allen Lane and Penguin Press.

Clogg, Richard, 1986, *Politics and the Academy: Arnold Toynbee and the Koraes Chair*, London: Frank Cass Publishers.

Clover, Charles, 2016, *Black Wind, White Snow: The Rise of Russia's New Nationalism*, New Haven, CT: Yale University Press.

Cobban, Alfred, 1964, *The Social Interpretation of the French Revolution*, Cambridge: Cambridge University Press.

Cochrane, Regina, 2007, 'Rural poverty and impoverished theory: Cultural populism, eco-feminism, and global justice', *The Journal of Peasant Studies*, Vol. 34, No. 2.

Cohn-Bendit, Daniel, and Gabriel Cohn-Bendit, 1968, *Obsolete Communism: The Left-Wing Alternative*, New York: McGraw-Hill Book Company.

Colley, Linda, 1992, *Britons: Forging the Nation, 1707–1837*, London: Pimlico.

Collini, Stefan, 2006, *Absent Minds: Intellectuals in Britain*, Oxford: Oxford University Press.

Collins, Henry, and Chimen Abramsky, 1965, *Karl Marx and the British Labour Movement: Years of the First International*. London: Macmillan & Co. Ltd.

Comninel, George C., 1987, *Rethinking the French Revolution: Marxism and the Revisionist Challenge*, London: Verso.

Conlin, Sean, 1974, 'Participation versus Expertise', in Pierre van den Berghe (ed.), *Class and Ethnicity in Peru*, Leiden: E.J. Brill.

Corbridge, Stuart, 1990 'Post-Marxism and Development Studies: Beyond the Impasse', *World Development*, Vol. 18, No. 5.

Corbridge, Stuart, 1994 'Post-Marxism and Post-Colonialism: The Needs and Rights of Distant Strangers', in David Booth (ed.), *Rethinking Social Development*, London: Longman Scientific & Technical.

Corbridge, Stuart, 1998 '"Beneath the Pavement Only Soil": The Poverty of Post-Development', *The Journal of Development Studies*, Vol. 34, No. 6.

Corbridge, Stuart, and Gareth A. Jones, 2005, 'The Continuing Debate About Urban Bias: Its Critics, Its Influence, and Implications for Poverty Reduction', Report for the Department for International Development (DfID), London.

Corbridge, Stuart, and John Harriss, 2000, *Reinventing India: Liberalization, Hindu Nationalism and Popular Democracy*, Oxford: Polity Press [see Review 1].

Costello, C., and M. Freedland (eds.), 2014, *Migrants at Work: Immigration and Vulnerability in Labour Law*, Oxford: Oxford University Press.

Coupland, R., 1933, *The British Anti-Slavery Movement*, London: Thornton Butterworth, Ltd.

Cox, C.B., and A.E. Dyson (eds.), 1969–77, *Black Papers on Education*, London: The Critical Quarterly Society.

Crabtree, John, 2003, 'The Impact of Neo-liberal Economics on Peruvian Peasant Agriculture in the 1990s', in Tom Brass (ed.), *Latin American Peasants*, London and Portland, OR: Frank Cass Publishers.

Craig, Wesley W., 1969, 'Peru: The Peasant Movement of La Convención', in Henry A. Landsberger (ed.), *Latin American Peasant Movements*, Ithaca, NY: Cornell University Press.

Cuadros, Carlos F., 1949, 'El arriendo y la reforma agraria en la provincia de La Convención', *Revista Universitaria de la Universidad Nacional de Cuzco*, Vol. XXXVIII, No. 96.

Daniel, E. Valentine, *et al.*, (eds.), 1992, *Plantations, Proletarians and Peasants in Colonial Asia*, London and Portland, OR: Frank Cass Publishers.

Danilov, V.P., 1988, *Rural Russia under the New Regime* (translated and introduced by Orlando Figes), London and Bloomington, IN: Hutchinson and Indiana University Press.

Darling, Malcom Lyall, 1925, *The Punjab Peasant in Prosperity and Debt*, London and Bombay: Oxford University Press.

Darling, Malcom Lyall, 1930, *Rusticus Loquitur, or the Old Light and the New in the Punjab Village*, London: Oxford University Press.

Darling, Malcom Lyall, 1934, *Wisdom and Waste in the Punjab Village*, London: Oxford University Press.

Darling, Malcom Lyall, 1949, *At Freedom's Door*, London: Oxford University Press.

Das, Arvind N., 1979, *Does Bihar Show the Way?* Calcutta: Research India Publications.

Das, Raju, 1996, 'State theories: A critical analysis', *Science & Society*, Vol. 60, No. 1.

Das, Raju, 2005, 'Rural society, the State and social capital in Eastern India: A critical investigation', *The Journal of Peasant Studies*, Vol. 32, No. 1.

Das, Raju, 2007, 'Looking, but not seeing: The State and/as class in rural India', *The Journal of Peasant Studies*, Vol. 34, Nos. 3–4.

Das, Raju, 2013, 'The Relevance of Marxist Academics', *Class, Race and Corporate Power*, Vol. 1, No. 1, Available at: http://digitalcommons.fiu.edu/classracecorporatepower/vol1/iss1/11.

Das, Raju, 2014, *A Contribution to the Critique of Contemporary Capitalism: Theoretical and International Perspectives*, New York: Nova Publishers [see Review 8].

David, Paul A., Herbert G. Gutman, Richard Sutch, Peter Temin, Gavin Wright, 1976, *Reckoning with Slavery: A Critical Study in the Quantitative History of American Negro Slavery*, New York: Oxford University Press.

de Kadt, Emmanuel, 1970, *Catholic Radicals in Brazil*, Oxford: Oxford University Press.

de Neve, Geert, 1999, 'Asking for and Giving *Baki*: Neo-bondage, or the Interplay of Bondage and Resistance in the Tamil Nadu Power-Loom Industry', in Jonathan Parry, *et al.*, (eds.), *The Worlds of Indian Industrial Labour*, London and New Delhi: Sage Publications.

de Neve, Geert, 2005, *The Everyday Politics of Labour: Working Lives in India's Informal Economy*, Delhi: Social Science Press.

de Ste Croix, G.E.M., 1981, *The Class Struggle in the Ancient Greek World*, London: Duckworth.

de Ste Croix, G.E.M., 1984, 'Class in Marx's Conception of History, Ancient and Modern', *New Left Review*, No. 146.

de Tocqueville, Alexis. 1850. *On the State of Society in France before the Revolution of 1789 and on the Causes which led to that Event*. London: John Murray, Albemarle Street.

de Vylder, Stefan, 1976, *Allende's Chile: The political economy of the rise and fall of the Unidad Popular*, Cambridge: Cambridge University Press.

Deere, C., Niurka Pérez, and Ernel Gonzales, 1994, 'The View from Below: The Cuban Agricultural Sector in the "Special Period in Peacetime"', *The Journal of Peasant Studies*, Vol. 21, No. 2.

Degler, C.N., 1976, 'The Irony of American Negro Slavery', in H.P. Owens (ed.), *Perspectives and Irony in American Slavery*, Jackson, MI: University of Mississipi Press.

Delande, Nicolas, 2013, 'Zomia, Land Without State', www.books&ideas.net/Zomia-Land-Without.

Desai, A.R., 1984, *India's Path of Development: A Marxist Approach*, Bombay: Popular Prakashan.

Dingwaney, Manjari, 1985, 'Unredeemed Promises: The Law and Servitude', in Utsa Patnaik and Manjari Dingwaney (eds.) *Chains of Servitude: Bondage and Slavery in India*, Madras: Sangham Books.

Dobb, M., 1955, *On Economic Theory and Socialism: Collected Papers*. London: Routledge & Kegan Paul.

Domike, Arthur L., 1973, 'The Politics of Land Reform', *Latin America Review of Books*, No. 1 (Spring).

Dorner, Peter, 1972, *Land Reform and Economic Development*, Harmondsworth: Penguin Books.

Dossani, Rafiq, 2008, *India Arriving: How This Economic Powerhouse is Redefining Global Business*, New York: American Management Association.

Douglass, Frederick, 1845, *Narrative of the Life of Frederick Douglass*, Boston, MA: Anti-Slavery Office.

Drèze, Jean, and Amartya Sen, 1989, *Hunger and Public Action*, Oxford: Clarendon Press.

Drieu la Rochelle, Pierre, 1958 [1939], 'The New Fact of the Twentieth Century', in Justin O'Brien (ed.), *From the Nouvelle Revue Français*, New York: Farrar, Straus and Cudahy.

Dummett, M., 2001, *On Immigration and Refugees*. London: Routledge.

Dumont, Louis, 1970, *Homo Hierarchicus*, London: Weidenfeld & Nicolson.

Duràn de Huerta, Marta, and Nicholas Higgins, 1999, 'An interview with Subcomandante Insurgente Marcos, spokesperson and military commander of the Zapatista National Liberation Army (EZLN)', *International Affairs*, Vol. 75, No. 2.

Eckstein, Schlomo, and Thomas F. Carroll, 1976, 'Peasant Cooperation in Land Reform Programs', in June Nash, Jorge Dandler, and Nicolas J. Hopkins (ed.), *Popular Participation in Social Change: Cooperatives, Collectives and Nationalized Industry*, The Hague and Chicago, IL: Mouton and Aldine Press.

Edelman, Marc and Carwil James, 2011, 'Peasants' rights and the UN system: quixotic struggle? Or emancipatory idea whose time has come?' *The Journal of Peasant Studies*, Vol. 38, No. 1.

Emmer, P.C., 1984, 'The Importation of British Indians into Surinam (Dutch Guiana), 1873–1916', in Shula Marks and Peter Richardson (eds.), *International Labour Migration: Historical Perspectives*, London: Maurice Temple Smith.

Emmer, P.C., 1987, 'Asians Compared: Some Observations regarding Indian and Indonesian Indentured Labourers in Surinam, 1873–1939', *Itinerario*, Vol. XI, No.1.

Emmer, P.C., 1992, 'The Price of Freedom: The Constraints of Change in Postemancipation America', in Frank McGlynn and Seymour Drescher (eds.), *The Meaning of Freedom: Economics, Politics, and Culture After Slavery*, Pittsburgh, PA: University of Pittsburgh Press.

Emmer, P.C., 1997a, 'European Expansion and Unfree Labour', *Itinerario*, Vol. XXI, No.1.

Emmer, P.C., 1997b, 'Caribbean Plantations and Indentured Labour, 1640–1917: A Constructive or Destructive Deviation from the Free Labour Market?' *Itinerario*, Vol. XXI, No.1.

Engels, Frederick, 1975 [1844], 'The Condition of the Working Class in England', *Karl Marx Frederick Engels Collected Works*, Vol. 4, London: Lawrence & Wishart.

Engels, Frederick, 1990 [1894], 'The Peasant Question in France and Germany', *Karl Marx and Frederick Engels Collected Works*, Volume 27, London: Lawrence and Wishart.

Epstein, A.L., 1992, *Scenes from African Urban Life: Collected Copperbelt Essays*, Edinburgh: Edinburgh University Press.

Erickson, Charlotte, 1994, *Leaving England: Essays on British Emigration in the Nineteenth Century*, London & Ithaca: Cornell University Press.

Evans, Richard J., 2014, *Altered Pasts: Counterfactuals in History*, London: Little, Brown.

Fanon, Franz, 1963, *The Wretched of the Earth*. New York: Grove Press.

Fielding, Nigel, 1981, *The National Front*, London & Boston, MA: Routledge & Kegan Paul.

Figueroa, Adolfo, 1984, *Capitalist Development and Peasant Economy in Peru*, Cambridge: Cambridge University Press.

Fioravanti, Eduardo, 1974, *Latifundio y Sindicalismo Agrario en el Peru*, Lima: Instituto de Estudios Peruanos.

Fisher, A.G.B., 1946, *International Implications of Full Employment in Great Britain*, London and New York: RIIA.

Fishlow, Albert, 2003, 'Review of Alexander Gerschenkron *Economic Backwardness in Historical Perspective*,' http://eh.net/bookreviews/library/fishlow.shtml.

Fitzgerald, E.V.K., 1983, 'State Capitalism in Peru: A Model of Economic Development and Its Limits', in Cynthia McClintock and Abraham F. Lowenthal (eds.), *The Peruvian Experiment Reconsidered*, Princeton, NJ: Princeton University Press.

Florescano, Enrique (ed.), (1975), *Haciendas, Latifundios y Plantaciones en América Latina*, México: siglo veintiuno editores, sa.

Fogel, Robert W., and Stanley M. Engerman, 1974, *Time on the Cross: Volume I – The Economics of American Negro Slavery*, London: Wildwood House.

Foner, Laura, and Eugene D. Genovese (eds.), 1969, *Slavery in the New World*, Englewood Cliffs, NJ: Prentice-Hall, Inc.

Ford, R., and M. Goodwin, 2014, *Revolt on the Right: Explaining support for the radical right in Britain*, London: Routledge.

Fortes, Meyer, 1945, 'An Anthropologist's Point of View', in Rita Hinden (ed.), *Fabian Colonial Essays*, London: George Allen and Unwin Ltd.

Frantz, Elizabeth, 2013, 'Jordan's Unfree Workforce: State-Sponsored Bonded Labour in the Arab Region,' *The Journal of Development Studies*, Vol. 49, No. 8.

Friedman, M., 1962, *Capitalism and Freedom*, Chicago, IL: University of Chicago Press.

Furedi, Frank, 2004, *Where Have All the Intellectuals Gone? Confronting 21st Century Philistinism*, London: Continuum.

Furnivall, J.S., 1944, *Netherlands India: A Study of Plural Economy*, New York: The Macmillan Company.

Galeski, Boguslaw, 1972, *Basic Concepts of Rural Sociology*, Manchester: Manchester University Press.

Gay, Peter, 1952, *The Dilemma of Democratic Socialism: Eduard Bernstein's Challenge to Marx*, New York: Columbia University Press.

Geras, Norman, 1998, *The Contract of Mutual Indifference*, London: Verso.

Gerschenkron, Alexander, 1943, *Bread and Democracy in Germany*, Berkeley, CA: University of California Press.

Gerschenkron, Alexander, 1955, 'The Problem of Economic Development in Russian Intellectual History of the Nineteenth Century,' in Ernest J. Simmons (ed.), *Continuity and Change in Russian and Soviet Thought*, Cambridge, MA: Harvard University Press.

Gerschenkron, Alexander, 1962, *Economic Backwardness in Historical Perspective*, Cambridge, MA: Harvard University Press.

Ghanshyam Shah, Mario Rutten, and Hein Streefkerk (eds.), (2002), *Development and Deprivation in Gujarat: In Honour of Jan Breman*, New Delhi: Sage [see Review 2].

Gibbon, Peter, and Michael Neocosmos, 1985, 'Some Problems in the Political Economy of "African Socialism"', in Henry Bernstein and Bonnie K. Campbell (eds.), *Contradictions of Accumulation in Africa: Studies in Economy and State*, Beverley Hills, CA: Sage Publications.

Giddens, A. (ed.), 2003, *The Progressive Manifesto: New Ideas for the Centre-Left*, Cambridge: Polity Press.

Gill, Sucha Singh, 1995, 'The Farmers' Movement and Agrarian Change in the Green Revolution Belt of Northwest India', in Tom Brass (ed.) *New Farmers' Movements in India*, London: Frank Cass Publishers (a special issue of *The Journal of Peasant Studies*).

Gilroy, Paul, Lawrence Grossberg, and Angela McRobbie (eds.), 2000, *Without Guarantees: In Honour of Stuart Hall*, London: Verso.

Gonzales, Alberto, and Germán Torre (eds.), 1985, *Las parcelaciones de las cooperativas agrarias del Peru*, Chiclayo: Centro de Estudios Sociales 'Solidaridad'.

Goodman, David, and Michael Redclift, 1981, *From Peasant to Proletarian: Capitalist Development and Agrarian Transitions*, Oxford: Basil Blackwell.

Goodwin, M., and C. Milazzo, 2015, *UKIP: Inside the campaign to redraw the map of British politics*, Oxford: Oxford University Press.

Gott, Richard, 1970, *Guerrilla Movements in Latin America*, London: Nelson.

Gould, Julius, 1977, *The Attack on Higher Education: Marxist and Radical Penetration*, London: Institute for the Study of Conflict.

Gouldner, Alvin W., 1979, *The Future of Intellectuals and the Rise of the New Class*, London: Macmillan.

Goyder, George, 1951, *The Future of Private Enterprise: A Study in Responsibility*, Oxford: Basil Blackwell.

Graeber, David, 2011, *Debt: The First 5,000 Years*, New York: Melville House Publishing [see Review 7].

Graeber, David, 2013, *The Democracy Project: A History, a Crisis, a Movement*, London: Allen Lane [see Review 7].

Grant, Andrew, 2013, 'Review: The Art of Not Being Governed', *Asian Highland Perspectives*, Vol. 28.

Graves, Adrian, 1993, *Cane and Labour: The Political Economy of the Queensland Sugar Industry, 1862–1906*, Edinburgh: Edinburgh University Press.

Griffin, Keith, 1970, 'Reform and Diversification in a Coffee Economy: The Case of Guatemala', in Paul Streeten (ed.), *Unfashionable Economics: Essays in Honour of Lord Balogh*, London: Weidenfeld and Nicolson.

Griffin, Keith, 1987, *World Hunger and the World Economy*, London: Macmillan.

Guérin, Isabelle, 2013, 'Bonded Labour, Agrarian Changes and Capitalism: Emerging Patterns in South India,' *Journal of Agrarian Change*, Vol. 13, No. 3.

Guérin, Isabelle, Augenda Bhukuth, Kamala Marius-Gnanou, and Govindan Venkatasubramanian, 2004, *Indebtedness, Vulnerability to Bondage, and Microfinance*, Geneva: ILO.

Guérin, Isabelle, Marc Roesch, Govindan Venkatasubramanian, and Bert D'Espallier, 2012, 'Credit for whom and for what? The diversity of borrowing sources and uses in rural southern India,' *Journal of International Development*, Vol. 24.

Guevara, Ernesto 'Che', 1967, *Episodes of the [Cuban] Revolutionary War*. Havana: Book Institute.

Guha, Ranajit, 1982, 'On Some Aspects of the Historiography of Colonial India', in Ranajit Guha (ed.), *Subaltern Studies I*, New Delhi: Oxford University Press.

Guha, Ranajit (ed.), 1982–89, *Subaltern Studies I–VI*, New Delhi: Oxford University Press.

Guillet, David, 1981, 'Surplus Extraction, Risk Management and Economic Exchange among Peruvian Peasants', *The Journal of Development Studies*, Vol. 18, No. 1.

Gutman, Herbert G., 1975, *Slavery and the Numbers Game: A Critique of Time on the Cross*, Urbana, IL: University of Illinois Press.

Hall, Derek, 2013, *Land*, Cambridge: Polity Press.

Hall, Stuart, 1960, 'The Supply of Demand,' in E.P. Thompson (ed.), *Out of Apathy*, London: New Left Books.

Hall, Stuart, 1977a, 'Rethinking the "Base-and-Superstructure" Metaphor', in Jon Bloomfield (ed.), *Class, Hegemony and Party*, London: Lawrence & Wishart.

Hall, Stuart, 1977b, 'The "Political" and the "Economic" in Marx's Theory of Classes,' in Alan Hunt (ed.), *Class and Class Structure*, London: Lawrence & Wishart.

Hall, Stuart, 1988, *The Hard Road to Renewal: Thatcherism and the Crisis of the Left*, London: Verso.

Hall, Stuart, 1989a, 'The Meaning of New Times,' in Stuart Hall and Martin Jacques (eds.), *New Times: The Changing Face of Politics in the 1990s*, London: Lawrence & Wishart.

Hall, Stuart, 1989b, 'Ethnicity: Identity and Difference,' *Radical America*, Vol. 23, No. 4.

Hamid, M., 2014, *Discontent and its Civilizations: Dispatches from Lahore, New York, London*, London: Hamish Hamilton.

Hardt, Michael, and Antonio Negri, 2001, *Empire*, Cambridge, MA: Harvard University Press.

Hardt, Michael, and Antonio Negri, 2005, *Multitude: War and Democracy in the Age of Empire*, London: Hamish Hamilton.

Harris, Marvin, 1969, 'The Myth of the Friendly Master', in L. Foner and E.D. Genovese (eds.), *Slavery in the New World*, Englewood Cliffs, NJ: Prentice-Hall, Inc.

Harris, Sir John, 1933, *A Century of Emancipation*, London: J.M. Dent & Sons, Ltd.

Harriss, John, 1982a, *Capitalism and Peasant Farming: Agrarian Structure and Ideology in Northern Tamil Nadu*, Bombay: Oxford University Press.

Harriss, John, 1982b, 'Introduction', in John Harriss (ed.), *Rural Development: Theories of peasant economy and agrarian change*, London: Hutchinson University Library.

Harriss, John, 1992, 'Does the "Depressor" Still Work? Agrarian Structure and Development in India – A Review of Evidence and Argument', *The Journal of Peasant Studies*, Vol. 19, No. 2.

Harriss, John, 1994, 'Between Economism and Postmodernism: Reflections on Research on "Agrarian Change" in India', in David Booth (ed.), *Rethinking Social Development*, London: Longman Scientific & Technical.

Harriss, John, 1997 'Rural Development and Agrarian Change in the "Post-Peasant" Era', unpublished paper presented to a LSE Workshop on Rural Labour in India Today, 19–20 June.

Harriss, John, 1998, 'Development Studies and the Development of India: An Awkward Case?' *Oxford Development Studies*, Vol. 26, No. 3.

Harriss, John, 2002b, *Depoliticizing Development: The World Bank and Social Capital*, London: Wimbledon Publishing Company.

Harriss, John, 2005, 'Great promise, hubris and recovery: a participant's history of development studies', in Uma Kothari (ed.), *A Radical History of Development Studies: Individuals, Institutions and Ideologies*, London: Zed Books [see Review Essay 11].

Harriss, John, 2009, *Power Matters: Essays on Institutions, Politics, and Society in India*, Delhi: Oxford University Press.

Harriss, John, Janet Hunter and Colin M. Lewis (eds.), 1995 *The New Institutional Economics and Third World Development*, London: Routledge.

Harriss-White, Barbara, 1981, *Transitional Trade and Rural Development: The Nature and Role of Agricultural Trade in a South Indian District*, New Delhi: Vikas Publishing House.

Harriss-White, Barbara, 1984, *State and Market: State Intervention in Agricultural Exchange in a Dry Region of Tamil Nadu: South India*, New Delhi: Concept Publishing Company.

Harriss-White, Barbara, 1991, 'Another Awkward Class: Merchants and Agrarian Change in India', in Henry Bernstein, Ben Crow, Maureen Mackintosh, and Charlotte Martin (eds.), *The Food Question*, London: Earthscan Publications, Ltd.

Harriss-White, Barbara, 1992, 'Real Foodgrains Markets and State Intervention in India', *European Journal of Development Research*, Vol. 4, No. 2.

Harriss-White, Barbara, 1996, *A Political Economy of Agricultural Markets in South India: Masters of the Countryside*, New Delhi: Sage Publications.

Harriss-White, Barbara, 1999, 'State, Market, Collective and Household Action in India's Social Sector', in Barbara Harriss-White and S. Subramanian (eds.), *Illfare in India*, New Delhi: Sage Publications.

Harriss-White, Barbara, 2003a, *India Working: Essays on Society and Economy*, Cambridge: Cambridge University Press.

Harriss-White, Barbara, 2003b, 'On Understanding Markets as Social and Political Institutions in Developing Economies', in Ha-Joon Chang (ed.), *Rethinking Development Economics*, London: Anthem.

Harriss-White, Barbara, and Nandini Gooptu, 2000, 'Mapping India's World of Unorganized Labour', in Leo Panitch and Colin Leys (eds.), *Socialist Register 2001*, London: The Merlin Press.

Harvey, David, 2003, *The New Imperialism*, Oxford: Oxford University Press.

Hasan, Zoya, 1995, 'Shifting Ground: Hindutva Politics and the Farmers' Movement in Uttar Pradesh', in Tom Brass (ed.) *New Farmers' Movements in India*, London: Frank Cass Publishers (a special issue of *The Journal of Peasant Studies*).

Haslam, Jonathan, 2000, *The Vices of Integrity: E.H. Carr, 1892–1982*, London: Verso.

Hawthorn, Geoffrey P., 1978, *Population and Development*, London: Frank Cass.

Hawthorn, Geoffrey P., 1991, *Plausible Worlds: Possibility and Understanding in History and the Social Sciences*, Cambridge: Cambridge University Press.

Hayek, F.A. (ed.), 1954, *Capitalism and the Historians*, London: Routledge & Kegan Paul Limited.

Hayek, F.A., 1960, *The Constitution of Liberty*, London: Routledge & Kegan Paul.

Henninger, Max, 2014, 'Poverty, Labour, Development: Towards a Critique of Marx's Conceptualisations,' in Marcel van der Linden and Karl Heinz Roth (eds.), *Beyond Marx: Theorising the Global Labour Relations of the Twenty-First Century*, Leiden: Brill.

Herring, Ronald J., and Rina Agarwala (eds.), 2008, *Whatever Happened to Class? Reflections from South Asia*, Delhi: Daanish Books.

Heuman, Gad, 1988, 'Runaway Slaves in Nineteenth Century Barbados', in L. Archer (ed.), *Slavery and Other Forms of Unfreedom*, London: Routledge.

Hewitt de Alcántara, C., 1984, *Anthropological Perspectives on Rural Mexico*, London: Routledge & Kegan Paul.

Hilton, Rodney (ed.), 1976, *The Transition from Feudalism to Capitalism*, London: New Left Books.

Hitchens, Christopher, 2000, *Unacknowledged Legislation*, London: Verso.

Hjejle, Benedicte, 1967, 'Slavery and Agricultural Bondage in South India in the Nineteenth Century', *The Scandanavian Economic History Review*, Vol.15, Nos.1 and 2.

Hobsbawm, Eric J., 1969a, 'A Case of Neo-Feudalism: La Convención, Peru', *Journal of Latin American Studies*, Vol. I, No. 1.

Hobsbawm, Eric J., 1969b, 'Maurice Dobb', in C.H. Feinstein (ed.), *Socialism, Capitalism and Economic Growth: Essays presented to Maurice Dobb*, Cambridge: Cambridge University Press.

Hobsbawm, Eric J., 1981, 'Observations on the Debate', in Martin Jacques and Francis Mulhern (eds.), *The Forward March of Labour Halted?* London: Verso.

Hobsbawm, Eric J., 1991, 'Out of the Ashes', in Robin Blackburn (ed.), *After the Fall: The Failure of Communism and the Future of Socialism*, London: Verso.

Hobsbawm, Eric J., 2009, 'Socialism has failed. Now capitalism is bankrupt. So what comes next?' *The Guardian* (London), 10 April.

Holbrook, David, 1994, *Even If They Fail*, London: Breese Books.

Horowitz, Irving Louis, Josué de Castro, and John Gerassi (eds.), 1969, *Latin American Radicalism*, London: Jonathan Cape Ltd.

Houben, Vincent J.H., and J. Thomas Lindblad (eds.), 1999, *Coolie Labour in Colonial Indonesia: A Study of Labour Relations in the Outer Islands, c.1900–1940*, Wiesbaden: Harrassowitz.

Houben, Vincent J.H., and J. Thomas Lindblad, 2002, 'Correspondence', *Journal of Southeast Asian Studies*, Vol. 33, No. 3.

Houellebecq, Michel, 2015, *Submission*, London: William Heinemann [see Review 9].

Houellebecq, Michel, and Bernard-Henri Levy, 2011, *Public Enemies*, London: Atlantic Books.

House of Commons Environment, Food and Rural Affairs Committee, 2003, *Gangmasters (Fourteenth Report of Session 2002–03)*, London: The Stationery Office Ltd.

Huizer, Gerrit, 1983a, 'The politics of rural development in Latin America: constraints on cooperatives and popular participation', *Boletín de Estudios Latinoamericanos y del Caribe*, No. 35.

Huizer, Gerrit, 1983b, 'Social polarization as a disruptive force in cooperatives: the case of the Te Huyro Central Cooperative in La Convención, Peru', *Boletín de Estudios Latinoamericanos y del Caribe*, No. 35.

Hussain, Athar, and Keith Tribe (eds.), 1984, *Paths of Development in Capitalist Agriculture: Readings from German Social Democracy, 1891–99*, London: Macmillan.

Hutton, J.H., 1929, 'Diaries of Two Tours in the Unadministered Area East of the Naga Hills,' *Memoirs of the Asiatic Society of Bengal*, Vol. XI, No. 1.

Hynes, James, 2001, *The Lecturer's Tale*, New York: Picador USA.

Ignatieff, Michael, 1998, 'Where Are They Now?' *Prospect/The London Observer*.

Im Thurn, Sir E.F. 1892, 'Notes on British Guiana', A paper read before The Royal Colonial Institute, 13 December, London.

International Labour Conference, 1929, *Forced Labour: Report and Draft Questionnaire*, Geneva: ILO.

International Labour Organization, 2001, *Stopping Forced Labour*, Geneva: ILO.

International Labour Organization, 2005, *A Global Alliance Against Forced Labour*, Geneva: ILO.

International Monetary Fund, 1998, *India: Recent Economic Developments*, Washington, DC: International Monetary Fund.

Isaac, Claudia B., 1995, 'Class Stratification and Cooperative Production among Rural Women in Central Mexico,' *Latin American Research Review*, Vol. 30, No. 2.

Isbell, Billie Jean, 1978, *To Defend Ourselves: Ecology and Ritual in an Andean Village*, Austin, TX: The University of Texas Press.

Ivanov, Y.M., 1979, *Agrarian Reforms and Hired Labour in Africa*, Moscow: Progress Publishers.

Jackson, Cecile, 1993, 'Women/Nature or Gender/History? A Critique of Ecofeminist "Development"', *The Journal of Peasant Studies*, Vol. 20, No. 3.

Jakobson, Roman, 1970, 'On Russian Fairy Tales', in Michael Lane (ed.), *Structuralism: A Reader*, London: Jonathan Cape.

James, C.L.R., 1938, *The Black Jacobins: Toussaint L'Overture and the Santo Domingo Revolution*, London: Secker and Warburg.

Jansen, Kees, and Esther Roquas, 2003, 'Devil Pact narratives in Rural Central America: Class, Gender and "Resistance"', in Tom Brass (ed.) *Latin American Peasants*, London: Frank Cass Publishers (a special issue of *The Journal of Peasant Studies*).

Jasny, Naum, 1972, *Soviet Economists of the Twenties*, Cambridge: Cambridge University Press.

Jodhka, Surinder S., 1994, 'Agrarian Changes and Attached Labour: Emerging Patterns in Haryana Agriculture', *Economic and Political Weekly*, Vol. XXIX, No. 39.

Jodhka, Surinder S., 1995, 'Agrarian Changes, Unfreedom and Attached Labour', *Economic and Political Weekly*, Vol. XXX, Nos. 30–31.

Jodhka, Surinder S., 1996, 'Interpreting Attached Labour in Contemporary Haryana', *Economic and Political Weekly*, Vol. XXXI, No. 21.

Jodhka, Surinder S., 1998, 'Attached Labour in Haryana', in J.S. Grewal and Hindu Banga (eds.), *Punjab in Prosperity and Violence*, Chandigarh: Institute of Punjab Studies.

Jodhka, Surinder S., 2004, 'Unfree Labour and "Postmodern Myths": Towards a Critical Re-examination', *Historical Materialism*, Vol. 12, No. 4.

Jodhka, Surinder S., 2007, 'The Other Side of Development: Poverty, Bondage and Marginalisation of the Rural Underclass', *Economic and Political Weekly*, Vol. XLII, No. 39.

Johnson, Heather, 2004, 'Subsistence and Control: The Persistence of the Peasantry in the Developing World', *Undercurrent*, Vol. 1, No. 1.

Johnson, Paul, 1996, *Intellectuals*, London: Phoenix.

Kapadia, Karin, and Jens Lerche, 1999, 'Introduction', in T.J. Byres, K. Kapadia and J. Lerche (eds.), *Rural Labour Relations in India*, London: Frank Cass.

Kapila, Raj, and Uma Kapila, 2002, *Economic Developments in India*, New Delhi: Academic Foundation.

Kapsoli, Wilfredo, *et al.*, 1974, *Régimen de hacienda y luchas campesinas: Huyro – La Convención*, Lima: Universidad Nacional de San Marcos.

Kautsky, Karl, 1988 [1899], *The Agrarian Question* (Introduction by Hamza Alavi and Teodor Shanin), Vols. 1 and 2, London and Winchester, MA: Zwan Books.

Kay, James Phillips, 1969 [1832], *The Moral and Physical Condition of the Working Classes employed in the Cotton Manufacture in Manchester*, Manchester: E.J. Morten (Publishers).

Kay-Shuttleworth, Sir James, 1973 [1873], *Thoughts and Suggestions on Certain Social Problems*, Manchester: E.J. Morten (Publishers).

Keen, B.A., 1946, *The Agricultural Development of the Middle East*, London: HMSO.

Klein, Naomi, 1999, *No Logo: Taking Aim at the Brand Bullies*, New York: St. Martin's Press.

Klinge, Gerardo, 1946, *Política Agrícola-Alimenticia*, Lima: Sociedad Nacional Agraria.

Kloosterboer, W., 1960, *Involuntary Labour since the Abolition of Slavery: A Survey of Compulsory Labour throughout the World*, Leiden: E.J. Brill.

Kofi, Tetteh A., 1978, 'Peasants and Economic Development: Populist Lessons for Africa', in Alan K. Smith and Claude E. Welch Jr. (eds.), *Peasants in Africa*, Waltham, MA: Crossroads Press for the African Studies Association, Brandeis University.

Kohli, Atul (ed.), 2001, *The Success of India's Democracy*, Cambridge: Cambridge University Press.

Korovkin, Tanya, 1990, *Politics of Agricultural Cooperativism: Peru, 1969–83*, Vancouver: University of British Columbia Press.

Kothari, Uma, 2005, *A Radical History of Development Studies: Individuals, Institutions and Ideologies*, London: Zed Books [see Review Essay 11].

Kothari, Uma, 2013, 'Geographies and Histories of Unfreedom: Indentured Labourers and Contract Workers in Mauritius,' *The Journal of Development Studies*, Vol. 49, No. 8.

Kremnev, I. [ps. A.V. Chayanov], 1977 [1920], 'The Journey of My Brother Alexei to the Land of Peasant Utopia', in R.E.F. Smith (ed.), *The Russian Peasant in 1920 and 1984*, London: Frank Cass Publishers.

Kritsman, L.N., 1984, 'Class Stratification of the Soviet Countryside', *The Journal of Peasant Studies*, Vol. 11, No. 2.

Kumar, Krishan, 2003, *The Making of English National Identity*, Cambridge: Cambridge University Press.

Kuper, Adam, 1973, *Anthropologists and Anthropology: The British School 1922–1972*, London: Allen Lane.

Kusuman, K.K., 1973, *Slavery in Travancore*, Trivandrum: Kerala Historical Society.

Lacey, Marian, 1981, *Working for Boroko: The Origins of a Coercive Labour System in South Africa*, Johannesburg: Ravan Press.

Lahr, John (ed.), 2002, *The Diaries of Kenneth Tynan*, London: Bloomsbury.

Lal, Deepak, 2004, *In Praise of Empires: Globalization and Order*, New York: Palgrave Macmillan.

Lamartine, Alphonse de, 1849, *History of the French Revolution of 1848*, London: Henry G. Bohn.

Langham, Ian, 1981, *The Building of British Social Anthropology: W.H.R. Rivers and his Cambridge Disciples in the Development of Kinship Studies, 1898–1931*, Dordrecht: D. Reidel Publishing Co.

Leach, Edmund, 1984, 'Notes on the Mythology of Cambridge Anthropology', *Cambridge Anthropology*, Vol. 9.

Leach, Edmund, 1988, *Noah's Second Son* (*Sermon before the University, King's College Chapel, 15 May 1988*), Cambridge: University Printing Services.

LeBaron, Genevieve, Forthcoming, 'Unfree Labor Beyond Binaries: Social Hierarchy, Insecurity, and Labor Market Restucturing,' *International Feminist Journal of Politics*.

Lebaron, Genevieve, and Alison J. Ayers, 2013, 'The Rise of a "New Slavery"? Understanding African unfree labour through neoliberalism,' *Third World Quarterly*, Vol. 34, No. 5.

Legassick, Martin, 1977, 'Gold, Agriculture, and Secondary Industry in South Africa, 1885–1970: From Periphery to Sub-Metropole as a Forced Labour System', in R. Palmer and N. Parsons (eds.), *The Roots of Rural Poverty in Central and Southern Africa*, London: Heinemann

Lele, Uma, 1981, 'Co-operatives and the Poor: A Comparative Perspective', *World Development*, Vol. 9, No. 1.

Lenin, V.I., 1961a [1901], 'The Agrarian Question and the "Critics of Marx"', *Collected Works*, Vol. 5, London: Lawrence & Wishart.

Lenin, V.I., 1961b [1902], 'What is to be Done?' *Collected Works*, Vol. 5, Moscow: Progress Publishers.

Lenin, V.I., 1962 [1907], 'Preface to the Russian Translation of *Letters by Johannes Becker, Joseph Dietzgen, Frederick Engels, Karl Marx, and Others to Friedrich Sorge and Others*', *Collected Works* 12, Moscow: Progress Publishers.

Lenin, V.I., 1964a [1899], 'The Development of Capitalism in Russia', *Collected Works*, Vol. 3, Moscow: Foreign Languages Publishing House.

Lenin, V.I., 1964b [1917], 'The Russian Revolution and Civil War', *Collected Works*, Vol. 26, Moscow: Progress Publishers.

Lenin, V.I., 1964c [1902], 'Revolutionary Adventurism', *Collected Works*, Vol. 6, London: Lawrence & Wishart.

Lenin, V.I., 1964d [1903], 'To the Rural Poor', *Collected Works*, Vol. 5, London: Lawrence & Wishart.

Lenin, V.I., 1964e, [1899], 'A Protest by Russian Social-Democrats', *Collected Works* 4, Moscow: Progress Publishers.

Lenin, V.I., 1966 [1923], 'On Co-operation', *Collected Works*, Vol. 33, Moscow: Progress Publishers.

Leons, William, 1982, 'Economic and Political Implications of a Rural Bolivian Cooperative', *International Social Science Review*, Vol. 57, No. 3.

Lerche, Jens, 1995, 'Is Bonded Labour a Bound Category? Reconceptualising Agrarian Conflict in India', *The Journal of Peasant Studies*, Vol. 22, No. 3.

Lerche, Jens, 1999, 'Politics of the Poor: Agricultural Labourers and Political Transformations in Uttar Pradesh', in T.J. Byres, K. Kapadia and J. Lerche (eds.), *Rural Labour Relations in India*, London: Frank Cass.

Lerche, Jens, 2007, 'An Alliance Against Forced Labour in India? Unfree Labour, Neoliberal Globalization and the International Labour Organization', http://www.qeh.ox.ac.uk/pdf-heyer07/lerche07-heyer-workshop.pdf.

Lévi-Strauss, Claude, and Didier Eribon, 1991, *Conversations with Claude Lévi-Strauss*, Chicago IL: The University of Chicago Press.

Lewin, M., 1968, *Russian Peasants and Soviet Power*, London: George Allen and Unwin Ltd.

Leys, Colin, 1996, *The Rise and Fall of Development Theory*, Oxford: James Currey.

Li, Huaiyin, 2005, 'Life Cycle, Labour Remuneration and Gender Inequality in a Chinese Agrarian Collective', *The Journal of Peasant Studies*, Vol. 32, No. 2.

Lichtenstein, A., 1996, *Twice the Work of Free Labor: The Political Economy of Convict Labor in the New South*, London: Verso.

Long, Norman, 1977, *An Introduction to the Sociology of Rural Development*, London: Tavistock Publications.

Long, Norman, 1988, 'Sociological Perspectives on Agrarian Development and State Intervention', in Anthony L. Hall and James Midgley (eds.), *Development Policies: Sociological Perspectives*, Manchester: Manchester University Press.

Long, Norman, 1989, 'The raison d'être for studying rural development interface', in Norman Long (ed.), *Encounters at the Interface: A Perspective on Social Discontinuities in Rural Development*, Wageningen, The Netherlands: Wageningen Studies in Sociology No. 27.

Lukács, Georg, 1972 [1919], '"Intellectual Workers" and the Problem of Intellectual Leadership', *Political Writings, 1919–1929*, (edited by Rodney Livingstone), London: NLB.

Luxemburg, Rosa, 1951 [1913], *The Accumulation of Capital* (translated from the German by Agnes Schwarzschild). London: Faber & Faber.

Luxemburg, Rosa, 1961, *The Russian Revolution and Leninism or Marxism?*, Ann Arbor, MI: University of Michigan Press.

Luxemburg, Rosa, 1970 [1915], 'The Junius Pamphlet: The Crisis in the German Social Democracy', in Mary-Alice Waters (ed.), *Rosa Luxemburg Speaks*, New York: Pathfinder Press, Inc.

Luxemburg, Rosa, 2013, *Complete Works – Volume I (Economic Writings 1)*, London: Verso.

MacLean y Estenós, Roberto, 1965, *La Reforma Agrarian en el Peru*, México, DF: Instituto de Investigaciones Sociales, UNAM.

Mahbubani, Kishore, 2008, *The New Asian Hemisphere: The Irresistible Shift of Global Power to the East*, New York: PublicAffairs.

Malamoud, C. (ed.), 1983, *Debts and Debtors*, New Delhi: Vikas Publishing House.

Mandel, E., 1980, *Long Waves of Capitalist Development: The Marxist Interpretation*, Cambridge: Cambridge University Press.

Mangru, Basdeo, 1987, *Benevolent Neutrality: Indian Government Policy and Labour Migration to British Guiana, 1854–1884*, London: Hansib Publishing.

Manickam, S., 1982, *Slavery in Tamil Country*, Madras: CLS.

Mann, Harold H., 1929, 'The Agriculture of India', *The Annals of the American Academy of Political and Social Science*, Vol. CXLV, Part II.

Mann, Harold H., 1967, *The Social Framework of Agriculture: India, Middle East, England* (edited by Daniel Thorner), Bombay: Vora & Co.

Manuel, Frank E., 1972, *Freedom from History, and Other Untimely Essays*, London: University of London Press, Ltd.

Manzo, Kate, 2005, 'Modern Slavery, Global Capitalism and Deproletarianisation in West Africa', *Review of African Political Economy*, Vol. 32, No. 106.

Marcuse, Herbert, 1970, *Five Lectures*. London: Allan Lane.

Maríategui, José Carlos, 1968 [1928], *Siete ensayos de interpretación de la realidad Peruana*, Lima: Biblioteca Amauta.

Marks, Shula, and Peter Richardson (eds.), 1984, *International Labour Migration: Historical Perspectives*, London: Maurice Temple Smith.

Marla, Sharma, 1981, *Bonded Labour in India*, New Delhi: Biblia Impex.

Marshall, P., 1992, *Demanding the Impossible: A History of Anarchism*, London: Fontana Press.

Martínez-Torres, María, and Peter M. Rosset, 2010, 'La Vía Campesina: the birth and evolution of a transnational social movement', *The Journal of Peasant Studies*, Vol. 37, No. 1.

Martins, José de Souza, 1997, 'The Reappearance of Slavery and the Reproduction of Capital on the Brazilian Frontier', in Tom Brass and Marcel van der Linden (eds.), *Free and Unfree Labour: The Debate Continues*, Bern: Peter Lang, AG.

Marx, Karl, 1969, *Theories of Surplus Value – Part II*, London: Lawrence & Wishart.

Marx, Karl, 1973a [1857–8], *Grundrisse* (translated by Martin Nicolaus), London: Penguin Books.

Marx, Karl, 1973b, *The First International and After* (edited by David Fernbach), London: Penguin Books.

Marx, Karl, 1975 [1844], 'Economic and Philosophical Manuscripts', in *Karl Marx – Early Writings* (Introduced by Lucio Colletti), Harmondworth: Penguin Books.

Marx, Karl, 1976, *Capital – Volume 1*, Harmondsworth: Penguin Books.

Marx, Karl, 1985 [1866], 'Instructions for the Delegates of the Provisional General Council: The Different Questions', Karl Marx Frederick Engels, *Collected Works*, Vol. 20, London: Lawrence & Wishart.

Marx, Karl, 1986 [1857–58], 'Economic Manuscripts of 1857–58', Karl Marx Frederick Engels, *Collected Works*, Vol. 28, London: Lawrence & Wishart.

Marx, Karl, and Fredrick Engels, 1934, *Correspondence 1846–1895*, London: Martin Lawrence Ltd.

Marx, Karl, and Frederick Engels, 1976a [1845], 'The German Ideology', *Collected Works*, Volume 5, London: Lawrence & Wishart.

Marx, Karl, and Frederick Engels, 1976b [1848], 'Manifesto of the Communist Party', *Collected Works*, Volume 6, London: Lawrence and Wishart.

Marxist Study Courses, 1932–33, *Marxist Study Courses 1–2 (History of the Working Class, Lessons I–IV; Political Economy, Lessons IV–XI)*, London: Martin Lawrence Ltd.

Mattick, Paul, 1971, *Marx and Keynes: The Limits of the Mixed Economy*, London: Merlin Press.

Mattick, Paul, 1978, *Anti-Bolshevik Communism*, London: Merlin Press.

Mattick, Paul, 1981, *Economic Crisis and Crisis Theory*, London: Merlin Press.

Mattick, Paul, 1983, *Marxism: Last Refuge of the Bourgeoisie?* (edited by Paul Mattick, Jr.), London: The Merlin Press.

Mayer, Peter, 1982, 'South India, North India: The Capitalist Transformation of two Provincial Districts', in H. Alavi *et al.*, *Capitalism and Colonial Production*, London & Canberra: Croom Helm.

Maynard, John, 1942, *The Russian Peasant: and Other Studies*, London: Victor Gollancz Ltd.

McClintock, Cynthia, 1981, *Peasant Cooperatives and Political Change in Peru*, Princeton, NJ: Princeton University Press.

McGlynn, Frank, and Seymour Drescher (eds.), 1992, *The Meaning of Freedom: Economics, Politics, and Culture After Slavery*, Pittsburgh, PA: University of Pittsburgh Press.

McMichael, Philip (ed.), 1994, *The Global Restructuring of Agro-Food Systems*, London and Ithaca, NY: Cornell University Press.

Meillassoux, C., 1975, *Maidens, Meal and Money*, Cambridge: Cambridge University Press.

Meillassoux, C., 1991, *The Anthropology of Slavery*, London: The Athlone Press.

Melmed-Sanjak, Jolyne S., and Michael R. Carter, 1991, 'The Economic Viability and Stability of "Capitalised Family Farming": An Analysis of Agricultural Decollectivisation in Peru', *The Journal of Development Studies*, Vol. 27, No. 2.

Mezzadra, S., 2006, *Diritto di fuga. Migrationi, Cittadinanza, Globalizzazione*, Verona: ombre corte.

Mezzada, S., 2011a, 'How many histories of labor? Towards a theory of postcolonial capitalism', *Postcolonial Studies*, Vol. 14, No. 2.

Mezzadra, S., 2011b, 'The gaze of autonomy: Capitalism, migration, and social struggles', in V. Squire (ed.), *The contested politics of mobility: borderzones and irregularity*, London: Routledge.

Mezzadra, S., and B. Neilson (eds.), 2013, *Border as Method, or the Multiplication of Labor*, Durham, NC: Duke University Press.

Miers, Suzanne, and Igor Kopytoff (eds.), 1977, *Slavery in Africa: Historical and Anthropological Perspectives*, Madison, WI: University of Wisconsin Press.

Mies, Maria, and Vandana Shiva, 1993, *Ecofeminism*, London: Zed Press.

Millar, J.P.M., c.1947, *What is Workers' Education?* Tillicoultry, Scotland: NCLC Publishing Society Ltd.

Mirsky, Dmitri, 1935, *The Intelligentsia of Great Britain* (translated by Alec Brown), London: Victor Gollancz Ltd.

Mitrany, David, 1951, *Marx against the Peasant*, Chapel Hill, NC: The University of North Carolina Press.

Moberg, Mark A., 1983, 'From Individuals to Class: The Dynamics of Peasant Cooperatives in Revolutionary Nicaragua', *Dialectical Anthropology*, Vol. 8, No. 3.

Montoya, Rodrigo, 1974, *La SAIS Cahuide y sus contradicciones*, Lima: Universidad Nacional de San Marcos.

Morand, Paul, 2002 [1971], *Venices*, London: Pushkin Press.

Moreno Fraginals, M., 1976, *The Sugarmill: The Socioeconomic Complex of Sugar in Cuba*, New York: Monthly Review Press.

Mörner, Magnus, 1991, 'The extent and limitations of change: Cuzco, Peru, 1895–1920', in Magnus Mörner and Thommy Svensson (eds.), *The Transformation of Rural Society in the Third World*, London: Routledge.

Mosley, Oswald, 1936, *Fascism: One Hundred Questions Asked and Answered*, London: BUF Publications.

Mukherji, Partha Nath, and Bhupati P. Sahoo, 1992, 'Agrarian Structure, Contradiction and Mobilization: A Framework for the Analysis of Emerging Rural Power', *Social Scientist*, Nos. 9–10.

Mundle, Sudipto, 1979, *Backwardness and Bondage*, New Delhi: Indian Institute of Public Administration.

Munslow, B., and H. Finch (eds.), 1984, *Proletarianisation in the Third World: Studies in the Creation of a Labour Force Under Dependent Capitalism*, London: Croom Helm.

Murra, John V., 1972, *El 'control vertical' de un máximo de pisos ecológicos en la economía de las sociedades Andinas,* Huanuco: Universidad Hermilio Valdizán.

Murra, John V., 1975, *Formaciones económicas y politicas del mundo andino,* Lima: Instituto de Estudios Peruanos.

Nader, Laura, 1997, 'The Phantom Factor: Impact of the Cold War on Anthropology', in André Schiffrin (ed.), *The Cold War and the University: Toward an Intellectual History of the Postwar Years,* New York: The New Press.

Nash, June, and Nicolas J. Hopkins, 1976, 'Anthropological Approaches to the Study of Cooperatives, Collectives, and Self-Management', in June Nash, Jorge Dandler, and Nicolas J. Hopkins (ed.), *Popular Participation in Social Change: Cooperatives, Collectives and Nationalized Industry,* The Hague and Chicago, IL: Mouton and Aldine Press.

Nayak, Satyendra S., 2008, *Globalization and the Indian Economy,* London and New York: Routledge.

Nayar, Baldev Raj (ed.), 2007, *Globalization and Politics in India,* New Delhi: Oxford University Press.

Neira, Hugo, 1968, *Los Andes: Tierra o Muerte,* Madrid: Editorial ZYX.

Newman, John Henry (Cardinal), 1899 [1838], 'Medieval Oxford', *Historical Sketches,* III, London, New York and Bombay: Longmans, Green, and Co.

Nisbet, Robert, 1971, *The Degradation of the Academic Dogma: The University in America 1945–1970,* New York: Basic Books.

Nock, A.J., 1935, *Our Enemy the State,* New York: W. Morrow & Company.

Nozick, R., 1975, *Anarchy, State and Utopia,* Oxford: Blackwell.

Nuijten, Monique, 2004, 'Peasant "Participation", Rural Property and the State in Western Mexico', *The Journal of Peasant Studies,* Vol. 31, No. 2.

O'Brien, Conor Cruise, 1969, 'Introduction', in Conor Cruise O'Brien and William Dean Vanech (eds.), *Power and Consciousness,* London and New York: New York University Press.

O'Meara, Dan, 1983, *Volkskapitalisme: Class, Capital and Ideology in the Development of Afrikaner Nationalism, 1934–1948,* Cambridge: Cambridge University Press.

Olmsted, Frederick Law, 1953, *The Cotton Kingdom: A Traveller's Observations on Cotton and Slavery in the American Slave States,* New York: Alfred A. Knopf.

Orde Browne, G. St. J., 1933, *The African Labourer,* London: Oxford University Press.

Orlove, Benjamin S., and Custred Glynn, 1980, 'The Alternative Model of Agrarian Society in the Andes: Households, Networks and Corporate Groups', in Benjamin S Orlove and Glynn Custred (eds.), *Land and Power in Latin America,* London and New York: Holmes & Meier Publishers, Inc.

Overton, James, 2000, 'Academic Populists, the Informal Economy and Those Benevolent Merchants: Politics and Income Security Reform in Newfoundland,' *The Journal of Peasant Studies,* Vol. 28, No. 1.

Owen, Roger, 1973, 'Imperial Policy and Theories of Social Change: Sir Alfred Lyall in India', in Talal Asad (ed.), *Anthropology and the Colonial Encounter*, London: Ithaca Press.

Oya, Carlos, 2004, 'The Empirical Investigation of Rural Class Formation: Methodological Issues in a Study of Large- and Mid-Scale Farmers in Senegal', *Historical Materialism*, Vol. 12, No. 4.

Panagaria, Arvind, 2008, *India: The Emerging Giant*, New York: Oxford University Press.

Panchamukhi, V.R., 2002, *Economic Development in India: Challenges and Perspectives*, Delhi: Bookwell Publications.

Panoff, Michel, 1994/5, 'Workers, Recruiters and Planters in the Bismark Archipelago, 1885–1914', *The Journal of Pacific Studies*, Vol. 18.

Patel, Raj, 2007, *Stuffed and Starved*, London: Portobello Books.

Patel, Raj, 2009a, *The Value of Nothing: How to reshape Market Society and Redefine Democracy*, London: Portobello Books Ltd.

Patel, Raj, 2009b, 'What does food sovereignty look like?' *The Journal of Peasant Studies*, Vol. 36, No. 3.

Patel, S.J., 1952, *Agricultural Labourers in Modern India and Pakistan*, Bombay: Current Book House.

Patel, Sujata, Jasodhara Bagchi, and Krishna Raj (eds.), 2002, *Thinking Social Science in India: Essays in Honour of Alice Thorner*, New Delhi: Sage [see Review 2].

Patnaik, Utsa, 1985, 'Introduction', in U. Patnaik and M. Dingwaney (eds.), *Chains of Servitude: Bondage and Slavery in India*, Madras: Sangham Books.

Patnaik, Utsa, 1995, 'On Capitalism and Agrestic Unfreedom', *International Review of Social History*, Vol. 40, Part 1.

Patnaik, Utsa, and Manjari Dingwaney (eds.), 1985, *Chains of Servitude: Bondage and Slavery in India*, Madras: Sangham Books.

Pattison, Mark, 1885, *Memoirs*, London: Macmillan & Co.

Paxman, Jeremy, 1999, *The English: A Portrait of a People*, London: Penguin.

Pearse, Andrew, 1980, *Seeds of Plenty, Seeds of Want: Social and Economic Implications of the Green Revolution*, Oxford: Clarendon Press.

Perlin, Ross, 2011, *Intern Nation: How to Earn Nothing and Learn Little in the Brave New Economy*, London: Verso [see Review 5].

Petras, James, 1969, *Politics and Social Forces in Chilean Development*, Berkeley, CA: University of California Press.

Petras, James, 1970, *Politics and Social Structure in Latin America*, New York: Monthly Review.

Petras, James, 1990, 'Retreat of the Intellectuals', *Economic and Political Weekly*, Vol. XXV, No. 38.

Petras, James, 1998, 'The Political and Social Basis of Regional Variation in Land Occupations in Brazil,' *The Journal of Peasant Studies*, Vol. 25, No. 4.

Petras, James, 2002, 'A Rose by Any Other Name? The Fragrance of Imperialism', *The Journal of Peasant Studies*, Vol. 29, No. 2.

Petras, James, 2003, *The New Development Politics: The Age of Empire Building and New Social Movements*, Aldershot: Ashgate.

Petras, James, 2006a, '"Centre Left" Regimes in Latin America: History Repeating Itself as Farce?' *The Journal of Peasant Studies*, Vol. 33, No. 2.

Petras, James, 2006b, *The Power of Israel in the United States*, Atlanta, GA: Clarity Press.

Petras, James, and Henry Veltmeyer, 1997, *Neoliberalism and Class Conflict in Latin America*, London and New York: Macmillan Press and St. Martin's Press.

Petras, James, and Henry Veltmeyer, 2001a, 'Are Latin American Peasant Movements Still a Force for Change? Some New Paradigms Revisited', *The Journal of Peasant Studies*, Vol. 28, No. 2.

Petras, James, and Henry Veltmeyer, 2001b, *Globalization Unmasked: Imperialism in the 21st Century*, London and Halifax: Zed Press and Fernwood.

Petras, James, and Henry Veltmeyer, 2003a, 'The Peasantry and the State in Latin America: A Troubled Past, an Uncertain Future,' in Tom Brass (ed.), *Latin American Peasants*, London and Portland, OR: Frank Cass Publishers.

Petras, James, and Henry Veltmeyer, 2003b, 'Whither Lula's Brazil? Neo-Liberalism and "Third Way" Ideology,' *The Journal of Peasant Studies*, Vol. 31, No. 1.

Petras, James, and Henry Veltmeyer, 2003c, *System in Crisis: The Dynamics of Free Market Capitalism*, London: Zed Books [see Review Essay 11].

Petras, James, and Henry Veltmeyer, 2005, *Social Movements and the State: Argentina, Bolivia, Brazil, Ecuador*, London: Pluto Press.

Petras, James, and Hugo Zemelman Merino, 1972, *Peasants in Revolt: A Chilean Case Study, 1965–71*, Austin, TX: The University of Texas Press.

Petras, James, and Morris Morley, 1990, *US Hegemony Under Siege: Class, Politics and Development in Latin America*, London and New York: Verso.

Petras, James, and Robert LaPorte Jr.,, 1971, *Cultivating Revolution: The United States and Agrarian Reform in Latin America*, New York: Random House.

Petras, James, Henry Veltmeyer and Luciano Vasapollo, 2005, *Empire and Imperialism*, London and Halifax: Zed Press and Fernwood.

Phelps Brown, E.H., 1962, *The Economics of Labor*, London & New Haven: Yale University Press.

Phillips, Nicola, 2011, 'Unfree labour and adverse incorporation in global production networks: comparative perspectives on Brazil and India,' *Chronic Poverty Research Centre*. Working Paper No. 176.

Phillips, Nicola, Stephanie Barrientos, John O'Neill, Wendy Olsen, Hillel Steiner and Karen Sykes, 2011, *Unfree Labour: Research Brief*, London: Economic and Social Research Council.

Piketty, Thomas, 2014, *Capital in the Twenty-First Century*, Cambridge, MA: Harvard University Press.

Piketty, Thomas, 2016, *Chronicles: On Our Troubled Times*, London: Viking.

Powderly, T.V., 1967 [1890], *Thirty Years of Labor, 1859–1889*, New York: Augustus M. Kelley Publishers.

Powell, Enoch, 1969, *Freedom and Reality*, London: B.T. Batsford Ltd.

Prakash, Gyan, 1990, *Bonded Histories: Genealogies of Labour Servitude in Colonial India*, Cambridge: Cambridge University Press.

Prakash, Gyan, 1992, 'The History and Historiography of Rural Labourers in Colonial India', in Gyan Prakash (ed.), *The World of the Rural Labourer in Colonial India*, Delhi: Oxford University Press.

Preobrazhensky, E.A., 1965, *The New Economics*, London: Oxford University Press.

Preobrazhensky, E.A., 1980, *The Crisis of Soviet Industrialization* (Edited by Donald A. Filtzer), London: Macmillan.

Ramachandran, V.K., and Madhura Swaminathan (eds.), 2003, *Agrarian Studies: Essays on Agrarian Relations in Less Developed Countries*, London: Zed Books [see Review Essay 11].

Rao, Mohan, 1999a, 'Agrarian Power and Unfree Labour', *The Journal of Peasant Studies*, Vol. 26, Nos. 2–3.

Rao, Mohan, 1999b, 'Freedom, Equality, Property and Bentham: The Debate over Unfree Labour,' *The Journal of Peasant Studies*, Vol. 27, No. 1.

Rawal, Vikas, 2004, 'Agricultural Labour and Unfreedom: Siri Workers in a Village in Western Haryana', accessed at http://www.cpim.org/marxist/200402_agri_labour_haryana.doc.

Reid, A. (ed.), 1983, *Slavery, Bondage and Dependency in Southeast Asia*, St Lucia: University of Queensland Press.

Renton, David, 2001, 'The Agrarian Roots of Fascism: German Exceptionalism Revisited', *The Journal of Peasant Studies*, Vol. 28, No. 4.

Richards, Paul, 2004, 'Private versus public? Agenda-setting in international agrotechnologies', in Kees Jansen and Sietze Vellema (eds.), *Agribusiness and Society: Corporate responses to environmentalism, market opportunities and public regulation*, London and New York: Zed Books.

Robbins, L., 1976, *Political Economy Past and Present: A review of leading theories of economic policy*, London: Macmillan.

Rodgers, Dennis, 1996, 'Rhetoric versus Reality: "Participatory Development," Cooperation and the Case of the AMUL Cooperative', *Cambridge Anthropology*, Vol. 19, No. 1.

Rodney, Walter, 1981, *A History of the Guyanese Working People, 1881–1905*, London: Heinemann.

Rosdolsky, R., 1977, *The Making of Marx's 'Capital'*, London: Pluto Press.

Rose, Jonathan, 2001, *The Intellectual Life of the British Working Classes*, New Haven, CT, and London: Yale University Press.

Rosset, Peter, 2013, 'Re-thinking agrarian reform, land and territory in La Vía Campesina', *The Journal of Peasant Studies*, Vol. 40, No. 4.

Roth, Karl Heinz, 1997, 'Unfree Labour in the Area under German Hegemony, 1930–1945: Some Historical and Methodological Questions', in Tom Brass and Marcel van der Linden (eds.), *Free and Unfree Labour: The Debate Continues*, Bern: Peter Lang, AG.

Rothbard, M., 1982, *The Ethics of Liberty*, Atlantic Highlands, NJ: Humanities Press.

Rothstein, Andrew, 1953, 'Marxism and "The Times Literary Supplement"', *The Modern Quarterly*, Vol. 8.

Rowbotham, Sheila, 1999, 'Locked in the Ivory Tower', *The Times Higher*, 13 November.

Rudra, Ashok, *et al.*, 1978, *Studies in the Development of Capitalism in India*, Lahore: Vanguard Books.

Ruskin History Workshop Students, 1981, 'Worker-Historians in the 1920s', in Raphael Samuel (ed.), *People's History and Socialist Theory*, London: Routledge & Kegan Paul Ltd.

Sahlins, Marshall, 1972, *Stone Age Economics*, Chicago and New York: Aldine Atherton, Inc.

Saintsbury, George, 1829/[1972], *East India Slavery*, Shannon: Irish University Press.

Salvadori, Massimo, 1979, *Karl Kautsky and the Socialist Revolution 1880–1938*, London: New Left Books.

Samuel, Raphael (ed.), 1989, *Patriotism: The Making and Unmaking of British National Identity – Vol. I (History and Politics)*, London: Routledge.

Sánchez, R., 1977, 'The Model of Verticality in the Andean Economy: A Critical Reconsideration', *Bulletin of the Society for Latin American Studies*, 27.

Sánchez, R., 1982, 'The Andean economic system and capitalism', in A.D. Lehmann (ed.), *Ecology and Exchange in the Andes*, Cambridge: Cambridge University Press.

Saradamoni, K., 1980, *Emergence of a Slave Caste*, New Delhi: People's Publishing House.

Saul, John S., 1969, 'Africa', in Ghiţa Ionescu and Ernest Gellner (eds.), *Populism: Its Meanings and National Characteristics*, London: Weidenfeld and Nicolson.

Saunders, Christopher, 1988, *The Making of the South African Past: Major Historians on Race and Class*, Cape Town & Johannesburg: David Philip.

Sawyer, Roger, 1986, *Slavery in the Twentieth Century*, London: Routledge & Kegan Paul.

Saxe-Fernandez, John, James Petras, Omar Nuñez, and Henry Veltmeyer, 2001, *Globalización, imperialismo y clase social*, Buenos Aires and Mexico City: Editorial Lumen.

Sayers, Sean, 2006, 'Marxist Philosophy in Britain: An Overview', Accessed at www.kent.ac.uk/secl/philosophy/staff/sayers.html.

Schiller, Otto M., 1969, *Cooperation and Integration in Agricultural Production*, London: Asia Publishing House.

Schlesinger, Rudolf, 1953, *Central European Democracy and its Background*. London: Routledge & Kegan Paul.

Schneider, Herbert W., 1928, *Making the Fascist State*, New York: Oxford University Press.

Scitovsky, T., 1958, *Economic Theory and Western European Integration*, London: George Allen & Unwin Ltd.

Scott, James C., 1976, *The Moral Economy of the Peasant: Rebellion and Subsistence in Southeast Asia*, New Haven, CT: Yale University Press.

Scott, James C., 1985, *Weapons of the Weak: Everyday Forms of Peasant Resistance*, New Haven, CT: Yale University Press.

Scott, James C., 1990, *Domination and the Arts of Resistance: Hidden Transcripts*, New Haven, CT: Yale University Press.

Scott, James C., 1998, *Seeing Like a State: How Certain Schemes to Improve the Human Condition Have Failed*, New Haven, CT: Yale University Press.

Scott, James C., 2009, *The Art of Not Being Governed: An Anarchist History of Southeast Asia*, London and New Haven, CT: Yale University Press [see Review Essay 12].

Scruton, Roger, 1985, *Thinkers of the New Left*, London: Claridge Press.

Scruton, Roger, 1987, *Untimely Tracts*, London: Macmillan Press.

Seligmann, Linda J., 1995, *Between Reform and Revolution: Political Struggles in the Peruvian Andes, 1969–1991*, Stanford, CA: Stanford University Press.

Sen, Amartya, 1975, *Employment, Technology and Development*, Oxford: Clarendon Press.

Sen, Amartya, 1980, 'Famine Mortality: A Study of the Bengal Famine of 1943', in E.J. Hobsbawm, Witold Kula, Ashok Mitra, K.N. Raj, and Ignacy Sachs (eds.), *Peasants in History: Essays in Honour of Daniel Thorner*, Delhi: Oxford University Press.

Sen, Amartya, 1981, *Poverty and Famines: An Essay on Entitlement and Deprivation*, Oxford: Clarendon Press.

Sen, Amartya, 1992, *Inequality Re-examined*, Oxford: Oxford University Press.

Sen, Amartya, 1999, *Development as Freedom*, Oxford: Clarendon Press.

Serge, Victor, 1963, *Memoirs of a Revolutionary 1901–1941*, London: Oxford University Press.

Shalin, Dmitri N., 1980, 'Marxist Paradigm and Academic Freedom', *Social Research*, Vol. 47.

Shanin, Teodor (ed.), 1988, *Peasants and Peasant Societies*, London: Penguin Books.

Shapiro, Karin A., 1998, *A New South Rebellion: The Battle against Convict Labor in the Tennessee Coalfields, 1871–1896*, Chapel Hill, NC, and London: The University of North Carolina Press.

Shepherd, C.Y., 1938, 'Farm Labour and Social Standards: Discussion', *Proceedings of the Fifth International Conference of Agricultural Economists*, London: Oxford University Press.

Shlomowitz, Ralph, Lance Brennan, and John McDonald, 1996, *Mortality and Migration in the Modern World*, Aldershot: Variorum.

Shoemaker, Robin, 1981, *The Peasants of El Dorado*, Ithaca, NY: Cornell University Press.

Simpson, Eyler N., 1937, *The Ejido: Mexico's Way Out*, Chapel Hill, NC: The University of North Carolina Press.

Skar, Harald O., 1982, *The Warm Valley People: Duality and Land Reform among the Quechua Indians of Highland Peru*, Oslo, Bergen and Tromsø: Universitetsforlaget.

Slobodin, Richard, 1978, *W.H.R. Rivers*, New York: Columbia University Press.

Smuts, J.C., 1930, *Africa and Some World Problems: Including the Rhodes Memorial Lectures delivered in the Michaelmas Term, 1929*, Oxford: Clarendon Press.

Solomon, S.G., 1977, *The Soviet Agrarian Debate: A Controversy in Social Science, 1923–1929*, Boulder, CO: Westview Press.

Sorj, Bernardo, 1977, 'The Dialectics of Class and State Apparatus: The Peruvian Case', *Dialectical Anthropology*, Vol. 2, No. 4.

Spencer, H., 1884, *Man versus the State*, London: Williams & Norgate.

Spencer, Sarah, 2007, 'Immigration', in Anthony Seldon (ed.), *Blair's Britain 1997–2007*, Cambridge: Cambridge University Press.

Srinivas, M.N., 1987, *The Dominant Caste and Other Essays*, Delhi: Oxford University Press.

Srivastava, G.P., 1962, *Traditional Forms of Cooperation in India*, New Delhi: Indian Cooperative Union.

Staudenmaier, Peter, and Janet Biehl, 1995, *Ecofascism: Lessons from the German Experience*, Edinburgh: AK Press.

Stauder, Jack, 1974, 'The "Relevance" of Anthropology to Colonialism and Imperialism', *Radical Science Journal*, Vol. 1.

Steinfeld, Robert J., 2001, *Coercion, Contract, and Free Labor in the Nineteenth Century*, Cambridge: Cambridge University Press.

Steinfeld, Robert J., and Stanley M. Engermann, 1997, 'Labor – Free or Coerced? A Historical Reassessment of Differences and Similarities', in Tom Brass and Marcel van der Linden (eds.), *Free and Unfree Labour: The Debate Continues*, Berne: Peter Lang AG.

Stelzer, I.M., 2001, *Immigration Policy for an Age of Mass Movement*, London: IEA.

Stern, Robert W., 2006, *Changing India: Bourgeois Revolution on the Subcontinent*, Cambridge: Cambridge University Press.

Stonor Saunders, Frances, 1999, *Who Paid the Piper? The CIA and the Cultural Cold War*, London: Granta Books.

Stowe, Harriet Beecher, 1853, *A Key to Uncle Tom's Cabin: Presenting the Original Facts and Documents upon which the Story is Founded*, London: Thomas Bosworth.

Suárez, Modesto (ed.), 1990, *Historia, Antropología y Política: Homenaje a Ángel Palerm* (Vol. I), Mexico, DF: Alianza Editorial Mexicana.

Sutch, Richard, 1975, 'The Treatment Received by American Slaves: A Critical Review of the Evidence Presented in *Time on the Cross*', *Explorations in Economic History*, Vol. 12, No.4.

Sweezy, P.M., 1946, *The Theory of Capitalist Development: Principles of Marxian Political Economy*, London: Dennis Dobson Limited.

Taine, H., 1872, *Notes on England* (Translated by W.F. Rae), London: Strahan & Co.

Taylor, Lewis, 2005, A review of *Latin American Peasants*, edited by Tom Brass, *Bulletin of Latin American Research*, Vol. 24, No. 3.

Temperley, Howard, 1972, *British Antislavery 1833–1870*, Columbia, SC: University of South Carolina Press.

Temperley, Howard (ed.), 2000, *After Slavery: Emancipation and its Discontents*, London: Frank Cass Publishers [see Review Essay 10].

Tendler, Judith, 1988, 'What to Think About Cooperatives: A Guide from Bolivia', in Sheldon Annis and Peter Hakim (eds.), *Direct to the Poor: Grassroots Development in Latin America*, Boulder, CO: Lynne Rienner Publishers.

Thackeray, W.M., 1855, *The Book of Snobs*, London: Bradbury & Evans.

Thawnghmung, Ardeth Maung, 2003, 'Rural Perceptions of State Legitimacy in Burma/ Myanmar', *The Journal of Peasant Studies*, Vol. 30, No. 2.

Thomas, W., and F. Znaniecki, 1958 [1918–20], *The Polish Peasant in Europe and America* (2 vols.), New York: Dover Publications.

Thompson, E.P., 1982, 'Notes on Exterminism, the Last Stage of Civilization', In E.P. Thomson *et al.*, (eds.), *Exterminism and Cold War*, London: Verso.

Thompson, E.P., 1991, *Customs in Common*, London: Merlin Press.

Thorner, Alice, 1982, 'Semi-Feudalism or Capitalism? Contemporary Debate on Classes and Modes of Production in India', *Economic and Political Weekly*, Vol. XVII, Nos. 49–51.

Thorner, Alice, 1982a, 'Excerpts from an FBI file', *Economic and Political Weekly*, Vol. XVII, No. 21.

Thorner, Daniel, 1964, *Agricultural Cooperatives in India: A Field Report*, New York: Asia Publishing House.

Thorner, Daniel, 1980, *The Shaping of Modern India*, New Delhi and Bombay: Allied Publishers.

Thorner, Daniel, and Alice Thorner, 1962, *Land and Labour in India*, Bombay: Asia Publishing House.

Thorp, Rosemary, and Geoffrey Bertram, 1978, *Peru 1890–1977: Growth and Policy in an Open Economy*, London: The Macmillan Press.

Tirrell, Sarah Rebecca, 1951, *German Agrarian Politics After Bismark's Fall: The Formation of the Farmers' League*, New York: Columbia University Press.

Tiwary, S.P., 1985, 'Bondage in Santal Parganas', in U. Patnaik and M. Dingwaney (eds.), *Chains of Servitude: Bondage and Slavery in India*, Madras: Sangham Books.

Todd, Emmanuel, 2015, *Who Is Charlie? Xenophobia and the New Middle Classes*, Cambridge: Polity Press.

Trevaskis, Hugh Kennedy, 1928, *The Land of the Five Rivers: An Economic History of the Punjab from the Earliest Times to the Year of Grace 1890*, London: Oxford University Press.

Trevaskis, Hugh Kennedy, 1931–32, *The Punjab of Today: An Economic Survey of the Punjab in Recent Years (1890–1925)*, Volumes I and II, Lahore: The Civil and Military Gazette Press.

Trias, C., 1975, 'La batalla decisiva', *Mundial*, No. 13.

Trollope, Anthony, 1971 [1875], *The Way We Live Now*, London: Oxford University Press.

Trotsky, Leon, 1925, *Literature and Revolution* (translated by Rose Strunsky), London: George Allen & Unwin, Ltd.

Trotsky, Leon, 1930, *My Life*, London: Thornton Butterworth Ltd.

Trotsky, Leon, 1936, *The Third International After Lenin*, New York: Pioneer Publishers.

Trotsky, Leon, 1959 [1910], *The Intelligentsia and Socialism* (translated by Brian Pearce), London: Fourth International.

Trotsky, Leon, 1962 [1929], *The Permanent Revolution and Results and Prospects*, London: New Park Publications.

Trotsky, Leon, 1967, *The Revolution Betrayed*, London: New Park Publications.

Trotsky, Leon, 1970, *Marxism in Our Time*, New York: Pathfinder Press.

Trotsky, Leon, 1971/1975, *The Struggle Against Fascism in Germany*, New York: Pathfinder Press/Harmondsworth: Penguin Books.

Trotsky, Leon, 1972, *1905* (translated by Anya Bostock), London: Allen Lane, The Penguin Press.

Trotsky, Leon, 1973 [1925], *Leon Trotsky on Britain*, New York: Pathfinder Press, Inc.

Tudor, H., and J.M. Tudor (eds.), 1988, *Marxism and Social Democracy: The Revisionist Debate*, 1896–1898, Cambridge: Cambridge University Press.

Tupayachi, Isaac, 1959, 'Un ensayo de econometría en La Convención', *Revista Universitaria de la Universidad Nacional de Cuzco*, Vol. XLVIII, No. 117.

Turner, F.S., 1949, 'The Significance of the Frontier in American History (1893)', in G.R. Taylor (ed.), *The Turner Thesis, Concerning the Role of the Frontier in American History*, Boston, MA: D.C. Heath and Co.

Turner, Stephen P., and Dirk Kasler (eds.), 1992, *Sociology Responds to Fascism*, London: Routledge.

Twain, Mark, 1875, 'The Facts Concerning a Recent Resignation', *Mark Twain's Sketches, New and Old*, Hartford, CT, and Chicago, IL: The American Publishing Company.

Ulyanovsky, R., 1974: *Socialism and the Newly Independent Nations*, Moscow: Progress Publishers.

United Nations Department of Economic Affairs, 1954, *Progress in Land Reform*, New York: United Nations.

United States Senate Commission, 1913, *Agricultural Cooperation and Rural Credit in Europe*, Washington, DC: Government Printing Office.
United States Senate Commission, 1913, *Agricultural Cooperation and Rural Credit in Europe*, Washington, DC: Government Printing Office.
Valderamma, Mariano, 1982, 'The Agrarian Reform: Continuity and Change in the Peruvian Rural Area', in Steve Jones, P.C. Joshi and Miguel Murmis (eds.), *Rural Poverty and Agrarian Reform*, New Delhi: Allied Publishers.

Valderrama, Mariano, and Patricia Ludmann, 1979, *La oligarquia terrateniente: Ayer y hoy*, Lima: Universidad Cátolica del Peru.

van den Berghe, Pierre L., 1970, *Academic Gamesmanship*, London and New York: Abelard-Schuman.

van den Berghe, Pierre L., and George Primov (eds.), 1977, *Inequality in the Peruvian Andes: Class and Ethnicity in Cuzco*, Colombia, MO: University of Missourie Press.

van der Haar, Gemma, 2007, 'Land Reform, the State, and the Zapatista Uprising in Chiapas', in Sarah Washbrook (ed.), *Rural Chiapas Ten Years after the Zapatista Uprising*, London and New York: Routledge.

van der Linden, Marcel, 2003a, 'Refuting Labour History's Occidentalism,' in Arvind N. Das and Marcel van der Linden (eds.), *Work and Social Change in Asia: Essays in Honour of Jan Breman*, New Delhi: Manohar.

van der Linden, Marcel, 2003b, 'Labour History as the History of Multitudes,' *Labour/ Le Travail* 52.

van der Linden, Marcel, 2008, *Workers of the World: Essays toward a Global Labor History*, Leiden: Brill.

van der Linden, Marcel, 2010, 'Foreword,' in Jairus Banaji, *Theory as History: Essays on Modes of Production and Exploitation*, Leiden: Brill.

van der Linden, Marcel, and Karl Heinz Roth (eds.), 2014, *Beyond Marx: Theorising the Global Labour Relations of the Twenty-First Century*, Leiden: Brill [see Review Essay 13].

van der Ploeg, Jan Douwe, 2009, *The New Peasantries: Struggles for Autonomy and Sustainability in an Era of Empire and Globalization*, London: Earthscan.

van Onselen, Charles, 1977, 'South Africa's Lumpenproletariat Army: "Umkosi Wa Ntaba" – "The Regiment of the Hills", 1890–1920.', *Collected Seminar Papers on the Societies of Southern Africa in the 19th and 20th Centuries*, London: Institute of Commonwealth Studies (University of London).

Varoufakis, Yanis, 2016, *And the Weak Suffer What They Must? Europe, Austerity and the Threat to Global Stability*, London: The Bodley Head.

Vásquez-León, Marcela, and Timothy J. Finan, 2007, 'Walking the Tight Rope: A Comparative Analysis of Small-scale Agricultural Cooperatives in Latin America', an unpublished study for the project *Development and Expansion of Economic Assistance Programs That Fully Utilize Cooperatives or Credit Unions*, USAID/ACDI/VOCA.

Veltmeyer, Henry, 1997, 'New Social Movements in Latin America: The Dynamics of Class and Identity', *The Journal of Peasant Studies*, Vol. 25, No. 1.

Veltmeyer, Henry, 1999, *The Labyrinth of Latin American Development*, New Delhi: APH Publications.

Veltmeyer, Henry, 2000, *América Latina: capital global y la perspectiva del desarrollo alternativo*, Zacatecas, Mexico: UAZ/UNESCO.

Veltmeyer, Henry, 2005, 'The Dynamics of Land Occupations in Latin America', in Sam Moyo and Paris Yeros (eds.), *Reclaiming the Land: The Resurgence of Rural Movements in Africa, Asia and Latin America*, London: Zed Books [see Review Essay 11].

Venkateshwarlu, Davaluri, and Lucia da Corta, 2001, 'Transformations in the Age and Gender of Unfree Workers on Hybrid Cotton Seed Farms in Andhra Pradesh', *The Journal of Peasant Studies*, Vol. 28, No. 3.

Villanueva, Victor, 1967, *Hugo Blanco y la rebelión campesina*, Lima: Libreria-Editorial Juan Mejía Baca.

Volin, Lazar, 1970, *A Century of Russian Agriculture: From Alexander II to Khrushchev*, Cambridge, MA: Harvard University Press.

Volkov, Shulamit, 1978, *The Rise of Popular Antimodernism in Germany*, Princeton, NJ: Princeton University Press.

Walinsky, Louis J. Jr. (ed.), 1977, *Agrarian Reform as Unfinished Business: The Selected Papers of Wolf Ladejinsky*, Washington, DC: The World Bank.

Walkin, Jacob, 1963, *The Rise of Democracy in Pre-Revolutionary Russia: Political and Social Institutions Under the Last Three Czars*, London: Thames and Hudson.

Wallerstein, Immanuel, 1979, *The Capitalist World Economy*, Cambridge: Cambridge University Press.

Walter, N., 1969, *About Anarchism*, London: Freedom Press.

Walvin, James, 1992, *Black Ivory: A History of British Slavery*, London: HarperCollins.

Warriner, Doreen, 1969, *Land Reform in Principle and Practice*, Oxford: Clarendon Press.

Washbrook, Sarah (ed.), 2005, *Rural Chiapas Ten Years After the Zapatista Uprising*, a special issue of *The Journal of Peasant Studies*, Vol. 32, Nos. 3–4.

Weitz, Raanan (ed.), 1965, *Rural Planning in Developing Countries*, London: Routledge and Kegan Paul.

West India Royal Commission, 1897, *Report of the West India Royal Commission* (Appendix C, Vols. I–III), London: Her Majesty's Stationery Office.

Wharton, Clifton R. (ed.), 1970, *Subsistence Agriculture and Economic Development*, London: Frank Cass & Co., Ltd.

Whetten, Nathan L., 1948, *Rural Mexico*, Chicago, IL: The University of Chicago Press.

Whiteside, A.G., 1962, *Austrian National Socialism before 1918*, The Hague: Martinus Nijhoff.

Whiteside, A.G., 1975, *The Socialism of Fools: Georg Ritter von Schönerer and Austrian Pan-Germanism*, Berkeley, CA: University of California Press.

Widgery, David (ed.), 1976, *The Left in Britain 1956–1968*, Harmondsworth: Penguin Books.

Wiener, Jon, 1991, *Professors, Politics and Pop*, London: Verso.

Wiener, Jon, 2005, *Historians in Trouble: Plagiarism, Fraud, and Politics in the Ivory Tower*, New York: The New Press.

Wiles, Peter, 1969, 'A Syndrome, Not a Doctrine: Some Elementary Theses on Populism', in Ghiţa Ionescu and Ernest Gellner (eds.), *Populism: Its Meanings and National Characteristics*, London: Weidenfeld and Nicolson.

Wilkie, Raymond, 1971, *San Miguel: A Mexican Collective Ejido*, Stanford, CA: Stanford University Press.

Willan, Brian, 1979, 'The Anti-Slavery and Aborigines' Protection Society and the South African Natives' Land Act of 1913', *Journal of African History*, Vol. 20, No.1.

Willan, Brian, 1984, *Sol Plaatje: South African Nationalist 1876–1932*, London: Heinemann.

Williams, Eric, 1966, *British Historians and The West Indies*, London: Andre Deutsch.

Williams, Eric, 1970, *From Columbus to Castro: The History of the Caribbean, 1492–1969*, London: Andre Deutsch.

Wilson, Monica, and Thompson Leonard (eds.), 1971, *The Oxford History of South Africa: II – South Africa 1870–1966*, Oxford: The Clarendon Press.

Wiser, W.H., 1936, *The Hindu Jajmani System*, Lucknow: Lucknow Publishing House.

Wolf, E.R., and E.C. Hanson, 1972, *The Human Condition in Latin America*, New York: Oxford University Press.

Wolpe, Harold, 1972, 'Capitalism and Cheap Labour Power in South Africa: From Segregation to Apartheid', *Economy and Society*, Vol.1, No.4.

World Bank, 1975a, *Rural Development (Sector Policy Paper)*, Washington, DC: World Bank Publications.

World Bank, 1975b, *Land Reform (Sector Policy Paper)*, Washington, DC: World Bank Publications.

World Bank, 1978, *Agricultural Land Settlement (Sector Policy Paper)*, Washington, DC: World Bank Publications.

World Bank, 1991, *Promoting Rural Cooperatives in Developing Countries: The Case of Sub-Saharan Africa*, Washington, DC: World Bank Publications.

Worsley, Peter (ed.), 1971, *Two Blades of Grass: Rural Cooperatives in Agricultural Modernization*, Manchester: Manchester University Press.

Worsley, Peter, 1984, *The Three Worlds: Culture and World Development*, London: Weidenfeld & Nicolson.

Wright, Thomas, 1969 [1873], *Our New Masters*, New York: Augustus M. Kelley.

Young, Crawford, Neal P. Sherman, and Tim Rose, 1981, *Cooperatives and Development: Agricultural Politics in Ghana and Uganda*, Madison, WI: University of Wisconsin Press.

Zaldívar, Ramón, 1974, 'Agrarian Reform and Military Reformism in Peru', in A.D. Lehmann (ed.), *Agrarian Reform and Agrarian Reformism*, London: Faber and Faber.

Žižek, Slavoj, 2014, *Trouble in Paradise: From the End of History to the End of Capitalism*, London: Penguin Books.

Žižek, Slavoj, 2016, *Against the Double Blackmail: Refugees, Terror and Other Troubles with the Neighbours*, London: Penguin Random House.

Author Index

Aguirre Beltrán, G. 149
Abramsky, C. 363
Agarwala, R. 343
Ahluwalia, I.J. 239
Alavi, H. 88
Albert, B. 102
Alderson-Smith, G. 217
Alfaro, J. 212
Allina-Pisano, J. 207
Amnesty International 184
Ampuero, I. 108, 133
Amsden, A.H. 239
Anderson, B. 375, 378
Anderson, P. 335–6
Angelo, L. 88
Annan, N. 312, 331–2
Anonymous 330
Apthorpe, R. 195
Arce, A. 217
Ariff, M. 239
Arndt, H.W. 104
Arnold, D. 95
Aron, R. 337
Aronna, M. 168
Ashley, M.P. 323
Assadi, M.H. 24, 172
Assies, W. 129
Attwood, D.W. 195
Awad, M. 271
Ayers, A.J. 292, 298ff., 309

Bagchi, A.K. 45
Bagchi, J. 44
Baldwin, E. 192
Bales, K. 90
Balibar, E. 376
Balogh, T. 194
Banaji, J. 8, 57, 160, 243, 266, 271, 276, 281ff., 297, 304, 309
Banerjee, D. 88
Baran, P. 143
Bardhan, P. 42
Barraclough, S.L. 192ff., 204, 210
Barrientos, S. 292 *passim*
Barthes, R. 342
Bauer, A.J. 194, 281
Bauer, P.T. 197, 337
Baviskar, B.S. 195
Beachey, R.W. 104
Becker, G.S. 369
Bedoya Garland, E. 129, 209
Bedoya Silva-Santisteban, A. 129, 209
Beer, M. 326
Beidelman, T.O. 275
Belfort Bax, E. 361
Belloc, H. 1, 69–70, 80
Benda, J. 82, 338
Berger, J. 374
Berlan, A. 292, 306
Berlin, I. 26, 62ff. 331–2
Bernstein, H. 22, 25, 56–58, 112, 114 *passim*, 124ff., 136ff., 199, 343
Bertram, G. 210
Beverley, J. 168
Bhaduri, A. 8
Bhagwati, J. 239, 369
Bhattacharya, N. 248
Bhukuth, A. 305
Biehl, J. 171
Bierce, A. 1, 239, 312
Blanco, H. 208, 211
Bloom, H. 342
Blum, J. 141
Boeke, J.H. 104
Booth, D. 36–7
Borras, S. 21
Bottomore, T. 344
Bowyer, T. 377–8
Bradby, B. 150, 339
Bragg, B. 15
Brass, T. 6ff., 18 *passim*, 47–8, 50, 55ff., 66, 75, 79, 82, 107, 109, 113, 116, 129, 149 *passim*, 160ff., 167, 181, 194, 211, 216, 219, 241 *passim*, 264 *passim*, 276 *passim*, 294 *passim*, 340, 349, 376
Brayne, F.L. 206
Brecht, B. 7
Breman, J. 8, 44ff., 96, 160, 239 *passim*, 251 *passim*, 262 *passim*, 272 *passim*, 290, 304

Brennan, L. 90
Brittain, J.J. 108, 133, 136
Broomfield, N. 51ff.
Browning, R. 88
Bücher, C. 319–20
Buck, S.J. 197–8
Bukharin, N. 121, 316, 320
Bush, M.L. 92
Byres, T. 8, 96, 119 *passim,* 126 *passim,* 135ff., 268, 275, 280ff., 294

Caballero, J.M. 208, 210, 213
Calleros-Rodríguez, H. 25
Callinicos, A. 338
Calvert, H. 206
Campbell, Sir G. 100–101
Canetti, E. 312
Cannadine, D. 335, 346
Canovan, M. 197
Carroll, T.F. 194
Carr-Saunders, A.M. 192–3
Carter, A. 145
Carter, M.R. 234
Castro Pozo, H. 149, 203–4
Catanach, I.J. 206
Caute, D. 62ff., 331, 333, 346
Chakravarti, U. 45
Chakravarty, S. 128
Chakravorty, S. 239
Chandra, U. 153
Chatterjee, P. 34
Chattopadhyay, B. 271
Chaturvedi, V. 116
Chayanov, A.V. 57, 115, 117, 125, 154, 170ff., 192, 198ff.
Chimhowu, A. 110
Chomsky, N. 64, 72
Chonchol, J. 202
Chopra, S. 260
Chossudovsky, M. 207
Chowdhry, P. 129, 265
Cleaves, P.S. 217, 218
Clegg, I. 207
Clogg, R. 321ff.
Clover, C. 153ff.
Cobban, A. 63, 332
Cochrane, R. 171
Cohn-Bendit, D. 336–7
Cohn-Bendit, G. 336–7
Collarte, J.C. 192, 193, 204, 210
Colley, L. 15
Collini, S. 313, 327, 340
Collins, H. 363
Comninel, G.C. 332
Conlin, S. 218–19
Corbridge, S. 33 *passim,* 108
Costello, C. 375
Coupland, R. 86, 93
Cox, C.B. 337
Crabtree, J. 210
Craig, W.W. 211
Cuadros, C.F. 211
Custred, G. 203

D'Espallier, B. 305
da Corta, L. 267
Dandler, J. 192
Daniel, E.V. 88
Danilov, V.P. 197–8
Darling, M.L. 206, 287
Das, A.N. 48, 205
Das, R. 73ff., 111
David, P.A. 97
de Castro, J. 109
de Kadt, E. 187
de Man, P. 342
de Neve, G. 243–44, 265ff., 272ff., 291
de Souza Martins, J. 307
de Ste Croix, G.E.M. 88
de Tocqueville, A. 4
de Vylder, S. 207
Deere, C. 207
Degler, C.N. 95
Delande, N. 153
Derrida, J. 16, 342
Desai, A.R. 241
Deutscher, I. 26, 62ff., 331–2
Dingwaney, M. 95, 294
Dobb, M. 63, 280, 307, 362, 364
Domike, A.L. 195, 205
Dorner, P. 192
Dossani, R. 239
Douglass, F. 102
Drèze, J. 257
Drieu La Rochelle, P. 82
Dummett, M. 356

Dumont, L. 267
Duràn de Huerta, M. 194
Dyson, A.E. 337

Eagleton, T. 331–2
Eckstein, S. 194
Edelman, M. 23
Emmer, P.C. 93, 96 *passim*
Engels, F. 3, 120, 171, 174, 280, 316, 325, 362, 363
Engerman, S.M. 86, 90, 97, 132, 257, 259, 281, 297, 308
Epstein, A.L. 65, 190
Epstein, T.S. 253
Eribon, D. 80
Erickson, C. 354
Evans, R.J. 67

Fanon, F. 157, 159
Fielding, N. 377
Figueroa, A. 217
Finan, T.J. 195
Finch, H. 88
Fioravanti, E. 211
Fisher, A.G.B. 364
Fishlow, A. 122
Fitzgerald, E.V.K. 208
Florence, P.S. 192, 193
Florescano, E. 88
Fogel, R.W. 90, 97, 132, 257, 259, 281, 297, 308
Ford, R. 377
Fortes, M. 20
Foucault, M. 16
Frank, A.G. 8, 135
Frantz, E. 292
Freedland, M. 375
Friedman, M. 144
Fukayama, F. 41
Furedi, F. 313
Furnivall, J.S. 104

Galeski, B. 192
Gasper, D. 195
Gay, P. 158
Geras, N. 313
Gerassi, J. 109
Gerschenkron, A. 121ff.
Gibbon, P. 116–18
Giddens, A. 33, 335, 375
Gill, S.S. 24, 165
Gilroy, P. 207
Gonzales, A. 234
Gonzales, E. 207
Goode, P. 344
Goodman, D. 196
Goodwin, M. 377
Gooptu, N. 262, 263
Gott, R. 211
Gould, J. 337
Gouldner, A.W. 338
Goyder, G. 368
Graeber, D. 68ff., 292, 299, 307
Grant, A. 153
Graves, A. 88, 102
Griffin, K. 132, 192, 194
Grossberg, L. 165
Guérin, D. 280
Guérin, I. 292, 298ff., 304ff., 309–10
Guevara, E. 'Che' 71
Guha, Ranajit 14, 157, 159, 168–9
Guillet, D. 217
Gulati, L. 45
Gumilev, L. 20, 153ff.
Gutman, H.G. 97

Hall, D. 25
Hall, S. 157, 159, 162ff.
Hamid, M. 372ff.
Hansen, E.C. 88
Hardiman, D. 45
Hardt, M. 69, 119, 157, 159, 165, 168ff.
Harris, M. 97
Harris, Sir J. 93
Harriss, J. 33 *passim*, 110ff., 118, 135, 138, 253, 343
Harriss-White, B. 240ff., 256, 260 *passim*, 276, 290–91, 343
Hartman, G. 342
Hasan, Z. 24
Haslam, J. 332
Hawthorn, G.P. 65ff.
Hayek, F. 144, 259, 337
Hegel, G.W.F. 296, 308
Henninger, M. 172
Herder, J.G. 154
Herring, R.J. 343

Heuman, G. 92
Hewitt de Alcántara, C. 149
Higgins, N. 194
Hillis Miller, J. 342
Hilton, R. 87, 334
Hirst, P. 39
Hirway, I. 46
Hitchens, C. 331
Hjejle, B. 95, 306
Hobsbawm, E.J. 63, 71, 181, 334
Holbrook, D. 345
Hopkins, N.J. 192
Horowitz, I.L. 109
Houben, V.J.H. 246
Houellebecq, M. 77ff.
House of Commons Environment, Food and Rural Affairs Committee 55
Hughes, V. 375
Huizer, G. 192, 213
Hunter, J. 41
Hussain, A. 158, 200
Hutton, J.H. 151, 323
Hynes, J. 345

Ignatieff, M. 313, 331
Im Thurn, Sir E.F. 86
International Labour Conference 99
International Labour Organization 270
International Monetary Fund 239
Isaac, C.B. 206
Isbell, B.J. 217
Ivanov, Y.M. 197

Jackson, C. 110
Jaffrelot, C. 45
Jakobson, R. 153–4
James, C. 23
James, C.L.R. 87
Jansen, K. 23
Jasny, N. 203
Jodhka, S.S. 243–44, 265ff., 272–3, 291, 304
Johnson, H. 117
Johnson, P. 337, 338, 349
Jones, G.A. 108

Kapadia, K. 276
Kapila, R. 239
Kapila, U. 239
Kapsoli, W. 213
Kasler, D. 330
Kautsky, K. 57, 58, 87, 119ff., 158, 174, 200
Kay, J.P. 325
Kay-Shuttleworth, J. 325
Keen, B.A. 193
Kerblay, B. 192
Klein, N. 105
Klinge, G. 212
Kloosterboer, W. 97
Kofi, T.A. 110
Kohli, A. 239
Kopytoff, I. 86
Korovkin, T. 195, 209, 211
Kothari, U. 48–49, 106, 108 *passim*, 125, 137, 292, 298 *passim*
Kremnev, I. 171
Kristeva, J. 16
Kritsman, L.N. 201
Kuczynski, J. 280, 307
Kumar, K. 15
Kuper, A. 323
Kusuman, K.K. 86, 95, 306

Lacan, J. 16
Lacey, M. 93
Laclau, E. 8
Lahr, J. 338
Lal, D. 133
Lall, S.V. 239
Lamartine, A. de. 173–4
Langham, I. 323
LaPorte, R. 134, 192, 205, 214
Leach, E. 323
LeBaron, G. 292, 298 *passim*
Legassick, M. 88
Lele, U. 195
Lenin, V.I. 34, 57, 58, 62, 87, 119ff., 126, 141, 174, 199ff., 280, 307, 314, 316–17, 320, 331, 337, 353, 372
Leons, W. 195
Lerche, J. 241ff., 265 *passim*, 275 *passim*, 291, 298, 304
Lévi-Strauss, C. 80
Levy, B.-H. 77ff.
Lewin, M. 198
Lewis, C.M. 41
Leys, C. 117
Li, H. 206
Lichtenstein, A. 88, 307

Lindblad, J.T. 246
Lipton, M. 114, 132
Little, I.M.D. 239
Long, N. 196, 217, 218
Ludmann, P. 211
Lukács, G. 314
Luxemburg, R. 1 *passim,* 20, 201–2, 316, 319–20, 362ff.

MacLean y Estenós, R. 211, 213, 217
Mahbubani, K. 239
Malamoud, C. 150
Mandel, E. 280, 307, 362, 365
Mangru, B. 103, 104
Manickam, S. 95
Mann, H.H. 137, 206, 287
Manuel, F. 44
Manzo, K. 279
Marcuse, H. 157, 159
Maríategui, J.C. 149, 203
Marius-Gnanou, K. 305
Markovits, C. 45
Marla, S. 268
Marshall, P. 145
Mártinez-Torres, M. 24
Marx, K. 7, 171, 173, 174, 272, 284, 326, 357ff., 360, 362–3, 380
Marxist Study Courses 326
Matchek, V. 166
Mattick, P. 14
Mayer, P. 95
Maynard, J. 197
McClintock, C. 196
McDonald, J. 90
McMichael, P. 195
McRobbie, A. 165
Meillassoux, C. 88
Melmed-Sanjak, J.S. 234
Mencher, J. 45
Mezzadra, S. 375–76
Miers, S. 86
Mies, M. 171
Milazzo, C. 377
Mill, J.S. 308
Millar, J.P.M. 327
Mirsky, D. 328
Mitra, A. 45
Mitrany, D. 197
Moberg, M.A. 203
Mohr, J. 374
Montoya, R. 228
Morand, P. 82
Moreno Fraginals, M. 88
Morley, M. 134, 135
Mörner, M. 211
Mosley, O. 198
Moulier-Boutang, Y. 307
Moyo, S. 106, 108, 114ff., 137
Mukherji, P.N. 129
Mundle, S. 241, 260, 268
Munslow, B. 88
Murra, J.V. 150, 166

Nader, L. 332
Nash, J. 192
Nayak, S.S. 239
Nayar, B.R. 239
Negri, A. 9, 69, 119, 157, 159, 165, 168ff.
Neilson, B. 376
Neira, H. 211, 212
Neocosmos, M. 116ff.
Newman, J.H. 315
Nisbet, R. 337
Nock, A.J. 144
Nozick, R. 144
Nuijten, M. 205
Nuñez, O. 134

O'Brien, C.C. 64, 331
O'Meara, D. 93
Olmsted, F.L. 102
Orde Browne, G. St. J. 98
Ore, T. 212
Orlov, B.S. 203
Orwell, G. 69
Overton, J. 134
Oviedo, J. 168
Owen, R. 323
Oya, C. 118

Palerm, A. 149
Panagaria, A. 239
Panchamukhi, V.R. 239
Panoff, M. 88
Patel, R. 22ff.
Patel, S. 44
Patel, S.J. 94, 247, 306
Patnaik, U. 8, 96, 268, 294, 298

Pattison, M. 321, 344
Paxman, J. 15
Pearse, A. 195
Peers, R. 192, 193
Pérez, N. 207
Perlin, R. 59ff.
Petras, J. 8, 106ff., 113, 119, 133 *passim,* 192, 205, 214, 307, 315, 348
Phelps Brown, E.H. 354
Phillips, N. 292, 298 *passim*
Piketty, T. 360, 377
Pouchepadass, J. 45
Powderly, T.V. 357
Powell, E. 368, 377
Prakash, G. 248
Prasad. P. 8
Preobrazhensky, E.A. 120, 121, 200, 316, 320
Primov, G. 219

Raj, K. 44
Ramachandran, V.K. 106ff., 132, 137
Rao, M. 273
Rawal, V. 129, 243, 244, 265, 267ff., 272, 274, 285, 291
Rawls, J. 41
Ray, A.K. 271
Redclift, M. 196
Reid, A. 141
Renton, D. 122
Richards, P. 217
Robbins, L. 364
Rodgers, D. 195
Rodney, W. 88, 104
Roemer, J. 41
Roesch, M. 305
Roquas, E. 23
Rosdolsky, R. 365
Rose, G. 66
Rose, J. 326
Rose, T. 195
Rosset, P.M. 24
Roth, K.H. 157–81
Rothbard, M. 144
Rothstein, A. 333
Rowbotham, S. 313
Rudra, A. 88, 241, 245, 252, 294, 307
Ruskin History Workshop Students 326
Rutten, M. 44, 46–48
Sahlins, M. 339
Sahoo, B.P. 129
Saintsbury, G. 95
Salvadori, M. 158
Samaddar, R. 376
Samuel, R. 15
Sánchez, R. 150
Saradamoni, K. 95
Saul, J.S. 110
Saunders, C. 93
Saunders, C.T. 323
Sawyer, R. 270
Saxe-Fernandez, J. 134
Sayers, S. 335
Schiller, O.M. 192
Schlesinger, R. 13, 14
Schneider, H.W. 198
Scitovsky, T. 364
Scott, J.C. 20, 26–27, 37, 71, 113, 115, 140 *passim,* 152ff., 196, 266–67
Scruton, R. 337–38
Scurrah, M.J. 217, 218
Seligmann, L.J. 203
Sen, Amartya 257ff.
Serge, V. 71
Shah, G. 44, 46–48
Shalin, D.N. 328
Shanin, T. 199, 241
Shapiro, K.A. 98
Sharma, S.C. 271
Shepherd, C.Y. 103
Sherman, N.P. 195
Shiva, V. 171
Shlomowitz, R. 90, 308
Shoemaker, R. 217
Simpson, E.N. 206
Skar, H.O. 217
Slobodin, R. 323–4
Smith, Adam 296, 308
Smuts, J.C. 147
Sorj, B. 208
Spencer, H. 144
Spencer, S. 377–78
Srinivas, M.N. 267
Srivastava, G.P. 192
Staudenmaier, P. 171
Stauder, J. 63, 323, 332–33
Steinfeld, R.J. 132, 281, 308

Stelzer, I.M. 369
Stern, R.W. 239
Stirner, M. 174
Stonor Saunders, F. 327
Stowe, H.B. 85, 102
Streefkerk, H. 44, 46, 49–50
Suárez, M. 449
Sutch, R. 97, 302
Swaisland, C. 93–4
Swaminathan, M. 106, 108, 132, 137
Sweezy, P.M. 358

Taine, H. 344
Taylor, L. 193–4
Temperley, H. 85, 86, 92 *passim*
Tendler, J. 195
Terhal, P. 46
Thackeray, W.M. 329
Thawnghmung, A.M. 205
Thomas, W. 374
Thompson, E.P. 334
Thompson, J. 66
Thompson, L. 93, 99
Thorner, A. 44, 45, 241, 247, 294, 307, 332
Thorner, D. 8, 45, 63, 195, 206, 241, 247, 307, 332
Thorp, R. 210
Tirrell, S.R. 122
Tiwary, S.P. 95, 260
Todd, E. 80
Torre, G. 234
Trevaskis, H.K. 287
Trias, C. 212
Tribe, K. 158, 200
Trollope, A. 328
Trotsky, L. 8, 13, 21–22, 35, 58, 62, 71, 121, 201, 239, 280, 307, 316, 318ff., 331, 333, 338, 362, 364–5
Tudor, H. 158
Tudor, J.M. 158
Tupayachi, I. 211
Turner, F.S. 148, 149
Turner, S.P. 330
Twain, M. 313

Uberoi, P. 45
Ulyanovsky, R. 197
United Nations Department of Economic Affairs 192
United States Senate Commission 122, 193, 201

Valderrama, M. 211
van den Berghe, P.L. 219, 345
van der Haar, G. 25, 205
van der Linden, M. 157–81, 241, 258, 307
van der Ploeg, J.D. 22
van Onselen, C. 175
Varga, E. 307
Varoufakis, Y. 360
Varshney, A. 34, 42
Vasapollo, L. 134
Vásquez-León, M. 195
Veltmeyer, H. 106, 107, 108, 133 *passim*
Venkatasubramanian, G. 305
Venkateshwarlu, D. 267
Villafuerte, D. 25
Villanueva, V. 211
Volin, L. 198
Volkov, S. 174

Walinsky, L.J. 192
Walkin, J. 198
Wallerstein, I. 298, 345
Walter, N. 145
Walvin, J. 105
Warriner, D. 192
Washbrook, S. 25, 172
Weitz, R. 192
West India Royal Commission 101, 102
Wharton, C.R. 241
Whetten, N.L. 206
Whitcombe, E. 45
Whiteside, A.G. 357
Widgery, D. 339
Wiener, J. 332, 345–6
Wiles, P. 197
Wilkie, R. 206
Willan, B. 93
Williams, E. 86, 101
Wilson, M. 93, 99
Wiser, W.H. 275
Wolf, E.R. 88
Wolpe, H. 88
Woodhouse, P. 110

World Bank 193, 195
Worsley, P. 81, 192
Wright, T. 173

Yeros, P. 106,108, 114ff., 137
Young, C. 195

Zaldivar, R. 233
Zemelman Merino, H. 134
Žižek, S. 9, 15–20
Znaniecki, F. 374

Subject Index

Abraham, David 63, 332
academia
  deradicalization and 28, 71
  festschrift 25, 44–45, 63, 165, 335
  katheder-socialism and 316–17
  Koraes Chair 321–22
  political exclusions from 62ff., 324, 331ff., 350
  research grants 74
  tolerance/pluralism in 63ff.
  troublemaking in 63, 332, 339
Africa 17, 26, 70, 86, 88, 93, 98ff., 110, 117–18, 146ff., 153, 160, 190, 192, 197, 259, 270, 279, 372. *See also* South Africa
  miners 190
  strikes 190
agrarian change 21, 39, 45ff., 56–58, 73, 113, 115, 240, 256, 268, 289, 303
agrarian myth 1, 70, 172, 342
agrarian populism 20ff., 43, 57, 58, 91, 115ff., 126, 149, 166ff., 343
agrarian question 26, 33, 34, 87, 108, 115, 116, 119 *passim*, 130 *passim*, 201, 209, 268
agrarian reform 134, 184, 187, 192, 195, 202 *passim*, 232, 237
agrarian transition 58, 73, 120 *passim*, 209, 241, 293, 295
agribusiness 9, 24, 28, 111, 115, 124, 129, 130, 136, 139, 177, 210, 242, 262, 271, 283, 290, 294, 366
Algeria 207
Allende, Salvador 202, 207, 210
anarchism 68, 144, 149, 152
ancient society 3, 4, 69, 87, 88, 148, 155
anthropology 80, 151, 166, 181, 190, 323, 324, 332, 333, 339. *See also* Leach, Edmund; methodology; Rivers, W.H.R.; State, the
  anthropologist-as-observer 27, 181, 186–7
  anthropologist-as-participant 27, 181
  ethnography 77, 80, 151, 256
Argentina 134
Asia 20, 26, 71, 88, 93, 97ff., 140 *passim*, 160, 166, 172, 240, 259, 293, 322, 341, 370
Australia 90, 279
Austria 318, 344, 357, 363
Austro-Marxism 318. *See also* academia, *katheder*-socialism and

Badiou, Alain 18
Baüer, Otto 126, 318
Belloc, Hilaire 1, 69, 70, 80
Benda, Julien 82, 338
Berlin, Isaiah 26, 62ff., 331–32
Bernstein, Eduard 157, 158, 316
Blair, Tony 165, 334, 378. *See also* political parties, New Labour
Blanco, Hugo 208, 211
Bolivia 129, 149, 190
Bolsheviks 71, 121, 153, 154, 192, 198, 338. *See also* Lenin, V.I.; Marxism; revolution; Russia; Trotsky, L.D.
bonded labour. *See* agrarian transition; capitalism; class, formation/struggle; debt-bondage; deproletarianization; semi-feudalism; unfree labour
bourgeoisie 34ff., 122, 127, 139, 143, 157, 169, 173, 174ff., 200, 288, 295, 310, 315ff., 328–9, 334, 336, 349, 363, 364, 379. *See also* capitalism; class; democracy
  as 'progressive' 288, 295, 328–9, 334
Brazil 69, 90, 95, 136, 187, 301
Brecht, Bertolt 7
Bulgaria 166
bureaucracy 27–8, 204ff., 216 *passim*, 227 *passim*, 259. *See also* State, the
Burma/Myanmar 146, 151, 197, 205

Campbell, Sir George 100–1
capital
  Confederation of British Industry 8, 369
  finance 59, 68–9, 122, 130, 158, 170, 177, 194, 197, 198, 262, 366, 370
  industrial 35, 49, 56, 68–9, 95, 98, 120, 124–5, 130, 132, 162, 176, 206, 210, 211, 257, 261, 278, 319, 349, 358, 359, 364, 367, 368
  Institute of Directors 369
  International Monetary Fund 239, 369

capitalism
as 'benign' 39, 40, 46, 48, 51, 60, 61, 64, 68, 81, 97, 98, 99, 103, 111, 126, 129, 133, 264, 269, 281, 289, 296, 320, 352, 372, 375
inequality and 14, 17, 26, 135, 141, 193, 213, 238, 259, 299, 377
multinational corporations and 8, 64, 69, 306, 345, 347, 366
poverty and 46, 47, 50, 55, 74, 105, 111, 112, 113, 135, 143, 193, 194, 240, 257, 258, 260, 299, 304–5, 340, 364
Caribbean ix, 26, 88, 92, 93, 96ff., 101ff., 279
Cuba 71, 207, 210
Grenada 101
Jamaica 102, 104
St Lucia 102
St Vincent 101
Trinidad 101
Carr, E.H., 63, 332
caste 33, 36, 42, 47, 48, 94, 169, 254, 261, 267, 268, 273, 285. *See also* debt-bondage, *jajmani*; labour, patronage
Chamars 270
dominant 47
Dublas 249, 251, 252
Halpati 48, 49, 253, 254
Patidars 48
Central Labour College 326
Chayanov, A.V. 57, 115, 117, 125, 154, 170ff., 192, 198ff.
Chesterton, G.K. 80
Chile 128, 134, 195, 202, 206, 207, 210
China 22, 51, 52, 53, 55, 58, 69, 206, 207, 324
Chomsky, Noam 64, 72
citizenship 29, 297, 355, 356, 371, 375ff., 379, 382, 383. *See also* human rights
civil society 34, 35, 118, 297. *See also* State, the
class. *See also* deproletarianization; proletarianization
collaboration 13, 82, 283, 328ff.
consciousness 3, 7, 13, 17, 39, 57, 81, 103, 122, 136, 154, 157, 158, 164, 177, 187, 188, 202–3, 209, 229–32, 238, 273, 292, 313, 317, 325, 342, 372–3, 380
formation 26, 33, 40, 57–8, 74, 104, 118, 154, 157–8, 188, 218, 237–8, 255, 272, 292, 298, 304, 308, 324, 356, 363
landlord 122, 123, 131, 172, 208, 211ff., 225, 232ff.
struggle 2, 3, 5ff., 9 *passim,* 23, 60–61, 74–5, 87, 88, 118, 128–9, 135, 139, 145, 155, 162, 163, 172ff., 181, 200, 202, 212, 255, 260, 263, 276 *passim,* 289ff., 292 *passim,* 310, 317, 342, 354 *passim,* 372, 378, 380, 383
working 3, 7, 13, 18, 19, 21, 35, 103, 122, 125, 126, 157 *passim,* 173 *passim,* 272–3, 317, 324 *passim,* 355 *passim,* 377ff.
Cobban, Alfred 63, 332
Colombia 133, 136
colonialism 5, 16, 17, 21, 26, 42, 45, 56, 86, 92, 93, 98, 100, 101, 120, 126, 147, 149, 151, 169, 190, 203–4, 206, 248, 249, 250, 253, 256, 286, 287, 290, 323, 345, 354
neo-colonialism 167 (*see also* imperialism)
community, rural 42, 203, 204
ayllu 204
conservatism ix, 1, 11, 16, 27, 35, 37, 53, 67, 70, 73, 74, 91, 100, 104, 107, 109, 112, 127, 135, 137, 146, 152, 153, 158, 172, 173, 289, 318–19, 323, 330, 332 *passim,* 348, 350ff., 368, 370, 377, 379.
contractor, labour 53, 209, 273, 274, 277–8, 305, 307. *See also* debt-bondage, *enganche*; gangmasters; unfree labour
maistry 273
Costa Rica 104
Croatia 166
culture
celebrity 15, 59, 340
Eurasianism 153, 156. *See also* Gumilev, Lev; Zomia
popular 88, 154, 165, 350
poverty as 13, 14, 27, 74, 112

David, Eduard 200
debt
agrarian 223, 225, 232ff., 236
loans 49, 50, 68, 122, 150, 201, 206, 223ff., 235, 236, 245–6, 269, 275, 277, 285, 287, 305, 307
productive/unproductive 269
debt-bondage 28, 39, 48, 49, 88–89, 95–6, 118, 131, 150, 194, 204, 206, 209, 213, 216, 237, 240, 245, 247, 249, 259, 260 *passim,* 273, 277, 282, 284, 287 *passim,* 305, 307. *See also* class, struggle; deproletarianization; labour, coercion; subsistence guarantee; unfree labour

capitalist/non-capitalist 28, 39, 96, 131, 209, 240, 245, 260ff., 288ff.
efficiency/inefficiency of 258, 263, 288, 294, 297
enganche 129, 193, 204, 209
hali system 47, 245, 248ff., 253
jajmani 245, 267
reverse bondage 274, 277
siri 268, 274, 285
democracy 3, 4, 11ff., 21, 26, 34–5, 68ff., 78, 81, 106, 120ff., 126, 127, 135, 138, 149, 153, 158, 174, 192, 193, 194, 196, 198, 200, 209, 217, 254, 283, 288, 295, 297, 316, 318, 319, 329, 351, 357, 361. *See also* bourgeoisie; capitalism; development theory; socialism
full employment 81, 161, 164, 364
welfare state 59, 80, 81, 144, 164, 260, 372
deproletarianization 6ff., 28, 41, 50, 74–5, 118, 129, 209, 241 *passim,* 255, 262–3, 268, 275, 279, 282, 284 *passim,* 296ff., 301 *passim,* 360. *See also* class, formation/struggle; debt-bondage; unfree labour
Derrida, Jacques 16, 342
Deutscher, Isaac 26, 62–5, 331, 332
Deutscher, Tamara 62, 63, 331
development theory 4, 27, 37, 47, 108, 109, 111 *passim,* 132 *passim,* 143, 167, 176, 193, 238, 257, 259, 296–7, 310, 359. *See also* capitalism; immigration; Marxism; economics, neoclassical; political economy; socialism
core/periphery 141, 142, 149, 298, 345, 374
dependency 95, 117, 297–8, 360
environmentalism 38, 110
and epidemiology 89–90
humanitarianism 15, 18, 29, 86, 356–7, 371–2, 379, 381ff.
impasse 19, 25, 36–7, 113
jobless growth 367
Keynesianism 14, 60, 240, 293, 364
and land grabbing 21ff.
as modernity ix, 1, 2, 12, 20, 33–4, 38, 40, 42, 80, 143, 152, 163, 167, 376
primitive accumulation 5, 9, 362
stages 10, 100, 210, 241, 295
Third Way 33, 80, 329
discourse, anti-capitalist 12, 14, 23, 24, 26ff., 70ff., 122, 158–9, 168, 170, 174, 176, 330, 351, 353. *See also* conservativism; Marxism; agrarian populism; socialism
Dobb, Maurice 63, 280, 307, 362, 364
Drieu la Rochelle, Pierre 82

ecology 21, 38, 110, 166. *See also* Zomia
Andean peasant economy 150, 166
verticality 150, 166
economics, neoclassical 9, 26, 55, 57, 88, 91, 133, 194, 205, 257, 259, 260, 264, 272, 281, 283, 284, 289, 297, 355b. *See also* capitalism; historiography, cliometric; immigration; market
Egypt 72, 81, 148, 318
England 26, 51, 53, 55, 62, 120, 316, 322, 329, 333, 334, 363
Enlightenment 16, 67, 77, 79, 153ff., 341
Epstein, A.L. (Bill) 65, 190
Eurasia 20, 153ff.. *See also* Zomia
Europe 3, 11 *passim,* 38, 54, 56, 59, 69, 77, 78, 81, 96, 135, 146, 148, 153, 165ff., 193, 198, 240, 259, 293, 316, 327, 337, 354, 357, 360, 371 *passim. See also* capitalism; industrial reserve army; immigration
European Union 5, 11, 354, 366, 369

famine 52, 94, 95, 100, 257, 340
farmers' movements 23, 24, 39, 41ff., 58, 166, 172, 268
Bharatiya Kisan Union 24
Green International 25, 166
Karnataka Rajya Ryota Sangham 24
Via Campesina 21, 23ff., 166
fascism 12, 13, 14, 35, 122, 156, 165, 166, 198, 365
BUF 198
Freikorps 175
Squadristi 175
Sturmabteilung 175
feudalism 69, 87, 125, 135, 143, 202. *See also* capitalism; semi-feudalism
film directors
Biberman, Herbert 51
Broomfield, Nick 51–55
Kubrick, Stanley 55
Palmer, Tony 330
Sen, Mrinal 52
Spielberg, Stephen 54
Watkin, Peter 52

films
  Clockwork Orange (1971) 55
  Culloden (1964) 51
  Ghosts (2006) 51–55
  In Search of Famine (1982) 52
  Indiana Jones and the Last Crusade (1989) 54
  Inside Job (2010) 73
  O Fortuna (2008) 330
  Raiders of the Lost Ark (1981) 54
  Salt of the Earth (1954) 51
  The War Game (1965) 51–2
  Two Days, One Night (2014) 73
food
  prices 55, 121, 124, 257
  regimes 56, 199, 260
  security 48, 95, 97, 98, 151
  sovereignty 20ff., 25, 143
football 220ff.
Foucault, Michel 16
foundation myth 143, 148, 166
France 22, 26, 67, 77–82, 120, 166, 172, 173, 316, 317, 336, 337
  Paris 78, 336
Freud, Sigmund 163
Fukayama, Francis 41

gangmasters 9, 52, 53, 55, 129
gender 22, 49, 59, 110, 169, 171, 206, 265, 268, 272, 349, 350, 360, 365
  ecofeminism 107, 171
Germany 7, 22, 35, 121, 122, 166, 174, 175, 199, 200, 316, 342, 369
  Junkers 35, 121–22, 139
  Nazism 35, 62, 330
  Prussia 35, 120, 121, 122, 126, 128, 209, 295
  Weimar Republic 121, 122
Gerschenkron, Alexander 122ff.
Ghana 306
Giddens, Anthony 33, 335, 375
Gramsci, Antonio 33
Greece 148
Guha, Ranajit 14, 157, 159, 168, 169. *See also* Subaltern Studies
Guiana, British 86, 103
Gumilev, Lev 20, 152–56
Gunder Frank, Andre 8, 135

Hall, Stuart 157, 162–5
Harris, Sir John 93
Hawthorn, Geoffrey 65–67
Heidegger, Martin 17
Herder, Johann Gottfried 154
Hirst, Paul 39
historiography 43, 57, 66, 67, 86, 90, 91, 142, 151ff., 159 *passim*, 245, 256, 257, 264, 274, 281, 289, 297, 308, 341
  cliometric 9, 26, 55, 57, 88, 90–91, 257, 264, 274, 281, 283, 297, 308
  counterfactual 66
  global labour history 157–77
  imperial 86, 169
  populist 27, 142, 144, 151–2
Hitler, Adolf 121–2
human rights 21, 90, 93, 145, 146, 255, 288, 297, 300, 303, 355, 356, 371, 375. *See also* justice; NGOs
Hungary 166
Hutton, J.H. 151, 323

identity
  agency and 7, 13, 23, 25, 27, 33, 36, 37, 47–48, 52, 74, 92, 107, 125–6, 135, 141, 144ff., 158–9, 168 *passim*, 196, 272, 314, 375–6
  belonginess 17, 165, 168
  Britishness 15, 163, 169, 322, 336, 372, 377, 379–80
  cultural ix, 58, 155, 163–4, 168, 176, 379–80
  Englishness 15, 163
  ethnic 47, 143, 153, 163, 167
  Ethnogenesis 155
  indigenista 149
  mestizo 219
  national 2, 15, 19, 20, 110, 149, 166, 342, 356, 372, 377, 383
  political 126, 186, 191
  religious 2, 12, 15, 17, 18, 19, 38, 40, 78, 80, 81, 153, 222, 337, 368
ideology 11, 14, 23, 40, 43, 70, 80, 81, 91, 100, 108, 126, 143, 146, 149, 164, 166, 168, 174, 175, 321, 333, 335, 336, 343, 350, 364, 368, 379, 380. *See also* class, consciousness/struggle; identity
immigration 8, 10, 11, 15 *passim*, 29, 53, 54, 102, 103, 354 *passim*, 365 *passim*, 374

passim. *See also* citizenship; class, formation; human rights; identity; industrial reserve army; justice; postmodernism, 'new' populist; racism; UKIP
benefits of 18, 356 *passim*, 375 *passim*
class struggle and 2, 7–12, 354ff., 357–61, 364, 372, 378, 380, 383
culture and 355ff., 368, 371ff., 377ff., 381ff.
employers and 354, 355, 356, 357, 360, 365ff., 370ff., 376, 381ff.
as 'escape' 375
Euroscepticism and 379
Marxism and 362–65, 380, 381, 382
open/closed-door 11, 17, 354, 356, 369ff., 377ff.
political economy and 355ff., 358, 361, 372–3, 377, 380, 382
regulation/control and 10, 11, 16, 29, 365, 371, 374, 379, 382
imperialism 3, 16, 21, 56, 100, 120, 124, 133, 134, 136, 139, 140, 167, 323, 327, 333, 341. *See also* capitalism; class, struggle; colonialism; nationalism
India 8, 14, 23, 24, 25, 26, 28, 33 *passim*, 44–50, 58, 69, 70, 73, 86, 88, 90, 93, 94ff., 98ff., 111, 113–14, 127ff., 136, 137, 141, 149, 150, 151, 166, 170ff., 195, 196, 205, 206, 217, 239 *passim*, 251ff., 256ff., 260ff., 267 *passim*, 276ff., 280 *passim*, 290–91, 293ff., 301ff., 312, 323, 332, 350
Andhra Pradesh 132–33
Bengal 52, 100, 102
Bihar 95, 205, 260, 279
Gujarat 44–50, 245 *passim*, 276
Haryana 128ff., 265, 267ff., 273–4, 279, 282, 285
Kerala 95
Malabar 95
Orissa 73
panchayat system 70
Punjab 128, 129, 132, 206, 279, 282, 287
Tamil Nadu 41, 113, 253
Tanjore 95
Trichinopoly 95
Uttar Pradesh 24, 128, 132, 269
industrial reserve army 5, 7, 8, 10, 11, 15, 18, 29, 54, 75, 150, 160, 175, 289, 354 *passim*, 362ff., 368ff., 376, 378ff., 381ff.. *See also* capitalism; class, struggle; deproletarianization; immigration; lumpenproletariat; unfree labour
Ireland 339, 340, 353
Italy 166, 175, 198, 342

James, C.L.R. 87
Japan 120, 128, 166, 342, 366
journals
Capital & Class 355
Charlie Hebdo 78, 80
Journal of Development Studies 292
Journal of Peasant Studies 21–25, 43, 57, 115, 116
Marxism Today 329
New Left Review 338
Slavery & Abolition 104
justice 29, 70, 71, 193, 208, 355, 356, 371, 375, 376, 382. *See also* human rights; NGOS

Kautsky, Karl 57, 58, 87, 119, 120, 121, 158, 174, 200. *See also* agrarian question; Marxism; socialism
Kristeva, Julia 16
Kritsman, L.N. 201
kulaks. *See* peasants, rich

La Convención 181, 201 *passim*, 222, 231, 232, 236ff.
Quillabamba 27, 181–2, 187, 213, 218
labour. *See also* capitalism; deproletarianization; industrial reserve army; labour process; proletarianization; unfree labour
age-specific 49, 60, 61, 85, 161, 171, 257, 272, 280, 299, 303, 306
agricultural 8, 27, 34, 36, 39, 46, 48, 49, 70, 89, 94, 95, 108, 111, 124, 129, 136, 137, 143, 152, 159, 167, 170, 172, 204, 205, 206, 208, 213, 215, 231, 236, 237, 240, 246, 249, 250, 253, 254, 267ff., 284, 286, 294
attached 48, 133, 265, 279
casual 7, 48ff., 60, 175, 245, 247, 268, 273–4, 284ff., 289, 295, 303, 348
coercion 5, 42, 52, 55, 88, 89, 97, 99, 123, 246ff., 260–61, 268ff., 275, 278, 281ff., 302, 306
contract 49, 59, 101, 122, 211, 215, 258, 262, 268, 274, 281ff., 297, 367
convict 6, 98, 101

labour (cont.)
coolie 46, 69, 86, 100ff., 299
corvée 141, 150
cost of 5, 6, 49, 60, 75, 89, 96ff., 103, 124, 129, 152, 242, 258, 262, 270, 279, 288, 308, 358 *passim*
daily 7, 49, 215
depatronization 47, 245, 249
flexible 54, 366
gender-specific 48, 49, 59, 78, 80, 81, 103, 110, 133, 150, 161, 171, 206, 265, 345, 356
indenture 26, 86, 88, 89, 96 *passim*, 169, 240, 264, 293, 297
intern 59ff.
neo-bondage 47, 244ff., 252, 263, 265, 275, 291
patronage 47, 48, 49, 88, 96, 118, 245, 247ff., 255, 261, 263, 265, 267, 270, 291, 305, 306, 344
permanent 6–7, 48, 49, 59–60, 129, 173, 191, 209, 229–30, 247, 251, 265, 273, 284ff., 289, 295, 301, 363
seasonal 7, 48, 129, 159, 209, 251, 273, 277, 282ff., 289, 295, 366
serf 44, 47, 69, 123, 159, 200, 259, 299
skilled/unskilled 6, 59, 220, 227ff., 294, 334, 355, 357ff., 360, 364, 367, 369, 370
social division of 223, 231, 232
zero-hours 367
labour process
decentralized 69
decomposition/recomposition 6, 60, 128, 158, 242, 262, 278, 279, 289, 294, 360
downsizing 69, 75, 81, 175, 359
outsourcing 59, 60, 69, 75, 81, 175, 240, 359, 365
restructuring 5, 6, 10, 24, 50, 53, 60, 75, 91, 103, 138, 160, 171, 175, 186, 262, 277ff., 289, 294, 300, 357, 359, 360, 380
sweatshops 59, 69, 345, 370
labour regime. *See* agrarian transition; capitalism; class; deproletarianization; labour; labour-power; proletarianization; State, the; unfree labour
labour-power
as commodity 6, 57, 97, 104, 151, 162, 217, 257, 264, 282, 284ff., 294, 296
exploitation 12, 14, 39–40, 50, 52, 55, 57, 60, 81, 88, 135, 198, 201, 232, 262, 270, 271, 289, 298, 300, 301, 308, 345, 362
sale/purchase 6, 10, 57, 99, 104, 119, 161–2, 203, 277, 282, 285, 302, 308, 310
supply/demand 9, 10, 11, 40, 41, 59, 60, 89, 95, 98ff., 103–4, 273, 277, 285, 355, 358ff., 366ff., 372
Lacan, Jacques 16
Laclau, Ernesto 8
land tenure
haciendas 192, 196
plantations 46, 85, 88, 90, 95ff., 100ff., 124, 161, 187, 204, 256, 257, 280, 281, 285, 302
sharecroppers 34, 159, 160, 176, 207, 264, 375
sub-tenants 204, 209, 211, 214, 215, 216, 233, 236
tenants 34, 100, 123, 204, 211, 212, 214, 215, 216, 233, 236
language 24, 46, 73–4, 128, 153ff., 164, 166, 255, 263, 341–2, 363
Latin America 8, 58, 88, 90, 128, 133ff., 139, 148, 149, 150, 160, 166, 169, 172, 192ff., 201ff., 210, 217, 241–2, 278–9, 294, 303, 304, 341, 348, 350
law 10, 51, 53, 59, 60ff., 78, 91, 93, 95, 100, 101, 145, 154, 200, 255, 272, 287, 318, 319, 324, 358, 362, 375, 382
Leach, Edmund 323
Leibknecht, Karl 158
Lenin, V.I. 34, 57, 58, 62, 87, 119, 120ff., 126, 141, 174, 199ff., 280, 307, 314, 316–17, 320, 331, 337, 353, 372
liberalism/neo-liberalism 10, 11, 18, 20, 27, 28, 33, 36, 39, 40, 41, 43, 59, 61, 63, 69, 70, 73, 106, 111, 118, 136, 137, 153, 165, 170, 238, 292, 329, 348, 353, 373
Lipton, Michael 114, 132
lumpenproletariat 19, 27, 157, 159, 161, 172ff., 177, 375. *See also* class, struggle; conservatism; industrial reserve army
strike-breaking 159, 173, 174
Luxemburg, Rosa 1 *passim,* 12, 20, 201, 316, 319–20, 362ff.

market. *See* capitalism; conservatism; labour; labour-power; Marxism; State, the
efficiency of 258
laissez-faire policy 357, 361, 369, 372, 374, 378, 380, 382
morality of 258

perfection/imperfection 205, 260, 261, 262, 263, 264
well-working 90
Marx, Karl 5, 7, 11, 17, 57, 87, 161, 162, 163, 171, 173ff., 272, 275, 280, 281, 284, 286, 296, 303, 307, 308, 316, 318, 326, 338, 349, 353, 357, 358, 360, 362ff., 380
Marxism 1 *passim,* 13 *passim,* 26ff., 36, 40ff., 47, 57, 58, 59, 62 *passim,* 73ff., 79, 82, 86ff., 106, 107, 113, 115 *passim,* 128, 132, 133, 135, 137ff., 143, 145, 146, 155 *passim,* 167, 168, 170 *passim,* 193ff., 197, 199, 202, 203, 252, 260, 263, 264, 271, 275–6, 279 *passim,* 292 *passim,* 303 *passim,* 312 *passim,* 326, 328 *passim,* 339, 341ff., 348ff., 355ff., 362, 364–5, 375, 377ff.. *See also* class, Lenin, V.I.; political economy; Preobrazhensky, Yevgeni; State, the; Trotsky, L.D.
Maoism 73
Stalinism 7, 22, 62, 280, 327, 331, 334, 336, 376
means of production
irrigation 199, 214
livestock 199, 214, 223, 224, 226, 227, 233, 234, 236
technology 41, 209, 358
media 51, 59, 72, 77, 183, 189, 340, 372, 373, 379. *See also* discourse, anti-capitalist; films
methodology 8, 9, 91, 120, 124, 149, 157, 160, 162, 217ff., 223, 241, 253, 254, 269, 273, 302, 314, 318, 321, 326, 346. *See also* anthropology
comparative 27, 86, 100, 120, 139, 153, 278
empiricist 26, 86, 104, 260, 304
Mexico 14, 58, 128, 135, 136, 172, 205, 206, 217
Middle East 5, 12, 148, 193
migrants
Chinese 26, 51, 52, 53, 55
Czech 357
European 11, 17
mode of production. *See* capitalism; feudalism; Marxism
money-lending 52, 150, 206, 260, 261, 286, 287
Morand, Paul 82

nationalism 3, 8, 14, 20, 26, 33, 37, 38, 41, 42, 74, 79, 91, 109, 116, 126, 138, 149, 155ff., 160, 163, 165, 169, 171, 175, 176, 193, 203, 288, 298, 322, 334, 348–49, 357, 368, 377, 379, 380, 381. *See also* conservatism; culture; identity; immigration; postmodernism, 'new' populist
as anti-globalization 14, 126
as barbarism 1 *passim,* 12, 14
Bharat 24, 35, 38, 43, 172
Hindu 24, 33, 35, 38, 39, 42, 43
hindutva 33, 35, 39, 42, 43
Nepal 150
Netherlands 45, 46, 104, 240, 256, 363, 379
new social movements
Landless Workers Movement (MST) 136
Occupy Wall Street (OWP) 26, 68ff.
Zapatista Army of National Liberation (EZLN) 136
NGOS
Aborigines Protection Society 93
Amnesty International 184, 379
Anti-Slavery Society 93, 270
Christian Aid 371
Friends of the Burma Hill People 146
Oxfam 371
Nicaragua 203

Pakistan 148
peasant movements
Cristeros 172
Sinarquistas 172
Vendee 141, 172
Zapatistas 25, 136, 194, 204
peasants. *See* agrarian populism; agrarian reform; depeasantization; peasants; peasant movements; property relations
depeasantization 21, 175, 176, 192, 198
differentiation 34, 39, 57, 58, 70, 114, 116, 118, 138, 141, 172, 202, 203, 211, 213
economy 17, 20, 22, 115, 117, 125, 126, 141, 143, 150, 154, 172, 198ff., 287, 288, 295, 341
family farm 20, 21, 57, 110, 115, 154, 169, 171, 193, 197 *passim,* 213, 375
middle 57, 115, 121, 166, 169, 202, 209, 212, 213, 216, 224, 225, 234, 235
pauperization 34, 95, 96, 174, 364
poor 42, 50, 57, 74, 111, 115, 130, 143, 145, 152, 167, 172, 177, 193, 200, 201, 202, 205, 206, 207, 209, 212, 213, 216, 225, 226, 234, 235, 237, 240, 253, 255, 257, 285, 287, 288, 289, 295

peasants (cont.)
- repeasantization 22, 295
- rich 23, 25, 39, 40, 42, 43, 57, 96, 115, 121, 128, 129, 130–31, 141, 169, 172, 200, 201 *passim*, 211ff., 216, 221, 225, 231, 234–5, 242, 271, 290, 294, 296

Peru 27, 128, 129, 149, 172, 181 *passim*, 192, 196, 203, 208 *passim*, 219, 232, 234, 236, 237, 279
- Cusco 27, 181, 182, 184, 189, 211, 218, 219, 224
- Lima 27, 181, 182, 185, 188, 189, 190, 191, 225

Petras, James 8, 106ff., 113, 119, 133ff., 139, 192, 205, 214, 307, 315, 348

petty commodity producers. *See* peasants

Philippines 148

Poland 363, 367

political economy 3, 11, 12, 13, 15, 16, 17, 18, 27, 28, 40, 73, 75, 106, 113, 120, 127, 128, 132ff., 138, 157ff., 168, 170ff., 175, 176, 240, 252, 264, 286, 292, 294, 299, 300, 303, 304, 307, 308, 310–11, 326, 329, 350, 355ff., 361, 372, 373, 377, 380, 382

political parties
- African National Congress (ANC) 93, 190
- Bharatia Janata Party (BJP) 24, 35, 43, 172
- Communist Party of Great Britain (CPGB) 88
- German Social Democracy (SDP) 3, 121, 158
- Indian National Congress 253
- Muslim Brotherhood 78ff.
- National Front 79
- New Labour 20, 59, 165, 334, 377, 378, 379
- Polish Communist Party 62
- Revolutionary Left Front 208–9
- United Kingdom Independence Party (UKIP) 368, 377, 379

postmodernism, 'new' populist 1, 12, 13ff., 19, 20, 24, 27, 28, 34, 36ff., 42, 58, 66, 67, 71, 74, 79, 82, 86, 88, 89, 90, 91, 106ff., 111ff., 115, 116, 119, 123ff., 127, 128, 134ff., 138, 140, 143, 144, 146, 152, 153ff., 158, 163ff., 167, 168, 172, 175, 176, 193, 194, 248, 314–15, 334ff., 340ff., 348ff., 353, 356, 357, 373, 376, 377, 379ff.. *See also* agrarian populism; culture; development theory; discourse, anti-capitalist; Enlightenment; historiography; identity; nationalism; new social movements; peasants; Subaltern Studies
- choice and 36, 141, 144, 146, 149, 165, 343, 349
- cultural turn 1, 12, 16, 20, 40, 58, 59, 107, 109, 115, 116, 135, 138, 164, 176, 337, 340, 341, 377, 379, 381
- decentering 163
- difference 36, 37, 38, 40, 42, 143, 163, 167, 350, 368, 380
- multitude 27, 119, 157ff., 168ff., 174, 176, 376
- New Left 157, 164, 338
- orientalism 38
- post-colonialism 37, 49, 107, 109, 345
- post-development 37, 40, 111, 117, 135
- post-Marxism 40, 73, 74, 107
- post-structuralism 40, 43, 116, 135
- proletarian multiverse 27, 158, 159, 162, 168ff., 173ff.

Preobrazhensky, Yevgeni 120, 121, 200, 316, 320

privatisation 59, 232, 234, 235, 237

production relations
- fictive kinship 201, 216, 225, 306, 376
- kinship 22, 42, 86, 141, 201, 202, 251, 268, 278, 302, 306, 376

proletarianization 10, 47, 48, 50, 198, 209, 244, 263, 264. *See also* agrarian question; capitalism; class; depeasantization; deproletarianization; Marxism; peasants, differentiation; political economy
- assertiveness as 36, 40, 47, 48, 49, 92, 153, 266
- freedmen and 86, 98, 99, 103, 104

property relations
- cooperatives 27, 192 *passim*, 203ff., 206 *passim*, 216 *passim*, 227 *passim*, 235ff.
- *ejidos* 194, 206
- estates 86, 88, 100, 101, 103, 122, 209, 210, 211, 212, 214, 215, 216, 219, 220, 223, 224, 226, 229, 231, 233, 234, 235, 237
- smallholdings 1, 21, 34, 57, 58, 110, 136, 137, 142, 148, 159, 166, 168, 171, 193, 195, 201, 203, 206, 209, 287, 341, 375

Puerto Rico 104, 279

racism 16, 77, 81, 102, 146–7, 356, 360. *See also* South Africa, apartheid system; immigration; industrial reserve army; South Africa
anti-semitism 77
Islamophobia 77, 78, 80
religion 2, 12, 15, 17, 18, 19, 38, 40, 69, 77ff., 153, 156, 166, 175, 222, 337, 349, 368. *See also* caste; culture; identity; nationalism; postmodernism, 'new' populist
Dalai Lama 78
fiesta system 222
Islam 18, 77, 78, 79, 80, 81, 82, 337
Roman Catholicism 69, 70, 79, 80, 190, 337
resistance. *See also* postmodernism, 'new' populist; State, the; Subaltern Studies; Zomia
as empowerment 26, 27, 35, 36, 47, 49, 52, 58, 59, 74, 88, 89, 92, 96, 100, 106, 117, 141, 143, 147, 148, 149, 152, 153, 165, 267, 341, 349, 350, 356, 361
everyday forms of 13, 37, 52, 88, 90, 92, 113, 144, 152, 153, 196, 207, 243, 254, 267, 351
as State-avoidance 71, 140 *passim*
revolution. *See also* agrarian question; class; Marxism; socialism
France 1789 332
France 1848 173, 363
Green 43, 282, 359
passive 33, 34
permanent 21, 201, 239
Russia 1917 4, 121, 153, 154, 319
Sonderweg thesis 122
Rivers, W.H.R. 323–24
Romania 166, 322
Rudé, George 63, 331–2, 335
Rushdie, Salman 78
Russia 4, 13, 20, 35, 58, 62, 70, 71, 117, 121, 122, 141, 148, 153, 154, 155, 156, 169, 171, 197, 198, 199, 200ff., 207, 317, 318, 319, 320, 322. *See also* agrarian question; class; Lenin, V.I.; Marxism

Sandinistas 203
Saussure, Ferdinand de 163
Schmoller, Gustav 316, 320
semi-feudalism 8, 9, 10, 34, 35, 55, 95, 96, 123ff., 129ff., 135, 138, 139, 209, 241, 245, 257, 259, 260, 267, 268, 272, 275, 280ff., 288ff., 294ff., 300, 307, 309ff., 319, 349, 360. *See also* agrarian transition; capitalism; class; debt-bondage; feudalism; peasants; proletarianization; unfree labour
slavery 9, 26, 85 *passim,* 96, 98, 101ff., 123, 124, 141, 142, 150, 240, 264, 271, 280ff., 293, 303, 304. *See also* capitalist; labour process; the Caribbean; colonialism; development theory; labour; labour-power; Marxism; unfree labour
abolition 48, 51, 90, 91, 95, 205
and emancipation 6, 26, 71, 85, 86, 87, 93, 95, 96, 97, 99, 100, 105, 243, 255, 266, 276, 289, 296, 297, 304, 330
Smuts, Jan Christian 147
social science 4, 20, 21, 27, 42, 67, 109, 113, 143, 159, 167, 313, 314, 320, 330, 334, 335, 336, 339, 343, 348, 349. *See also* academia; anthropology; political economy
socialism 1 passim, 14 passim, 25ff., 58ff., 71 *passim,* 96, 106, 107, 118, 120ff., 124ff., 132 *passim,* 145, 147, 156 *passim* 165 *passim,* 175, 176, 177, 192, 198 *passim,* 207, 208, 209, 258, 259, 283, 286, 288, 292, 293, 295, 296, 304, 310, 311, 312 *passim,* 321 *passim,* 332 *passim,* 340 *passim,* 350ff., 355 *passim,* 374 *passim. See also* academia; agrarian question; capitalism; class; democracy; development theory; historiography; Lenin, V.I.; labour process; market; Marxism; nationalism; peasants; proletarianization; revolution; Trotsky, L.D.
Sol Plaatje 93
Sombart, Werner 316, 319
South Africa 17, 26, 70, 88, 93, 99, 147, 153, 270, 279, 372. *See also* identity; racism
apartheid system 17, 70, 71, 88, 93147, 153, 270, 372
Bantustans 147
Natives Land Act 1913, 93
South Korea 120, 128
Spain 22, 35, 71, 166

State, the
- arrest by 27, 72, 181 *passim,* 330
- Department for International Development (DFID), 304
- Economic and Social Research Council (ESRC) 304
- expulsion by 27, 185, 189, 190
- Foreign and Commonwealth Office (FCO) 188, 189, 190, 191
- *Guardia Civil* (GC) 181, 182, 183
- *Guardia Republicana* (GR) 184

Stauder, Jack 63, 323, 332–33
Stirner, Max 174. *See also* anarchism
Subaltern Studies 13, 14, 34, 113, 153, 164, 169, 170, 171, 194, 341. *See also* identity; India; Latin America; nationalism; postmodernism, 'new' populist; Guha, Ranajit
subsistence guarantee 39, 47, 48, 88, 89 *passim,* 105, 245, 249, 250, 265, 267, 302, 305–6. *See also* debt-bondage; labour, patronage; unfree labour
Switzerland 174

Taiwan 120, 128
taxation 8, 19, 53, 59, 141, 144, 145, 366, 367
Thorner, Alice 44, 45, 241, 247, 294, 307, 332
Thorner, Daniel 8, 45, 63, 195, 206, 241, 247, 307, 332
Toynbee, Arnold 321, 322, 323
trade unions 48, 49, 53, 54, 59, 60, 61, 91, 98, 166, 181, 188, 211, 212, 214, 222, 224, 278, 317, 324, 325, 357, 360, 361, 363, 364, 365, 370, 373, 376, 381. *See also* capitalism; class struggle; capitalist; labour process; democracy; farmers' movements; labour
tribe
- Karen 145–6
- Naga 151

Trotsky, L.D. 9, 13, 21, 22, 35, 58, 62, 71, 121, 201, 239, 280, 307, 316, 318, 319, 320, 331, 333, 338, 362, 364, 365. *See also* agrarian question; class struggle; Lenin, V.I.; Marxism, peasants; revolution; Russia

unfree labour 1 *passim,* 26, 28, 41, 47, 51, 57, 75, 86, 87 *passim,* 98, 99, 102, 103, 105, 122, 123 *passim,* 138 139, 150, 158, 160, 161, 162, 172, 175, 176, 204, 208, 209, 213, 216, 240 *passim,* 252 *passim,* 264 *passim,* 275 *passim,* 286, 288ff., 292 *passim,* 303 *passim,* 360. *See also* agrarian question; capitalism; class; debt-bondage; deproletarianization; development theory; economics, neoclassical; historiography, cliometric; labour; labour-power; labour process; Marxism; slavery
- as 'adverse incorporation' 298, 308
- changing masters 285, 286
- as a 'continuum' 300, 301, 302, 310
- entry-into, exit-from 282, 297, 301, 304
- and 'fresh perspectives' 299, 301, 308, 311
- as 'neo-liberal governance' 298
- as 'non-standard work' 298
- as 'precarity' 298
- as 'social reproduction' 298
- as 'voluntary' 248, 249, 250, 282
- as 'vulnerability' 298
- withholding wages 101, 270, 277

United States 12, 13, 26, 69, 90, 120, 122, 139, 148, 166, 167, 193, 198, 201, 328, 333, 348, 357, 373
- Antebellum South 85, 90, 97, 102, 123, 257, 280, 302

Universities
- Amsterdam 45
- Cambridge 63, 65, 66, 151, 323, 324, 329, 332, 344, 345, 351
- Durham 339
- *La Católica* 181
- London 72, 322, 334
- London School of Economics (LSE) 33
- New York 44
- Oxford 315, 319, 321, 323, 324, 329, 331, 338, 346
- Sussex 27, 62, 63, 190, 331, 339

Venice 82
Vichy 82
Vietnam 141
Vollmar, Georg von 157, 158

wages 7, 9, 22, 49, 53, 54, 64, 88, 89, 94 *passim,* 124, 130, 135, 152, 164, 173, 208, 216, 254, 265, 270, 277, 284, 286, 295, 305, 309, 310, 358, 360 *passim,* 370 *passim*
- undercutting 53, 360, 363, 371, 376

Wagner, Adolf 316, 319

war
1914–18 3, 122, 193
1939–45 13, 14, 69, 166, 168, 240, 293, 364
American Civil 257
Cold 62, 165, 259, 327, 330, 333, 338

World Bank 111, 119, 193, 195

Zomia 20, 26–7, 140 *passim*, 152ff.. *See also* Eurasia

www.ingramcontent.com/pod-product-compliance
Lightning Source LLC
Chambersburg PA
CBHW072000110726
47910CB00005B/1600
9781608469284